World History
Volume II
1500 to 20th Century

Editor

David McComb
Colorado State University

David McComb received his Ph.D. from the University of Texas and is currently a professor of history at Colorado State University. He has written five books, numerous articles and book reviews, and teaches courses in the history of technology, cities, sport, and the world. He has traveled twice around the world as a Semester at Sea faculty member of the University of Pittsburgh, and spent additional time in India.

Annual Editions
A Library of Information from the Public Press

Cover illustration by Mike Eagle

The Dushkin Publishing Group, Inc.
Sluice Dock, Guilford, Connecticut 06437

The Annual Editions Series

Annual Editions is a series of over forty volumes designed to provide the reader with convenient, low-cost access to a wide range of current, carefully selected articles from some of the most important magazines, newspapers, and journals published today. Annual Editions are updated on an annual basis through a continuous monitoring of over 200 periodical sources. All Annual Editions have a number of features designed to make them particularly useful, including topic guides, annotated tables of contents, unit overviews, and indexes. For the teacher using Annual Editions in the classroom, an Instructor's Resource Guide with test questions is available for each volume.

VOLUMES AVAILABLE

- Africa
- Aging
- American Government
- American History, Pre-Civil War
- American History, Post-Civil War
- Anthropology
- Biology
- Business and Management
- China
- Comparative Politics
- Computers in Education
- Computers in Business
- Computers in Society
- Criminal Justice
- Drugs, Society, and Behavior
- Early Childhood Education
- Economics
- Educating Exceptional Children
- Education
- Educational Psychology
- Environment
- Geography
- Global Issues
- Health
- Human Development
- Human Sexuality
- Latin America
- Macroeconomics
- Marketing
- Marriage and Family
- Middle East and the Islamic World
- Nutrition
- Personal Growth and Behavior
- Psychology
- Social Problems
- Sociology
- Soviet Union and Eastern Europe
- State and Local Government
- Third World
- Urban Society
- Western Civilization, Pre-Reformation
- Western Civilization, Post-Reformation
- Western Europe
- World History, Pre-Modern
- World History, Modern
- World Politics

Library of Congress Cataloging in Publication Data.
Main entry under title: Annual editions: World history, vol. II: 1500 to 20th Century.
1. World history—Periodicals. 2. Civilization, Modern—Periodicals. 3. Social problems—Periodicals. I. McComb, David, comp. II. Title: World history, vol. II: 1500 to 20th Century.
905   ISBN: 0-87967-736-8

©1988 by The Dushkin Publishing Group, Inc. Annual Editions is a Trade Mark of The Dushkin Publishing Group, Inc.

Copyright ©1988 by The Dushkin Publishing Group, Inc., Guilford, Connecticut 06437

All rights reserved. No part of this book may be reproduced, stored, or transmitted by any means—mechanical, electronic, or otherwise—without written permission from the publisher.

First Edition

Manufactured by The Banta Company, Harrisonburg, Virginia 22801

Editors/Advisory Board

EDITOR
David McComb
Colorado State University

Members of the Advisory Board are instrumental in the final selection of articles for each edition of Annual Editions. Their review of articles for content, level, currency, and appropriateness provides critical direction to the editor and staff. We think you'll find their careful consideration well reflected in this volume.

ADVISORY BOARD

Beverly Blois
Northern Virginia Community College

Howard C. Giles
Murray State University

Craig E. Harline
University of Idaho

William Hughes
Essex Community College

Wallace Hutcheon
Northern Virginia Community College

Elliot Lefkovitz
Loyola University

Vivian L. Munson
University of Wisconsin
La Crosse

Wei-Ping Wu
University of Bridgeport

Martin Yanuck
Spelman College

STAFF

Rick Connelly, Publisher
Ian A. Nielsen, Program Manager
Celeste Borg, Editor
Addie Kawula, Administrative Editor
Brenda S. Filley, Production Manager
Cheryl Nicholas, Permissions Editor
Charles Vitelli, Designer
Jean Bailey, Graphics Coordinator
Lynn Shannon, Graphics
Libra A. Cusack, Typesetting Coordinator
Diane Barker, Editorial Assistant

To The Reader

In publishing ANNUAL EDITIONS we recognize the enormous role played by the magazines, newspapers, and journals of the *public press* in providing current, first-rate educational information in a broad spectrum of interest areas. Within the articles, the best scientists, practitioners, researchers, and commentators draw issues into new perspective as accepted theories and viewpoints are called into account by new events, recent discoveries change old facts, and fresh debate breaks out over important controversies.

Many of the articles resulting from this enormous editorial effort are appropriate for students, researchers, and professionals seeking accurate, current material to help bridge the gap between principles and theories and the real world. These articles, however, become more useful for study when those of lasting value are carefully *collected, organized, indexed,* and *reproduced* in a *low-cost format,* which provides easy and permanent access when the material is needed. That is the role played by *Annual Editions.* Under the direction of each volume's *Editor,* who is an expert in the subject area, and with the guidance of an *Advisory Board,* we seek each year to provide in each ANNUAL EDITION a current, well-balanced, carefully selected collection of the best of the public press for your study and enjoyment. We think you'll find this volume useful, and we hope you'll take a moment to let us know what you think.

After 1500 the world was increasingly taken up with the power and problems of the West. Europe and its offspring in North America experienced a unique transformation with the industrial and scientific revolutions. The technology it generated allowed a global extension of its culture. Ideas, not only about science and technology, but also about liberalism, socialism, capitalism, Christianity, democracy, and nationalism, followed in the wake of caravels and steamboats. It was the Europeans who dispelled the myth of the "sea of pithy darkness" in the ocean below the western hump of Africa, who discovered a New World, and who carried trade to the mysterious orient. It was not a Chinese mariner who sailed up the Hudson River, nor an African who forced the Japanese at gunpoint to open their ports. For all their faults it was the Europeans and, later, Americans who ventured forth around the globe and on to the surface of the moon.

The history of the world in the modern period, therefore, vitally concerns the circumstances of the West and the ambitions of its people. As taught by William H. McNeill and L.S. Stavrianos in their texts, the West expanded into the rest of the world and the peoples there reacted in one way and another. First there was a time of colonialism. Then, after the disasters of two world wars and a depression in the twentieth century, the West retreated. It left behind a residue of ideas, an interest in technology, and the English language.

Annual Editions: World History, Volume II follows that same general pattern. The articles are meant to give you an idea of what was happening in the world, but they are intended as a supplement for other course material. The selections generally reflect the more recent thinking on a subject. They were chosen for their readability and ability to provoke a response. Because of the topical approach, the chronology might not be suitable for some teachers. The Topic Guide may be useful to correlate topics with another approach. It is impossible to cover all subjects everywhere on earth. World history by its nature must be selective. You may have suggestions for improving this edition, and may have some articles you think would be useful. Please use the article rating form at the back of this volume to submit your thoughts and ideas.

David McComb

Editor

Contents

Unit 1

The Industrial and Scientific Revolutions

Nine selections discuss the revolutions in the industrial and scientific world. Topics include the change from cottage industry to factory, the impact of the Copernican revolution, the importance of Galileo, Darwin's effect on the scientific community, the effect of agriculture on world development, and the role of the computer in modern society.

To the Reader	iv
Topic Guide	2
Overview	4

1. **Cottage Industry and the Factory System,** Duncan Bythell, *History Today,* April 1983.   6
   There was no sudden displacement of the cottage industry by the factories of the **Industrial Revolution**. The change was gradual, lasting as long as three generations, and the shift was beneficial in the long run.

2. **From Astronomy to Astrophysics,** James Trefil, *The Wilson Quarterly,* Summer 1987.   13
   The Copernican revolution altered people's view of the cosmos and inspired a **scientific** inquiry about the nature of the universe which continues to the present.

3. **Galileo's Science and the Trial of 1633,** William A. Wallace, *The Wilson Quarterly,* Summer 1983.   18
   Galileo stands as a transitional figure between the crumbling truth of medieval Europe and the power of the new **science**. His arguments for the Copernican system which placed him at the court of the inquisition, however, were weak and based more on intuition than on scientific proof.

4. **Halley and Post-Restoration Science,** Noel Coley, *History Today,* September 1986.   24
   Edmund Halley was an astronomer, mathematician, classicist, inventor, sea captain, diplomat, and friend of Isaac Newton. He represents the breadth and vigor of the seventeenth-century **scientific mind**.

5. **Darwin as a Geologist,** Sandra Herbert, *Scientific American,* May 1986.   31
   Even though Charles Darwin is known as a biologist today, he saw himself as a geologist. **Scientific** observations about gradual changes in land elevations led him to the idea of gradual changes in species.

6. **Life's Recipe,** *The Economist,* May 30-June 5, 1987.   37
   Understanding the genetic code is considered one of the great achievements in **science**. It not only explains how life reproduces, but also promises improvement of animal and plant life.

7. **The Green Revolution,** Robert E. Huke, *Journal of Geography,* November/December 1985.   40
   New plant types, fertilizer, and water control can dramatically improve crop yields. Application of this **scientific agriculture** has produced such varied results, however, that its impact is difficult to evaluate.

The concepts in bold italics are developed in the article. For further expansion please refer to the Topic Guide and the Index.

8. **Artificial Intelligence: A New Reality,** Joseph J. Kroger, *The Futurist,* July/August 1987. 47
What role should the computer play in society? Modern **technology** is developing computers that may even have emotions, high levels of **artificial intelligence**, and abilities adaptable to areas that up to now have been reserved for humans.

9. **Scientists Go North,** Anthony de Souza, *The Geographical Magazine,* April 1986. 50
National development depends to a certain extent on a commitment to basic scientific effort. Regardless of where they are from, talented **scientists** tend to concentrate in the northern part of the world, thereby widening the gap between rich and poor nations.

Unit 2

The Cultural Ferment of the West

Seven articles examine the cultural development of the West including such topics as early religious thinking, early economic interpretations of capitalism, music, women in eighteenth-century society, and the importance of the American Constitution in world events.

Overview 52

10. **Luther: Giant of His Time and Ours,** *Time,* October 31, 1983. 54
In 1517 Martin Luther began his protestations against the corruption of the Roman Catholic Church. His action started a landslide of **religious thinking** within Christianity which started the Protestant movement, developed new theologies, and, perhaps, saved Christianity as well.

11. **Scotland's Greatest Son,** John Kenneth Galbraith, *Horizon,* Summer 1974. 59
Adam Smith, with his book *The Wealth of Nations*, became the first of the great **economists** and interpreters of capitalism. Although he is still revered, much of what he said must be understood in the context of his times and must be modified by present circumstances.

12. **Marx: His Death and Resurrection,** Louis J. Halle, *Encounter,* January 1970. 65
There are two sides to the **economist** Karl Marx. One boasts of the legend and his role in the Communist revolution; the other criticizes his chaotic and unsuccessful personal life.

13. **The Body of Bach,** Edward Rothstein, *The New Republic,* June 24, 1985. 69
While leading a mundane life—fathering twenty children, smoking his pipe, and drinking large amounts of port wine—Johann Sebastian Bach created immortal **music**.

The concepts in bold italics are developed in the article. For further expansion please refer to the Topic Guide and the Index.

14. **Freudian Myths and Freudian Realities,** Peter F. Drucker, 74
from *Adventures of a Bystander,* Harper and Row, 1979.
Sigmund Freud was one of the towering intellects of **science** in the twentieth century. He encouraged myths about himself, however, which were far from reality.

15. **The First Feminist,** Shirley Tomkievicz, *Horizon,* Spring 1972. 81
She did not hate men, nor did she deny the traditional role of **women** as wives and mothers. However, in the late eighteenth century, Mary Wollstonecraft pursued a successful writing career and argued that the female had as good a mind as the male.

16. **Making It Work,** A.E. Dick Howard, *The Wilson Quarterly,* Spring 1987. 86
Once completed there was a scramble to ratify the Constitution of the **United States**. Over time the Supreme Court has interpreted this **political** document to protect the rights of minorities and women, and to extend the powers of the federal government.

Unit 3

The Extension and Domination of the West

Six articles show how the West extended and dominated much of the world. Topics include the emergence of Western colonial powers, the importance of the Anglo-Zulu War, the domination of India by England, feudal Japan, and the cultural importance of early twentieth-century Paris.

Overview 90

17. **The Emergence of the Great Powers,** Gordon A. Craig 92
and Alexander L. George, *Force and Statecraft: Diplomatic Problems of Our Times,* Oxford University Press, 1983.
Between 1600 and 1815 **Great Britain**, **France**, **Austria**, **Prussia**, and **Russia** came forth as the great powers which would dominate the world up until World War I. This was accomplished through war, diplomacy, an efficient bureaucracy, and an attitude which held that the state was more important than any group, individual, or leader.

18. **The Struggle for Land,** Frank Emery, *The Geographical Magazine,* June 1986. 99
The Anglo-Zulu War of 1879 is the best known **war** of imperialism in **Africa**. Although **British** arms eventually prevailed, the Zulu nation survived and, in retrospect, British policy seems pointless.

19. **West Africa's Mary Kingsley,** Deborah Birkett, *History Today,* May 1987. 102
In the 1890s Mary Kingsley, a middle-class English woman, traveled through **West Africa** as a trader and anthropologist. She returned to England and argued that scholars should live with the people they intend to study and learn to "think in black." Moreover, she spoke against the colonial system and proposed a relationship based upon commerce.

The concepts in bold italics are developed in the article. For further expansion please refer to the Topic Guide and the Index.

Unit 4

War and Depression

Seven articles examine the effect of war and depression on modern world history. Topics include the causes of war, the impact of the First World War, the rise of Hitler, the Vietnam War, and the seemingly historical inevitability of a cold war.

20. **The East India Company and the Emperor Aurangzeb,** Bruce Lenman, *History Today,* February 1987.   109

   In the 1680s Sir Josiah Child used **warfare** to further the **colonization** and trade objectives of the East India Company. The Mogul Emperor, however, defeated the **British** and the plans failed. A later attempt under Robert Clive in 1757 succeeded and resulted in English domination of **India**.

21. **Southern Barbarians and Red Hairs in Feudal Japan,** C.R. Boxer, *History Today,* October 1981.   116

   During the seventeenth and eighteenth centuries, Westerners were by and large banned from **Japan**. The Portuguese and Dutch confined to small posts, however, remained. The letters and observations of the time describe their life, especially in regard to acquired Japanese **women**.

22. **Sarah Bernhardt's Paris,** Christopher Hibbert, *Mankind,* October 1982.   119

   At the turn of the century, Paris was at the center of life and **culture** in Western civilization. Its rich existence is symbolized in the career of the actress Sarah Bernhardt.

Overview   128

23. **The Causes of Wars,** Michael Howard, *The Wilson Quarterly,* Summer 1984.   130

   Throughout history, **wars** have started when both sides have reasoned that they will gain more through fighting than through peace. Atomic warfare is a new element in the decision-making process.

24. **Sarajevo: The End of Innocence,** Edmund Stillman, *Horizon,* Summer 1964.   137

   The goals of the various nations involved in **World War I** were pitiously small compared to ten million dead soldiers. We have yet to recover from the chaos and barbarity of the war.

25. **The Dangerous Summer of 1940,** John Lukacs, *American Heritage,* October/November 1986.   141

   In five weeks during the spring of 1940, Hitler's armies conquered **Europe**. The Germans were close to winning the **war**, but Churchill and the English resisted until the United States could be aroused to turn the tide of battle.

The concepts in bold italics are developed in the article. For further expansion please refer to the Topic Guide and the Index.

26. **Social Outcasts in Nazi Germany,** Jeremy Noakes, *History Today,* December 1985. 146

The holocaust against the Jews has rightly demanded the most attention from the public, but there were also others whom the Nazis attacked and eliminated in the gas chambers and work camps. Of the 30,000 gypsies living in Germany in 1939, only 5,000 survived the *war*. They were subject to the infamous medical experiments at Auschwitz where 11,000 gypsies were murdered.

27. **Reborn from Holocaust,** Michael Dillon, *The Geographical Magazine,* August 1985. 151

Although Hiroshima has recovered from the 1945 atom bomb blast of *World War II*, the author describes some long-term scars and sadness which remain.

28. **Lessons from a Lost War,** *Time,* April 15, 1985. 153

The *United States* has been reluctant to face questions about the Vietnam War. Who lost? Was the *war* inevitable? Could it have been won? Was it fought for the right reasons? Did it prove the domino theory? All of these questions are important if the United States is to send troops abroad again.

29. **The Two Thousand Years' War,** Walter Karp, *Harper's,* March 1981. 157

There are parallels between the ancient *war* between Sparta and Athens, and the *cold war* between the *United States* and the *Soviet Union*. Technologies have changed, but many aspects of human nature and ambition have remained the same.

Unit 5

The Retreat of the West

Seven articles discuss how Western colonialism has impacted on the world. Topics include African independence, South Africa, Gandhi, the Middle East, Stalin, and the legacy of English colonization.

Overview 160

30. **Whose Dream Was It Anyway? Twenty-Five Years of African Independence,** Michael Crowder, *African Affairs,* January 1987. 162

The current judgments about *African* political failure have been made in a framework of European hopes. There have been African accomplishments worth noting, while the failures must be shared between the African leaders and their colonial forebears.

31. **Visit to South Africa,** Bhupinder Singh Liddar, *International Perspectives,* March/April 1986. 170

A dark-skinned Canadian journalist traveled through *South Africa* to witness apartheid first-hand. He concluded that the nation is on the brink of a bloodbath.

32. **Gandhi: A Twentieth-Century Anomaly?** John Broomfield, *LSA (University of Michigan),* Winter 1984. 174

Compared to contemporary revolutionaries who advocated violence, Gandhi appears to be an anomaly. His calculated methods of non-violence were different, but Gandhi, like others, hoped to build a new political and economic order for *India*.

The concepts in bold italics are developed in the article. For further expansion please refer to the Topic Guide and the Index.

33. **The Vatican, Israel and the Jerusalem Question (1943-1984),** Silvio Ferrari, *The Middle East Journal,* Spring 1985.   180

    The problems of the ***Middle East*** are often seen as a split between Jew and Arab. What is forgotten are the interests of Christians in the Holy Lands. At the time of the creation of Israel, the Vatican wanted international control of the area under United Nations jurisdiction.

34. **Islam: Religion Has Potential to Reshape World,** Tom Hundley, *Fort Collins Coloradoan,* February 15, 1987.   188

    A resurgence of Islamic religious fervor is offering an alternative to the capitalism of the West and the "godless communism" of the Soviet Union. There is a dream of making Islam a superpower in the ***Middle East***.

35. **Stalin's Afterlife,** Stephen F. Cohen, *The New Republic,* December 29, 1979.   190

    Joseph Stalin, who ruled the ***Soviet Union*** from 1929 to 1953, represents the greatest unresolved problem in Soviet political history. His mountain of accomplishments stands next to his mountain of crimes, and a reconciliation has not been reached.

36. **The New English Empire,** *The Economist,* December 20, 1986.   195

    Four centuries ago, seven million people spoke English. Today there are 330 million who use it as a mother tongue and close to one billion who use it as a second language. One of the legacies of ***colonization*** and ***technology*** is that English has become a world language.

Unit 6

World Problems and Interdependence

Eight selections examine the effects of interdependence on some world problems including population growth, Chinese urbanization, Brazil, the conservation organization "Greenpeace," Japanese women, divorce in China, the history of Acquired Immune Deficiency (AIDS), and the importance of education.

Overview   200

37. **Population and Economic Growth: The Third World,** Nick Eberstadt, *The Wilson Quarterly,* Winter 1986.   202

    An examination of the ***population*** problem and the various theories about it reveals that size and growth rate are not so important for prosperity. More significant are the reactions of leaders and people to change.

38. **China Goes to Town,** Richard Kirkby, *The Geographical Magazine,* October 1986.   213

    In the past decade Chinese ***urbanization*** has moved rapidly. Since 1953 the number of cities over one million in population have increased from nine to twenty. Due to ***China's*** commitment to welfare, however, mass urban squalor is absent.

39. **Capital of Dreams,** Paul Forster, *The Geographical Magazine,* September 1986.   217

    Built almost three decades ago, the futuristic Brasilia failed to live up to expectations of ***urbanization*** in Brazil. The author explains why it has not been a total failure, either.

The concepts in bold italics are developed in the article. For further expansion please refer to the Topic Guide and the Index.

40. **The Zeal of Disapproval,** Michael Brown, *Oceans,* May/June 1987.   **221**
Greenpeace is a small, sometimes outrageous, but effective **conservation** organization dedicated to a peaceful, healthy world. Its actions against pollution and nuclear tests, and its work for the salvation of whales and seals is well known.

41. **Japanese Women in a Male Society,** Nobuko Hashimoto, *The Christian Science Monitor,* January 10, 1985.   **225**
In 1980 **Japan** endorsed the United Nations pledge to eliminate **discrimination against women**. Yet, because of age-old traditions the quality and condition of women's jobs have remained poor, and wages amount to about one-half the amount paid to men.

42. **Divorce, Chinese Style,** Tamara K. Hareven, *The Atlantic,* April 1987.   **228**
Socialist **China** wants marriage based upon free choice, love, and equality, but there are no role models nor dating customs. The divorce courts reflect the clash between traditions and an emergent individualism.

43. **The Natural History of AIDS,** Matthew Allen Gonda, *Natural History,* May 1986.   **234**
No one yet knows the origin of the AIDS virus, but it may have long existed in isolated **African** villages. The disease may have become epidemic when infected individuals moved to cities following the breakdown of tribal and geographic boundaries.

44. **The Importance of Learning About the Rest of the World: What Would Emerson Say Today?** Lewis Hanke, *American Studies International,* October 1986.   **239**
It is wisdom to learn what outsiders think about your **culture** and your nation when the world is filled with perils.

Index   **242**
Article Rating Form   **245**

The concepts in bold italics are developed in the article. For further expansion please refer to the Topic Guide and the Index.

Topic Guide

This topic guide suggests how the selections in this book relate to topics of traditional concern to World History students and professionals. It is very useful in locating articles which relate to each other for reading and research. The guide is arranged alphabetically according to topic. Articles may, of course, treat topics that do not appear in the topic guide. In turn, entries in the topic guide do not necessarily constitute a comprehensive listing of all the contents of each selection.

TOPIC AREA	TREATED AS AN ISSUE IN:	TOPIC AREA	TREATED AS AN ISSUE IN:
Africa	18. The Struggle for Land 19. West Africa's Mary Kingsley 30. Whose Dream Was It Anyway? 31. Visit to South Africa 37. Population and Economic Growth 43. The Natural History of AIDS	Economics	11. Scotland's Greatest Son 12. Marx 19. West Africa's Mary Kingsley 20. The East India Company 37. Population and Economic Growth 41. Japanese Women in a Male Society
Agriculture	7. The Green Revolution	Europe	1. Cottage Industry and the Factory System 3. Galileo's Science and the Trial of 1633 4. Halley and Post-Restoration Science 5. Darwin as a Geologist 10. Luther 11. Scotland's Greatest Son 12. Marx 13. The Body of Bach 14. Freudian Myths and Freudian Realities 15. The First Feminist 17. The Emergence of the Great Powers 22. Sarah Bernhardt's Paris 24. Sarajevo 25. The Dangerous Summer of 1940 26. Social Outcasts in Nazi Germany 35. Stalin's Afterlife
Americas	9. Scientists Go North 16. Making It Work 39. Capital of Dreams		
Asia	7. The Green Revolution 21. Southern Barbarians and Red Hairs 27. Reborn from Holocaust 28. Lessons from a Lost War 37. Population and Economic Growth: The Third World 38. China Goes to Town 41. Japanese Women in a Male Society 42. Divorce, Chinese Style		
China	12. Marx 39. China Goes to Town 42. Divorce, Chinese Style		
Colonization	18. The Struggle for Land 19. West Africa's Mary Kingsley 20. The East India Company 30. Whose Dream Was It Anyway? 31. Visit to South Africa 32. Gandhi 36. The New English Empire	Great Britain	1. Cottage Industry and the Factory System 4. Halley and Post-Restoration Science 5. Darwin as a Geologist 11. Scotland's Greatest Son 12. Marx 15. The First Feminist 17. The Emergence of the Great Powers 18. The Struggle for Land 19. West Africa's Mary Kingsley 20. The East India Company 32. Gandhi 36. The New English Empire
Conservation	40. The Zeal of Disapproval		
Culture	13. The Body of Bach 15. The First Feminist 21. Southern Barbarians and Red Hairs 22. Sarah Bernhardt's Paris 26. Social Outcasts in Nazi Germany 33. The Vatican, Israel and the Jerusalem Question 34. Islam 35. Stalin's Afterlife 36. The New English Empire 39. Capital of Dreams 41. Japanese Women in a Male Society 42. Divorce, Chinese Style 44. The Importance of Learning About the Rest of the World	India	20. The East India Company 32. Gandhi
		Industrial Revolution	1. Cottage Industry and the Factory System 11. Scotland's Greatest Son 12. Marx

TOPIC AREA	TREATED AS AN ISSUE IN:	TOPIC AREA	TREATED AS AN ISSUE IN:
Japan	21. Southern Barbarians and Red Hairs 27. Reborn from Holocaust 41. Japanese Women in a Male Society	Soviet Union/Russia	12. Marx 17. The Emergence of the Great Powers 29. The Two Thousand Years' War 35. Stalin's Afterlife
Middle East	33. The Vatican, Israel and the Jerusalem Question 34. Islam	Techology	7. The Green Revolution 8. Artificial Intelligence 29. The Two Thousand Years' War
Politics	3. Galileo's Science and the Trial of 1633 16. Making It Work 17. The Emergence of the Great Powers 19. West Africa's Mary Kingsley 23. The Causes of Wars 28. Lessons from a Lost War 30. Whose Dream Was It Anyway? 32. Gandhi 33. The Vatican, Israel and the Jerusalem Question 34. Islam 37. Population and Economic Growth 40. The Zeal of Disapproval	Terrorism	26. Social Outcasts in Nazi Germany 34. Islam 35. Stalin's Afterlife
		United States	9. Scientists Go North 16. Making It Work 28. Lessons from a Lost War 29. The Two Thousand Years' War
		Urbanization/Cities	1. Cottage Industry and the Factory System 27. Reborn from Holocaust 38. China Goes to Town 39. Capital of Dreams
Pollution	40. The Zeal of Disapproval	Warfare	17. The Emergence of the Great Powers 18. The Struggle for Land 20. The East India Company 23. The Causes of Wars 24. Sarajevo, the End of Innocence 25. The Dangerous Summer of 1940 26. Social Outcasts in Nazi Germany 27. Reborn from Holocaust 28. Lessons from a Lost War 29. The Two Thousand Years' War
Population	9. Scientists Go North 26. Social Outcasts in Nazi Germany 37. Population and Economic Growth: The Third World 38. China Goes to Town 43. The Natural History of AIDS		
Religion	3. Galileo's Science and the Trial of 1633 10. Luther 33. The Vatican, Israel and the Jerusalem Question 34. Islam	Women	15. The First Feminist 16. Making It Work 19. West Africa's Mary Kingsley 21. Southern Barbarians and Red Hairs 22. Sarah Bernhardt's Paris 41. Japanese Women in a Male Society 42. Divorce, Chinese Style
Science	2. From Astronomy to Astrophysics 3. Galileo's Science and the Trial of 1633 4. Halley and Post-Restoration Science 5. Darwin as a Geologist 6. Life's Recipe 7. The Green Revolution 9. Scientists Go North 14. Freudian Myths and Freudian Realities 19. West Africa's Mary Kingsley 43. The Natural History of AIDS		

The Industrial and Scientific Revolutions

Revolutions are generally thought to be sudden and violent affairs. The revolutions in industry and science were gradual, however, as Duncan Bythell indicates in his article about the cottage and factory systems. At the time, neither system was particularly pleasant for the workers, and on occasion there was violence. English textile workers, the Luddites, from 1811 to 1816 attracted severe repression after destroying factory machinery. In the long run the Industrial Revolution brought cheap consumer goods, a higher standard of living, and increased leisure. This required, however, a century and a half of rising social awareness, democracy, labor unrest, and social legislation.

Leading the way in the scientific revolution were the astronomers who followed the revelation of Copernicus about the nature of the solar system. Human beings were no longer at the center of the universe, but their minds were opened to an intellectual questing which continues to the present. This is the theme of James Trefil's article on astronomy. Galileo, who combined his technical skills of telescope construction with his scientific curiosity, discovered four new planets, the stars of the Milky Way, eighty stars in the constellation Orion, the mountains of the moon, and the moons of Jupiter, which suggested that Copernicus was correct. Galileo was a transitional man, however, with one foot in the Medieval world and the other in the modern. His arguments for the Copernican system, as William A. Wallace points out, were based more on intuition than fact.

Typical of the seventeenth-century scientist was Edmund Halley whose curiosity led him in many directions, not just to astronomy and the comet which bears his name. Noel Coley writes about Halley.

Sandra Herbert points out that although Charles Darwin gave us the theory of evolution, he thought of himself as a geologist. The curiosity and breadth of Darwin's mind contributed to this disturbing concept that heaven and earth were not created as the Bible had dictated. Ever since Darwin, there has been an unhealed split between science and religion.

In our own time biologists have unraveled nature's secret of reproduction by understanding the genetic codes of living beings. "Life's Recipe" summarizes the history of this discovery and points out the promise it holds for the improvement of life. Such benefit takes place when the findings of science can be applied (some people refer to applied science as technology). The green revolution reported by Robert E. Huke is an example of this powerful combination of science and technology. In this instance, because of uncontrolled conditions the impact on the production of food is hard to measure.

A similar combination of science and technology produced the computer which now is creating what some writers call the second industrial revolution. The first revolution substituted inanimate power and mechanization for muscle power and human dexterity; the second revolution replaced the control function of humans with automatic machines which could analyze and make decisions. This has raised the question about artificial intelligence and whether or not computers can think like human beings. Joseph Kroger explores the "new reality" of artificial intelligence. Behind the inquiries lies the foreboding possibility that human beings may have doomed themselves to obsolescence.

An issue for world history in this thrust of science and technology involves the conditions necessary to nurture it. The industrial and scientific revolutions took place in the civilization of the West. Why? Part of the reason is the intellectual ferment that bubbled after the Protestant Reformation broke the hammerlock of the Catholic Church on the minds of Europeans. Part of the reason is the growth of capitalism which provided monetary resources for investment in trade, new ideas, and inventions. Part of the reason can also be found in the development of liberal and egalitarian ideals which served to expand the opportunities of people. Being skeptical yet open seems to be an important ingredient in the success of the West.

Scientists and innovators tend to gather together in order to enjoy the stimulation of each other's thought. It might actually be a necessity for the advance of science and technology. Isaac Newton once commented, "If I have seen further it is by standing on the shoulders of giants." The article by Anthony de Souza demonstrates this phenomenon. Not only are there heavy concentrations of scientists in the United States, but also in the northern half of the globe. This underscores in a special way the growing split between the rich and poor nations, a split that also seems to cut between the north and the south.

Following 1500, the West began to reach out around the world. At the moment there was nothing particularly unique about the civilization with the exception of the scientific and technological attitude which was still unfolding. This

Unit 1

was the characteristic, however, which brought the West to global dominance.

Looking Ahead: Challenge Questions

What were the characteristics of the cottage industry and why was it replaced by the factory system?
Why was astronomy the leading area of scientific inquiry?
How "scientific" was the science of Galileo?
Why did Halley and Darwin succeed?
Why is the understanding about the genetic code considered an important discovery?
What is the green revolution and what happened to it?
Can a computer think?
Should a computer be allowed to think?
In regard to science, will the rich become richer? Why? What might be done about it? Should anything be done about it?

Article 1

COTTAGE INDUSTRY AND THE FACTORY SYSTEM

Duncan Bythell

AT THE CENTRE OF MOST PEOPLE'S picture of Britain's industrial revolution in the nineteenth century stands the dark, satanic mill, where an exploited and dispirited army of men, women and children is engaged for starvation wages in a seemingly endless round of drudgery: the pace of their labour is determined by the persistent pulse of the steam engine and accompanied by the ceaseless clanking of machines; and the sole beneficiary of their efforts is the grasping, tyrannical, licentious factory master, pilloried by Charles Dickens in that loud-mouthed hypocrite and philistine, Mr. Bounderby. Crude and exaggerated though this image is, it depicts very clearly the main features of the pattern of production which became widespread in the manufacturing industries, not only of Britain, but also of the other advanced countries, by the end of the nineteenth century. For it highlights the emergence of the factory, where hundreds labour together under one roof and one direction, as the normal type of work-unit; it stresses the new importance of complex machine-technology in the process of production; and it emphasises that, because ownership of these machines, of the building which houses them and the engine which drives them, rests with the private capitalist, there exists an unbridgeable gulf between him and his property-less wage-earning employees.

This system of production, which is usually assumed to have been pioneered and rapidly adopted in Britain's textile industries around the end of the eighteenth century, did not, of course, emerge in a wholly non-industrial world. The popular picture suggests that it replaced – or rather, brutally displaced – an earlier type of organisation, variously referred to as 'the domestic system', the 'outwork system', or simply as 'cottage industry', which differed totally from the factory system. Whereas the latter concentrates workers under one roof in an increasingly urban enviroment, the former disperses employment into the homes of the workers, most of whom live in the countryside. Although the modern mill is filled with the factory master's costly machinery, the domestic workshop houses simple and traditional hand-tools – the spinner's wheel, the weaver's loom, the cordwainer's bench, the nail-maker's forge, and the seamstress' humble pins and needles – which actually belong to the worker. And whilst the factory system implies clear class division, with the wage-earner firmly subordinated to, and perpetually at odds with, his employer, the domestic system gives the head of the household an independent, quasi-managerial status, which enables him to control his own time and to direct, in a 'natural' fatherly way, the efforts of his family team.

The unspoken assumption is that, in the undisciplined, fulfilling, and relatively classless world of cottage industry, the common man was certainly happier, even if he was materially worse off, than his grandson. Only in the last desperate phase, when the dwindling band of domestic handworkers found themselves competing hopelessly against the new generation of factory machine-minders, is the idyllic image tarnished; and the haunting picture of the doomed handloom weaver, striving in his cellar to match the output of his wife and children who have been forced into the factory, reinforces the notion that, between old and new systems, there is nothing but contrast, conflict, and competition.

Any concept of historical change based on snapshots taken on separate occasions tends to emphasise differences and discontinuities. In the caricature of the domestic and factory systems just presented, they appear to be completely antithetical. Yet on closer examination, the story of most industries which 'modernised' in the course of the nineteenth century is full of important elements of *continuity* and *complementarity* between the factory and the pre-factory stages of their development; and it is on these two dimensions, rather than on the stark contrasts suggested by the traditional stereotype, that I want to focus attention.

Let us consider continuity first. A number of historians have recently suggested that the existence of the domestic system of production in such industries as textiles was one of the main features

Factory spinning

1. Cottage Industry and the Factory System

distinguishing the pre-industrial economies of Europe from the Third World countries of today; and although they prefer the abstract concept of 'proto industrialisation' to the well-established and perfectly adequate term 'domestic system', they are essentially claiming that the industrial revolutions of the nineteenth century could not have taken place without the prior development of a form of production which, in their view, was to provide both the capital and the labour needed for modern industrial development.

In making this claim, proponents of the theory of 'proto industry' are drawing attention to one of the most important, but often misunderstood, features of the classic domestic system – the fact that it already showed a clear distinction between the capitalists who controlled it and the wage-earners who depended upon it for their livelihood. For the domestic system, no less than the factory system which replaced it, was a method of mass-production which enabled wealthy merchant-manufacturers to supply not only textile fabrics, but also items as diverse as ready-made clothes, hosiery, boots and shoes, and hardware, to distant markets at home and abroad. In order to do so, they, like the factory masters who followed them, bought the appropriate raw materials and hired wage-labour to convert them into finished products. The pay roll of some of these merchant-manufacturers could run into many hundreds: in the late 1830s, for example, Dixons of Carlisle, cotton manufacturers, employed 3,500 handloom weavers scattered over the border counties of England and Scotland and in Ulster; a decade or so later, Wards of Belper, hosiers, provided work for some 4,000 knitting frames in the counties of Derbyshire, Nottinghamshire, and Leicestershire; and as late as the 1870s, Eliza Tinsley and Co. put out work to 2,000 domestic nail- and chain-makers in the west Midlands.

To service and co-ordinate such large and scattered forces required an elaborate system of communication and control in which the key figures were the agents – variously known as 'putters-out', 'bagmen', and 'foggers' – who were the equivalents of the modern supervisor or shop-floor manager. Certainly, the workers whom these great men employed generally owned their own tools, although in the case of an elaborate piece of machinery like the knitting frame they often had to hire it; and most of them worked on their own premises – although, again, it was by no means rare for the individual weaver, knitter, or nail-maker to rent space and tools in another man's shop. But except in a few minor rural trades like straw-plaiting and lace-making in the south and east Midlands, they neither provided their own raw materials, nor had they any interest in marketing the goods they helped to make. They were, in short, wage-earners who happened to own some of the tools of their trade. But the trade in which they worked was organised by capitalists; and far from making goods to sell to local customers, they were often, all unknowing, supplying the wants of West Indian slaves and North American frontiersmen.

The crux of the argument about continuity between domestic and factory systems of mass-production turns on whether it was actually the case that the firms which set up the first modern factories in a particular industry were already active in it on a putting-out basis, and whether the last generation of domestic workers transformed themselves into the new race of factory hands. Of course, no one is maintaining that continuity was direct and complete in every single industry or region where such a transition occurred: indeed, there were areas such as East Anglia or the Cotswolds where the change-over simply did not take place, and where a once important industry gradually vanished as the old domestic system dwindled and died. But where 'modernisation' did happen in traditional outwork industries in the course of the nineteenth century, as it did in the textile industries of Lancashire and Yorkshire and in the hosiery trade of the east Midlands, historians seem to be agreed that it was existing firms which played a leading role, albeit cautiously and belatedly in some instances, in setting-up the factory system and in embodying some of their capital in buildings and machines; in other words the fortunes made, and the expertise in marketing and managing acquired, in the old system of production were important in enabling the new system to develop.

There is less agreement, however, as to how far the existing hand-workers in any particular industry really did shift over to the factory. The theory of 'proto industry' suggests that the domestic system had created a country-dwelling but landless proletariat in many ways at odds with the traditional rural society around them: they had only a minimal involvement in the agrarian economy, and were therefore rootless and prone to migration; they possessed manual skills irrelevant to farming activities; and as wage-earners, they were obliged to respond to the pressures and the opportunities of a market economy in which the price of survival was adaptability. In terms of both work-skills and mental outlook, that is to say, they were already well-equipped to form the first generation of the modern industrial labour force.

But did this actually happen? The traditional picture suggests not, because it depicts a stubborn refusal to come to terms with changed circumstances and, indeed, a downright hostility to 'machinery' which, in the Luddite movement of 1811-16 in the Midlands and the various outbreaks of loom-smashing in Lancashire and elsewhere, sometimes erupted in violence. Clearly, the worker's readiness to change with the times depended partly on age, and partly on opportunity. Case studies based on census returns for Lancashire weaving villages during the crucial phase of transition in the middle of the nineteenth century suggest that, once a powerloom shed had been started locally, the younger married men were ready enough to take work in it, but that the elderly were either reluctant to do so, or were debarred by the employer, and therefore stuck to the handloom. But until there was a mill virtually on the spot, most of these villagers believed they had little option but to stick to the handloom, and for want of other opportunity they continued to bring their children up to it. Probably the most important strand of continuity in the labour force was in fact provided by the children of the last generation of handworkers: by and large, a trade dies out because it stopped recruiting sometime before; and the demise of occupations like handloom weaving was finally assured when families were willing and able to put their offspring into something different, instead of forcing them to follow automatically in father's footsteps.

By highlighting the division between capital and labour which characterised the domestic no less than the factory system of production, and by considering the continuity which this engendered, the new theory of 'proto industry' has pinpointed certain popular misconceptions about the nature of cottage

1. THE INDUSTRIAL AND SCIENTIFIC REVOLUTIONS

industry. First of all, it must be clear that when economic historians refer to 'outwork' or 'cottage industry' they are *not* talking about a world where each family simply makes manufactured goods for its own use – although in even the most advanced societies elements of the home-made and the do-it-yourself survive. Nor are they discussing the self-employed craftsman or genuine artisan – the village shoe-maker and tailor, or the more sophisticated urban wig-maker or cabinet-maker – who produced and sold 'one-off' goods directly to the order of their local customers, and whose successors are still to be found in some parts of the modern economy. Indeed – and this is a second error which needs to be corrected – in the strict sense they are not dealing with 'skill' or 'craft' at all. As a method of mass-production, the greater part of cottage industry involved the making of plain, simple, inexpensive goods by hands which, although they became more nimble and adept with experience, had neither needed nor received much initial training. Weaving heavy woollens and hammering nails and chains required a certain strength; but weaving plain calico, knitting coarse stockings, sewing buttons on shirts, plaiting straw, and sticking matchboxes together with glue called for neither brain nor brawn. A seven-year apprenticeship to learn the 'mysteries' of most domestic industries was unnecessary, when the work merely involved the monotonous repetition of a few simple movements of the fingers; and because the work was unskilled and undemanding it was considered particularly suitable for women and children. Domestic industry, like factory industry, involved the worker in much mindless drudgery; the chief difference was that, in working at home with hand-tools, the wage-earner could go at his or her own pace, instead of having to keep up with the steam engine.

Thirdly, just as we need to abandon the notion that the domestic system was all about skilled craftsmen, so we must reject the idea that it was predominantly about 'men' at all. One of the advantages which the old terms 'domestic system' and 'cottage industry' have over 'proto industry' is that they suggest an important feature which old-style mass-production shared with the early textile mills: a domestic or cottage workshop called on the efforts of housewife, grandparents, and children of both sexes, as well as those of the household's head. Thus the average weaving or knitting family would run two or three looms or frames, and in addition would operate any ancillary machinery needed to prepare or finish the work. Because it worked as a team, the domestic work unit could also practice division of labour, so that each member could specialise on just one stage in the sequence of production. Like any other family business, a workshop involved in the domestic system was a collective enterprise to which all contributed who could: and only when the household included no children old enough to do even the simplest tasks did it depend for its income on what a man could earn by his own unaided efforts. Because the capitalist-controlled outwork industries made particular use of women's and children's labour in this way, female workers were generally in a clear majority in the work force; and in the mass-production section of the needlework trades, where outwork remained particularly important until late in the nineteenth century, and which included men's tailoring and shirt-making as well as dress-making and lace stitching, the preponderance of women was especially striking.

Fourthly, we must not imagine that, in a capitalist controlled industrial system such as outwork was, relations between masters and operatives were marked by much sweetness and light. Since the main tie between them was the cash nexus, disputes about wages could be frequent and bitter. Most employers in the industries which used the domestic system operated in a tough competitive environment, and their likely reaction to a spell of bad trading conditions would be to cut the piece-rates they paid their workers. Most of the scattered rural outworkers were disorganised and docile, and could offer little, if any, resistance; and in any case, for women and children a pittance was deemed better than no work at all. But the adult men – especially those who lived in the towns, and did the better-class work which needed more strength or skill – were another matter. They had a clear

The weaver at his domestic hand loom (above) contrasts sharply with work on a factory power loom (below).

1. Cottage Industry and the Factory System

conception of the work and wages proper for a man, and they were better able to take collective action against underpaying masters and weak-willed blacklegs who broke the conventional rules.

As a result, at different times in the late eighteenth and early nineteenth centuries, fierce strikes broke out in such towns as Manchester, Coventry, Barnsley and Norwich, major centres of handloom weaving; among the urban framework knitters of Nottingham and Leicester; and among the nail-makers of the Black Country. At a time when formal trade unionism was a shadowy affair, and in difficult political and economic circumstances, some at least of Britain's industrial outworkers played their part in sustaining patterns of collective bargaining which, *faute de mieux*, sometimes involved great violence; whilst the support these disgruntled men gave to the various campaigns for parliamentary reform between the 1790s and the 1850s has been frequently noted by historians.

Once we have abandoned such misconceptions about the nature of the domestic system as it had come to exist by the end of the eighteenth century, it is easier to see the similarities and the points of continuity between it and the factory system which was eventually and gradually to supersede it. And when we realise that the domestic system, far from being some prehistoric monster which expired when the first cotton factory was built, actually expanded and persisted in many industries and regions until well into the second half of the nineteenth century, we become aware, not only that the two types of mass-production overlapped in time, but also that they complemented each other,

(Above left) The Domestic Rope Maker; from *The Book of Trades*, 1804. (Above right) Making ropes by Huddart's Machinery.
(Below left) An outworker making pins at home: (below right) a needle pointer at work in a factory in Redditch, Worcester.

1. THE INDUSTRIAL AND SCIENTIFIC REVOLUTIONS

rather than competed. The textile industries usually occupy the forefront of any discussion of the domestic and factory systems; and in view of their wide geographic dispersal, their rapid expansion, and the hundreds of thousands they had come to employ by the late eighteenth century, this is entirely appropriate. But because, starting with the spinning branch of the British cotton industry in the 1770s, it was in these industries that the complete triumph of the factory system was achieved earliest, attention has been deflected from the many other trades – particularly shoe-making, clothing, and some branches of hardware – where the domestic system actually became more, rather than less, important. For although the first half of the nineteenth century saw the disappearance into the factory first of spinning and then of weaving in Lancashire and Yorkshire, it also witnessed the expansion of mass-production by outwork methods in the ready-made clothing trades and in the boot and shoe industries. And apart from the fact that these growing industries increased output by traditional rather than modern methods, there were other, less expansionary trades – such as Midlands hosiery and Black Country nail-making – which remained fossilised at the 'domestic' stage of development until well after 1850. In addition, the latter part of the nineteenth century actually saw a number of new, small-scale manufactures, such as paperbag and cardboard-box making, establish themselves as cottage industries. Thus, if outwork had more or less disappeared from the staple textile industries by the 1850s, it was more firmly entrenched than ever in and around many of the industrial towns of the Midlands and the south of England, and, above all, in what were to become known as the 'sweated trades' of London. Why was this?

The pioneering experience of the textile industries suggests some of the answers. Contrary to popular belief, even in the cotton industry, the transition from the domestic to the factory system was a slow, piecemeal affair, which took three generations; and in wool, linen and silk, the process was even more protracted. The reason was simple: the first power-driven machines of the 1770s revolutionised *spinning* only; and by making it possible to produce thread on a scale and at a price which would have been inconceivable in the days of the spinning wheel, they simply created a good deal more work for a great many more workers – in this case, the weavers – at the next stage in the production process. And so long as enough extra weavers could be found at wages the employers were prepared to pay, there was no need to think of replacing the handloom with some labour-saving device, as yet uninvented. Thus between 1780 and 1820, the growth of spinning factories marched *pari passu* with a vast increase in the number of handloom weavers' shops; and technical progress in one section of the industry merely led to the multiplication of traditional handwork in associated sections.

The Croppers of the West Riding of Yorkshire were much involved in the machine-wrecking Luddite movement of 1812.

The same thing was to happen in other industries later: when lace-making was mechanised in Nottingham from the 1820s, there was a consequent increase in the amount of stitching, finishing and mending for hand-sewers in their homes; when machines were first used to cut out the components of a stock-sized shoe or coat, they made more unskilled assembly work for domestic workers; and even when the sewing machine had transformed the traditional needlework trades, it did not necessarily drive them out of the home into the factory, because, as a compact, hand-powered, and relatively inexpensive tool, it could be used in a domestic workshop as effectively as in a large factory. In all these ways, factory and domestic systems often co-existed and complemented each other in a given industry. Since it was rarely either possible or necessary for new techniques to be introduced simultaneously at every stage in the process of manufacture, flexible combinations of centralised factory work at one stage, and cottage industry at the next, were perfectly practicable.

There was often a regional dimension to the co-existence of these two types of mass-production, and it was here that elements of competition emerged between them. In the classic case of cotton weaving, for example, the handloom survived as the dominant machine in some parts of Lancashire for almost a generation after it had largely given way to the powerloom in others: in large towns such as Stockport, Oldham and Blackburn, factory production was taken up in the 1820s by manufacturers who already operated spinning mills; but it made little progress in the small towns and villages of north-east Lancashire, such as Padiham, Colne and Haggate before the 1840s. In part, this reflected local differences in the availability of labour and capital, for the more remote rural areas were richer in the former than in the latter. But independent of such regional differences, there was also a qualitative side to this 'staggered' adoption of the powerloom, because the early, clumsy factory looms could cope better with the plain types of cloth than with fancy or patterned goods. Other industries were later to show similar disparities in the rate at which different districts and sections adopted new techniques: for example, the boot and shoe industry of Leicester

1. Cottage Industry and the Factory System

Merchants in the Cloth Hall, Leeds in 1814. Merchants used cottage industries as a method of mass-production to supply their buyers.

seems to have relied more on factory production and less on outwork than did that of Northampton in the second half of the nineteenth century; whilst in the 1890s, cottage industry was more apparent in the ready-made clothing trade of London than in that of Leeds.

In short, the domestic system of mass-production in British industry took a long time a-dying during the nineteenth century. It might expand in one trade at the very time that it was contracting in another; in some industries, it could enjoy a harmonious co-existence with factory production for many years, whilst elsewhere it might struggle on in arduous competition for a generation or more. Why was this? How could this technically primitive form of large-scale production remain viable for so long in important parts of the world's first industrial economy?

To find the answer, we must try to fathom the minds of the entrepreneurs in the different industries, as they calculated how best, in a complex and competitive world, to get their goods to market with least cost and least trouble to themselves. A manufacturer who had grown up with the domestic system as the dominant mode of production in his trade would need strong inducements to abandon it, because under normal circumstances it offered him many advantages. If his employees provided their own tools and workrooms, he himself was spared the need to tie up his own capital in bricks and mortar and in machinery; and in times of periodic trade depression or slack seasonal demand – and most of these industries were subject to one or other of these risks, if not, indeed, to both of them – it was the worker, not his employer, who suffered when plant and equipment were standing idle. It was not that these great merchant-manufacturers lacked capital – indeed it required remarkably little fixed capital in most of these industries to build or rent a small factory and fill it with new or second-hand machinery; nor was it generally the case that appropriate new techniques were not available – the time-lag between invention and adoption of a new machine is a recurrent feature in many of these trades; it was rather the case that their capital under the domestic system was embodied in unused raw materials, goods 'in the make', and stocks in the warehouse.

Nevertheless, because it involved more sophisticated machinery, the application of power, and the construction of large, purpose-built work premises, the factory system of production was capital-intensive, rather than labour-intensive. By contrast, what an employer had to rely on to keep cottage industry viable was an abundance of cheap, unskilled, and unorganised labour. So long as he could find enough workers who had no choice but to take his work at the wages he was prepared to offer – no matter how low these might be – he could meet his production targets and reap his expected profits. From the late eighteenth to the late nineteenth centuries, there were many regions of Britain which could provide just such supplies of labour: a high and sustained rate of population increase, together with the greater commercialisation of agriculture, tended to create pools of unemployed or under-employed workers in many rural areas; and in so far as these impoverished country people moved off to the towns in search of more work and better wages, they often merely added to the chaos and confusion in the unskilled urban labour markets.

But what kept the domestic system alive after the mid-nineteenth century more than anything else was the continued availability – long after most adult men had deserted these low paid, dead-end jobs – of female and child labour: incapable of collective self-defence, and often deliberately ignored by their better organised menfolk; accustomed to regarding any earnings, however minute, as a worthwhile contribution to family income; and often only able to work on a part-time or casual basis – they were ideal for many employers' purposes. And in a perverse way, because it thrived on family labour, the domestic system actually helped to perpetuate its own labour force: because cottage industry, by enabling the whole household to earn, acted as a great inducement to early marriages and large families, and thus contributed to the 'population explosion' which was so important a feature of Britain's industrial revolution.

Because labour could be much cheaper in one part of the country than in another, an old-fashioned employer who stuck to outwork could still hope to compete with his more ambitious and enterprising fellows elsewhere who had switched over to factory production. Only in the last quarter of the nineteenth century did a combination of new circumstances – including rural depopulation, compulsory schooling (which both kept young children out of the labour market and widened their horizons), rising real incomes (which made small supplementary earnings less essential to a family), and more 'chivalrous' male

11

1. THE INDUSTRIAL AND SCIENTIFIC REVOLUTIONS

Gathering Teasels in the West Riding of Yorkshire, an aquatint after George Walker. Teasels are still used to raise the nap on woollen cloth.

(Below) The Preemer Boy, 1814; aquatint after George Walker. 'Preeming' is detaching, with an iron comb, the bits of wool on the teasel.

only stay in business if they themselves adopted American methods of production. Both the cotton manufacturers of the 1820s and the boot and shoe manufacturers of the 1890s had to overcome strong opposition from workers still suspicious of machinery and still attached (in spite of the precarious economic position in which it left them) to the domestic system: but once the entrepreneurs in any industry had concluded, for whatever reasons, that the disadvantages of cottage industry outweighed the benefits, its days were numbered.

From the worker's point of view, even if we forget the caricature, the dark satanic mill offered an uninviting prospect; but it is hard to escape the conclusion that the domestic system was in many ways even less agreeable. Even where cottage workers were not directly competing with factory workers – and I have suggested that it would be wrong to put too much emphasis on this side of the story – most of them were poorly paid, and likely to be alternately overworked and under-employed. Worst of all, they were subject to all kinds of abuses, not only from employers and their agents, but often from heads of households and fathers of families who connived, however reluctantly, in the exploitation of their own wives and children. Men may have been unwilling to accept the separation of home and workplace which the gradual replacement of the domestic system by the factory system involved: but in its long-term implications for family life, it was probably one of the most beneficial, as well as one of the most fundamental, of all the changes brought about by the industrial revolution.

attitudes towards women as workers – help gradually to eliminate some of the sources of cheap labour and thus undermine one of the domestic system's chief props.

Changes in market conditions, as well as the increasing difficulty of finding suitable labour, could also be instrumental in persuading entrepreneurs to abandon old-style mass-production in favour of the factory. When, for example, attractive new export markets opened up for the English cotton industry in Latin America in the early 1820s, Lancashire manufacturers knew that they would be better able to increase output by introducing powerlooms than by seeking out more handloom weavers at higher wages; and when, more than two generations later, British boot and shoe manufacturers were faced with an 'invasion' of their own home market by cheap mass-produced, factory-made American imports, they recognised that they could

FOR FURTHER READING:
D. Bythell, *The Sweated Trades* (Batsford, 1978); J. L. and B. Hammond, *The Skilled Labourer* (London, 1919); G. Stedman Jones, *Outcast London* (Oxford University Press, 1971); P. Kriedte, H. Medick and J. Schlumbohm, *Industrialization before Industrialization* (Cambridge University Press, 1981); D. Levine, *Family Formation in an Age of Nascent Capitalism* (Academic Press, 1977); J. M. Prest, *The Industrial Revolution in Coventry* (Oxford University Press, 1960); E. P. Thompson, *The Making of the English Working Class* (Gollancz, 1963; Penguin Books).

FROM ASTRONOMY TO ASTROPHYSICS

James Trefil

James S. Trefil, is professor of physics at the University of Virginia. Born in Chicago, Illinois, he received a B.S. (1960) from the University of Illinois, a B.A. and an M.A. (1962) from Oxford University, and an M.S. (1964) and a Ph.D. (1966) from Stanford University. He is the author of Meditations at Ten Thousand Feet *(1986).*

Nicolaus Copernicus (1473–1543) was a Pole, a churchman, an intellectual recluse, and a somewhat enigmatic figure. Much is unknown about him, yet he sparked a scientific revolution that powerfully influenced the subsequent five centuries. Today, looking back at his life and work, it is difficult to comprehend the magnitude of the Copernican Revolution, how momentous a change it really was for 16th-century Europe. But altering civilized man's view of the cosmos is exactly what he did.

Guided by his uncle, a Roman Catholic bishop, Copernicus was elected to a position as canon (business manager) at the Cathedral of Frauenburg in his native Poland. He traveled widely, studied in Italy, and was a model scholar and churchman. From roughly 1512 on, he developed a scheme of a planetary system in which the planets moved and the Sun stood still. He confided his manuscript to a printer only in 1540, at age 67. As the story goes, he received a copy of his published book on the day he died, three years later.

The book, *On the Revolutions of the Celestial Spheres*, is an odd mixture of revolutionary and traditional ideas. Since Claudius Ptolemy (circa A.D. 100–178), the ancient Greek astronomer who advocated a geocentric model of the universe, Europeans had envisioned the Sun, stars, and planets embedded in concentric spheres around the Earth, with God, in effect, cranking the mechanism from the outside.

Copernicus realized that the daily motion of the stars across the sky resulted from the Earth's rotation, and that the complex motions of planets were the natural effect of their movement around the Sun. His system, of course, was not identical to the modern one. To account for the true planetary orbits, Copernicus had to put his planets on epicycles (small circles centered on the rims of larger ones). The centers of the larger circles lay not in the Sun, but at a point in space between the Sun and the Earth. Even if it could not be proved, his view had an immense allure for adventuresome minds.

Copernicus's scheme was only somewhat simpler than Ptolemy's, but it prompted astronomy students (at least from 1543 on) to realize that they could question traditional wisdom. Human reason was freeing itself from burdens of the past—another major step for Europeans who had just experienced the throes of the Reformation, Martin Luther's break with the monolithic authoritarianism of Rome.

Another consequence of the Copernican system—one often overlooked—is that it expanded mankind's concept of the universe. Formerly, with a seemingly stationary Earth, the realm of the stars lay just beyond Saturn's orbit; the entire universe seemed only as big as the solar system. But with Earth orbiting the Sun, the stars had to

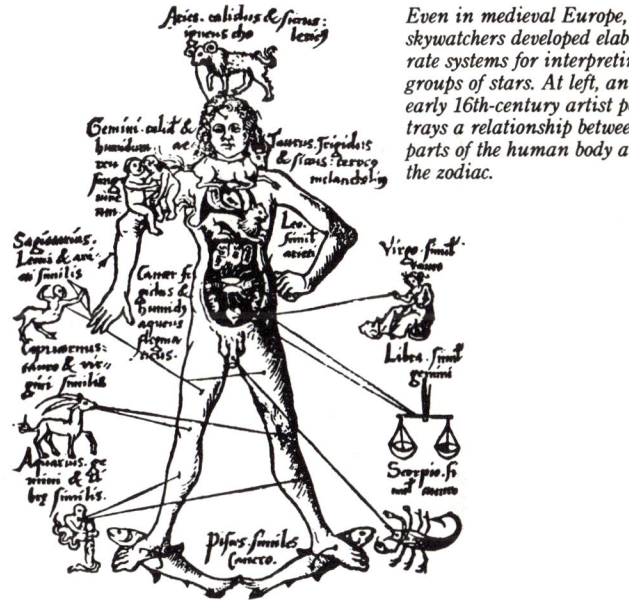

Even in medieval Europe, skywatchers developed elaborate systems for interpreting groups of stars. At left, an early 16th-century artist portrays a relationship between parts of the human body and the zodiac.

be far away to appear stationary. In one fell swoop, Copernicus moved the Earth from the center and set it moving in a new heaven of wider horizons. He and Christopher Columbus were contemporaries. Each man revealed a new world to Europe—but Copernicus was charting a realm whose outer boundaries have yet to be discovered.

As it happened, *On the Revolutions of the Celestial Spheres* spread quickly throughout Europe, encountering far less ecclesiastical opposition than Galileo would later face. For one thing, Copernicus was well connected in the church. For another, the unsigned preface of his book presents the Copernican system as a mathematical exercise, not necessarily a statement about the real world. This pretension left plenty of maneuver room for theologians and scholars.

Among Copernicus's readers was the Danish nobleman Tycho Brahe (1546–1601), who had a lifelong obsession with measuring the heavens accurately. During the 16th century, observation was not much more accurate than it had been during the time of Ptolemy. Tycho, born before the invention of the telescope, pushed the accuracy of naked-eye astronomy to its limit. He built astronomical instruments, such as a huge brass quadrant and a four-cubit sextant, to reduce errors associated with reading small scales. He compensated for the expansion and shrinkage of his brass instruments due to temperature changes, devising tables to correct for these effects. He even built an underground observatory to reduce wind vibrations.

1. THE INDUSTRIAL AND SCIENTIFIC REVOLUTIONS

In part, the quest for precision grew out of the desire to distinguish between the Copernican and Ptolemaic systems, and because people of the mid-16th century had witnessed some unusual events in the heavens. On November 11, 1572, for instance, a new star appeared in the constellation of Cassiopeia—one so bright that during the next month it could be seen in daylight. Repairing to his beautifully crafted instruments, Tycho took a series of readings. He established beyond a doubt that the object (now called Tycho's supernova) moved less than the most distant planet in the sky and was therefore beyond the sphere of the stars. This feat established the 25-year-old Dane as one of Europe's premier astronomers.

So impressed was King Frederick II of Denmark that he installed Tycho on the Baltic island of Hven and provided the money to construct the world's largest astronomical observatory. There Tycho built instruments and gathered data unprecedented in both volume and accuracy.

All was well, until Tycho ran afoul of Frederick's successor, Christian IV, over a number of issues—such as whether or not Tycho had the right to throw peasants into his private dungeon. So the astronomer packed up his data, instruments, and court jester, and quit Hven for the court of Emperor Rudolf II in Prague.

Tycho's Undoing

All told, Tycho lived an unusual life. At an early age, he was kidnapped by his wealthy and childless uncle Jorgen, who raised him in a castle in Tostrup. Sent to the University of Copenhagen to study jurisprudence, Tycho—profoundly impressed by an eclipse of the Sun in 1560—instead spent his time studying the stars. Prone to emotional outbursts, at the age of 20 he dueled a fellow student over the question of who was a better mathematician. During the battle, Tycho lost a piece of his nose and had to wear a gold alloy prosthesis. Even his death was bizarre. At a banquet attended by much of Prague's nobility, he partook copiously of Bohemian beer. Not wishing to appear impolite—so the story goes—he ate and drank without excusing himself. Bladder stones may have been his undoing; he fell into a fever that night and died 11 days later.

Tycho's data tables went to an impecunious Austrian mathematician he had hired after his arrival in Prague—Johannes Kepler.

Kepler (1571–1630) was a mystic by nature. But, when confronted with all the data that Tycho had collected over a lifetime, he felt compelled to question some of his basic assumptions. Instead of trying to force Tycho's data into preconceived patterns, Kepler returned to the basics and considered which shapes best described the motions of the known planets.

Galileo as Martyr

Kepler's results are stated in what are now known as Kepler's first and second laws of planetary motion. The first law says that a planet's orbit assumes the shape of an ellipse—rather than a circle—with the Sun at one focus; the second law indicates that planets move faster when near the Sun than they do when farther away. In other words, as a planet passes near to the Sun it "swings around," speeding up as it does so.

Kepler published these two laws in 1609. A third and final law was published in 1619, relating the length of a planet's "year" to its distance from the Sun. Thus it became possible to shed excess conceptual baggage that scientists had developed to justify a false notion, namely, that celestial objects move along circular orbits.

Following the observational work of Copernicus, Tycho, and Kepler, Galileo Galilei (1564–1642) was the first to study the sky through a telescope.

Ironically, Galileo is one of those men in history who is famous for the wrong reasons. Because of his notorious trial in 1633 by the Roman Inquisition he has, perhaps undeservedly, become enshrined as a "martyr of science." Legend has it that he stood alone as a champion of the heliocentric universe against the forces of dogma-

---

GOING BACK TO STONEHENGE

Today most people take the sky for granted. Not so the ancients. They used the sky as clock, calendar, navigational aid, and oracle.

Among the oldest observatories, according to British astronomer Gerald S. Hawkins, is Stonehenge—a series of concentric circles, marked by large stones, standing on a plain near Salisbury, England. In 1963, Hawkins argued that Stonehenge enabled skywatchers, perhaps as early as 3100 B.C., to mark the solstices (when viewed correctly, the Sun rises over a 35-ton Heel Stone), the lunar cycles, and eclipses. Similar ruins stand around the world, in places as disparate as Scotland, Kenya, and the central United States.

Cro-Magnon people were probably the first humans to note the stars. Animal bones with markings that correspond to lunar phases, dated 9,000 to 30,000 years old, have been found in Europe. Between 3000 B.C. and 2000 B.C., Babylonians in Mesopotamia devised the first systematic calendar, based on 235 lunar months (29.5 days apiece) in 19 solar years. Between 1646 and 1626 B.C., they made the first detailed astronomical records, and later (circa 400 B.C.) used mathematics to predict celestial events. They were astrologers too. Atop immense, stepped, mud-brick towers, such as the ziggurat of Ur in southeastern Iraq (construction began in 2100 B.C.), Babylonian priests prayed to the Moon god Nanna-Sin while surveying stars.

•

Ancient Egyptians also were stargazers. Many of their great monuments—such as the Great Pyramid of Cheops and the temple at Karnak—are aligned with key positions of the Sun, Moon, and stars. Yet, despite Egypt's creation of a "modern" calendar (12 30-day months, plus five extra days), the Babylonians surpassed the Egyptians in astronomical sophistication.

The Greeks were the first scientists, not only recording celestial motion but wondering why stars and planets moved along particular paths. They sought physical rather than religious explanations. Thales of Miletus (circa 585 B.C.) predicted eclipses; Pythagoras (circa 580–500 B.C.) and his school deduced that the Earth is round, and Eratosthenes of Cyrene (circa 276–194 B.C.) devised a method for measuring its circumference at the equator—250,000 stadia (the width of a stadium, 607 feet), a figure quite close to the actual 24,902 miles. By the second century A.D., Claudius Ptolemy summarized four centuries of Greek astronomy in his treatise *Almagest*. As early as 720 B.C., Chinese astronomers kept watch for "portentous" events: eclipses, comets, meteors, planetary alignments. But their observations were not "scientific"; they tended simply to record, not analyze, unusual phenomena.

The Mayan Caracol of Chichén Itzá, as it may have appeared circa 1000 A.D.

In Central America, circa 1000 A.D., Mayan astronomers on the Yucatán Peninsula constructed an observatory, the Caracol of Chichén Itzá. It demonstrates in its architecture alone—through alignments with certain stars and planets—a knowledge of solstices, lunar cycles, and the motions of the Morning and Evening Star (Venus). Their astronomical records, detailed on the bark leaves of an almanac called the Dresden Codex (it is now in a Dresden museum), reveal great sophistication: They calculated the length of a 365-day solar year, a 29.5 day lunar cycle, and the cycles of Venus within minutes of their true periods.

Throughout North America, Indian tribes, too, practiced astronomy. Atop Medicine Mountain, in Wyoming's Bighorn Range, lies a circular arrangement of "loaf-sized" rocks. This "medicine wheel," in which 28 35-foot-long lines of rocks, seemingly spokes, reach out from a central hub to a surrounding circle of rocks, is believed to have been used for astronomical purposes. Similarly, the Hohokam Indian structure at Casa Grande near Phoenix, Arizona, contains 14 windowlike openings, eight of which are aligned with the rising and setting Sun during solstices and equinoxes. Other Sun-marking sites exist at Chaco Canyon, New Mexico, and Hovenweep, Utah. And, at Cahokia, Illinois, the American "woodhenge"—concentric circles comprised of 49 poles, with the largest circle measuring 410 feet across—is thought to have been a tool for measuring solstices and equinoxes, and possibly to predict eclipses.

2. From Astronomy to Astrophysics

tism and authority. This is unfortunate, because Galileo did many other things during his lifetime that were worthy of lasting fame. He was, for example, the founder of modern experimental physics. He also made the first break with naked-eye astronomy by starting a systematic study of the heavens with a telescope. He was largely responsible for bringing the ideas of Copernicus to the attention of the intellectual community of 17th-century Europe. It was this seemingly heretical activity, of course, that eventually caused him to draw the attention of the Inquisition.

The son of a musician in Pisa, Galileo studied at the local university and embarked on a career teaching mathematics. As the story goes, his early interest in physics is associated with observations conducted at the Pisa cathedral. He noted that a cathedral lamp required the same amount of time to complete a swing no matter how wide the range of the swing. Later, Galileo suggested that this principle could be used to develop a pendulum clock. His studies of physics and mathematics helped him to win a position in the Medici court in Florence in 1610.

While in Venice in 1609, Galileo learned of the recent invention of the telescope in the United Netherlands. He devised a superior lensmaking technique and produced a telescope capable of magnifying an image 32 times. It was an immense step forward. Astronomers could thereupon examine the heavens with more than the power of the unaided human eye. He opened a window on the cosmos and was not slow to exploit it.

During the years after the building of his telescope, Galileo and others saw many new things. Mountains loomed on the Moon where no mountains were supposed to be. The apparently unblemished Sun had spots. Venus was seen to go through phases as does the Moon. Galileo observed the four largest moons of Jupiter and caught a hint of Saturn's rings. As has happened ever since, whenever a new window on the sky is opened, the first glimpse shows an undreamed-of richness and complexity.

Why were these discoveries so important? The first two—lunar mountains and sunspots—showed that the Greek ideal of heavenly perfection was incorrect. Also, the fact that Venus could be observed to pass through Moonlike phases proved that at least one other planet orbited the Sun. And Jupiter's four moons belied the assumption that everything orbited Earth. These facts had enormous psychological impact during the 17th century.

Enter Newton

Galileo announced the first of these findings in his book *The Starry Messenger*. He called Jupiter's satellites the Sidera Medici (Medicean Stars), attempting to flatter his hoped-for patrons, the Medici family. The ploy worked. He received support from Florence, and today those satellites are called the Galilean Moons.

Furthermore, the maestro had a way with words, writing—unlike Copernicus and Kepler—in the vernacular, Italian in this case. Through his writings, Copernican ideas spread throughout Europe. Galileo's trial did not curb the spread of these ideas—indeed, its only effect was to guarantee that the center of astronomical studies would move across the Alps to the Protestant countries of Europe and eventually to England.

In the same year that Galileo died, 1642, Isaac Newton was born. It is a coincidence, of course, but one that symbolizes the continuity of the development of scientific ideas about the universe during the 17th century.

The scientific revolution of the 17th century culminated in the work of Isaac Newton, who developed a view of the universe still held today. His most important contribution to astronomy is the law of universal gravitation, which states that any two objects in the universe will experience a force of attraction proportional to their masses and to the distance between them. The laws that Kepler deduced from Tycho's data can also be derived from Newton's work.

In later years, a legend grew about how Newton realized that one gravitational law governed the entire universe. The part that sticks in the public fancy is the fall of an apple in an orchard.

To understand Newton's insight in that orchard, one must remember that, until his time, the science of astronomy and the science of mechanics (which dealt with the motions of things on Earth) were totally separated. No one had yet connected the stately turning of the planets with the fall of an apple on Earth. Newton's gift to humanity

17th-century Chinese skywatchers at the Imperial Observatory observed the stars with astronomical instruments, some imported from Europe.

was to show that such artificial distinctions do not hold in nature—that the universe is a single, seamless web, and that the forces guiding the Moon also cause apples to fall.

To demonstrate the unity of the gravitational force, Newton imagined what would happen if a cannon were placed on a mountaintop, firing successive projectiles, with an increase in the charge of each shot. Eventually, with just enough gunpowder, the cannonball would fly around the world, overcoming gravity's downward pull and maintaining a constant altitude.

This hypothetical missile, he concluded, was behaving like the Moon, or any other satellite. In his own words, "[I] compared the force requisite to keep the Moon in her Orb with the force of gravity at the surface of the Earth, and found them to answer pretty nearly." In effect, Newton had seen that the Moon and the Earth continually fall toward each other, offset by their orbital motion. With this realization, any simple distinction between terrestrial and celestial science—a notion accepted since ancient Greece—crumbled. Using calculus, a method that he originated, Newton worked out the planets' orbits and demonstrated that they followed Kepler's laws.

His vision of the solar system in perpetual motion led naturally to a model of the universe resembling a geared clock. Once the solar system had been created, its future history lay ordained. But a debate ensued along these lines: mathematician G. W. Leibniz argued that God had made an automated universe; theologian Samuel Clarke contended that God was continually adjusting the works. Either way, the Creator had more leisure than with Ptolemy's system, which ascribed to God (or appointed angels) the turning of cranks. Newton believed that God created a mechanistic universe and then fine-tuned the machinery while it operated.

It is difficult to overemphasize the importance of this new scientific movement, and of Newton's place as its prime mover. He completed the work begun by Copernicus and his successors.

In fact, the Newtonian Synthesis gave rise to another powerful idea: Events anywhere in the universe can be studied in laboratories on Earth. And, if nature's laws are constant, then all events of the past—right back to the creation of the universe—are accessible to investigation.

It is comforting, in the face of such advances in scientific knowledge, to reflect on how it all started. An obscure Polish scholar was able to set in motion a scientific revolution capped by, of all things, a view of space and time based on an inspired interpretation of a fallen apple in an English orchard.

On to Mount Palomar

During the 200 years that followed Newton's discovery of the workings of the solar system, astronomers developed two improved tools. First, bigger, and sometimes better, telescopes allowed astron-

1. THE INDUSTRIAL AND SCIENTIFIC REVOLUTIONS

omers to collect more light from objects farther away. And second, improved theoretical tools, based on calculus and Newton's laws, enabled scientists to analyze (and therefore predict) the behavior of more complex celestial phenomena. The delicate interplay of instrumental and theoretical advances was like a waltz through history—first one partner would lead, then the other.

Galileo turned a primitive telescope toward the heavens. But to go beyond Galileo, it was necessary to build better telescopes. This was no easy task.

Newton saw no future in the type of telescope used by Galileo. Called the refractor, it uses a series of lenses to collect and focus incoming light. Unfortunately, it also suffers from a defect known as "chromatic aberration," in which colored fringes appear around an image's edges. Consequently, Newton built a telescope without lenses. Such a *reflector* telescope uses curved mirrors, made of polished metal, to focus light at the back of the instrument. However, his first models had little more power than did Galileo's refractor.

By the mid-18th century, techniques for fashioning mirrors from metal had been perfected. By the 20th century, mirrors were ground from glass and then coated with reflective metal. Today, such highly efficient light collectors are the workhorses of astronomy. The most famous (and most productive) of these giants is the 200-inch telescope located at the Hale Observatory on Mount Palomar near San Diego, California.

Completed in 1948, Hale's main mirror is 17 feet (five meters) across and weighs 14.5 tons. Technicians ground away more than five tons of glass from the original 20-ton disk to form a concave surface, which became reflective when polished and coated with a thin layer of aluminum. To construct the immense disk, molten Pyrex glass was poured into a form, then allowed to cool for eight months to keep the glass from cracking.

The telescope itself is so big that at one time an astronomer sat inside it to observe the stars. Today, however, a computer monitors observations. It is so well balanced that an electric motor no more powerful than one found in a food processor can rotate it. Although the Soviets now have a larger optical telescope operating in the Caucasus Mountains, technical troubles have limited its usefulness.

Improved telescope designs enabled astronomers to expand their inventory of the solar system. William Herschel (1738–1822), born in Germany, was a musician-turned-astronomer who lived in England during the 18th century. He built his own reflecting telescopes because he could not afford to buy one made by craftsmen. Believing that studying the heavens was one way to peer into the mind of God, Herschel set out to catalogue everything in the sky.

Finding Neptune

On March 13, 1781, Herschel observed a fuzzy object, hitherto unknown. His telescope allowed him to see that this new object was not just a point (as most stars appear), but something with an extended structure. Since the object moved against a background of fixed stars, it had to be a planet or a comet. And, given that 2,000 years of skywatching had turned up only six planets, European astronomers looked carefully before concluding that Herschel really had found another planet—one located too far from the Sun to be seen by the naked eye. It was christened Uranus, and became the first planet discovered in modern times.

Astronomers throughout Europe worked to chart its orbit. It quickly became apparent that applying Newton's law of gravitation to the new planet did not give a correct description of its path in the sky. Working independently, an English and a French astronomer came to the same conclusion. In 1845, John Couch Adams and Urbain-Jean-Joseph Le Verrier showed that this orbital discrepancy could be explained if there were yet another planet beyond Uranus. On September 23, 1846, astronomers in Berlin saw it—the planet we now call Neptune.

While the discovery of Uranus depended on the development of better telescopes, the discovery of Neptune depended on the ability

---

NEW EFFORTS IN ASTRONOMY

Since the discovery in 1932 that radio waves emanate from the Milky Way's center, astronomers have been scanning the "invisible" universe. That task requires special instruments. Because only visible light, radio waves, and some infrared radiation can penetrate the atmosphere, special devices are sent into space aboard satellites. Below, some details about the latest efforts to analyze specific kinds of electromagnetic radiation:

• RADIO WAVES (wavelength: one millimeter to 10 meters): The first radio telescope—a bowl-shaped antenna measuring 9.4 meters across—was built in Illinois in 1937. Today, "interferometry"—a computerized system that merges signals from an array of radio telescopes—allows astronomers to simulate one enormous dish. The Very Large Array in New Mexico synchronizes 27 radio telescopes to form images equivalent to those of one 24-kilometer dish. Currently, the National Science Foundation is building the Very Long Baseline Array; with 10 antennas spanning Hawaii to St. Croix, its "baseline" will measure 7,500 kilometers.

• INFRARED RADIATION (wavelength: one micron to one millimeter): Infrared radiation carries crucial data about star and planet formation. NASA's Kuiper Airborne Observatory, a 0.9 meter telescope aloft at 41,000 feet, has charted infrared sources since 1975. More impressive, the joint U.S.–Dutch–British Infrared Astronomical Satellite mapped more than 250,000 sources during 1983. On the drawing board for the 1990s are two space-based observatories: NASA's $600 million Shuttle Infrared Telescope Facility and the European Space Agency's Infrared Space Observatory.

• VISIBLE LIGHT (wavelength: 300 nanometers to one micron): Delayed because of space shuttle troubles, NASA's $1.5 billion Hubble Space Telescope awaits launch in 1988. Its 2.4-meter telescope will capture visible, infrared, and ultraviolet radiation, detecting objects 50 times fainter and seven times farther away than those detectable by Earth's best telescopes. Still, ground-based observatories with larger apertures remain important in spectral analysis. By the mid-1990s, Hawaii may house two giant optical telescopes; the $87 million Keck Telescope, using a honeycomb design, will join 36 mirrors into a single 10-meter mirror, while the proposed $125 million National New Technology Telescope will achieve a 15-meter aperture—the world's largest.

• ULTRAVIOLET RADIATION (wavelength: 10–300 nanometers). The first ultraviolet telescopes were hoisted aloft on high-altitude balloons. Today, the International Ultraviolet Explorer, a U.S.–European satellite launched in 1978, examines radiation from intergalactic matter and the outer layers of stars. Soon, NASA's Extreme Ultraviolet Explorer, now being developed, will study high-energy ultraviolet rays, so far uncharted.

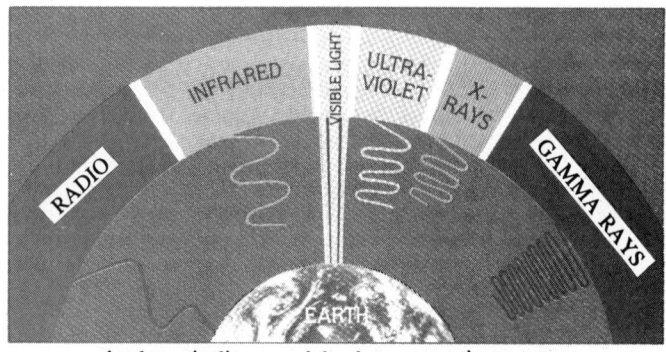

A schematic diagram of the electromagnetic spectrum.

• X-RAYS (wavelength: .01–10 nanometers). So energetic are x-rays that studying them requires a unique telescope design: cylindrical mirrors to deflect x-rays into focus. Between 1978 and 1981, the orbiting Einstein Observatory satellite used this method (as did its European counterpart, Exosat) to collect data on pulsars, neutron stars, and galactic nuclei. The latest x-ray space observatory is Japan's Astro-C, launched in February 1987 (approximate cost: $40 million). By 1995, NASA hopes to place in orbit the Advanced X-Ray Astrophysics Facility, a $1 billion telescope 100 times more sensitive than the Einstein Observatory.

• GAMMA RAYS (wavelength: less than .01 nanometers): Gamma rays are more energetic than x-rays, and difficult to measure. Thus the European gamma ray observatory, Cos-B, took seven years (1975–82) to make a gamma ray chart of the sky. In 1990, NASA plans to launch a $500 million space-based Gamma Ray Observatory, 10 times more sensitive than Cos-B, which will carry instruments supplied by the United States and Germany.

2. From Astronomy to Astrophysics

of theoreticians to predict the orbit of the new planet. In fact, once told of its general location, observers at Berlin took less than one night to pinpoint Neptune. The ninth planet, Pluto, was also found through computation and observation.

About the same time that Herschel was expanding our perception of the solar system, the return of a comet in 1758 as predicted served to provide dramatic confirmation of the clockwork universe developed by Newton. In 1682, Edmund Halley (1656–1742) had observed a large comet approach the Sun and swing away. Looking at historical records, he found that a bright comet with roughly the same orbit had appeared in 1531 and 1607. Using Newton's laws and the positions of the planets, Halley calculated the orbit of the comet and predicted that it would again be near the Sun in 1758. Its appearance, on Christmas Day of that year, provided a major verification of Newton's description of the universe.

With telescopes and satellites routinely probing the farthest reaches of the universe, one would expect few surprises in the relatively mundane study of our own neighborhood in space. Not so. In 1978, scientists at the U.S. Naval Observatory in Flagstaff, Arizona, obtained high-grade photographs of Pluto, showing that the planet has a moon. It was christened Charon, after the boatman charged with conducting souls of the dead to the underworld, Pluto's realm. This discovery allowed astronomers to estimate the mass of Pluto, a value insufficient to explain all of the vagaries of the orbits of Neptune and Uranus. Thus, there still may be pages to be written in the story of the solar system—a possible 10th planet.

Seeing the Spectrum

Beyond our own star system lie other stars, perhaps with their own planets. From a science concerned with determining *where* stars and planets are, the new discoveries changed the focus of astronomy to the question of *what* they are. A new science, astrophysics, emerged as a complement to astronomy. It seeks to reveal the nature of the stars through an understanding of the laws of physics.

The basis for this new departure in man's view of the heavens was a famous experiment by Isaac Newton. He noted that a glass prism held up to a beam of sunlight broke the light into its constituent colors—a "spectrum" of sunlight.

For a long time, this peculiar property of light was merely a nuisance to lensmakers. Then, in 1802, physician William Hyde Wollaston found narrow bands of missing color in the spectrum of sunlight. By 1814, a physicist, Joseph von Fraunhofer, made the first map of these lines, which now bear his name. Their origin remained a mystery until 1859, when Gustav Kirchhoff, working with Robert Bunsen at Heidelberg, showed that the lines were caused by familiar chemical elements in the Sun's outer atmosphere that absorb certain wavelengths of light.

Such "spectral analysis" works something like this: Each kind of element (e.g., hydrogen, nitrogen), when pushed to an "excited" state, emits a unique spectrum of light—a kind of atomic fingerprint.

In fact, burning an element gives off a specific "emission spectrum," while passing light *through* an element causes certain colors to be absorbed, creating an "absorption spectrum." The correspondence between atoms and their unique spectra is daily evident: A neon light glows red; sodium-vapor street lamps emit yellow light; mercury-vapor lamps are bluish-white. Each element has its own colors.

Discovering this connection between atoms and light was enormously important. As early as 1868, bright lines were observed in the Sun's spectrum—lines that had no counterpart in any known element on Earth. Scientists concluded that a new element was present on the Sun, one that they named helium (from the Greek word for Sun, *helios*).

There was, as far as anyone could tell, no helium on the Earth. In 1895, however, helium was discovered in certain uranium-bearing minerals. Once again, it turned out that the Earth was not as different from the rest of the universe as some people had thought.

From these early days, the technique of identifying chemicals by their light spectra has penetrated every corner of modern technology. Spectroscopy is today used in industrial quality control (to monitor the presence of impurities), in medicine (to identify substances taken from the body), and in many other areas where one must determine the chemical constituents of materials. It even figures in courtroom dramas, where substances identified by this sort of analysis are accepted as legal evidence.

Once scientists had proven that known elements make up the Sun and other stars, another question arose: How could the stars shine so brightly for so long? Astrophysicists had calculated that, even if the Sun were made of pure anthracite coal, it could have shone for only 20,000 years—instead of the 4.5 billion years so far.

Throughout the last decades of the 19th century, scientists tried to determine the Sun's fuel source. The answer came from a completely unexpected quarter—the study of radioactive materials. By the 1930s, a number of things had become clear: First, certain nuclear processes alter the weight of atoms; second, the weight change is related to energy by means of Einstein's famous formula, $E = mc^2$. Arthur (later Sir Arthur) Eddington, working in England during the 1920s, had suggested that the conversion of mass to energy might be the process that provided the Sun's energy. But no one knew enough about nuclear physics at that time to consider Eddington's suggestion as anything more than an educated guess.

In fact, the Sun shines through a fusion process in which lighter elements are transmuted into heavier ones, liberating energy. Detailed knowledge of this phenomenon grew out of a small conference held in Washington, D.C., in April 1938. The gathering had aimed to unite astrophysicists and nuclear physicists. The former knew about stellar structure; the latter understood something of the reactions taking place in stars. The interchange must have been extraordinarily effective: Shortly thereafter Hans Bethe of Cornell University worked out the earliest model of fusion in stars.

The theory was so successful that Bethe was awarded a Nobel Prize for physics in 1967. His idea of nuclear reactions in our Sun allowed scientists to begin to understand the very fires of creation.

Article 3

Galileo's Science And the Trial of 1633

"Nature . . . is inexorable and immutable; she never transgresses the laws imposed upon her." Thus did Galileo argue in 1615 for the authority of science over that of Scripture in the physical world. The Catholic Church's 1633 condemnation of Galileo is popularly seen as the response of theological dogmatism. But the issue debated by scholars today is whether Galileo actually *proved* that the Earth revolves around the sun. Here, as he analyzes Galileo's ordeal, historian William A. Wallace explores the complexities of demonstrating truth in science.

William A. Wallace

William A. Wallace, O.P., is professor of philosophy and history at the Catholic University of America (CUA). Born in New York City, he received a B.E.E. from Manhattan College (1940), an M.S. from CUA (1952), and a Ph.D. from University of Fribourg, Switzerland (1959). He was ordained in 1953, and his most recent book is Prelude to Galileo: Medieval and 16th-Century Sources of Galileo's Thought *(1981).*

The casual tourist in Rome, should he climb the Spanish Steps and approach the imposing palace to which they lead, might notice a green marble pillar bearing an inscription in Italian that translates as follows:

The next palace is the Trinità dei Monti, once belonging to the Medici; it was here that Galileo was kept prisoner of the Inquisition when he was on trial for seeing that the Earth moves and the sun stands still.

The first part of that inscription is undoubtedly true, but less certain is the claim that Galileo was brought to trial "for seeing that the Earth moves and the sun stands still." One cannot actually observe the Earth's movement; proof of this now commonplace notion is considerably more complex.

Notwithstanding the conservatism, overzealousness, and incompetence of the Catholic Church officials who prosecuted him, Galileo's defense, scientifically speaking, was not nearly so strong as is commonly thought. All of the evidence marshalled *after* his time distorts modern judgments of the trial. We must return to Galileo's assessment of his own work to appreciate his real achievements.

Polish astronomer Nicolaus Copernicus (1473–1543) brought the theory of a rotating Earth that revolved around the sun into public discourse with the publication in 1543 of *On the Revolutions of the Heavenly Spheres*. But it was Galileo's work that sparked debate, almost 70 years later, over this heliocentric theory.

Galileo Galilei was born at Pisa on February 15, 1564, and in his early years he apparently thought of becoming a monk. His father persuaded him to study medicine instead, and he pursued courses at the University of Pisa with that intention from 1581 to 1585, when he dropped out, without a degree, and devoted himself increasingly to the study of mathematics.

Such was his competence in mathematics, both pure and applied, that the University of Pisa called him back in 1589 to teach courses in geometry and astronomy. In 1592, he was offered a more prestigious position at the University of Padua, and there, for the next 18 years—which Galileo recalled as "the happiest of my life"—he flourished as professor of mathematics. He taught courses in astronomy; experimented with pendulums, inclined planes, and falling bodies; and perfected the telescope as a reliable instrument for astronomical observations.

On the basis of such observations, he published his *Sidereus nuncius (The Starry Messenger)* in Venice in 1610, and soon won acclaim throughout Europe as the foremost astronomer of his time.

Galileo's teaching notes from his stays at Pisa and Padua have survived, and from these we know that he was aware of the Copernican theory. But he preferred to teach the geocentric theory of Ptolemy (second century A.D.), which at the time was the dominant theory in the universities. Half a century after the appearance of Copernicus's book, only a few scholars had seriously entertained his views.

One such scholar was the German astronomer Johann Kepler (1571–1630), who corresponded with Galileo, and to whom Galileo wrote in 1597 that he himself had become a committed Copernican. Recent research suggests, however, that Galileo wavered in his commitment; his treatises on astronomy published during the early 1600s show him still arguing for the Ptolemaic system. What transformed Galileo after 1610 into an enthusiastic supporter of the Polish astronomer were his own discoveries with the telescope.

Between 1609 and 1611, he discovered the moons of Jupiter, which showed that not all motions in the heavens had to be around the Earth as a center. He saw mountains on Earth's moon, which suggested that Earth and moon were made of the same material and possibly under-

3. Galileo's Science

went similar motions. He discerned the phases of Venus, which showed that its orbit had to be around the sun, not around the Earth as had previously been supposed.

Citing the Cardinal

On the strength of the publication of *Sidereus nuncius*, Galileo obtained the patronage of the Grand Duke of Tuscany, Cosimo II de Medici. He gave up his teaching duties at Padua and moved to Florence where he served as mathematician and philosopher to the Grand Duke.

His advocacy of the Copernican theory as the true explanation of the universe soon came under attack from two camps. On the one hand, Italian philosophers were concerned over the Copernican system's apparent violation of the principles of Aristotelian physics. Theologians, on the other hand, claimed that Copernicanism violated Scripture, notably the Old Testament's assertions that the sun moves across the heavens (e.g., Joshua commanded the sun to stand still, Josh. 10:12), and that the Earth is the immovable center around which God made the heavenly luminaries rotate (e.g., Ps. 93:1).*

Encouraged, it seems, by his patron, Galileo responded to both parties: to the conservative Aristotelian philosophers with a *Discourse on Floating Bodies* (1612), and to the theologians with a *Letter to Castelli*, later enlarged as the *Letter to Christina* (1615), wherein he suggested that the Scriptures could be reconciled with the Copernican system by interpreting the Bible allegorically rather than literally. He cited Caesar Cardinal Baronius, a contemporary who said: "The intention of the Holy Spirit is to teach us how one goes to heaven, not how heaven goes."

Meanwhile, a Carmelite friar, Paolo Foscarini, had published in 1615 a theological treatise in which he interpreted the Scriptures in a fashion similar to Galileo's. The works of both men were brought to the atten-

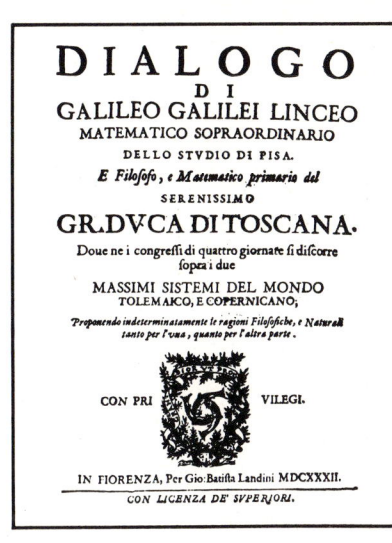

---

*According to Aristotelian physics (which St. Thomas Aquinas and other Scholastics had followed), the Earth's position in the center of the universe explained local motions such as the downward fall of bodies. Further, the heavenly bodies appeared to be immutable; such perfect spheres, it was thought, could only move in circles. The Earth appeared to be so unlike the celestial luminaries that it seemed impossible to attribute to it the same heavenly motion. Even before Galileo's time, astronomical observations had cast some doubt on some features of this cosmology, and philosophers were divided into those committed to preserving it (the Peripatetics) and those willing to revise it (the more progressive Scholastics).

Aristotle, Ptolemy, and Copernicus (left to right) are depicted in the frontispiece to the first edition of Galileo's Dialogue (1632).

tion of Robert Cardinal Bellarmine, a learned Jesuit in Rome who at that time was investigating the criticisms of the Reformers and what the Roman church regarded as their heretical interpretations of Scripture.

In April 1615, Bellarmine wrote to both Foscarini and Galileo, advising them that the Copernican system was as yet only a hypothesis, since the motion of the Earth had not been conclusively demonstrated. He cautioned that until such time as solid proof was offered, the commonly accepted interpretation of Scripture was to be preserved.

Shortly thereafter, in 1616, the Congregation of the Index (a church agency that judged works as heretical or correct) published a decree against the Copernican teaching, condemning Foscarini's book outright and suspending publication of Copernicus's work of 1543 pending correction of its text.

Necessary Demonstrations

Oddly enough, in his *Letter to Christina*, Galileo had agreed with Bellarmine that the traditional interpretation of Scripture was to stand unless the new system could be "well founded on manifest experiences and necessary demonstrations." He apparently felt that he would soon provide such evidence. But, as we shall see, he subsequently ran into difficulties.

In February 1616, when he was in Rome, Galileo had an important meeting with Cardinal Bellarmine. In the files of the Holy Office, a much-discussed document is preserved, dated February 26, which states that Galileo, while in Bellarmine's household, was enjoined not to hold, teach, or defend the Copernican system "in any way whatever."

The document seems to be a record of an injunction that was to be served on Galileo should he not agree to Bellarmine's instructions. It appears that the injunction was never actually served on Galileo, and thus there is some doubt whether he was told that he could teach the Copernican system as a mathematical *hypothesis* that simplified astronomical predictions, or whether he was told that he was not to hold, teach, or defend it in any way whatsoever.

I will return to this matter later, for the question of whether the injunction was actually served on Galileo assumed some importance at the trial of 1633.

Difficult Dialogue

Galileo's early relations with the papacy and the Jesuits were, on the whole, good. Cardinal Bellarmine had questioned the Jesuit astronomers at the Collegio Romano about the accuracy of the new observations with the telescope; they had promptly confirmed Galileo's findings. The Collegio's greatest mathematician, Christopher Clavius, knew of Galileo's work and had helped him get his teaching positions.

Clavius died in 1612, however, and soon after, Galileo got into a nasty dispute with a German Jesuit, Christopher Scheiner, over the nature and motion of sunspots. The situation worsened a few years later, in 1618,

1. THE INDUSTRIAL AND SCIENTIFIC REVOLUTIONS

when Galileo launched another attack on one of Clavius's successors at the Collegio, Orazio Grassi, over the paths and appearances of comets.

While this argument was raging, in 1621 three important figures died: Pope Paul V, Cardinal Bellarmine, and Galileo's patron, Cosimo de Medici. Fortunately, Paul V was succeeded by a Florentine cardinal, Matteo Barberini, who had been sympathetic to Galileo during the troubles of 1616 and who generally took Galileo's side in his battles with the more orthodox Jesuits.

When Barberini assumed the papacy in 1623 as Urban VIII, Galileo took the opportunity to dedicate his definitive answer to Grassi on comets, *The Assayer*, to the new pope. No doubt Urban VIII was pleased and flattered by this action; Galileo was granted the favor of six papal audiences. Most scholars agree that Galileo secured some kind of permission from Urban to resume work on the Copernican system.

By 1630, he had finished his great work, the *Dialogue on the Two Chief Systems of the World*. In it he evaluated all of the evidence and arguments for and against the Ptolemaic and Copernican systems, coming down rather hard on the side of the Copernicans and making the Ptolemaists and the Aristotelians look somewhat foolish in the process. Galileo caricatures their positions through a fictional character, the inept Simplicio, a Peripatetic who finds his philosophy in the text of Aristotle rather than in the book of nature.

The importance of the *Dialogue* is twofold. It was the first frontal attack on the whole of Aristotelian physics. It focused on the weakest point of Aristotelian physics—its account of the motions of bodies.

Galileo had difficulty obtaining permission to have the *Dialogue* published. The Dominican Niccolò Riccardi, charged with censoring the work, was mindful of the decree against Copernicanism handed down in 1616. But, by doctoring the manuscript, Galileo was able to get Riccardi's approval, and his book was printed by Landini at Florence in 1632. He had added a preface and a note at the end, wherein he disclaimed giving any actual proof of the Copernican system and labeled it a pure mathematical hypothesis.

The "dialogue" takes place over four days among the fictional characters Salviati, Sagredo, and Simplicio, with a different series of

Portrait by Flemish painter Justus Susterman of Galileo, who was elected in 1611 to the Academy of the Lynx-eyed, Europe's first scientific society.

arguments being developed in the course of each day. On the first day, Salviati, Galileo's mouthpiece, argues that there is no clear dichotomy between the celestial and terrestrial regions, a central tenet of Aristotelian cosmology. He says the world is one, probably constructed of the same kind of material (e.g., the mountains on the moon, just like those on Earth) and probably undergoing the same kinds of motion.

On the second day, the main topic is the rotation of the Earth on its axis. Here Galileo rebuts most of the proofs that the Earth is at rest (such as the fact that a stone dropped from a tower always falls at its foot) and shows that, if one knows the proper principles of mechanics, the proofs offered yield the same results whether the Earth is still or turning.

Rejecting Kepler

The arguments, he admits, do not *prove* that the Earth is rotating. They simply destroy the proofs of his adversaries that it must be at rest. The Earth's diurnal rotation is thus left an open question.

The third day is devoted to a more difficult problem: whether the Earth is immobile in the center of the universe or actually travels in a large, annual orbit around the sun. Arguing by analogy, Galileo asks: Since the other planets revolve around the sun, why should not the Earth do likewise? Further, earthly revolution can explain the movement of sunspots.

Finally, on the fourth day, Galileo puts together the conclusions of the second and third days' discussions, showing how they provide a simple explanation of a universally observed phenomenon, the motion of the tides.

His argument, in summary, is that the combination of the Earth's daily rotation on its axis with its annual revolution around the sun results in unequal forces being exerted daily on the waters on the Earth's surface. These unequal forces give rise to the tides.

To make his point, Galileo had to reject Kepler's theory of tides—that they are caused by lunar attraction —the theory that is accepted by scientists today. In the preface, Galileo himself refers to his argument on tides as an "ingenious fantasy"; he labored over it for years without removing all its flaws.

Coming to Trial

With the publication of the *Dialogue* in 1632, Galileo found himself in deeper trouble than he had ever imagined. Pope Urban VIII was furious, probably because he felt Galileo had betrayed his earlier pledge that he would write impartially, and almost certainly because he felt that Galileo had misused, and ridiculed, Urban's own preferred answer to the Ptolemaic-Copernican controversy, namely that it could not be definitively resolved by human intellect.

In August 1632, all further publication and sales of the book were prohibited by the Holy Office. Galileo

3. Galileo's Science

was summoned to Rome from Florence to be tried by a tribunal of 10 cardinals on the charge that he had willfully taught the Copernican doctrine despite its condemnation as contrary to Scripture. In preparing for the trial, the clerical prosecutors discovered the written injunction that had putatively been given to Galileo on February 26, 1616, enjoining him not to hold, teach, or defend the Copernican system in any way.

Accordingly, a number of theologians examined the *Dialogue* to ascertain whether Galileo had or had not actually held, taught, or defended Copernicanism in that work. The results were, predictably, that Galileo had undoubtedly *taught* the motion of the Earth and the immobility of the sun in the *Dialogue*, and that he had also *defended*, without a doubt, the same teaching.

House Arrest

But had Galileo actually *held* a belief in this teaching? Basing their judgment on the preface Galileo had written (presumably to please Riccardi and so get his work approved for publication), the theologians gave him the benefit of the doubt and decided that he might not have proffered the work as a statement of his own personal conviction.

During the course of the trial, Galileo, for whatever motive, took the obvious way out and said that the theologians' finding on the third point was correct. As a devout son of the church, he would not personally believe anything that was contrary to sacred Scripture. He was made to swear that he did not believe in the Earth's motion, and on this basis he was given a salutary penance ("for the spiritual benefit of former heretics who had returned to the faith") and confined to house arrest. The *Dialogue* was banned, and Galileo was forbidden to write any more on Copernicanism.

Galileo then retired to his villa at Arcetri, outside Florence, and there spent the remaining years of his life studying and writing. In 1638 (four years before his death), he published *Two New Sciences*, a work regarded by scientists as laying out the principles of the modern science of mechanics. It has earned him the title "Father of Modern Science."

The work is replete with claims that the author has founded a "new science," that he has provided demonstrations or strict proofs pertaining to the motions of earthly bodies. Such claims are conspicuously absent from the earlier *Dialogue on the Two Chief Systems of the World*, and their absence, I argue, necessitates reevaluation of what Galileo did and thought he did in *that* book, and of why he recanted.

Return to the inscription on the pillar in Rome and its implication that Galileo actually *saw* the Earth's motion, i.e., that he was able to prove, on the basis of incontrovertible evidence, that the Earth was rotating on its axis and revolving in a closed orbit around the sun. Did Galileo believe he had done this? To answer this, one must know precisely what he took to be scientific proof.

Galileo's Sources

Unfortunately, this has proved difficult for historians of science to discover. My study, over the past 15 years, of three notebooks that Galileo composed while he was a young math professor at Pisa, has turned up an unsuspected possibility. These notebooks, now in the Biblioteca Nazionale Centrale in Florence, cast an entirely new light on the way Galileo structured his *Dialogue*.

What is surprising about the notebooks is that they summarize and explore the logical and physical treatises of Aristotle, not in the conservative and textual style of the Peripatetics in the Italian universities, but rather in a progressive application of Aristotle's principles to current problems. For example, in the third notebook, Galileo applies Aristotelian principles to the motions of heavy bodies.

Even more surprising are the sources on which the notebooks draw, since Galileo has been so often cast in opposition to both the church and the Aristotelians. The first two volumes were drawn from Latin notes used by Jesuit lecturers at the Collegio Romano on logic and natural philosophy, respectively. The third is an adaptation of the same materials to Galileo's own study of the motion of projectiles and falling bodies. Galileo apparently obtained the lecture notes through his correspondence with the Jesuit Clavius.

Using Suppositions

The key to my solution is an expression that occurs repeatedly throughout Galileo's writings from his earliest to his last years, namely, the Latin term *suppositio*, especially as applied to a type of demonstration. Reasoning *ex suppositione* is rarely discussed in the present day, but it assumed considerable importance at the end of the 16th century among progressive Aristotelians. It is in these notebooks that the clearest statement of Galileo's methodology, that of *ex suppositione*, is found, and its debt to Aristotle is unmistakable.

Identifying the Jesuit Aristotelian precursors of his thought gives us a new appreciation of Galileo's later contacts with Jesuits such as Bellarmine, Scheiner, and Grassi, particularly in evaluating Galileo's claims for demonstration and proof. All of these men used precisely the same terminology employed in Galileo's early notebooks. When we reread the *Dialogue*, we can assume that his later Jesuit protagonists understood and to some extent shared both the concept of *ex suppositione* and the methods for evaluating such reasoning as applied therein.

What is reasoning *ex suppositione*? Unlike the hypothetico-deductive method scientists use today (which denies that there can be positive, incontestable proof of any conclusions based on hypotheses), it allows the possibility of *demonstrating* the truth and certainty of some results through the use of appropriate suppositions. Both Galileo and the Jesuits recognized that there were two types of *suppositiones:* some would be merely imagined situations that could not be verified, whereas others would be capable of verification, either by induction from sense experience or by measurement to within a specified degree of accuracy.*

In all of Galileo's serious scientific writings up to, but not including, the *Dialogue*, he is at pains to identify and verify the suppositions on which his reasoning is based, to justify his claims for strict proof. He follows the same procedure in *Two New Sciences*, where the new science of local motion is finally worked out. But in the *Dialogue*, such claims are strangely absent. Thus one must wonder whether Galileo really did think in 1632 that he had proved the Earth's motion. Was the question, in his own eyes, still debatable?

My suspicion is that Galileo himself was aware, in 1632, that he lacked rigorous proof of the Earth's motion. He supported the Coperni-

---

*For example, the supposition of epicycles in the geocentric theory was postulated *merely* for predicting planets' positions—not because it was believed to be physically true. On the other hand, Galileo's supposition in the *Two New Sciences* that a body falls with uniformly increasing velocity is mathematically formulated in terms of time and distance; this formula he then verifies experimentally.

1. THE INDUSTRIAL AND SCIENTIFIC REVOLUTIONS

THE COPERNICAN CHALLENGE... VS. THE TYCHONIAN COMPROMISE...

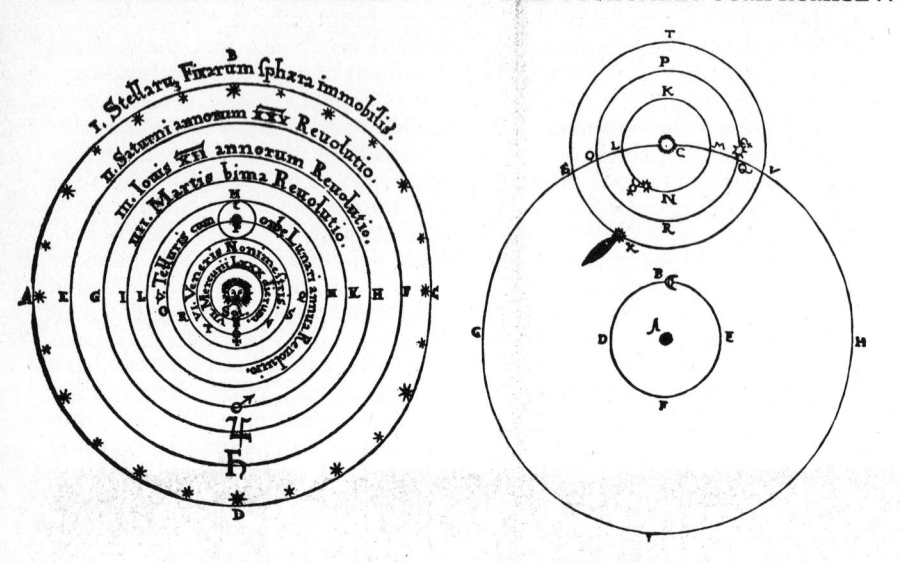

VS. THE MEDIEVAL WORLDVIEW

The Copernican system's (above left) main attraction was its mathematical simplicity. Galileo sought the same simplicity in motions on Earth. The Tychonian system (above right) appealed to those who believed the Earth could not possibly move as fast as Copernicus's theory required. It, too, simplified the Aristotelian model (right), whose defects Ptolemy had sought to remedy with complex devices such as epicycles and equants.

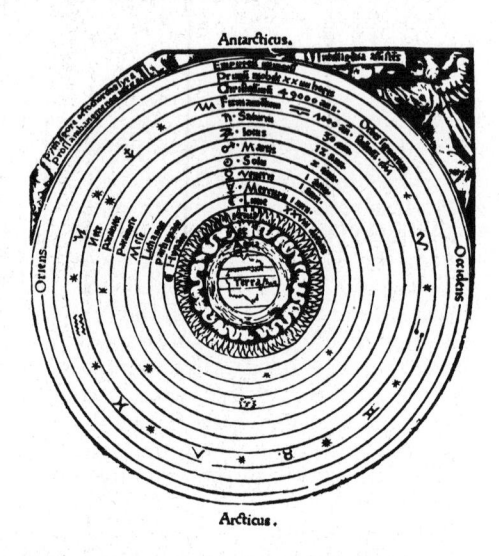

can system anyway on the grounds that the arguments he had been able to muster, though not conclusive, were better than his opponents'.

We now know that during his 1592–1610 stay at Padua, Galileo continued to work on problems of motion and mechanics and that he made drafts of proofs and demonstrations on which his "science of motion" would one day be erected. By 1609, when he started to work with the telescope, he had completed all the investigations that would be required to write the *Two New Sciences*—a book that would not be published for another 30 years.

Galileo's familiarity with the subject was such that in 1609 he had implicitly grasped the demonstrative force of the arguments he would later formalize in the *Two New Sci-*

ences. He had already experimentally validated the *suppositiones* (e.g., the definition of accelerated motion; the negligible effects of friction) on which his work would be based, and he spoke with confidence of the book's imminent appearance.

It was a confident Galileo, then, who gazed through the telescope, and his intuition was this: If he could systematize his new observations, and couple these with the principles of motion he was soon to formulate, he could quickly extend his demonstrations to cover the Earth's motion—not only in its diurnal rotation but in its revolution around the sun as well. Such a comprehensive system would be an imposing rival to Aristotelian physics.

It was the prospect of these demonstrations that led him to make the

extravagant claims in the *Letter to Christina*. And it was the same prospect that was to haunt him when he came to write his definitive treatise defending the Copernican system. He had to cast it as a dialogue precisely because the proof of the suppositions on which the reasoning was based (i.e., the Earth's rotation and revolution, and the sun's immobility) still eluded him in 1632.

Both before and after the publication of the *Dialogue*, then, Galileo gives abundant evidence of his awareness of and adherence to the canons of demonstrative proof as required by the method of reasoning *ex suppositione*. In the *Dialogue* itself, persuasive argumentation is used, not demonstration, and no mention is even made of the Tychonian system, favored by Galileo's real opponents, which could just as readily explain all of the observational evidence provided with the telescope.*

Finally, as if to add insult to injury, the rebuttal to Galileo's proof of the tides—perhaps dictated by Urban VIII—is voiced at the end of the work by Simplicio, the "simpleton," whose judgment and credibility have already been questioned at every turn. Urban's argument was that God in his infinite power could effect the tidal motion in many ways beyond the reach of man's intellect, and thus that no human explanation, however ingenious, should be regarded as true and conclusive.

But the rebuttal also leads one to wonder whether Galileo was really forced to make the statements in the preface and endnote. Did he use them freely, aware that his arguments for the Earth's motion had barely progressed beyond the level of hypothetical reasoning, appealing enough, but still short of incontestable proof? More important, did he perjure himself when he swore after his trial that he personally did not believe in the Earth's motion?

If his concept of proof was indeed the one outlined of necessity *ex suppositione*, then one must conclude that he did not verify the mathematical principles on which the *Dialogue* was based. And only if one concludes that Galileo himself was aware of this shortcoming, do we give proper credit to his intelligence and to his

---

*Danish astronomer Tycho Brahe (1546–1601) maintained that the other planets circled the sun, and that this system as a whole revolved around the Earth, thus preserving the geocentric theory of the universe.

character, to both his brilliance and his will. He was perceptive enough to recognize the limitations of his argument, skillful though it was, and he was honest enough, as a believer, to acquiesce in the church's interpretation of the Scriptures when he lacked the "necessary demonstrations" to show it was otherwise.

Such a resolution of the problem posed by Galileo's abjuration of Copernicanism is not easy to grasp in the late 20th century, when there is no clear and accepted demarcation between the provinces of faith and reason. But in Galileo's day, in the Italy of the late 16th and early 17th centuries, an important teaching of Aquinas prevailed: Faith and reason have radically different spheres.

This means that a person cannot assent to one and the same truth by faith and by reason at the same time. If one *knows* something by reason, for example, one cannot assent to it by faith. If one *believes* something, on the other hand, one does so only because one's *reason* is unable to decide whether it is true or not.

In light of this teaching, the human intellect can go only so far in penetrating the secrets of the universe. Yet reasoning does not exhaust the sphere of the knowable, as it can be supplemented by faith—in those instances where God chooses to reveal something important.

Galileo, on such an accounting, would have two options on the matter of the Earth's motion: either he could *prove* it, and so *know* the truth of the proposition "the Earth moves" on the basis of his own reasoning; or he could *not prove* it, leaving it an open question which could still be decided by faith.

Early on in his investigations, if my analysis is correct, Galileo thought that convincing proof of the Earth's motion was within his grasp. Later, he saw the difficulty and complexity of the situation and came to admit, begrudgingly, that the opposite conclusion would have to be accepted on faith—because the church was proposing it to him as something beyond man's knowing powers and directly revealed by God.

Galileo's only "crime," to use historian Giorgio de Santillana's term, was that he was too precipitate in urging his intuitions on others, too presumptuous in expecting others to "see" what he could "see." Very human are faults such as these. But we need not add to these the further charges of arrogance and insincerity, of stubborn adherence to a position he was finally unable to defend, of swearing under oath that he did not believe what he truly believed.

It is much better, in my view, to see him as a true son of his church, willing to accept its teachings when his reason—despite its strong intuitions—was unable to establish their opposite. And, as a true scientist, he not only admitted that he failed to meet the standards of his profession but also persevered during his last years in the quest for a new science that would, one day, be able to furnish the proofs that eluded his grasp.

Article 4

HALLEY & POST-RESTORATION SCIENCE

Not just 'the Comet man' — Halley's achievements as a polymath testify to the breadth and vigour of English scientific enquiry and experiment in the years after 1660.

Noel Coley

AMONG MEN OF SCIENCE IN THE post-Restoration period, it would be difficult to find one more talented than Edmond Halley. For diversity of scientific interests he was the equal of Robert Hooke. For practical inventiveness he could rival Wilkins, Petty or Wren. His grasp of the theory of gravitation and his ability in calculating the motions of the heavenly bodies was second only to that of Isaac Newton, whilst in his understanding of the wider implications of gravitational theory and in the boldness of his adventurous spirit, Halley surpassed them all. His eventful career stirs the imagination and yet his genius and contributions to science are not well known and he is remembered today only for the comet which bears his name.

Born about 1656, the son of a soap-boiler in the City of London, Halley was educated at St Paul's School. Whilst he was a pupil there he made his first recorded observation on the variation of the magnetic compass needle from true North – a subject which was later to lead him into some of his most remarkable adventures. In 1673 he entered Queen's College, Oxford, and whilst still an undergraduate his first three scientific papers, all on astronomical subjects, were published in the *Philosophical Transactions* of the Royal Society. Two of these were in collaboration with his friend John Flamsteed, the first Astronomer Royal.

The rapid increase in maritime activity in the seventeenth century made the problem of determining longitude at sea ever more pressing, and this was one of the chief aims proposed for the Royal Observatory, founded by Charles II at Greenwich in 1675. Flamsteed's idea was to use the Moon's motion across the heavens as a great clock, but in order to do this it was necessary to determine the positions of the principal stars and the motion of the Moon more accurately than they were then known. Halley often assisted Flamsteed or competed in friendly rivalry. But eager as he was to make his name as an astronomer, he was even keener to see that his work would be *useful*.

At that time there were three outstanding astronomers in Europe. Besides Flamsteed at Greenwich, there was Johannes Hevelius in Danzig and the Italian astronomer, Giovanni Domenico Cassini, working in Paris. All three were improving the reliability of astronomical observations in the Northern hemisphere and Halley realised that he could not hope to compete successfully with them:

> ...If I were to attempt anything of the same kind, I know I should be as one stupidly quacking amongst such matchless swans.

A better prospect of making a **useful**

4. Halley and Post-Restoration Science

The interior of the Octagon Room in the Royal Observatory at Greenwich, showing observations with quadrant and telescope; Charles II, patron of the Observatory, looks down from the wall-portrait.

contribution to astronomy lay in observing the stars of the Southern hemisphere about which much less was known. So, before the end of 1676, Halley had left Oxford and set off for St Helena, the lonely island in the South Atlantic, then the most southerly British territory, governed by the East India Company. The king commanded the Company to convey Halley and a friend, together with all their equipment, on the first ship bound for St Helena and to provide them with free accommodation on the island throughout their stay.

As soon as he was sure of going, Halley had a large sextant made in iron and brass, fitted with the latest telescopic sights and mounted so that it could be adjusted with great precision. He also took a two-foot quadrant and several accurate telescopes. During his expedition, which lasted a full two years, Halley determined the positions of over 340 stars in the Southern hemisphere, each correlated with at least two others in Tycho Brahe's catalogue. This meant that any improvements in the accuracy of the Northern star-positions resulting from Flamsteed's or Hevelius' observations could be used to produce corresponding improvements in Halley's results.

Within a few months of his return Halley published the first catalogue of telescopically determined stars of the Southern hemisphere. He also dedicated a planisphere of these stars to Charles II, whilst Flamsteed called him 'Our Southern Tycho' and the Royal Society honoured him with its Fellowship – he was just twenty-two.

Throughout his long life Halley formed many friendships with leading men of science, but there can be no doubt that the most important of these was his connection with Isaac Newton. It was Halley who recognised Newton's progress towards the law of universal gravitation; it was he who persuaded Newton to complete his work, but most of all it was Halley who ultimately saw Newton's *Principia* through the press and even paid the printer's bill out of his own pocket, despite the fact that following his father's death in 1684 he was himself in financial difficulties. He not only read and corrected the proofs, showing that he fully understood Newton's work, but he also tactfully defused a dispute over priority between Newton and Hooke, persuaded Newton to complete Book III and himself supplied some of the data for this. The

1. THE INDUSTRIAL AND SCIENTIFIC REVOLUTIONS

work issued from the press in July 1687 with the imprimatur of the President of the Royal Society (at that time Samuel Pepys) and Halley heralded its appearance with a generous review in the *Philosophical Transactions* of which he was then editor.

Written in Latin and full of sophisticated arguments, the *Principia* was far beyond the mathematical competence of many potential readers. Thus it fell to Halley to provide a simpler explanation of its more difficult parts. For King James II who was an experienced seaman, Halley gave an explanation of Newton's theory of the tides, showing how they arise naturally from gravitational principles. Some years later this paper was published for those who might be curious about the causes of the tides, but unable to follow Newton's reasoning.

Halley has often been rated second only to Newton amongst the British men of science of his time and his achievements in the theory of gravitation fully justify this judgement, but like many of his contemporaries his range of interests was wide. He studied the mechanics of the atmosphere and estimated its height to be about forty miles above the earth. He investigated the distribution of solar heat and the broad pattern of winds over the oceans of the world. In astronomy he endeavoured to estimate the size of the solar system by observing transits of the planet Mercury across the sun's disc. He was also interested in physics, the age of the earth and natural history. Add to that his abilities in mathematics and classical scholarship and Halley appears as a polymath of phenomenal diversity, even by comparision with his contemporaries.

In the late seventeenth century there was no certainty about the best way of proceeding in science and the relative merits of different methods were vigorously debated. Fellows of the Royal Society often adopted the principles proposed by Francis Bacon earlier in the century, by which large numbers of observations were collected from many sources and conclusions were drawn by induction. Bacon had aimed to place all learning on a more progressive footing than that formerly provided by the authority of ancient learning. In his scheme, however, mathematics played no part, whereas Galileo, Kepler and the French mathematician-philosopher René Descartes all based their scientific conclusions firmly upon mathematics. It was Cartesian descriptive cosmology which commanded widespread support, especially amongst Descartes' countrymen, far into the eighteenth century and offered strong opposition to the Newtonian experimental philosophy.

Friend and associate of Newton though he was, Halley yet managed to avoid the arguments which grew up about Newton's work. He was himself

Tycho Brahe, sixteenth-century exponent of Copernican cosmology, with his great mural quadrant.

prepared to use whatever ideas seemed most appropriate in each problem – gravitational theory and mathematics in astronomy, Bacon's method of data collection for his work on magnetic variation, or Cartesian imagery to explain the aurora.

As mentioned, Flamsteed had begun to improve observations on the moon and stars in order to solve the problem of determining longitude at sea, but there would however be difficulties in using such a method, not least the need for clear skies. Practical

4. Halley and Post-Restoration Science

Chester, before Halley could at last set sail in October 1698.

Halley was no stranger to the sea. On his voyage to St Helena he had become acquainted with the methods of navigation used by seamen and had made some improvements to their instruments. He had also invented a new type of ship's log for determining speed through the water. He had written papers on tidal phenomena, charted the Thames estuary and Sussex coast and advised Pepys on nautical matters.

The *Paramour* was to carry out a survey of the magnetic variation in the South Atlantic and to determine the latitude and longitude of all ports and islands visited. On his first voyage Halley met with various difficulties. The most serious was the disobedience of his first lieutenant who, unknown to Halley, had himself written a book on the problem of longitude and resented being commanded by a landsman. Halley therefore returned to England where this officer faced a court-martial and the *Paramour* again set sail (this time without a first lieutenant) on September 16th, 1699. Reaching latitude 52° South they encountered large icebergs and, fearing for the safety of his ship and crew, Halley decided to turn back. After calling at Tristan de Cunha, St Helena, Barbados and Newfoundland, they arrived in Plymouth Sound on August 27th, 1700. In the course of his voyages, Halley had determined the exact locations of many places, visited unfamiliar islands and made observations of all kinds, including unusual species of birds, marine creatures and plants. But above all, he had collected the data needed for his chart of the variation of the compass.

Adding his new observations to his already large collection of data on the magnetic variation, Halley put it all together on two charts, one of the Atlantic Ocean alone with the course taken by the *Paramour* clearly shown and the other of all the oceans of the world. Isogonic, or Halley-lines, joining points of equal magnetic variation were drawn on these charts. Although today we are familiar with contour lines, isotherms and isobars on maps, this was then a new principle and Halley's charts are believed to be the earliest printed examples of such annotated maps. They were fre-

'Matchless swans'; Hevelius and his wife measuring distances between stars by sextant; from a 1673 German engraving.

as ever, Halley sought a method which could be used in all weathers by unlettered seamen.

He had long been collecting all the reliable observations of the variations of the compass he could get from mariners. His idea was to use these to construct lines joining points of equal variation on charts of the oceans. These lines would cut the parallels of latitude and so by two ordinary nautical observations – determinations of latitude and magnetic variation – it would be possible to estimate the position of a ship to within a few miles. This plan proved attractive to the Admiralty and it was in order to follow it up that a pink (a flat-bottomed sailing vessel), the *Paramour*, was built and Halley was commissioned as a naval captain in command of the very first scientific expedition to the South Atlantic. Unfortunately there were several delays, including a two-year spell as Deputy Warden of the Royal Mint at

1. THE INDUSTRIAL AND SCIENTIFIC REVOLUTIONS

quently published and widely used during the eighteenth century.

Following these voyages of discovery in the Atlantic, Halley went on to chart the tides, depths of the sea, currents and winds in the English Channel using the *Paramour*. The results of this survey were set out on another valuable chart.

In the late seventeenth century the mapping of the heavens and charting of the earth's surface were still very closely linked; star-charts and terrestial maps were often printed side-by-side in atlases of the period.

Ever since its foundation in 1662 the Royal Society had promoted the utility of science. Some of the early Fellows had studied traditional trades and crafts with an eye to improving their efficiency, although the proposals of the intellectuals were not always welcomed by the artisans who were supposed to benefit. Other Fellows concentrated on improving the scientific instruments of the day, or invented new ones. Indeed, many of them had useful inventions to their credit, from devices like Petty's double-bottomed boat to scientific apparatus such as the air-pump, or Newton's reflecting telescope. In this tradition, Halley improved the practicability of the diving bell.

The idea of descending into the sea inside a large barrel which would allow a diver to remain under water for a longer time than was possible by simply holding the breath, had been thought of already in the sixteenth century. This was not very practical however, since the pressure forced water into the vessel so that the diver was half-submerged, whilst the air compressed into the upper part of the vessel was soon vitiated. It was to these two problems that Halley addressed himself.

Halley's diving bell was a large conical vessel, open at the base, weighted with a covering of lead and having a seat about a foot from the bottom and a valve in the crown. It was lowered into the water fifteen feet at a time and at each stage a forty-gallon iron bound cask full of air was lowered down to the bell. Each cask was fitted with a stop-cock at the top and a bung at the base. The divers opened the cock under the bell and removed the bung so that water rushing into the cask would expel fresh air into the bell. By opening the valve, vitiated air could be released from the top of the bell and thus the supply of fresh air could be constantly replenished. Not content with merely describing such a device, Halley had a prototype constructed and tested it himself. He describes how he spent over an hour and a half with three other divers in such a bell at a depth of ten fathoms (sixty feet). In a clear sea it was possible to use the diving bell to study marine life, and by the aid of light through a window in the top of the bell, or by a candle, notes could be written. Halley also invented a diving helmet connected to the air supply in the bell by a leather hose which enabled a diver to leave the bell and walk on the sea bed for short distances. Wrecked ships could be examined in this way and he suggested that it might be possible to raise wrecks by attaching several such diving bells filled with air to them. So confident was he in these inventions that he set up a public company to exploit them. The shares were quoted regularly between 1692 and 1696 and it would appear that Halley's diving bell was both more practical and more successful than some other inventions of the time.

Halley, who strove himself for accuracy and reliability as well as usefulness, was always self-critical and could sometimes be critical of others. This attitude was in keeping with the objectives of the Royal Society, but not all the early Fellows were able to accept criticism of their work and some bitterly resented it. John Flamsteed, for instance, could never bear to be shown in the wrong. He was a dour, unhappy man, often ill, and always struggling to carry out his work at the Royal Observatory with inadequate funds. Royal patronage did not provide much financial support and Flamsteed is said to have spent at least £2,000 of his own fortune whilst being forced to take pupils to supplement his income. Most of the astronomical instruments in the Observatory had been provided by Flamsteed and he therefore, not unnaturally, regarded the observations he made with them as his own property, despite the fact that by his appointment he was a public servant.

Both Newton and Halley complained about Flamsteed's slowness in publishing his results and when, in 1686, Halley was able to show that some figures Flamsteed *had* published predicting the times of high tides at Dublin were wrong, Flamsteed was greatly offended and the earlier friendly relations between them were at an end. Flamsteed began to accuse Halley of plagiarism and where before he had hailed the younger astronomer's observations in the Southern hemisphere, he now began to find fault with them and hint that they were not Halley's own work. This sorry affair dragged on for some years. Halley's main concern was for the advancement of science; he showed no desire to quarrel with Flamsteed and wished 'all personal reflexion to bee forborn', but in 1692 was driven to make a public declaration that his observations were indeed his own and exactly what he had always claimed them to be.

Flamsteed died on December 31st, 1719, and in the following February Halley was appointed Astronomer Royal in his place. He was then sixty-four, yet he at once prepared to resume his observations on the Moon which he had been forced to break off in 1684. His objective was to observe the motion of the Moon through a full cycle of eighteen years and it is a tribute to his dedication that he was prepared at his age to begin a task of such magnitude which he could hardly expect to complete. In the end he did complete the full cycle, but unfortunately his observations were less precise than was needed to solve the long-standing problem of longitude.

Ever since he had worked on Newton's *Principia*, Halley had been interested in the wider significance of the theory of universal gravitation and at the beginning of his tenure as Astronomer Royal in 1720, he wrote two pioneering papers on cosmology in which he discussed the general nature of the Universe and the distribution of stars throughout infinite space. This was the first attempt to apply the new physical theory to the Universe as a whole. It shows Halley's profound grasp of Newtonian ideas and pre-dates Thomas Wright's *Original Theory of the Universe* by thirty years.

During this period there were many who continued to accept older traditions and beliefs; curiosities and monstrosities of all kinds attracted great interest, even amongst the Fellows of

4. Halley and Post-Restoration Science

the Royal Society who began to make a collection of useful and curious items. In 1683 Nehemiah Grew produced a catalogue of this collection which by then contained an Egyptian mummy, the tanned skin of a Moor, human skulls and a bone from a mermaid's head. Accounts of dramatic events such as earthquakes or volcanic eruptions and other traveller's tales were also sought by the Society and recorded in the *Philosophical Transactions*. Superstitions too were common. Belief in witchcraft, magic, sympathetic healing, the weapon salve, astrology, alchemy and other similar irrationalities were widespread. Nor were these confined to the common people. Isaac Newton, for instance, worked for over a quarter of a century on alchemy and his library contained more than a hundred books on the subject. In an age when such credulity was abroad, it is not surprising that any new or unusual object in the sky should be generally accepted as an omen of some impending calamity.

Of all the celestial phenomena which had from time immemorial struck awe into simple minds, none were more significant than the comets. Until the late sixteenth century these objects had been thought to occur in the earth's atmosphere below the moon, but observations by Tycho Brahe on the comet of 1577 had shown that it was much further away. Many comets had been observed since that time, but it remained for Halley, using Newton's gravitational principles, to show that comets are ordinary members of the solar system moving in elongated eliptical orbits and that they must therefore return periodically. This was arguably his greatest achievement. Halley observed the paths of several comets in the 1680s and, using data recorded in earlier times, he showed that in some cases the same comet had reappeared. This led him to predict that the comet he had observed in 1683 would return after an interval of seventy-five years and when it duly reappeared near the end of 1758, his theory of cometary motions was vindicated. It was able to explain the periodic appearance of comets as normal events and so lay the foundations for dispelling superstitions about them.

However, there were other celestial phenomena which needed similar rational treatment. It happened that in the five years preceding Halley's appointment as Astronomer Royal, several such unusual phenomena occurred. In each case Halley seized the opportunity to explain them in scientific terms.

In the spring of 1715 European astronomers were preparing to observe a total eclipse of the Sun due on April 22nd. It would be visible in many parts of England and the Royal Society instructed Halley to arrange for observations to be made from the roof of their house in Crane Court, Fleet Street. In preparation for the event, Halley published a map of England showing the path of the Moon's shadow so that:

> ...the suddain darkness wherein the Stars will be visible about the sun may give no surprise to the People, who would if unadvertized be apt to look upon it as Ominous...

In good Baconian style, he also solicited careful observations from 'the curious' so that the precise path of the shadow could be plotted and after the event he published a paper in which were incorporated his own and others' observations, giving at the same time very detailed descriptions of the Sun's corona and solar prominences.

The aurora borealis, or 'Northern lights' was another celestial apparition often considered an evil omen. When in March 1716 a brilliant display of the Northern lights occurred, it was thought to be a consequence of the execution of the Jacobite nobleman, Lord Derwentwater, two weeks earlier. Descriptions of this phenomenon were received by the Royal Society from many parts of Britain and Halley was asked to draw up a general account of it. The most interesting part of his paper is his theory of the cause of the aurora, based on the Cartesian notion of 'magnetic efluvia' emanating from the poles of the Earth. Halley suggested that in certain circumstances the streams of magnetic corpuscles could emit light as 'electric bodies' do under friction. This linking of the auroral light with the forces of magnetism and static electricity clearly shows the power of Halley's original mind and his scientific imagination. About the same time he also explained the nature of meteors and the sight of the planet Venus in the daytime sky, dispelling the super-

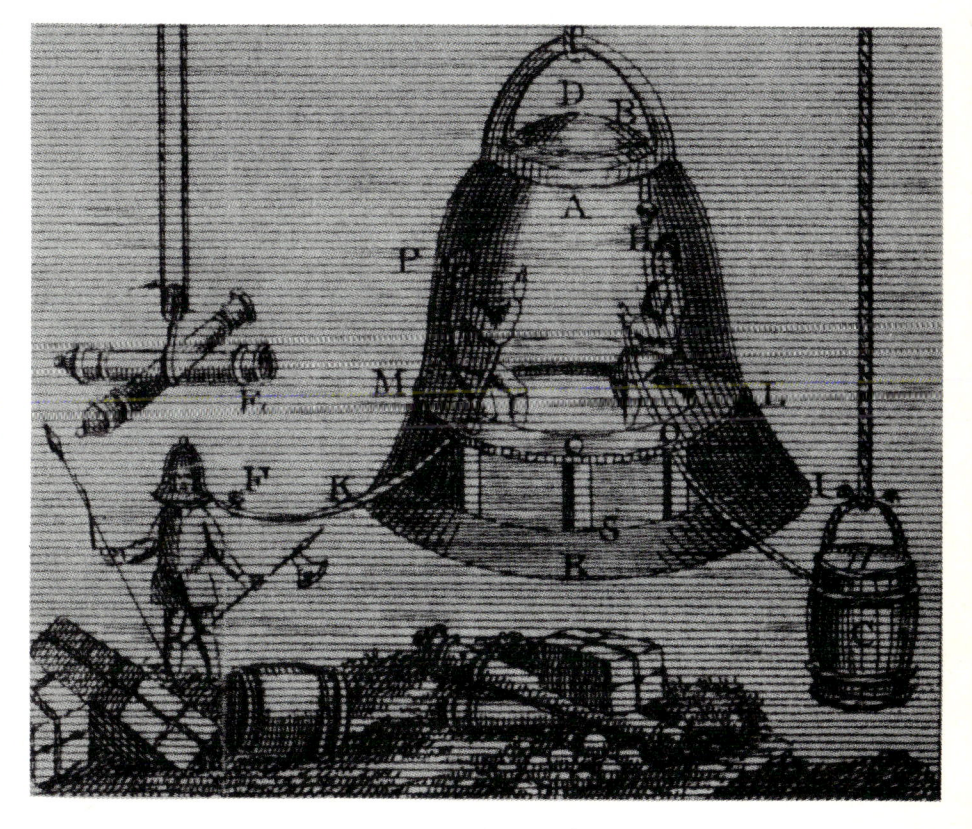

Halley's diving bell and helmet; the figures in the bell and outside have air replenished through tubes from the barrel (from Hooper's Rational Recreations, 1782).

1. THE INDUSTRIAL AND SCIENTIFIC REVOLUTIONS

stitious awe surrounding these phenomena.

Halley's rational outlook and rejection of supernatural powers in common with some of his contemporaries, resulted in accusations of atheism, charges which he was unable to shake off successfully. In 1691 whilst he was engaged on experiments with the diving bell in Pagham Bay near Chichester, the Savilian chair of Astronomy at Oxford fell vacant but Halley, suspected of atheism, was passed over. Twelve years later when John Wallis, the veteran mathematician, died, Halley was appointed Savilian Professor of Mathematics in his place although, according to Flamsteed, he '...now talks, swears and drinks brandy like a sea-captain'. Halley occupied this post for the rest of his life and his contributions to mathematics were considerable. His most remarkable feat was the translation of the works of Apollonius of Perga (especially the famous work on conic sections) from Arabic into Latin. Despite the fact that he knew no Arabic when he embarked upon this task Halley's translations were to be hailed by Arabic scholars for their elegance and accuracy.

Politically Halley was a Tory and a Royalist. He made no secret of his gratitude to the Stuarts even after the Revolution of 1688 and yet, recognising his loyalty to the Crown, William granted him command of a warship and Queen Anne sent him on several delicate diplomatic missions. Despite these favours Halley did not seek Royal patronage and never exploited the financial potential of his work on the improvement of navigation. His chief aim it seems, was not so much personal gain as a wish to serve the interests of society through the practical applications of science and, in the best traditions of post-Restoration science, to leave behind '...Observations that may be confided in and...hypotheses which after Ages may examine, amend or confute'.

FOR FURTHER READING:
Angus Armitage, *Edmond Halley*, (Thomas Nelson & Sons, 1966); Colin A. Ronan, *Edmond Halley; Genius in Eclipse*, (Macdonald & Co, 1970); Colin A. Ronan in *Dictionary of Scientific Biography*, edited by C.C. Gillispie, 16 Vols., New York, Charles Scribner's Sons, 1970-76, Vol. 6, (1972). Michael Hunter, *Science and Society in Restoration England*, (Cambridge University Press, 1981); A. Rupert Hall, *The Revolution in Science, 1500-1750*, (Longman, 1983), Lesley Murdin, *Under Newton's Shadow: Astronomical Practices in the Seventeenth Century*, (Adam Hilger, 1985); Frank Manuel, *A Portrait of Isaac Newton*, (Harvard University Press, 1986); M. Espinasse, *Robert Hooke*, (Heinemann, 1956).

Darwin as a Geologist

He tends to be viewed now as a biologist, but in his five years on the Beagle *his main work was geology, and he saw himself as a geologist. His work contributed significantly to the field*

Sandra Herbert

SANDRA HERBERT ("Darwin as a Geologist") is associate professor of history at the University of Maryland at Baltimore County. She has a B.A. in interdisciplinary studies from Wittenberg University and a Ph.D. in the history of ideas from Brandeis University. Before taking her current position she taught at the University of Maryland at College Park and at Princeton University and also served for a year as a visiting curator at the Smithsonian Institution.

One tends to see Charles Darwin today essentially as a biologist, concerned with the origin and evolution of plant and animal species. Yet it was as a geologist even more than as a naturalist that he took part in the famous voyage of the *Beagle* from 1831 to 1836, and it was as a geologist that he saw himself in the years immediately following the voyage. His contributions to geology were significant. His meticulous fieldwork on the voyage produced collections of material that remain valuable. His insights on the origin of coral reefs laid the basis for today's view of the matter. Finally, in large part it was his geological work that led him to his views on evolution, or "transmutation" as the vocabulary of the time had it.

Darwin's interest in geology during the voyage did not stem from long involvement with the subject. Indeed, at the outset of the voyage he was better prepared to collect insects and invertebrate animals; he had been an amateur entomologist since his youth and had been well trained in the study of invertebrates during the two years he spent as a medical student at the University of Edinburgh.

Geology took precedence on the voyage for several reasons. First, the Admiralty wanted a man trained in geology to make the voyage, and that must have affected the way Darwin presented himself to Robert FitzRoy, commander of the vessel, in their initial discussions. FitzRoy was aware of the economic interests served by geology. In 1830, after an earlier mission to South America with the *Beagle,* he had pointed out that a geologist or a mineralogist would be able to ascertain, for example, whether the mountains of Tierra del Fuego did indeed contain metal. Similarly, when it came time to commission the *Beagle* for its second voyage, Francis Beaufort, the hydrographer to the British navy, stressed the importance of a geological investigation of coral islands. He noted that they "occasionally afford excellent landlocked harbours," and he also pointed out that they were currently of interest to geologists.

The second reason for Darwin's bending toward geology during the *Beagle's* voyage had to do with the particularly attractive state of the field at the time. The 1830's were a golden decade for geology. It was the decade in which English geologists established the Cambrian, Silurian and Devonian systems and in so doing completed in global outline the basic sequence of geologic strata. It was also the decade in which most English geologists abandoned the attempt to synchronize biblical and geologic history.

The person who put Darwin in touch

1. THE INDUSTRIAL AND SCIENTIFIC REVOLUTIONS

with the new developments in the field was John Stevens Henslow, professor of botany at the University of Cambridge (which Darwin had entered after leaving Edinburgh), fellow of the Geological Society in London and Darwin's mentor. It was in 1831, at Henslow's instigation, that Darwin first began serious study in the field. Until then he had avoided the subject, having been disappointed in the geological lectures of Robert Jameson at Edinburgh.

Through arrangements made by Henslow, Darwin did fieldwork in the summer of 1831 with Adam Sedgwick, Woodwardian professor of geology at Cambridge. This was the work that led Sedgwick to define the Cambrian system. So it was that Darwin, only a few months before embarking on the *Beagle,* was trained in field methods by the most distinguished geological fieldworker in England, who was at the time engaged in his greatest work. On arriving home from his travels with Sedgwick, Darwin found the letter containing the offer to join the *Beagle* awaiting him.

The third reason Darwin chose geology was surely its suitability to his own makeup. Geology in the 1830's combined the traditional emphasis of natural history on the particularity of things with an openness to theorizing—a combination that suited Darwin's abilities and tastes extremely well. In a short autobiographical note written soon after the voyage he recalled a childhood desire "of being able to know something about every pebble in front of the hall door—it was my earliest and only geological aspiration at that time." His talent for abstraction led him to write of his interest in "recording the stratification and nature of the rocks and fossils at many points, always reasoning and predicting what will be found elsewhere."

Darwin's decision to focus on geology came early in the voyage. What seems to have caused the forces from within and without to coalesce was the prospect of authorship. As he prepared for the voyage he noted that he was afraid of "being overwhelmed with the number of subjects which I ought to take into hand." While the *Beagle* was in its first port, São Tiago in the Cape Verde Islands, a plan occurred to him that had the effect of ordering his activities for the rest of the voyage: he would write a book on the geology of the points visited. In his autobiography he wrote that after he had deduced the geologic history of São Tiago Island by studying its rocks "it then first dawned on me that I might perhaps write a book on the geology of the various countries visited, and this made me thrill with delight."

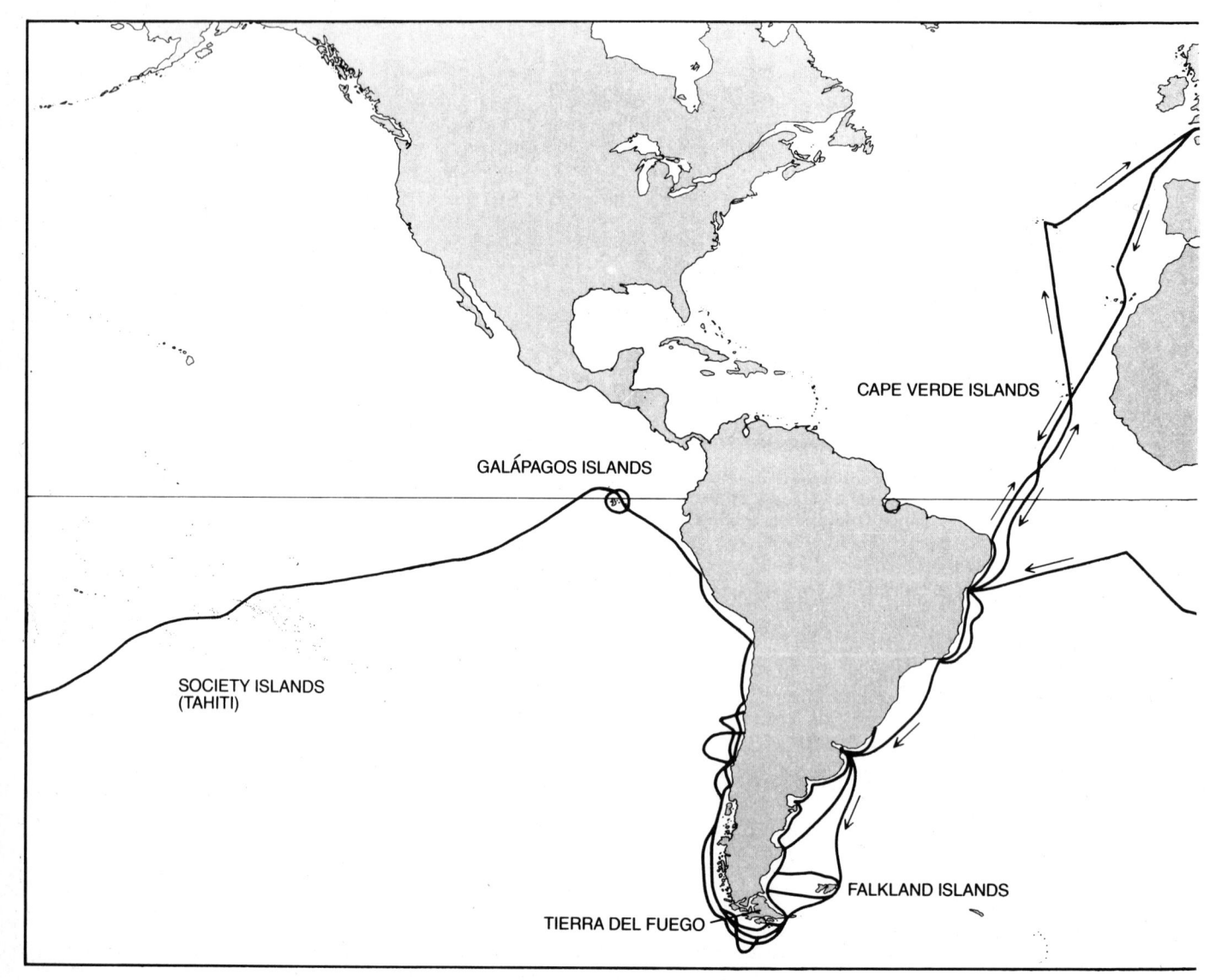

VOYAGE OF *BEAGLE* from 1831 to 1836, with Darwin aboard as scientific investigator, is charted on the basis of records kept by Robert FitzRoy, the commander of the ship. In a book FitzRoy published in 1839 on two of his voyages he included a similar map

5. Darwin as a Geologist

That Darwin should have thought of himself as the author of a major geological work at such a young age—he was nearing his 23rd birthday—is surely a sign of a powerful ambition at work. It was, however, a realistic ambition, because Darwin knew that the geology of South America, particularly the southern extremities of the continent, was so little explored that his work could not fail to be original. Moreover, he had the influence and inspiration of two recently read masterpieces before him: Alexander von Humboldt's *Personal Narrative* of his travels in South America, which was heavily geological but dealt mainly with the northern portion of the continent, and Charles Lyell's *Principles of Geology,* the first volume of which had appeared in 1830 and appealed to Darwin for its bold style and provocative content.

With future publication in his mind, then, Darwin set out from Cape Verde to collect thoroughly in geology and to observe as completely as he could. As he wrote to Henslow in August, 1832, "I have endeavoured to get specimens of every variety of rock, and have written notes upon all." Eventually his work led to a three-part publication on the geological findings of the voyage: *The Structure and Distribution of Coral Reefs* (1842), *Geological Observations on the Volcanic Islands Visited during the Voyage of H.M.S. Beagle, together with Some Notices of the Geology of Australia and the Cape of Good Hope* (1844) and *Geological Observations on South America* (1846).

In the course of collecting during the voyage and of writing up his findings Darwin became a geologist. That was how he viewed himself and that was how others viewed him. At the end of the voyage he referred to himself in a private notebook as "I, a geologist." His identity had formed around his ambition.

It was typical for him that his ambition operated on more than one level. Each day he pursued his original intention to systematically collect and observe. Here his methodical habits stood him in good stead. As a sportsman he had recorded his quarry; as a geologist he was equally diligent in numbering his specimens, recording their locations and keeping up with his note-taking. On quite another level he pondered the significance of his findings and developed the hypotheses that have led to his enduring reputation as a profoundly original thinker.

Darwin's notes from the voyage, which are in the Cambridge library, reveal his daily habits of work. Unlike his peers in England, who often

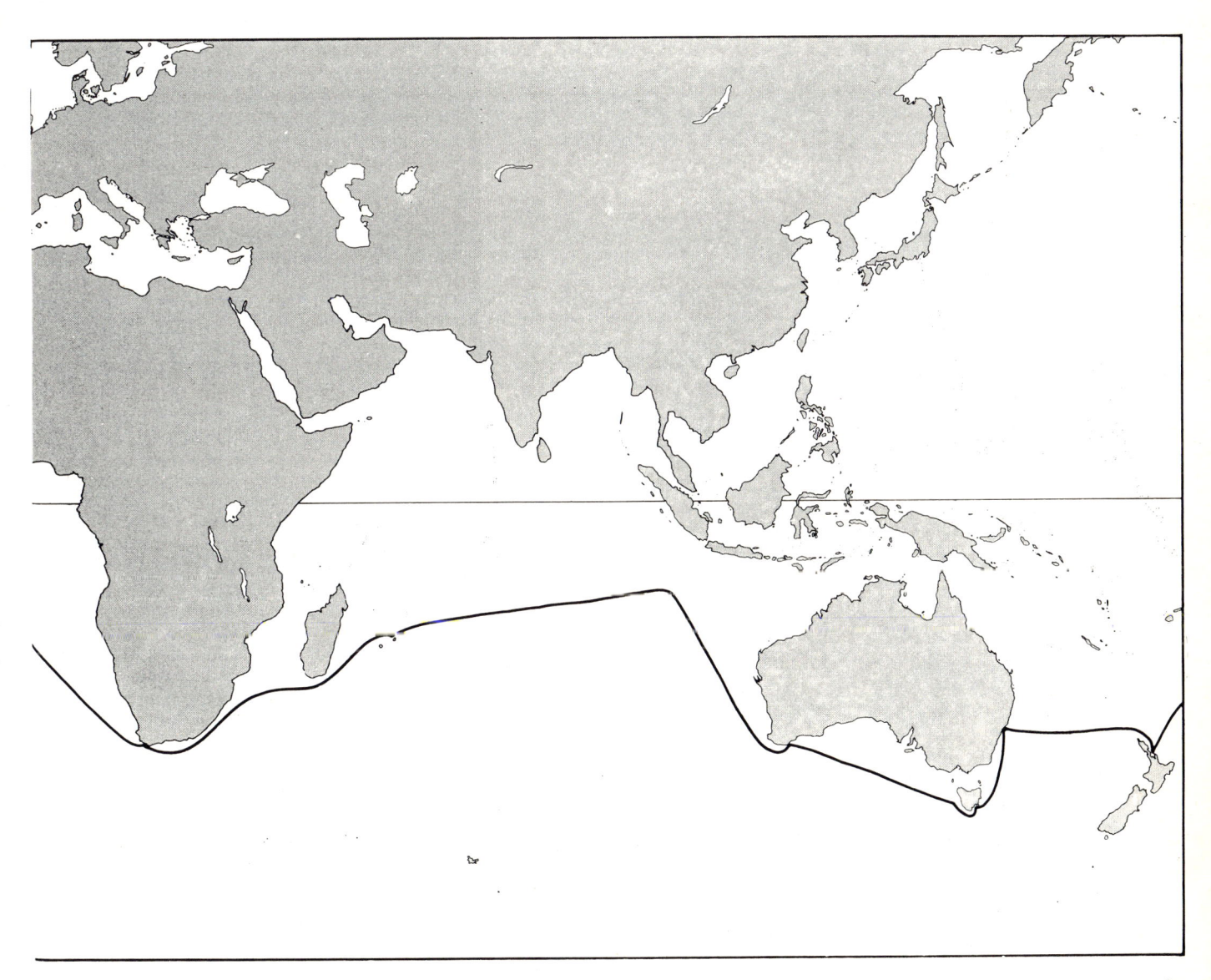

that he described as a "general chart shewing the principal tracks of H.M.S. *Beagle.*" Because FitzRoy's concern was with the "principal tracks," the map does not show all the ship's movements in such cases as the numerous trips to and from the Falkland Islands.

1. THE INDUSTRIAL AND SCIENTIFIC REVOLUTIONS

returned each summer to the same site, Darwin usually had to get what he wanted the first time through an area. The notes he made during the voyage on his first geological excursion illustrate his approach. On January 17 and 18, 1832, the stop was at tiny Quail Island (now Ilhéu de Santa Maria) in the harbor of Praia in São Tiago. The notes begin:

"Quail island a small desolate spot lying close to Porto Praya.—Its shape is oval from N. to S. & barely a mile in circumference. There are round Porto Praya several truncate conical hills: this island may be considered one of the set, but with sea instead of a sandy valley at its foot.—The washing of the sea round its base affords a good section & I thought by studying this island attentively, I might find a good keystone for the neighbouring country.—I will begin by the lowest beds & describe the whole succession with minuteness."

Accompanying the detailed description of the beds were rock samples. In examining his specimens Darwin relied on simple devices: a lens for magnification; an acid bottle for testing alkalinity; a blowpipe for testing the reaction of a specimen to heat; a goniometer for measuring angles, and a magnet. He was careful to label each specimen with a number keyed both to his specimen book and to his notes. As a result virtually his entire collection was and still is usable, unlike many collections rendered fruitless by poor accompanying data.

Besides describing beds and collecting rocks, Darwin speculated on the origin of what he saw. Of Quail Island, for example, he concluded: "Upon the whole I should think it probable [he crossed out *clear*] that after the marine beds had been quietly deposited on the inferior Volcanic rocks, a sheet of melted matter was spread over them: that the whole mass was then raised, since which or at the time there has been a *partial sinking*."

Notwithstanding Darwin's skills as a collector and an observer, it is on his theorizing that his reputation as a geologist rests. What set him apart from most of his colleagues was his ability to treat abstract questions of structure and causation together with questions of detailed observation, and to move back and forth between the two levels with ease. His theoretical impulse, accompanied by a willingness to take on controversial issues, was displayed in his earliest notes on Quail Island. Moreover, his ambition as a geologist grew as the voyage stretched to five years from the two initially planned. With the contemporary geological literature as a guide, he allowed himself to become more speculative in his approach to the subject.

Darwin's growth as a theorist is best illustrated by examining the two largest themes he pursued: vertical movements of the earth's crust and transmutation, or the evolution of species. The first theme came to him from his reading. He picked an idea from his predecessors and then expanded it beyond the dimensions they had given it. The second theme, which he pursued later in the voyage and more circuitously, also came from his predecessors, but in this case he had to overcome their influence, since most of them had viewed evolution negatively.

Darwin's first theme was set in his mind by the end of the voyage. In his "Red Notebook" he wrote in 1836, on the last leg of the voyage, that the "Geology of whole world will turn out simple.—" He alluded to the notion that world geology was governed by simple upward and downward motion, that is, by the elevation and subsidence of land. He believed a balance of these two forces was the key to determining the main features of the earth's surface.

In taking up this theme Darwin was continuing work begun by other geologists. The one person whose thinking influenced him most profoundly was Lyell. Following in a tradition established in the late 1700's by the Scottish geologist James Hutton, Lyell argued in *Principles of Geology* that the earth's surface is perpetually in motion. Like most of the contemporaneous geologists, he believed positing changes in the level of the land was a simpler way to account for the presence of marine remains inland than positing worldwide changes in sea level. Unlike many of his peers, he believed changes in land level took place gradually. He opposed the view held by many geologists that the earth went through periods of stability followed by periods of upheaval.

Darwin approached the phenomena he saw on the voyage with Lyell's views in mind. Whereas Lyell's fieldwork was done in fairly confined areas of Europe, Darwin did his over several oceans and continents. His different experiences affected the way he applied Lyell's ideas. The major change he made in Lyell's notion of elevation and subsidence was to work with it on a larger scale, that of continents rather than that of a confined area.

When he explored what is now Argentina, Darwin was impressed by the immensity of the plains and by the persistence for great distances along the coast of raised beaches of nearly identical height. He inferred from these observations the operation of an elevatory force acting over a large geographic area and working so slowly that it did not disturb the continuity in the height of the plains and the raised beaches. When he got to the Andes, he was impressed by their scale compared with the mountains in Europe. Near Valparaíso in Chile he found evidence of a rising coastline: the presence of recent marine shells well inland and above the high-water mark on the coast. On February 20, 1835, he witnessed an earthquake at Valparaíso accompanied by a land rise of several feet.

All these observations combined to lead him to the conclusion that the entire continent of South America was rising. He saw the creation of the Andes and the occurrence of earthquakes and volcanic eruptions in South America as side effects of the motion.

In his next application of Lyell's notion of elevation and subsidence Darwin made his most lasting contribution to geology outside his work on evolution. This was his theory of the origin of coral reefs, published fully in 1842 as *The Structure and Distribution of Coral Reefs*.

It may seem puzzling that, as the geologist H. W. Menard once put it, "at times, Darwin seems to be concerned with the origin of coral reefs only so far as it gives evidence for regional subsidence of the sea floor." There is no puzzle, however, if one realizes that Darwin formulated his theory as a corollary to his understanding of crustal motion. For him as for Hutton and Lyell, the rise of one area of the earth's surface had to be balanced by the fall of another area. Once he had arrived at the conclusion that all of South America, and even presumably all of North America as well, was rising he looked for a corresponding area of subsidence elsewhere. "Does not the great extent of the Northern & Southern Pacifick include this corresponding Area?" he asked.

Once again Lyell had given Darwin the fundamental points of his argument. In *Principles of Geology* Lyell suggested the Pacific Ocean as an area of subsidence. He also offered an explanation for the shapes of various kinds of coral reef. His argument was that since corals do not grow above the surface of the water and reef-forming corals grow only at shallow depths, reefs must form on preexisting submarine platforms such as subsided mountaintops or volcanic craters. Coral islands must rest on the former, coral atolls on the latter.

5. Darwin as a Geologist

Darwin thought Lyell's explanation of the origin of coral reefs was ingenious but believed Lyell had taken insufficient account of the vastness of the Pacific Ocean. In his view such a large area must have experienced correspondingly extensive subsidence. Therefore it was erroneous to posit the existence of barely submerged mountains and volcanoes simply to account for the presence of coral reefs in mid-ocean. It was better, Darwin thought, to imagine reefs forming on platforms they themselves had built as the floor of the ocean subsided below them. In Darwin's view—which was not finally confirmed until the 1950's—coral reefs might be of great thickness.

What of the various forms of reef? Here Darwin's earliest sighting of a coral reef was instructive. The *Beagle* stopped at Tahiti in November, 1835. Darwin climbed some 2,000 to 3,000 feet up a mountain and gazed toward the beautiful reef-encircled island of Eimeo (now called Moorea). As he looked at it rising out of its "glassy lake" (as he wrote later) he thought, "Remove the central group of mountains, and there remains a Lagoon Is^d." But how could a subsiding mountain leave a ring-shaped reef rather than a disk-shaped island? Because, Darwin maintained, the lagoon that formed where the mountain had once stood held still water and was too shallow to provide a good environment for the growth of reef-forming corals.

On the way back to England, Darwin generalized his insight. He divided reefs into three classes: fringing, barrier and atoll. Fringing reefs (slightly separated from land by shallow water) would occur where the reef simply grew outward from the shore. Darwin believed such reefs must form when the land is stable or rising. Barrier reefs (separated from the land by a deep channel) would be formed when a fringing reef subsided. Coral grew best in full surf, and the outer edge of the fringing reef would form the barrier. The channel would be formed as the interior landmass sank. An atoll reef would be formed if the landmass sank entirely but slowly; otherwise the coral would drown.

Interestingly, Darwin's theory entailed the conclusions that one form of reef evolved into another, that the rate of motion of the ocean floor was sufficiently gradual to not drown a good number of reefs and that by noting the presence of one or another class of reefs one might identify the areas of the ocean floor that were either rising or subsiding. (Fringing reefs would indicate stability or elevation, barrier and atoll reefs subsidence.)

Although Darwin's theory of the structure and distribution of coral reefs has subsequently been challenged at specific points, it is nonetheless held in high regard. Judged as a theory, it remains a model of simplicity and explanatory power.

Darwin came to his second grand ambition in geology more circuitously, but once he was there the work led ultimately to his most famous publication: *On the Origin of Species*. He did not begin the *Beagle* voyage with the intention of writing on that subject. Nor did his peers in science expect it of him.

In hindsight one can identify certain circumstances in his background that prepared him to pursue such a goal, notably the tradition of free thought that existed in his family and the example of his grandfather, Erasmus Darwin, who had written a developmental cosmology. Nevertheless, for Darwin to espouse a transmutationist hypothesis (holding that new species arise from preexisting ones) in the 1830's required him to break with the majority of his peers. His new ambition required a rupture with tradition.

Ironically Lyell was once again the major influence on Darwin. Lyell had devoted most of the second volume of *Principles of Geology* to an attack on the transmutationist hypothesis of the French writer Jean Baptiste de Lamarck. In the course of attacking the hypothesis, however, Lyell gave his readers a clear statement of it. When Darwin received the volume in November, 1832, while the *Beagle* was at Montevideo, he had at hand an up-to-date and well-informed presentation of both sides of the controversy. Hence early in the voyage he knew what the tradition of interpretation regarding species was and what breaking with it would require. Moreover, in arguing against transmutation Lyell had presented an enormous amount of information on the geographic distribution of species and on nature's economy, or what would now be called ecology. Later Darwin would draw on this information for his own purposes.

The central issue that had brought the question of transmutation to the fore in geology was extinction. In 1796 the French naturalist Georges Cuvier had stated that the bones of a large fossil found in Paraguay belonged to an unknown animal. He invented a name for the new form: *Megatherium* (large beast). Because the continents had been fairly well explored by his day and no such animal had ever been sighted, Cuvier concluded that the animal had become extinct. Before long the remains of other large animals without living representatives (*Mastodon* and *Palaeotherium*) were identified. By the early 19th century the case for extinction was so strong that it was regarded as fact.

Darwin confronted the extinction issue as both collector and interpreter. As collector he took pains on the voyage to pick up specimens of the great extinct land animals. Eventually he had partial specimens of about a dozen different forms.

As interpreter Darwin's main concern with fossils during the voyage was to determine their geologic association, that is, their position in a particular stratum and the relation of that bed to the surrounding beds. His aim was to determine the conditions under which the bones had been deposited and from that knowledge to gain some understanding of the causes of extinction. He was aware of the split in English geology between those (including Lyell) who believed species became extinct gradually and those (including William Buckland, reader in geology at the University of Oxford) who believed species died out rather suddenly, presumably as a result of dramatic changes in living conditions arising from, say, a flood or an abrupt change in temperature.

Darwin decided in favor of the gradualist view, partly because of the gradual nature of the land elevations he thought were taking place in South America. As he wrote while he was in Chile in 1835: "With respect to the *death* of species of Terrestrial Mammalia in the S. part of S. America I am strongly inclined to reject the action of any sudden debacle.—"

Then, like Lyell, he went on to assert that extinct species must have been replaced by new species. His reason may surprise the present-day reader, because it was drawn from theology. "The fitness which the Author of Nature has now established," he argued, would be contradicted if extinct species were not replaced. In 1835, then, he believed he had theological grounds for considering how replacements might arise.

When Darwin returned to England in October, 1836, he turned his fossil bones over to Richard Owen, anatomist at the Royal College of Surgeons and a disciple of Cuvier. By the end of January, Owen had completed a preliminary examination of the bones.

1. THE INDUSTRIAL AND SCIENTIFIC REVOLUTIONS

Some he declared belonged to known species of extinct animals, but others were completely new. What particularly impressed Darwin were the connections Owen pointed out between the fossil bones and various living animals peculiar to South America. One specimen, later named *Toxodon Platensis*, had affinities to the modern capybara. Another, later named *Macrauchenia Patachonica*, had affinities (eventually questioned) to the modern llama, or guanaco. Lyell himself called attention to this striking pattern of geologic succession in the forms of South American animals soon after Owen had pronounced on Darwin's specimens.

To a present-day reader such a pattern might seem to demand a transmutationist explanation; in 1837 an insuperable difficulty intervened. However many points of similarity there were between ancient and modern forms, there were still many points of difference, and various lines existed along which one might draw affinities. Furthermore, no series of intermediate forms connecting ancient and modern forms were known. Hence the fossil evidence, although it was suggestive, was insufficient to support a transmutationist hypothesis. Another element was needed.

That element was supplied by facts drawn from the present geographic distribution of species. The advantage of living forms was that they had fine gradations. Darwin, relating how he adopted a transmutationist hypothesis, wrote in his autobiography he was struck "by the manner in which closely allied animals replace one another in proceeding southwards over the Continent" and also "by the South American character of most of the Galapagos archipelago, and more especially by the manner in which they differ slightly on each island of the group."

One of Darwin's key examples of the replacement of a species by a closely allied species involved the two rheas: the greater or common rhea, found from northeastern Brazil to the Río Negro in central Argentina, and the lesser or Darwin's rhea, found in the Patagonian lowlands. His key example of island-by-island variation in form was provided by the Galápagos mockingbirds. Three islands, Charles, Albemarle and Chatham, each had its own mockingbird, barely distinguishable from one another by eye but nonetheless separate species according to the ornithologist John Gould.

Rheas, mockingbirds and similar examples made transmutation seem possible to Darwin. Clearly it was easier to imagine a living form transmuting into a slightly different living form than it was to imagine the passage of an extinct animal into a related but still markedly different living animal. Once he had grasped the transmutation potential of living species, Darwin quickly read it back into the past. As he observed in the "Red Notebook" in March, 1837: "The same kind of relation that common ostrich [the large rhea] bears to [the small one]: extinct Guanaco to recent: in former case position, in latter time... being the relation." In the notebook he went on to consider the possibility that one species can change into another. He had become a transmutationist.

Thus did Darwin's second grand ambition in geology crystallize in March, 1837, when he drew an analogy comparing the distribution of species in space to their distribution in time. This same ambition was fully realized in 1859, when he published *On the Origin of Species*. In the intervening 22 years he remained faithful to his vocation as a geologist, but he worked primarily as an author, writing up material for which the fieldwork had already been done. Both as field-worker and author, however, his legacy as a geologist was assured.

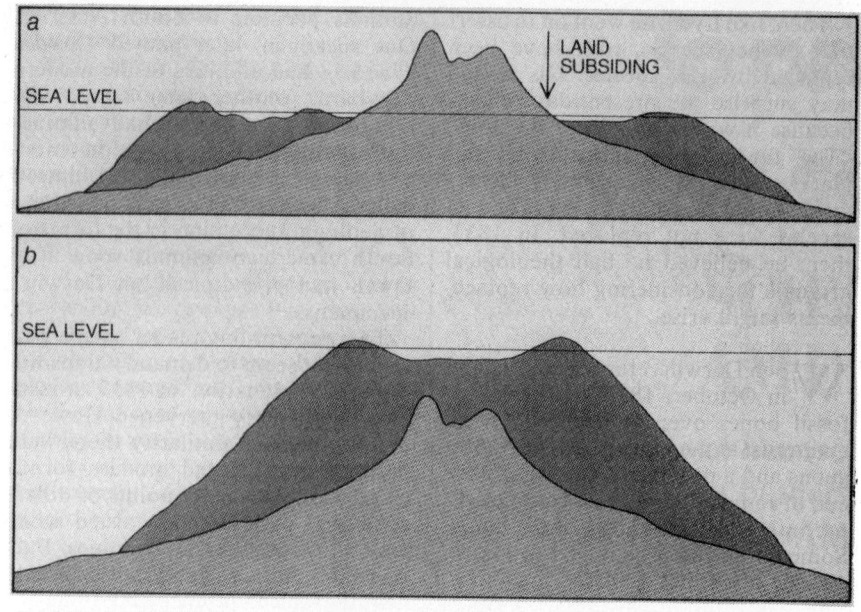

DARWIN'S THEORY on the formation of coral reefs rested on the concept that corals grow on land that is slowly sinking. Here corals (dark gray) build up in shallow water over land that was once the above-water perimeter of a sinking island (*a*). Eventually the entire island subsides and the corals form an atoll: a reef around a lagoon that lies over what was the highest part of the island (*b*). Darwin explained correctly that corals do not grow in a lagoon because they need moving water in order to flourish, and lagoon water is too still.

Article 6

Life's recipe

This brief is about genes and science's greatest achievement this century: deciphering the code in which are written the instructions for building, running and reproducing bodies. The text is still being read.

In the 1940s and 1950s, several clever physicists turned themselves into biologists. Flushed with their success within the atom, they decided the next problem to be solved was life itself. It was a shrewd move. Between 1944 and 1972, discoveries came thick and fast: first, the nature of hereditary material, called genes; then the ingenious molecular structure of genes; then the code in which their hereditary message was written; and then a way to tinker with that code.

Since then, genetics has become a significant part of the biotechnology industry. It has also invaded the rest of biology as a tool. Medicine, agriculture and the study of evolution have all adopted the techniques and insights of molecular biology, along with its jargon of clones, sequences and mutants.

Since 1972, genetics has made few big breakthroughs. This is not because it has nothing left to discover. Progress is being held up because scientists now know practically all there is to know about bacteria (the simple one-cell creatures on which early genetic studies were done), but little about man and other animals.

In the past few years, however, biotechnology has given scientists the tools to explore the genes of mice and even men. Molecular biologists now hope they can tackle two pressing questions: how does a fertilised egg manage to turn into a human being, and how does a healthy cell turn into a cancer tumour?

Before 1860, ideas about heredity were few and vague. Charles Darwin, for example, thought that a child somehow inherited a blended mixture of vital fluid from its father and mother. Then Gregor Mendel, a Bohemian monk, crossed some pea plants and showed that the offspring were not blended versions of their parents, but that they inherited discrete "factors" from each parent and passed those factors on unchanged to their offspring in predictable ratios.

Mendel's experiments, rescued from obscurity by British and American biologists in the early part of the twentieth century, seemed to prove that heredity relied on particles carried within eggs and sperm. The particles became known as genes.

In 1871, a substance called deoxyribonucleic acid (DNA) was found to be common in the sperm of trout from the river Rhine. It, too, had to be rescued from obscurity by a series of elegant experiments in the 1940s by a Canadian physician, Oswald Avery, and his colleagues. They proved, to the surprise of most biologists, that genes are made of DNA and not, as expected, of protein—out of whose molecules most of the body's machinery and structure are made.

Yet DNA was known to be just a long, thin molecular string, made of a repeating sequence of sugars, phosphates and chemical bases. How could it possibly carry the instructions for building and running bodies? Clearly, its secret must lie in its structure. In 1953, the race to work out the structure of DNA was won by two young Cambridge scientists, Mr James Watson and Dr Francis Crick, working largely in their spare time. The ingenuity of the structure was immediately obvious: it was Mendel's factors made flesh.

Two intertwined helices of DNA are linked by weak bonds between the bases. The bases come in four kinds (A, C, G and T) and links can be made only between given pairs of them: G to C and A to T (see chart on this page). Thus a sequence of bases can spell out a code and that code can be faithfully passed on to offspring by untwining the two helices and copying them.

Code crackers

Next, to crack the code. Were it not for some great leaps of imagination, mainly on the part of Dr Crick, this problem might have remained intractable for decades. It was already fairly widely agreed that the code must be principally a set of instructions for making proteins. Proteins depend largely on their shapes to do their jobs, so somehow the code must spell out that shape. Proteins, like DNA, are made of long unbranching strings. Dr Crick realised that the protein shape was determined by the sequence of amino acids in the strings, and he guessed that the sequence was somehow determined directly by the sequence of bases (letters) on the DNA.

He was right. By 1970, the last letter of the code had been cracked: the code is written in three-letter words (called codons), each of which specifies one of the 20 amino acids in the protein alphabet, except for a few which act as signals to the copying machinery to start and stop. Each gene is faithfully transcribed to make a temporary single-stranded copy from a material called RNA (which is very like DNA, except that it is unable to form double helices).

This transcript, known as the messenger, is then used as the blueprint for building a protein by a neat little machine tool in the form of a cell called a ribosome (see diagram on next page). The ribosome reads the messenger by moving from codon to codon along it.

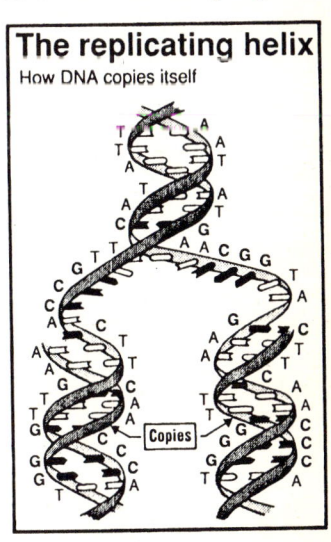

The replicating helix
How DNA copies itself

From *The Economist*, May 30, 1987, pp. 84-85. © 1987 The Economist, reprinted by permission of The New York Times Syndicated Sales Service.

6. Life's Recipe

At each stop, a small tug-like RNA molecule called transfer-RNA brings along the appropriate amino acid to attach to a growing protein chain: each transfer molecule has on its head the three-letter word corresponding to the code for the amino acid it carries. The code is the same in man, mouse and all living creatures—with one exception found so far, a tiny slipper-shaped protozoan (called Paramecian) that uses different words for certain amino acids.

One big problem remained—and it has not been fully solved to this day. Every cell in the human body contains the complete recipe for the whole body. Yet cells differ in their sizes, shapes, biochemistry and abundance. Skin cells, blood cells, nerve cells, muscle cells—all must somehow receive instructions to differentiate in the growing embryo. How?

The first part of that question is, how do the cells switch on different sets of genes and so produce different sets of proteins? The hunt for gene switches began in bacteria. A common bacterium like *E. coli*, from the human gut, is able to switch on the gene for an enzyme called beta-galactosidase when lactose sugar (essentially its food) is present, and switch it off when there is no lactose. The enzyme breaks down the lactose into simpler sugars on which the bacteria can feed.

In the 1960s, two French scientists, Jacques Monod and François Jacob, worked out how the gene is switched on and off. Lactose itself boosts the amount of beta-galactosidase by somehow increasing the activity of another enzyme that transcribes the beta-galactosidase gene. Lactose thus speeds up the production of messenger RNAs and hence of beta-galactosidase protein which, in turn, digests the lactose. Its abundance controls the means of its own destruction.

However, certain mutant bacteria can produce lots of enzyme whether their lactose food supply is there or not. Jacques Monod came up with an explanation: a specific repressor molecule attaches itself to the DNA, blocking the transcription of the beta-galactosidase gene. Lactose unblocks it by attaching itself to the repressor and putting it out of action. In mutant bacteria, the genes to which the repressor molecule attaches itself do not work, so the main gene is always switched on.

This may sound complicated, but it was in fact the system's simplicity that excited scientists. Similar switches have been found to control most bacterial genes. Do the same mechanisms control human genes? Dr Monod, in a fit of optimism, declared that "what is true for *E. coli* is also true for an elephant."

Unfortunately, it is not. Elephant and human genes turn out to be much more complicated—which is not surprising, since bacteria are single cells. Elephants are made up of billions of different sorts of cells.

The first thing scientists found about switches in human cells was that a short distance "upstream" of a gene (ie, at the end that is transcribed first), there usually lies a short sequence of four bases, TATA. This turned out to be a red herring. The TATA grouping is merely a signal to tell the transcribing mechanism where the gene starts; it is not the switch itself.

To find the switches, scientists had to isolate pure genes in test tubes, add basic ingredients such as the transcribing enzyme and any other proteins necessary to switch on the gene, and then try to work out where the proteins attached to the DNA. In theory, these points could be where the switches are.

What scientists found was a series of short sequences (or "boxes") upstream of the gene and a series of new proteins that attach to these boxes. For example, one gene, to be switched on, requires two proteins called SP1 to attach to boxes that read GGGCGG, and one other protein to attach to a third box between those boxes reading GCCAAT.

Moreover, these boxes (known as promoters) have to be in exactly the right place relative to the gene. Other sequences, known as enhancers, can be anywhere, not even close by, and still control the gene. This gap between the gene and an enhancer took some explaining, until experiments revealed that the protein that attaches to the enhancer can cause the DNA to bend into a loop, bringing the enhancer into contact with the gene.

So some switches have been found. Nobody knows how the proteins that control the switches are themselves controlled, and nobody knows exactly how switches control development. There are tantalising clues, though. One comes from fruit flies, in which certain genes cause young flies to develop abnormally: to grow a leg instead of an antenna, for example.

In 1984, several scientists discovered that such genes all had a single sequence of 180 DNA letters in them. Even more remarkable, these sequences (called homeo-boxes) were found in the genes that affect development in mice and even human beings. It was as if this sequence were somehow a universal switch for genes that control growth and differentiation.

Sceptics point out, however, that the universality of the homeo-box is likely to mean that it is the least interesting part of the machinery. All computers use the same plugs to plug into the electricity supply. Perhaps the homeo-box is the developmental gene's plug.

To understand embryonic development is one of the reasons for studying gene switches. The other is to understand cancer. The discovery that healthy cells harbour special genes called oncogenes that can cause cancer has transformed the way scientists think about this disease.

It now looks as if the proteins made by oncogenes control a series of master switches that are responsible for controlling the cell's growth. Cancer, which is nothing more than a cell gone berserk, growing and dividing continuously, is therefore caused by somebody leaving the growth genes switched on.

Scientists realised this in 1983, when they read the sequence of bases in one human oncogene. It turned out to resemble closely the sequence of a human gene that encoded a protein called a growth factor. In healthy cells, growth factors set off a chain of events via so-called receptors on the cell's surface, so that the cell reproduces itself—for instance, when blood clots, healing cells multiply. Normally, the cells that make a growth factor do not respond to it, and vice versa. If a cell that responds to a growth factor switches on the gene for that factor, it tells itself continuously to grow and multiply. It becomes a cancer.

Two other kinds of oncogenes work in similar ways. One makes a faulty version of the receptor for the growth factor—faulty in the sense that it acts as if it were continuously receiving the factor. Again, it continuously tells the cell to grow. A third class of oncogenes encodes proteins that are themselves switches for other genes.

Gene dreams

These discoveries were quite unexpected. Before 1982, when the first human oncogene was found, nobody expected cancer to be so readily explicable through genetics. Thanks to molecular biology, cancer is now understood, though not conquered. The aim of most molecular biologists is to uncover enough information so that cures can be found to treat hitherto intractable diseases. One possibility is that agents could be developed which block the binding of the growth factors to the receptor. They could turn out to be promising anti-cancer drugs.

These are distant dreams, but they are not fantasies. Already molecular biology has begun to transform medicine in many different ways. It has enabled scientists to track down the genes responsible

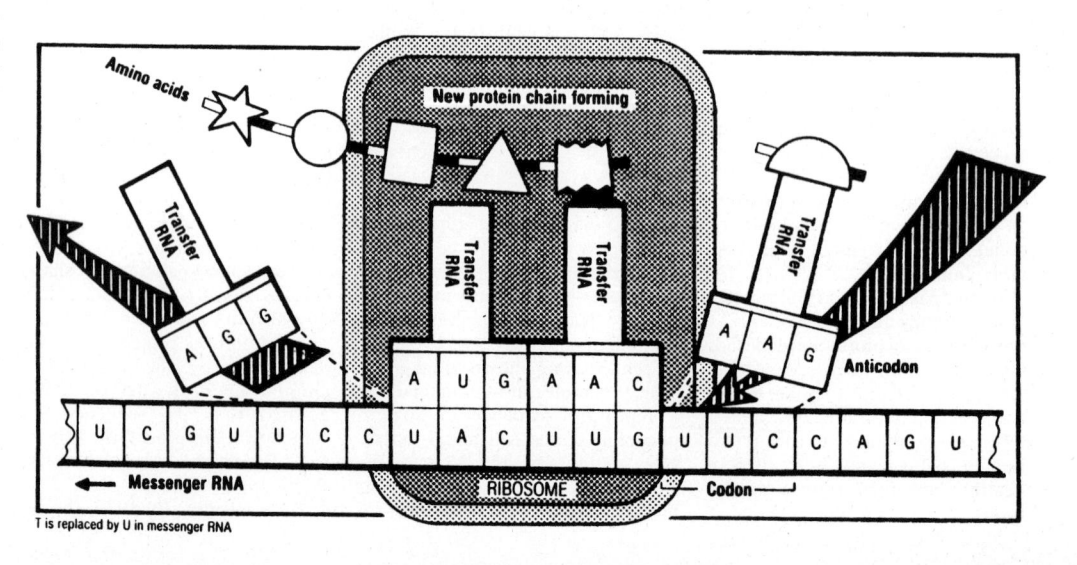

T is replaced by U in messenger RNA

1. THE INDUSTRIAL AND SCIENTIFIC REVOLUTIONS

for inherited diseases like cystic fibrosis. It has enabled them to find the cause of diseases like AIDS and to design drugs and vaccines that fight disease.

Molecular biology has given scientists two especially useful tools: sequencing and genetic engineering. Sequencing is a clumsy term for reading the sequence of letters in a gene and translating it to work out what protein it spells out. As the cancer story illustrates, it is useful mainly because of the coincidences it reveals: a computer first spotted that oncogenes are like the genes which code for growth-factor proteins by comparing their sequences.

In 1986, encouraged by the recent invention of a machine to read the sequences of genes automatically, a bold plan was aired by a group of American scientists: to read the sequences of the entire set of 50,000 human genes (called the genome).

The result would be a list of bases 3.5 billion characters long—or enough characters to fill about 5,000 average-sized books. Even with the new machines, it would take about ten years and $1 billion a year to do the job. Moreover, genomes are as idiosyncratic as people: whose would you choose to read?

Genetic engineering means taking a gene from one creature and putting it in another. It was first invented in 1972 and perfected during the late 1970s, for transferring genes from human cells to bacteria. The advantage of doing this is that the bacteria can then be encouraged to churn out large amounts of some human protein that can then be used as a drug.

Insulin for diabetics and growth hormone for young dwarfs are both made this way. Drugs to fight cancer and heart disease have also been mass-produced in bacteria—without any great success, as yet, simply because scientists do not know enough about the body's biochemistry to predict which proteins they want to mass-produce.

Genes can now also be put into plants and even animals. For example, a gene was taken from a bacterium that kills insects and put into a tobacco plant. That plant was then left alone by insects. Putting genes into animals is less easy, but it has been done. Human globin genes, which encode the protein responsible for carrying oxygen in the blood, have been transferred to mice. Scientists hope this will reveal how the switches controlling globin genes work. But they could, conceivably, have more practical ambitions—to make cattle grow wool, for instance.

The most ambitious scheme is to put human genes into other human beings. The point would be to cure certain inherited diseases, such as Huntington's chorea, that are caused by the absence of a working copy of the gene. "Gene therapy" would add a working copy of the gene using a special virus called a retrovirus that inserts its genes into human DNA when it infects a cell.

The virus would first be disarmed by removing the genes that enable it to make more viruses, and the experiment would be done only on the bone marrow, not on the germ cells that carry genes to the next generation. Nonetheless, the idea of playing with human genes and retroviruses—AIDS is a retrovirus—alarms people. The alternative, though, for diseases like Huntington's chorea, is to do nothing.

The Green Revolution

Robert E. Huke

Robert E. Huke was educated at Dartmouth College and Syracuse University, and he is currently Professor of Geography, Dartmouth College, Hanover, NH 03755. His teaching and research interests focus on agriculture, especially in South and Southeast Asia where he has completed a number of village and regional level research projects. A second major interest lies with the development of computer-assisted instruction modules for use in teaching and in training agricultural extension workers.

The Green Revolution refers to a complex package that includes improved seeds and a wide range of management practices. The new plant types show a strong positive response to fertilizer because of a high leaf area index, short stature, and stiff straw that resists lodging. These plant varieties have resistance to many insect pests and plant diseases. The management package is concerned with timing; rate and method of application of various inputs; appropriate spacing of plants; thorough weeding; careful monitoring and control of pests; and improved harvesting, drying, and threshing methods. Of all the management practices, the control of water is perhaps the most important, because its timely application is essential to efficient utilization of fertilizer and the attainment of high yields (Anderson et al. 1982).

The Green Revolution is not a miracle of modern agricultural technology, but rather an evolution that differs only in time and place from earlier developments in industrialized countries. In both cases, the route to significant yield improvements involved plant materials having high genetic potential farmed with improved management practices that included considerably increased levels of input.

This paper provides a brief historic and geographic

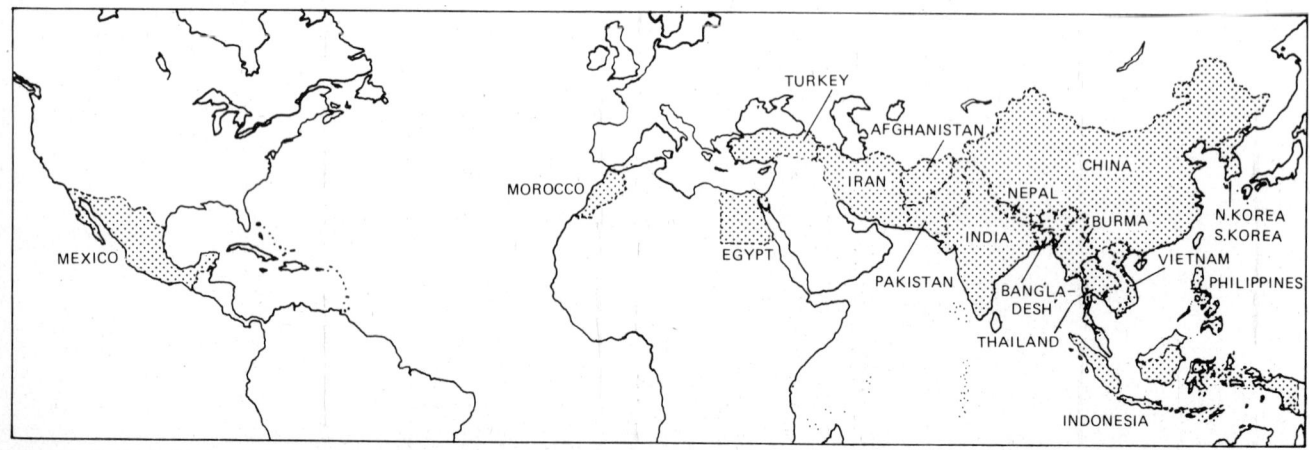

Figure 1. Chief benefiting countries. Source: Author.

7. The Green Revolution

view of the genetic and technological developments that led to the Green Revolution. It describes some of the characteristics of the area where these developments were most readily applied and raises questions concerning the unequal impact of the revolution.

Targeted Areas

Yield increases and improved food availability have been particularly important in a group of eighteen heavily populated countries where wheat and/or rice are major food crops. These countries, which are the chief beneficiaries of the Green Revolution, extend across the subtropical part of the world from Korea in the east to Mexico in the west (Figure 1). Fifteen of these countries are contiguous, describing an arc in southern Asia, and are characterized by high rural and farming populations. The benefiting countries include eighteen percent of the earth's land surface, thirty-two percent of its cultivated area, and are home to fifty-six percent of the world's population. Except for China, their population numbers are increasing at a markedly higher rate than that for the world as a whole, and population density is already at extraordinary levels. In mid-1985, there were 290 persons per square mile (750 per square kilometer) compared to forty-nine (127) for the remainder of the world. Population density is almost six times higher than that of the rest of the world; and the nutritional density, or population per square mile of cultivated land, is over 1,500.

The high population-to-land ratio helps to explain other characteristics of the area as well. Grain is raised chiefly on small farms without mechanization and often in monocultivation. The annual crop provides a major portion of the total farm income, and frequently a significant portion of the crop stays on the farm to provide food for the coming year. The farm population dependent on either wheat or rice as a major crop totals at least 1.7 billion people, or 320 million families. Many of these families have no land at all and depend on farm employment for their income. Even those who own or rent land have an average of less than 2.5 acres (about one hectare) per family. The vast majority of these Third World farmers live close to the margin of existence. Surpluses of food and money are minimal.

Unfortunately for these and other underdeveloped countries, the Green Revolution promises more than it can deliver. The term "Green Revolution" implies that a solution has been found for the problem of providing adequate food for a population that grows exponentially. A solution has not been found. The Green Revolution has provided for a quantum leap in food production per unit area, but further increases will be slower, smaller, and probably more expensive. What the Green Revolution has done is to provide time—a breathing space—for people to find a more permanent solution to the population-food problem.

Genetic History: The Green Evolution

The term, "Green Revolution," was originally inspired by work with wheat and rice during the late 1960s, but today is applied to developments in a broad range of food crops throughout the tropics and subtropics. Much of the fundamental research is done at a series of international centers that conduct basic research and train scientists from and in underdeveloped countries. National research centers adapt this research to local needs.

The genes that sparked the Green Revolution were brought to the attention of the post-World War II scientific community by S.C. Salmon who carried seeds of an obscure, short, stiff-strawed, heavy-seeded Japanese wheat (Norin No. 10) to the US in 1946. In 1953 a small packet of second-generation seeds (Norin crossed with a tall North American wheat) was received in Mexico and became the foundation for a breeding program that eventually resulted in a Nobel Peace Prize for Norman Borlaug. In 1962 the first few of Borlaug's Mexican semi-dwarf, rust-resistant seeds were matured in New Dehli. M.S. Swaminathan, then head of the Indian Agricultural Research Institute's Division of Genetics, was so impressed that Borlaug was invited to India where the two scientists launched a program of agricultural innovation in the subcontinent (CIMMYT Economics Program 1983).

Also in 1962, Peter Jennings at the International Rice Research Institute in the Philippines crossed Peta (a tall Indonesian rice variety) with Dee-geo-woo-gen (a short statured variety from Taiwan) (Chandler 1982), and 130 seeds were formed. From these seeds, IR8 (the first of the IRRI modern high-yielding varieties) was identified and named. IR8 was short and sturdy, tillered well, had great seedling vigor, responded well to fertilizer, had moderate seed dormancy, was reasonably resistant to tungro virus, and was essentially insensitive to photoperiod. (Varieties that are insensitive to photoperiod can be planted and harvested in any season without regard to the number of hours of daylight.) IR8 produced record yields almost everywhere it was tested. Unfortunately, it also had several disadvantages. The grain was bold and chalky in appearance, which detracted from its value; it was subject to considerable breakage in the milling process; and the amalose content of its starch was so high as to cause a hardening after cooking and cooling (a distinct handicap for sales to Asian consumers). It was also susceptible to bacterial blight and several races of rice blast. IR8 was soon replaced by a sequence of newer varieties that overcame IR8's disadvantages but maintained most of its yield advantage.

Contact with rice scientists in China was difficult and limited until the 1970s. Nonetheless, a small but steady exchange of genetic material and published research was maintained through Hong Kong and East Pakistan (now called Bangladesh). In China the breeding efforts in rice were divided between the development of improved varieties and hybrids, for which new seeds had to be developed for each planting. The emphasis on hybrids was so strong that by the early 1980s almost twenty percent of China's total rice area was planted to hybrids (Huke 1982). In other rice growing countries, the cost and effort of raising hybrid seed was not considered worth the gains to be realized from hybrid vigor until recently.

Innovations Through Breeding

The breeding of rice and wheat in the mid-twentieth century developed along three distinctive and equally important lines. The first innovation was the introduction of the dwarfing gene that allowed plants to use high levels of fertilizer and achieve yield levels far above those previously possible. Along with this change came the elimination of photoperiod sensitivity. This innovation was of greatest benefit to farmers on the highest quality land that could be irrigated year round. But even for farmers on rainfed land, it allowed increased flexibility and the opportunity to adjust planting dates to the soil moisture levels of individual seasons. It also allowed some spreading out of labor demands in areas where monocultivation was the normal mode of operation and, therefore, moderated the "boom" and "bust" character of the labor market.

1. THE INDUSTRIAL AND SCIENTIFIC REVOLUTIONS

The second innovation was the genetic capability to resist attacks by various insect pests and diseases. One reason for the rapid and widespread acceptance of wheat varieties from Mexico in the early 1960s was a strong resistance to various rusts. With rice, early releases were not as resistant to attack. In many parts of Asia, losses to insects and diseases were often severe, especially during the monsoon season. Several early varieties produced yields up to their genetic potential only with heavy and frequent application of chemical insect controls. Farmer resistance to the use of expensive systemics, inappropriate use of sprays, increasing environmental concerns, and the development of resistant genotypes among insect populations hastened the development of grain types with genetic resistance. Newer varieties of both rice and wheat require smaller amounts of pesticides than varieties used in the 1970s.

The third innovation was the development of plants with much shorter growing seasons. Before this innovation, the normal practice in Asia was for farmers to plant rice with the first monsoon rains in June and to harvest in mid-December. A 180-day growing season was common. The growing season, however, was reduced to 150 days with IR8 and 110 days with IR36. The adoption of IR36 allows farmers in areas subject to erratic, early rains to evade moisture problems by planting late, and it allows farmers more favorable conditions to supplement the rice crop with an early planting or post-rice planting of a vegetable or a pulse.

The importance of these innovations may be appreciated with reference to wheat in Bangladesh, where output increased from 100,000 metric tons to over 1,000,000 metric tons in twelve years. When the country was established as an independent nation in 1971, many writers believed the problem of producing sufficient food for over 90,000,000 people on a land area the size of New York State, and whose farm base is subject to annual deep flooding as well as to periodic devastation by typhoons, was close to hopeless. Rice is the major food crop, and wheat a secondary crop used chiefly for making chapatis. The environment for rice production is probably the most difficult of any rice-growing country. Of 24.7 million acres (ten million hectares) planted annually, only ten percent is irrigated; twelve percent is flooded to a depth of greater than three feet (one meter); almost ten percent is dryland, lacking even bunds to pond rainfall; and the remainder is rainfed, frequently subject to massive but temporary flooding. Despite such handicaps, Bangladesh has converted about fifteen percent of its rice area to modern varieties and has improved its national rice yield by almost thirty percent. At the same time, wheat acreages, yields, and production increased sharply (Figure 2). This shift came about only after changes had been made in rice and wheat seeds. The shortened rice growing season provided a window of opportunity for Bangladeshi farmers; and the rust-resistant, short growing season wheat allowed farmers to take advantage of the opportunity. Wheat is now grown as a winter season crop on large areas that previously produced only a rainy season, long-duration rice crop.

It is improbable, however, that wheat expansion would have taken place rapidly were it not for the fact that farmers had prior experience with modern rice varieties and had received help from extension agents. In less than fifteen years, wheat yields more than doubled. The area planted to wheat expanded five times, and wheat production increased ten times (CIMMYT 1982). In the world's most crowded country where food shortages and natural disasters occur frequently, the food situation by mid-1985 in Bangladesh was marginally better than it was a decade earlier. In Bangladesh, modern agricultural technology has already proven that it can provide the time for the country to tackle the population-food problem.

Inputs and Yield

Modern plant varieties give higher yields than do traditional ones. They are planted on the best land, tend to occupy irrigated or at least reliable water control areas, receive

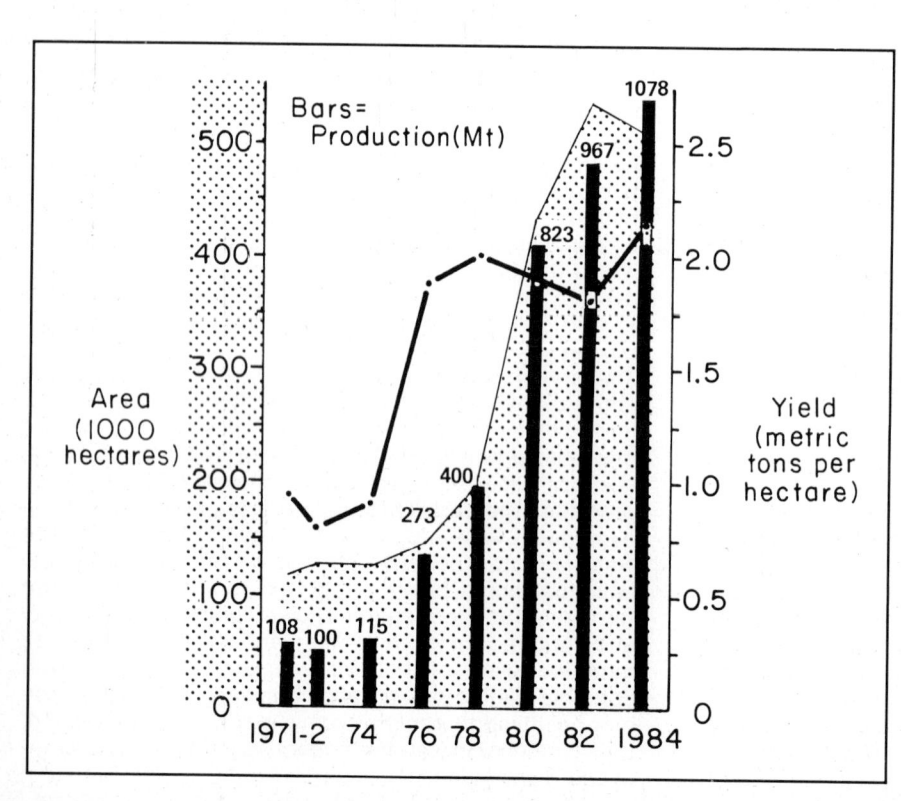

Figure 2. Bangladesh wheat: area, yield, production. Source: US Department of Agriculture (1984).

7. The Green Revolution

Table 1.

Percentage Change in Area, Production, and Yield of Rice: 1965-67 to 1982-84

Country	Change in rice area million hectares	percentage	Change in rice production million metric tons	percentage	Change in rice yield metric tons per hectare	percentage
China	3.1	10	67.9	73	1.76	57
India	4.0	11	31.5	69	0.66	51
Indonesia	1.6	21	18.8	122	1.72	83
Bangladesh	1.4	15	7.0	46	0.44	27
Thailand	2.8	43	5.2	42	−0.02	−1
Burma	0.1	2	7.0	97	1.45	94
Vietnam	0.9	19	5.3	60	0.66	75
Philippines	0.3	10	3.8	93	0.99	75
S. Korea	<.1	0	2.3	45	1.96	47
Pakistan	0.6	43	3.2	160	1.20	83
N. Korea	0.2	33	2.7	117	2.47	66
Total	+15.0	+14	+154.7	+74	+1.05	+52
World less 11 above	+3	+15	+5.3	+11	−0.10	−4

Source: Palacpac (1982) and US Department of Agriculture (1984).

Table 2.

Percentage Change in Area, Population, and Yield of Wheat: 1965-1984

Country	Change in wheat area thousands of hectares	percentage	Change in wheat production thousands of metric tons	percentage	Change in wheat yield metric tons per hectare	percentage
Egypt	47	+9	728	+57	1.08	+45
Morocco	318	+19	874	+80	.34	+52
Afghanistan	294	+13	800	+36	.20	+21
Bangladesh	405	+405	960	+813	.96	+81
China	4106	+17	51671	+173	1.63	+135
India	9685	+72	25900	+156	.61	+50
Iran	2000	+50	2582	+66	.10	+10
Pakistan	2052	+39	6284	+103	.54	+47
Turkey	1574	+22	3264	+33	.12	+9
Total	20481	+39	93063	+131	.82	+66
World less 9 above		−4		+24		+29

Source: US Department of Agriculture (1984) and FAO (1967).

higher levels of fertilizer, and are often more carefully weeded than traditional varieties. Plant protection is more commonly extended to modern varieties; the net labor input is higher, and the modern varieties are first adopted by the most innovative farmers. For almost every input controlled by farmers, modern varieties have an advantage over traditional ones.

Changes in area planted, production, and yield for rice and wheat for Green Revolution countries are shown in Tables 1 & 2. In the case of rice, area increased by a modest fifteen percent over eighteen years, reflecting the fact that land was already at a premium and that the best land had already been developed. The new area was land previously avoided for rice because of poor soils, excessive flooding, excessive drainage, remoteness, or some other physical or locational handicap. Despite this modest increase in area, the production of rice rose by seventy-four percent over the same period because of a remarkable increase in yield per unit area.

Output of modern grain varieties increases sharply with the application of the first unit of a new input, but an additional unit of that same input results in a lower additional increase. For example, a first weeding may result in a yield increase of fifteen percent over that of no weeding, but a second weeding may result in only a ten percent additional increase. Eventually, one further weeding will cost more than the value of the resulting yield increase. With chemical fertilizers, the response will be more dramatic. At some level, a point will be reached where one additional unit of input will result in a decrease in yield. Nonetheless, at all levels of fertilizer input, the expected yield of modern varieties exceeds that of traditional varieties. The general formula describing this relationship is:

Final Yield = Base Yield + A(Fertilizer) − B(Fertilizer)^2.

The case of Indonesia provides an example of the differential impact of high nitrogen fertilizer on irrigated rice (Figure 3). The coefficients for (Fertilizer) and

1. THE INDUSTRIAL AND SCIENTIFIC REVOLUTIONS

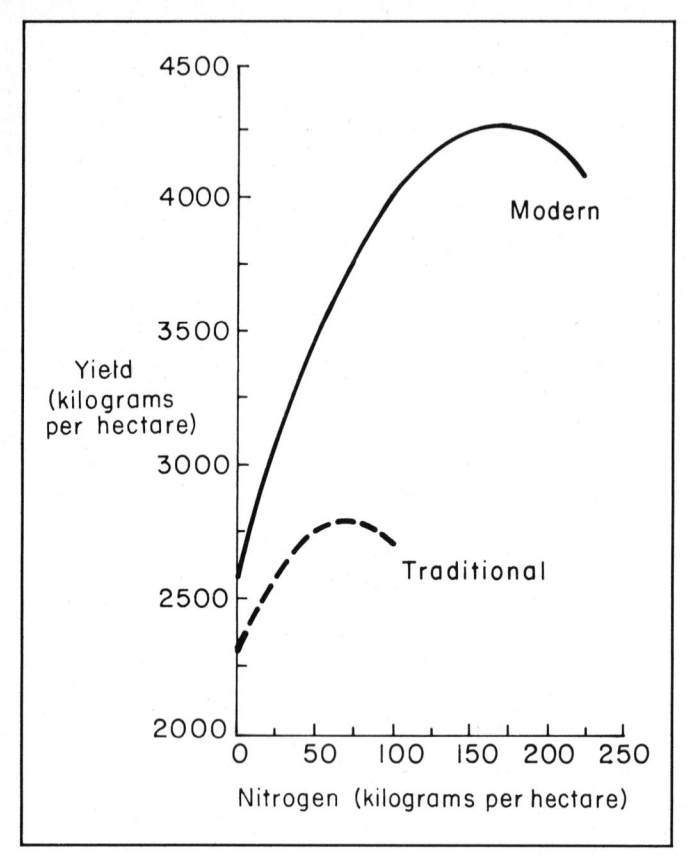

Figure 3. Yield response of nitrogen on irrigated rice in Indonesia. Source: Herdt and Capule (1983).

(Fertilizer)[2] vary with rice variety, water control, soil character, and season but always show a more rapid response on the part of improved grain types. The observation that modern varieties require more fertilizer is only partly correct. Although they do require more fertilizer to reach their maximum potential, modern varieties outyield traditional types even without the application of fertilizer (Barker and Herdt 1985).

Impact of the Green Revolution

From 1965 through 1983, underdeveloped countries outperformed developed countries in terms of the rate of increase in food production (Figure 4). Unfortunately, population growth was so high in underdeveloped countries that their per capita gain was no more than in developed countries, about one percent per year.

On a regional scale, the impact of the improved technology is illustrated in Tables 1 & 2. In the case of rice, the benefiting countries increased their average yield by an impressive fifty-two percent between 1965 and 1983, representing almost 2.5 percent per year. In the same period, their total production went up by seventy-

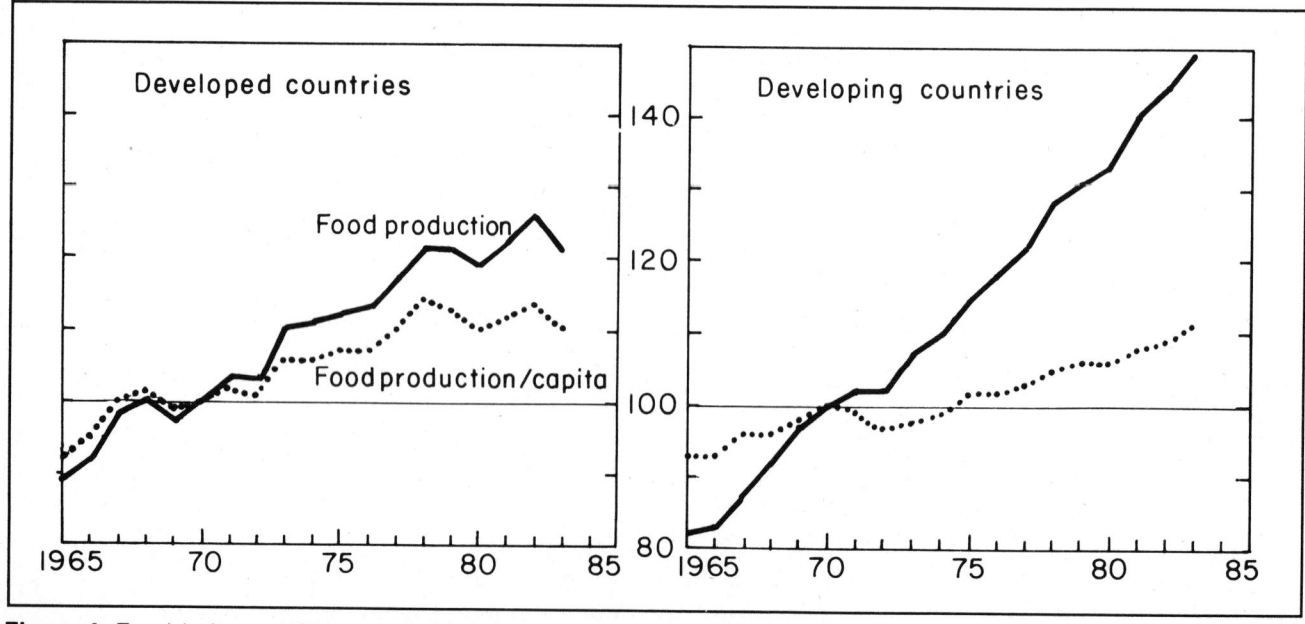

Figure 4. Food indexes (1970 = 100 percent). Source: After FAO (1984).

7. The Green Revolution

Table 3.

Rice Area and Nitrogen Used 1979-1980

Country	Rice area planted thousand hectares	Nitrogen kilograms per hectare	Yield rough rice metric tons per hectare
Burma	5,013	11	2.19
Bangladesh	10,308	21	2.02
India	40,200	19	2.01
Pakistan	2,026	52	2.37
Indonesia	8,495	73	3.29
Philippines	3,543	33	2.15
Thailand	8,288	10	1.82
S. Korea	1,314	131	5.90

Source: Martinez and Diamond (1982) and FAS (1983).

four percent. For the rest of the world, yield decreased by four percent, and production advanced by only eleven percent. Higher yields among the beneficiaries were related to improved irrigation, increased use of fertilizers, better weeding, and plant protection, all applied to a stronger genetic stock.

High yielding modern varieties of wheat and rice have not been universally adopted, nor have their full potentials been realized by the farmers using them. On experimental farms, the new seeds commonly produce four times the yield of traditional varieties, but on farmers' fields the advantage is far smaller. The difference is often called the "yield gap" and probably occurs because the environment on the farmers' fields is less ideal than on experimental farms where neither flood nor drought is a problem, where soil conditions are most favorable, where each field is carefully monitored by specialists, and where the level of inputs, especially fertilizer, is well above that used by farmers. On experimental farms, the new varieties maximize their yield on most soil types at levels of nitrogen ranging from 130 to 200 pounds per acre (150 to 225 kilograms per hectare). Depending on the relative price of fertilizer and the market value of rough rice, the optimum level of application to maximize returns without measurable damage to the ecosystem is between ninety and 130 pounds per acre (100 to 150 kilograms per hectare). These levels are seldom achieved in Third World countries.

In South and Southeast Asia, modern wheat seeds have been planted to roughly eighty percent of the wheat area compared to under fifty percent for rice. The lower figure for rice is related to the character of the new seed and the physical geography of Asia's rice lands. The seed produces a plant about three feet (about one meter) tall that matures in roughly 110 days. The plant does poorly when subject to submergence, and it does not have time to recover from drought stress that may occur early in the growing season. Modern rice cannot be grown at all on areas normally subject to more than three feet (about one meter) of standing water during the wet season. Rice varieties also provide only modest yield advantage under saline conditions or in high sulfate soils (IRRI 1985). Large areas of the great delta regions of South and Southeast Asia, therefore, are unsuitable for today's modern rice varieties. With this in mind, the fifty-two percent mean yield increase already achieved is even more remarkable.

Figure 5. Percentage adoption of modern wheat and rice in Asia. Source: Dalrymple (1978, 1985a, 1985b).

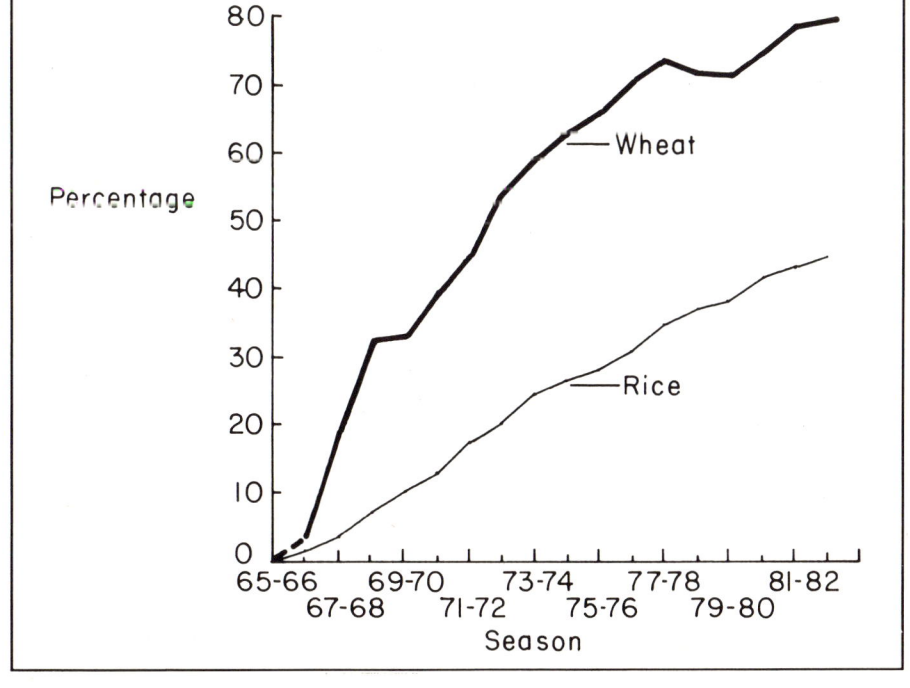

1. THE INDUSTRIAL AND SCIENTIFIC REVOLUTIONS

It is difficult to identify and document those factors beyond the physical environment that have contributed directly to unequal benefits, and many questions have been raised. Has the Green Revolution resulted in unfair advantages accruing to the already well-to-do, or have the poor benefited as well? Do farmers with large holdings reap disproportionately more profit than those with small holdings? Do owners of land prosper while tenants and the landless become poorer?

In 1982, The American Association for the Advancement of Science published the results of a symposium devoted to discussing these questions (Anderson et al. 1982). The publication consists of eighteen well-documented papers that provide different answers to these fundamental questions. In a much briefer report, more than 100 sources reporting on modern rice varieties in Asia are analyzed for answers to the same questions (Herdt and Capule 1983). The evidence is strongly conflicting across time, place, and cultural setting and, therefore, the authors conclude that there are no consistent findings relating successful adoption of the Green Revolution package to either farm size or tenure.

In a report on two Indonesian and two Philippine villages, strong evidence was found supporting the environment as the principal determinant of success in adoption.

> The four village cases invariably show that farm size was not a factor in the adoption of MV [modern varieties]. In the three villages with environmental conditions suitable for MV, both large and small farmers planted MV in nearly 100% of their paddy areas. On the other hand, both large and small farmers rejected MV when they found the MV to be unsuited to their environment. In neither case was a significant difference observed in the levels of either yield or application of modern inputs such as fertilizers (Hayami and Kikuchi 1982, pp. 212-13).

Conclusion

In the years ahead, there are two groups of challenges facing agricultural scientists and social scientists in regard to the Green Revolution. The first is to continue research on breeding and farm systems. The objective of breeding should be to develop plants that will adapt more readily to the less than ideal environments where most of the poorest farmers of the world live. The objective of farming systems research should be to maximize year-round food production on a given plot of land and to substitute home-grown or home-produced inputs for purchased industrial inputs where possible.

The second objective is to continue to extend the improved technology to those farmers who have not yet participated and to encourage those who have adopted one-half the package to intensify their operations. For example, a majority of farmers in Asia apply very low levels of nitrogen to their crop. In environments as different as Indonesia and South Korea where nitrogen levels are high, yields are significantly above those of neighboring countries. For the other countries, much unexploited potential remains to be developed through fertilizers and other management inputs.

Success in these broad research objectives holds promise for possibly a fifty percent increase in yields. Such a result would provide the world with two or three decades to find a more permanent solution to the population-food question.

References

Anderson, R.S., ed. et al. 1982. *Science, Politics and the Agricultural Revolution in Asia.* Boulder, CO: Westview Press.

Barker, R., and Herdt, R.V. 1985. *The Rice Economy of Asia.* Resources for the Future Series. Baltimore: Johns Hopkins University Press, forthcoming.

Chandler, R.F., Jr. 1982. *An Adventure in Applied Science: A History of the International Rice Research Institute.* Manila, Philippines: International Rice Research Institute.

CIMMYT. 1982. "Wheat in Bangladesh." *CIMMYT Today No. 15.* Mexico, D.F. Mexico: Centro Internacional de Mejoramiento de Maiz y Trigo.

CIMMYT Economics Program. 1983. *World Wheat Facts and Trends.* Report 2: An Analysis of Rapidly Rising Third World Consumption and Imports of Wheat. Mexico, D.F. Mexico: Centro Internacional de Mejoramiento de Maiz y Trigo.

Dalrymple, D.G. 1978. *Development and Spread of High-Yielding Varieties of Wheat and Rice in the Less Developed Nations.* Report No. 95. Washington, DC: US Department of Agriculture.

_____. 1985a. *Development and Spread of High Yielding Rice Varieties in the Developing Countries.* AID Technical Bulletin Series. Washington, DC: United States Agency for International Development.

_____. 1985b. *Development and Spread of High Yielding Wheat Varieties in the Developing Countries.* AID Technical Bulletin Series. Washington, DC: United States Agency for International Development.

FAO. 1967. *FAO Production Yearbook 1967.* Rome.

_____. 1984. *FAO Production Yearbook 1984.* Rome.

FAS. 1983. *Foreign Agriculture Circular FG-26-83 World Rice Reference Tables.* Washington, DC: US Department of Agriculture.

Hayami, Y., and Kikuchi, M. 1982. *Asian Village Economy at the Crossroads: An Economic Approach to Institutional Change.* Baltimore: Johns Hopkins Press.

Herdt, R.V., and Capule, C. 1983. *Adoption, Spread, and Production Impact of Modern Rice Varieties in Asia.* Manila, Philippines: International Rice Research Institute.

Huke, R.E. 1982. *Rice Area by Type of Culture: South, Southeast and East Asia.* Manila, Philippines: International Rice Research Institute.

IRRI. 1985. *International Rice Research: 25 Years of Partnership.* Manila, Philippines: International Rice Research Institute.

Martinez, A., and Diamond, R.B. 1982. *Fertilizer Use Statistics in Crop Production.* Muscle Shoals, AL: International Fertilizer Development Center.

Palacpac, A.C. 1982. *World Rice Statistics.* Los Banos, Philippines: IRRI, Department of Agricultural Economics.

US Department of Agriculture. 1984. *Agriculture Statistics 1984.* Washington, DC: US Government Printing Office.

Article 8

Artificial Intelligence

A New Reality

Artificial intelligence is already moving into the factory and the workplace and helping solve problems that until now were beyond the computer's range. It may be in widespread use by the year 2000.

Joseph J. Kroger

Joseph J. Kroger is vice-chairman of Unisys Corporation, P.O. Box 500, Blue Bell, Pennsylvania 19424.

Science writers love terms that connote mystery. "Artificial intelligence" is one of their favorites. It has a futuristic, Flash Gordon-ish ring to it. But AI — which can be defined simply as the capability of a machine to mimic intelligent behavior — is really neither far off nor far out. It's here, now, and it's beginning to change the way we live.

Artificial intelligence (AI) is beginning to offer business and industry a vast array of new tools. Already helping to uncover subterranean oil deposits and design computer chips, AI is expected to be in general use among companies and government agencies virtually everywhere by the end of this century.

Though AI may still be misconstrued by some as a dangerous toy, it is basically nothing more than sophisticated electronic circuitry rigged up to manipulate symbols in the same way that people do when they reason through problems and come up with feasible solutions.

For example, AI technology is now making possible a sophisticated type of problem-solving activity called rapid prototyping, which involves simulation based so closely on reality that users can visualize real-life implementation. NASA scientists turned to rapid prototyping after spending eight years trying to eradicate carbon dioxide from space shuttles and solved the problem in four weeks.

A major U.S. airline has developed an AI system that optimizes seat revenue by analyzing such factors as capacity versus tickets sold, allocation of full fares and discounted ones, number of days until departure, competitive airlines' seats available, and so forth. For the airline, the benefits are significant: increased profit, more efficient use of personnel and facilities, and a competitive advantage.

An AI system called "Just In Time Manufacturing" aims at reducing costs and improving quality on factory production lines by virtually eliminating the need for inventory and storage. The "Just In Time" system simulates a factory's entire production flow via representations of various workstations and tools that appear in "windows" on a video screen. It shows not only the functions and relative speed of each tool, but also how much lead time is needed to order parts for each step along the way. The system also suggests ways to correct bottlenecks by moving people and machines around to change the product flow, thus indicating which configuration is most productive.

Another AI system being developed takes aim at automating the diagnosis of printed-circuit-board failures. The system has already demonstrated its ability to pinpoint faulty devices with a minimal number of probes, while it

1. THE INDUSTRIAL AND SCIENTIFIC REVOLUTIONS

Computers with Emotions

Computers may express love, hate, and other emotions in the future.

Can computers be made to love, hate, show compassion, or be creative? Should they? Lawrence Stevens explores these questions in his book *Artificial Intelligence: The Search for the Perfect Machine*. The important task now facing artificial-intelligence researchers, says Stevens, is to produce machines that can duplicate the psychological activities that allow people to reason effectively.

The fact that many great leaders and thinkers are emotional, creative people lends support to the importance of emotions and creativity for problem solving. For a machine to make decisions on a par with those of leading thinkers, it must be programmed to make use of psychological factors, Stevens claims.

Computers will interact more frequently with humans in the future, so emotional understanding by the computers will be necessary, says Stevens. A computer may need to make decisions for its human master based on emotional responses of love, hate, or compassion.

Stevens writes that emotions are based on rules — certain things make us happy, while other things make us frightened, depending on the situation. For example, a person would probably not be afraid of a nip from his own dog, but he might be afraid of a nip from a strange dog. Stevens writes that these situational factors can be converted into a series of rules — if/then statements — that can be programmed into a computer.

"Ironically, here in the emotional center of man, in the one area that many people predict no machines can imitate, is a behavior source that is very closely related to a computer program," says Stevens.

Stevens also writes that there is no evidence that even sudden personality changes — such as those brought on by prayer or meditation — are not also rule-based (though governed by rules not yet understood). These rules, once understood, presumably could be programmed, so that an intelligent computer might undergo a similar transformation.

Another possibility is programming imagination. Stevens writes that the ability of programs to make guesses about what would occur under a given set of circumstances can be viewed as rudimentary imagination. For example, a computer program on architectural design could "imagine" how a particular structure might be built, finding shortcuts and pitfalls before construction begins.

Computer programs could even use "pleasure" or "satisfaction" as a means of determining what to do, says Stevens. The computer could exhibit pleasure by exploring imaginative possibilities in detail and by working out possible variations and ramifications. If a ramification produces a negative emotion, the program would — as a human would — explore another possibility that might have more "satisfying" consequences. A program with "imagination" could be said to be a very efficient daydreamer, imagining for the sake of pleasurable solutions.

Source: *Artificial Intelligence: The Search for the Perfect Machine* by Lawrence Stevens. Hayden Book Company, 10 Mulholland Drive, Hasbrouck Heights, New Jersey 07604. 1985. 177 pages. Paperback. $14.95.

frees up valuable human resources. The potential cost savings are dramatic: Conventional testing uses hardware that costs $1.5 million and is operated by a highly skilled technician, while the AI approach uses a program that costs less than $100,000 and can be run by someone with just two weeks of training.

Expert Systems

Programs like the ones described above are called expert systems — so named because they contain the collected, computer-stored knowledge of specialists in a given field. An expert system can draw on mountains of data to make a decision based on its stored knowledge about a given task. Industry insiders are so bullish about the future of expert systems that they're forecasting $1.2 billion in sales by 1990. And by 1990, the total market for AI applications will grow to $5 billion.

Artificial intelligence's scope also encompasses natural-language processing, robotics, and vision and speech recognition. But — at least for the moment — the most promising advances are in the expert systems area. Potential applications for expert systems are in such diverse areas as health and human services administration, communications systems simulation, electronic data processing audit, natural-language interface, and airline pilot assistance.

Pilot assistance, or flight management, offers another good illustration of AI's practicality. Think of all the cockpit gadgetry with which a pilot has to contend. Some newer planes have more than a hundred computers spewing information onto the instrument panel. It's all important, but it can also be pretty confusing

8. Artificial Intelligence

The Implications of Super Intelligence

Will the widespread use of artificial intelligence bring a technotopia or an Orwellian nightmare? Derek Partridge, an associate professor in computer science at New Mexico State University, says that this new technology has the potential to cause cataclysmic social change.

For example, AI's boost to automation — with the robot takeover of hazardous, repetitive, and menial tasks — could bring increased unemployment along with increased leisure time. A new socioeconomic system might separate income from employment, with most income being derived from a return on capital investment. Alternatively, employers could shrink the workweek, or governments might develop more automation-resistant human service jobs.

Partridge foresees the possibility of human and artificial intelligence forming a "partnership to super intelligence," composed of "the global knowledge and broad association abilities of human beings, together with the exhaustive rigour and depth of machines."

Advanced AI systems will adapt to the user, Partridge claims. Thus, AI holds the promise of customized mass production, with a wealth of cheap expertise and assistance that also embodies a sensitive treatment of people as individuals. Computer-aided instruction, for example, could be responsive to a student's particular strengths, weaknesses, general level of competence, and preferred style of interaction. Each copy of the system could build up a "model" of each student that has interacted with it and treat each one as an individual.

An especially promising type of AI technology — natural-language processing — could make sophisticated computer technology readily available to almost anyone. Natural-language systems are computers that possess some understanding of, say, English in the same way people do. Thus, one could give commands to one's computer in conversational English.

Source: "Social Implications of Artificial Intelligence" by Derek Partridge in *Artificial Intelligence: Principles and Applications*, edited by Masoud Yazdani. 1986. Chapman and Hall, 29 West 35th Street, New York, New York 10001. Paperback. 348 pages. $22.

when a sudden problem demands an immediate response. But AI programs now being perfected will someday, when presented with an emergency, significantly reduce the complexity of the data, isolate and display critical information, and tell the pilot what options are available for corrective action.

Ultimately, that is just what AI lets the user do: obtain useful information from huge data banks faster, perform certain crucial tasks better by precisely narrowing down the available options, develop rapid prototype solutions for complex problems, and improve the users' understanding of what their computers are doing for them.

Power Packs

Another promising development in AI is the creation of "power packs" — specialized AI tools, or system "drivers" — which contain generic knowledge that can provide solutions to specific problems found in particular industries or fields of endeavor. One such "power pack" is already helping the utilities industry to design and build new plants. What it does, in effect, is allow users to place simulated boilers and pipes and valves in various configurations on a video screen while a software program runs fail-safe checks on the design.

Any company serious about participating in the AI revolution must be willing to invest heavily in R&D to make sure that its expert systems and other AI programs operate directly with data already held in traditional information-processing systems and that the programs keep up with software innovations. In addition, such a company must be willing to initiate extensive training programs, increase support for university research projects, and team up with other companies to undertake joint ventures so that products can be delivered in a smooth, timely fashion.

Artificial intelligence is an exciting development with enormous potential. As it moves out of the laboratory and into the marketplace, AI is solving problems that until now were beyond even the computer's grasp.

SCIENTISTS GO NORTH

Anthony de Souza

Anthony R. de Souza is professor of geography at the University of Wisconsin-Eau Claire and editor of the Journal of Geography (USA).

THE contrast between the rich, developed 'North' and the poorer developing 'South' is nowhere wider than in scientific research. The scientific divide is so enormous that it is tempting to argue that countries must have vigorous and productive scientific communities if they are to develop.

The development potential of a country may be measured by the size of its pool of publishing scientists. This measure is crude because it does not take into account country-by-country variations in the quality of work published, yet it is an easier base from which to make comparisons than one which is dependent on budget data, such as the proportion of GNP a country spends on science.

Data on the number of publishing scientists in 164 countries, produced by the Institute for Scientific Information in Philadelphia show a remarkable imbalance: 47 countries account for 99 per cent of scientific authorship. Within this, the USA alone accounts for 36 per cent and 10 countries produce 80 per cent.

Industrial market economies and East European non-market economies have nearly 95 per cent of all publishing scientists. India, which has a venerable history of technical and scientific education and which is one of the biggest contributors of scientists in the world, is home to nearly 50 per cent of all the publishing scientists of the South. China and a handful of newly industrializing and oil-exporting countries such as Singapore, Nigeria and Mexico, account for much of the remainder.

The information that is so vital to the conduct of scientific research is most abundant in major metropolitan areas and specialized science centres. And, although it can be communicated to scientists elsewhere by various methods, there are inherent advantages in personal exchanges. However, the geographical concentration of scientists may often operate against such exchanges since it varies considerably both within the 'North' and between the 'North' and 'South'.

In the USA, patterns of communication and cooperation among scientists are informal and no single city or region has a monopoly of talented scientists. New York is the leading US scientific city and has universities, medical centres, industrial laboratories, zoological and botanical parks, and museums. Yet it has only three per cent of the publishing scientists.

Outside the USA, scientific effort tends to be more concentrated geographically. Moscow, the world's largest scientific city, supports 38 per cent of the USSR's publishing scientists. Moscow, Leningrad, and Kiev together have 55 per cent of the country's scientific capacity.

The concentration of scientists in most West European countries and Japan falls somewhere between that of the USA and East Europe.

Largest scientific cities of the 'South' in 1984		
city	number of publishing scientists	percentage share of national scientific effort
Beijing	2334	38.0
Buenos Aires	2109	59.1
Bombay	1539	8.0
Santiago	1496	71.1
New Delhi	1292	6.7
Cairo	1266	60.0
Calcutta	1221	6.3
Mexico City	1211	70.2
Shanghai	1143	18.6
Sao Paulo	1079	23.2

Largest scientific cities in 1984		
Moscow	25,511	37.8
London	25,511	37.8
London	14,784	23.7
Tokyo	10,875	18.9
Paris	10,707	23.3
New York	8994	3.1
Boston	7300	2.5
Washington	6982	2.4
Philadelphia	6275	2.1
Los Angeles	6183	2.1
Leningrad	6120	9.1
Chicago	5777	2.0
Bethesda, Maryland	5443	1.9
Kiev	5431	8.1
Houston	5106	1.7
Toronto	4143	13.4

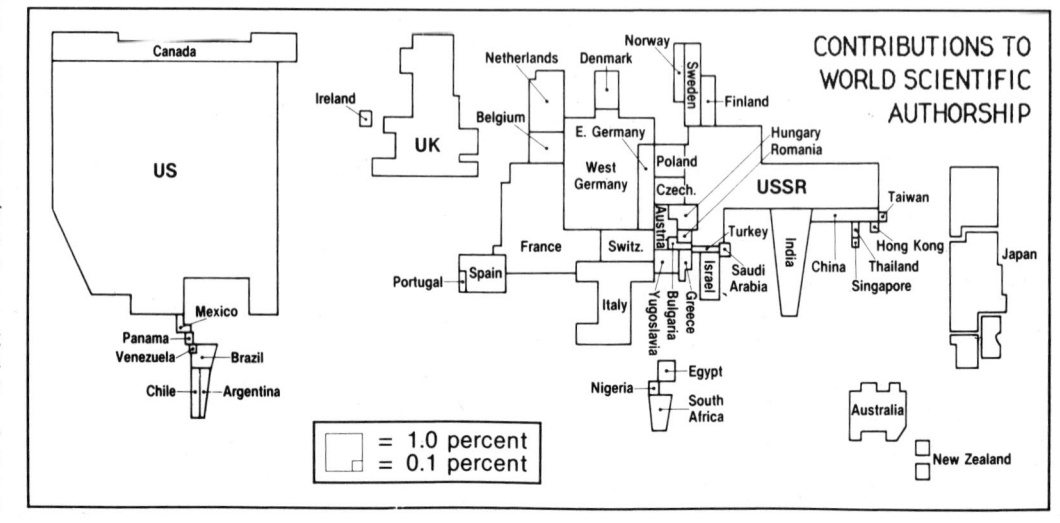

CONTRIBUTIONS TO WORLD SCIENTIFIC AUTHORSHIP

□ = 1.0 percent
▫ = 0.1 percent

9. Scientists Go North

London has 24 per cent of Britain's publishing scientists; Paris 23 per cent of France's; and Tokyo, 19 per cent of Japan's. London has more than five times the number of scientists of Britain's second- and third-ranked scientific cities — Cambridge and Oxford.

In the 'South', scientific research is concentrated in a few institutions in capital cities. For example, Mexico City boasts 70 per cent of Mexico's scientific community. India is among the few countries of the poor 'South' where scientific effort is dispersed among a number of regional centres. Only 21 per cent of India's publishing scientists live in Bombay, New Delhi and Calcutta.

Countries with a large pool of publishing scientists have a high technological potential. If countries are classified by technological levels, high technology countries with industries such as aeronautics and aerospace, telecommunications and telematics, nuclear energy, computers and bio-industry, account for 80 per cent of all scientific authorship. The USA, Canada, Japan, Sweden, Denmark, Italy, Switzerland, West Germany, Netherlands, Belgium, UK, Australia, USSR, and East Germany fall into this category. In only two of these, USSR and East Germany, is science highly regulated by government. The countries with a classic technology, that is all the remaining countries in the study except for Panama, Nigeria, and Saudi Arabia, account for 19 per cent of scientific authorship. The vast majority of the third group of technologically dependent countries do not appear in the statistics because they have too few publishing scientists.

Development is not primarily a scientific but a political and social process. Nonetheless, a commitment to basic scientific effort appears to be necessary for development to succeed. Unfortunately the opportunities for talented scientists from developing countries are mainly in the universities, research institutes, and industrial laboratories of the 'North'. This drain of intellectual resources from the 'South' helps to widen the North-South intellectual gap so that the 'South' looks likely to remain scientifically undermanned and technologically dependent in the foreseeable future.

The Cultural Ferment of the West

The same milieu which produced the new attitudes of science and technology fired other intellectual explorations. In religion, Martin Luther started the Protestant Reformation with his protests against the excesses of the Roman Catholic Church. As the first article in this section describes, Luther started a landslide of religious thinking which not only contributed to theology, but also served to feed the skepticism of the time. If people could doubt the church fathers, they could challenge the status quo elsewhere as well.

Beginning with the work of Adam Smith in the eighteenth century, the study of economics emerged as a dis-

Unit 2

cipline and as an explanation of life. He gave a rationale and interpretation to the capitalism of England, the birthplace of the industrial revolution. Laissez faire and the invisible hand in the marketplace would work to supply the goods people demanded. Smith, as described by John Kenneth Galbraith, became the godfather of capitalism, the economic system adopted by the West.

Smith's capitalism has been much modified by changing conditions—the regulations of government, social welfare, large multinational corporations—but it was not destroyed in a turnover by downtrodden workers. This is what Karl Marx thought would happen in the middle of the nineteenth century. He described a new order of state-directed socialism which would work for the benefit of the total population, not just for the rich. This thought found fertile ground not in the West, but in the Soviet Union and, later, China—places Marx would never have predicted. His personal life, described by Louis J. Halle, was unsuccessful and chaotic, but, nevertheless, his ideas about communism became one of the most revolutionary political and economic doctrines exported to the world from the West.

The West also produced more than its quota of prominent composers and artists. Michelangelo, Leonardo da Vinci, Titian, Rembrandt, Van Dyke, Hogarth, and, later, Delacroix, Goya, Monet, and Picasso are but a few of the artists. In music, the classical tradition began in the eighteenth century and continued into the twentieth. It included composers such as Mozart, Beethoven, Paganni, Schubert, Chopin, Tchaikovsky, Rimsky-Korakov, Puccini, and Rachmaninov. In his description of Bach, Edward Rothstein reveals that great musicians, like others, have their share of the cares of the world.

In yet another area, psychology, the West led the way. Sigmund Freud was one of the great intellects of the twentieth century. He displayed a whole new dimension of human existence when he opened the door to the recesses of the mind. According to Peter F. Drucker, Freud fooled himself about the realities of his own life. Freud was also famous for the question, "What do women want?"

Mary Wollstonecraft, characterized by writer Shirley Tomkievicz as the first feminist, had an answer. She wanted recognition that the female mind was just as good as the male mind. Through much of history women had groaned under the weight of the patriarchal attitudes which confined them in space and action. During the American Revolution and Constitutional period, women hoped for greater freedoms. In the nineteenth century women agitated for suffrage and property rights. In the twentieth century the women of the West won equality before the law and the right to vote, but still the age-old patriarchy continued in employment, politics, and public attitudes.

Late in the eighteenth century, the young United States reconstructed its government to gain greater efficiency and to state with clarity the thought of the patriots about the relationship of government to the people. Freedom, federalism, control of the economy, democracy, and property rights were all topics involved in the discussions at Philadelphia. A.E. Dick Howard reveals how the Constitution has been adjusted over time to protect minorities. The Constitution inspired imitation and might be considered the country's most important export.

Women's rights and the United States Constitution fall into a category of liberalism, a movement and concern for the freedom of the individual. Liberalism, socialism, capitalism, democracy, communism, Christianity, and science were products of the Western mind. They were carried to the rest of the world as part of the intellectual baggage as European merchants, soldiers, and diplomats set forth to conquer the world.

Looking Ahead: Challenge Questions

Why are the people featured in this section considered "great?"

Do great people make history, or does history produce great people?

Why did Luther's protest have an effect?

How have Adam Smith's ideas been modified by subsequent conditions?

Why did the Communist revolution not occur in Western Europe?

What is the significance of music in a culture? Does it merely reflect the nature of society, or does it have the power to shape it?

How do you define "feminist"? How does Mary Wollstonecraft fit into the definition?

Luther: Giant of His Time and Ours

Half a millennium after his birth, the first Protestant is still a towering force

It was a back-room deal, little different from many others struck at the time, but it triggered an upheaval that altered irrevocably the history of the Western world. Albrecht of Brandenburg, a German nobleman who had previously acquired a dispensation from the Vatican to become a priest while underage and to head two dioceses at the same time, wanted yet another favor from the Pope: the powerful archbishop's chair in Mainz. Pope Leo X, a profligate spender who needed money to build St. Peter's Basilica, granted the appointment—for 24,000 gold pieces, roughly equal to the annual imperial revenues in Germany. It was worth it. Besides being a rich source of income, the Mainz post brought Albrecht a vote for the next Holy Roman Emperor, which could be sold to the highest bidder.

In return, Albrecht agreed to initiate the sale of indulgences in Mainz. Granted for good works, indulgences were papally controlled dispensations drawn from an eternal "treasury of merits" built up by Christ and the saints; the church taught that they would help pay the debt of "temporal punishment" due in purgatory for sins committed by either the penitent or any deceased person. The Pope received half the proceeds of the Mainz indulgence sale, while the other half went to repay the bankers who had lent the new archbishop gold.

Enter Martin Luther, a 33-year-old priest and professor at Wittenberg University. Disgusted not only with the traffic in indulgences but with its doctrinal underpinnings, he forcefully protested to Albrecht—never expecting that his action would provoke a sweeping uprising against a corrupt church.

A statue of the reformer stares defiantly across Eisenach, East Germany

To some Catholic scholars, he has even become a "father in the faith."

10. Luther

Luther's challenge culminated in the Protestant Reformation and the rending of Western Christendom, and made him a towering figure in European history. In this 500th anniversary year of his birth (Nov. 10, 1483), the rebel of Wittenberg remains the subject of persistent study. It is said that more books have been written about him than anyone else in history, save his own master, Jesus Christ. The renaissance in Luther scholarship surrounding this year's anniversary serves as a reminder that his impact on modern life is profound, even for those who know little about the doctrinal feuds that brought him unsought fame. From the distance of half a millennium, the man who, as Historian Hans Hillerbrand of Southern Methodist University in Dallas says, brought Christianity from lofty theological dogma to a clearer and more personal belief is still able to stimulate more heated debate than all but a handful of historical figures.

Indeed, as the reformer who fractured Christianity, Luther has latterly become a key to reuniting it. With the approval of the Vatican, and with Americans taking the lead, Roman Catholic theologians are working with Lutherans and other Protestants to sift through the 16th century disputes and see whether the Protestant-Catholic split can some day be overcome. In a remarkable turnabout, Catholic scholars today express growing appreciation of Luther as a "father in the faith" and are willing to play down his excesses. According to a growing consensus, the great division need never have happened at all.

Beyond his importance as a religious leader, Luther had a profound effect on Western culture. He is, paradoxically, the last medieval man and the first modern one, a political conservative and a spiritual revolutionary. His impact is most marked, of course, in Germany, where he laid the cultural foundations for what later became a united German nation.

When Luther attacked the indulgence business in 1517, he was not only the most popular teacher at Wittenberg but also vicar provincial in charge of eleven houses of the Hermits of St. Augustine. He was brilliant, tireless and a judicious administrator, though given to bouts of spiritual depression. To make his point on indulgences, Luther dashed off 95 theses condemning the system ("They preach human folly who pretend that as soon as money in the coffer rings, a soul from purgatory springs") and sent them to Archbishop Albrecht and a number of theologians.*

*Despite colorful legend, it is not certain he ever nailed them to the door of the Castle Church.

The room where Luther translated the New Testament; title page of his Bible

The response was harsh: the Pope eventually rejected Luther's protest and demanded capitulation. It was then that Luther began asking questions about other aspects of the church, including the papacy itself. In 1520 he

2. THE CULTURAL FERMENT OF THE WEST

charged in an open letter to the Pope, "The Roman Church, once the holiest of all, has become the most licentious den of thieves, the most shameless of brothels, the kingdom of sin, death and hell." Leo called Luther "the wild boar which has invaded the Lord's vineyard."

The following year Luther was summoned to recant his writings before the Diet of Worms, a council of princes convened by the young Holy Roman Emperor Charles V. In his closing defense, Luther proclaimed defiantly: "Unless I am convinced by testimony from Holy Scriptures and clear proofs based on reason—because, since it is notorious that they have erred and contradicted themselves, I cannot believe either the Pope or the council alone—I am bound by conscience and the Word of God. Therefore I can and will recant nothing, because to act against one's conscience is neither safe nor salutary. So help me God." (Experts today think that he did not actually speak the famous words, "Here I stand. I can do no other.")

This was hardly the cry of a skeptic, but it was ample grounds for the Emperor to put Luther under sentence of death as a heretic. Instead of being executed, Luther lived for another 25 years, became a major author and composer of hymns, father of a bustling household and a secular figure who opposed rebellion—in all, a commanding force in European affairs. In the years beyond, the abiding split in Western Christendom developed, including a large component of specifically "Lutheran" churches that today have 69 million adherents in 85 nations.

The enormous presence of the Wittenberg rebel, the sheer force of his personality, still broods over all Christendom, not just Lutheranism. Although Luther declared that the Roman Pontiffs were the "Antichrist," today's Pope, in an anniversary tip of the zucchetto, mildly speaks of Luther as "the reformer." Ecumenical-minded Catholic theologians have come to rank Luther in importance with Augustine and Aquinas. "No one who came after Luther could match him," says Father Peter Manns, a Catholic theologian in Mainz. "On the question of truth, Luther is a lifesaver for Christians." While Western Protestants still express embarrassment over Luther's anti-Jewish rantings or his skepticism about political clergy, Communist East Germany has turned him into a secular saint because of his influence on German culture. Party Boss Erich Honecker, head of the regime's *Lutherjahr* committee, is willing to downplay Luther's antirevolutionary ideas, using the giant figure to bolster national pride.

Said West German President Karl Carstens, as he opened one of the hundreds of events commemorating Luther this year: "Luther has become a symbol of the unity of all Germany. We are all Luther's heirs."

After five centuries, scholars still have difficulty coming to terms with the contradictions of a tempestuous man. He was often inexcusably vicious in his writings (he wrote, for instance, that one princely foe was a "fainthearted wretch and fearful sissy" who should "do nothing but stand like a eunuch, that is, a harem guard, in a fool's cap with a fly swatter"). Yet he was kindly in person and so generous to the needy that his wife despaired of balancing the household budget. When the plague struck Wittenberg and others fled, he stayed behind to minister to the dying. He was a powerful spiritual author, yet his words on other occasions were so scatological that no Lutheran periodical would print them today. His writing was hardly systematic, and his output runs to more than 100 volumes. On the average, Luther wrote a major tract or treatise every two weeks throughout his life.

The scope of Luther's work has made him the subject of endless reinterpretation. The Enlightenment treated him as the father of free thought, conveniently omitting his belief in a sovereign God who inspired an authoritative Bible. During the era of Otto von Bismarck a century ago, Luther was fashioned into a nationalistic symbol; 70 years later, Nazi propagandists claimed him as one of their own by citing his anti-Jewish polemics.

All scholars agree on Luther's importance for German culture, surpassing even that of Shakespeare on the English-speaking world. Luther's masterpiece was his translation of the New Testament from Greek into German, largely completed in ten weeks while he was in hiding after the Worms confrontation, and of the Old Testament, published in 1534 with the assistance of Hebrew experts. The Luther Bible sold massively in his lifetime and remains today the authorized German Protestant version. Before Luther's Bible was published, there was no standard German, just a profusion of dialects. "It was Luther," said Johann Gottfried von Herder, one of Goethe's mentors, "who has awakened and let loose the giant: the German language."

Only a generation ago, Catholics were trained to consider Luther the arch-heretic. Now no less than the Vatican's specialist on Lutheranism, Monsignor Aloys Klein, says that "Martin Luther's action was beneficial to the Catholic Church." Like many other Catholics, Klein thinks that if Luther were living today there would be no split. Klein's colleague in the Vatican's Secretariat for Promoting Christian Unity, Father Pierre Duprey, suggests that with the Second Vatican Council (1962–65) Luther "got the council he asked for, but 450 years too late." Vatican II accepted his contention that, in a sense, all believers are priests; while the council left the Roman church's hierarchy intact, it enhanced the role of the laity. More important, the council moved the Bible to the center of Catholic life, urged continual reform and instituted worship in local languages rather than Latin.

One of the key elements in the Reformation was the question of "justification," the role of faith in relation to good works in justifying a sinner in the eyes of God. Actually, Catholicism had never officially taught that salvation could be attained only through pious works, but the popular perception held otherwise. Luther recognized, as University of Chicago Historian Martin Marty explains, that everything "in the system of Catholic teaching seemed aimed toward appeasing God. Luther was led to the idea of God not as an angry judge but as a forgiving father. It is a position that gives the individual a great sense of freedom and security." In effect, says U.S. Historian Roland Bainton, Luther destroyed the implication that men could "bargain with God."

Father George Tavard, a French Catholic expert on Protestantism who teaches in Ohio and has this month published *Justification: an Ecumenical Study* (Paulist; $7.95), notes that "today many Catholic scholars think Luther was right and the 16th century Catholic polemicists did not understand what he meant. Both Lutherans and Catholics agree that good works by Christian believers are the result of their faith and the working of divine grace in them, not their personal contributions to their own salvation. Christ is the only Savior. One does not save oneself." An international Lutheran-Catholic commission, exploring the basis for possible reunion, made a joint statement along these lines in 1980. Last month a parallel panel in the U.S. issued a significant 21,000-word paper on justification that affirms much of Luther's thinking, though with some careful hedging from the Catholic theologians.

There is doubt, of course, about the degree to which Protestants and Catholics can, in the end, overcome their differences. Catholics may now be permitted to sing Luther's *A Mighty Fortress Is Our God* or worship in their native languages, but a wide gulf clearly remains on issues like the status of Protestant ministers and, most crucially, papal authority.

During the futile Protestant-Catholic reunion negotiations in 1530 at the Diet of Augsburg, the issue of priestly celibacy was as big an obstacle as the faith *vs.* good works controversy. Luther had married a nun, to the disgust of his Catholic contemporaries. From the start, the marriage of clergy was a sharply defined difference between Protestantism and Catholicism, and it remains a key barrier today. By discarding the concept of the moral superiority of celibacy, Luther established sexuality as a gift from God. In general, he was a lover of the simple pleasures, and would have had little patience with the later Puritans. He spoke offhandedly about sex, enjoyed good-natured joshing, beer drinking and food ("If our Lord is permitted to create nice large pike and good Rhine wine, presumably I may be allowed to eat and drink"). For his time, he also had an elevated opinion of women. He cherished his wife and enjoyed fatherhood, siring six children and rearing eleven orphaned nieces and nephews as well.

But if Luther's views on the Catholic Church have come to be accepted even by many Catholics, his anti-Semitic views remain a problem for even his most devoted supporters. Says New York City Rabbi Marc Tanenbaum: "The anniversary will be marred by the haunting specter of Luther's devil theory of the Jews."

Luther assailed the Jews on doctrinal grounds, just as he excoriated "papists" and Turkish "infidels." But his work titled *On the Jews and Their Lies* (1543) went so far as to advocate that their synagogues, schools and homes should be destroyed and their prayer books and Talmudic volumes taken away. Jews were to be relieved of their savings and put to work as agricultural laborers or expelled outright.

Fortunately, the Protestant princes ignored such savage recommendations, and the Lutheran Church quickly forgot about them. But the words were there to be gleefully picked up by the Nazis, who removed them from the fold of religious polemics and used them to buttress their 20th century racism. For a good Lutheran, of course, the Bible is the sole authority, not Luther's writings, and the thoroughly Lutheran Scandinavia vigorously opposed Hitler's racist madness. In the anniversary year, all sectors of Lutheranism have apologized for their founder's views.

Whatever the impact of Luther's anti-Jewish tracts, there is no doubt that his political philosophy, which tended to make church people submit to state authority, was crucial in weakening opposition by German Lutherans to the Nazis. Probably no aspect of Luther's teaching is the subject of more agonizing Protestant scrutiny in West Germany today.

Luther sought to declericalize society and to free people from economic burdens imposed by the church. But he was soon forced, if reluctantly, to deliver considerable control of the new Protestant church into the hands of secular rulers who alone could ensure the survival of the Reformation. Luther spoke of "two kingdoms," the spiritual and the secular, and his writings provided strong theological support for authoritarian government and Christian docility.

The Lutheran wing of the Reformation was democratic, but only in terms of the church itself, teaching that a plowman did God's work as much as a priest, encouraging lay leadership and seeking to educate one and all. But it was Calvin, not Luther, who created a theology for the democratic state. A related aspect of Luther's politics, controversial then and now, was his opposition to the bloody Peasants' War of 1525. The insurgents thought they were applying Luther's ideas, but he urged rulers to crush the revolt: "Let whoever can, stab, strike, kill." Support of the rulers was vital for the Reformation, but Luther loathed violent rebellion and anarchy in any case.

Today Luther's law-and-order approach is at odds with the revolutionary romanticism and liberation theology that are popular in some theology schools. In contrast with modern European Protestantism's social gospel, Munich Historian Thomas Nipperdey says, Luther "would not accept modern attempts to build a utopia and would argue, on the contrary, that we as mortal sinners are incapable of developing a paradise on earth."

Meanwhile, the internal state of the Lutheran Church raises other questions about the lasting power of Luther's vision. Lutheranism in the U.S., with 8.5 million adherents, is stable and healthy. The church is also growing in Third World strongholds like racially torn Namibia, where black Lutherans predominate. But in Lutheranism's historic heartland, the two Germanys and Scandinavia, there are deep problems. In East Germany, Lutherans are

2. THE CULTURAL FERMENT OF THE WEST

under pressure from the Communist regime. In West Germany, the Evangelical Church in Germany (E.K.D.), a church federation that includes some non-Lutherans, is wealthy (annual income: $3 billion), but membership is shrinking and attendance at Sunday services is feeble indeed. Only 6% of West Germans—or, for that matter, Scandinavians—worship regularly.

What seems to be lacking in the old European churches is the passion for God and his truth that so characterizes Luther. He retains the potential to shake people out of religious complacency. Given Christianity's need, on all sides, for a good jolt, eminent Historian Heiko Oberman muses, "I wonder if the time of Luther isn't ahead of us."

The boldest assertion about Luther for modern believers is made by Protestants who claim that the reformer did nothing less than enable Christianity to survive. In the Middle Ages, too many Popes and bishops were little more than corrupt, luxury-loving politicians, neglecting the teaching of the love of God and using the fear of God to enhance their power and wealth. George Lindbeck, the Lutheran co-chairman of the international Lutheran-Catholic commission, believes that without Luther "religion would have been much less important during the next 400 to 500 years. And since medieval religion was falling apart, secularization would have marched on, unimpeded."

A provocative thesis, and a debatable one. But with secularization still marching on, almost unimpeded, Protestants and Catholics have much to reflect upon as they scan the five centuries after Luther and the shared future of their still divided churches.

—By Richard N. Ostling. Reported by Roland Flamini and Wanda Menke-Glückert/Bonn, with other bureaus.

Scotland's Greatest Son

In *The Wealth of Nations* Adam Smith gave the world a new
and witty and literate perception of
the dismal science. But what would he have said about ITT?

JOHN KENNETH GALBRAITH

In June of 1973 economists gathered from all over the world in the Royal Burgh of Kirkcaldy, immediately across the Firth of Forth from Edinburgh, to celebrate the two hundred and fiftieth anniversary of the birth of the town's — most would say Scotland's — greatest son. That was Adam Smith, who was born there in 1723, the son of the local collector of customs, and who, after study at the evidently excellent local school, went on to the University of Glasgow and then to Balliol for six years. Returning to Scotland, he became, first, professor of logic and then, in 1752, professor of moral philosophy at Glasgow. This chair he resigned in 1764 to travel on the Continent as the well-paid tutor of the young Duke of Buccleuch, a family possessed to this day of a vast acreage of dubious land on the border. In Europe Smith made the acquaintance of the physiocratic philosophers and economists Quesnay and Turgot, as well as Voltaire and other notable contemporaries, and used his time and mind well. He then returned to Kirkcaldy where, for the next twelve years, subject to lengthy sojourns in London and to the despair of some of his friends who feared he would never finish, he engaged himself in the writing of *The Wealth of Nations*.

This great book was published in 1776, a few weeks before the Declaration of Independence, and if there is coincidence in the dates, there was also association in the events. Unlike his friend David Hume (who died that August), Smith deplored the separation. He had wanted instead full union, full and equal representation of the erstwhile colonies in Parliament, free trade within the Union, equal taxation along with equal representation, and the prospect that, as the American part developed in wealth and population, the capital would be removed from London to some new Constantinople in the West. Practical men must have shuddered.

However, *The Wealth of Nations*, at least among the knowledgeable, was an immediate success. Gibbon wrote, "What an excellent work is that with which our common friend Mr. Adam Smith has enriched the public . . . most profound ideas expressed in the most perspicacious language." Hume, in a much quoted letter, was exuberant:

Euge! Belle! Dear Mr. Smith. I am much pleased with your performance, and the perusal of it has taken from me a state of great anxiety. It was a work of so much expectation, by yourself, by your friends, and by the public, that I trembled for its appearance, but am now much relieved . . . it has depth and solidity and acuteness, and is so much illustrated by curious facts that it must at last attract the public attention.

The public response — to two volumes costing £1 16s., the equivalent of perhaps thirty dollars today — was also good. The first edition was soon sold out, although this intelligence would be more valuable were the size of the edition known. Smith spent the next couple of years in London being, one gathers, much fêted by his contemporaries for his accomplishment, and then, having been appointed Commissioner of Customs in Edinburgh, an admirable sinecure, he returned to Scotland. He died in Edinburgh in 1790.

By this time, *The Wealth of Nations*, though at first ignored by politicians, was having an influence on men of affairs. A year and a half after Smith's death, Pitt, introducing his budget, said of Smith that his "extensive knowledge of detail and depth of philosophical research will, I believe, furnish the best solution of every question connected with the history of commerce and with the system of political economy." Not since, in the nonsocialist world at least, has a politician committed himself so courageously to an economist.

Smith has not been a popular subject for biographers. He was a bachelor. His best-remembered personal trait was his absent-mindedness. Once, according to legend, he fell into deep thought and walked fifteen miles in his dressing gown before regaining consciousness. His manuscripts, by his instruction, were destroyed at his death. He disliked writing letters, and few of these have survived. The papers of those with whom he did correspond, or which reflected his influence, were destroyed, mostly because of lack of interest, and some, it appears, as late as 1941 or 1942. Adam Smith's only other major published work, *The Theory of Moral Sentiments*, reflects in-

2. THE CULTURAL FERMENT OF THE WEST

terests antecedent to those in political economy. It is often cited by scholars but little read. No biography of Adam Smith has superseded that by John Rae, published nearly eighty years ago.

If Smith's life has attracted little attention, perhaps it is because so much attention has centered on *Inquiry into the Nature and Causes of the Wealth of Nations*, to give the title of his masterpiece its full resonance. With *Das Kapital* and the Bible, *Wealth of Nations* enjoys the distinction of being one of the three books that people may refer to at will without feeling they should have read it. Scholarly dispute over what is Smith's principal contribution has gone on endlessly. This is partly because there is so much in the book that every reader has full opportunity to exercise his own preference.

Exercising that preference, I have always thought that two of Smith's achievements have been neglected. One, mentioned by Gibbon, is his gift for language. Few writers ever, and certainly no economist since, have been as amusing, lucid, or resourceful—or on occasion as devastating. Most rightly remember his conclusion that "People of the same trade seldom meet together, even for merriment and diversion, but the conversation ends in a conspiracy against the public, or in some contrivance to raise prices." There are many more such gems. He noted that "The late resolution of the Quakers in Pennsylvania to set at liberty all their negro slaves may satisfy us that their number cannot be very great." And, anticipating Thorstein Veblen, that "With the greater part of rich people, the chief enjoyment of riches consists in the parade of riches." On the function or nonfunction of stockholders, no one in the next two centuries was more penetrating in however many words: "[Stockholders] seldom pretend to understand anything of the business of the company, and when the spirit of faction happens not to prevail among them, give themselves no trouble about it, but receive contentedly such half-yearly or yearly dividend, as the directors think proper to make to them." One of Smith's most famous observations, it may be noted, is not in *Wealth of Nations*. On hearing from Sir John Sinclair in October, 1777, that

MARY EVANS PICTURE LIBRARY, LONDON

Gussied up and properly shod (he usually wore his bedroom slippers), Smith appears in an engraving of 1790, the year of his death.

Burgoyne had surrendered at Saratoga and of his friend's fear that the nation was ruined, Smith said, "There is a great deal of ruin in a nation."

Also neglected now are the "curious facts" that enchanted Hume and of which *Wealth of Nations* is a treasure house. Their intrusion has, in fact, been deplored. As a writer Smith was a superb carpenter but a poor architect. The facts appear in lengthy digressions that have been criticized as such. But for any discriminating reader it is worth the interruption to learn that the expenses of the civil government of the Massachusetts Bay Colony "before the commencement of the present disturbances," meaning the Revolution, were only £18,000 a year and that this was a rather sizable sum compared with New York and Pennsylvania at £4,500 each and New Jersey at £1,200. (These and numerous other details on the Colonies reflect an interest John Rae believes was stimulated by Benjamin Franklin, with whom Smith was closely acquainted.)

Also, were it not for Smith we might not know that after a bad storm, or "inundation," the citizens of the Swiss canton of Underwald (Unterwalden) came together in an assembly where each publicly confessed his wealth to the multitude and was then assessed *pro rata* for the repair of the damage. Or that, at least by Smith's exceptionally precise calculation, Isocrates earned £3,333 6s. 8d. (upward of 50,000 dollars) for what "we would call one course of lectures, a number which will not appear extraordinary from so great a city to so famous a teacher, who taught, too, what was at that time the most fashionable of all sciences, rhetoric." Or that Plutarch was paid the same. Or, continuing with professors, that those who are subject to reward unrelated to their capacity to attract students will perform their duty in "as careless and slovenly a manner" as authority will permit and that in "the university of Oxford, the greater part of the public professors [those with endowed chairs] have, for these many years, given up altogether even the pretence of teaching."

So no one should neglect Smith's contribution to expository prose and "curious facts." Now as to economic thought and policy. Here a sharp and

11. Scotland's Greatest Son

ADAM SMITH ON SELF-INTEREST:

"It is not from the benevolence of the butcher, the brewer, or the baker that we expect our dinner but from their regard to their self-interest. We address ourselves not to their humanity, but to their self-love, and never talk to them of our necessities, but of their advantages."

obvious distinction must be made between what was important in 1776 and what is important now. The first is very great; the second, save in the imagination of those who misuse Smith as a prophet of reaction, is much less so. The business corporation, which Smith deplored, and the wealth that accumulated in consequence of his advice combined against him. But first we must consider his meaning in 1776.

Smith's economic contribution to his own time can be thought of as falling into three categories—method, system, and advice. The second, overflowing onto the third, is by far the most important.

As to method, Smith gave to political economy, later to become economics, the basic structure which was to survive almost intact at least for the next hundred and fifty years. This structure begins with the problem of value—how prices are set. Then comes the question of how the proceeds are shared—how the participants in production are rewarded. This latter involves the great trinity of labor, capital, and land. Along the way is the role of money. Thereafter come banking, international trade, taxation, public works, defense, and the other functions of the state. Other writers, notably the physiocrats, had previously given political economy a fairly systematic frame, although, as Alexander Gray observed, they had "embellished it with strange frills." But it was Smith who, for the English-speaking world, provided the enduring structure.

The structure, in turn, was more important than what it enclosed. Although Smith's treatment of value, wages, profits, and rents was suggestive and often incisive, it was, in all respects, a beginning and not an end. So it was regarded by Ricardo, Malthus, and the two Mills. Thus, as one example, Smith held that the supply of workers would increase *pari passu* with an increase in the sustenance available for their support. Ricardo translated this thought into the iron law of wages—the rule that wages would tend always to fall to the bare minimum necessary to sustain life. And Malthus, going a step further, adduced his immortal conclusion that people everywhere would proliferate to the point of starvation. Subsequent scholars —the marginal-utility theorists, Alfred Marshall, others—added further modifications to the theory of prices, wages, interest, profits, and rent, and yet further transmutations were of course to follow. Smith was left far behind.

For Smith, the structure he gave to economics and the explanation of economic behavior that it contained were only steps in the creation of his larger system—his complete view of how economic life should be arranged and governed. This was his central achievement. It provides a set of guiding rules for economic policy that are comprehensive and consistent without being arbitrary or dogmatic.

The Smithian system requires that the individual, suitably educated, be left free to pursue his own interest. In doing so, he serves not perfectly, but better than by any alternative arrangement, the common public purpose. Self-interest or selfishness guides men, as though by the influence of an unseen hand, to the exercise of the diligence and intelligence that maximize productive effort and thus the public good. Private vice becomes a public virtue.

In pursuit of private interest, producers exploit the opportunities inherent in the division of labor—in, broadly speaking, the specialized development of skill for the performance of each small part of a total task of production. Combined with the division of labor is the natural propensity of man "to truck, barter or exchange." The freedom of the individual to do his best both in production and in exchange is inhibited by regulation and taxation. Thus the hand of the state should weigh on him as lightly as possible. The limiting factor on the division of labor—roughly, the scale of specialized productive activity —is the size of the market. Obviously, this should be as wide as possible.

There follows Smith's special case against internal, monopolistic, or international restrictions on trade. The case against international barriers gains force from the fact that both well-being and national strength derive not from the accumulation of precious metal, as Smith's mercantilist precursors had held, but—as one would now say and as Smith in effect did say—from the productivity of the labor force. Given an industrious and productive labor force, in the most majestic of Smith's arguments, the supply of gold will take care of itself.

Such, in greatest compression, is the Smithian system—the one that Pitt proclaimed as "the best solution of every question connected ... with the system of political economy."

Smith's third contribution was in the field of practical policy. His advice—on banking, education, colonies, taxation (including the famous canons and extending even to recommendations for the reform of taxation in France), public works, joint-stock companies, agriculture—was infinitely abundant. It could be that no economist since has offered so much. With many exceptions and frequent modifications to fit the circumstance, it is in keeping with Smith's system. The bias in favor of freeing or unburdening the individual to pursue his

61

2. THE CULTURAL FERMENT OF THE WEST

ADAM SMITH ON CHILDBEARING:

"Poverty, though it no doubt discourages, does not always prevent marriage. It seems even to be favourable to generation. A half-starved Highland woman frequently bears more than twenty children, while a pampered fine lady is often incapable of bearing any, and is generally exhausted by two or three.... But poverty ... is extremely unfavourable to the rearing of children. The tender plant is produced, but in so cold a soil and so severe a climate, soon withers and dies."

interest is omnipresent, and so is his belief that men will toil effectively only in the pursuit of pecuniary self-interest. There will be occasion for a further word on this advice; now we must see what of Smith survives.

Needless to say, the mordant language and the curious facts survive; it is too bad they are not more read and enjoyed. Also, Smith's concept of the economic problem—and the division of the subject between value and distribution—are still to be found in that part of the textbooks that economists call microeconomics (and those given to tasteless insider abbreviation call "micro"). His particular conclusions as to how prices, wages, rents, and return to capital are determined, and his views on gold, paper currency, banks, and the like, are now only of antiquarian interest.

Nor does much of the abundant advice just mentioned have modern meaning. It better illuminates life in the eighteenth century than any current problems. Until recently the textbooks on taxation included reverent mention of Smith's four great canons. But no one now coming to them without knowledge of their author would think them very remarkable. That taxes should be certain or predictable and arbitrary in their bite; that they should be so levied and collected as to fit the reasonable convenience of the taxpayer; and that the cost of collection should be a modest part of the total take was important in 1776. But these three things are pretty well accepted now.

Smith's fourth canon, that the "subjects of every state ought to contribute towards the support of the government, as nearly as possible, in proportion to their respective abilities; that is, in proportion to the revenue which they respectively enjoy under the protection of the state," could be taken as an enduring prescription for a proportional (i.e., fixed percentage) as distinct from a progressive income tax. Some beleaguered rich have so argued. In fact, Smith was speaking only of what seemed possible and sensible in his own time. He would have moved with the times. It might be added that his modest prescription gives no comfort to tax shelters, special treatment of state and municipal bonds, the oil-depletion allowance, or those who believe that they were intended by nature to be untroubled by the IRS. Numerous of the big rich in the United States would find even Adam Smith's proportional prescription rather costly as compared with what they now pay.

The next and more interesting question concerns Smith's system—his rules for guiding economic life. What of that survives? Is economic life still guided in appreciable measure by the unseen hand of self-interest—in modern language, by the market? What has happened to the notion of the minimal state, and is it forever dead? And what of Smith's plea for the widest possible market both within and between nations?

In truth, time has dealt harshly with Smith's system. On one important matter he was simply wrong. Further damage was done by an institution, the business corporation, for which he saw little future and which, on the whole, he deplored. And his system was gravely impaired by the very success of the prescription that he offered.

Smith's error was his underestimate of man's capacity, perhaps with some social conditioning, for co-operation. He thought it negligible. Men would work assiduously for their own pecuniary advantage; on shared tasks, even for shared reward, they would continue to do as little as authority allowed. Only in defeating or circumventing that authority—in minimizing physical and intellectual toil, maximizing indolence and sloth—would they bring real effort and ingenuity to bear. But not otherwise. People work only if working for themselves. There is no more persistent theme in *Wealth of Nations*. It is why government tasks are poorly performed. It is why civil servants are an uncivil and feckless crew. It is his case against the British bureaucracy in India. It is why the Oxford professors lapse into idleness. And it is why, in Smith's view, joint-stock companies, except for routine tasks, have little to commend them. Their best chance for survival, one to which the minds of the directors almost invariably turn, is to obtain a monopoly of their industry or trade, a tendency to which Smith devotes some of his finest scorn. Otherwise, their employees or servants devote themselves not to enriching the company but to enriching themselves or not enriching anyone.

In fact, experience since Smith has shown that man's capacity for co-operative effort is very great. Perhaps this was the product of education and social conditioning, something that no one writing in the eighteenth century could have foreseen. Perhaps Smith, handicapped by his environment, judged all races by the Scotch (as we are correctly called). Most likely he failed to see the pride people could have in their organi-

11. Scotland's Greatest Son

zation, their desire for the good opinion or esteem of their co-workers, maybe what Veblen called their instinct to workmanship.

In any case, governments in the performance of public tasks, some of great technical and military complexity, corporations in pursuit of growth, profit, and power, and socialist states in pursuit of national development and power have been able to enlist a great intensity of co-operative effort. And both corporate and socialist economic activities have been able to unite an instinct to co-operation with a promise of individual economic reward and gain from both. At least in the industrialized world, highly organized forms of economic activity enlist a great intensity of co-operative effort.

The most spectacular example of co-operative effort—or perhaps, to speak more precisely, of a successful marriage of co-operative and self-serving endeavor—has, of course, been the corporation. This, for the reasons just noted, Smith did not think possible. And the development of the corporation, in turn, was destructive of the minimal state that Smith prescribed.

For this there were several reasons. The corporation had needs—franchises, rights-of-way, capital, qualified manpower, technical support, highways for its motor cars, airways for its airplanes—which only the state could supply. A state that served its corporations satisfactorily quickly ceased, except in the hopes of truly romantic conservatives, to be minimal.

Also, a less evident point, the economy of the great corporation, when combined with that of the unions (which were in some measure the response to it), was no longer stable. The corporation retained earnings for investment; there was no certainty that all of such savings would be invested. The resulting shortage of demand could be cumulative, for wages and prices would no longer adjust to arrest the downward spiral. And in other circumstances wages and prices might force each other up to produce an enduring and cumulative inflation. The state was called upon to offset the tendency to recession by stabilizing the demand for goods. This was the message of Keynes. And the state had to intervene to stabilize prices and wages if inflation were to be kept within tolerable limits. Both actions were heavy blows at the Smithian state.

The corporation, as it became very large, also ceased to be subordinate to the market. It fixed prices, sought out supplies, influenced consumers, and otherwise exercised power not different in kind from the power of the the state itself. As Smith would have foreseen, this power was exercised in the interest of its possessors, and on numerous matters—the use of air, water, and land—the corporate interest diverged from the public interest. It also diverged where, as in the case of the weapons firms, the corporation was able to persuade the state to be its customer. Corporate interest did not coincide with the public interest as the Smithian system assumed. And there were yet further appeals to the government for redress and further enhancement of the state. This development, on which I will have a later word, has proceeded with explosive speed, especially since World War II.

Finally, Smith's system was destroyed by its own success. In the nineteenth century and with a rather deliberate recognition of their source, Britain was governed by Smith's ideas. So, though more by instinct than by deliberate philosophical commitment, was the United States. And directly, or through such great disciples as the French economist J. B. Say, Smith's influence extended to Western Europe. In the context of time and place, the Smithian system worked; there was a vast release of productive energy, a great increase in wealth, a large though highly uneven increase in living standards. Then came the corporation with its superior access to capital (including that reserved from its own earnings), its great ability to adapt science and technology to its purposes, and its strong commitment to its own growth through expanding sales and output. This, and by a new order of magnitude, added to the increase in output, income, and consumption.

This was the next nail. It is not possible to combine a highly productive economy with a minimal state. Public regulation had to develop in step with private consumption; public services must bear some reasonable relationship to the supply of private services and goods. Both points are accepted in practice if not in principle. A country cannot have a high consumption of automobiles, alcohol, medication, transportation, communications, or even cosmetics, without rules governing their use. The greater the wealth, the more men needed to protect it, and the more required to pick up the discarded containers in which so much of it comes. And in rough accord with increased private consumption goes an increased demand for public services—for education, health care, parks and public recreation, postal services, and the infinity of other things that must be provided, or are best provided, by the state.

Among numerous conservatives there is still a conviction that the society of the minimal state was deliberately destroyed by socialists, planners, *étatists,* and other wicked men who did not know what they were about, or knew all too well. Far more of the responsibility lies with Smith himself. Along with the corporation, his system created the wealth that made his state impossible.

In one last area, it will be insisted, Adam Smith does survive. Men still respect his inspired and inspiring call for the widest possible market, one that will facilitate in the greatest degree the division of labor. And after two centuries the dominant body of opinion in industrial nations resists tariffs and quotas. And in Europe the nation-states have created the ultimate monument to Adam Smith, the European Economic Community. In even more specific tribute to Smith, it is usually called the Common Market.

2. THE CULTURAL FERMENT OF THE WEST

Even here, however, there is less of Smith than meets the eye. Since the eighteenth century, or, for that matter, in the last fifty years, domestic markets have grown enormously. That of insular Britain today is far greater than that of imperial Britain at the height of empire. The technical opportunities in large-scale production have developed enormously since 1776. But national markets have developed much, much more. Proof lies in the fact that General Motors, IBM, Shell, Nestlé, do not produce in ever larger plants as would be the case if they needed to realize the full opportunities inherent in the division of labor. Rather, they produce the same items in numerous small plants. Except perhaps in the very small industrial countries — Holland, Belgium, Luxembourg — domestic markets have long been large enough so that even were they confined to the home market, producers would realize the full economies of scale, the full technical advantages of the division of labor.

The Common Market, and the modern enlightenment on international trade, owe much more to the nontechnical needs of the modern multinational corporation than they do to Adam Smith. The multinational corporation stands astride national boundaries. Instead of seeking tariff support of the state against countries that have a comparative advantage, it can go to the advantaged countries to produce what it needs. At the same time, modern marketing techniques require that it be able to follow its products into other countries to persuade consumers and governments and, in concert with other producers, to avoid the price competition that would be disastrous for all. So, for the multinational corporation, tariffs, to speak loosely and generally, are both unnecessary and a nuisance. It would not have escaped the attention of Adam Smith, although it has escaped the attention of many in these last few years, that where there are no corporations, the Common Market is less than common and very much less than popular. The tariff enlightenment following World War II has resulted not from a belated reading of *Wealth of Nations* but from the much more powerful tendency for what serves the needs of large enterprises to become sound public policy.

But if time and the revolution that he helped set in motion have overtaken Smith's system and Smith's advice, there is one further respect in which he remains wonderfully relevant. That is in the example he sets for professional economists — for what, at the moment, is a troubled, rather saddened discipline. Smith is not a prophet for our time, but, as we have seen, he was magnificently in touch with his own time. He broke with the mercantilist orthodoxy to bring economic ideas abreast of the industrial and agricultural changes that were only then just visible on the horizon. His writing in relation to the Industrial Revolution involved both prophecy and self-fulfilling prophecy. He sensed, even if he did not fully see, what was about to come, and he greatly helped to make it come.

The instinct of the economist, now as never before, is to remain with the past. On that, there is a doctrine, a theory — one that is now wonderfully refined. And there are practical advantages. An economist's capital lies in what he knows — sometimes what he learned in graduate school. Or he has investment in a textbook. To adhere to and articulate the accepted view protects this investment. It also keeps a scholar clear of controversy, something that is usually regarded as a trifle uncouth or indecent. To stay with what is accepted is also consistent with the good life — with the fur-lined comfort of the daily routine between suburb, classroom, and office. To this blandishment, economists are no more immune than other people. The tragedy lies in their resulting obsolescence. As the economic world changes, that proceeds relentlessly, and it is a painful thing.

Remarkably, the same institution, the corporation, which helped to take the economic world away from Adam Smith, has, in its explosive development in modern times, taken it away from the mature generation of present-day economists. As even economists in their nonprofessional life concede, the modern corporation controls prices and costs, organizes suppliers, persuades consumers, guides the Pentagon, shapes public opinion, buys presidents, and is otherwise a dominant influence in the state. It also, alas, in its modern and comprehensively powerful form, figures not at all in the accepted economic theory. That theory still holds the business firm to be solely subordinate to the market, solely subject to the authority of the state, and ultimately the passive servant of the sovereign citizen. There is no ITT in the system. So there is no control of prices, no weapons culture, no dangerously laggard industries, no deeply endemic inequality — there is only incidental damage to the environment arising from minor and hitherto uncelebrated defects (what are called external diseconomies) in the price system. To have to lose touch with reality is the tragedy. And matters are made worse by a younger generation of scholars that accepts and explores the problem of economic power and struggles, sometimes rather crudely, to come to terms with it. Older scholars are left with the barren hope that they can somehow consolidate their forces and thus exclude the threat. It is a fate that calls less for criticism than for compassion.

It is not a fate that Adam Smith would have suffered. Given his avid empiricism, his deep commitment to reality, his profound concern for practical reform, he would have made the modern corporation and its power, and the related power of the unions and the state, an integral part of his theoretical system. His problem would have been different. With his contempt for theoretical pretense, his intense interest in practical questions, he might have had trouble getting tenure in a first-rate modern university.

Marx: His Death & Resurrection

Louis J. Halle

All great men must be viewed in two distinct aspects. There is the limited aspect in which they are great, and there is the other aspect in which they are ordinary human beings like the rest of us. The greatness of most truly great men resides in some quality of vision that on occasion exalts them, and that exalts those to whom it is communicated. No great man, however, lives constantly on the level of his vision. Like the rest of us, in their daily lives all are largely preoccupied with petty concerns; they are prone to be moved by jealousy or bad temper, to say foolish things, to act meanly, and to behave inconsiderately toward those who are close to them.

Our need for heroes to worship, however, generally makes us disregard or deny what is ordinary in a great man. For the man as he was we substitute, sometimes while he is still alive, a legend. Even while Gandhi, for example, was still alive, there was a legendary Gandhi different from the real one: for the real Gandhi was an advocate of the use of violence when, as it seemed to him, the occasion allowed of no good alternative, while the legendary Gandhi is an absolute pacifist. The real Gandhi advocated economic policies or practices that had no relevance to the requirements of reality, or offered such impractical advice as that all the Jews under Hitler should commit suicide, while the legendary Gandhi is perfect in understanding and counsel.

The disparity between legend and reality seems to me greater in the case of Karl Marx than in that of any other modern figure. In legend he is an infallible prophet, basing his prophecies on an empirical science unknown before him. But one has only to read his writings to see for oneself that, in addition to being romantic rather than empirical or scientific, the whole body of prediction they contain was long ago proved wrong by the course history actually took. (I assume that fewer and fewer persons still believe that the Russian *coup d'etat* of October 1917 bore any resemblance to the Revolution predicted in *The Communist Manifesto,* or that what followed was a "dictatorship of the proletariat.") This presents a full contrast to the predictions of his contemporary, Alexis de Tocqueville, which have in fact been borne out; yet de Tocqueville, who never acquired a legendary persona, has no reputation as a prophet remotely comparable to that of Marx.

For years I have had a frustrated curiosity about Karl Marx as a human being, a curiosity left totally unsatisfied by such biographies as that of Franz Mehring, which depict Marx as if he were God the Father, perfect in his wisdom, infallible in his utterance, but persecuted throughout his life on earth as God the Son had been persecuted. One finds nothing about his ordinary day-to-day life, since eating, sleeping, and the involvements of family living are not for gods.

At last, however, I have found a biography that deals with the human Marx and, in fact, goes to the other extreme from Mehring's. Robert Payne's *Marx*[1] concentrates on his daily life, with special emphasis on such activities as pub-crawling in London, drunken binges, and whatever else may serve to diminish the man and discredit the legend. It is a hostile biography, in some ways petty, meretricious, and unscholarly, but I found it satisfying in a way that I daresay Mr. Payne would not have expected. To the extent that it makes Marx human it provides grounds for viewing him with the compassion proper to all us pitiful mortals, caught up as we all are in the tragedy of life.

I admit that my own attitude toward Marx, both as a person and as a writer, has always been hostile. I have credited him with an epic albeit fictional vision of history,[2] but I have always abhorred the style of writing that represents the main Marxist tradition and has its origin in Marx's own work: the *ex-cathedra* dogmatism, the overstatement, the crude vituperation, and the screaming hatred that dominates so much of it. Marx appears to have had no love for his fellow men, no compassion, no humanitarianism, and little concern for

---

[1] Robert Payne, *Marx* (W. H. Allen, 70s.).
[2] See my article, "Marx's Religious Drama" in Encounter, October 1965.

2. THE CULTURAL FERMENT OF THE WEST

the sufferings of anyone but himself. Men did not exist for him as individual human beings of flesh and blood but as abstract social classes or statistics. His entire career was nominally dedicated to the working class, yet he showed no interest in working men and had virtually no contact with them. His "Proletariat" was simply an epic hero of the imagination. He represented the German philosophical tradition in which grandiose abstractions take the place of existential realities, and are even dealt with as if they were actual persons possessed of mind and will. The extremism of Marx, represented as well by the line of Marxist tradition that passes through Lenin, has always been extraordinarily callous to the sufferings of real human beings; and there is no doubt that Marx, himself, occasionally revelled in the dream of wholesale massacres, with blood flowing in the streets. One is tempted to believe, uncharitably, that his consistent opposition to improving the lot of the workers by progressive reforms, rather than by violent revolution, had at least some of its roots in this dream. Lenin, Stalin, and Mao Tse-tung, although not representing Marx's thinking in other respects, have been representative of him in the same lack of concern for real people, in their disposition to cure the evils of society by subjecting actual flesh-and-blood to suffering and death on a scale that no one else in history except Hitler has ever approached. All this, as I say, has always made Marx's writings, and those of his successors, repulsive to me.

There was also the fact that Marx's first book, *On the Jewish Question,* had been an anti-Semitic polemic in which he poured his vituperation over the people (again, regarded as a class or collectivity) from whom he had himself sprung, but from whom he dissociated himself with the hatred that the book manifests. It is extraordinary how those who have cultivated the Marxian legend have succeeded in keeping the existence or nature of this book quiet, or in explaining it away by pretending that he was using the terms "Jew" and "Judaism" in a metaphorical sense only.

I admit, as well, that my curiosity about Marx's personal life was not the expression of a favourable disposition. I could not understand how a man could allow his wife and children to live in the most humiliating misery, his children dying and his wife suffering mental and physical agonies for want of proper medical care, rather than subject himself to the normal discipline of working to support his family. Did he never feel a twinge of conscience over this? One could hardly admire the way he sponged all his life on his friends and relatives, even exploiting their labour, as when he got Engels, a man who was busy as he was not, to write many of the columns for *The New York Tribune* that appeared under Marx's name and for which he pocketed the pay. A puritan streak in my nature and inheritance (which, like grey hair, begins to show itself with age) aroused in me incredulity, even more than disapproval, of a life so lived.

It is a paradox that the reading of the Payne biography has had the effect of softening my standing hostility toward Marx. This is partly because Payne is himself so unfair and so unpitying in his treatment of what is, after all, a long record of human suffering that the reader at last tends to rebel against the writer and to make compensating judgments.

One example will suffice. It is virtually beyond doubt that Marx was the father of Helene Demuth's illegitimate son. Helene Demuth had been a servant girl in the household of Marx's father-in-law, the Baron von Westphalen. When Marx's wife, Jenny, was expecting her second child, the Baroness had sent Lenchen, as she was called, to help out, and Lenchen had remained with the Marxes for the rest of their lives. There is not a wisp of evidence to indicate the circumstances in which Marx fathered her child. Nevertheless, on page 260 Mr. Payne allows himself to speculate on whether it was a case of seduction or rape, suggesting that it was most likely the latter, and by page 266 he is referring to the "rape" as if the matter were settled.

Now the fact is that at this period Karl and Jenny Marx, Lenchen, and the three Marx children were all living together in two rooms in Soho, a general-purpose room and a "tiny bedroom." They had no bathroom and they had to go downstairs to the common rooming-house toilet. Since the general-purpose room was also Marx's study, where he habitually worked through a large part of the night, one wonders where Lenchen could have slept. In any case, the circumstances could not have permitted what most of us would consider the normal requirements of privacy. Presumably it was hardly practicable for the members of the household even to dress and undress in private. Marx was still a young man, his wife was four years older than he, bedridden with illness much of the time, afraid of becoming pregnant, and sometimes away from London for weeks at a stretch. Lenchen was young and pretty. Various persons are bound to react differently to the event in question, but my own reaction is: what else could one expect? Marx and Lenchen were living together in the closest quarters during long periods when Mrs. Marx was away. Surely the circumstances call for a compassionate attitude, not for an unsupported accusation of rape! The biographer sometimes seems as lacking in human understanding as ever his subject was. So it is that his hostile animus has the effect of arousing sympathy for his subject even in a reader whose basic disposition is hostile.

The statement that my own hostility was softened by reading the biography must be qualified. For the young Marx I feel no sympathy. From his university days he appears to have combined a monumental intellectual arrogance with a disposition to admire whatever was Satanic—to see himself, in fact, as another Satan destroying the hated creation of his celestial opponent, which he looked forward to seeing washed away in its own blood. His consequent destructive animus does not appear to have been devoid of what is the corrupting element in almost all revolutionaries, the desire for personal power. Rather than join the established society, earning his bread and making his career in it, he would overthrow it, and in the vaguely imagined society that he would erect on its ruins he would be top man.

Until Marx was well into middle-age he generally expected the Revolution he predicted to occur imminently. Perhaps he had to believe this, for it was the entire justification of what was otherwise simply a self-indulgent way of life that kept his family in destitution. He was repeatedly assuring himself and his associates that any day now the Revolution would come which would vindicate him and, one surmises, elevate him to his rightful place as the hero of the world.

This is familiar and plausible to one who remembers the intellectual circles of New York in the 1930s, when a standard conversational phrase in serious use was: "Come the Revolution. . . ." The commonly accepted belief, after the Great Depression began, was that what had happened in Russia in 1917 was about to happen in the United States and, indeed, all over the world. I knew many typical intellectuals of the time well enough to know that, whether consciously or unconsciously, their active support of the Communist line was not disinterested. They were making a place for themselves on the band-wagon of history. Some of them were manoeuvring actively so that, "come the Revolution," they would find themselves in positions similar to those of Lenin and his associates after October 1917—positions from which they would watch us others, who had not had the sense to see what was coming, passing through the streets in the equivalent of tumbrels on our way to some modern version of the guillotine. Remembering all this, I think I understand Marx's mind through these years of his life better than I would otherwise, but without sympathy.

Engels, whose name is indissolubly linked with that of Marx, also arouses no sympathy in me. He rose in the management and at last became part owner of his father's textile factory in Manchester. I can find no evidence that he ever took any interest in the condition of the workers in that factory. What occupied a good part of his personal life was pretty women, good food and wines, fox-hunting, and other amenities of a *bon-vivant's* life; and when he died in 1895 he left a personal estate worth £25,267—presumably representing his appropriation of the "surplus value" produced by the labour he exploited. He too lived most of his life in a position to make a satisfactory adjustment to the Revolution when and if it came, although in his later years he tended to become cynical about the whole Marxist movement, even going so far as to denigrate the doctrine of "historical materialism" on which it was based.

Given the personal attitude I have set forth here, I might have been expected to be among the most uncritical readers of the Payne biography. Nevertheless, there comes a time in the tale of Marx's life, even as related by a hostile biographer, when one's compassion begins to be stirred. Out of the *hubris* of a very young man, he had committed himself to an undisciplined and irresponsible career, based on the false premise that he had it within his power to turn the world upside-down. But by the time he was in his mid-fifties and the premise had been reduced to a pipe-dream it was too late for him to choose another direction. He had for so long lived a life of doing as he pleased, within the limits of such shake-downs as he could subject Engels and others to, that he had at last become genuinely unemployable. In fact, he was gradually becoming incapable of any work at all. It is true that in his old age he was finally put on a comfortable pension by Engels; but by then he was suffering from painful ailments too unpleasant to think about, his wife who had been born to the elegant life of the German aristocracy had been simply burned out by the years of horror, during which for long periods she had wondered how she could survive from day to day. Of their six children three, including the only two boys, had died. The tale of human suffering in the life of this family builds up until at last any faults in those who suffer become irrelevant. Beyond a certain point it would be both pharisaical and cruel to suggest that such agony was deserved. What does it matter, any longer, that the young Marx had thought he had the world by the tail, and had looked forward to the torment he would inflict on it? The prematurely old Marx, although he still cultivates hatred and arrogant language, is essentially a broken man. The hope of revolution and personal power is gone, and all he has left to feed his self-esteem is a rare mention of himself in a newspaper.

As for Johanna Bertha Julie Jenny Marx, *née* von Westphalen, history can provide no greater example of a woman's dedication to the man to whom she has given her life. Here no one could make a case that she deserved the horror of those thirty-eight years of marriage. One can only hope, if one wishes to believe in some ultimate justice, that there were compensations in those inner recesses of the mind to which no outsider can ever penetrate.

The whole tale, as Mr. Payne tells it, ends at last like the final scene of *Hamlet* with death piled on death. The aged Jenny, who has been declining throughout all the years of her marriage, dies with her hand in her husband's, her last words, spoken in English, being: "My strength is broken. . . ." The old man lasts for another fourteen months, cared for by his daughter Eleanor, trying to recover his health by going from one resort or watering place to another, but stricken by news of his favourite daughter's death. Then one day, in his London house, Lenchen "went upstairs to see him and returned two minutes later. 'Come up,' she said. 'He is half asleep.'" Eleanor, Lenchen, and Engels "then went to the bedroom and found him sitting in his armchair. He was dead at the age of sixty-five."

The next to die, in the ugliness and agony of a painful

2. THE CULTURAL FERMENT OF THE WEST

ailment, is Lenchen, now an old woman who had moved into Engels' household after Marx's death. "We were the last two of the pre-1848 old guard," Engels wrote to his friend Friedrich Sorge. He, himself, was to die a few years later of cancer of the throat.

It remains to mention only that each of the two surviving daughters, Laura and Eleanor, after long years of unhappiness and hopes that all came to nothing, ended her life by suicide.

This history of the House of Marx, taking its departure from the *hubris* of the young Karl, matches that of the House of Atreus.

The epilogue is well known. Karl Marx never became a great public figure in his life-time, as he had expected he would; and in the end, after years of retirement and inactivity, he was a pitiful old man who had been all but forgotten. However, the alienated intellectuals of the succeeding generation would feel the need of a Prophet of the Industrial Age to take the place of the Christ, born into a pastoral society, who had come to seem irrelevant in the circumstances of the new times. So when Engels, who had no illusions about Marx's limitations, set out to create a legendary Marx the conditions were propitious. Marx had always spoken in the voice of prophecy, as if he had been Jehovah handing down the Tablets of the Law, and this counted where the question of whether the prophecies had been confirmed by the course of history did not. By contrast with Marx, de Tocqueville had prophesied truly, but because he had not presented himself as if speaking out of the thunder, and because his vision had no quality of epic drama, he had no qualifications for the role.

Marx's burial was postponed in order to enable any following on the Continent to come to England for it; but in the end there were only eleven persons who attended the funeral, six of them members of the immediate family, if one includes Engels as an honorary member. Engels began his funeral oration to the other ten with the words: "On March 14, at a quarter to three in the afternoon, the greatest living thinker ceased to think." So the legend was launched. After Marx's death he was born again, this time as another Mahomet—except that, unlike Mahomet, he was a Prophet without a God.

By a caprice of history that the real Marx did not live to see, and that Engels viewed with becoming irony, the Prophet needed by the new Industrial Age was the unhappy old man whose life had been a failure and to whose graveside only eleven mourners could be gathered. All history is tragic as well as ironic; and great men, even though we know they are not good men, may still be deserving of compassion.

The pipe-smoking man and his heavenly music.

THE BODY OF BACH

Edward Rothstein

THERE would seem to be very little mysterious about Bach. He has reached his 300th birthday with a reputation unmatched in the musical pantheon. He is neither neglected nor overrated; no revisions of the repertory are taking place; no discoveries are changing our understanding of his achievement. There is, simply, the music itself, extravagant in its range and invention: the *Goldberg Variations*, the *St. Matthew Passion*, the *B minor Mass*, the cantatas, the *Well-tempered Clavier*, the cello suites, the violin sonatas, assorted toccatas and suites and fugues and partitas.

The man behind the music also would seem to offer few secrets—no hints of syphilis as with his Romantic successors, no passionate letters like Beethoven's to his "Immortal Beloved," no arcane musical programs with autobiographical clues buried in scores as with Berlioz or Elgar or Berg. Bach simply looked at himself as a craftsman. "I was obliged to work hard," he said; "whoever is equally industrious will succeed just as well." We know him through that industry—a cantata written every week for two years, a set of collected works that took more than 50 years to edit. He was part of a dynasty of musicians who were so influential that in Eisenach the family name became generic; town musicians were called "die Baache." And Johann Sebastian embodied in his career the variety of that dynasty's social roles. He was a virtuoso organist, a court composer, a church composer, a teacher, a producer of secular concerts. The facts about his life are known through those roles, in public documents, city records, petitions, announcements, resignations. The private man is seemingly irrelevant: he worked hard, married twice, and in domestic harmony fathered 20 children.

But there is something missing in this apparently clear portrait. We are used to enshrining composers as gods in a temple of art, divorcing earthly facts from our understanding of the music. But in no other composer is the disparity between the man and his work so immense. Bach's life is considered stupefyingly ordinary, but his music is divine, dealing in essence rather than in accident, in being rather than in appearance. Indeed, who can listen to the *D sharp minor Fugue* in Book I of the *Well-tempered Clavier* and not feel, in the ways in which a single theme is contemplated, combined with itself, inverted, expanded, contracted, and dissected, that this work has transcendent concerns? Even the turns of the melodic theme, which hint at something vulnerable, even melancholy, ultimately become aspects of architecture rather than of sentiment. Albert Schweitzer, who wrote one of the more profound studies of the composer, put it this way: "The artistic personality exists independently of the human, the latter remaining in the background as if it were something almost accidental. Bach's works would have been the same even if his existence had run quite another course." As a man, he remains mundane; his music, meanwhile, dwells in the eternal.

It is remarkable how consistent this view of Bach has been. Even during the years of Bach's supposed eclipse just after his death, when his works were not performed and were compared unfavorably with Handel's, he still had a profound impact on music's greatest practitioners—on Mozart, Haydn, Beethoven, and even Chopin. Bach's son, Carl Philipp Emanuel, made money by renting unpublished scores of his father's works; his wife continued the tradition, and so did Bach's granddaughter.

And, soon enough, devotion to Bach as transcendent artist entered the heart of German musical and intellectual life. On hearing the *Well-tempered Clavier* for the first time on June 21, 1827, Goethe felt, he wrote, "as if the eternal harmony were communing with itself, as might have happened in God's bosom shortly before the creation of the world. It was thus that my inner depths were stirred, and I seemed neither to possess nor to need ears, still less eyes, or any other sense." Wagner presented Bach as a musical savior of the German people itself:

> If we would comprehend the wonderful originality, strength, and significance of the German mind in one incomparably eloquent image, we must look keenly and discerningly at the appearance, otherwise almost inexplicably mysterious, of the musical marvel Sebastian Bach. . . . Look at this head, hidden in its absurd French full-bottomed wig, look at this master, a miserable cantor and organist in little Thuringian towns whose names we hardly know now, wearing himself out in poor situations, always so little considered that it needed a whole century after his death to rescue his works from oblivion; even in his music taking up with an art-form

2. THE CULTURAL FERMENT OF THE WEST

which externally was the complete likeness of his epoch, dry, stiff, pedantic, like perruques and pigtails in notes; and see now the world the incomprehensibly great Sebastian built up out of these elements!

The amazement and worship endure even in the most scholarly musicological circles of this century. Bach has always been at the center of the "authenticity" movement, which attempts to reconstruct the instruments, ensembles, and performance practice of Bach's time. Arguments over "authentic performance" can resemble disputations over holy texts; they have split the musical community along more than scholarly lines. "You play Bach your way," the harpsichordist Wanda Landowska commented to a colleague, "I will play him his way."

Behind these invocations of the sacred there was, however, a man whose life and character must have been bound up in his music. Even the physical traces of Bach are suggestive. His skeleton was found in 1894 in an oak coffin, with its skull bearing—in Schweitzer's words—a "prominent lower jaw, high forehead, deep-set eyesockets, and marked nasal angle." He continues: "Among the interesting peculiarities of Bach's skull may be mentioned the extraordinary toughness of the bone of the temple that encloses the inner organ of hearing, and the quite remarkable largeness of the fenestra rotunda." The skull bears some resemblance to the only two portraits of Bach that have been authenticated. Both were probably painted by Elias Gottlieb Haussmann, the later (1748) a copy of the earlier (1746). A few years before his death the composer is shown holding, angled against his stomach, the score of a puzzle canon: the canon challenges the player to figure out how and when and where a version of the theme is to be played against itself. Bach's right hand is fleshy, feminine, delicately proffering the sheet of paper, while the rest of his body takes no cognizance of his presented art. He stares directly out at the viewer, bewigged in perruques and pigtails, his face as well fed as his belly, the mouth in a pose of slight tension, neither a smile nor a sneer, possessing some degree of self-satisfaction. His left eyebrow is raised, as if in inquiry, his right brow slightly lowered. It is not quite what we expect of the composer either of the canon or the great *Passions*. The body is so solidly there, the eyes so surely presenting a claim, their glance so skeptical—and so ambiguous—that the gentility of the musical offering seems posed, unconvincing, artificial.

WAS THAT the pose in which he made his true "Musical Offering" to King Frederick II, based on a theme that the king composed? With a slight irony, and more than a slight ego? When Bach visited Potsdam, the king had presented him with a theme on which to improvise. Most immodestly, Bach improvised extravagantly, and just two months later had engraved two fugues, ten canons, and a trio sonata based upon the king's theme. This is surely the gesture of a man at once making an effusive offering while raising his eyebrow in pride over his invention and his powers. As in the portrait, this is not a man out of touch with his surroundings. Bach is very much in control, choosing to write his puzzle canons, knowing full well how they will be received, and how anomalous such taut structures are in a world beginning to love sentimental novels.

THERE IS also something in the composer's thick neck and corpulent chest covered in white silk and a gold-buttoned coat that suggests a physical body that can be sensed even in Bach's most abstract music—in its dance rhythms, surprising accents, and swirl of figuration. Bach was, in fact, hot-tempered and stubborn. He was censured for getting into a sword fight after calling one of his players a "nanny-goat bassoonist." His taste for wine is evident in the substantial sums that appear on many of his accounts. But in Haussmann's portrait there is also that feminine hand, so split apart in manner from the physically commanding pose of the man. Indeed, in dealing with those in authority, those who controlled the means of patronage, Bach presented that most fleshy delicate hand, the pinky lightly floating in deference. Bach *served* all his life. Servile epistolary salutations were, for example, conventions of the time, but Bach never missed an opportunity to exploit the style when approaching patrons. There is this remarkable opening to an argumentative missive:

Their Magnificences, the Most Noble, Most Reverend, Most Distinguished, Respected and Most Learned Members of the Most Worshipful Royal and Electoral Saxon Consistory at Leipzig, My Most Honored Masters and High and Mighty Patron. YOUR MAGNIFICENCES, MOST NOBLE, MOST REVEREND, MOST DISTINGUISHED, RESPECTED AND MOST LEARNED, MOST HIGHLY ESTEEMED MASTERS AND HIGH PATRONI!

But after that very salutation comes the stern and skeptical glance, a demand, an appeal, a complaint—a man discontent with his place and his role.

The letter following that fawning address was, in fact, to Bach's masters at Leipzig, the city where Bach spent most of his mature musical life, from 1723 to 1750. There he produced his great sacred works, including five complete cycles of cantatas, the *Mass* and *Passions*, and the great fugues and canons of his late years. It was the place, in other words, where the transcendental Bach took shape, after he had written most of his organ and keyboard masterpieces. As Kantor of the Thomaskirche and Director Musices, he was the most important musician in Leipzig, responsible for the music in the four principal churches, and for the town's musical life. These were the years of musical grandeur, in which Bach, one would assume, had the religious and public support of Leipzig behind him.

STILL, as any number of his letters to the Leipzig Council indicate, the situation was in fact far different. Before going to Leipzig, Bach was remarkably content at Köthen, where he was a court composer to a prince who loved music. Then the prince married a rather unmusical woman. Sensing the change in his status, Bach made inquiries in other towns. Kuhnau, who held the position at Leipzig, had died. Telemann, then the most renowned musician in Germany, was first offered the position; next in line was Christoph Graupner, who was something of an alumnus. Only when they both declined was Bach considered. To the councillors Bach was a mediocrity and, conversely, the position was a compromise for Bach. From his place at the center of court life with a sensitive prince, he moved to Leipzig, where he had to answer to several dozen civic and church superiors, who included the 15 members of the city council who hired him, the ecclesiastical authority of the consistory, which supervised the church services, and the rector of the school itself, within which Bach had to teach Latin

13. The Body of Bach

along with music. Bach was paid less than a quarter of what he had received at Köthen, living expenses were higher, and he was dependent upon "freelance" playing at funerals and weddings. (Bach later complained that a "healthy wind was blowing" one year in Leipzig so he made almost nothing from funerals.)

Bach's new position also demanded rising at four or five in the morning to maintain discipline in the school until the students retired at eight in the evening. He was expected to write and prepare music for all the church services; he composed a cantata every week for the first two years. Moreover, as soon as he arrived in Leipzig, Bach was embroiled in a dispute over whether he would have charge of the music at St. Paul's, the university church. Bach needed the income and pressed his case. In 1725 he went over his superiors' heads and wrote three petitions to the Elector of Saxony, pleading a tightly argued case. This did not make for good relations with the council; Bach lost his appeal, and the composer found commissions passing him by, leading to other conflicts. In 1729, just after his first performance of the *St. Matthew Passion*, the council ignored both Bach's selections of new pupils and his musical priorities. At a council meeting, according to the minutes, Bach was called "incorrigible." The council decided "he must be reproached and admonished."

Eschewing his usual salutation, Bach sent a memo to the council, biting in its graciousness and title: "Short but most necessary draft for a well-appointed church music; with certain modest reflections on the decline of the same." The climactic conflict, lasting more than two years, came in 1734, when Johann August Ernesti was appointed rector of the school. One historical account, dating from 1776, describes how the men became bitter enemies: "Bach began to hate those students who devoted themselves completely to the *humaniora* and treated music as a secondary matter, and Ernesti became a foe of music. When he came upon a student practicing on an instrument he would exclaim, 'What? You want to be a beer-fiddler too?'" Finding deaf ears at the council with more than four lengthy complaints and responses, Bach again appealed over their heads, "To His Most Serene Highness, the Mighty Prince and Lord, Frederick Augustus, King in Poland," etc., etc.

These confrontations, which occurred earlier in Bach's career as well, show a keen sense of political hierarchy in Bach's language, along with a peremptory dismissal of political manners in his actions. When it came to musical matters, there was no compromise. Yet Bach came to Leipzig at a moment when music was becoming less and less important in schools and the community, ironically, because of the dawn of the Enlightenment, which Ernesti represented. Bach's role was peculiar; he was even dependent at the end of his life on contributions from the community, because he essentially had no social position. When he died, one member of the council cautioned against replacing him with anyone resembling a "Kapellmeister." His successor gave his first performance in a concert hall, not a church.

Christoph Wolff, the distinguished Bach scholar, points out that Bach understood these matters quite well. In the cantata of homage to the municipal council (BWV 216a), Mercury, the god of commerce, declares his gift to the council: "My trade, which here / I firmly plant, / shall provide you with / the greatest part of your lustre." That trade, and the world of the bourgeoisie that developed in its wake, did indeed leave the Kantor and Director Musices looking somewhat quaint. Haussmann's portrait captures the paradox, in Bach's face and body and hand, the gracious offer of music, and the ironic awareness that the music was posing more than a trivial puzzle to its listeners.

The biggest puzzle is that this most contentious man working at this peculiar historical moment produced such works as the *St. Matthew Passion* and the *B minor Mass*—music that seems to speak without ambiguities about faith and belief, in a tone of voice and with a technical assurance that make the music seem not just pre-modern, but otherworldly. There would seem to be scarcely a hint of Bach treating the religious realm as he did the political, of offering praise out of duty rather than belief, or of demonstrating the raised eyebrow and ambiguous lips of the Haussmann portrait. There is a certainty in Bach's harmonies. However much they meander into painful realms, the foundation is never left behind.

Moreover, the texts themselves are never subordinate to technical aspects of the music. In fact, they determine the music's central figurations. In the common practice of the period, the music *paints* the texts being set, illustrating them, commenting upon them, knowing its own laws are subordinate to the word. This means that words like "descent" are illustrated with descending melodic lines. Relations between meaning and musical sign can become still more intricate. Sometimes the music intentionally bears mystical or numerological meanings—a bass line, for example, repeated 13 times, underscoring the tragedy of the "Crucifixus" in the *Mass*. And always in the vocal music, there are the chorales—the heart of Lutheran music—which Bach harmonizes and re-harmonizes, treating them with as much care as if they too were sacred texts. Scores also bear dedicatory abbreviations, wholly sincere, like "S.D.G." ("Soli Deo Gloria," To god alone be praise) or "J.J." ("Jesu juva," Help me, Jesus). Bach writes that even so rudimentary an element of music as the figured bass—the fundamental bass line to be filled in by the player—merits attention. In instructing his pupils, he wrote: "Like all music, the figured bass should have no other end and aim than the glory of God and the recreation of the soul; where this is not kept in mind there is no true music, but only an infernal clamor and ranting."

WHAT THEN of the clamor and ranting that comes of Bach's own life? And what are its echoes in the music itself? Theodor Adorno noted that if we treat Bach simply as an archaic man of faith, we have missed the most important aspect of his music: it is a product of its time, anticipating the Enlightenment even as it seems to nestle itself in formal rigors.

Even the work that would seem furthest from the Enlightenment—the *B minor Mass*—acknowledges the new age by attempting to swerve away from it. The *Mass* was written over a period of 20 years; its Credo is now believed to be one of Bach's final works. It is deliberately archaic, orthodox, exaggerating aspects of formality and faith. Bach di-

2. THE CULTURAL FERMENT OF THE WEST

vided the Credo text into nine sections, grouped into a trinity of three parts each. There is also a formal symmetry around the center group of three, with the Crucifixus lying at its heart. That tripartite center is framed by two arias: "Et in unum Deum" (I believe in one Lord Jesus Christ) and "Et in Spiritum sanctum" (And I believe in the Holy Ghost). Each chorus is suffused with numerical symbolism and pictorial references, so that in "Et incarnatus," for example, the pulsing three tones of the bass line shift upon the words "and was made man"; the breathing sighs of the violins descend, and become incarnated, musically, in that low-pitched earthly realm, like the described movement of the Holy Ghost. Such a musical symbol is not subliminal. It can, in performance, elicit a gasp, as if the music itself had incarnated a spiritual idea and was presenting it, not for appreciation, but as the simple truth.

This gives the Credo an orthodoxy and a seriousness far more extreme than the most impassioned cantatas. But even in this case, the effect of the music is far different from a simple assertion of faith. As the arias and the instrumental solos make clear, there is an *interior* world being presented as well. The communal fugues and proclamations of the choruses are contrasted with the meditative arias of personal belief that frame the central section of the Credo. "Et in unum Deum" is a duet in which the proclamation of belief in one god becomes a sensuous intertwining of imitative voices; similarly, the oboe duet in "Et in Spiritum" is lyrically intimate. The choruses of the central section—the Incarnation, Crucifixion, and Resurrection—also convey a sense of human drama, sounding hushed and eerie at first and finally blazing forth with communal force.

All is so tightly controlled here that the tensions between individual and community, will and authority, sentiment and law, feeling and faith—all the tensions so evident elsewhere in Bach's music—are muted. The cantatas, though, celebrate those tensions, placing them at the core of Bach's religious music. The erotic arias between the soprano soul and bass Christ in *Cantata No. 140*, the variations on the single chorale theme in *Cantata No. 4*, the sharp contrasts between choral fugues and mellifluous arias in nearly all of the cantatas, show Bach moving constantly between the public demands of faith and its interior trials. In these works, as in the *Passions*, the style becomes almost operatic, dramatic, very different from earlier sacred works. The subject in much of Bach's sacred music is man—man in the particular—represented religiously in the figure of Christ. This shares certain elements with Pietism—the movement that attacked Lutheran orthodoxy, stressing personal and mystical devotion. There are anticipations of similar attitudes in other Baroque composers such as Heinrich Schütz, now celebrating his quadricentennial. But this religious emphasis on the individual links Bach more to the world that came after him than to the world that came before.

THIS IS TRUE even in the most serious secular works. The *Goldberg Variations*, as Glenn Gould pointed out, does not guide the listener through a structure or a narrative that develops in a certain direction. Instead, said Gould, it seems, despite its intricate architecture, to be "a community of sentiment" possessing "a fundamental coordinating intelligence which we [label] ego." It is the path of an individual will at play in the realm of musical structure. Bach is so sure of musical law that it grants him freedom. The canons at each interval are as ecstatic in spirit as the regularly appearing dance movements. And the *Variations*' piety is limited: the return of the magisterial theme at the end is preceded by a "quodlibet"—a playful interweaving of popular songs of the period, "*Ich bin so lang nicht bei dir g'west*" (Long have I been away from you) and "*Kraut und Rüben haben mich vertrieben*" (Cabbage and turnips have put me to flight). It has even been suggested that these songs refer to the theme itself. First heard at the beginning of the work, it returns an hour later; its foundations—its bass line and harmonies—have been transmuted and transformed, put in flight with sophisticated techniques that Bach may have modestly considered as commonplace as cabbages and turnips.

BACH'S musical style, in fact, may almost be defined as the play of an ego in a highly structured world. Such, for example, is the texture of the fugue, which seems to govern every note Bach penned. His fugues construct musical orders in which each individual voice is playfully free—maintaining its identity but capable of the most fantastical diversions—while having its position verified and reinforced by other voices. The fugue establishes a community of like minds and distinct parts, very different from the polyphony of the Renaissance, where the focus is less on individual voices than on the overall texture. It also contrasts with earlier Baroque fugues, where propriety and sobriety govern the behavior of the voices. Bach's achievement is to make each voice seem completely independent, while showing again and again their links, and even identities, with other free voices. Bach turned the Baroque fugue into a sign of the Enlightenment.

The fugue as used by Bach presents an order known not through faith, but through persistent examination and exploration. His themes are not mere organizations of musical material; instead they venture forth into the fugue fully formed, with shape and character and tensions all their own. Bach, it was said, could glance at a theme and, as if judging its character, tell immediately how it should be treated in a fugue—whether there should be stretti (multiple entrances overlapped in a short time), inversion (the theme played upside down), retrogression (the theme played backward), and so on.

The theme's character is defined as a character by no other composer before Bach. The fugue thus becomes reflective as well as rational. A single voice explores and creates its own musical universe. The fugue as a style can be seen as a prelude, historically, to its own extinction in a style of "feeling," where one voice finds itself thoroughly alone, without such mirrorings and reflections and architectural structures; it wanders through sentiment and fantasy. The fugue and the canon began to seem archaic in the rococo world of Bach's sons. The canon could even seem, as C. P. E. Bach told Charles Burney, a "certain proof to him of a total want of genius." But C. P. E. Bach's successors in the Romantic era understood quite clearly the powers of canon and fugue. The most autobiographical music of the 19th century invokes the fugue in attempts to turn personal feeling into something more metaphysical, as in Beethoven's last piano sonatas or the finale to Liszt's piano sonata.

There is indeed something metaphysical about Bach's concern with the fugue: the belief that the world and the self are images of each other, that the word and music and the world are linked in their structure and their substance. Hence the nearly mystical concern with musical signs and symbols, from the most mundane illustration of joy with dotted rhythms to the use of themes with notes corresponding to the letters of Bach's name.

There is no way in this metaphysical vision to separate the world of daily life from a transcendent spiritual realm. So Bach did not think it at all peculiar to include in a book of music composed and collected for his wife, Anna Magdalena, a poem (attributed to him) about a most mundane pleasure. It is entitled "Edifying Thoughts of a Tobacco Smoker":

> Whene'er I take my pipe and stuff it
> And smoke to pass the time away,
> My thoughts, as I sit there and puff it,
> Dwell on a picture sad and gray;
> It teaches me that very like
> Am I myself unto my pipe.

Like the pipe, he is made of but earth and clay; like the pipe, which glows leaving ash, so will his fame pass and his body turn to dust.

> Thus o'er my pipe, in contemplation
> Of such things, I can constantly
> Indulge in fruitful meditation,
> And so, puffing contentedly,
> On land, on sea, at home, abroad,
> I smoke my pipe and worship God.

Similar speculation suffuses Bach's musical universe. In his compositions, with their word-painting and affects and symbolism, metaphoric and metaphysical links are made between the most mundane and the most spiritual. The world is full of echoes and allusions. Nothing is arbitrary. Into this world comes the ego, the musical subject, Bach himself, whose work is craft rather than art because he does not create a world, he attempts to mirror it. In doing so, of course, he also catches part of himself. His presence slightly disrupts that metaphysical mirror because he begins to sense in his own peculiar position something awry—earthly hierarchies and authorities not quite matching the heavenly. So there is a double perspective: Bach serves, but he also serves himself. "J.J." (Help me, Jesus), he writes, but he also inscribes his own name musically in his final work. He is the voice in the fugues, the solitary individual ironically sensing his own freedom while remaining linked to a larger order. We can see him in the Haussmann portrait questioning, daring, stern and patient, and we can imagine him relishing his glass of port as well as his own skills, smoking his pipe and worshiping God.

13. The Body of Bach

BACH ON RECORD

Most Bach playing may still be execrable: consider the "spinning wheel" textures of the most publicly acclaimed modern virtuosos (Jean-Pierre Rampal, Alexis Weissenberg, Pinchas Zukerman, virtually any conductor with any symphony orchestra). But Bach has become the most well-performed composer on record. Herewith, a prejudiced selection on the occasion of Bach's tricentenary:

In the last six months, Archiv has released a generous selection of its Bach recordings dating as far back as the 1950s, on budget-priced disks that lack only English liner notes. The selections range from the large-scale, subtly detailed cantata performances of Karl Richter and the classic organ playing of the great blind virtuoso Helmut Walcha to Nathan Milstein's noble version of the violin sonatas and partitas, and lyrical, idiosyncratic chamber performances by the Musica Antiqua Köln. Most are lush, modern performances; nearly all are elegantly musical, some profoundly so.

Teldec has similarly repackaged for budget collecting its important recordings of the authentic performances of Nikolaus Harnoncourt. These include an introspective *B minor Mass*, plangent *Easter cantatas*, the *Brandenburg concertos*, the *St. John Passion*. Harnoncourt is at once orthodox and impassioned.

Pro Arte records is releasing here the "Leipzig Bach Edition" of recordings from East Germany. Some are distressingly unfocused (Max Pommer leading *Cantatas 56* and *82*—M CP27062). Others are unusually rewarding, including "Music in the Bach Household" (M CP27065), and a recording of Hannes Kästner playing a recently built organ in Bach's own Thomaskirche (M CP27069). East Germany's musicians are traditional in style—living near the source and rarely traveling beyond it.

The Cantatas: Nikolaus Harnoncourt and Gustav Leonhardt have been involved in a nearly 20-year project, recording the complete 200-some cantatas in authentic performances, packaged with complete scores. Now well past the halfway mark, the recordings have helped redefine Bach performance style, bringing introspection and sentiment into the authenticity movement.

The Goldberg Variations: Glenn Gould (CBS M3X-38610). Here, in a boxed set, are two important performances, Gould's 1955 debut recording along with his 1982 rethinking of the work. These should stand alongside Wanda Landowska's grandly scaled performance (RCA AGM1-5251), and all of Gould's other Bach recordings.

The Well-tempered Clavier: Edwin Fischer (Vol I: EMI GR-70028-29—imported from Japan). This important piano performance from the 1930s is full of character and inauthentic nuance—a complement to Gould's pianistic Bach.

Ralph Kirkpatrick (five disks, available only through Quarry Communications, P.O. Box 3168, Stony Creek, Connecticut 06405). This re-release of the Deutsche Grammophon harpsichord version is transparent, restrained, and illuminating. The performance by Kirkpatrick's teacher, Wanda Landowska, is no longer available (originally RCA).

The Brandenburg concertos: Christopher Hogwood and the Academy of Ancient Music (L'Oiseau-Lyre 414 187-1) and Ton Koopman and the Amsterdam Baroque Orchestra (Erato 751342) present two newly recorded authentic performances; parts of each would form a single collection giving brio and tension to these worn divertimenti.

The Violin sonatas and partitas: Sigiswald Kuijken (Harmonia Mundi 1C 3LP 157). This first successful authentic Baroque interpretation should be heard alongside Milstein's modern renderings.

Other recordings of note include: Karl Münchinger's lush, pre-authentic string version of the "Musical Offering" (London STS-15063); the Anna Magdalena Notebooks with Igor Kipnis and Judith Blegen (Nonesuch DB-79020), showing Bach as pedagogue; and recordings by harpsichordist, organist, and conductor Trevor Pinnock, whose freewheeling energy and rigorous authentic style exemplify the qualities that mark a renaissance in Bach performance.

E.R.

Freudian Myths and Freudian Realities

Peter F. Drucker

If Sigmund Freud had not been so visible and prominent in the Vienna of my childhood, I would never have paid attention to the glaring discrepancy between the Freudian myths and the Freudian realities.

My parents had both known Freud for many years. But Freud was more than twenty years older than my father. And so my father would bow with great respect when he encountered Freud on the paths around the Alpine lake on which the Freuds had their summer villa, next to Genia Schwarzwald's resort. And Freud would bow back. My mother had had an interest in psychiatry as a medical student, and had worked for a year in the Psychiatric Clinic in Zurich headed by Bleuler, a psychiatrist whom Freud greatly respected. She had bought Freud's books as a young woman, well before her marriage. I own her copy of the first edition, dated 1900, of *Die Traumdeutung (The Interpretation of Dreams)*—one of the pitiful 351 copies which was all the first edition sold—and her copy of the definitive 1907 edition of *Zur Psychopathologie des Alltagslebens (Psychopathology of Everyday Life)* with its famous analysis of the "Freudian slips"—both with bookmarks still in my mother's maiden name. Before her marriage, she also attended one of his lecture series, whether at the University or at the Psychoanalytic Society I do not know, where she apparently was the only woman; she used to recount with some amusement how her presence embarrassed Freud in discussing sex and sexual problems.

I myself had been introduced to Dr. Freud when I was eight or nine years old. One of Genia Schwarzwald's co-op restaurants during World War I was in the Berggasse, next to the Freud apartment. In those hunger years in Vienna Dr. Freud and his family sometimes ate lunch there—and so did we. On one of those days the Freuds' and we sat at the same table. Dr. Freud recognized my parents and I was presented and asked to shake hands.

But this was my only contact with Dr. Freud. And the only reason why I even remember it when I have, of course, forgotten all the other adults with whom I had to shake hands as a boy, is that my parents afterwards said to me: "Remember today; you have just met the most important man in Austria, and perhaps in Europe." This was apparently before the end of the war, for I asked, "More important than the Emperor?" "Yes," said my father, "more important than the Emperor." And this so impressed me that I remembered it, even though I was still quite a small child.

This is the point. My parents were not disciples of Freud—indeed, my mother was quite critical of both the man and his theories. But they still knew that he was "the most important man in Austria and perhaps in Europe."

Three "facts" about Sigmund Freud's life are accepted without question by most people, especially in the English-speaking world: That all his life Freud lived with serious financial worries and in near-poverty; that he suffered greatly from anti-Semitism and was denied full recognition and the university appointments that were his due, because he was a Jew; and that the Vienna of his day, especially medical Vienna, ignored and neglected Freud.

All three of these "facts" are pure myths. Even as a youngster Freud was well-to-do; and from the beginning of his professional life as a young doctor he made good money. He never suffered from discrimination as a Jew until Hitler drove him into exile at the very end of his life. He received official recognition and academic honors not only earlier than almost any person in Austrian medical history; he received at an early age honors and recognition to which, according to the fairly strict Austrian canon, he was not entitled at all. Above all, medical Vienna did not ignore or neglect Freud. It took him most seriously. No one was discussed as much, studied as much, or argued about more. Medical

"Freudian Myths and Freudian Realities," from ADVENTURES OF A BYSTANDER by Peter F. Drucker, pp. 83-99. Copyright © 1978, 1979 by Peter F. Drucker. Reprinted by permission of Harper & Row, Publishers, Inc.

14. Freudian Myths

Vienna did not ignore or neglect Freud, it *rejected* him. It rejected him as a person because it held him to be in gross violation of the ethics of the healer. And it rejected his theory as a glittering half-truth, and as poetry rather than medical science or therapy.

The myths about Freud and his life in Vienna of his days would be trivial and quite irrelevant to the man and to psychoanalytic theory but for one fact: Freud himself believed them. Indeed he invented them and publicized them. In his letters, above all, these myths are stressed again and again. And it was in his letters that the proud, disciplined, and very private man unburdened himself of his own concerns. These myths, in other words, were extremely important to Freud himself. But why?

Freud was a stoic who never complained, abhorred self-pity, and detested whiners. He bore great physical pain without a sound of complaint. And he was equally stoical about sufferings in his private and family life. But he complains incessantly about imaginary sufferings—lack of money, anti-Semitic discrimination, and being ignored by the Viennese physicians.

Freud was in everything else ruthlessly candid, above all with himself. He was merciless in his own self-examination and tore out root and branch what to an ordinary mortal would have been harmless self-indulgence. It is inconceivable that Freud could have knowingly created and propagated fairy tales and myths about himself. But it seems equally inconceivable that Freud could not have been known that these assertions and complaints were not "facts," but pure myths. Everyone else in the Vienna of Freud's time knew it and commented on Freud's strange "obsessions."

The only answer is a Freudian one: these myths are "Freudian slips." They are symptoms of deep existential realities and traumas that Freud could not face despite his self-analysis, his uncompromising truthfulness, his stoic self-discipline. And it is Freud who has taught us that "Freudian slips" are never trivial. The Freud of official legend is a stern monolithic god—a Zeus on Olympus or an Old Testament Jehovah. The Freud of his own "Freudian slips" is a tormented Prometheus. And it was Prometheus who of all the gods of classical mythology is mentioned most often in Freud's works.

The Freuds were not "Rothschild-rich," to use the Viennese term for the super-rich. They were comfortable middle class. Freud's father was a fairly successful merchant. In the Vienna of Freud's youth—he was born in 1856, just when the rapid growth of Vienna into a metropolis began—this meant a high-ceilinged apartment in one of the new four- or five-story apartment buildings just outside the old "Inner City": fairly spacious though dark, overcrowded with furniture, and with one bathroom only. It meant two or three servants, a weekly cleaning woman, and a seamstress every month, a summer vacation in a spa near Vienna or in the mountains, Sunday walks in the Vienna Woods for the whole family, high school (Gymnasium) for the children, books, music, and weekly visits to opera and theaters. And this is precisely how the Freuds lived. Freud's brother, Alexander—he published a reference book on railroad freight tariffs for the Ministry of Commerce when my father was the ministry's head—always resented Sigmund's insistence on the dire poverty in which he grew up as maligning their dead father's memory, "who was such a good provider." All the sons got university educations, he would point out. Young Sigmund was being supported in considerable comfort in Paris for three or four more years of study, even after he had finished both his medical and his speciality training; and the young Freuds always had enough pocket money to buy books and tickets to opera and theater. Of course, they kept no horse and carriage—that was being "Rothschild-rich." But they rented one when they went for their summer vacation to Baden or Voeslau, the two popular spas near Vienna. And from the day on which Freud went into practice after his return from Paris, he had patients. For his skill in treating neuroses was immediately recognized.

But he also received official recognition very early. The title "Professor" given to an Austrian physician was a license to coin money; the holder automatically tripled or quadrupled his fees. For that reason alone, it was almost never given to a physician before he was in his late fifties. Freud had it in his late forties. A firm rule reserved this title to the medical directors of major hospitals as a way to compensate them for the substantial income they gave up in treating hospital and charity patients for free. Freud received the title, even though he held no hospital appointment and treated only private and paying patients.

But what of his oft-repeated complaint about "anti-Semitic discrimination," in that he was not going to have the title of "full professor" but only that of "extraordinary" or "associate professor" when offered the chair of neurology at the University's medical school? The fact is that the university chairs at the medical school were established by law and required an act of Parliament for any change. The only clinical chairs in the medical school that carried a "full professorship" were the ones in the "old," i.e., eighteenth-century disciplines—in internal medicine, obstetrics, and surgery. Every other chair was an "extraordinary professorship." Any such professor who headed a university hospital, such as the neurological unit that was offered to Freud—again at an earlier age than a university hospital had been offered to a Viennese physician before—received, however, within a year or two, the "personal" rank and title of "full professor." Freud was going to receive it too, had he accepted the offer instead of turning it down and then complaining that "anti-Semitism" had denied him a full professorship.

However strong anti-Semitism was becoming among the small shopkeepers and craftsmen of Vienna in the late 1800s, it was frowned upon at the Imperial court, in the government service, among "educated" people, and above all in the Viennese medical community. In the very years of Freud's professional growth, from 1880 through 1900 or so, the majority of the leadership positions in Viennese medicine were taken over by men who were Jews, if not by religion, then by birth. In 1881, at the time when Freud started on his professional career, more than 60 percent of Veinna's physicians were already Jewish, according to C. A. McCartney, the leading historian of Austria-Hungary. By 1900, Jews held the great majority of clinical chairs at the University's medical school, of the medical directorships in the

2. THE CULTURAL FERMENT OF THE WEST

major hospitals, and such positions as surgeon-general of the Army, personal physician to the Emperor, and obstetrician to the ladies of the Imperial family. "Anti-Semitism" was not the reason why Freud did not have the professorship in neurology; it played altogether no role in his practice, in his standing in official medicine, or in his acceptance by a Viennese medical community that was as Jewish as he was.

Indeed a main reason why this Viennese medical community found Freud unacceptable was that it was Jewish. For the first criticism of Freud, voiced even by believers in psychoanalysis, was always that Freud violated the basic Jewish ethics of the healer. Freud did not accept charity patients, but taught instead that the psychoanalyst must not treat a patient for free, and that the patient will benefit from treatment only if made to pay handsomely. This was absolutely "unethical" to the Jewish tradition out of which so many of Vienna's physicians came. There were of course plenty of physicians, Jewish ones included, who were out for the buck. They were called "rippers"—"*Reisser.*" A physician might have to refer patients to a "ripper" if they needed the special skill of one of them—if, for instance, they suffered from some sort of skin problem or some kind of stomach ailment. But the "rippers" were held in contempt. And even the most outrageous "ripper" would serve as medical director of a hospital or as department head in one of the university clinics, and thus take care of the indigent sick. And all of them, for all their greed, would at least preach the traditional ethic of the healer, the ethic of selfless giving. Not Freud, however: he spurned it. And thus he challenged head-on the deepest, most cherished values of the Jewish tradition of the healer. He made medicine a *trade*. Worse still, the Veinnese doctors came to suspect that Freud might be right. At least for emotional and psychic ailments, insistence by the physician on a good fee was therapeutic and selflessness did damage.

Even more disturbing was Freud's insistence on emotional detachment of physician from patient. The physicians knew of course that the doctor has to learn to be hard-skinned and to get used to suffering, death, and pain. They knew that there were good reasons for the rule that physicians do not treat members of their own families. But central to their creed was the belief that tender, loving care is the one prescription that fits all symptoms. Admittedly, a broken bone would knit without it—though still better with it. But the wounded *person* needed a caring physician above all. And here was Dr. Freud demanding that the physician divest himself of sympathy for—indeed of human interest in— the patient, and that for the physician to become involved with the human being meant damaging the patient, made him or her dependent, and inhibited recovery and cure. Instead of being a brother, the suffering patient became an object.

That however was tantamount to degrading the physician from healer to mechanic. To all those Jewish physicians of Vienna—and not only to the Jewish ones—this was express denial of the very reasons why they had become physicians, and an affront to what they respected in themselves and in their calling. What made this doubly offensive was again that many suspected Freud might be right, at least with respect to psychoanalysis. "But," once said the elder of Vienna's Jewish surgeons at our dinner table—Marcus Hajek, the head of the University's ear, nose, and throat hospital and one of those "extraordinary" professors with the "personal" title of full professor—"if Freud is right, then psychoanalysis is a narcotic; and for a physician knowingly to create addiction—or even the risk thereof—is both a crime and a breach of his sacred duty."

There was even more discussion of psychoanalysis as therapy and scientific method than of its ethics. Freud belonged to the second generation of "modern" medicine in Vienna. "Modern" medicine, after a century or more of slow gestation, had finally emerged fully developed—at Vienna—only a few years before Freud was born. Freud's medical generation was therefore conscious of what had made possible the giant step from "prescientific" medicine—the medicine of the contemptible quacks of Molière's plays—to medicine that could diagnose, could heal, could be learned, and could be taught. And during this generation's own lifetime "modern" medicine had yielded its greatest gains, in the development of bacteriology, for instance, and with it in the capacity to prevent and to treat infectious diseases; in anesthesia that made surgery bearable; or in the antisepsis and asepsis that made surgery possible without killing the patient through subsequent infection.

The fundamental step from quackery to medicine—the step first taken by such revered ancestors as Boerhave in Holland or Sydenham in England around 1700—had been abstention from big theory and from global speculation. Diseases are specific, with specific causes, specific symptoms, and specific cures. The great triumph of the bacteriologist—that is, of Freud's own generation—was precisely that he showed that every infection is specific, each with its specific bacterial cause carried and spread by its own unique carriers, whether flea or mosquito, and each acting in its own specific way on specific tissue. And whenever anyone in the history of modern medicine had forgotten the lesson of Boerhave and Sydenham as, for instance, the homeopathic school of Hahnemann had done (Hahnemann was only recently dead when Freud was born), his teachings immediately degenerated into the quackery of the "humors" and "vapors." Yet here was psychoanalysis, which postulated one universal psychological dynamism for *every* emotional disorder; and many of its practitioners (though not Freud himself) even claimed that many psychoses too were "emotional" rather than "physical," caused by the same forces of ego, id, and superego acting out sexual repression in the subconscious. Around 1900, I was once told, the Vienna Medical Society put on a skit at one of its parties. It was a parody of Molière's *Le Malade Imaginaire* in which the scurrilous quack was made to say: "If the patient loved his mother, it is the reason for this neurosis of his; and if he hated her, it is the reason for the same neurosis. Whatever the disease, the cause is always the same. And whatever the cause, the disease is always the same. So is the cure: twenty one-hour sessions at 50 Kronen each." Of course, that was gross caricature of psychoanalytic theory and practice. But it was close enough to bring the house down; even the psychoanalysts in the audience, I was told by one of them who had been there as a medical student, laughed until the tears came.

But if the basic method was so controversial to anyone familiar with the history of medicine, what about results? The leaders of the medical fraternity had seen enough to know that medicine is not entirely rational and that things do work which no one can explain. Hence their emphasis on demonstrable results and on the controlled test. But when the Viennese physicians asked for the results of psychoanalysis, they found themselves baffled. That Freud himself was a master healer was beyond doubt. But the results of psychoanalysis were something else again. In the first place Freud and the Freudians refused to define "results." Was it restoration of ability to function? Or relief from anxiety? Was psychoanalysis "curing" anybody? If so, what explained the obvious fact that so many of its patients became permanent patients, or at the least came back to the psychoanalyst again and again? Was it alleviation of a chronic condition—and was it then good enough that the patient became addicted to the treatment and "felt better" for it? And however one defined the "results" of this strange therapy, what was the appropriate control to test its results? Every Viennese doctor saw obviously "neurotic" people in his practice; a large number of them got better without any treatment—especially, of course, adolescents. At least the symptoms disappeared or changed quite drastically. What was the natural rate of remissions in neuroses, and how significantly better did the patient of the psychoanalyst do? It was not only that all the data were lacking. The psychoanalysts, beginning with Freud, refused to discuss the question.

And then it seemed that all methods of psychotherapy had the same results, or non-results. There were some rivals in the field by 1910, offsprings of the Freudian school, Alfred Adler, for instance, or Carl Jung. There was also, in Germany, Oskar Kohnstamm—the forerunner of today's "humanist" psychologists, a respected and successful psychotherapist, and totally non-Freudian in his approach in that he stressed the therapist's personal involvement in the life and problems of the patient. But there were also all kinds of assorted faith healers and "consciousness-raisers" around: spiritualists, hypnotists, people with mysterious magnetic boxes, not to mention pilgrimages to Lourdes and Hassidic "miracle rabbis." The studies of the results of psychotherapies which began to be done around 1920 always showed the same results and still do: psychotherapies might have significant results. The data are inconclusive; but no one method has results that are significantly better than or different from any other. This can mean two things: Freud's psychoanalysis is a specific treatment for some, but not for all, emotional disorders; or emotional problems improve or are even cured by having a fuss made over them. Either conclusion was, of course, unacceptable to Freud and the psychoanalysts; it was a rejection of Freud's entire claim.

I recall a discussion of a big study of the results of psychotherapy—again at our dinner table—between Karl Buehler, a moderately pro-Freudian, who taught psychology at the University (and whose wife, Charlotte, was a Freudian psychoanalyst), and, as I recall it, Oskar Morgenstern, then probably still a student and later, at Princeton, to become the foremost authority on statistical theory. Buehler argued that the results indicated that psychoanalysis is powerful and specific therapy for a fairly wide range of psychic ailments, and that there was need to do research as to what that range encompassed. "Not so," said Morgenstern; "if you go by the figures, then there are either no emotional illnesses at all or the trust of the patient in any method makes the patient feel better, regardless of method." "In either case," said another dinner guest, an eye surgeon, "there is as yet no valid Freudian psychotherapy which a physician can recommend or use in good conscience."

But most bothersome of all for the Viennese physician was that you could never know whether Freud and his disciples talked healing the sick or "art criticism." One minute they were trying to cure a specific ailment, whether fear of crossing the street or impotence. The next moment they were applying the same method, the same vocabulary, the same analysis to Grimm's *Fairy Tales* or *King Lear*. The physicians were perfectly willing to concede that, as Thomas Mann put it in his speech at Freud's eightieth birthday, "Psychoanalysis is the greatest contribution to the art of the novel." Freud as the powerful, imaginative, stimulating critic of culture and literature, of religion and art, was one thing; it was readily conceded by a good many that he had opened a window on the soul that had long been nailed shut. This is what made him "the most important man in Austria." But was psychoanalysis then likely to be therapy, any more than were Newton's physics or Kant's metaphysics or Goethe's aesthetics? Yet this was precisely what Freud and his followers claimed. It was a claim the Viennese physicians, by and large, could not accept.

Freud himself was deeply hurt by any hint that his theory was "poetry" rather than "science." He is known to have bitterly resented Thomas Mann's birthday speech even though he himself had asked Mann to be the speaker. But, of course, whatever the validity of psychoanalysis as science, Freud was a very great artist. He was probably the greatest writer of German prose in this century—it is so clear, so simple, so precise as to be as untranslatable as first-rate poetry. His anonymous case histories portray a whole person in two paragraphs better than many long novels, including, I would say, those of Thomas Mann himself. The terms he coined—whether "anal" and "oral" or "ego" and "superego"—are great poetic imagery. Yet this made "scientific medicine" only more uncomfortable, while praising Freud as a poet and artist infuriated him and his followers.

All these things were being discussed and debated endlessly even in my childhood, and far more so, I believe, in earlier years, in the years between 1890 and 1910 when Freud's great books came out and when he moved from being a first-rate neurologist with remarkable clinical results, especially with women, to becoming the leader of a "movement." Again and again the questions came up: of Freud's ethics and of the ethics of psychoanalysis; of its results and how they should be judged or measured; and of the compatibility of cosmic

2. THE CULTURAL FERMENT OF THE WEST

philosophy and clinical therapy. One thing is crystal clear: Freud was not ignored. He was taken very seriously and then rejected.

The emergence of psychoanalysis is often explained, especially in America, as a reaction to the "Victorian repression of sex." Maybe there was such "repression" in America but it is even doubtful whether there was any such phenomenon in England, except for a few short years. It did not exist in the Austria in which young Sigmund Freud grew up and in which he started to practice. On the contrary, late-nineteenth-century Vienna was sexually permissive and sex flourished openly everywhere. The symbol of Freud's Vienna was Johann Strauss's comic opera *Die Fledermaus (The Bat)*, which had its first performance in 1874 when Freud was eighteen. It is an opera of lover-swapping and open sexual pairing in which the wife jumps into the arms of her old boyfriend the moment she thinks her husband is out of the way; in which the maid, one of the main stars, sneaks off to the masked ball to pick up a rich sugar-daddy who will set her up as his mistress and finance her theatrical career; in which another main character—Prince Orlofsky, who gives the ball where all this takes place—is a homosexual whose main aria, in which he invites his guests to love "each to his own taste," must have been understood by every adult in the audience as "gay liberation." This plot might not be "X-rated" should it come up for approval now; but it certainly would not be classed as healthy family fare. Yet it was set in the resort in which the prudish Austrian Emperor spent his summers rather than in some mythical never-never land. And no one was shocked!

The popular playwright a little later, in the Vienna of the 1880s and 1890s, was Freud's former fellow medical student, Artur Schnitzler, whose best-known and most popular play *La Ronde (Der Reigen)* can be described as a game of musical beds, in which everything but the sex act itself takes place on stage.

To be sure, a woman was not supposed to have affairs before her marriage—though it was the fear of unwanted pregnancy far more than morality that underlay that rule. She married young, of course; but then she was on her own, and only expected to be reasonably discreet. And that no restriction on premarital sex was applied to men was not so much because of the "double standard"—though it did exist—as because men had to postpone marriage until they could support a wife and children, and no one had the slightest illusion that they would remain chaste until then, or that such abstinence would be desirable.

Indeed what created sexual anxieties in so many of the middle-class women, and especially the Jewish middle-class women who were Freud's early patients, was Vienna's openness of sex and its sexually supercharged atmosphere. These women came, for the most part, from the ghettos of small Jewish towns, like the Freuds themselves, whose roots were in one of the small Jewish settlements in Moravia—now a part of Czechoslovakia. In these small ghettos, sex was indeed repressed—for both men and women. Marriages were arranged by a middleman when both bride and groom were children. They married as soon as they reached sexual maturity—and until then they had never seen each other. From then on, the woman lived a domestic life in which she saw her family but few other people, and no men. Sex was deemphasized—in the synagogue, in the family, in the community. But out of this sexless atmosphere the young Jewish woman was, as the century wore on, increasingly projected without preparation into the erotic whirlpool of Vienna, with its constant balls, its waltzes, its intense sexual competition, its demand that she prove herself sexually all the time, that she be "attractive" and attract, and that she be "sexy." No wonder that these women suffered anxieties and became neurotic over their sex life and sexual roles. Freud himself never referred to the alleged "sexual repression" of Viennese society. That explanation came much later and is, incidentally, of American manufacture. No Viennese would have fallen for it.

Freud was, clearly, not in favor of "sexual freedom." He would have repudiated paternity for the sexual liberation of this century that is so often ascribed to him. He was a puritan and suspected that sex, while inevitable, was not really good for the human race. As for the claim that men have made women into "sex objects," he would have thought it a very poor joke. He was familiar with the old Jewish legend of the evil Lilith, Adam's second wife, and considered it symbolic truth. Lilith seduces Adam away from Eve and makes a sex object out of the male by changing woman into the one female among the higher animals that is at all times sexually available—whereas the females of other higher animals are in heat only a few days each month and are otherwise sexless for all practical purposes. Altogether the Freudian sex drives that create repression and neuroses are independent of culture and mores; they are structured into the relationship between adults and children rather than into the relationships between the sexes in a particular society.

Still, in the Freudian literature a constant theme is sexual anxiety, sexual frustration, sexual malfunction. But the one neurosis that is stressed in every other record of late-nineteenth-century Vienna—or indeed late-nineteenth-century Europe—is totally absent: the money neurosis. It was not sex that was repressed in Freud's Vienna. It was money. Money had come to dominate; but money had also come to be unmentionable. Early in the century, in Jane Austen's novels, money is open—almost the first thing Jane Austen tells the reader is how much annual income everybody has. Seventy-five years later, by the time young Freud begins his adult life, the novelist's characters are consumed with concern for money and wealth—and never discuss it. Dickens still talks about money quite openly, just as he talks about sex quite openly, about illegitimate children and illicit liaisons, about the haunts of vice and the training of young girls to be prostitutes. Trollope, only three years Dickens's junior but already a "mid-Victorian," is still fairly explicit about sex—far more explicit than a "proper Victorian" is supposed to be. Yet most of his novels are about money, and about money which the hero or anti-hero (or, as in *The Eustace Diamonds*, the anti-heroine) has to have but cannot mention. And in the novels of Henry James, Freud's closest contemporary among the novelists of society, money and the secrecy surrounding the lack thereof, is as much the subject as the

14. Freudian Myths

tension between American and European.

In the Vienna of Freud's time no respectable parent discussed his income with his children; it was a carefully avoided topic. Yet money had become the preoccupation of both. This, as we now know, happens in every society where there is rapid economic development.

In Jane Austen's England—still presumed to be quite static—one's money income was a fact. It could be changed only by marriage or by the right aunt's dying at the right time—the change agents in Jane Austen's books. It could not be changed by individual effort. Seventy years later economic development had made incomes highly mobile. At the same time, however, as in any society in the early stages of rapid economic development, there were now "winners" and "losers." A fairly small group profited mightily and became rich. A much larger group, but still a minority, reached precarious affluence—the Freuds in Sigmund's youth were just a cut above that level, I imagine. A majority had suddenly much greater expectations and were torn out of the static poverty of their small-town lives; but their incomes either did not go up at all or far less than their expectations had risen. It was Adlai Stevenson who first talked of the "rising tide of expectations." But the phenomenon antedates him by 150 years. The classical treatment of it is Thackeray's *Vanity Fair*, written well over a century before Stevenson's phrase and dealing with that "less developed country," the England of 1820 rather than with Asia or South America.

No European country in the last decades of the nineteenth century developed faster—and from a lower base at that—than Austria, and especially the Czech areas (Bohemia and Moravia) from which the Freuds had come and from which the Jewish middle class in Vienna was largely recruited. Thus the secret and suppressed obsession with money—the "poorhouse neurosis," it was commonly called—had become a major affliction, and a common one among the older middle-class people of my young years. (The young people were far less prone to it, for by then Austria was no longer developing and was indeed shrinking economically; the younger people were not obsessed with becoming poor, they were poor.) The poorhouse neurosis showed itself in a constant fear of ending up poor, a constant nagging worry about not earning enough, of not being able to keep up with the social expectations of oneself and one's family—and one's neighbors—and, above all, in constant obsessive talking about money while always claiming not to be interested in it.

Freud clearly suffered from the "poorhouse neurosis"; it is etched even into the letters he wrote his betrothed from Paris while still a young man. Yet for all his ruthless honesty with himself, he never could face up to it. That he misrepresented his professional life as being underpaid, under constant financial pressure, and in financial anxiety—these were misrepresentations that evinced the anxiety neurosis which he could not and did not face and which, in a Freudian slip mechanism, he repressed. This also explains why he did not notice it in his patients and leaves it out of his case histories. It had to be a "non-fact," for the fact itself was much too painful for him.

Freud's complaints about being the victim of anti-Semitic persecution similarly covered up and, at the same time, betrayed another fact Freud could not face: his inability to tolerate non-Jews.

Freud's generation of Central European (and especially Austrian) Jews had wholeheartedly and with a vengeance become German nationalists—in their culture, in their self-identification, and in their political affiliation and leanings. And no one was more consciously a German in his culture than Sigmund Freud. Yet there were no non-Jews in psychoanalysis, or at least no non-Jewish Austrians and Continental Europeans. Freud tried hard to attract them. But those who joined were always driven out.

In the "Heroic Age" of psychoanalysis, between 1890 and 1914, Freud repudiated every one of his non-Jewish followers or associates who was Austrian, German or German-speaking, or even a Continental European male. That he broke with Carl Jung and forced Jung in turn to break with him is one example. He could tolerate non-Jews only if they were foreigners, and even then he preferred women like the French Princess Bonaparte—for women did not, of course, rank as equals in Freud's world. For all their German culture—their constant references to German poets and writers, their humanist culture of the German Gymnasium, their strong Wagnerianism, and their aesthetics of the educated German "humanist" whose taste had been formed by Jakob Burckhart's *Culture of the Renaissance in Italy*—the members of the Freud circle could not rid themselves of their intense Jewishness. Their jokes were Jewish, and it is a Freudian tenet, after all, that jokes speak the truth of the heart. The non-Jew was irksome, difficult, a stranger, an irritation—and soon gotten rid of.

This, however, Freud, grand master of non-Jewish German culture, could not admit, least of all to himself. He needed an explanation that would put the blame on others, hence the Freudian slip of "anti-Semitic discrimination" and near-persecution. It was well known, for instance, that both Wagner-Jauregg, the eminent psychiatrist who headed one neuropsychiatric hospital at the University, and the head of the other neuropsychiatric hospital at the University, and the head of the other neuropsychiatric university hospital—the one that had been offered to Freud but was turned down by him—had wanted to attend the meetings of Freud's Psychoanalytical Society. Both were non-Jews, and both were made decidedly unwelcome. But in Freud's version these two men had rejected him and denied him recognition because he was a Jew. Freud needed a Freudian slip because the reality, that is, the fact of his not being able to break out of his Jewishness, was much too painful for him to face and to accept. And finally, of course, he had to make Moses into an Egyptian who was not a Jew at all—in *Moses and Monotheism*, one of his last major works.

But most important and most revealing is Freud's "Freudian slip" in respect to his being "ignored" by the Viennese physicians. He had to suppress their rejection of him; and he could do it only by pretending, above all to himself, that they were not discussing him, not doubting him, not rejecting him, but ignoring him. I

2. THE CULTURAL FERMENT OF THE WEST

suspect that Freud in his heart shared a good many of their doubts about the methodology of psychoanalysis. But he could not even discuss these doubts. For to do so would have forced him to abandon the one central achievement of his: a theory that was both strictly "scientific" and rationalist, and yet went beyond rationalism into the "subconscious," into the inner space of dream and fantasy and, in Thomas Mann's words, into the unscientific experience of the "novel," that is, into fiction.

Freud was led to psychoanalysis by his realization that the prevailing rationalism of the Enlightenment—of which modern scientific medicine was a distinguished and most successful child—could not explain the dynamics of the emotions. Yet he could not abandon the world and world view of science. To his dying day he maintained that psychoanalysis was strictly "scientific"; he maintained that the workings of the mind would be found to be capable of explanation in rational, scientific terms, in terms of chemical or electrical phenomena and of the laws of physics. Freudian psychoanalysis represents a giant effort to hold together in one synthesis the two worlds of scientific reason and nonrational inner experience. It represents a giant effort to hold together in one person the ultra-rationalist Freud, the child of the Enlightenment, and Freud the dreamer and poet of the "dark night of the soul." This synthesis made psychoanalysis so important, and yet so fragile. It gave psychoanalysis its impact. It made it timely. The systems of the nineteenth century that have had a major impact on the Western world—Marx, Freud, and Keynes—all have had in common the synthesis between the scientific and the magical, and the emphasis on logic and empirical research leading to the *credo quia absurdum*—"I believe because it makes no rational sense."

Freud clearly realized how narrow his footing was. Give one inch and you descend into the Eastern mysticism of Jung, with his invocation of myth as the experience of the race, his reliance on the magical sticks of the *I Ching* and on the fairy tales of shamans, sorcerers, and sybils. And there was the descent into the "orgone box" of another ex-disciple, Otto Reich. Give one inch the other way and you descend into the trivialities of another renegade disciple, Alfred Adler, with his arithmetic of "overcompensation" and his petty envies such as the "inferiority complex" as a substitute for the passion of the Prophets and the *hubris* of the Greek dramatists. Freud had to maintain the synthesis where he had carefully and precariously balanced it, otherwise he would have had either the pure magic of the faith healer or the pure and futile mechanism of those children of the ultra-rationalist eighteenth century, the phrenologists or the Mesmerians with their electric rods. Freud had to have in one statement both "scientific" method for clinical therapy *and* "cosmic philosophy."

Just how precarious the balance was we know today. For by now it has disintegrated. There is on the one hand the scientific, rationalist clinical exploration of the brain—and indeed, Freud's prediction that the brain and its diseases would be shown to be subject to the same approaches of chemotherapy, diet, surgery, and electrotherapy as the rest of the body is well on its way to being proven. But the phenomena with which Freud dealt—we call them "emotional" today—are increasingly being tackled by methods that do not even pretend to belong to the realm of science, but are clearly in Freud's terms "superstition": transcendental meditation, for instance, or the instant "consciousness-raising" psychodynamic techniques. Whether this is good or bad, I do not know. For unlike Freud's generation, we seem to be able to accept a split of the world into incompatible universes.

However, Freud had to hold the precarious balance. I do not know whether he thought it through. Freud was not given to writing his thought processes down for others to read; no other major thinker so carefully dismantled the scaffolding of his thoughts before presenting the finished building to public view. But he knew that he needed the synthesis. And he must have realized, if only subconsciously, that it would collapse the moment he even discussed the questions the critics raised: the question of methodology; the definition of "results" and the matter of control tests; the problem of getting the same—or similar—therapeutic results from any psychotherapy, including purely magical ones; and the hybrid character of psychoanalysis as both scientific theory and therapy, and myth of personality and philosophy of man. He could only maintain the synthesis by ignoring these questions. And so he had to pretend, above all to himself, that the Viennese physicians ignored psychoanalysis so as to be able to ignore them.

The Freud of the Freudian realities is a much more interesting man, I submit, than the Freud of the conventional myth. He is also, I think a much bigger man—a tragic hero. And while a Freudian theory that can only maintain the synthesis between the world of Cartesian rationality and the world of the dark night of the soul by ignoring all inconvenient questions may be a much weaker theory—and one that cannot ultimately stand—it is also, I submit, a more fascinating and more revealing theory, and a humanly moving one.

The First Feminist

In 1792 Mary Wollstonecraft wrote
a book to prove that her sex was as intelligent
as the other: thus did feminism
come into the world. Right on, Ms. Mary!

SHIRLEY TOMKIEVICZ

The first person—male or female—to speak at any length and to any effect about woman's rights was Mary Wollstonecraft. In 1792, when her *Vindication of the Rights of Woman* appeared, Mary was a beautiful spinster of thirty-three who had made a successful career for herself in the publishing world of London. This accomplishment was rare enough for a woman in that day. Her manifesto, at once impassioned and learned, was an achievement of real originality. The book electrified the reading public and made Mary famous. The core of its argument is simple: "I wish to see women neither heroines nor brutes; but reasonable creatures," Mary wrote. This ancestress of the Women's Liberation Movement did not demand day-care centers or an end to woman's traditional role as wife and mother, nor did she call anyone a chauvinist pig. The happiest period of Mary's own life was when she was married and awaiting the birth of her second child. And the greatest delight she ever knew was in her first child, an illegitimate daughter. Mary's feminism may not appear today to be the hard-core revolutionary variety, but she did live, for a time, a scandalous and unconventional life—"emancipated," it is called by those who have never tried it. The essence of her thought, however, is simply that a woman's mind is as good as a man's.

Not many intelligent men could be found to dispute this proposition today, at least not in mixed company. In Mary's time, to speak of *anybody's* rights, let alone woman's rights, was a radical act. In England, as in other nations, "rights" were an entity belonging to the government. The common run of mankind had little access to what we now call "human rights." As an example of British justice in the late eighteenth century, the law cited two hundred different capital crimes, among them shoplifting. An accused man was not entitled to counsel. A child could be tried and hanged as soon as an adult. The right to vote existed, certainly, but because of unjust apportionment, it had come to mean little. In the United States some of these abuses had been corrected—but the rights of man did not extend past the color bar and the masculine gender was intentional. In the land of Washington and Jefferson, as in the land of George III, human rights were a new idea and woman's rights were not even an issue.

In France, in 1792, a Revolution in the name of equality was in full course, and woman's rights had at least been alluded to. The Revolutionary government drew up plans for female education—to the age of eight. "The education of the women should always be relative to the men," Rousseau had written in *Emile*. "To please, to be useful to us, to make us love and esteem them, to educate us when young, and take care of us when grown up, to advise, to console us, to render our lives easy and agreeable: these are the duties of women at all times, and what they should be taught in their infancy." And, less prettily, "Women have, or ought to have, but little liberty."

Rousseau would have found little cause for complaint in eighteenth-century England. An Englishwoman had almost the same civil status as an American slave. Thomas Hardy, a hundred years hence, was to base a novel on the idea of a man casually selling his wife and daughter at public auction. Obviously this was not a common occurrence, but neither is it wholly implausible. In 1792, and later, a woman could not own property, nor keep any earned wages. All that she possessed belonged to her husband. She could not divorce him, but he could divorce her and take her children. There was no law to say she could not grow up illiterate or be beaten every day.

Such was the legal and moral climate in which Mary Wollstonecraft lived. She was born in London in the spring of 1759, the second child and first daughter of Edward Wollstonecraft, a prosperous weaver. Two more daughters and two more sons were eventually born into the family, making six children in all. Before they had all arrived, Mr. Wollstonecraft came into an inheritance and decided to move his

©1972 American Heritage Publishing Company, Inc. Reprinted by permission from HORIZON (Spring, 1972).

2. THE CULTURAL FERMENT OF THE WEST

family to the country and become a gentleman farmer. But this plan failed. His money dwindled, and he began drinking heavily. His wife turned into a terrified wraith whose only interest was her eldest son, Edward. Only he escaped the beatings and abuse that his father dealt out regularly to every other household member, from Mrs. Wollstonecraft to the family dog. As often happens in large and disordered families, the eldest sister had to assume the role of mother and scullery maid. Mary was a bright, strong child, determined not to be broken, and she undertook her task energetically, defying her father when he was violent and keeping her younger brothers and sisters in hand. Clearly, Mary held the household together, and in so doing forfeited her own childhood. This experience left her with an everlasting gloomy streak, and was a strong factor in making her a reformer.

At some point in Mary's childhood, another injustice was visited upon her, though so commonplace for the time that she can hardly have felt the sting. Her elder brother was sent away to be educated, and the younger children were left to learn their letters as best they could. The family now frequently changed lodgings, but from her ninth to her fifteenth year Mary went to a day school, where she had the only formal training of her life. Fortunately, this included French and composition, and somewhere Mary learned to read critically and widely. These skills, together with her curiosity and determination, were really all she needed. The *Vindication* is in some parts long-winded, ill-punctuated, and simply full of hot air, but it is the work of a well-informed mind.

Feminists—and Mary would gladly have claimed the title—inevitably, even deservedly, get bad notices. The term calls up an image of relentless battle-axes: "thin college ladies with eyeglasses, no-nonsense features, mouths thin as bologna slicers, a babe in one arm, a hatchet in the other, grey eyes bright with balefire," as Norman Mailer feelingly envisions his antagonists in the Women's Liberation Movement. He has conjured up all the horrid elements: the lips with a cutting edge, the baby immaculately conceived (one is forced to conclude), the lethal weapon tightly clutched, the desiccating college degree, the joylessness. Hanging miasmally over the tableau is the suspicion of a deformed sexuality. Are these girls man-haters, or worse? Mary Wollstonecraft, as the first of her line, has had each of these scarlet letters (except the B.A.) stitched upon her bosom. Yet she conformed very little to the hateful stereotype. In at least one respect, however, she would have chilled Mailer's bones. Having spent her childhood as an adult, Mary reached the age of nineteen in a state of complete joylessness. She was later to quit the role, but for now she wore the garb of a martyr.

Her early twenties were spent in this elderly frame of mind. First she went out as companion to an old lady living at Bath, and was released from this servitude only by a call to nurse the dying Mrs. Wollstonecraft. Then the family broke up entirely, though the younger sisters continued off and on to be dependent on Mary. The family of Mary's dearest friend, Fanny Blood, invited her to come and stay with them; the two girls made a small living doing sewing and handicrafts, and Mary dreamed of starting a primary school. Eventually, in a pleasant village called Newington Green, this plan materialized and prospered. But Fanny Blood in the meantime had married and moved to Lisbon. She wanted Mary to come and nurse her through the birth of her first child. Mary reached Lisbon just in time to see her friend die of childbed fever, and returned home just in time to find that her sisters, in whose care the flourishing little school had been left, had lost all but two pupils.

Mary made up her mind to die. "My constitution is impaired, I hope I shan't live long," she wrote to a friend in February, 1786. Under this almost habitual grief, however, Mary was gaining some new sense of herself. Newington Green, apart from offering her a brief success as a schoolmistress, had brought her some acquaintance in the world of letters, most important among them, Joseph Johnson, an intelligent and successful London publisher in search of new writers. Debt-ridden and penniless, Mary set aside her impaired constitution and wrote her first book, probably in the space of a week. Johnson bought it for ten guineas and published it. Called *Thoughts on the Education of Daughters*, it went unnoticed, and the ten guineas was soon spent. Mary had to find work. She accepted a position as governess in the house of Lord and Lady Kingsborough in the north of Ireland.

Mary's letters from Ireland to her sisters and to Joseph Johnson are so filled with Gothic gloom, so stained with tears, that one cannot keep from laughing at them. "I entered the great gates with the same kind of feeling I should have if I was going to the Bastille," she wrote upon entering Kingsborough Castle in the fall of 1786. Mary was now twenty-seven. Her most recent biographer, Margaret George, believes that Mary was not really suffering so much as she was having literary fantasies. In private she was furiously at work on a novel entitled, not very artfully, *Mary, A Fiction*. This is the story of a young lady of immense sensibilities who closely resembles Mary except that she has wealthy parents, a neglectful bridegroom, and an attractive lover. The title and fantasizing contents are precisely what a scribbler of thirteen might secretly concoct. Somehow Mary was embarking on her adolescence—with all its daydreams—fifteen years after the usual date. Mary's experience in Kingsborough Castle was a fruitful one, for all her complaints. In the summer of 1787 she lost her post as governess and set off for

15. The First Feminist

London with her novel. Not only did Johnson accept it for publication, he offered her a regular job as editor and translator and helped her find a place to live.

Thus, aged twenty-eight, Mary put aside her doleful persona as the martyred, set-upon elder sister. How different she is now, jauntily writing from London to her sisters: "Mr. Johnson . . . assures me that if I exert my talents in writing I may support myself in a comfortable way. I am then going to be the first of a new genus . . ." Now Mary discovered the sweetness of financial independence earned by interesting work. She had her own apartment. She was often invited to Mr. Johnson's dinner parties, usually as the only female guest among all the most interesting men in London: Joseph Priestley, Thomas Paine, Henry Fuseli, William Blake, Thomas Christie, William Godwin—all of them up-and-coming scientists or poets or painters or philosophers, bound together by left-wing political views. Moreover, Mary was successful in her own writing as well as in editorial work. Her *Original Stories for Children* went into three editions and was illustrated by Blake. Johnson and his friend Thomas Christie had started a magazine called the *Analytical Review*, to which Mary became a regular contributor.

But—lest anyone imagine an elegantly dressed Mary presiding flirtatiously at Johnson's dinner table—her social accomplishments were rather behind her professional ones. Johnson's circle looked upon her as one of the boys. "Wollstonecraft" is what William Godwin calls her in his diary. One of her later detractors reported that she was at this time a "philosophic sloven," in a dreadful old dress and beaver hat, "with her hair hanging lank about her shoulders." Mary had yet to arrive at her final incarnation, but the new identity was imminent, if achieved by an odd route. Edmund Burke had recently published his *Reflections on the Revolution in France,* and the book had enraged Mary. The statesman who so readily supported the quest for liberty in the American colonies had his doubts about events in France.

Mary's reply to Burke, *A Vindication of the Rights of Men,* astounded London, partly because she was hitherto unknown, partly because it was good. Mary proved to be an excellent polemicist, and she had written in anger. She accused Burke, the erstwhile champion of liberty, of being "the champion of property." "Man preys on man," said she, "and you mourn for the idle tapestry that decorated a gothic pile and the dronish bell that summoned the fat priest to prayer." The book sold well. Mary moved into a better apartment and bought some pretty dresses—no farthingales, of course, but some of the revolutionary new "classical" gowns. She put her auburn hair up in a loose knot. Her days as a philosophic sloven were over.

Vindication of the Rights of Woman was her next work. In its current edition it runs to 250-odd pages; Mary wrote it in six weeks. *Vindication* is no prose masterpiece, but it has never failed to arouse its audience, in one way or another. Horace Walpole unintentionally set the style for the book's foes. Writing to his friend Hannah More in August, 1792, he referred to Thomas Paine and to Mary as "philosophizing serpents" and was "glad to hear you have not read the tract of the last mentioned writer. I would not look at it." Neither would many another of Mary's assailants, the most virulent of whom, Ferdinand Lundberg, surfaced at the late date of 1947 with a tract of his own, *Modern Woman, the Lost Sex.* Savagely misogynistic as it is, this book was hailed in its time as "the best book yet to be written about women." Lundberg calls Mary the Karl Marx of the feminist movement, and the *Vindication* a "fateful book," to which "the tenets of feminism, which have undergone no change to our day, may be traced." Very well, but then, recounting Mary's life with the maximum possible number of errors per line, he warns us that she was "an extreme neurotic of a compulsive type" who "wanted to turn on men and injure them." In one respect, at least, Mr. Lundberg hits the mark: he blames Mary for starting women in the pernicious habit of wanting an education. In the nineteenth century, he relates, English and American feminists were hard at work. "Following Mary Wollstonecraft's prescription, they made a considerable point about acquiring a higher education." This is precisely Mary's prescription, and the most dangerous idea in her fateful book.

"Men complain and with reason, of the follies and caprices of our Sex," she writes in Chapter 1. "Behold, I should answer, the natural effect of ignorance." Women, she thinks, are usually so mindless as to be scarcely fit for their roles as wives and mothers. Nevertheless, she believes this state not to be part of the feminine nature, but the result of an equally mindless oppression, as demoralizing for men as for women. If a woman's basic mission is as a wife and mother, need she be an illiterate slave for this?

The heart of the work is Mary's attack on Rousseau. In *Emile* Rousseau had set forth some refreshing new ideas for the education of little boys. But women, he decreed, are tools for pleasure, creatures too base for moral or political or educational privilege. Mary recognized that this view was destined to shut half the human race out of all hope for political freedom. *Vindication* is a plea that the "rights of men" ought to mean the "rights of humanity." The human right that she held highest was the right to have a mind and think with it. Virginia Woolf, who lived through a time of feminist activity, thought that the *Vindication*

2. THE CULTURAL FERMENT OF THE WEST

was a work so true "as to seem to contain nothing new." Its originality, she wrote, rather too optimistically, had become a commonplace.

Vindication went quickly into a second edition. Mary's name was soon known all over Europe. But as she savored her fame—and she did savor it—she found that the edge was wearing off and that she was rather lonely. So far as anyone knows, Mary had reached this point in her life without ever having had a love affair. Johnson was the only man she was close to, and he was, as she wrote him, "A father, or a brother—you have been both to me." Mary was often now in the company of the Swiss painter Henry Fuseli, and suddenly she developed what she thought was a Platonic passion in his direction. He rebuffed her, and in the winter of 1792 she went to Paris, partly to escape her embarrassment but also because she wanted to observe the workings of the Revolution firsthand.

Soon after her arrival, as she collected notes for the history of the Revolution she hoped to write, Mary saw Louis XVI, "sitting in a hackney coach . . . going to meet death." Back in her room that evening, she wrote to Mr. Johnson of seeing "eyes glare through a glass door opposite my chair and bloody hands shook at me . . . I am going to bed and for the first time in my life, I cannot put out the candle." As the weeks went on, Edmund Burke's implacable critic began to lose her faith in the brave new world. "The aristocracy of birth is levelled to the ground, only to make room for that of riches," she wrote. By February France and England were at war, and British subjects classified as enemy aliens.

Though many Englishmen were arrested, Mary and a large English colony stayed on. One day in spring, some friends presented her to an attractive American, newly arrived in Paris, Gilbert Imlay. Probably about four years Mary's senior, Imlay, a former officer in the Continental Army, was an explorer and adventurer. He came to France seeking to finance a scheme for seizing Spanish lands in the Mississippi valley. This "natural and unaffected creature," as Mary was later to describe him, was probably the social lion of the moment, for he was also the author of a best-selling novel called *The Emigrants*, a farfetched account of life and love in the American wilderness. He and Mary soon became lovers. They were a seemingly perfect pair. Imlay must have been pleased with his famous catch, and—dear, liberated girl that she was—Mary did not insist upon marriage. Rather the contrary. But fearing that she was in danger as an Englishwoman, he registered her at the American embassy as his wife.

Blood was literally running in the Paris streets now, so Mary settled down by herself in a cottage at Neuilly. Imlay spent his days in town, working out various plans. The Mississippi expedition came to nothing, and he decided to stay in France and go into the import-export business, part of his imports being gunpowder and other war goods run from Scandinavia through the English blockade. In the evenings he would ride out to the cottage. By now it was summer, and Mary, who spent the days writing, would often stroll up the road to meet him, carrying a basket of freshly-gathered grapes.

A note she wrote Imlay that summer shows exactly what her feelings for him were: "You can scarcely imagine with what pleasure I anticipate the day when we are to begin almost to live together; and you would smile to hear how many plans of employment I have in my head, now that I am confident that my heart has found peace . . ." Soon she was pregnant. She and Imlay moved into Paris. He promised to take her to America, where they would settle down on a farm and raise six children. But business called Imlay to Le Havre, and his stay lengthened ominously into weeks.

Imlay's letters to Mary have not survived, and without them it is hard to gauge what sort of man he was and what he really thought of his adoring mistress. Her biographers like to make him out a cad, a philistine, not half good enough for Mary. Perhaps; yet the two must have had something in common. His novel, unreadable though it is now, shows that he shared her political views, including her feminist ones. He may never have been serious about the farm in America, but he was a miserably long time deciding to leave Mary alone. Though they were seprated during the early months of her pregnancy, he finally did bring her to Le Havre, and continued to live with her there until the child was born and for some six months afterward. The baby arrived in May, 1794, a healthy little girl, whom Mary named Fanny after her old friend. Mary was proud that her delivery had been easy, and as for Fanny, Mary loved her instantly. "My little Girl," she wrote to a friend, "begins to suck so manfully that her father reckons saucily on her writing the second part of the Rights of Woman." Mary's joy in this child illuminates almost every letter she wrote henceforth.

Fanny's father was the chief recipient of these letters with all the details of the baby's life. To Mary's despair, she and Imlay hardly ever lived together again. A year went by; Imlay was now in London and Mary in France. She offered to break it off, but mysteriously, he could not let go. In the last bitter phase of their involvement, after she had joined him in London at his behest, he even sent her—as "Mrs. Imlay"—on a complicated business errand to the Scandinavian countries. Returning to London, Mary discovered that he was living with another woman. By now half crazy with humiliation, Mary chose a dark night and threw herself in the Thames. She was nearly dead when two rivermen pulled her from the water.

15. The First Feminist

Though this desperate incident was almost the end of Mary, at least it was the end of the Imlay episode. He sent a doctor to care for her, but they rarely met again. Since Mary had no money, she set about providing for herself and Fanny in the way she knew. The faithful Johnson had already brought out Volume I of her history of the French Revolution. Now she set to work editing and revising her *Letters Written during a Short Residence in Sweden, Norway, and Denmark,* a kind of thoughtful travelogue. The book was well received and widely translated.

And it also revived the memory of Mary Wollstonecraft in the mind of an old acquaintance, William Godwin. As the author of the treatise *Political Justice,* he was now as famous a philosophizing serpent as Mary and was widely admired and hated as a "freethinker." He came to call on Mary. They became friends and then lovers. Early in 1797 Mary was again pregnant. William Godwin was an avowed atheist who had publicly denounced the very institution of marriage. On March 29, 1797, he nevertheless went peaceably to church with Mary and made her his wife.

The Godwins were happy together, however William's theories may have been outraged. He adored his small stepdaughter and took pride in his brilliant wife. Awaiting the birth of her child throughout the summer, Mary worked on a new novel and made plans for a book on "the management of infants"—it would have been the first "Dr. Spock." She expected to have another easy delivery and promised to come downstairs to dinner the day following. But when labor began, on August 30, it proved to be long and agonizing. A daughter, named Mary Wollstonecraft, was born; ten days later, the mother died.

Occasionally, when a gifted writer dies young, one can feel, as in the example of Shelley, that perhaps he had at any rate accomplished his best work. But so recently had Mary come into her full intellectual and emotional growth that her death at the age of thirty-eight is bleak indeed. There is no knowing what Mary might have accomplished now that she enjoyed domestic stability. Perhaps she might have achieved little or nothing further as a writer. But she might have been able to protect her daughters from some part of the sadness that overtook them; for as things turned out, both Fanny and Mary were to sacrifice themselves.

Fanny grew up to be a shy young girl, required to feel grateful for the roof over her head, overshadowed by her prettier half sister, Mary. Godwin in due course married a formidable widow named Mrs. Clairmont, who brought her own daughter into the house—the Claire Clairmont who grew up to become Byron's mistress and the mother of his daughter Allegra. Over the years Godwin turned into a hypocrite and a miser who nevertheless continued to pose as the great liberal of the day. Percy Bysshe Shelley, born the same year that the *Vindication of the Rights of Woman* was published, came to be a devoted admirer of Mary Wollstonecraft's writing. As a young man he therefore came with his wife to call upon Godwin. What he really sought, however, were Mary's daughters—because they were her daughters. First he approached Fanny, but later changed his mind. Mary Godwin was then sixteen, the perfect potential soul mate for a man whose needs for soul mates knew no bounds. They conducted their courtship in the most up-to-the-minute romantic style: beneath a tree near her mother's grave they read aloud to each other from the *Vindication.* Soon they eloped, having pledged their "troth" in the cemetery. Godwin, the celebrated freethinker, was enraged. To make matters worse, Claire Clairmont had run off to Switzerland with them.

Not long afterward Fanny, too, ran away. She went to an inn in a distant town and drank a fatal dose of laudanum. It has traditionally been said that unrequited love for Shelley drove her to this pass, but there is no evidence one way or the other. One suicide that can more justly be laid at Shelley's door is that of his first wife, which occurred a month after Fanny's and which at any rate left him free to wed his mistress, Mary Godwin. Wife or mistress, she had to endure poverty, ostracism, and Percy's constant infidelities. But now at last her father could, and did, boast to his relations that he was father-in-law to a baronet's son. "Oh, philosophy!" as Mary Godwin Shelley remarked.

If in practice Shelley was merely a womanizer, on paper he was a convinced feminist. He had learned this creed from Mary Wollstonecraft. Through his verse Mary's ideas began to be disseminated. They were one part of that vast tidal wave of political, social, and artistic revolution that arose in the late eighteenth century, the romantic movement. But because of Mary's unconventional way of life, her name fell into disrepute during the nineteenth century, and her book failed to exert its rightful influence on the development of feminism. Emma Willard and other pioneers of the early Victorian period indignantly refused to claim Mary as their forebear. Elizabeth Cady Stanton and Lucretia Mott were mercifully less strait-laced on the subject. In 1889, when Mrs. Stanton and Susan B. Anthony published their *History of Woman Suffrage,* they dedicated the book to Mary. Though Mary Wollstonecraft can in no sense be said to have founded the woman's rights movement, she was, by the late nineteenth century, recognized as its inspiration, and the *Vindication* was vindicated for the highly original work it was, a landmark in the history of society.

MAKING IT WORK

A. E. Dick Howard

A. E. Dick Howard, a former Wilson Center Fellow, is White Burkett Miller Professor of Law and Public Affairs at the University of Virginia. Born in Richmond, Virginia, he is a graduate of the University of Richmond (1954) and received his law degree from the University of Virginia (1961). A former law clerk to Mr. Justice Hugo L. Black, Professor Howard was the chief architect of Virginia's current (1971) constitution. His books include The Road from Runnymede: Magna Carta and Constitutionalism in America *(1968) and* Commentaries on the Constitution of Virginia *(1974).*

By dint of his strong personality and powerful intellect, John Marshall, fourth chief justice of the U.S. Supreme Court (1801-35), laid the foundation of American constitutional law.

"We the People," read the first words of the new Constitution. As the former Colonies debated the Constitution after the Philadelphia Convention's adjournment, even these seemingly unexceptionable words came under attack. Who, demanded Virginia's Patrick Henry, had authorized the Convention to "speak the language of *We the People*, instead of *We the States*?" In the Continental Congress, Richard Henry Lee of Virginia thundered against the document's backers, a coalition, he said, "of monarchy men, military men, aristocrats and drones, whose noise, impudence and zeal exceed all belief."

The real battle began after September 27, 1787, when the Continental Congress in New York City sent the new Constitution to special ratifying conventions to be held by the 13 states.

At first, the Federalists—the Constitution's supporters—held the initiative. During the Convention, they had managed to avoid the crippling precedent of the old wartime Articles of Confederation, which could not be altered without the unanimous consent of the states. The Constitution, by contrast, would become effective after only nine states had ratified it.

During the autumn of 1787, James Madison, the Convention's political maestro, brought his tactical skills to bear on ratification. He kept up a steady correspondence with allies around the country, gathering intelligence, coordinating campaigns, and offering advice on such crucial matters as the precise timing of the state conventions. To explain the Constitution to his countrymen, Madison contributed to a series of 85 essays that ran under the pseudonym "Publius," which he shared with Alexander Hamilton and John Jay, in several New York City newspapers. Published in book form as *The Federalist* (1788), they were hailed by Thomas Jefferson as "the best commentary on the principles of government which ever was written."

The Antifederalists, on the other hand, were in disarray. They advanced no positive alternatives. They disagreed even among themselves about the vices and virtues of the new Constitution. At first, they fell back on obstructionism. In September, Antifederalist legislators boycotted the Pennsylvania Assembly, denying it the quorum needed to authorize a convention. The tactic worked until a Federalist mob descended on the homes of two Antifederalist legislators and hustled them off to the State House. A quorum thus secured, the Assembly voted to call a convention.

Nationwide, early returns were favorable to the Federalists. Delaware moved swiftly, becoming the first state to ratify, on December 7, 1787. Pennsylvania quickly followed, joined soon thereafter by New Jersey, Georgia, and Connecticut. By January 1788, five of the nine needed states had ratified.

The contest was closer in Massachusetts. However, on February 5, after the Federalists agreed to support a measure calling upon Congress to consider nine amendments (later partially incorporated into the Bill of Rights) limiting the new government's powers, the Constitution was approved by a vote of 187 to 168.

Meanwhile, the Antifederalists, led by Virginia's Patrick Henry and Governor George Clinton of New York, among others, had begun their counterattack. In newspapers around the country, they warned that a "consolidated" national government would impose onerous taxes and wipe out the liberties won by the Revolution.

Nevertheless, in April 1788, Maryland joined the fold, followed late in May by South Carolina. Only one more state was needed to ratify. The Rhode Islanders, who chose to hold a statewide referendum on the Constitution, rejected it by a vote of 2,708 to 237.

Attention turned to Virginia, the largest and wealthiest state. "That overwhelming torrent, Patrick Henry," as General Henry Knox called him, was the leading orator of his day, and in Richmond he summoned all of his powers. For three weeks, day after day, he flung invective at the Constitution and its "chains of consolidation." The authority conferred upon the president, Henry declared, "squints towards monarchy." Madison's checks and balances he dismissed as "your specious, imaginary balances, your rope-dancing, chain-rattling, ridiculous ideal checks and contrivances."

It took all of Madison's cool reason and tactical acumen, reinforced by the support of such prominent Virginians as Governor Edmund Randolph and John Marshall, to prevail. On June 27, 1789, Virginia ratified, 89 to 79. Again, the delegates petitioned Congress for amendments.

Unbeknownst to the Virginians, the ninth state, New Hampshire, had approved the Constitution four days earlier. Success in Virginia, however, was a special cause for celebration. John Quincy Adams noted in his diary that when Boston heard the news from Richmond, enthusiastic Federalists took to the streets, firing muskets into the air for hours on end.

16. Making It Work

EXPORTING THE CONSTITUTION

"The most wonderful work ever struck off at a given time by the brain and purpose of man." That was British prime minister William Gladstone's generous assessment of the U.S. Constitution in 1878.

Around the world, many political leaders before and after Gladstone shared his admiration, borrowing liberally from America's founding document for their own constitutions. The U.S. prototype may be, as Rutgers's Albert Blaustein says, "the nation's most important export."

Ironically, Britain is one of only six nations in the world today that have not followed the U.S. example of adopting a "written" constitution. Like Britain, New Zealand and Israel are committed to unwritten constitutions that can be altered by simple acts of parliament; Saudi Arabia, Oman, and Libya claim the Koran as their supreme law.

Historically, writing constitutions has proved far easier than preserving them. In 1791, Polish politicians authored the world's second written national constitution, echoing the Americans in their claim that "all authority in human society takes its beginning in the will of the people." But Russia's Catherine the Great saw the Polish experiment as a threat; a Russian invasion killed the plan before it could be implemented.

•

Constitutionalism fared little better in France. During the summer of 1791, reformers including the Marquis de Lafayette, George Washington's old comrade-in-arms, drafted a charter providing for a limited monarchy under King Louis XVI. Owing to the immense popularity of Benjamin Franklin, U.S. envoy to Paris during 1776–85, the French borrowed much more from the constitution of Pennsylvania (e.g., a unicameral legislature) than from the work of the Framers. But the 1791 plan lasted only a year before it was swept away in the nation's continuing revolutionary turmoil. Subsequent charters did not survive much longer; the French drew up more than a dozen before writing their most recent one for General Charles de Gaulle in 1958. To the French, historian C. F. Strong wrote some years ago, a constitution is "a work of art . . . the order and symmetry must be perfect."

The U.S. example had a more direct impact in Latin America. The early constitutions of Venezuela (1811), Mexico (1824), and Argentina (1853) leaned heavily on the U.S. model. Results were mixed. The Mexicans, unfamiliar with self-government, failed at their first try at a federal system. Their unhappy experience led Tocqueville to compare the U.S. Constitution to "those exquisite productions of human industry which ensure wealth and renown to their inventors, but which are profitless in any other hands."

More successful was Brazil's homegrown constitution of 1824. It combined a monarchy with limited popular rule, surviving until 1889.

•

Ever since Thomas Jefferson and Thomas Paine advised the French in 1791, American consultants have spread the gospel abroad. By and large, they have recognized that American-style institutions often do not work in other lands. For example, when lawyers on the staff of General Douglas MacArthur drafted (in only one week) a new plan of government for occupied Japan in 1946, they outlined a *parliamentary* democracy.

The world's longest (300 pages) and possibly most complicated constitution is the product of its largest democracy. India's 1949 constitution, prepared with the help of U.S. advisers, includes not only fundamental rights, which correspond almost exactly to the provisions of the U.S. Bill of Rights (revised to reflect U.S. Supreme Court interpretations), but also several "positive" rights. Long-oppressed castes, for example, are guaranteed fixed percentages of the parliamentary seats in New Delhi.

India's is one of only 29 national constitutions (out of 162) that are more than 26 years old. But neither the longevity of a charter nor the mere fact of its existence is always cause for celebration. Argentina's 1853 constitution, for example, has simply been ignored during some harsher periods of the nation's history. And many constitutions, notably those in the Soviet bloc and some in the Third World, make no provision for democratic government, or proclaim rights, such as free speech, that citizens have no real prospect of exercising.

Still, 200 years after the Framing, the democratic constitutions of Nigeria (1979), El Salvador (1983), and the Philippines (1987)—all prepared with U.S. help—testify to the continuing appeal of the American experiment.

Accepting the New Order

On July 4, towns and cities around the country celebrated the ratification with elaborate "federal processions." Philadelphia's was the grandest of all. A mile and a half long, it was crowned by the "Grand Foederal Edifice," an imposing structure supported by 13 Corinthian columns, three left unfinished, borne through the streets on a carriage pulled by 10 white horses.

Still, without New York, the Union would suffer a fatal geographic split. And the Antifederalists there enjoyed a two to one edge in the state convention, held in Poughkeepsie. On July 26, the Constitution was put to a vote. It squeaked by, 30 to 27. The prospect of later amendments and the last-minute support of Governor Clinton, who feared secession by New York City and the southern counties if his state failed to ratify, provided the margin of victory.

North Carolina and Rhode Island, the last holdouts, finally ratified in 1789 and 1790.

Almost everywhere, acceptance of the Constitution was attended by a spirit of reconciliation. At a raucous meeting of "Henryites" in Richmond, the great orator told his followers that he had done his best to defeat the document "in the proper place." He added: "As true and faithful republicans you had all better go home." Some Antifederalists would remain bitter foes of the new order, but they kept their dissent within bounds—an important political success for the young Republic.

When the first Congress under the new Constitution met in New York City in March 1789, Representative James Madison redeemed the Federalists' pledge, drawing up nine amendments based on proposals by the states and on existing provisions of various state constitutions. Ultimately, Congress submitted 12 amendments to the states. Ten were ratified by December 1791; two were rejected.*

Midnight Appointments

The Constitution created a distinctively American array of legal and political arrangements to combat what Madison called (in his famous Federalist No. 10) the "mischief of factions." The formulas that the Framers designed—federalism, the separation of powers, and checks and balances—work to ensure that no social class or interest group can entirely control the government. Each of these devices plays a part in dispersing or containing power while permitting effective government; for almost two centuries, the system has proved to be, as Madison predicted, "a Republican remedy for the diseases most incident to Republican Government."

The Framers also recognized the need for what Madison called "useful alterations [to the Constitution] suggested by experience."

One vehicle for such change is the formal amendment. Article V provides that amendments may be proposed by a two-thirds vote of both houses of Congress or, upon application by two-thirds of the states, by a national convention.† To take effect, an amendment must be agreed to by three-fourths of the states. This arrangement, Madison argued, "guards equally against that extreme facility, which would render the Constitution too mutable; and that extreme difficulty, which might perpetuate its discovered faults."

Since the first Congress, more than 5,000 bills proposing constitutional amendments have been introduced, providing for everything from public ownership of the telegraph system to the restoration of prayer in the public schools. Only 33 proposed amendments have won enough votes in Congress to be sent to the states for their approval, and only 26 of these have been ratified.*

While few in number, the 26 amendments have dramatically transformed the constitutional landscape. The Bill of Rights has not

---

†Congress is required to call a constitutional convention if two-thirds (34) of the states request it. Between 1975 and 1983, 32 states petitioned Congress for a convention to consider a balanced-budget amendment. It is uncertain, however, whether such a convention's agenda could be restricted to only one amendment.

*Of the seven rejected amendments, two—described earlier—were proposed as part of the Bill of Rights. The other amendments would have stripped Americans who accepted foreign titles of nobility of their citizenship (1811); banned future amendments empowering Congress to interfere with "states' rights" (1861); authorized Congress to regulate child labor (1924); guaranteed absolute legal equality for women (1972); and granted the District of Columbia elected representation in Congress (1978).

---

*One of the failed amendments would have increased the membership of the House of Representatives. The other would have required the approval of two successive Congresses before the legislators could increase their own pay.

only worked to limit federal power, but, through judicial interpretation, has come (with limited exceptions) to apply to the states as well. Following the Civil War, the Reconstruction Amendments—the Thirteenth, Fourteenth, and Fifteenth—were added to protect the newly freed slaves. No constitutional amendment has been the vehicle for more judicial interpretation than has the Fourteenth, with its guarantees of "due process of law" and "equal protection of the laws."

The courts have taken on a central role in interpreting and enforcing the Constitution. Indeed, in many ways, the history of the Constitution since 1789 is that of the Supreme Court. In creating the federal courts, the Framers did not explicitly confer upon them the power of judicial review—the authority to declare a law unconstitutional. Article VI of the Constitution, however, states that the Constitution and laws "which shall be made in Pursuance thereof" shall be the "supreme Law of the Land."

In 1803, in *Marbury* v. *Madison*, the Supreme Court, under Chief Justice John Marshall, used the logic of Article VI formally to lay claim to the power of judicial review.

The case arose under unusual conditions. After Jefferson's Democratic-Republican Party swept to victory in the election of 1800, despairing Federalists looked to the judiciary as the country's last bastion against "mob" rule. In a series of midnight appointments just before leaving office, President John Adams named several new judges to the federal bench. But one of them, William Marbury, was never presented with his commission, and Jefferson's secretary of state, James Madison, refused to deliver it.

The immediate issue in *Marbury*—whether the writ that William Marbury sought could properly issue from the Supreme Court—was a narrow one. But Marshall seized the opportunity to criticize Jefferson's administration for actions "not warranted by law." Then, he wheeled around and ruled that the act of Congress under which Marbury was seeking a writ was unconstitutional. "It is," Marshall declared, "emphatically the province and duty of the judicial department to say what the law is."

'A Drag upon Democracy'

Marshall's deft handling of the case disarmed his critics. He asserted the Court's right to judicial review, but voided the congressional statute on the grounds that it had granted the Court *too much* power, thus averting a confrontation with Jefferson that the Court would have been sure to lose.

But, after *Marbury*, the Court often found that exercising its powers aroused wrathful opposition. In 1821, in *Cohens* v. *Virginia*, Marshall rejected the state of Virginia's claim that the Supreme Court lacked the authority to review the Cohens brothers' conviction, under Virginia state law, for illegally selling lottery tickets. In a twist reminiscent of *Marbury*, Marshall then upheld the Virginia conviction, sending the Cohenses to jail. This did not quiet Marshall's critics. Judge Spencer Roane of Virginia denounced *Cohens* as "a most monstrous and unexampled decision," which could only be explained by "that love of power which all history informs us infects and corrupts all who possess it, and from which even the upright and ermined judges are not exempt."

Although it is most often attacked for arrogating power to itself, the Supreme Court has also greatly expanded the authority of the other branches of the national government, especially that of Congress. In Article I of the Constitution, the Framers enumerated 17 legislative powers, from levying taxes to establishing post offices. To that list they added the seemingly innocuous authorization for Congress to make such laws as were "necessary and proper" for executing the stated powers.

Thomas Jefferson compared the potential mischief of this clause to children playing at "This is the House that Jack Built." "Under such a process of filiation of necessities," he wrote, "the sweeping clause makes clean work." As the subsequent expansion of government interests and activities indicates, his fears were not groundless. In *McCulloch* v. *Maryland* (1819), Chief Justice Marshall rejected a challenge by the state of Maryland to Congress's authority to create a Bank of the United States. The "necessary and proper" clause, he wrote for the unanimous Court, does not limit Congress to "absolutely indispensable" legislation. "We must never forget," he wrote with a flourish, "that it is a *constitution* we are expounding."

During the first 70 years after *Marbury*, the Supreme Court

One of many early controversies: Do states have the right to nullify parts of the Constitution? This 1833 cartoon attacks South Carolina's John C. Calhoun for his advocacy of the nullification doctrine.

availed itself of judicial review on relatively few occasions, overturning, for example, only 10 acts of Congress. By the late 19th century, however, during the heyday of laissez-faire capitalism in America, conservative lawyers and judges were regularly using the commerce clause and the due process clause of the Fourteenth Amendment to defeat the work of reformist federal and state legislators.*

In *Lochner* v. *New York* (1905), for example, the Court struck down a protective state labor law that forbade bakers to work more than 60 hours per week, declaring it an abridgment of what it called the "liberty of contract." Justice Rufus W. Peckham, for the majority, dismissed New York's statute as "mere meddlesome interference with the rights of the individual" to work whatever hours he chooses.

In one of the most famous dissents in the Court's history, an exasperated Justice Oliver Wendell Holmes, alluding to the leading conservative thinker of the day, reminded his brethren that the Fourteenth Amendment "does not enact Mr. Herbert Spencer's *Social Statics*." Outside the Court, frustrated liberals assailed the Court's "judicial activism." In 1922, Senator Robert LaFollette, the Wisconsin Progressive, argued that the Court had secured the power of judicial review by "usurpation"; as late as 1943, historian Henry Steele Commager called judicial review "a drag upon democracy."

New Protections

The inevitable showdown came in 1937, the sesquicentennial year of the Constitution's drafting. Chief Justice Charles Evans Hughes and his colleagues had invalidated several major elements of President Franklin D. Roosevelt's New Deal, including the National Industrial Recovery Act. In February, Roosevelt presented Congress with his famous "Court-packing" plan, asking, in the name of helping the Court to clear its crowded docket, for the authority to appoint an additional justice for each member of the Court over 70 years of age.** To FDR's surprise, even many of his allies in Congress opposed the measure. "Too clever—too damned clever," said one pro–New Deal newspaper. Roosevelt never got his wish.

In the meantime, however, the Supreme Court appeared to experience a sea change in attitude—what one wag called "the switch in time that saved nine." On April 12, 1937, the Court upheld, against a commerce clause challenge, the National Labor Relations Act. It signaled the beginning of a new era.

---

*The commerce clause (Article I, Section 8) grants Congress the power to "regulate Commerce with foreign Nations, and among the several States, and with the Indian Tribes." The due process clause of the Fourteenth Amendment states: "nor shall any State deprive any person of life, liberty, or property, without due process of law."

**The Constitution does not fix the size of the Supreme Court. In 1789, Congress established a six-member Court, and it subsequently moved the number up and down six times before finally arriving, in 1869, at nine, the present composition. FDR's plan would have added six justices to the Court.

During the half-century since those New Deal cases, the Court has left state and federal legislators free to experiment very much as they chose with solutions to economic problems. Justice Hugo L. Black's opinion in *Ferguson* v. *Skrupa* (1963) sums up the modern Court's attitude: "We refuse to sit as a super-legislature to weigh the wisdom of legislation. Whether the legislature takes for its textbook Adam Smith, Herbert Spencer, or Lord Keynes or some other is no concern of ours."

Although the Court has abandoned "judicial activism" in the economic sphere, it has made vigorous use of the Constitution to police governmental acts in other areas. In a sense, it has turned its attention from "property rights" to "human rights."

The first hint of this new approach came in 1938. In a famous footnote in *United States* v. *Carolene Products*, Justice Harlan F. Stone suggested that there might be "more exacting judicial scrutiny" of legislation that restricted the political process or that reflected prejudice against "discrete and insular minorities."

The paradigm of judicial intervention to protect a racial minority is the Court's 1954 decision in *Brown* v. *Board of Education*. The Court held that "separate but equal" public schools for blacks and whites violated the Fourteenth Amendment's equal protection clause. *Brown* encouraged the emerging civil rights movement, as blacks sought equal treatment beyond the schoolroom. The Court consistently supported them. In 1955–56, Martin Luther King, Jr., emerged as a national leader when he led a boycott of the segregated city bus system in Montgomery, Alabama. In November 1956, the Court ruled that segregation of public transportation was unconstitutional. Congress's major civil rights initiatives—the Civil Rights Act of 1964 and the Voting Rights Act of 1965—were a decade away.

The example of *Brown* was not lost on other groups. By the late 1960s, feminists, the handicapped, prisoners, environmentalists, and other groups that had failed to achieve all of their goals through the political process began to take their grievances to the federal courts. The women's movement, for example, pursued its agenda on several fronts: constitutional amendment (the Equal Rights Amendment), legislation ("equal pay for equal work"), and litigation.

The Fourteenth Amendment was designed to protect the interests of the slaves freed by the Civil War. But it does not speak in terms of race. No state, it says, shall "deny to any person within its jurisdiction the equal protection of the laws." Thus, beginning in the early 1970s, the Supreme Court used the equal protection clause to strike down both state and federal measures found to discriminate against women. In 1971, it overturned an Idaho law that gave preference to men in naming administrators of estates; in 1973, it ruled unconstitutional a federal statute that automatically provided married men in the U.S. armed forces with allowances for dependents but required service*women* to prove that their families were dependent.

Searching for Meaning

In 1973, Justice William J. Brennan, Jr., argued that gender discrimination ought to be tested by the same standard of "strict scrutiny" that the Court applied in race cases. A majority of the justices would not go that far, choosing instead an "intermediate" level of scrutiny.

These decisions were handed down by a Supreme Court presided over by Chief Justice Warren Burger, one of four justices appointed by President Richard M. Nixon to halt the Court's much-criticized "activism." But the Burger Court proved to be as willing as its famous predecessor, the Warren Court (1953–69), to find creative uses for the Constitution. To be sure, the Court during the Burger years did modify some of the Warren Court's more liberal judgments, notably those broadly construing the Fourth Amendment's ban on unreasonable searches and seizures. But the Burger Court rediscovered, and found new uses for, the Fourteenth Amendment's due process clause.

Indeed, the Burger Court's far-reaching decision in *Roe* v. *Wade* (1973) sparked more public outrage than any other Supreme Court ruling in recent memory. Dissenting justices Byron R. White and William H. Rehnquist (now chief justice) branded *Roe* an "extravagant exercise" of "raw judicial power." In *Roe*, the Court said that the due process clause implies a constitutional "right to privacy" that protects a woman's right to have an abortion during the first two trimesters of pregnancy without interference by the state. In other decisions, the Court has taken steps that enlarge the "right to privacy," striking down state laws that restrict access to contraceptives, or that overregulate marriage and divorce.

These decisions, too, sparked controversy. In a dissent against another "privacy" case in 1965, Justice Black wrote that the Court's talk of a "right to privacy" reminded him of the "natural law–due process" philosophy that the Court had used 60 years earlier in *Lochner*. Black's statement underscored the perpetual dilemma of the Supreme Court. Must it judge solely on the basis of what is written in the Constitution and what is recorded of the original debates over it and its amendments? Or can it refer to overarching natural law, enforcing "principles of liberty and justice," as Stanford's Thomas Grey writes, even when they are "not to be found within the four corners of our founding document"?

The Court has often split the difference. It grounds some of its decisions, such as those interpreting the First Amendment's establishment of religion clause, in the thinking of the Framers. Other judgments seem to reflect contemporary attitudes. Thus, the modern Court has extended the First Amendment's protection of free speech to "symbolic" speech (e.g., burning draft cards) and to commercial speech (advertising).

It is hard to know what the Framers would have made of all this. When the delegates met at Philadelphia in 1787, they knew that they were embarking upon a great experiment. Obviously, they did not intend the Constitution to be infinitely elastic; the rule of law could not survive such malleability. The barriers they erected against facile amendments testify to that. But they also knew, as Chief Justice Marshall later put it, that the Constitution was "intended to endure for ages to come, and, consequently, to be adapted to the various crises of human nature." And so it has been.

The Extension and Domination of the West

In the fifteenth century the Portuguese and the Spanish began to reach out with their great explorations. Under the Spanish flag, Columbus discovered America, and the nations of Europe shortly joined the great adventure of exploration motivated by God, gold, glory, and greed. The initial leaders, however, gave way to other nations. Between 1600 and 1815 Great Britain, France, Austria, Prussia, and Russia became the great powers which would dominate the West and much of the world until World War I. Gordon A. Craig and Alexander L. George describe this transition and stress diplomacy, warfare, bureaucracy, and dedication as the keys to supremacy.

The conquest of the world by the West, however, was not a sudden nor a quickly successful venture. Exceptions might be the quick collapse of the Aztec and Inca Empires after a flash of the Spanish sword, but elsewhere it was not so easy. In Africa there was the barrier of waterfalls in the rivers and malarial mosquitos. Penetration beyond the coastline had to await the invention of steamboats and the discovery of quinine as a prophylactic for malaria in the nineteenth century. The development of superior firearms also aided the Europeans when the conquest of Africa finally arrived. Even then it was not easy since some of the native groups resisted.

One of the most famous campaigns of imperialism was the Anglo-Zulu War in 1879 in South Africa. The Zulus fought with shields and spears, the British with rifles and cannons. There is no doubt of the Zulu courage, but modern firearms prevailed and Redcoats subdued the Zulu nation. Considering the current troubles in South Africa, the eventual loss of the empire, and the survival of the Zulus, Frank Emery raises a question about the pointless nature of imperialism.

The article by Deborah Birkett on Mary Kingsley, an English trader and anthropologist who traveled through West Africa in the 1890s, reveals not only how Western culture was taken to Africa, but also how the native culture affected Westerners. Kinglsey developed a great sympathy and respect for African life and fought for a change in imperial policy. She also is an example of an intrepid woman venturing forth where others feared to go.

In the subcontinent of India, initial attempts by British traders at conquest in the 1680s ended in failure. Bruce Lenman describes this defeat. The Mogul Empire was too strong and conquest had to wait until 1757 when internal affairs made India vulnerable. The subcontinent had possessed one of the early riverine civilizations, and since the days of Alexander had been partially ruled by a series of empires and invaders. When the British took over, their influence on Indian life penetrated into the village, something others had not accomplished.

The Chinese developed a unique and self-contained society over four millennia. Their first contact with the West came when Portuguese merchants appeared on the southeast coast in 1514. After this came the British and the Dutch by sea, and the Russians by land. The Chinese resisted the penetration, but lost their autonomy in the nineteenth century in three disastrous wars. The Japanese likewise resisted foreign influence and remained as a closed society for two-hundred years until forced by the threat of warships to open their ports to the United States in the middle of the nineteenth century. The isolation of Japan is described by C.R. Boxer. Interestingly, unlike the Chinese, the Japanese used Western technology to become strong enough to resist Western civilization and maintain their own culture and independence.

By the end of the nineteenth century, the West was predominant and Paris was the center of civilization. The article about Sarah Bernhardt describes life in this global capital. But it did not last; the West lost its hegemony in the twentieth century. As historian William H. McNeill has suggested, the rise of the West and its subsequent decline

Unit 3

can be interpreted as another in a series of empires which have come and gone in world history.

Looking Ahead: Challenge Questions
What are the essential elements characteristic of the great powers after 1815?

What makes a great power "great?"
How did the British defeat the Zulus?
How do Mary Kinglsey and Sarah Bernhardt compare as feminists?
Was there anything beneficial that Europeans gave to other peoples during their time of imperialism?

The Emergence of the Great Powers

I

Although the term *great power* was used in a treaty for the first time only in 1815, it had been part of the general political vocabulary since the middle of the eighteenth century and was generally understood to mean Great Britain, France, Austria, Prussia, and Russia. This would not have been true in the year 1600, when the term itself would have meant nothing and a ranking of the European states in terms of political weight and influence would not have included three of the countries just mentioned. In 1600, Russia, for instance, was a remote and ineffectual land, separated from Europe by the large territory that was called Poland-Lithuania with whose rulers it waged periodic territorial conflicts, as it did with the Ottoman Turks to the south; Prussia did not exist in its later sense but, as the Electorate of Brandenburg, lived a purely German existence, like Bavaria or Württemberg, with no European significance; and Great Britain, a country of some commercial importance, was not accorded primary political significance, although it had, in 1588, demonstrated its will and its capacity for self-defense in repelling the Spanish Armada. In 1600, it is fair to say that, politically, the strongest center in Europe was the old Holy Roman Empire, with its capital in Vienna and its alliances with Spain (one of the most formidable military powers in Europe) and the Catholic states of southern Germany—an empire inspired by a militant Catholicism that dreamed of restoring Charles V's claims of universal dominion. In comparison with Austria and Spain, France seemed destined to play a minor role in European politics, because of the state of internal anarchy and religious strife that followed the murder of Henri IV in 1610.

Why did this situation not persist? Or, to put it another way, why was the European system transformed so radically that the empire became an insignificant political force and the continent came in the eighteenth century to be dominated by Great Britain, France, Austria, Prussia, and Russia? The answer, of course, is war, or, rather more precisely, wars—a long series of religious and dynastic conflicts which raged intermittently from 1618 until 1721 and changed the rank order of European states by exhausting some and exalting others. As if bent upon supplying materials for the nineteenth-century Darwinians, the states mentioned above proved themselves in the grinding struggle of the seventeenth century to be the fittest, the ones best organized to meet the demands of protracted international competition.

The process of transformation began with the Thirty Years War, which stretched from 1618 to 1648. It is sometimes called the last of the religious wars, a description that is justified by the fact that it was motivated originally by the desire of the House of Habsburg and its Jesuit advisers to restore the Protestant parts of the empire to the true faith and because, in thirty years of fighting, the religious motive gave way to political considerations and, in the spreading of the conflict from its German center to embrace all of Europe, some governments, notably France, waged war against their own coreligionists for material reasons. For the states that initiated this wasting conflict, which before it was over had reduced the population of central Europe by at least a third, the war was an unmitigated disaster. The House of Habsburg was so debilitated by it that it lost the control it had formerly possessed over the German states, which meant that they became sovereign in their own right and that the empire now became a mere adjunct of the Austrian crown lands. Austria was, moreover, so weakened by the exertions and losses of that war that in the period after 1648 it had the greatest difficulty in protecting its

17. The Emergence of the Great Powers

eastern possessions from the depredations of the Turks and in 1683 was threatened with capture of Vienna by a Turkish army. Until this threat was contained, Austria ceased to be a potent factor in European affairs. At the same time, its strongest ally, Spain, had thrown away an infantry once judged to be the best in Europe in battles like that at Nördlingen in 1634, one of those victories that bleed a nation white. Spain's decline began not with the failure of the Armada, but with the terrible losses suffered in Germany and the Netherlands during the Thirty Years War.

In contrast, the states that profited from the war were the Netherlands, which completed the winning of its independence from Spain in the course of the war and became a commercial and financial center of major importance; the kingdom of Sweden, which under the leadership of Gustavus Adolphus, the Lion of the North, plunged into the conflict in 1630 and emerged as the strongest power in the Baltic region; and France, which entered the war formally in 1635 and came out of it as the most powerful state in western Europe.

It is perhaps no accident that these particular states were so successful, for they were excellent examples of the process that historians have described as the emergence of the modern state, the three principal characteristics of which were effective armed forces, an able bureaucracy, and a theory of state that restrained dynastic exuberance and defined political interest in practical terms. The seventeenth century saw the emergence of what came to be called *raison d'état* or *ragione di stato*—the idea that the state was more than its ruler and more than the expression of his wishes; that it transcended crown and land, prince and people; that it had its particular set of interests and a particular set of necessities based upon them; and that the art of government lay in recognizing those interests and necessities and acting in accordance with them, even if this might violate ordinary religious or ethical standards. The effective state must have the kind of servants who would interpret *raison d'état* wisely and the kind of material and physical resources necessary to implement it. In the first part of the seventeenth century, the Dutch, under leaders like Maurice of Nassau and Jan de Witt, the Swedes, under Gustavus Adolphus and Oxenstierna, and the French, under the inspired ministry of Richelieu, developed the administration and the forces and theoretical skills that exemplify this ideal of modern statehood. That they survived the rigors of the Thirty Years War was not an accident, but rather the result of the fact that they never lost sight of their objectives and never sought objectives that were in excess of their capabilities. Gustavus Adolphus doubtless brought his country into the Thirty Years War to save the cause of Protestantism when it was at a low ebb, but he never for a moment forgot the imperatives of national interest that impelled him to see the war also as a means of winning Swedish supremacy along the shore of the Baltic Sea. Cardinal Richelieu has been called the greatest public servant France ever had, but that title, as Sir George Clark has drily remarked, "was not achieved without many acts little fitting the character of a churchman." It was his clear recognition of France's needs and his absolute unconditionality in pursuing them that made him the most respected statesman of his age.

The Thirty Years War, then, brought a sensible change in the balance of forces in Europe, gravely weakening Austria, starting the irreversible decline of Spain, and bringing to the fore the most modern, best organized, and, if you will, most rationally motivated states: the Netherlands, Sweden, and France. This, however, was a somewhat misleading result, and the Netherlands was soon to yield its commercial and naval primacy to Great Britain (which had been paralyzed by civil conflict during the Thirty Years War), while Sweden, under a less rational ruler, was to throw its great gains away.

The gains made by France were more substantial, so much so that in the second half of the century, in the heyday of Louis XIV, they became oppressive. For that ruler was intoxicated by the power that Richelieu and his successor Mazarin had brought to France, and he wished to enhance it. As he wrote in his memoirs:

> The love of glory assuredly takes precedence over all other [passions] in my soul.... The hot blood of my youth and the violent desire I had to heighten my reputation instilled in me a strong passion for action.... *La Gloire,* when all is said and done, is not a mistress that one can ever neglect; nor can one be ever worthy of her slightest favors if one does not constantly long for fresh ones.

No one can say that Louis XIV was a man of small ambition. He dreamed in universal terms and sought to realize those dreams by a combination of diplomatic and military means. He maintained alliances with the Swedes in the north and the Turks in the south and thus prevented Russian interference while he placed his own candidate, Jan Sobieski, on the throne of Poland. His Turkish connection he used also to harry the eastern frontiers of Austria, and if he did not incite Kara Mustafa's expedition against Vienna in 1683, he knew of it. Austria's distractions enabled him to dabble freely in German politics. Bavaria and the Palatinate were bound to the French court by marriage, and almost all of the other German princes accepted subsidies at one time or another from France. It did not seem unlikely on one occasion that Louis would put himself or his son forward as candidate for Holy Roman emperor. The same method of infiltration was practiced in Italy, Portugal, and Spain, where the young king married a French princess and French ambassadors exerted so much influence in internal affairs that they succeeded in discrediting the strongest antagonist to French influence, Don Juan of Austria, the victor over the Turks at the battle of Lepanto. In addition to all of this, Louis sought

3. THE EXTENSION AND DOMINATION OF THE WEST

to undermine the independence of the Netherlands and gave the English king Charles II a pension in order to reduce the possibility of British interference as he did so.

French influence was so great in Europe in the second half of the seventeenth century that it threatened the independent development of other nations. This was particularly true, the German historian Leopold von Ranke was to write in the nineteenth century, because it

> was supported by a preeminence in literature. Italian literature had already run its course, English literature had not yet risen to general significance, and German literature did not exist at that time. French literature, light, brilliant and animated, in strictly regulated but charming form, intelligible to everyone and yet of individual, national character was beginning to dominate Europe.... [It] completely corresponded to the state and helped the latter to attain its supremacy, Paris was the capital of Europe. She wielded a dominion as did no other city, over language, over custom, and particularly over the world of fashion and the ruling classes. Here was the center of the community of Europe.

The effect upon the cultural independence of other parts of Europe—and one cannot separate cultural independence from political will—was devastating. In Germany, the dependence upon French example was almost abject, and the writer Moscherosch commented bitterly about "our little Germans who trot to the French and have no heart of their own, no speech of their own; but French opinion is their opinion, French speech, food, drink, morals and deportment their speech, food drink, morals and deportment whether they are good or bad."

But this kind of dominance was bound to invite resistance on the part of others, and out of that resistance combinations and alliances were bound to take place. And this indeed happened. In Ranke's words, "The concept of the European balance of power was developed in order that the union of many other states might resist the pretensions of the 'exorbitant' court, as it was called." This is a statement worth noting. The principle of the balance of power had been practiced in Machiavelli's time in the intermittent warfare between the city states of the Italian peninsula. Now it was being deliberately invoked as a principle of European statecraft, as a safeguard against universal domination. We shall have occasion to note the evolution and elaboration of this term in the eighteenth century and in the nineteenth, when it became one of the basic principles of the European system.

Opposition to France's universal pretensions centered first upon the Dutch, who were threatened most directly in a territorial sense by the French, and their gifted ruler, William III. But for their opposition to be successful, the Dutch needed strong allies, and they did not get them until the English had severed the connection that had existed between England and France under the later Stuarts and until Austria had modernized its administration and armed forces, contained the threat from the east, and regained the ability to play a role in the politics of central and western Europe. The Glorious Revolution of 1688 and the assumption of the English throne by the Dutch king moved England solidly into the anti-French camp. The repulse of the Turks at the gates of Vienna in 1683 marked the turning point in Austrian fortunes, and the brilliant campaigns of Eugene of Savoy in the subsequent period, which culminated in the smashing victory over the Turks at Zenta and the suppression of the Rakoczi revolt in Hungary, freed Austrian energies for collaboration in the containment of France. The last years of Louis XIV, therefore, were the years of the brilliant partnership of Henry Churchill, Duke of Marlborough, and Eugene of Savoy, a team that defeated a supposedly invulnerable French army at Blenheim in 1704, Ramillies in 1706, Oudenarde in 1708, and the bloody confrontation at Malplaquet in 1709.

These battles laid the basis for the Peace of Utrecht of 1713–1715, by which France was forced to recognize the results of the revolution in England, renounce the idea of a union of the French and Spanish thrones, surrender the Spanish Netherlands to Austria, raze the fortifications at Dunkirk, and hand important territories in America over to Great Britain. The broader significance of the settlement was that it restored an equilibrium of forces to western Europe and marked the return of Austria and the emergence of Britain as its supports. Indeed, the Peace of Utrecht was the first European treaty that specifically mentioned the balance of power. In the letters patent that accompanied Article VI of the treaty between Queen Anne and King Louis XIV, the French ruler noted that the Spanish renunciation of all rights to the throne of France was actuated by the hope of "obtaining a general Peace and securing the Tranquillity of *Europe* by a Ballance of Power," and the king of Spain acknowledged the importance of "the Maxim of securing for ever the universal Good and Quiet of Europe, by an equal Weight of Power, so that many being united in one, the Ballance of the Equality desired, might not turn to the Advantage of one, and the Danger and Hazard of the rest."

Meanwhile, in northern Europe, France's ally Sweden was forced to yield its primacy to the rising powers of Russia and Prussia. This was due in part to the drain on Swedish resources caused by its participation in France's wars against the Dutch; but essentially the decline was caused, in the first instance, by the fact that Sweden had too many rivals for the position of supremacy in the Baltic area and, in the second, by the lack of perspective and restraint that characterized the policy of Gustavus Adolphus's most gifted successor, Charles XII. Sweden's most formidable rivals were Denmark, Poland, which in 1699 acquired an ambitious and unscrupulous new king in the person of Augustus the Strong of Saxony, and Russia, ruled since 1683 by a young and vigorous

17. The Emergence of the Great Powers

leader who was to gain the name Peter the Great. In 1700, Peter and Augustus made a pact to attack and despoil Sweden and persuaded Frederick of Denmark to join them in this enterprise. The Danes and the Saxons immediately invaded Sweden and to their considerable dismay were routed and driven from the country by armies led by the eighteen-year-old ruler, Charles XII. The Danes capitulated at once, and Charles without pause threw his army across the Baltic, fell upon Russian forces that were advancing on Narva, and, although his own forces were outnumbered five to one, dispersed, captured, or killed an army of forty thousand Russians. But brilliant victories are often the foundation of greater defeats. Charles now resolved to punish Augustus and plunged into the morass of Polish politics. It was his undoing. While he strove to control an intractable situation, an undertaking that occupied him for seven years, Peter was carrying through the reforms that were to bring Russia from its oriental past into the modern world. When his army was reorganized, he began a systematic conquest of the Swedish Baltic possessions. Charles responded, not with an attempt to retake those areas, but with an invasion of Russia—and this, like other later invasions, was defeated by winter and famine and ultimately by a lost battle, that of Pultawa in 1709, which broke the power of Sweden and marked the emergence of Russia as its successor.

Sweden had another rival which was also gathering its forces in these years. This was Prussia. At the beginning of the seventeenth century, it had, as the Electorate of Brandenburg, been a mere collection of territories, mostly centered upon Berlin, but with bits and pieces on the Rhine and in East Prussia, and was rich neither in population nor resources. Its rulers, the Hohenzollerns, found it difficult to administer these lands or, in time of trouble, defend them; and during the Thirty Years War, Brandenburg was overrun with foreign armies and its population and substance depleted by famine and pestilence. Things did not begin to change until 1640, when Frederick William, the so-called Great Elector, assumed the throne. An uncompromising realist, he saw that if he was to have security in a dangerous world, he would have to create what he considered to be the sinews of independence: a centralized state with an efficient bureaucracy and a strong army. The last was the key to the whole. As he wrote in his political testament, "A ruler is treated with no consideration if he does not have troops of his own. It is these, thank God! that have made me *considerable* since the time I began to have them"—and in the course of his reign, after purging his force of unruly and incompetent elements, Frederick William rapidly built an efficient force of thirty thousand men, so efficient indeed that in 1675, during the Franco-Swedish war against the Dutch, it came to the aid of the Dutch by defeating the Swedes at Fehrbellin and subsequently driving them out of Pomerania. It was to administer this army that Frederick William laid the foundations of the soon famous Prussian bureaucracy; it was to support it that he encouraged the growth of a native textile industry; it was with its aid that he smashed the recalcitrant provincial diets and centralized the state. And finally it was this army that, by its participation after the Great Elector's death in the wars against Louis XIV and its steadiness under fire at Ramillies and Malplaquet, induced the European powers to recognize his successor Frederick I as king of Prussia.

Under Frederick, an extravagant and thoughtless man, the new kingdom threatened to outrun its resources. But the ruler who assumed the throne in 1715, Frederick William I, resumed the work begun by the Great Elector, restored Prussia's financial stability, and completed the centralization and modernization of the state apparatus by elaborating a body of law and statute that clarified rights and responsibilities for all subjects. He nationalized the officer corps of the army, improved its dress and weapons, wrote its first handbook of field regulations, prescribing manual exercises and tactical evolutions, and rapidly increased its size. When Frederick William took the throne after the lax rule of his predecessor, there were rumors of an impending coup by his neighbors, like that attempted against Sweden in 1700. That kind of talk soon died away as the king's work proceeded, and it is easy to see why. In the course of his reign, he increased the size of his military establishment to eighty-three thousand men, a figure that made Prussia's army the fourth largest in Europe, although the state ranked only tenth from the standpoint of territory and thirteenth in population.

Before the eighteenth century was far advanced, then, the threat of French universal dominance had been defeated, a balance of power existed in western Europe, and two new powers had emerged as partners of the older established ones. It was generally recognized that in terms of power and influence, the leading states in Europe were Britain, France, Austria, Russia, and probably Prussia. The doubts on the last score were soon to be removed; and these five powers were to be the ones that dominated European and world politics until 1914.

II

Something should be said at this point about diplomacy, for it was in the seventeenth and eighteenth centuries that it assumed its modern form. The use of envoys and emissaries to convey messages from one ruler to another probably goes back to the beginning of history; there are heralds in the *Iliad* and, in the second letter to the Church of Corinth, the Apostle Paul describes himself as an ambassador. But modern diplomacy as we know it had its origins in the Italian city states of the Renaissance period, and particularly in the republic of Venice and the states of Milan and Tuscany. In the fourteenth and fifteenth centuries, Venice was a great commercial power whose prosperity depended

3. THE EXTENSION AND DOMINATION OF THE WEST

upon shrewd calculation of risks, accurate reports upon conditions in foreign markets, and effective negotiation. Because it did so, Venice developed the first systemized diplomatic service known to history, a network of agents who pursued the interests of the republic with fidelity, with a realistic appraisal of risks, with freedom from sentimentality and illusion.

From Venice the new practice of systematic diplomacy was passed on to the states of central Italy which, because they were situated in a political arena that was characterized by incessant rivalry and coalition warfare, were always vulnerable to external threats and consequently put an even greater premium than the Venetians upon accurate information and skillful negotiation. The mainland cities soon considered diplomacy so useful that they began to establish permanent embassies abroad, a practice instituted by Milan and Mantua in the fifteenth century, while their political thinkers (like the Florentine Machiavelli) reflected upon the principles best calculated to make diplomacy effective and tried to codify rules of procedure and diplomatic immunity. This last development facilitated the transmission of the shared experience of the Italian cities to the rising nation states of the west that soon dwarfed Florence and Venice in magnitude and strength. Thus, when the great powers emerged in the seventeenth century, they already possessed a highly developed system of diplomacy based upon long experience. The employment of occasional missions to foreign courts had given way to the practice of maintaining permanent missions. While the ambassadors abroad represented their princes and communicated with them directly, their reports were studied in, and they received their instructions from, permanent, organized bureaus which were the first foreign offices. France led the way in this and was followed by most other states, and the establishment of a Foreign Ministry on the French model was one of Peter the Great's important reforms. The emergence of a single individual who was charged with the coordination of all foreign business and who represented his sovereign in the conduct of foreign affairs came a bit later, but by the beginning of the eighteenth century, the major powers all had such officials, who came to be known as foreign ministers or secretaries of state for foreign affairs.

From earliest times, an aura of intrigue, conspiracy, and disingenuousness surrounded the person of the diplomat, and we have all heard the famous quip of Sir Henry Wotton, ambassador of James I to the court of Venice, who said that an ambassador was "an honest man sent to lie abroad for the good of his country." Moralists were always worried by this unsavory reputation, which they feared was deserved, and they sought to reform it by exhortation. In the fifteenth century, Bernard du Rosier, provost and later archbishop of Toulouse, wrote a treatise in which he argued that the business of an ambassador is peace, that ambassadors must labor for the common good, and that they should never be sent to stir up wars or internal dissensions; and in the nineteenth century, Sir Robert Peel the younger was to define diplomacy in general as "the great engine used by civilized society for the purpose of maintaining peace."

The realists always opposed this ethical emphasis. In the fifteenth century, in one of the first treatises on ambassadorial functions, Ermalao Barbaro wrote: "The first duty of an ambassador is exactly the same as that of any other servant of government: that is, to do, say, advise and think whatever may best serve the preservation and aggrandizement of his own state."

Seventeenth-century theorists were inclined to Barbaro's view. This was certainly the position of Abram de Wicquefort, who coined the definition of the diplomat as "an honorable spy," and who, in his own career, demonstrated that he did not take the adjectival qualification very seriously. A subject of Holland by birth, Wicquefort at various times in his checkered career performed diplomatic services for the courts of Brandenburg, Lüneburg, and France as well as for his own country, and he had no scruples about serving as a double agent, a practice that eventually led to his imprisonment in a Dutch jail. It was here that he wrote his treatise *L'Ambassadeur et ses fonctions*, a work that was both an amusing commentary on the political morals of the baroque age and an incisive analysis of the art and practice of diplomacy.

Wicquefort was not abashed by the peccadilloes of his colleagues, which varied from financial peculation and sins of the flesh to crimes of violence. He took the line that in a corrupt age, one could not expect that embassies would be oases of virtue. Morality was, in any case, an irrelevant consideration in diplomacy; a country could afford to be served by bad men, but not by incompetent ones. Competence began with a clear understanding on the diplomat's part of the nature of his job and a willingness to accept the fact that it had nothing to do with personal gratification or self-aggrandizement. The ambassador's principal function, Wicquefort wrote, "consisted in maintaining effective communication between the two Princes, in delivering letters that his master writes to the Prince at whose court he resides, in soliciting answers to them, . . . in protecting his Master's subjects and conserving his interests." He must have the charm and cultivation that would enable him to ingratiate himself at the court to which he was accredited and the adroitness needed to ferret out information that would reveal threats to his master's interests or opportunities for advancing them. He must possess the ability to gauge the temperament and intelligence of those with whom he had to deal and to use this knowledge profitably in negotiation. "Ministers are but men and as such have their weaknesses, that is to say, their passions and interests, which the ambassador ought to know if he wishes to do honor to himself and his Master."

In pursuing this intelligence, the qualities he should

17. The Emergence of the Great Powers

cultivate most assiduously were *prudence* and *modération*. The former Wicquefort equated with caution and reflection, and also with the gifts of silence and indirection, the art of "making it appear that one is not interested in the things one desires the most." The diplomat who possessed prudence did not have to resort to mendacity or deceit or to *tromperies* or *artifices,* which were usually, in any case, counterproductive. *Modération* was the ability to curb one's temper and remain cool and phlegmatic in moments of tension. "Those spirits who are compounded of sulphur and saltpeter, whom the slightest spark can set afire, are easily capable of compromising affairs by their excitability, because it is so easy to put them in a rage or drive them to a fury, so that they don't know what they are doing." Diplomacy is a cold and rational business, in short, not to be practiced by the moralist, or the enthusiast, or the man with a low boiling point.

The same point was made in the most famous of the eighteenth-century essays on diplomacy, François de Callières's *On the Manner of Negotiating with Princes* (1716), in which persons interested in the career of diplomacy were advised to consider whether they were born with "the qualities necessary for success." These, the author wrote, included

> an observant mind, a spirit of application which refuses to be distracted by pleasures or frivolous amusements, a sound judgment which takes the measure of things, as they are, and which goes straight to its goal by the shortest and most neutral paths without wandering into useless refinements and subtleties which as a rule only succeed in repelling those with whom one is dealing.

Important also were the kind of penetration that is useful in discovering the thoughts of men, a fertility in expedients when difficulties arise, an equable humor and a patient temperament, and easy and agreeable manners. Above all, Callières observed, in a probably not unconscious echo of Wicquefort's insistence upon moderation, the diplomat must have

> sufficient control over himself to resist the longing to speak before he has really thought what he shall say. He should not endeavour to gain the reputation of being able to reply immediately and without premeditation to every proposition which is made, and he should take a special care not to fall into the error of one famous foreign ambassador of our time who so loved an argument that each time he warmed up in controversy he revealed important secrets in order to support his opinion.

In his treatment of the art of negotiation, Callières drew from a wealth of experience to which Wicquefort could not pretend, for he was one of Louis XIV's most gifted diplomats and ended his career as head of the French delegation during the negotiations at Ryswick in 1697. It is interesting, in light of the heavy reliance upon lawyers in contemporary United States diplomacy (one thinks of President Eisenhower's secretary of state and President Reagan's national security adviser) and of the modern practice of negotiating in large gatherings, that Callières had no confidence in either of these preferences. The legal mind, he felt, was at once too narrow, too intent upon hair-splitting, and too contentious to be useful in a field where success, in the last analysis, was best assured by agreements that provided mutuality of advantage. As for large conferences—"vast concourses of ambassadors and envoys"—his view was that they were generally too clumsy to achieve anything very useful. Most successful conferences were the result of careful preliminary work by small groups of negotiators who hammered out the essential bases of agreement and secured approval for them from their governments before handing them over, for formal purposes, to the *omnium-gatherums* that were later celebrated in the history books.

Perhaps the most distinctive feature of Callières's treatise was the passion with which he argued that a nation's foreign relations should be conducted by persons trained for the task.

> Diplomacy is a profession by itself which deserves the same preparation and assiduity of attention that men give to other recognized professions.... The diplomatic genius is born, not made. But there are many qualities which may be developed with practice, and the greatest part of the necessary knowledge can only be acquired, by constant application to the subject. In this sense, diplomacy is certainly a profession itself capable of occupying a man's whole career, and those who think to embark upon a diplomatic mission as a pleasant diversion from their common task only prepare disappointment for themselves and disaster for the cause which they serve.

These words represented not only a personal view but an acknowledgment of the requirements of the age. The states that emerged as recognizedly great powers in the course of the seventeenth and eighteenth centuries were the states that had modernized their governmental structure, mobilized their economic and other resources in a rational manner, built up effective and disciplined military establishments, and elaborated a professional civil service that administered state business in accordance with the principles of *raison d'état.* An indispensable part of that civil service was the Foreign Office and the diplomatic corps, which had the important task of formulating the foreign policy that protected and advanced the state's vital interests and of seeing that it was carried out.

BIBLIOGRAPHICAL ESSAY

For the general state of international relations before the eighteenth century, the following are useful: Marvin R. O'Connell, *The Counter-Reformation, 1559–1610* (New York, 1974); Carl J. Friedrich, *The Age of the Baroque, 1610–1660* (New York, 1952), a brilliant volume; C. V. Wedgwood, *The Thirty Years War* (London, 1938, and later

3. THE EXTENSION AND DOMINATION OF THE WEST

editions); Frederick L. Nussbaum, *The Triumph of Science and Reason, 1660–1685* (New York, 1953); and John B. Wolf, *The Emergence of the Great Powers, 1685–1715* (New York, 1951). On Austrian policy in the seventeenth century, see especially Max Braubach, *Prinz Eugen von Savoyen*, 5 vols. (Vienna, 1963–1965); on Prussian, Otto Hintze, *Die Hohenzollern und ihr Werk* (Berlin, 1915) and, brief but useful, Sidney B. Fay, *The Rise of Brandenburg-Prussia* (New York, 1937). A classical essay on great-power politics in the early modern period is Leopold von Ranke, *Die grossen Mächte*, which can be found in English translation in the appendix of Theodore von Laue, *Leopold Ranke: The Formative Years* (Princeton, 1950). The standard work on *raison d'état* is Friedrich Meinecke, *Die Idee der Staatsräson*, 3rd ed. (Munich, 1963), translated by Douglas Scott as *Machiavellianism* (New Haven, 1957).

On the origins and development of diplomacy, see D. P. Heatley, *Diplomacy and the Study of International Relations* (Oxford, 1919); Leon van der Essen, *La Diplomatie: Ses origines et son organisation* (Brussels, 1953); Ragnar Numelin, *Les origines de la diplomatie*, trans. from the Swedish by Jean-Louis Perret (Paris, 1943); and especially Heinrich Wildner, *Die Technik der Diplomatie: L'Art de négocier* (Vienna, 1959). Highly readable is Harold Nicolson, *Diplomacy*, 2nd ed. (London, 1950). An interesting comparative study is Adda B. Bozeman, *Politics and Culture in International History* (Princeton, 1960).

There is no modern edition of *L'ambassadeur et ses fonctions par Monsieur de Wicquefort* (Cologne, 1690); but Callières's classic of 1776 can be found: François de Callières, *On the Manner of Negotiating with Princes*, trans. A. F. Whyte (London, 1919, and later editions).

THE STRUGGLE FOR LAND

Frank Emery looks at the causes and consequences of the Anglo-Zulu War

Dr Frank Emery is lecturer in historical geography at University of Oxford

THE Anglo-Zulu War of 1879 is the best known of all the many wars of dispossesion fought in colonial Africa. It retains a clear-cut image because it was marked by dramatic military events that sank deep into public awareness at the time, and they have been remembered to a surprising degree. Three of them were, and still are, outstanding. Not long after the British forces invaded Zululand, one entire column was decimated by the Zulu warriors at Isandlwana. Upwards of 1000 imperial troops, mostly seasoned campaigners, were cut to pieces by what was then usually described as a savage, barbarous foe armed mainly with spear and shield. It had never happened before, and the mother country was shocked to the core. As one survivor said, with masterly understatement, 'there will be an awful row at home about this'.

Then on the same day, as if by right of natural justice, a handful of soldiers defending the base hospital and stores at Rorke's Drift mission station did heroic deeds by beating off 3000 Zulu who attacked it before dusk and through the night of January 22-23, 1879. 'Here they come', shouted the look-out as the *impi* came in sight, 'black as hell and thick as grass'. It is rightly remembered as an epic defensive action against all the odds, packed with tension as the Zulu repeatedly stormed the makeshift barricades. When eventually they drew off after suffering heavy casualties, there was precious little ammunition left with the exhausted troops, 11 of whom were awarded the Victoria Cross. Without this victory the shambles at Isandlwana would have been all the heavier to bear.

As the campaign dragged on under the feeble generalship of Lord Chelmsford, ultra-cautious of Zulu military strength after seeing his men lying dead and ritually disembowelled at Isandlwana, another dire episode filled the headlines. Attached to the British staff was the Prince Imperial of France, Louis Napoleon, a young officer who led a mounted patrol through hostile territory on June 1, 1879. Bold and impetuous, heir to the Bonapartist faction in French politics and carrying the sword of his great-uncle Napoleon, he was ambushed by the Zulu and speared to death. The dismay at this was felt internationally, and it did little good for morale before the Zulu army was eventually defeated in pitched battle at Ulundi on July 4. Superior rifle power, Gatling guns, artillery and cavalry proved too strong for them.

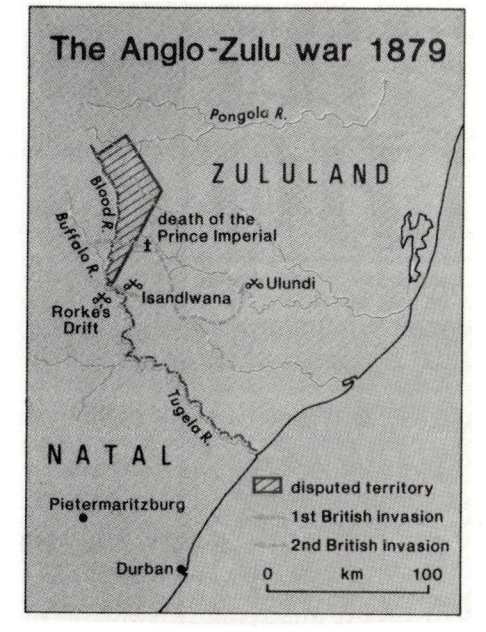

So much for the pattern of military events. The causes of the war are far more difficult to analyze, and historians' interpretations have shifted in emphasis over time. What is undisputed is that a key figure in the path to conflict was Sir Bartle Frere (1815-84), a Proconsul of Empire with a high reputation for his work in India before he went to South Africa in 1877 as Governor of the Cape Colony and High Commissioner. Frere was also a prominent geographer, serving as the President of the Royal Geographical Society in 1873, and publishing some excellent research on both Indian and African themes. In February 1874 he lectured publicly on Africa, with the confidence of a man who had recently negotiated the anti-slavery treaty at Zanzibar, and as a friend of David Livingstone. Frere argued the case for a more active exploitation of African resources. The external trade of the entire continent, he claimed, was less than that of a third rate European power, a paradox he explained as 'a defect of political cohesion'.

IN his view the best prospects for commercial initiative lay in the equatorial coastlands and again so far as Britain was concerned especially in the southern 'temperate' belt reaching to the Cape. Here powerful inducements to economic growth and European settlement lay in its mineral riches: diamonds, gold, and particularly to his way of thinking, the coalfields of Natal and Zambezia. These fields could supply fuel for steamships in the Indian Ocean and for future railways within the sub-continent. But in order to exploit these resources it was first necessary to create what Frere called 'a welding together of the loose elements of a great South African empire'. He advocated a policy of confederating the British colonies of the Cape and Natal with the Boer republics of the Transvaal and Orange Free State, incidentally expanding their territories as need be at the expense of African indigenous societies. Confederation was to be the mainspring of official British policy in South Africa after 1877, and it became a material reason for the destruction of the Zulu kingdom.

Traditionally the war was seen by historians as due to nothing more than the incompatibility of having such a 'primitive' and warlike people as the Zulu co-existing alongside civilized, peaceful states like Natal and the Transvaal. It is true that earlier in the 19th century under Shaka's leadership the Zulu were the most expan-

3. THE EXTENSION AND DOMINATION OF THE WEST

sionist and aggressive Black force in southern Africa. They ruthlessly established their own dominance over neighbouring groups, and created a system of relatively centralized control within the Zulu kingdom. Memories of all this influenced the attitudes of the White south, even though they were scarcely justified by the actions of Cetshwayo kaMpande, the king who was attacked by an imperial British army in 1879. Occupying the throne since 1872, he did little to threaten the status quo or to arouse fears along his borders. Psychologically, however, the recollection of savage conflict involving the Zulu strengthened the general view that war with them was inevitable at some stage, particularly when they began equipping themselves with firearms in the 1870s.

A liberal school of historians since the 1960s has developed a revisionist interpretation based on the specific circumstances that gave rise to the war. The only possible source of friction was an unresolved border dispute with the Transvaal over claims to a strip of land along the Blood River, coveted by both sides. The pastoralist Boers as much as the Zulu were dependent on their great herds of cattle as a mainstay of life, and this contested land was valued for its grazing potential during the dry winter season. Similar frontiers of settlement, in which Black territory was sought by intrusive Whites, were common enough in South Africa at this period. Early in 1878 the dispute was investigated by a boundary commission, and the Transvaal's case was found to rest on dubious evidence. Confirmation of Zulu rights over most of the debatable territory was therefore recommended, thus defusing their apparently hostile stance.

Here the spotlight has to be focused on Frere's decision not to use British power to restore these Zulu rights, but instead to embark on a course of action that brought them to war. It has long been known that Frere deliberately precipitated the Anglo-Zulu War in defiance of the British government's expressed desire to avoid military entanglement in South Africa at that moment. But why exactly did he decide to go it alone? Evidence shows that he exaggerated, for other motives, a sense of concern about the imminence of the Zulu 'menace'. His real aim was to press on with creating a great new British dominion in the form of confederation of the South African states and colonies. He saw it as a personal challenge that could bring him fame and fortune, and he was determined to do all in his power to bring it about.

It was a delicate and difficult task due to local and external complications. In 1877 Britain annexed the Transvaal, a major blunder because it suggested that a confederation strategy was to be forced through by high-handed acts of power politics. It also brought the border dispute with the Zulu fully within British responsibility, at a time when Disraeli's government was distracted from the ideal of confederation by a fresh crisis in Afghanistan. Before moving to Natal, in 1877-78 Frere willingly directed a war in the Transkei that effectively closed the frontier in the Eastern Cape by defeating the Xhosa. With that done, he even drew inspiration from British forward policies in Afghanistan to fuel his own designs on Zululand. It is no exaggeration to say that he tried to emulate the British invasion of Afghanistan in his own machinations against Cetshwayo and in preparation for war.

Frere refused to implement the report on the Transvaal-Zulu border dispute because, having found for the Zulu, it would place Britain in the role of patron of Black rights, not as benefactor of settler interests. White opinion would be alienated, and hopes for confederation dealt a serious blow. From July 1878, therefore, Frere suddenly began to paint a picture of Zulu aggressiveness, with Cetshwayo conspiring to unleash his army of 40,000 warriors, reviving the Zulu military machine as a potential danger to the whole region. Frere needed a war to break Zulu independence, because once the Zulu kingdom was defeated and demolished its territorial rights would cease to be an issue, and prospects for confederation enhanced.

WITHIN this new order, as the radical historians now argue, the way would also be opened for the advance of capitalist production in Southern Africa, an objective of which Frere and his associates were naturally well aware. Given such political and economic imperatives, it explains why Frere manipulated the long delays in telegraphic communication between Natal and London (the cable reached from London only to the Cape Verde Islands at this date, and the gap was bridged by steamship) to forge ahead, despite the known opposition of his masters at Whitehall. He presented Cetshwayo with an ultimatum in December 1878 that he knew the Zulu king could not accept, knowing too that before Disraeli could cable an order to stop the invasion, it would have already begun. A month later the troops went in to start what should really be known as Frere's war. There followed a bitter conflict costing thousands of Zulu and British lives, as well as a bill to the Treasury for over £5 million.

The aftermath of this unjustified and mismanaged war was equally disgraceful, because the post-war settlement imposed by Britain held the seeds of inevitable disruption. Cetshwayo was sent in exile to Cape Town. Zululand was split into 13 chiefdoms, some of them old pre-Shakan units, others newly demarcated. The chiefs were all opponents of the royal house; Cetshwayo's son and brother found themselves under the hostile authority of Zibhebhu, leader of the Ndwandwe clan, who treated them harshly. It was a woeful prescription for divide and misrule.

CETSHWAYO still had a powerful following among his Usuthu clan, and external supporters. He was brought to London in 1882 to put his case to the government (incidentally having lunch with Queen Victoria at Osborne), and he was allowed to return to Zululand in 1883. His status as paramount chief was far from secure, and Zibhebhu's party sparked off a vicious civil war. Cetshwayo was defeated in battle and he died, possibly poisoned, in 1884. White interventionism of the worst kind then followed. Boer and other mercenaries had taken a helping hand in Cetshwayo's overthrow; other Boers now came to help Dinuzulu, the royal heir, in recapturing the lost Usuthu territory. Having succeeded in this, under Lukas Meyer they grabbed for themselves as reward virtually all the old Disputed Territory along the Blood River, and much more, to create their New Republic, which was absorbed into the South African Republic (Transvaal) in 1887.

In that same year Britain annexed Zululand, allowing Zibhebhu back from exile and so undermining Dinuzulu's authority. Entrenched inter-tribal tensions broke out afresh. Civil war followed once again, with Dinuzulu eventually being sent to St Helena for 10 years for high treason. Before his return in 1897, Zululand was incorporated with the self-governing colony of Natal. For a while it was safe from encroachment, due largely to the distractions of the rinderpest pandemic of 1897-8 that wiped out millions of cattle, and of the second Anglo-Boer War of 1899-1902.

The inevitable step was taken of setting up a commission of delimitation, in other words dispossession, which reported in 1905. As a result of its findings more than one-third of Zululand, more than one million hectares, was released for purchase, leaving 1.6 million hectares in Zulu hands. The land was bought by Whites who converted it into sugar and timber plantations along the coastal plain, and cattle farms in the interior. Resentment over this restructuring of their hereditary lands, and other matters, flared up in refusal to pay taxes, and the Zulu broke out into open revolt in 1906. The Bambata Rebellion was brief but bloody, being crushed by the colonial authorities.

Who, then, won the Anglo-Zulu War? On the surface it was a military victory for Britain, however clumsily achieved, but victory was negated because confederation policies, the chief pretext for waging the war, were abandoned after 1879. For the Zulu nation the war was a harsh experience of defeat but, as their own historical perception of it makes clear, they suffered even more from the traumatic civil wars within the Zulu polity that continued for 10 years

18. The Struggle for Land

after 1879. The Transvaal Boers did well out of it after they regained their independence in 1881, resting secure from any kind of Zulu threat, real or imagined, as well as acquiring Zulu territory for themselves. In the long term the colony of Natal also benefited by getting their hands on Zulu labour, land, and trade. Those who contributed least to the conflict, in terms of lives and money, gained most, at the expense of dispossessing the Zulu of their kingdom.

Such calculations do not tell the whole story, for the reality is that despite all the pressures placed on them since Frere's ultimatum, the Zulu people survive undaunted. They are now the largest self-identifying 'nation' within the Republic of South Africa, at six million strong outnumbering any other ethnic group, White or non-White. More than this, they are vigorous, well organized politically, and confident. They have come to draw strength from their past.

The Chief Minister of KwaZulu is among the best known spokesmen for the Black majority in their struggle against apartheid. Chief Mangosutho Gatsha Buthelezi is a direct descendant of Chief Mnyamana Buthelezi, commander-in-chief of the Zulu army in 1879; he also has royal blood on his mother's side. He leads Inkatha, a powerful politico-cultural organisation largely, but not wholly, of Zulu membership. Although criticized by the African National Congress and others for his gradualist and non-violent views of negotiating for political change (ironic in such a warrior race as the Zulu), it is inconceivable that Inkatha could be omitted from any serious dialogue on the future of South Africa.

IN 1979 Chief Buthelezi opened a centenary conference at Durban on the history of the Anglo-Zulu War, appearing in all the finery of traditional Zulu dress. Relating the days of his people's despair to the present, he explained the deep difference between Black and White views of South Afrian history. 'A White perspective looks at yesterday as it leads to today. In the Black perspective, we see yesterday and today leading to tomorrow'. Nor are these empty words, because he could fairly claim, in a policy speech to his Legislative Assembly in April 1985, to have brought the region of KwaZulu-Natal to the very threshold of achieving real progress in the politics of power-sharing between Whites and Blacks. In March 1986 a multi-racial *indaba* or debate began in Durban to reach consensus on the creation of a single legislative body to govern the combined area of Natal and KwaZulu. Plans for a joint executive authority with statutory powers are already being considered by Pretoria. It makes Frere's war-mongering in 1879 look all the more sordid and pointless.

Article 19

WEST AFRICA'S MARY KINGSLEY

Deborah Birkett

'England... requires markets more than colonies.' Mary Kingsley's espousal of the African cause was founded on the empathy between second-class citizens in a white, male-dominated society.

IN 1893, FOR A THIRTY-YEAR-OLD British spinster to take a cargo vessel to West Africa was an extraordinary step. The unorthodoxy of Mary Kingsley's response to her stifling domestic life has cast her in the mould of an isolated heroine, removed from the cultural milieu of late nineteenth-century Cambridge in which she was raised. But the long voyage from the confines of her mother's sickroom to the Ogooué rapids was a psychological as well as physical journey. Its roots lay in the dreams and aspirations shared by many middle-class Victorian women who responded in less dramatic and memorable ways. Mary Kinglsey's contribution to the nineteenth-century image of Africa, her work as advisor and campaigner on colonial affairs, and the connections she made between theories of sexual and racial determinism, all reveal a woman firmly rooted in her time, not an individual divorced from it. Her very ordinary ambitions and desires are sometimes swamped amid the foreignness of the landscape in which they were realised.

Mary Kingsley in 1897, '... a maiden aunt dressed as a woman far beyond her mid-thirties'.

19. West Africa's Mary Kingsley

Her gender was also responsible for the hidden, and now largely forgotten, methods through which she expressed and exercised her power. Although by the time of her death in 1900, while nursing Boer prisoners of war in South Africa, she was considered the leading Africanist of her time, as a Victorian woman she was excluded from many of the forums concerned with African affairs. Her informal and behind-the-scenes politicking has lain buried under the greater weight of government reports and public records.

Although bearing the name of Kingsley, Mary had neither the education, money, nor established class status her literary uncles and cousins enjoyed. Born only four days after Dr George Kingsley married his housekeeper, Mary Bailey, in October 1862, Mary's first thirty years were consumed in tending to her sickly mother and acting as secretary to her father's amateur anthropological work.

When both parents died within weeks of each other in 1892, she felt like 'a boy with a new half crown'. Enticed by the tales of travel and adventure in her father's library, and with the intention of collecting 'fish and fetish', she sailed for West Africa – 'the white man's grave'. But alongside the spirits and jars for preserving her specimens packed in her large black waterproof bag, she took her cultural baggage. The isolation of Mary's early life had forced her onto the companionship of books, and from these she culled an image of the 'Dark Continent' and its exotic 'savage' inhabitants prevalent in both the academic and popular press. So strong were these images, that when the SS Lagos drew towards the West African Coast in August 1893, it all seemed so familiar.

Canoeing down the Ogooué rapids and climbing 13,000 foot Mount Cameroon by a route unconquered by any other European brought not only physical but psychological challenges. Her passionate desire to 'penetrate the African mind-forest' made her travel as a trader, living as her African companions and depending entirely upon them for her safety and well-being. In a land where she was first of all white, and only secondly a woman, she found a new kind of freedom which 'took all the colour out of other kinds of living'.

By 1896, after two journeys to West Africa, Mary Kingsley was a celebrity, a regular presence in the daily press and an enormously popular lecturer. Her quest in search of 'fish and fetish' had led her into more far-reaching discoveries, and what she saw and recorded questioned the images she had taken with her. 'One by one I took my old ideas derived from books and thoughts based on imperfect knowledge and weighed them against the real life surrounding me, and found them either worthless or wanting... the greatest recantation I had to make was my idea of the traders.' Popularly derided as the palm oil ruffians, the European traders in West Africa were mostly single men, some with African wives, caricatured in the British press as debauched and drunken rogues who had reluctantly given up dealing in slaves when 'legitimate trade' offered greater financial inducements. For Mary Kinglsey, however, they were men she was 'proud to be allowed to call friends and know were fellow-countrymen'.

It was not only her trader friends she believed were maligned. Africans, at the hands of the missionary party – eager 'not to tell you how the country they resided in was but how it was getting towards being what it ought to be' – were portrayed unfairly. Kingsley challenged:

> ...the stay at home statesmen, who think that Africans are awful savages or silly children – people who can only be dealt with on a reformatory penitentiary line. This view is not mine... but it is the view of the statesman and the general public and the mission public in African affairs.

Looking for consistency, practicality and humanity to be understood and explained, rather than vices and immorality to be manipulated and eradicated, she argued for a new approach to anthropological study by looking at African societies from the inside out, to 'think in black'. Long before anthropologists had developed the idea of fieldwork, she argued:

> ...unless you live among the natives you can never get to know them. At first you see nothing but a confused stupidity and crime; but when you get to see – well!... you see things worth seeing.

Although questioning many of the popular images of Africa, Mary Kingsley was steeped in the racial theories used to justify and support the expansion of British interests in West Africa. She espoused a by now out of fashion polygenesist outlook, believing that Africans and Europeans, as men and women, were essentially rather than evolutionary different. 'I feel certain that a black man is no more an undeveloped white man than a rabbit is an undeveloped hare, and the mental difference between the races is very similar to that between men and women among ourselves'. The fault of the missionary endeavour, she believed, was in trying to Europeanise Africans. Missionary-educated Africans were the curse of the Coast, embracing a secondhand rubbishy white culture rather than traditional African social customs. When writing about her travels, she focused on her contacts with the Fang people of Gabon, 'unadulterated Africans', as she called them, 'in the raw state'.

Her attitude towards women's rights shared this conservative and separatist philosophy. When approached by petitioners for women's admission to the learned societies she brushed aside their entreaties. 'These androgynes I have no time for', she complained. Women and men were different in kind rather than degree, as Africans to Europeans, and these differences should be recognised and encouraged rather than glossed over. While not denying a hierarchy within these differences constructed on racial and sexual lines, she nevertheless argued for areas of specialist knowledge, in line with the popular doctrine of 'separate spheres'. Opposed to the admission of women to societies of travellers, she argued for a separate women's meeting where things could be discussed without the presence of men. 'Women like myself know many things no man can know about the heathen' she told the Secretary of the Royal Geographical Society, 'and no doubt men do ditto'. On her return from West Africa in December 1895, her first venture into print was not, as commonly believed, in defence of European traders or 'real Africans' but in response to an article in the Daily Telegraph describing her as a New Woman. Infuriated by this label, she wrote to the Editor denying any such allegiance. 'I did not do anything', she wrote, 'without the assistance of the superior sex' denying the independence she had so desperately sought.

3. THE EXTENSION AND DOMINATION OF THE WEST

Calabar 1899; Mary Kingsley (centre front) with front-line representatives of the 'pen-pushers and ostrich feathers' of colonialism.

Claude Macdonald, Consul General of the Niger Territories, with his wife, Ethel, and staff — which included Roger Casement (right).

Mary Kingsley's philosophy of separate development of the races and sexes led her into direct opposition to the missionary party and their stress on a common humanity. Her defence of polygamy, domestic slavery, and even cannibalism as appropriate social forms in West Africa, shocked the conservative press and quickly brought her notoriety. But with this came a popular platform from which to air her views. Her first book, *Travels in West Africa*, published in January 1897, was an immediate bestseller. Based on an account of her second journey, its vast amount of new anthropological material established her as the leading West Africanist of the time. But Mary Kingsley was no longer content with confining herself to the issue of enthnology. Soon she was arguing for the recognition of anthropology as a tool of imperialist expansion; to govern the African, she argued, you must first know him. She wrote to the eminent Oxford anthropologist E.B. Teylor:

> ...I will force upon the politicians the recognition of anthropology if I have to do it with the stake and thumbscrew. Meanwhile the heathen unconsciously keeps on supporting anthropology gallantly, and officialdom says it won't have anything but its old toys – missionaries, stockbrokers, good intentions, ignorance and maxim guns. Well we shall see.

The imperial expansion Mary Kingsley envisioned was of a very different kind to that the new Colonial Secretary, Joseph Chamberlain, had in mind. In opposition to his plans for administrative intervention in West Africa and the establishment of the Crown Colony system, supported by the missionary parties, Mary Kingsley advocated informal economic imperialism, looking back to a mythical golden era when British interests in West Africa were protected by European traders and fair commerce between African and European flourished. Economic ties under British merchants rather than administrative control under 'pen-pushers and ostrich feathers' was her aim. She argued:

> England is the great manufacturing country of the world, and as such requires markets, and requires markets far more than colonies. A colony drains from the mother country, yearly, thousands of the most able and energetic of her children, leaving behind them their aged incapable relations. Whereas the holding of the West African markets drains a few hundred men, only too often for ever; but the trade they carry on and develop enables thousands of men, women and children to remain safe in England in comfort and pleasure, owing to the wages and profits arising from the manufacture and export of articles used in that trade.

Only this system – eventually outlined in her 'Alternative Plan' – would, she claimed, also benefit Africans, by

19. West Africa's Mary Kingsley

leaving their cultural and social organisations intact.

Mary Kingsley's means of raising support and realising her plans were limited, for her gender excluded her from the burgeoning number of forums concerned with African affairs. The admission of women to the Royal Geographical Society in 1892 had drawn such fierce opposition that the decision was hastily rescinded. Other societies of travellers were equally hostile to women's participation. Outspoken women's activities were confined to the field of missionary and philanthropic work, but even here public speaking could be frowned upon. For a woman to actively campaign against the missionary endeavour and on behalf of the palm oil ruffians and heathen Africans threatened her feminity in a way less controversial standpoints would not have done. Mary Kingsley's response was to emphasise her ladyhood, almost to the point of caricature, reminding her audience at public lectures that she appeared as their maiden aunt, dressed as a woman far beyond her mid-thirties. She appealed to a close friend to help her in the maintenance of this public persona, 'I implore if you hear it said in Society that I appear on platforms in African native costume, a billy cock hat, and a trade shirt, to contradict it', she wrote, 'honour bright I'd got my best frock on'.

As the corridors of official power were closed to her, she began to exploit unofficial methods and behind-the-scenes networks. Soon earning the name of 'Liverpool's hired assassin' for her pro-trader politics and clandestine ways of operating, in private she asserted pressure on individual politicians, exploited old networks and created new ones, and encouraged new venturers into the political arena. Her political development was inextricably knitted to the ways and means through which she could work. It is this informal, behind-the-scenes, nature of her politics that has often led to an underestimation of her influence in West African affairs.

Mary Kingsley felt bound to defend the European traders, Africans, and her own reputation against the allegations being paraded in the press. The first public debate in which she became involved was over the 'liquor traffic'. In 1895 a combination of factors – humanitarian and commercial – launched the 'liquor traffic' debate into a new phase, to which Kingsley's own efforts would soon be added. The British fear of the domination of the West African spirit trade by Hamburg firms reached a new height. The return to power of Salisbury in June, with the temperance supporter Joseph Chamberlain as his Colonial Secretary, was cited by Colonel Frederick Lugard, commissioner for the hinterland of Nigeria, as giving 'hope to those interested in the question that the time had at last come when effective steps would be taken to deal with this evil'. The language of the 'liquor traffic' debate became the 'demoralisation of the native' and 'the evil trade' versus 'legitimate commerce' – all reminiscent of earlier anti-slavery arguments – rather than profit and administrative control.

Sir John Kirk's enquiry following the 1895 Brass uprising had reopened the debate around the future control of the Niger Delta, and different interests were vying for influence in the area – the Royal Niger Company under the persuasive leadership of Sir George Goldie, the Niger Coast Protectorate government, Liverpool and Manchester trading houses, the Colonial Office, and the missionary bodies. The liquor traffic was, to a large extent, a pawn in this contest, a highly emotional issue which could be used to draw public support in the propaganda war.

For Mary Kingsley, the temperance party's argument had two main fallacies. Firstly, it painted a picture of an African population easily manipulated and less able to resist the enticements of alcohol than Europeans. Secondly, the curtailment on the importation of trade alcohol to West Africa would inhibit the 'free-trading' practices of the Liverpool merchants, who used it as a form of currency to obtain the palm oil and other raw materials of their trade. The pro-liquor lobby, however, had little ability to raise the sympathies of the general public against the appeal of the temperance party's tales of the degradation wrought by 'trade gin'. In Kingsley, the pro-liquor party found an advocate who could couch their economic arguments in terms more acceptable to the popular palate. While the leading Liverpool merchant John Holt had earlier complained that the anti-liquor leaders were 'professional agitators and old women', within a few years he would be extremely grateful that someone conforming to this image had come over to the traders' side.

The debate took place as much in extra-governmental forums as behind the walls of the Colonial Office. Lugard spoke to the Colonial Institute, the letters pages of *The Times* were dominated by the altercation between West African bishops and Governors, and missionary societies hosted public discussions. The thrashing out of the issue in these unofficial forums allowed Kingsley, excluded from the official arena, to be fully immersed in the centre of the debate.

Mary Kingsley's first attacks on the temperance party were made from her position as an ethnologist, to counter the image of the African as a 'drunken child'. She was drawn into the fray by an article appearing in the *Spectator* accusing Africans of being 'a people abnormally low, evil, cruel... It is in Africa that the lowest depth of evil barbarism is reached, and that we find the races with the least of humanity about them except the form... they are all degraded'. Kingsley's reply argued for an understanding of African culture:

> I do not believe the African to be brutal, degraded, or cruel. I know from wide experience with him that he is often grateful and faithful, and by no means the drunken idiot his so-called friends, the Protestant missionaries, are anxious, as an excuse for their failure in dealing with him, to make out.

Although a reluctant speaker, Kingsley embarked upon a vigorous and exhausting programme which took her throughout the country, from local geographical societies to 'magic lantern at YMCA'. The popular image of an intrepid lady explorer in the jungle which had initially so angered her could draw large crowds who would then receive political statements sugared in tales of African adventure.

While the propoganda war was being fought out in the pages of the press and on the public platform, in private the correspondence between Kingsley and her temperance adversaries was more wordy and considered. 'I am going for this mission

3. THE EXTENSION AND DOMINATION OF THE WEST

'Mavungu', the three-foot nail fetish brought back from West Africa on Mary Kingsley's first, 1893, journey, and which stood in her South Kensington flat.

party with feminine artfulness, not like a bull at a gate', she told Holt. As Lugard's damning account of the 'witty and amusing Miss Kingsley' appeared in *The Nineteenth Century*, in private his correspondence with her was a more mutual exchange of information and opinion. And while *The Times* paid her the ultimate insult and ignored the publication of her book, widely reviewed elsewhere, she met the editors for dinner. In this manner she hoped to exert private influence where public access was denied.

Kingsley was building up a network of contacts throughout the political spectrum, exploiting the social sphere controlled by women. Her first approach to her Liverpool ally Holt was made by writing to his wife, who had invited her to attend a meeting of the local Literary and Scientific Society. The wife of the Assistant Under Secretary at the Colonial Office, Reginald Antrobus, provided her with invaluable information and insight into Colonial Office wranglings by spying on her husband's papers. The leading Anglo-Irish social hostess Alice Stopford Green's ability to speak French enabled Kingsley to keep in contact with members of the French embassy in London.

Communications with West Africa were also developed, as Kingsley kept in regular contact with Africans on the Coast and hosted them on their visits to London. 'I have quantities of blacks here', she wrote to Holt – including the leading lawyer Samuel Lewis and Edward Blyden, editor of the *Sierra Leone Weekly News*.

The value of this diverse network of contacts would prove itself in the 'hut tax' controversy in the Protectorate of Sierra Leone. The British merchants had always opposed a tax on African property, accurately predicting that the resulting opposition would disrupt trade. When the first outbreak of resistance to payment occurred in early 1898 their fears were proved founded, but a wavering Colonial Secretary was reluctant to remove a tax in the face of persistent support for its implementation by the Governor of Sierra Leone and allegations by humanitarian pressure groups that clamping down on slavery had caused the rebellion. Realising she had once again to fight opponents who appeared to have humanitarian concerns entirely on their side, Kingsley pleaded for an understanding of Africans – sympathy for the black man as she put it, 'not emotional but common sense sympathy and honour and appreciation'.

But the sympathy she invoked also recalled earlier arguments with the temperance lobby over their misunderstanding of the African situation. The pro-hut taxers, she believed, suffered from a similar ignorance of African society, though a different aspect – not the misrepresenation of the African as a 'drunken child', but of the nature and value of indigenous African legal systems. The hut tax, Kingsley argued, offended African law. 'One of the root principles of African law is that the thing that you pay any one a regular fee for is a thing that is not your own – it is a thing belonging to the person to who you pay the fee'. But behind these initial objections lay her deeper objections to an interventionist policy in West Africa. The real cause of the rebellion was the 'reasonable dislike to being dispossessed alike of power and property in what they regard as their own country'. While publicly sticking to her claim that the tax was the root cause of the disturbances, in private she admitted that it was 'merely the match to a train of gunpowder'. By 'sticking severely to native law' however, other arguments would 'come by and by'.

How can the influence of someone who operated in such a behind-the-scenes and informal way be measured? Her prominent position on African affairs led the Colonial Secretary to write to her at this critical time. But he was reluctant to be seen to countenance the opinion of such a controversial figure. He sought her advice, therefore, as covertly as possible. 'He is horribly frightened of being known to communicate with the witch of Endor', Kingsley told Holt. She responded in kind, marking all her letters to him 'Private' and 'Strictly Confidential' – doubly underlined. When Sir David Chalmers was sent out to Freetown as Special Commissioner to investigate the cause of the disturbances, Chamberlain first briefed him on Kingsley's views. Governor Cardew of Sierra Leone paid her frequent visitors on his return to London, and the Acting-Governor Matthew Nathan, sent out in his place, zealously courted her friendship before his departure. His reading on board ship from Liverpool to Sierra Leone was Mary Kingsley's second book, *West African Studies*. In this manner she was in touch with all those involved in policy-making around the hut tax.

As her political experience grew, her methods of politicking became more sophisticated, subtle and therefore hidden from subsequent history. Not wanting to appear as an one-woman opponent to the hut tax, she encouraged others to commit themselves to print. Using her contacts with leading pressmen such as St Loe Strachey, editor of the *Spectator* and,

JOURNAL OF THE AFRICAN SOCIETY

FOUNDED IN MEMORY OF
MARY KINGSLEY

1901—1902

LONDON: MACMILLAN AND CO., LIMITED
NEW YORK: THE MACMILLAN CO.

Kingsley thought, a 'backstairs to Chamberlain, she introduced young journalists into print, most notably E.D. Morel, correspondent for the *Pall Mall Gazette*. She encouraged Holt to write to the papers, but warned him 'don't for goodness gracious sake let the mention of me occur'. As her contacts grew, she increasingly relied on these methods. 'The truth is Mr Holt', she wrote in 1899, 'every bit of solid good work I have done has been done through a man. I get more and more fond of doing things this way. It leaves me a free hand to fight with'. To St Loe Strachey she wrote, 'In the seclusion of private life, in the gentle course of private friendship, I shall do my best in language worse than you have ever heard from me, to weld my

19. West Africa's Mary Kingsley

men together and I'll fight to the last shot in my locker against the existing system'. Soon the Colonial Office christened her 'the most dangerous person on the other side'.

Her book, *West African Studies*, published in early 1899, contained a strong attack on the Crown Colony system. 'The sooner the Crown Colony system is removed from the sphere of practical politics and put under a glass case in the South Kensington Museum, labelled Extinct, the better for everyone', she wrote. She described its system of government as a waste of life and money, and a destroyer of African social organisations on which peace and prosperity depended. In its place she drew up an 'Alternative Plan'. This was innovative firstly, in giving governmental and administrative control to European trading interests in West Africa embodied in a Grand Council who appointed a Governor General of West Africa, and secondly, by officially incorporating African opinion – filtered through a council of chiefs – into the administrative network. But although the 'Alternative Plan' was presented as a new option for British control of West Africa, in fact it looked back to a former era rather than forward to a new one. The informal economic ties which Kingsley hoped would form the basis of British imperialism were central to this plan, as was their implementation by a European trading class. The failure of this scheme would depend not only on the impracticality of re-establishing an informal empire in a time of increasing European intervention in West Africa, but also the reluctance of British trading interests to take on the added responsibilities of government. British traders also wanted a non-trading European administrative class to run West African affairs and protect their markets from European and African rivals.

While on the public platform Kingsley appeared as the professional politician, in private she felt more and more drawn to the Africa she had left behind. While maintaining a professional façade of feminine conformity, in the privacy of her Kensington home she decorated her rooms with souvenirs from her journeys – enormous wooden drums and a yard-high nail fetish – and jangled about in her African bangles. To a

107

3. THE EXTENSION AND DOMINATION OF THE WEST

childhood friend she wrote of the stresses of her two personalities, the public politician and the private African:

> The majority of people I shrink from, I don't like them, I don't understand them and they most distinctly don't understand me... I cannot be a bushman *and* a drawing-roomer. Would to Allah I was in West Africa now, with a climate that suited me and a people who understood me, and who I could understand.

She longed to return to 'skylark' in West Africa and experience a freedom 'this smug, self-satisfied, sanctimonious, lazy, *Times*-believing England' could never give.

Her identity with the African had been strong and heartfelt since her return from West Africa. Emotional revelations of this personal sympathy to close friends found more public expression in the use of terms usually reserved for non-European peoples to describe her own experience. Calling herself a savage and a 'member of the tribe of women', she would even describe herself as 'an African'. 'We Africans are not fit for decent society', she told Alice Stopford Green, and to the Indianist Sir Alfred Lyall, she wrote 'I am a firm African'. She compared her beliefs to those of Africans. 'I desire to get on with the utter Bushman', she declared, 'and never sneer or laugh at his native form of religion, a pantheism which I confess is a form of my own religion'.

This identity was also an expression of her own philosophy of polygenesism and separate development. Arguing for the promotion of women's traditional sphere and African traditional life (although not always consistent in the definition of either), she said the 'African is a feminine race' – misunderstood by a dominant culture. The most candid revelation of these feelings was to Nathan, with whom she was unhappily in love:

> I will import to you, in strict confidence, for if it were known it would damage me badly, my opinion on the African. He is *not* 'half devil and half child', anymore than he is 'our benighted brother' and all that sort of thing. He is a woman... I know those nigs because I am a woman, a woman of a masculine race but a woman still.

Kingsley became increasingly dissatisfied with the isolation of her outspoken position, and the lack of support from disunited traders, and complained to Holt of loneliness. She secretly applied to nurse in South Africa, hoping to cover the Boer War for the *Morning Post* and travel northwards across the Orange River and far away from European settlements to her 'beloved South West Coast'. Letting only a few friends know of her imminent departure, she ended her final lecture at the Imperial Institute with the words 'Fare ye well, for I am homeward bound'. On arriving at the Cape at the end of March 1900, the medical conditions horrified her, and soon she was absorbed in the immediate needs of hospital work. 'All this work here, the stench, the washing, the enemas, the bed pans, the blood, is my world', she wrote to Alice Stopford Green, 'not London Society, politics, that gallery into which I so strangely wandered – into which I don't care a hairpin if I never wander again'. Within two months the typhoid fever that was daily killing four to five of her patients struck Mary, and on June 3rd she died. She was buried, at her own request, at sea. Full military and naval honours accompanied the funeral.

Commentators on Mary Kingsley's life and work have often accredited her with laying the political foundations for the introduction of indirect rule in Northern Nigeria. But it is in the informal sector, and not Colonial Office policy making, that we must look for her political legacy. Morel drew upon her inspiration, and continually agitated against Colonial Office politics, later leading the Congo Reform Movement, an informal pressure group relying on press coverage and public speaking in the Kingsley style. Alice Stopford Green, inheritor of Kingsley's behind-the-scenes politicking, formed the African Society in her memory, as a forum for the exchange of information between traders, academics, and officials involved in West African affairs. John Holt said, 'Miss Kingsley discovered me and made me think'.

FOR FURTHER READING:
Mary Kingsley *Travels in West Africa* (London, 1897; reprinted Virago, 1982); Catherine Barnes Stevenson, 'Female Anger and African Politics' the Case of Two Victorian "Lady Travellers"' *Turn-of-the-Century Woman* (1985); K. D. Nworah, 'The Liverpool Sect and British West African Politics 1895-1915' in *African Affairs* (1971); A. Olorunfemi 'The Liquor Traffic Dilemma in British West Africa: The Southern Nigerian Example 1895-1918' in *International Journal of African Historical Studies* (1984). The most recent biography of Kingsley is Katherine Frank *A Voyager Out* (Houghton and Mifflin, 1986).

THE EAST INDIA COMPANY AND THE EMPEROR AURANGZEB

'Trade follows the flag' is a truism of imperial expansion but in the 1680s it was the other way round, as East India Company entrepreneurs made an ambitious and abortive attempt to challenge the might of the Moghul empire.

Bruce Lenman

The first East India House in Leadenhall, c.1711.

THE ENGLISH EAST INDIA COMPANY was chartered by Elizabeth I on the last day of 1600. With the benefit of hindsight we know that it was destined to win for itself a spectacular territorial empire in India, and that the decisive step towards that empire was the seizure of power in the two great provinces of Bengal and Bihar by one of the Company's military servants, Robert Clive, in 1757. By his victory in a battle at Plassey which cost less than twenty English lives, Clive laid the foundations of a British Raj in India which lasted until 1947. It is a platitude amongst historians of the expansion of Europe that, compared with their achievements in the Americas, Europeans built their territorial empires in Asia belatedly. If all Europeans had been expelled from the Orient as late as 1750, they would have left precious little trace behind them, except in the Philippines, where, alone, the Spaniards had managed to rerun something like their dramatic conquests of non-European peoples in Mexico and Peru. The British are generally thought not even to have considered the forcible acquisition of a territorial

3. THE EXTENSION AND DOMINATION OF THE WEST

base in India until the unexpected success of French attacks on their position in south India in the 1740s and 1750s compelled them to create the military machine in India which Clive then turned against Bengal.

This is, however, not so. Clive was the second Englishman to lead a powerful force of troops and ships to Bengal. In the late 1680s, the English East India Company, under the leadership of a formidable City financier, Sir Josiah Child, embarked on a deliberate policy of using armed force to achieve its objectives in India. This extraordinary episode deserves more attention than it has hitherto been given, for two main reasons. One is the inherent difficulty of explaining why an East India Company founded by cautious merchants determined to stick to business and spurn conquest, ended up declaring war on the vast Moghul Empire which, under its last great sovereign, the Emperor Aurangzeb, had, by 1700, extended its formal boundaries over virtually the whole sub-continent. By implication we might hope in the course of probing this question to gain an insight into the aggressive and authoritarian spirit of late Stuart England, for the underlying thrust of a regime is often more apparent at the periphery of its power than at its centre. The second reason for studying this episode is the comparative material it provides for analysing the eventual transition to British supremacy in Bengal. The explanation of Child's failure must throw into high relief some of the reasons for Clive's success.

The early history of the East India Company certainly showed no hint of its future territorial greatness in India. It was founded as a strictly business enterprise to gain access to the lucrative oceanic commerce in spices from the Moluccas and other islands in what is now Indonesia. Queen Elizabeth, who chartered it, left not an inch of new colony to her sucessor James VI and I. It is true that under James an infant British overseas empire was born, but it was a sickly child struggling for survival in the 1620s when Spaniards ravaged its Caribbean toeholds, American Indians mauled Virginia, and the English colony in Newfoundland entered on a terminal decline. When William Alexander, Earl of Stirling, tried to create a North American colony for Scotland in Nova Scotia, it proved impossible, economically and politically, to maintain a settlement in such bleak northern latitudes, and in 1632 Charles I surrendered what there was of Nova Scotia as part of a peace settlement with France.

The East India Company made a profitable enough start in a series of voyages aimed primarily at the Spice Islands rather than India. Indeed, it was not until 1608 that one of its ships, on the third organised voyage, touched at the Indian port of Surat in Gujerat on the western or Malabar coast. The Company went through what has been called a 'hard infancy': the Dutch pursued a vendetta against their English rivals in the Spice Islands, culminating in the 1623 Massacre of Amboyna in which they executed several English merchants on trumped-up charges and, in the words of Henry Robinson (writing in 1649), 'by which strategem of theirs they have almost worried us out of the East India trade'. That was an exaggeration, but the East India Company turned increasingly to India, and tried to tailor its coat according to its shrinking cloth. Between 1610 and 1619 the Company built and used large vessels like the *Trades Increase* and the *Great James* of around a thousand tons burthen. Since its exports were mainly bullion and its imports, although high in value, were modest in bulk, it did not need such ships. (In a year the Company brought home perhaps one or two thousand tons of pepper, about the same of salt, and a few hundred tons of silks, cottons, and dyestuffs.) The 1620s saw a sensible halving of the tonnage of the average Company ship.

The Company was always deeply averse to becoming involved in local politics and wars; even a policy of seizing and fortifying bases was financially impractical. It had to be prepared to fight at sea, as its ships did in 1612 and 1615 to crack the Portuguese protection racket on the Malabar coast, but it knew that war ate up profit. Between 1615 and 1618 the East India Company financed the embassy of Sir Thomas Roe from James VI and I to the court of the Emperor Jahangir. Roe achieved little, but he summed up received wisdom when he wrote:

It is the beggering of the Portugall... that he keepes souldiers that spendes it; yet his garisons are meane. He never Profited by the Indyes, since he defended them. Observe this well. It hath beene also the error of the Dutch, who seek Plantation heere by the sword.

The establishment of Fort St George (the embryonic future city of Madras) on the eastern or Coromandel coast of India in the 1640s was not proof that the Company had changed its mind. Its London directorate was, in fact, angry that its local servants had accepted the invitation from a weak local rajah to build a fort, and even angrier when the rajah failed to honour an undertaking to pay for it.

It was only with the restoration of Charles II in 1660 that the Company entered a phase of sustained growth. Under Charles I it had nearly collapsed; with the Restoration its days of prosperity and grandeur could be said to begin. Yet this is unfair to the Cromwellian regime which in 1657 rechartered the Company as a united joint stock to which three-quarters of a million pounds were promptly subscribed. The roots of the social conservatism and aggressive commercial imperialism which were so characteristic of Restoration England are to be found in the Cromwellian Protectorate, and of this fact there is no better example than the man who came to dominate the Restoration East India Company – Sir Josiah Child.

Born in London in 1630, the second son of a merchant with East and West Indian interests, Josiah Child rose to prominence as a victualler and deputy naval treasurer to Cromwell's fleet in Portsmouth, where he gained access to the ruling town oligarchy by his marriage in 1654 to Hannah Boate, daughter of a Portsmouth master shipwright. By 1658, Child had become mayor of Portsmouth. The town corporation was puritanical and republican in sympathy, backing Sir Arthur Heselrige and the Rump Parliament in 1659 against the grandees of the Commonwealth army. With the return of Charles II in 1660 the republican oligarchy was soon purged by a visiting commission enforcing the terms of the Corporation Act of 1661. Mayor John Tippets and other prominent figures like Josiah Child were deprived and disenfranchised and, after his wife's death in the same year, Child returned to London.

20. The East India Company

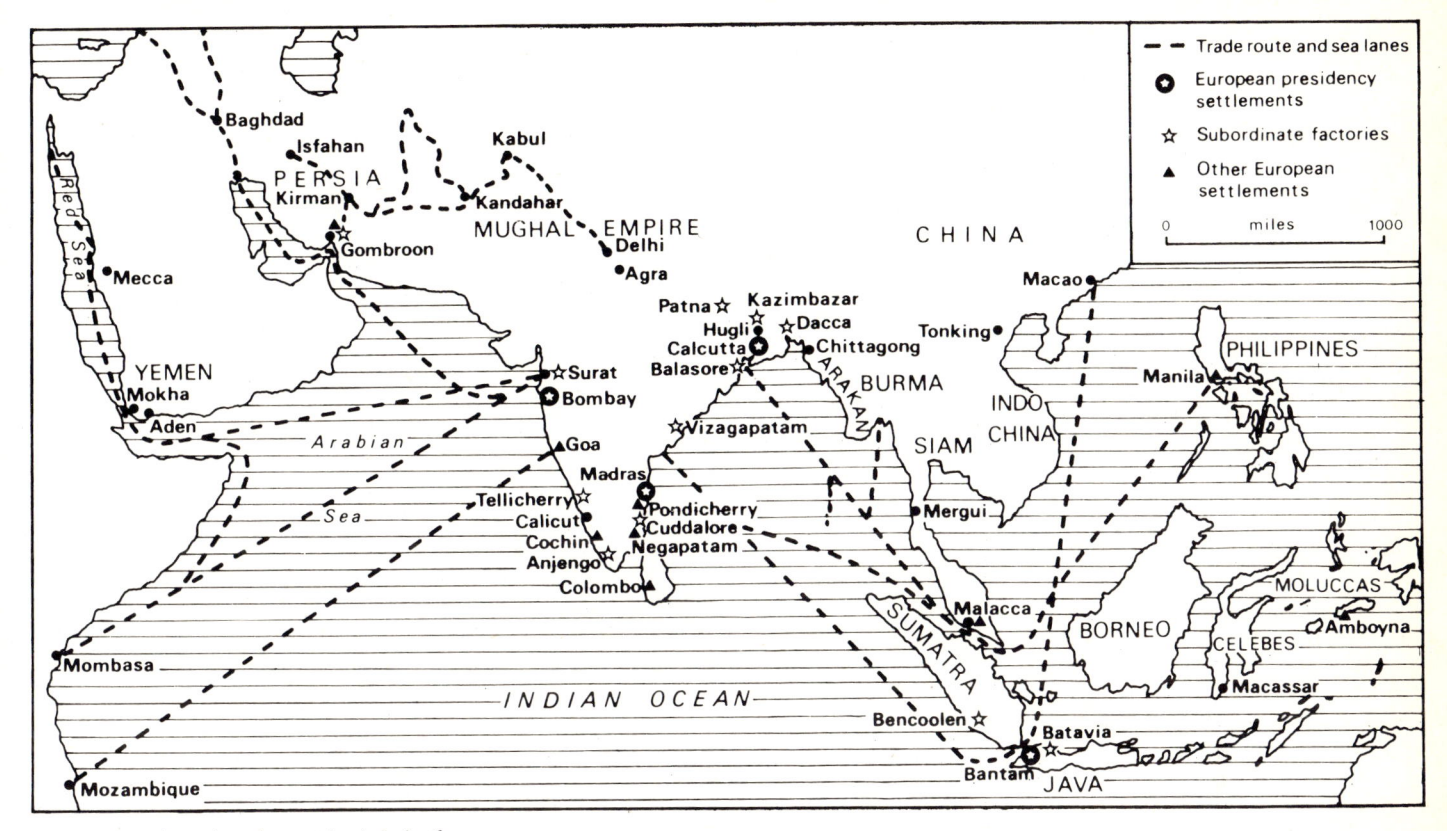

European trade and settlement in Asia in the late seventeenth century.

They both recovered fast. The Restoration regime continued the Cromwellian tradition of maritime and commercial imperialism with an Act of Navigation and predatory wars against the Dutch. Tippets, a master shipwright, was a useful man to Charles II. (Until 1669, when it was taken over by a clique of émigrés whose outlook was scarcely English, that monarch's government was really a coalition of returned Royalists and former Cromwellians.) Tippets became a Commissioner of the Navy in 1668 and was knighted in 1675. Josiah Child needed longer to worm his way into royal favour, but he never lost his knack for making money.

He had been provisioning East India Company ships in Portsmouth as early as 1659, so it was only natural that he should continue to do so after his return to London. Whether he was technically 'free of the Company' (that is to say a member of it) was a matter of some debate amongst the 'committees' or directors in 1664. He was certainly a major bidder for Company provision contracts in the later 1660s.

Marriage had helped Child in Portsmouth, and after his remarriage in 1663 to a lady who was both the daughter and the widow of London merchants, Child built a brewery in Southwark. His beer was said to be terrible, but he sold it to the navy, to whom he also sold mast timbers from America. Indeed, he was turning into an all-round commercial imperialist. He was also co-owner of 1,330 acres in Jamaica, and a founder member of the Royal Africa Company, which was sponsored by the Duke of York, heir presumptive to Charles II. As Member of Parliament for Dartmouth from 1673, Child had enough political influence to form a syndicate with Thomas Papillon and Sir Thomas Littleton and force his way into a major share of naval victualling contracts despite the hostility of the Secretary of the Admiralty, Samuel Pepys.

Child bought his way into the East India Company; by December 31st, 1675, he was the biggest investor in the New General Stock, with £12,000 out of the total stock balance of £369,891 divided among 554 adventurers. He had been elected to the Court of Committees (the directorate) in April 1674 and was active as a representative of the Company in the negotiations which concluded the unpopular and unsuccessful Third Dutch War of 1672-74. Partly because of his sustained sniping at Charles II's great minister Danby, whose aggressive Anglicanism did not appeal to the old Cromwellian in Child, Josiah Child was still not acceptable to his sovereign. When Charles heard in April 1676 that the East India Company was on the verge of electing Child and his close associate Thomas Papillon 'Governor and Sub-Governor for the year ensuing', he had Secretary of State, Sir Joseph Williamson, convey his displeasure, saying 'His Majesty should take it very ill of the Company if they should chuse them'.

It was too late to stop Child's election to the directorate, but the royal veto on his leadership was accepted until Child made his peace with the Crown, which he did in two ways. He

3. THE EXTENSION AND DOMINATION OF THE WEST

did not join in the attack on the Roman Catholic Duke of York's right to succeed his brother during the Exclusion Crisis. For that he was rewarded with a baronetcy. In 1679 he had been given general oversight of the affairs of 'the coast and the bay' (Madras and Bengal in modern parlance), and 1682 saw Sir Josiah persuade the General Court of stockholders that it was 'consistent with the Company's duty and interest to make a present to His Majesty of 10,000 guineas'. A smaller payment went to York, and the royal brothers came to rely on their annual Christmas presents from the East India Company. Child duly became Deputy Governor in 1684 and Governor in 1686.

Circumstances were changing in India, too. The Moghul Empire never really recovered from the wars of succession in 1657-60 between the sons of the Emperor Shahjahan, and though the victor, the Emperor Aurangzeb, proved a great ruler, he failed to check, indeed did much to provoke, the militant Hindu revivalism of the Maratha people. Led by the great warrior-king Sivaji, who died in 1680, Maratha armies rampaged along the Malabar Coast, raiding Surat, the principal East India Company trading port in India, in 1664 and 1667. Sir George Oxenden, President of the East India Company Council in Surat, helped the Moghul Governor fend off the 1664 assault. Oxenden had only a handful of Europeans and a few mercenaries to guard his warehouses, but Aurangzeb noticed and honoured his valour.

The European garrison at Fort St George on the Coromandel Coast had by 1655 fallen as low as twenty-five men, so nobody could accuse the English of plans of conquest. They did acquire Bombay in 1661 as part of the dowry for Catherine of Braganza, the Portuguese bride of Charles II, but the King regarded this island base as an expensive pest, so he wished it on the East India Company in 1668 for an annual rent of £10. In December 1667 his royal garrison there had numbered ninty-three English, forty-two Portuguese and French, and 150 men recruited from the great south India plateau of the Deccan.

The directors of the East India Company were still in 1681 emphatic that 'all war is... contrary to our constitution as well as our interest'. Geral Aungier, who between 1669 and 1677 governed Bombay with great ability for them, did not argue with the principle, but he was clear that:

> The state of India is much altered to what it was; that justice and respect, wherewith strangers were wont to be treated with, is quite laid aside, ... The times now require you to manage your general commerce with your sword in your hands.

The Emperor Aurangzeb on the battlefield; from Ogilby's 'Asia' (1673).

The Maratha warrior-king, Sivaji opponent of Moghul expansion.

20. The East India Company

Sir Josiah tied the East India Company to the chariot of late Stuart imperialism, and that imperialism was extremely assertive.

In India Sir Josiah's protegé John Child (who was not a relative, despite his name) had been rapidly rising in the East India Company hierarchy at Surat. From the lucrative post of factor he moved into the council which advised the Company President at Surat, and in 1680 he became Deputy-Governor of Bombay. The directorate still operated on the assumption that the East India Company was a purely private body whose job was to cut costs and make profits for stockholders, so they pressed for reductions in military pay and allowances. John Child tried to enforce these cuts on an already discontented Bombay garrison, provoking a rebellion led by Captain Richard Keigwin, the dashing commander of a miniscule force of cavalry raised to repel hit-and-run raids on the few square miles of English territory. In 1683 Keigwin arrested Ward, the resident Governor of Bombay, and repudiated Company authority, claiming to rule directly on behalf of Charles II.

The monarch was, however, much more open to suggestions from Sir Josiah Child than from Keigwin. Charles was persuaded to issue a commission under the Great Seal making John Child, now Sir John, Captain General and Admiral of all East India Company forces, with Sir Thomas Grantham, as his Vice-Admiral. Grantham had had experience of such affairs – having been sent to Virginia in 1676 to suppress a local rebellion. After the arrival of a flotilla of ten ships led by Grantham's HMS *Phoenix* in November 1684, Keigwin prudently surrendered and Sir John was annoyed to find that in exchange 'that notorious naughty rascal' was to be pardoned for his rebellion. Charles II could use his talents. Keigwin was to die gallantly in action fighting for the Crown. However, Charles did insist that the Company keep a minimum of three infantry companies at Bombay in future, and move its headquarters from Surat to Bombay since 'we are positively resolved never to be enslaved by the Moor's Government hereafter'. It was an indirect but real challenge to Moghul authority by a Company which now had in India precisely the sort of incipient sub-imperialism which it used to be thought only emerged in the mid-eighteenth century. Assertive Company magnates in London, like Sir Josiah, had intimate links with aggressive Company officers in India, like Sir John, and the latter had access to royal naval and military power. That still did not make Sir John a trained soldier. Robert Clive was not a trained professional, but he proved in the 1750s to be a natural soldier. Sir John had neither training nor talent. As a contemporary said:

> He was a General but no soldier; and better skilled at his pen than his sword; and more expert in casting an account than in martialling [sic] and conducting an army.

Yet as Sir Josiah progressed to Deputy Governor of the East India Company in 1684 and Governor in 1686, he embarked with Sir John and their mutual patron the Duke of York (James VII and II from 1685) on a policy which was bound to lead to armed conflict in India. Restoration England conducted much of its foreign business with an arrogant style and a militarised personnel. Thus the Earl of Carlisle, a soldier-bureaucrat who learned his trade under Cromwell, had been sent by Charles II to demand exemption from customs dues for English merchants in Russia, and when the Tsar declined on the reasonable grounds that he needed the money, Charles II toyed briefly with the idea of attacking Russia in alliance with Sweden. Any payments to the Moghul Empire were, of course, liable in this atmosphere to be seen as 'unreasonable'. Some exactions by Moghul officials no doubt were excessive, but all and every payment was resented.

Thereafter the directorate of the East India Company took a conscious decision to concentrate its activities in India in a series of heavily-fortified port centres over which it would exercise absolute authority. Innocent as this preference for fortified entrepôts might look at first sight, it threatened the sovereignty of any local ruler in two ways. First, it involved flouting any authority not prepared to grant permission to fortify. Secondly, it threatened the large customs component in a maritime region's state income. The shift of emphasis from Surat to Bombay was a shift from a Moghul city to an (inadequately) fortified English sovereign enclave. Madras was already fortified. The flashpoint was therefore bound to be the great and rich province of Bengal, which was emerging as the most lucrative area for European commerce in India, mainly because of the abundance and low prices of its principal export goods. The East India Company had several trading posts in the Ganges delta including factories (secure warehouse-complexes) at Kazimbazar, Patna and Hugli. The Council of the Bay, which ruled them, was in 1686 presided over by the formidable Job Charnock who was

Big trees from little acorns... (above) Moghul brush drawing of East India Company ships at the port of Surat; (below) the English fort at Bombay c.1720.

3. THE EXTENSION AND DOMINATION OF THE WEST

already on bad terms with the Moghul viceregal administration in India over disputed debt, cases involving local merchants, and Charnock's physical resistance to the officers of the *foujdar* or criminal magistrate of Hugli, who tried to distrain his assets. By April 1686 Charnock, using troops which had been unexpectedly sent out by the court of directors, trounced the police forces of the *foujdar*.

The very able Moghul Viceroy of Bengal, Shaista Khan, had made his name by dealing with one set of European ruffians. These were slavers and pirates from the so-called 'shadow empire' of Portugal on the Coromandel Coast: men of mixed blood who acknowledged the Archbishop of Goa, but not the Portuguese Viceroy there. Operating from a base in the Ganges delta, their slaving galleys had terrorised the peasantry until the Viceroy built forts on the Ganges and overwhelmed their ill-defended township by sheer weight of numbers. Some Portuguese renegades continued their activities from refuge in the Buddhist kingdom of Arakan, whose ruler had pretensions to the conquest of Bengal. Indeed the English in 1686-87 offered assistance against the Arakanese to Shaista Khan as an incentive to accept their demands.

There were in the end four points of conflict. One was the old East India Company centre of Surat where relations with the Moghul governor deteriorated when he tried to raise dues on British trade from 2½ per cent to a more realistic four. That conflict eventually bred violence at Bombay. Simultaneously, the East India Company managed to become involved in a naval war in the Bay of Bengal with the Kingdom of Siam, whose Greek foreign minister, one Phaulkion, was accused of intriguing with Louis XIV of France and of opening Siamese ports like Mergui to renegades from Company service who then violated its trade monopoly. Certainly, one of these men, Samuel White, known as 'Siamese White', was governor of Mergui. In 1688 the East India Company sent two frigates to attack Mergui, and a war of attacks on trading vessels spluttered and flared until the fall of Phaulkion in 1688.

By this time war in Bengal had been going on for some while. After William Hedges, the Company's special envoy to the Viceroy, had failed to secure satisfaction, Job Charnock demanded 'a place or Town by Salt Water for the building of a strong or fortified Factory' where he could 'Negotiate free of all duties'. Charnock's hand had been strengthened by the despatch of a flotilla of ten ships from England, carrying six companies of infantry to reinforce the few hundred European and mixed-blood troops which the Company kept to police rather than defend its Bengal establishments. The flotilla had a royal commission from James VII and II, but this hardly compensated for the loss of three ships on the way out, or the lack of any officers above the rank of lieutenant. Charnock and the merchants of his council were to assume the senior commands, despite their lack of professional training. They were able to expel the Moghul forces from Hugli in October 1686 by means of a surprise assault backed by a naval bombardment, but then they made the fatal mistake of negotiating with local Moghul officials. They would have been wiser to implement the orders which the directorate of the East India Company had sent out with the flotilla. These envisaged the seizure and fortification of Chittagong, a port on the east coast of Bengal. It is true that the second phase of operations envisaged by the orders – an attack on the regional capital of Dacca – would certainly have proven counter-productive, but no more so than staying in Hugli, a town well within reach of the army of the Viceroy of Bengal, and on a river which enabled him easily to concentrate troops and supplies.

The army of the Viceroy (whose Indian title was Nawab) was still built round a cavalry force. It had plenty of irregular infantry, many of them matchlock men, and could deploy a ponderous seige-train of very heavy cannon, but its essence lay in its sabre-wielding troopers. Charnock's forces could not generate enough fire-power to stop their charge. They lacked adequate mobile field artillery like the quick-firing six-pounders whose grapeshot were to serve Clive so well. Above all, the English soldiers of 1686-88 needed a fair proportion of their ranks (a minimum of a third) to wield pikes to protect the musketeers from cavalry whilst they went through the slow process of reloading their matchlock muskets which used a smouldering cord to fire the propellant. Effective bayonets were not really available until the 1690s. Driven from Hugli, Charnock retreated, destroying Moghul river forts, granaries and salt stores on his way. He was chased from his refuge at Sutanati, near a convenient deep anchorage, and ended up on the insalubrious island of Hijli where he repulsed an attack, but lost most of his surviving men to fever. He wisely started to negotiate a compromise settlement, aided by the effectiveness of his naval blockade, which was depriving the Nawab of customs revenue, when the arrival of Captain Heath from England with a sixty-four-gun man o' war, a frigate, and 160 soldiers wrecked hopes of compromise. Heath bombarded the town of Balasore, wisely jibbed at attacking a well-defended Chittagong, and then evacuated all English to Madras, where the council was busy urging its London masters to stop fighting two pointless wars.

For the Emperor Aurangzeb, Balasore was the last straw. Busy campaigning in the Deccan, he had treated the antics of the East India Company as an irrelevance, but Sir John Child's interference with the pilgrim traffic from Surat to Mecca vexed the pious emperor, and Captain Heath's behaviour enraged him. Sir John had retreated from Surat to Bombay in 1687. By 1688 the Moghul authorities had arrested English goods and merchants in Surat, while Sir John boasted that if their admiral attacked Bombay he would 'blow him off again with the wind of his Bum'. Alas, when the Moghul admiral Sidi Yakub Khan did land on Bombay with 20,000 men, Sir John was rapidly chased into Bombay Castle, which was inadequately fortified due to his previous ill-judged economies, and commanded by a hill on which the Sidi mounted a battery which pounded Bombay Castle with huge stone cannon balls or tossed mortar bombs (made from hollowed-out stones) over its parapets. There was no alternative to abject capitulation to the Emperor Aurangzeb, who might then call off the siege. It had not been particularly bloody. Casualties on the East India Company side were 104 killed, 130 wounded and 116 'run away', but the Company was in deep political trouble back home where the Glorious Revolution of 1688 had ousted its patron James II, and given those parliamentarians who had always detested its monopoly of English trade in the East a chance to win the ear of the new monarch, William III. In a shrewd career move, Sir John Child died and retired to a splendid tomb before the final peace terms, which involved his permanent exclusion from India, were put into force.

A contemptuous Imperial *Firman* or decree of the Emperor Aurangzeb in February 1690 readmitted the East India Company to trade in his dominions as before the war in exchange for a grovelling admission of guilt and a stiff fine of 150,000 rupees (at the time about £15,000). To Aurangzeb the Company was still a mere flea on the back of his imperial elephant. The Company was chastened. News of the decree's terms sharpened the crisis it faced in London, a crisis culminating in 1698 in Parliament chartering a General Society designed to supersede it. It may be argued that the Childs and James II never aimed at direct rule in Bengal, but then neither did Clive in 1757. What was at stake both times was military and commercial ascendancy. There is no reason to believe that victory for the Childs would have had results any different from those which followed Clive's triumph: subversion of indigenous institutions, leading to direct rule. What changed between 1686 and 1757 was English military capacity, and the cohesion of the Moghul Empire.

FOR FURTHER READING:
James P. Lawford, *Britain's Army in India from its Origins to the Conquest of Bengal* (Allen & Unwin, 1978); David Chandler, *The Art of Warfare in the Age of Marlborough* (B.T. Batsford Ltd., London 1976); K.N. Chaudhuri, *The Trading World of Asia and the English East India Company 1660-1760* (Cambridge University Press, 1978); Vincent A. Smith, *The Oxford History of India*, 3rd edn, ed Percival Spear (Oxford University Press, 1958); Percival Spear, *Penguin History of India*, Vol II; Arnold Wright, *Annesley of Surat* (London, 1918); W. Irvine, *The Army of the Indian Moghuls: Its Organisation and Administration* (London, 1903).

SOUTHERN BARBARIANS AND RED-HAIRS IN FEUDAL JAPAN

C.R. Boxer

'This government of Japan may well be accounted the greatest and powerfullest Tyranny, that ever was heard of in the world; for all the rest [of the people] are as slaves to the Emperor (or great commander as they call him), who upon the least suspicion (or jealousy) or being angry with any man (be he never so great a man) will cause him upon the receipt of his letter to cut his belly, which if he refuse to do, not only he, but all the rest of their race shall feel the smart thereof.' (Richard Cocks, chief of the English 'Factory' or trading-agency at Hirado, to the Earl of Salisbury, December 10th, 1614).

The rightful Emperor of Japan was an ostensibly highly venerated but powerless ruler at Kyoto, who claimed unbroken descent from the Sun-Goddess. He was called by foreigners the *Dairi*, or *Mikado*, and was sometimes described as a 'Pope' or spiritual monarch. The real power rested with the Shogun, or Generalissimo (originally, *sei-i-tai-shogun*, or 'barbarian-subduing generalissimo'). This title of 'great commander' as Cocks termed it, was hereditary in the House of Tokugawa, since the unification of the island-empire, after centuries of internecine warfare, by Tokugawa Ieyasu in 1600. Europeans who had resided for any length of time in Japan knew the true state of affairs; but they invariably referred to the incumbent Shogun as the Emperor, since he was the supreme executive ruler, and styled himself as such in correspondence with foreigners. The 'belly-cutting' mentioned by Cocks was the long-established Japanese custom of ritual suicide by *seppuku*, or *hara-kiri*, as it is more commonly termed in Europe.

All the Europeans who visited feudal Japan were impressed by the readiness with which capital punishment was inflicted on all and sundry for the most trifling offences. The celebrated English pilot, Will Adams, who lived in Japan from 1600 until his death in 1620, wrote that the Japanese were 'in justice very severe, having no respect of persons. . . . No thief for the most part put in prison, but presently executed'. Another contemporary, the Spaniard, Bernardino de Avila Girón, observed: 'Name a Japanese and you name an executioner; and yet they say it is cruel to punish children'—a contrast which significantly illustrates the difference between Japanese and European attitudes. Richard Cocks, after passing the mutilated corpses of criminals on a roadside journey in 1616, commented, 'If it were not for this strict justice, it were no living among them, they are so villainous desperate.'

Westerners who came to Japan from the time of its 'discovery' by three Portuguese castaways in 1543 until the expulsion of all foreigners save the Dutch and the Chinese in 1639, can be divided into two main categories. Those who visited the country briefly or for long periods, but who did not marry and settle down there; and those who became 'naturalised Japaners'. This latter category included the English pilot, Will Adams, with his homes at Hirado and Yokosuka, the Portuguese pilot, Balthazar de Sousa, 'who had a fine house with spacious and pleasant grounds' at Nagasaki in 1626, and the Dutch shipmates of Will Adams, Melchior van Sandvoort and Jan Joosten.

Before their official expulsion from the country in 1613-14, some of the missionaries, both Jesuits and friars, had lived in Japan for many years and acquired an excellent knowledge of the people, the language, and the country. The most remarkable among them was Padre João Rodriques *circa* 1562-1633, nicknamed *Tçuzzu*, or 'the Interpreter'. He lived in Japan from 1577 to 1610, acting as a confidential interpreter to the *Taiko*, Toyotomi Hideyoshi, 1536-1598, who first unified Japan, and later to the Shogun, Tokugawa Ieyasu, 1542-1616, until he fell out of favour, was banished to Macao, and was replaced by Will Adams. His membership of the Church Militant prevented Rodriques from giving objective accounts of Buddhism and Shinto. But his appreciation of Japanese art and literature in all their forms, his expert knowledge of the tea-ceremony and of many other distinctive aspects of Japanese culture, were not to be attained by any other Westerner in Japan until Von Siebold,

21. Southern Barbarians and Red Hairs

B.H. Chamberlain and E.M. Satow in the nineteenth century.

Another long-time resident of Japan with an excellent knowledge of the language, the culture, and the people, was the Italian Jesuit priest, Organtino Gnecchi-Soldi, 1533-1609. Within thirty years of his death, he entered into Japanese folklore in an anonymous chapbook entitled *Kirishitan Monogatari* (*Tale of Christianity*). He was described as being 'somewhat similar in shape to a human being, but more like a long-nosed goblin, seven feet high, with a black skin, large protruding red nose shaped like a conch-shell and with teeth longer than those of a horse'. Under the name of *Urugan Bateren* (Padre Organtino), he figures in modern Japanese literature, including Akutagawa Ryunosuke's short story 'When the Gods Smile'. After being proscribed on pain of death for centuries, the Jesuits and their religion are now in high favour in contemporary Japan. Many streets in Nagasaki have been given names evocative of 'the Christian Century'; and *Kirishitan* souvenirs are mass-produced for the tourist market.

The Japanese authorities at first showed themselves strangely reluctant to proceed to extremes against the European missionaries who had clearly and deliberately flouted the laws, manners, and customs of the 'Land of the Gods'. After the Shogun's proscription of Christianity and banishment of the missionaries in 1614, many of the Jesuits and friars thought that the *Bakufu* ('curtain government') would not enforce the death-sentence against such European missionaries as they found in hiding, but would merely deport them to Manila or to Macao. Even unconverted Japanese had often told them that Hideyoshi had been criticised by many of the *daimyo* (feudal lords) for crucifying some Spanish Franciscan missionary-friars in 1597. These critics had included Tokugawa Ieyasu; so it was widely assumed that the death-penalty would not be enforced against those who were caught in hiding. No missionary was in fact executed in Ieyasu's lifetime; but after his death, his son and successor, Hidetada, ordered the execution of four European missionary-priests in 1617. This marked an intensification of the persecution, which became yearly more wide-ranging, thorough, and severe. The problem of Christianity in Japan was no longer one of acceptance by the 'blind heathen', but the necessity for clandestine and underground adaption and survival.

During the years when the Portuguese were established at Nagasaki and the trade with Macao was maintained by an annual 'Great Ship' (*Náo* in Portuguese; carrack in English), Japanese painters of the Kano School produced richly decorated *byobu*, or folding-screens. These screens made a 'most delightful show', as an English traveller noted in 1637; and many of them were exported to Macao and to Goa, whence a few reached Europe. They depicted the *Nambanjin* (literally 'Southern Barbarians'), arriving in their huge *Kurofune* ('Black Ship'), and disembarking at Nagasaki. The Portuguese traders from Macao were depicted in their exotic costumes of richly embroidered Chinese silks, tailored after the Indo-Portuguese fashions prevailing at Goa. The black African slaves, servants and sailors were also richly dressed, but went barefoot as a mark of their servile status. They are shown performing acrobatic feats in the shrouds and rigging, holding sunshades over their masters ashore, or leading exotic animals for presentation to Japanese dignitaries. Portuguese Jesuits and Spanish friars also figure in these screens, accompanied by their Japanese acolytes, but it is the black slaves who steal the show. The Japanese were clearly fascinated by these tall, jet-black Negroes, mostly from Mozambique.

Black slaves were even able to buy—or otherwise acquire—Japanese girls to take back with them to Macao; much to the disgust of the Jesuit missionaries, who strongly denounced but failed to stop the practice. These girls were mostly sold into servitude for a trifling sum by their own parents. Many of them came from the Shimabara Peninsula near Nagasaki, where the peasantry lived on the barest subsistence-line or below it. The Italian merchant-adventurer, Francesco Carletti, who visited Japan in 1597/98, was (or professed to be) horrified by this 'most shameless immorality" of the Portuguese. They hired the girls by the day, or the week, or the month, or for years on end, as they felt inclined, 'and in some cases married them themselves'. The Dutch and English who traded at Hirado from 1609 onwards, behaved in the same way. The *Diary* of Richard Cocks, 1614-1623, is replete with references to these women.

The English voluntarily left Hirado in 1623, since they could not cover their expenses. The Portuguese were expelled from Japan in 1639, on pain of death if they tried to return. They did return next year, and they were all executed save for thirteen of the lowest members of the crew, who were spared to take back to Macao the news of the execution of sixty-one members of the Embassy in August 1640. In 1641 the Dutch were removed from Hirado to Deshima, a small artificial fan-shaped islet joined by a bridge to the town of Nagasaki, which had been built for the confinement of the Portuguese in 1635. Here they remained until after the opening of the country to foreigners in 1853-68.

The Dutch on Deshima have often been criticised for their real or alleged indifference to the rich cultural panorama of Tokugawa Japan, and for concentrating on balance-sheets rather than on artistic and intellectual interests. But what else could have been expected from the representatives of a monopolistic commercial company which confessedly had 'trade as its compass and profit as its lodestar'? Moreover, not all of the Dutch on Deshima were merely dollar-grubbing and dollar-grinding merchants, whose only diversions were the pipe and the bottle. Many of them were just that. But there was also a fair number of intelligent men, who took some interest in Japanese culture. They made the best of their very restricted opportunities, which were compounded by the fact that they were strictly forbidden to learn the language.

Engelbert Kaempfer, a German physician who was in the country in 1690-92, produced a remarkably accurate description of Japan, which was published posthumously in English in 1728, under the rather misleading title of *A History of Japan*. A Japanese author, writing in 1804, commented: 'The existence of this Holland Factory at Deshima has called into being books like Kaempfer's, which depicts our country's situation so well, that I, never having been in the Kwanto, still know what that district is like, because I have read this Dutch book. And so the Europeans know. Is this not terrible?' Nowadays, Japanese

3. THE EXTENSION AND DOMINATION OF THE WEST

historians avidly study the records of the Dutch East India Company from Hirado and Deshima, still preserved in the archives at the Hague, in order to glean information about social and other conditions in Tokugawa Japan, which the more percipient Dutch observers noted, but which are not available in Japanese sources since they were taken for granted by indigenous contemporaries.

The Japanese showed themselves to be as complaisant about providing the Dutch on Deshima with women, as they had originally been with the Portuguese. Kaempfer took a rather jaundiced view of the system as operated by the Nagasaki officials, although he did not object to much to the immorality involved as to the prices charged. 'They also take care to furnish our people on demand with whores; and truly our young sailors unacquainted as they commonly are with the virtues of temperance, are not ashamed to spend five or six dollars for one night's pleasure, and with such wenches too, whom a native of Nagasaki could have for two or three *mas* [small silver coin], they being none of the best and handsomest'. As the average Dutch sailor's basic pay was then the equivalent of five or six dollars a month, this was certainly not a cheap night's 'rest and recreation' for Jan Maat (Jack Tar).

Needless to say, it was not only young sailors who patronized these prostitutes; their clients included respectable middle-aged Dutch merchants, as no foreign women were allowed on Deshima. The Swedish botanist and traveller, C.P. Thunberg noted that in his time (1775-76), 'One of these female companions cannot be kept for less than three days, but she may be kept as long as one pleases, a year, or even several years together.' Most of the daily fee was paid to the brothel-keeper; but the girls sometimes got rich presents from their Dutch lovers, whom they in turn obliged by smuggling expensive goods, such as watches, into the town for sale at high prices. Children were seldom born of these unions. When they did produce offspring, the fathers were allowed to provide for the education of their children, but could not take them out of Japan. Thunberg adds in this connection: 'During my stay in this country, I saw a girl of about six years of age, who very much resembled her father, a European, and remained with him on our small island, the whole year through.' These romances were sometimes continued by correspondence, long after the lovers had parted with no hope of seeing each other again. Some of these letters from Japanese prostitutes to their former Dutch lovers are still preserved in the Netherlands.

The Dutch did not employ Negro slaves, but they did have Indonesian slaves and servants on Deshima. These likewise intrigued the Japanese, and are often depicted in colour-prints of the so-called *Nagasaki-e*, a form of Pop-Art produced for sale to Japanese tourists. These Indonesians were also allowed to have the services of prostitutes if they could afford to pay them. On one occasion, these ladies smuggled out some of their patrons, disguised in women's clothes, and took them to the brothel-quarter of Maruyama, where a good time was had by all until they were discovered and severely disciplined. One of the questions most commonly asked of Western men in Japan is "What do you think of Japanese women?" There has never been any doubt about the answer since the first Southern Barbarian to land at Tanegashima in 1543 asked for and received the local swordsmith's daughter in exchange for his own arquebus.

NOTES ON FURTHER READING

C.R. Boxer, *The Christian Century in Japan, 1549-1650.* (University of California Press, 1951, 1981); *Jan Compagnie in War and Peace, 1602-1799* (Heinemann (Asia), Hong Kong, 1979). Michael Cooper, S.J., *They Came to Japan. An Anthology of European Reports on Japan, 1543-1640* (Thames and Hudson, and University of California Press, 1965). George Elison, *Deus Destroyed. The Image of Christianity in Early Modern Japan* (Harvard University Press, 1973).

Sarah Bernhardt's Paris

Christopher Hibbert

CHRISTOPHER HIBBERT is a prize-winning British author of more than 30 books of history, military history and biography. They include *The Days of the French Revolution; The Great Mutiny: India 1857; Versailles; The Court of St. James's; The House of the Medici; Disraeli and His World;* and biographies of Charles I, George IV and Edward VII.

In the summer of 1862 an astonishingly thin young girl with a pale face, frizzy reddish hair, intense blue eyes and a prominent nose stood on the corner of the Rue Duphet and the Rue St. Honore in Paris looking at the yellow playbills which were pasted up to advertise forthcoming productions at the Theatre Francais. *Iphigenie by Jean Racine,* one of these playbills announced, *For the Debut of Mademoiselle Sarah Bernhardt.* "I have no idea how long I stood there, fascinated by the letters of my name," she recorded years later. "But I remember that it seemed to me as though every person who stopped to read the poster looked at me afterwards."

Sarah Bernhardt was then just eighteen. Her mother, a beautiful woman of Jewish Dutch descent, had once been a milliner and was now a highly successful courtesan with an apartment in the Rue St. Honore where, so it was said, attractive women of her calling could command a hundred thousand francs a month and enjoy the use of two carriages and the services of a footman and a chef. Certainly Julie Bernhardt lived well, and in her comfortable apartment received a succession of generous friends, protectors and lovers, bankers and noblemen, musicians and writers. They included the Italian composer Gioacchino Rossini, who had settled in Paris some years before, Alexandre Dumas, the prodigal, exuberant author of *The Three Musketeers,* who believed that in fiction as in life the two most important ingredients were "*l'action et l'amour,*" and Charles Auguste-Louis-Joseph, Duc de Morny, the half-brother of the Emperor Napoleon III whose *coup d'etat* he had helped to engineer.

Napoleon III had been born in Paris in 1808, the third son of a younger brother of Napoleon I. Adventurer and idealist—though with his waxed moustache and half-closed eyes, looking, as Theophile Gautier said, "more like a ringmaster who has been sacked for getting drunk"—he believed himself to be a man of destiny, bound to follow his star. After the overthrow of the Orleans monarchy in 1848 he was elected Prince President of the Second Republic, and four years later, following the *coup d'etat* by which he forcibly dissolved the *Assemblee Nationale Legislative,* he was proclaimed Emperor. Since then, with the help of Baron Haussmann, Prefet de la Seine, he had been transforming Paris, intent not only upon freeing the fine monuments of the past from the jumble of buildings that enclosed them on every side, and upon creating a modern dazzling *ville lumiere* with wide, gaslit boulevards and magnificent perspectives, but also upon ensuring that it became a capital city which artillery could overawe with clear fields of fire against revolutionary mobs.

Under Haussmann's ruthless direction pavements were torn up and narrow streets demolished; grandiose apartment blocks took the place of huddled houses whose poor occupants were forced out into the suburbs. Five hundred miles of water mains were laid, over 200 miles of sewers; more than 30,000 gas lamps replaced the ancient lanterns; railway stations were constructed close to the heart of the city. Imposing new thoroughfares were driven through the gardens of the Luxembourg Palace; the Boulevard de Sebastopol made its way through a populous district beside the cast-iron and glass food markets known as Les Halles; the Boulevard Haussmann pushed east from the Place de l'Etoile; the Boulevards Saint-Germain and St. Michel and the Rue de Rennes appeared on the Left Bank. The Ile de la Cite was transformed and its greatest pride, Notre-Dame, restored under the direction of Eugene-Emmanuel Viollet-le-Duc. The Tuileries and the Cour Carree were joined by a new gallery along a lengthened Rue de Rivoli. The Bois de Boulogne was laid out with artificial lakes and carriage drives. In 1861 the foundation stone of a vast opera house, which was to occupy almost three acres, was laid to the north of the Boulevard des Italiens; and here, after fourteen years' work, Charles Garnier's extravagant edifice, decorated with 33 varieties of marble and the works of 73 sculptors, was opened at last, a fitting tribute to the pomp and opulent display of the Second Empire.

In this prosperous and rapidly changing city of 1,825,000 people, the cosmopolitan capital of the world, the working day of the poor began as those more fortunate were going to bed after a night of pleasure. Before dawn *chiffonniers* appeared with lanterns and forks and with baskets on their backs to poke through the piles of rubbish which had been thrown out into the streets, searching for rags and bones, bottles and jars, hoping to find, and sometimes finding, an article more valuable before the rubbish wagons trundled along to cart the mounds away. And then, as the sun came up,

3. THE EXTENSION AND DOMINATION OF THE WEST

bootblacks came out with scissors as well as brushes for they were as expert at clipping poodles as they were at polishing shoes; women who sold sweetmeats in the streets prepared their trays of cakes and chocolates, while soup and coffee vendors took up their places on the Pont Notre-Dame; *marchands de coco,* relics of the time of King Louis Philippe, wearing cocked hats and little bells, chopped up lemons and sticks of licorice to flavor the water they carried on their backs in highly polished ornamental tanks to offer for sale in goblets to thirsty passers-by; mechanics greased the wheels of the roundabouts in the Champs Elysees where gardeners watered the exotic flowers; and waiters scattered damp sand under the tables of cafes where clerks and laborers called for coffee and croisettes, brandy plums, absinthe or cheap Orleans wine as they streamed down on their way to work from the heights of Montmartre and La Chapelle, smoking clay pipes, toolbags slung on their backs and loaves of bread under their arms—masons in white jackets, locksmiths in blue overalls, tilers in blouses and small round caps, painters in long smocks swinging their pots, bricklayers with hods on their shoulders, chimney-sweepers harnessed to their barrows of soot.

After their *petit dejeuner* visitors from the country and foreign tourists emerged from their hotels, from the Hotel de Helder; the Hotel Louvre in the Place du Palais Royal which the enterprising Pereire brothers, Emile and Isaac, had built for the Paris Exhibition of 1855; from the even larger Grand Hotel on the Boulevard des Capucines which, with its 750 rooms was the largest in Europe; and from the Ambassade, the Ritz, and the Bristol which, patronized by the Prince of Wales who stayed there, ineffectively incognito, as the Duke of Lancaster, was to become the most fashionable of all.

The doors of the shops now opened, of the smaller, smarter boutiques whose prices varied in accordance with the apparent wealth or gullibility of their customers; of Denton's bookshop in the Palais-Royal where 6,000 copies of the Goncourt brothers' *La Lorette* had been sold in a single week in 1853; and of those recent phenomena, the large department stores, the Maison du Bon Marche, which had been founded by Norman Boucicaut in 1852, Chaucard's Louvre in the Rue de Rivoli and Jaluzot's Au Printemps on the Boulevard Haussmann. Their shopping done, mothers and nurses took their children and charges out to play with hoops and balls and wooden horses on wheels by the sparkling fountains in the gardens of the Tuileries, wearing billowing, brilliantly colored and intricately embroidered crinolines and flowered hats, while men walked past on their way to the Jockey Club, the Club de L'Union or Le Cercle Agricole, resplendent in shining silk hats, long, narrow-waisted coats, elaborate cravats and tight trousers with buttons down the seams.

By midday the boulevards were crowded with horse-drawn *imperiale* omnibuses, with phaetons and *voitures a laquais,* cockaded coachmen and footmen sitting on the boxes. Smaller equipages, fiacres, traps, landaus and tandems rattled down the Champs Elysees towards the Bois de Boulogne to parade around the lakes and along the Allee des Poteaux. Soon the green iron chairs beneath the striped awnings of the cafes and restaurants were occupied; and familiar faces could be seen at the Cafe de Cardinal on the corner of the Rue Richelieu, at Tortoni's on the Boulevard des Italiens, next door to the Restaurant de la Maison Doree, at the Cafe de Paris which was the favorite haunt of Eugene Sue, Heinrich Heine and Balzac, and at the Moulin Rouge, a smart restaurant on the Champs Elysees where "at the bottom of the garden, at all the windows on every floor, in the lighted depths of private rooms, just as in boxes at the theater, women's heads could be seen nodding left and right to former companions of their nights." In the evenings, as guests set out for fancy dress balls and private dinner parties and the cafe-concerts and the theaters began to fill, crowds collected outside the Theatre Francais to watch the fashionable and famous go into the House of Moliere.

Here it was that Sarah Bernhardt had decided to become an actress. She had been taken by her mother and three of her mother's friends—Regis Lavolie, a rich banker, Dumas and the Duc de Morny—to see a performance of Racine's *Britannicus*. She had found it so moving that she had burst into tears and then into sobs so loud that her mother blushed scarlet in embarrassment, other members of the audience had turned round calling "Sh! Sh!" and Lavolie had stalked out of the box in disgust, slamming the door behind him.

On their return to Julie Bernhardt's apartment, Sarah had been sent to bed in disgrace. But Dumas had kindly gone up with her and, kissing her at her door, had whispered in her ear, "Good night, little star." Her chance of being a star had come in 1862 with her performance of *Iphigenie*. She had worked hard for the opportunity. With the influential help of the Duc de Morny, she had been granted an audition at the Conservatoire; then, having attended the classes there with enthusiastic assiduity, she had been taken on as a *pensionnaire* by the Comedie Francaise.

Overcome by stage fright, she gabbled her words throughout the first act, and although she recovered her confidence later on, neither audience nor critics were favorably impressed. Her subsequent performances were equally disappointing, and it was widely felt that the Comedie-Francaise had been ill-advised to take her on in the first place. There was little regret when, after breaking her parasol over the head of the stage doorkeeper for some imagined slight and punching an elderly actress in the face during a violent quarrel, she was told to resign from the company. At least she could comfort herself with the thought that she had made a name for herself. Caricatures and stories about her appeared in the newspapers; and her mother's friend, Lavolie, had little difficulty in persuading the directors of the Gymnase, a theater which specialized in popular comedies, to give the now notorious young actress another chance. She did not flourish at the Gymnase either, though, and after one particularly disastrous performance, which reduced her to thoughts of suicide, she decided to follow Dumas' advice and go abroad for a time. According to her own account she went to Spain. But, since her own accounts were always flavored by a reckless indifference to truth, she may well have gone no further than Brussels. Certainly she returned to Paris pregnant

22. Sarah Bernhardt's Paris

by a Belgian aristocrat, the paternity of whose child she ascribed at various times to Leon Gambetta, Victor Hugo, General Boulanger and even to the infant Duke of Clarence who was, in fact, born a fortnight before his alleged progeny.

Within a few weeks of Maurice Bernhardt's birth, his mother went back to work, this time at the Porte-Saint-Martin, a theater renowned for its melodramas and *vaudevilles feeriques.* Here yet again she proved a disappointment. And it was not until—once more with the help of one of her mother's friends—she signed a contract at the Odeon, a national theater on the Left Bank near the Jardin du Luxembourg, that she made her mark at last. Here, in the leading female role in a revival of Dumas' *Kean,* she enjoyed her first unalloyed success. Thereafter triumph followed triumph. Her name on the playbills was sure to fill the theater. She became the darling of the Left Bank. After her portrayal of the minstrel boy Zanetto in Francois Coppee's *Le Passant* in 1868, the Emperor's cousin, Princess Mathilde, arranged for a command performance at the Tuileries where she so impressed the Emperor himself that he gave her a splendid brooch blazing with diamonds. She moved into a large apartment in the Rue Auber; and here, in an untidy clutter of furniture and ornaments, over which turtles with gold-plated shells crawled to escape from barking dogs, she received an assortment of friends and lovers even more varied and distinguished than those who had paid court to her mother.

She entertained Leon Gambetta, then a young barrister and leading member of the political opposition, who was one day to become President of the Chamber of Deputies. She welcomed Princess Mathilde's brother, Prince Napoleon, like his sister a patron of literature and the arts, and a patron, too, of Cora Pearl, the saucy, irresistible English courtesan who was known to have presented herself to her admirers wearing nothing but a sprig of parsley. Sarah Bernhardt also welcomed Theophile Gautier, *"le bon Theo,"* whose praise of her art had done much to further her career. And, with particular pleasure, she opened her arms to Gautier's friend, George Sand, who, many years before, had left her husband, Baron Dudevant, to lead an independent, unconventional life in Paris, writing novels, wearing trousers, smoking incessantly, nursing Alfred de Musset through an illness before deserting him for his doctor, then going to live with Chopin. She was in her mid-sixties now, but working as hard as ever: Sarah Bernhardt appeared in two of her plays and grew to admire and to love her.

Both Gautier and George Sand were members of that coterie of writers and artists who, during these final years of the Second Empire, met regularly at Magny's, the restaurant in the Rue Contrescarpe-Dauphine which was run by Modeste Magny, an exceptionally gifted restaurateur from the Marne. George Sand had been one of his earliest customers, preferring his restaurant to the Pinson in the Rue de l'Ancienne-Comedie which she had previously patronized, despite the row made next door to Magny's by the performers and spectators at Aublin's *Les Folies Dauphine,* a *boui-boui* or music-hall known more familiarly as *Le Beuglant* because of the bellowing sounds that burst from its windows.

George Sand had not, however, been present at the inauguration of the dining club at Magny's on November 22, 1862. On this Saturday evening among those present had been the once lively but now rather morose lithographer and caricaturist Gavarni, whose sketches of Parisian life had been one of the most notable features in the satirical paper, *Le Charivari*; Gavarni's friends and future biographers, the two inseparable brothers, Edmond and Jules de Goncourt, novelists, social historians, diarists and men of letters, who spoke alternately, the one elaborating, complementing and developing the remarks of the other; and the great critic, Sainte-Beuve, an ugly, fat little man with a black skull-cap on his bald head, now nearing the end of his life but seeming to enjoy it as much as in those earlier days when he had been the lover of Victor Hugo's wife and had dined in a private room every Saturday night at Magny's with other women friends. On later occasions these four had been joined by Gustave Flaubert, the robust though syphilitic author of *Madame Bovary* and *Salammbo*; by the philogist and historian, Ernest Renan whose influential and controversial *Vie de Jesus* cost him the professorship of Hebrew at the College de France; the towering, bearded Ivan Turgenev, out of favor with the rulers of his native Russia; and Hippolyte Taine, critic and philosopher, whose *Histoire de la litterature anglaise* had appeared in three volumes in 1862.

They dined in one of the seven private rooms on the first floor, served by the head waiter, Charles Labran, who was to remain at Magny's until his master's death. And, as the Goncourts wrote in their journal after their first dinner there, they enjoyed "an exquisite meal, perfect in every respect, a meal such as [they] had thought impossible to obtain in a Paris restaurant." The *specialites de la maison* were *tournedos Rossini, chateaubriand, petites marmites, puree Magny* and *becasses a la Charles,* all of which the proprietor had contrived himself. Also exquisitely cooked at Magny's were *pieds de mouton a la poulette,* and *ecrevisses a la Bordelaise* which, as one customer said, "once you had begun eating there was no reason to stop, and you didn't stop either, unless there was a revolution or an earthquake."

With such dishes Magny gained for himself a special commendation in Adolphe Joanne's guide to the restaurants of Paris which, dividing them all into six categories, considered only a few worthy of being listed in the first class. Apart from Magny's and Philippe's in the Rue Montorqueil, the knowledgeable *bon viveur* recommended Brebant's, haunt of the racing people from Longchamps and Chantilly; Vefour's for Rhenish carp, baked and stuffed and surrounded by soft roe; Ledoyen's for salmon with a green sauce the secret of which was unknown to other establishments; Aux Trois Freres Provencaux for cod with garlic; the Cafe Riche for *sole aux crevettes*; the Maison Doree for fillet steak, braised with tomatoes and mushrooms and served with "a veritable gravy of truffles"; and Bignon's for *barbue au vin rouge* and *filet Richelieu.* But though there were so few restaurants which Joanne could recommend without reserve, he calculated that there were 4,000 pot-houses which were "frequented only by workmen and coachmen." And even in

3. THE EXTENSION AND DOMINATION OF THE WEST

these cheaper places the food was generally good and the service excellent, for in a city where prosperity had created an apparently insatiable demand for pleasure, those in search of it had learned to be discriminating.

"Civility appears to be the motive power of his life," an English visitor wrote of the Parisian waiter. "That wonderful fleetness with which he dashes through the cafe into the open air, and threads his way through rows of lounging customers at the green tables, carrying on the tops of his four fingers and thumb an immense pile of cups, liqueur glasses, bottles of iced water, and lumps of sugar . . . appears to be the noble effort of a chivalrous nature. Ask him for a light and he produces lucifers from any pocket. Although people are calling him or hissing to him in various directions, he finds time to light two or three lucifers and even to hold them till the fumes of the sulphur have passed away before he presents them to you . . . He is free with you; he has a light retort for any attempted joke; but he is never familiar—never rude . . . The reader who wishes to study the Parisian waiter in perfection, should choose a fine summer's night, and take his seat outside the rotunda in the Palais Royal about eight o'clock, in the midst of about 300 people, served by about eight waiters, who caper, loaded with crockery and newspapers with an activity that any Harlequin might envy."

There were numerous cafes in the Palais Royal, mostly expensive and respectable. But for those who preferred less decorous establishments there were even more of these elsewhere. Paris, indeed, was a very *embarras de richesse* of cafes, cafe-concerts, taverns, *bouillons, cremeries, brasseries, pensions bourgeoises, assommoirs* and *estaminets* as well as brothels, *cabinets particuliers* and licentious dance-halls. One on the best known brothels was Farcy's where, in the drawing-room, sprawling on red velvet divans around the floral-papered walls, the girls smiled and cooed and asked for drinks. One of the most expensive *cabinets particuliers* was the Grand Seize, an exotic private room at the Cafe Anglais hung with red wallpaper and gold hieroglyphics, furnished with gilt chairs and a crimson sofa, where Sarah Bernhardt was herself to be entertained by the Prince of Wales. And one of the most lively and wanton dance-halls was Mabille's in the Allee des Veuves where an orchestra of 50 played in a Chinese pavilion surrounded by artificial palm trees with gas globes hanging from the leaves; where, as a guidebook warned, "the limits of propriety [were] frequently passed"; and where parlor-maids, *grisettes* and milliners could find men willing to pay them twenty francs for a night of pleasure, more than they could otherwise earn in a month.

In the summer of 1870 the carefree frivolity of the Second Empire came suddenly to a close. Napoleon III declared war on Prussia, and a few weeks later his army was crushingly defeated at Sedan. The confidence of the Parisians, who had never believed in the remotest possibility of such a catastrophe, was shattered overnight.

"Who can describe the consternation written on every face," wrote Edmond de Goncourt as his fellow citizens pondered on the consequences of the fall of the imperial government, "the sound of aimless steps pacing the streets at random, the anxious conversations of shopkeepers and *concierges* on their doorsteps, the crowds collecting at street-corners, the siege of the newspaper kiosks, the triple line of readers gathering around every gas-lamp."

At news of the German army's approach, preparations for the expected siege of Paris gathered momentum. Mines were laid, woods chopped down, road blocks thrown up, road and river approaches obstructed, monuments protected by sandbags and boarding; and the capital's extensive defensive system of bastions, walls, moats and forts—which Adolphe Thiers had had constructed in 1840 but which had subsequently been neglected—was hastily restored and strengthened. Railway stations were converted into balloon factories or cannon-foundries, theaters into hospitals; couturiers' workshops began to make military uniforms, the Louvre to turn out armaments. Regular troops, marines and sailors marched into the city; conscripts and volunteers paraded through the streets; thousands of heavy guns were dragged out to the forest, while herds of cattle and sheep were driven into the Bois de Boulogne.

In the excitement of all this activity the morale of the Parisians rose. On September 13, a few days before the last mail-train left the city and the one remaining telegraph line to the west was cut, a review of the defenders was held by General Louis-Jules Trochu, president of the newly formed Government of National Defense, who galloped onto the scene to the rattle of drums and to shouts of *"Vive la France! Vive la Republique! Vive Trochu!"* Tens of thousands of soldiers lined the boulevards from the Place de la Bastille to the Arc de Triomphe. The National Guard, some in frock-coats, others in workmen's smocks, marched past to the strains of the *Marseillaise,* their rifles decorated with flowers and ribbons, children holding their fathers' hands.

Poets declaimed their verses; journalists issued proclamations; politicians harangued the crowds; priests preached sermons. Adelaide de Montgolfier, daughter of the great balloonist, watched the *Neptune,* the first postal balloon to leave Paris, soar into the sky above the Place Saint-Pierre in Montmartre, shouts of *"Vive la Republique!"* ringing in her ears, proud to think that her "dear father's invention [was] now proving of such great value to his country."

Enthusiasm was not matched, though, by achievement. Outside the city the French troops proved no match for the German invaders. Dejected and dispirited soldiers returned disconsolately from the front to the streets of Paris where already long queues were to be seen outside the butchers' shops as early as two o'clock in the morning and the restaurants started to serve beef that looked suspiciously like horse flesh. Looking for scapegoats, the Parisians turned on foreigners, particularly on the English residents who were believed to share their Queen's sympathetic attitude towards Germany: *Les Nouvelles* proposed that the best way to settle the question as to whether the British were spies or not was to shoot the lot of them. "Anyone who did not speak French with purity was arrested," commented Trochu's aide-de-camp, Maurice d'Herisson. "Englishmen, Americans, Swedes, Spaniards and Alsatians were arrested alike. A similar fate befell all those who, either in dress

22. Sarah Bernhardt's Paris

or manner, betrayed anything unusual. Stammerers were arrested because they tried to speak too quickly; dumb people because they did not speak at all; and the deaf because they did not seem to understand what was said to them. The sewermen who emerged from the sewers were arrested because they spoke Piedmontese."

The people turned, too, on Trochu and his government whom they accused of not facing the crisis with sufficient determination. Demonstrations were held in the Place de la Concorde; marches made to the Hotel de Ville; demands presented for a *levee en masse* and a *sortie en masse,* the election of a Municipal Commune, the formation of a corps of Amazons, the manufacture of "guns, more guns and still more guns." At the end of October news reached the capital that Marshal Bazaine had surrendered Metz to the enemy and that Le Bourget, a village north of Paris which had been captured by the Prussians, had been retaken by them. There were also rumors that Leon Gambetta, who, with a basket of homing pigeons, had left Paris by balloon at the beginning of the month to join the elderly members of the Delegation of Tours, was inclining to their view that surrender was inevitable.

Incensed by all this, a crowd of about 15,000 demonstrators advanced on the Hotel de Ville, shouting "No armistice!" and "The Commune forever!" Several hundred of them burst inside the building, demanding the resignation of all the members of the Government of National Defense and calling out the names of men whom they wished to replace them. Their leaders—with Gustave Flourens, a revolutionary member of the National Guard, well to the fore—climbed onto the baize covered table of the council-chamber and strode along it, trampling on papers and notebooks, knocking over inkstands and sandboxes, crushing pens and pencils, their voices lost in the clangor of shouts, drums and trumpets, while General Trochu calmly smoked his cigar.

Trochu's apparent indifference to these agitators was justified: an energetic colleague, Ernest Picard, called upon the more constructive leaders of the National Guard for help, and a bourgeois battalion marched to the Government's rescue. While Flourens went into hiding, Parisians were asked to answer the following question in a plebiscite: "Does the population of Paris wish to maintain the powers of the Government of National Defense? *Oui ou Non*?" Overwhelmingly the answer was yes.

So Trochu continued in office; his forces remained on the defensive; and Paris grew more and more to resemble a beleagured city. Many shops put up their shutters, having nothing to sell; others filled their windows with telescopes, knives, revolvers and brandy-flasks. Fashionable clothes were no longer conspicuous on the boulevards: men wore makeshift uniforms, women their oldest dresses or nurses' aprons.

As Henry Labouchere, Paris correspondent of the London *Daily News,* recorded on November 15, Paris' mood now veered wildly "from the lowest depths of despair to the wildest confidence. Yesterday afternoon a pigeon arrived covered with blood, bearing on his tail a despatch from Gambetta, announcing that the Prussians had been driven out of Orleans ... The despatch was read at the Mairies to large crowds, and in the cafes by enthusiasts who got up on the tables. I was in a shop when a person came in with it. Shopkeepers, assistants and customers immediately performed a war dance round a stove."

This festive mood was short-lived. People were soon complaining again about the National Guard, who performed very confidently on parade but showed little inclination to fight the enemy, and about General Trochu who, so one junior officer said, had associated so much with lawyers that he had become to resemble one himself: "He has dipped his pen in his scabbard and his sword in his inkstand, and when he finally attempts to draw the sword, he'll unsheath a penholder." Hopes were raised at the end of November by rumors of a great sortie involving 150,000 men who were to cross the Marne and occupy the enemy's positions at Champigny. But these hopes were dashed when the crowds, which had gathered at Pont d'Austerlitz and along the Avenue du Trone, learned that the sortie had ended in tragic failure. Hard upon this reverse came news of the defeat of the Army of the Loire and the recapture of Orleans. Less than a fortnight later the spirits of the people were revived again by an optimistic message from Gambetta published in the *Journal Officiel,* only to be dampened soon afterwards by the failure of another sortie.

In common with most other theaters and many hotels, the Odeon was converted into a hospital. Assuming the responsibility for organizing it, Sarah Bernhardt rushed from one admirer to another, asking for supplies, obtaining brandy from Baron Rothschild, chocolate from Meunier, sardines from the rich grocer, Felix Potin, outside whose store in the Boulevard de Strasbourg long queues stood throughout the night. Acting as nurse as well as storekeeper, she dressed wounds, assisted at operations, carried food to the helpless and brandy to the dying; and as the weeks passed and the supplies of food grew ever more depleted, often went without meals herself so that the patients might be fed.

By the end of the year the shortage of food in Paris had become acute. Beef and mutton, at first severely rationed, now disappeared from the shops altogether. Cab-horses and race-horses were sold by the butchers instead, then cats, rats and dogs. Eels and gudgeons from the Seine fetched their weight in silver.

"People talk of nothing but what is eaten, can be eaten, or is there to be eaten [wrote Edmond de Goncourt]. Conversation has come down to this:

" 'You know, a fresh egg costs twenty-five sous.'

" 'It appears there's a fellow who buys up all the candles he can find, adds some coloring, and produces that fat which sells at such a price.'

" 'Mind you don't buy any coconut butter. It stinks a house out for three days at least.'

" 'I've had some dog chops, and found them really very tasty: they look just like mutton chops.'

" 'Who was it who told me he had eaten some kangaroo?' "

As well as kangaroo, the director of the zoo sold all manner of animals for slaughter—buffaloes and zebras, reindeer and camels, yaks and elephants. But these animals were soon consumed. And "failing meat," one com-

3. THE EXTENSION AND DOMINATION OF THE WEST

mentator observed, "you cannot fall back on vegetables: a little turnip costs eight sous and you have to pay seven francs for a pound of onions. Nobody talks about butter any more, and every other sort of fat except candle-fat and axle-grease has disappeared too. As for the two staple items of the diet of the poor—potatoes and cheese—cheese is just a memory, and you have to have friends in high places to obtain potatoes at twenty francs a bushel. The greater part of Paris is living on coffee, wine and bread." And even bread, a hard black substance made principally of bran, rice and starch, was scarce.

Hunger was not the only privation. By the end of the year the temperature had fallen to twelve degrees below zero. While sentries froze to death, orders were given for the felling of six square miles of trees in the Bois de Boulogne and the Bois de Vincennes and along the city's boulevards. But the people could not wait: fences, trellises, benches and telegraph poles were cut up as well and dragged away to their homes.

To cold and hunger and the attendant sickness and disease was added the horror of bombardment. At first it was only the forts that were shelled. But at the beginning of January 1871, shells began also to burst in the city itself, mainly on the poorer houses on the Left Bank where the people bore the cannonade with stoic courage. "On every doorstep, women and children stand, half frightened, half inquisitive," wrote Edmond de Goncourt, "watching the medical orderlies going by, dressed in white smocks with red crosses on their arms and carrying stretchers, mattresses and pillows."

Before long most people grew quite accustomed to the bombing. Children, hearing an explosion, would say, "That was a shell," and then calmly continue with their game. And street urchins on seeing a well dressed person walk by, so Henry Labouchere observed, would cry out, "Flat! Flat! A shell—a shell—*a plat ventre!* Down on your faces!" "The man, gorgeous in fur, falls flat on the ground—perhaps in the gutter—and the Parisian urchin rejoices with exceeding great joy."

Despite all the hardships, Labouchere continued, the Parisians behaved with remarkable resignation. They criticized Trochu and the government endlessly, denouncing their mistakes and blunders; but, they made "no complaint about their miseries," accepting them "with an unpretending fortitude which no people in the world could surpass." By the end of January, however, it was clear that resistance could not much longer be maintained. Men and women were falling down dead in food queues; the death rate rose to almost 4,500 a week, many of these being children. "At every step," one survivor wrote, "you met an undertaker carrying a little deal coffin."

Edmond de Goncourt was struck by the deathly silence that had fallen over the city. You could no longer hear Paris living, he noted in his journal. Every face looked liked like that of a sick person or convalescent. You saw "nothing but thin, pallid features, faces as pale and yellow as horseflesh." One day a prostitute, splashing along behind him in the Rue Saint-Nicholas, called out pathetically, "Monsieur, will you come up to my room, for a piece of bread?"

On January 23, Jules Favre, the Foreign Minister, left Paris for the German headquarters at Versailles to open negotiations for surrender. "A tall, thin, stooping, miserable-looking lawyer," as his secretary described him, "with his wrinkled frock-coat and his white hair falling over his collar," he seemed no match for Count Bismarck, the robust, broad-chested Iron Chancellor, who received Favre in the tight, white tunic and yellow-banded cap of the White Cuirassiers. Yet Favre's apparent weakness, real dignity and "good old French manners" worked to his advantage. "It is very difficult for me to be as hard with him as I have to be," Bismarck told his wife. "The rascals know this, and consequently push him forward." The terms imposed upon them were, therefore, not as hard as the French had feared they might be. But they were nevertheless obliged to agree to the German army's ceremonial march into the capital. So, on Wednesday, March 1, German troups escorted by blaring bands and by cavalry with drawn swords, paraded through the Arc de Triomphe and down the Champs Elysees.

Parisians, their houses shuttered and their shops closed, were now in a bitter mood, harboring resentment not only against the Germans but also against the Government and the generals who, they felt, had failed them, as well as against the rich who, during the siege, had been able to pay for the food and warmth denied to others and who, now that it was over, had left for the country. There was resentment, too, against the provinces which, having escaped most of the horrors of the war, chose to elect a predominantly royalist assembly. In protest a *Federation Republicaine de la Garde Nationale* was formed; and insurgents established the Commune of Paris.

Civil war was now inevitable. On the orders of Adolphe Thiers, soon to be President of the Third Republic, an army of regulars was collected at Versailles under General MacMahon and marched into Paris. The subsequent slaughter was fearful. Prisoners taken by the Versailles forces were shot out of hand; in retaliation the Commune seized hostages, including the Archbishop of Paris and the Presiding Judge of the Court of Appeals, and executed them. In the Rue Haxo scores of other hostages, among them several priests, were shot by a frenzied crowd of men and women. Street battles raged and the pavements ran with blood; numerous public buildings were destroyed. The Palais des Tuileries and the Hotel de Ville, the Palais Royal and the Louvre, the Ministry of Finance and the Prefecture de Police were all set on fire. By the time the last defenders of the Commune had been shot down in the Pere Lachaise cemetery nearly 20,000 people, men, women and children, had lost their lives—more than the total number who had perished in the whole of France throughout the six years of the Revolution of 1789-95.

During the days of the Commune Bernhardt had left Paris to escape from the vindictive Prefect of Police whom she had much offended in the past by contemptuously returning to him a play he had written which she had said was "unworthy to touch let alone to read." But as soon as the troubles were over she returned to her

22. Sarah Bernhardt's Paris

apartment over which she splashed bottles full of her favorite scent to disperse the smell of smoke from the still smoldering buildings on every side. Victor Hugo had also returned from exile in Guernsey to what he himself described as "an indescribable welcome" from fellow republicans who elected him a senator. Although he was now in his seventies his career as poet, novelist and dramatist was far from over; but it was in a play which he had written over 30 years before, *Ruy Blas,* that Bernhardt, as the Queen of Spain, was to achieve the greatest triumph she had yet enjoyed. After the first night Hugo knelt before her to kiss her hand; cheering crowds filled the Rue Vaugirard; and a band of admiring young men unharnessed the horses of her carriage to drag it back themselves to her apartment, excitedly shouting "Make way for our Sarah!"

A few weeks later she was invited to return to the Theatre Francais. And here, in *Britannicus,* in Voltaire's *Zaire,* above all in Racine's *Phedre,* which some critics thought she played even more movingly than Rachel, she established herself as the most powerful dramatic actress of her time, mesmerizing her audiences, as Arthur Symons thought, "awakening the senses and sending the intelligence to sleep," interpreting her parts instinctively rather that intellectually with a kind of hypnotic fervor, and speaking in a voice in which, as Lytton Strachey said, "there was more than gold, there was thunder and lightning, there was heaven and hell."

As well as a great actress, Bernhardt also become known as a most outlandishly eccentric showman about whom stories—many invented, others that were not, yet seemed so—filled column after column in newspapers and magazines. Her apartment in the Rue de Rome and the house she later built on the corner of the Rue Fortury and the Avenue de Villiers, were furnished and decorated in the most bizarre manner, with a satin-lined resewood coffin in which she sometimes slept and a canopied fur-strewn divan prominent amidst the medley of ill-matched chairs, tables, cupboards, carpets, a stuffed vulture, a leering skeleton and works of art of extraordinarily uneven quality. Visitors were likely to be accosted by an alarming variety of strange animals, wild cats, hawks, a baby tigress, a puma that ate Dumas *fils'* straw boater and a boa constrictor that devoured its owner's cushions.

They were also likely to meet many of the most famous and notorious people in Paris, from actors and actresses such as the lovable comedian Constant Coquelin whose creation of *Cyrano de Bergerac* was to become legendary, Sophie Croizette in whose company Bernhardt used to stuff herself with cakes and chocolates in Chiboust's *patisserie,* and the alluring Jean Mounet-Sully, to exotic aesthetes like Robert de Montesquiou and Oscar Wilde, the composer Gounod, Ferndinand de Lesseps and Louis Pasteur. She would hold court on her divan, Persian hangings and the leaves of jungle plants framing her intense, pale, quizzically seductive face, a vast Russian wolfhound sprawled by the fur hem of a dress raised slightly to reveal a pretty, provocative white-stockinged ankle. It was in this pose that one of her numerous lovers, the painter Georges Clairin, portrayed her in a picture which was the principle talking-point of the Academy's 1876 exhibition in the Salon d'Apollon in the Louvre.

Those interested more in art than in iconography, however, were discussing another exhibition that year, the second held by the so-called Impressionists. The growing dissatisfaction of these artists with academic teaching had been brought to a head in 1863 when an exhibition of works rejected by the Salon, including Manet's *Dejeuner sur l'herbe,* was ridiculed by traditionalists. Four of them, Renoir, Sisley, Bazille and Monet were fellow-students at the studio of Marc Charles Gabriel Gleyre. They remained friends after leaving Gleyre's studio and used to meet regularly at the Cafe de la Nouvelle-Athenes in Montmartre, where they were often joined by Pisarro, Cezanne, Degas, Manet and Berthe Morisot. In 1873, after works by several of these artists were turned away by the Salon, they decided to hold an exhibition of their own; and the next year they did so in the studio of Nadar, the aeronaut, caricaturist and photographer. One of the pictures shown was Manet's *Impression, soleil levant* which led a mocking journalist from *Le Charivari* to deride the whole movement as Impressionism, a term which the artists themselves accepted as applying to them all. For, although their school was never a homogeneous one with a jointly recognized purpose, they did share a common belief that painting and its techniques should not be restricted in the way that the Salon seemed to prescribe. "One does not paint a landscape, a seascape, a figure," Manet declared in a summary of the Impressionists's view: "one paints the impression of one hour of the day in a landscape, in a seascape, upon a figure." The Impressionists' exhibition of 1876 was followed by six others in which Caillebotte, Forain and the American exile, Mary Cassatt, also showed their work.

But none of them aroused any interest in Sarah Bernhardt. She far preferred the traditional style of Georges Clairin and the sweetly Romantic pictures of her Lesbian friend, Louise Abbema; and in her own watercolors and facile sculptures, which she occasionally exhibited at the Salon, she displayed no sign of willingness to depart from the accepted Academy style. Discerning critics did not take her work seriously, agreeing with Rodin—whose masterpiece of 1877, *The Age of Bronze,* was condemned by Academicians as scandalous—that it was nothing but "old-fashioned tripe." Bernhardt, however, had one powerful apologist, a moody art critic, the first of whose great cycle of twenty *naturaliste* novels, *Les Rougon-Macquart,* had just been published. This was Emile Zola.

The Paris which Zola described in some of these novels was a far cry from the fashionable restaurants of the Boulevard des Italiens. It was a Paris where life was hard and the working day long, the Paris of the poor as depicted by Honore Daumier, a sad contrast to that of the elegant dandy as sketched by Constantin Guys. Here, in those mean streets northwest of the Gare du Nord, streets of crumbling, leaking tenement buildings and lodging-houses with rotting, rain-sodden shutters, scraggy hens scratched for worms between the pavements; colored streams of water poured from dye-works; butchers in bloodstained aprons stood before the doors of slaughter-houses;

3. THE EXTENSION AND DOMINATION OF THE WEST

men dragged beds and mattresses to pawnshops from which they emerged to get drunk in wine shops, to eat six-sous meals in *bistingos* or to take home paper bags of chipped potatoes or cans of mussels; and, as the factory bells summoned their husbands to work, women carried their dirty clothes to the wash-house where, in steamy air, smelling of sweat and soda and bleach, they banged shirts and trousers against their washboards, their red arms bare to the shoulders, their skirts caught up to reveal darned stockings and heavy laced boots, shouting to each other above the din. This is the world of *L'Assommoir,* of Coupeau, the roofer, and Gervaise, the laundry-woman, and of their daughter, Nana, whose career Zola later unfolded in his great novel of 1880.

The year before *Nana* was published Bernhardt left Paris for the first of those foreign tours which were to make her as celebrated abroad as she was at home. She returned from America in 1881 at the age of 36 to find Zola the most discussed and widely read author in France. She also found herself far from popular with her fellow Parisians who were resentful of her having abandoned their theaters for more lucrative appearances overseas and who were assured by various hostile journalists that she was becoming a prima donna of the most selfish, pretentious and avaricious kind. Her electrifying recitation of the *Marseillaise* at the end of a gala performance of the Opera on the glorious 14th of July, however, followed by a magnificent performance in Victorien Sardou's *Fedora*—whom she portrayed, in Maurice Baring's words, with "such tigerish passion and feline seduction which, whether it be good or bad art, nobody has been able to match since"—restored her to her former preeminence. She followed her Fedora with other equally brilliant performances—as Marguerite Gauthier in Dumas *fils' La Dame aux camelias,* as the Empress in Sardou's even more melodramatic *Theodora,* and as the heroine of Sardou's *Tosca.*

There were failures, too, though, and her private life was unhappy. Her sister, whom she loved dearly and had helped to bring up, died a drug addict. The Greek diplomat and would-be actor, the arrogant, selfish, compulsively satyric Aristide Damala, whom she found sexually enchanting and married, also became a morphine and cocaine addict, shamelessly injecting himself through his trouser leg in front of her friends, and further humiliating her by spending the money she gave him on other women before dying at the age of 34. Her former friend and colleague, Marie Colombier, of whom Manet painted a delightful portrait, revenged herself upon her for a professional slight by writing an obscene and libelous book, *The Memoirs of Sarah Barnum,* which induced Bernhardt to burst upon the author in her apartment, brandishing a dagger in one hand and a riding crop in the other, committing a violent assault which furnished journalists and caricaturists with irresistible copy. Finally, Bernhardt's beloved son, as costly an expense as her husband, quarrelled bitterly with his mother over the Dreyfus case and took himself off with his wife and daughter to the South of France where he remained for over a year, refusing to communicate with her.

Captain Alfred Dreyfus, a Jewish officer of unsullied reputation, was court-martialled in December 1894, found guilty of having passed military secrets to the German Embassy, and sentenced to life imprisonment on Devil's Island. It later appeared that the German's informant was not Dreyfus but another officer, Major Esterhazy. But the War Office suppressed this damaging discovery; and, when Esterhazy was himself court-martialled, he was acquitted. The resultant uproar divided France into rival factions of furiously antagonistic *Dreyfusards* and *anti-Dreyfusards.* Sarah Bernhardt was as violent a champion of Dreyfus as her son was a denigrator of the "Jewish traitor." It is said that it was she who approached her friend Zola and persuaded him to write the celebrated letter, *J'Accuse,* to the President, denouncing the Army's disgraceful behavior. Certainly she proclaimed her sympathies loudly and publicly; professed her horror when Dreyfus, despite all the evidence, was found guilty after a fresh trial; and rejoiced when at last he was pardoned.

The quarrels over the Dreyfus affair were still raging when Bernhardt appeared as the Duc de Reichstadt in Edmond Rostand's *L'Aiglon* which night after night filled the large theater in the Place Chatelet that she had recently taken over at the age of 55 on a 25-year lease, restored and redecorated at immense expense, and renamed the Theatre Sarah Bernhardt. The play opened in March 1900 and was still running to packed houses in the summer when the Great Exhibition of that year filled Paris with visitors from all over the world.

This Exhibiton was one of several which Paris had seen in Sarah Bernhardt's lifetime. The first had been in 1855 when a huge Palais de l'Industrie had been built beside the Champs Elysees and when Gustave Courbet had defiantly held a private exhibition of his work, entitled *Le Realisme,* immediately opposite the Palais des Beaux Arts where the more respectable paintings of Delacroix, Ingres, Vernet and Winterhalter had been shown. The next had been in 1867 when, in an immense brown and gold palace covering 40 acres on the Champ de Mars, the pictures of Jean Francois Millet had been displayed together with numerous marvels of modern science.

"A day at the Exhibition seems a mere hour," wrote Ludovic Halevy, who with Henri Meilhac wrote the libretto for Offenbach's *La Grande-Duchesse de Gerolstein* in which Hortense Schneider appeared at Varietes during the Exhibition's course. "How many things there are to see! . . . There are two miles or so of cafes and restaurants . . . You can eat and drink in every language . . . And the park round the palace, the houses from every land, the factories for glass-blowing and diamond-cutting, the bakery, the machine for making hats, and the machine for making shoes, and the machine for making soap . . . They make everything, these damned machines. I looked everywhere for the machines that turned out plays and novels. They are the only ones that are missing. They will be there at the next Exhibition."

The next Exhibition, the Universal Exhibition, had been held in 1878 to celebrate Paris' quick recovery from the horrors of the Commune. Another Palais de l'Industrie had appeared on the Champ de Mars, and Davioud's ornate palace on the Trocadero; and electric light had illuminated the Avenue de l'Opera. Eleven years later, an-

22. Sarah Bernhardt's Paris

other Universal Exhibition was held on the anniversary of the Revolution. And in that year visitors to Paris had their first sight of what was to become one of Paris' most familiar landmarks, the 300-meters-high iron tower constructed to the designs of Gustave Eiffel. And then in 1900 this new Universal Exhibition attracted over 50,000,000 visitors who visited the fine art shows in the new cast-iron halls by the Pont Alexandre III, who went for rides on the vast great wheel, and admired the immense metal bouquet glittering with electric lights near the Ecole Militaire.

Paris was now a modern city. Horse-drawn vehicles still trotted down the busy streets, but motor cars and electric trams were also to be seen, and the underground metropolitan railway was spreading fast beneath the pavements. *Haute couture* had become a large and thriving industry, enormously expanded since the days when the rich, following the example of the beautiful Empress Eugenie, had gone to the rooms in the Rue de la Paix where the Englishman, Charles Frederick Worth, held sway as the acknowledged arbiter of fashion. Now the firm founded by the banker Isadore Paquin and his wife alone employed nearly 3,000 people. Yet, for all the city's change and growth, its traditional pleasures remained unaltered. The essence of that Paris, to which King Edward VII made his famous and triumphant state visit in 1903, was the same as it had been when he was first captivated by its charm half a century earlier. The cafes of Montmartre, where Paul Verlaine had sat in slippered feet drinking hard until his death in 1896, were little different from those the Goncourts had known a generation before; the performers at the Moulin Rouge, where La Goulue, plump and lascivious, and the pale, thin-legged Jane Avril kicked out their legs in the cancan, were as lively and exciting as Rigolette and Mogador and those other polka dancers at the Mabille in the days of Bernhardt's childhood. The brothels of the Rue des Moulins and Rue d'Amboise, where the ugly, crippled Comte de Toulouse-Lautrec sat closely observing the naked women through his pince-nez and portraying them with realistic sincerity, were much the same as those that Baudelaire had known at the time of the Second Empire.

When Toulouse-Lautrec died in 1901, Bernhardt was approaching her 57th birthday. But age meant nothing to her. She dismissed all thoughts of retirement, putting on play after play, some successful, others not, choosing them for the roles they offered her genius. In 1904 she was still "highly triumphant over time," in the words of Max Beerbohm, who was a professed "lover of Sarah's imcomparable art," though he had derided her Hamlet which had made him wonder if she would next play Othello opposite the booming voiced Mounet-Sully as Desdemona. So little regard did Bernhardt pay to her age, in fact, that when she was 65 she took the leading role in Emile Moreau's *Proces de Jeanne d'Arc* in which she turned with serene confidence to the audience, when the Grand Inquisitor asked Joan her age, to answer in her still beautifully clear, silvery voice, *"Dix-neuf ans"* (19). Night after night the audience broke into rapturous applause.

Not long after the finish of this play's run the Great War broke out. Bernhardt announced her intention of remaining in Paris as she had done in 1870; but she was persuaded to leave by Clemenceau himself who told her that, as she was likely to be on a list of possible hostages, the Government did not want to be responsible for her safety.

She asked to be taken to the station by way of the Champs Elysees which she feared she might never see again. And as she drove into it she was amazed to come upon long lines of taxis, nose to tail and packed with soldiers, stretching as far as the eye could reach. These were the famous *Taxis de la Marne*, rushing troops to the front to reinforce the French 5th and 6th Armies which were making what was to prove a successful counterattack against the German forces on the River Marne.

Bernhardt had left Paris with her right leg in a plaster cast. She had injured it some time before, and by the time she reached the villa in the Bay of Arcachon where she was to stay, gangrene had set in. In February 1915 the leg was amputated in a hospital in Bordeaux. Yet even this did not destroy her determination to continue on the stage. By the end of the year she was back in Paris, appearing in Eugene Moraud's patriotic piece *Les Cathedrales,* balancing on one leg as she supported herself on the arm of a chair. She protested that she would carry on thus until she died, having herself strapped to the scenery if necessary. "Madame," she said to Queen Mary during a visit to England, "I shall die on the stage. It is my battlefield."

The prediction was almost fulfilled. On the night of a dress rehearsal of a play in which she was to appear with her old friend Lucien Guitry, his son Sacha and his daughter-in-law, Yvonne Printemps, she collapsed in a coma. Some weeks later, on May 26, 1923, her doctor opened a window of her house in the Boulevard Pereire and announced to the crowds below, "Messieurs, Madame Bernhardt is dead."

"Bernhardt is dead" one Parisian said, passing on the sad news to another. "How dark it seems all of a sudden."

War and Depression

Unit 4

L.S. Stavrianos in his *Global History* blames the two world wars and the depression for the decline of Western influence in the world. The loss of life, the violence, the cost, and the view of internecine fighting among the nations of the West took their toll. After 1945 the empires broke up.

Given the history of conflict in the world, people sometimes wonder if warfare is an inborn part of human nature. We excuse ourselves at times by saying that warfare represents a loss of good sense, but Michael Howard, author of "The Causes of Wars," argues that wars start when both sides think that there is an advantage in fighting. Going to war, therefore, is a rational act. Yet, as Edmund Stillman says about World War I, the goals of the warring nations were very questionable compared to the cost of ten million dead soldiers and a legacy of barbarism.

The war left not only the dead young men, but also a disillusioned younger generation which supported the excesses of the Jazz Age and the cynicism of the "lost generation." The collapse of the economy in the 1930s was an additional blow, and skeptics could readily question the older ethic of progress in human life. The depression was cured only by the huge spending of World War II.

It is also difficult to believe in the rationality of war when you consider the career of Adolph Hitler. In 1940, however, according to John Lukacs, Hitler almost won the war. There was even talk of a negotiated peace, but the fighting continued. the British under Churchill's leadership hung on, and the United States entered the war at the end of 1941.

World War II was interpreted by the Allies as a just war, a fight between good and evil. This was confirmed toward the end of the fighting when Allied soldiers overran the Nazi death camps where six million Jews has been exterminated. The holocaust is justly condemned and remembered, but others suffered too. Jeremy Noakes points out that some 25,000 gypsies were likewise executed and subjected to infamous medical tortures with other prisoners. The gypsies are such a vagabond people that no one has paid much attention to their suffering. Only 5,000 of them survived the conflict.

The Japanese underwent a nuclear holocaust at Hiroshima and Nagasaki. In earlier wars, even World War I to an extent, it was a part of military ethics to safeguard women, children, and noncombatants. With the advent of submarine warfare in World War I and bombing raids in World War II, such ethics could no longer be sustained. It became total war—one nationality against another. The American Air Force did ostensibly chose military targets for the atom bombs, but obliterated the entire cities. In the forty years after the dropping of the atom bomb, Hiroshima has recovered and looks like many other modern cities. Michael Dillon notes, however, that long-term scars and sadness remain.

Warfare, of course, has continued. The United States, the most powerful nation emerging from World War II, has been involved in Korea and Vietnam. It fought both wars while espousing limited goals, and managed to battle the Chinese and North Koreans to a standstill without escalating into a world war. In Vietnam a decade later, the US again fought a limited war, but this time lost to a determined enemy using guerilla tactics. The selection from *Time*, a retrospective article written twenty years after the fall of Saigon, claims that Americans have yet to face the critical questions of the war.

There are lessons to be learned from the analysis of the past. In the case of Vietnam we must understand what happened or we may blunder again in the future. Walter Karp draws parallels between the ancient war between Athens and Sparta, and the cold war between the United States and the Soviet Union. Something can be gained by looking at the motives and what happened. Today, as the author points out, the technologies have changed but human nature has not. The author of the first article in this unit notes that the technology of atomic warfare is a major consideration in any decision for war. President Dwight D. Eisenhower, the successful general of the Allies in World War II, said that in the atomic world there was no alternative to peace.

Looking Ahead: Challenge Questions

What are the causes of war?
Can war be prevented? How?
How has technology influenced the nature of warfare?
Has anything worthwhile been achieved in fighting wars?
What can be gained by an analysis of past wars, even those from 2,000 years ago?

The Causes of Wars

Michael Howard

Michael Howard, a Wilson Center Fellow, holds the Regius Chair of Modern History at Oxford University. He was born in London, England. Before receiving his B.A. from Oxford (1946), Howard served in the Coldstream Guards in Italy during World War II, was twice wounded, and was awarded the Military Cross. He received his Litt. D. from Oxford in 1976. Among his many works, he has written War in European History *(1976) and* War and the Liberal Conscience *(1978), and he has translated, with Peter Paret of Stanford, Karl von Clausewitz's classic study* On War *(1976).*

Since the mid-18th century, many European and American theorists have attempted to explain war as an aberration in human affairs or as an occurrence beyond rational control. Violent conflicts between nations have been depicted, variously, as collective outbursts of male aggression, as the inevitable outcome of ruling-class greed, or as necessary, even healthy, events in the evolutionary scheme. One exception to the general trend was the 19th-century Prussian strategist Karl von Clausewitz, who declared, in an oft-quoted dictum, that war was the extension of politics "by other means." Here, historian Michael Howard argues further that war is one of Reason's progeny—indeed, that war stems from nothing less than a "superabundance of analytic rationality."

No one can describe the topic that I have chosen to discuss as a neglected and understudied one. How much ink has been spilled about it, how many library shelves have been filled with works on the subject, since the days of Thucydides! How many scholars from how many specialties have applied their expertise to this intractable problem! Mathematicians, meteorologists, sociologists, anthropologists, geographers, physicists, political scientists, philosophers, theologians, and lawyers are only the most obvious of the categories that come to mind when one surveys the ranks of those who have sought some formula for perpetual peace, or who have at least hoped to reduce the complexities of international conflict to some orderly structure, to develop a theory that will enable us to explain, to understand, and to control a phenomenon which, if we fail to abolish it, might well abolish us.

Yet it is not a problem that has aroused a great deal of interest in the historical profession. The causes of specific wars, yes: These provide unending material for analysis and interpretation, usually fueled by plenty of documents and starkly conflicting prejudices on the part of the scholars themselves.

But the phenomenon of war as a continuing activity within human society is one that as a profession we take very much for granted. The alternation of war and peace has been the very stuff of the past. War has been throughout history a normal way of conducting disputes between political groups. Few of us, probably, would go along with those sociobiologists who claim that this has been so because man is "innately aggressive." The calculations of advantage and risk, sometimes careful, sometimes crude, that statesmen make before committing their countries to war are linked very remotely, if at all, to the displays of tribal "machismo" that we witness today in football crowds. Since the use or threat of physical force is the most elementary way of asserting power and controlling one's environment, the fact that men have frequently had recourse to it does not cause the historian a great deal of surprise. Force, or the threat of it, may not settle arguments, but it does play a considerable part in determining the structure of the world in which we live.

I mentioned the multiplicity of books that have been written about the causes of war since the time of Thucydides. In fact, I think we would find that the vast majority of them have been written since 1914, and that the degree of intellectual concern about the causes of war to which we have become accustomed has existed only since the First World War. In view of the damage which that war did to the social and political structure of Europe, this is understandable enough. But there has been a tendency to argue that because that war caused such great and lasting damage, because it destroyed three great empires and nearly beggared a fourth, it must have arisen from causes of peculiar complexity and profundity, from the neuroses of nations, from the widening class struggle, from a crisis in industrial society. I have argued this myself, taking issue with Mr. A. J. P. Taylor, who maintained that because the war had such profound consequences, it did not necessarily have equally profound causes. But now I wonder whether on this, as on so many other matters, I was not wrong and he was not right.

■

It is true, and it is important to bear in mind in examining the problems of that period, that before

1914 war was almost universally considered an acceptable, perhaps an inevitable and for many people a desirable, way of settling international differences, and that the war generally foreseen was expected to be, if not exactly brisk and cheerful, then certainly brief; no longer, certainly, than the war of 1870 between France and Prussia that was consciously or unconsciously taken by that generation as a model. Had it not been so generally felt that war was an acceptable and tolerable way of solving international disputes, statesmen and soldiers would no doubt have approached the crisis of 1914 in a very different fashion.

But there was nothing new about this attitude to war. Statesmen had always been able to assume that war would be acceptable at least to those sections of their populations whose opinion mattered to them, and in this respect the decision to go to war in 1914—for continental statesmen at least—in no way differed from those taken by their predecessors of earlier generations. The causes of the Great War are thus in essence no more complex or profound than those of any previous European war, or indeed than those described by Thucydides as underlying the Peloponnesian War. "What made war inevitable was the growth of Athenian power and the fear this caused in Sparta." In Central Europe, there was the German fear that the disintegration of the Habsburg Empire would result in an enormous enhancement of Russian power—power already becoming formidable as French-financed industries and railways put Russian manpower at the service of her military machine. In Western Europe, there was the traditional British fear that Germany might establish a hegemony over Europe which, even more than that of Napoleon, would place at risk the security of Britain and her own possessions, a fear fueled by the knowledge that there was within Germany a widespread determination to achieve a world status comparable with her latent power. Considerations of this kind had caused wars in Europe often enough before. Was there really anything different about 1914?

■

Ever since the 18th century, war had been blamed by intellectuals upon the stupidity or the self-interest of governing elites (as it is now blamed upon "military-industrial complexes"), with the implicit or explicit assumption that if the control of state affairs were in the hands of sensible men—businessmen, as Richard Cobden thought, the workers, as Jean Jaurès thought—then wars would be no more.

By the 20th century, the growth of the social and biological sciences was producing alternative explanations. As Quincy Wright expressed it in his massive *A Study of War* (1942), "Scientific investigators ... tended to attribute war to immaturities in social knowledge and control, as one might attribute epidemics to insufficient medical knowledge or to inadequate public health services." The Social Darwinian acceptance of the inevitability of struggle, indeed of its desirability if mankind was to progress, the view, expressed by the elder Moltke but very widely shared at the turn of the century, that perpetual peace was a dream and not even a beautiful dream, did not survive the Great War in those countries where the bourgeois-liberal culture was dominant, Britain and the United States. The failure of these nations to appreciate that such bellicist views, or variants of them, were still widespread in other areas of the world, those dominated by Fascism and by Marxism-Leninism, was to cause embarrassing misunderstandings, and possibly still does.

For liberal intellectuals, war was self-evidently a pathological aberration from the norm, at best a ghastly mistake, at worst a crime. Those who initiated wars must in their view have been criminal, or sick, or the victims of forces beyond their power to control. Those who were so accused disclaimed responsibility for the events of 1914, throwing it on others or saying the whole thing was a terrible mistake for which no one was to blame. None of them, with their societies in ruins around them and tens of millions dead, were prepared to say courageously: "We only acted as statesmen always have in the past. In the circumstances then prevailing, war seemed to us to be the best way of protecting or forwarding the national interests for which we were responsible. There was an element of risk, certainly, but the risk might have been greater had we postponed the issue. Our real guilt does not lie in the fact that we started the war. It lies in our mistaken belief that we could win it."

■

The trouble is that if we are to regard war as pathological and abnormal, then all conflict must be similarly regarded; for war is only a particular kind of conflict between a particular category of social groups: sovereign states. It is, as Clausewitz put it, "a clash between major interests that is resolved by bloodshed—that is the only way in which it differs from other conflicts." If one had no sovereign states, one would have no wars, as Rousseau rightly pointed out—but, as Hobbes equally rightly pointed out, we would probably have no peace either. As states acquire a monopoly of violence, war becomes the only remaining form of conflict that may legitimately be settled by physical force. The mechanism of legitimization of authority and of social control that makes it possible for a state to moderate or eliminate conflicts within its borders or at very least to ensure that these are not conducted by competitive violence—the mechanism to the study of which historians have quite properly devoted so much attention—makes possible the conduct of armed conflict with other states, and on occasion—if the state is to survive—makes it necessary.

These conflicts arise from conflicting claims, or interests, or ideologies, or perceptions; and these perceptions may indeed be fueled by social or psychologi-

4. WAR AND DEPRESSION

cal drives that we do not fully understand and that one day we may learn rather better how to control. But the problem is the control of social conflict *as such,* not simply of war. However inchoate or disreputable the motives for war may be, its initiation is almost by definition a deliberate and carefully considered act and its conduct, at least at the more advanced levels of social development, a matter of very precise central control. If history shows any record of "accidental" wars, I have yet to find them. Certainly statesmen have sometimes been surprised by the nature of the war they have unleashed, and it is reasonable to assume that in at least 50 percent of the cases they got a result they did not expect. But that is not the same as a war begun by mistake and continued with no political purpose.

■

Statesmen in fact go to war to achieve very specific ends, and the reasons for which states have fought one another have been categorized and recategorized innumerable times. Vattel, the Swiss lawyer, divided them into the necessary, the customary, the rational, and the capricious. Jomini, the Swiss strategist, identified ideological, economic, and popular wars, wars to defend the balance of power, wars to assist allies, wars to assert or to defend rights. Quincy Wright, the American political scientist, divided them into the idealistic, the psychological, the political, and the juridical. Bernard Brodie in our own times has refused to discriminate: "Any theory of the causes of war in general or any war in particular that is not inherently eclectic and comprehensive," he stated, ". . . is bound for that very reason to be wrong." Another contemporary analyst, Geoffrey Blainey, is on the contrary unashamedly reductionist. All war aims, he wrote, "are simply varieties of power. The vanity of nationalism, the will to spread an ideology, the protection of kinsmen in an adjacent land, the desire for more territory . . . all these represent power in different wrappings. The conflicting aims of rival nations are always conflicts of power."

In principle, I am sure that Bernard Brodie was right: No single explanation for conflict between states, any more than for conflict between any other social groups, is likely to stand up to critical examination. But Blainey is right as well. Quincy Wright provided us with a useful indicator when he suggested that "while animal war is a function of instinct and primitive war of the mores, civilized war is primarily a function of state politics."

Medievalists will perhaps bridle at the application of the term "primitive" to the sophisticated and subtle societies of the Middle Ages, for whom war was also a "function of the mores," a way of life that often demanded only the most banal of justifications. As a way of life, it persisted in Europe well into the 17th century, if no later. For Louis XIV and his court war was, in the early years at least, little more than a seasonal variation on hunting. But by the 18th century, the mood had changed. For Frederick the Great, war was to be pre-eminently a function of *Staatspolitik,* and so it has remained ever since. And although statesmen can be as emotional or as prejudiced in their judgments as any other group of human beings, it is very seldom that their attitudes, their perceptions, and their decisions are not related, however remotely, to the fundamental issues of *power,* that capacity to control their environment on which the independent existence of their states and often the cultural values of their societies depend.

■

And here perhaps we do find a factor that sets interstate conflict somewhat apart from other forms of social rivalry. States may fight—indeed as often as not they do fight—not over any specific issue such as might otherwise have been resolved by peaceful means, but in order to acquire, to enhance, or to preserve their capacity to function as independent actors in the international system at all. "The stakes of war," as Raymond Aron has reminded us, "are the existence, the creation, or the elimination of States." It is a somber analysis, but one which the historical record very amply bears out.

It is here that those analysts who come to the study of war from the disciplines of the natural sciences, particularly the biological sciences, tend, it seems to me, to go astray. The conflicts between states which have usually led to war have normally arisen, not from any irrational and emotive drives, but from almost a superabundance of analytic rationality. Sophisticated communities (one hesitates to apply to them Quincy Wright's word, "civilized") do not react simply to immediate threats. Their intelligence (and I use the term in its double sense) enables them to assess the implications that any event taking place anywhere in the world, however remote, may have for their own capacity, immediately to exert influence, ultimately perhaps to survive. In the later Middle Ages and the early Modern period, every child born to every prince anywhere in Europe was registered on the delicate seismographs that monitored the shifts in dynastic power. Every marriage was a diplomatic triumph or disaster. Every stillbirth, as Henry VIII knew, could presage political catastrophe.

Today, the key events may be different. The pattern remains the same. A malfunction in the political mechanism of some remote African community, a coup d'état in a minuscule Caribbean republic, an insurrection deep in the hinterland of Southeast Asia, an assassination in some emirate in the Middle East—all these will be subjected to the kind of anxious examination and calculation that was devoted a hundred years ago to the news of comparable events in the Balkans: an insurrection in Philippopoli, a coup d'état in Constantinople, an assassination in Belgrade. To whose advantage will this ultimately redound, asked the worried diplomats, ours or *theirs?* Little enough in itself, perhaps, but will it not precipitate or strengthen a trend, set in motion a tide whose melancholy withdrawing roar will strip us of our friends and influence and leave us isolated in a world dominated by adversaries deeply hostile to us and all that we stand for?

There have certainly been occasions when states have gone to war in a mood of ideological fervor like the French republican armies in 1792; or of swaggering aggression like the Americans against Spain in 1898 or the British against the Boers a year later; or to make more money, as did the British in the War of Jenkins' Ear in 1739; or in a generous desire to help peoples of similar creed or race, as perhaps the Russians did in helping the Bulgarians fight the Turks in 1877 and the British dominions certainly did in 1914 and 1939. But, in general, men have fought during the past two hundred years neither because they are aggressive nor because they are acquisitive animals, but because they are reasoning ones: because they discern, or believe that they can discern, dangers before they become immediate, the possibility of threats before they are made.

■

But be this as it may, in 1914 many of the German people, and in 1939 nearly all of the British, felt justified in going to war, not over any specific issue that could have been settled by negotiation, but *to maintain their power;* and to do so while it was still possible, before they found themselves so isolated, so impotent, that they had no power left to maintain and had to accept a subordinate position within an international system dominated by their adversaries. "What made war inevitable was the growth of Athenian power and the fear this caused in Sparta." Or, to quote another grimly apt passage from Thucydides:

> The Athenians made their Empire more and more strong... [until] finally the point was reached when Athenian strength attained a peak plain for all to see and the Athenians began to encroach upon Sparta's allies. It was at this point that Sparta felt the position to be no longer tolerable and decided by starting the present war to employ all her energies in attacking and it possible destroying the power of Athens.

You can vary the names of the actors, but the model remains a valid one for the purposes of our analysis. I am rather afraid that it still does.

Something that has changed since the time of Thucydides, however, is the nature of the power that appears so threatening. From the time of Thucydides until that of Louis XIV, there was basically only one source of political and military power—control of territory, with all the resources in wealth and manpower that this provided. This control might come through conquest, or through alliance, or through marriage, or through purchase, but the power of princes could be very exactly computed in terms of the extent of their territories and the number of men they could put under arms.

In 17th-century Europe, this began to change. Extent of territory remained important, but no less important was the effectiveness with which the resources of that territory could be exploited. Initially there were the bureaucratic and fiscal mechanisms that transformed loose bonds of territorial authority into highly structured centralized states whose armed forces, though not necessarily large, were permanent, disciplined, and paid.

■

Then came the political transformations of the revolutionary era that made available to these state systems the entire manpower of their country, or at least as much of it as the administrators were able to handle. And finally came the revolution in transport, the railways of the 19th century that turned the revolutionary ideal of the "Nation in Arms" into a reality. By the early 20th century, military power—on the continent of Europe, at least—was seen as a simple combination of military manpower and railways. The quality of armaments was of secondary importance, and political intentions were virtually excluded from account. The growth of power was measured in terms of the growth of populations and of communications; of the number of men who could be put under arms and transported to the battlefield to make their weight felt in the initial and presumably decisive battles. It was the mutual perception of threat in those terms that turned Europe before 1914 into an armed camp, and it was their calculations within this framework that reduced German staff officers increasingly to despair and launched their leaders on their catastrophic gamble in 1914, which started the First World War.

But already the development of weapons technology had introduced yet another element into the international power calculus, one that has in our own age become dominant. It was only in the course of the 19th century that technology began to produce weapons systems—initially in the form of naval vessels—that could be seen as likely in themselves to prove decisive, through their qualitative and quantitative superiority, in the event of conflict. But as war became increasingly a matter of competing technologies rather than competing armies, so there developed that escalatory process known as the "arms race." As a title, the phrase, like so many coined by journalists to catch the eye, is misleading.

■

"Arms races" are in fact continuing and open-ended attempts to match power for power. They are as much means of achieving stable or, if possible, favorable power balances as were the dynastic marriage policies of Valois and Habsburg. To suggest that they in themselves are causes of war implies a naive if not

4. WAR AND DEPRESSION

totally mistaken view of the relationship between the two phenomena. The causes of war remain rooted, as much as they were in the preindustrial age, in perceptions by statesmen of the growth of hostile power and the fears for the restriction, if not the extinction, of their own. The threat, or rather the fear, has not changed, whether it comes from aggregations of territory or from dreadnoughts, from the numbers of men under arms or from missile systems. The means that states employ to sustain or to extend their power may have been transformed, but their objectives and preoccupations remain the same.

"Arms races" can no more be isolated than wars themselves from the political circumstances that give rise to them, and like wars they will take as many different forms as political circumstances dictate. They may be no more than a process of competitive modernization, of maintaining a status quo that commands general support but in which no participant wishes, whether from reasons of pride or of prudence, to fall behind in keeping his armory up to date. If there are no political causes for fear or rivalry, this process need not in itself be a destabilizing factor in international relations. But arms races may, on the other hand, be the result of a quite deliberate assertion of an intention to *change* the status quo, as was, for example, the German naval challenge to Britain at the beginning of this century.

This challenge was an explicit attempt by Admiral Alfred von Tirpitz and his associates to destroy the hegemonic position at sea which Britain saw as essential to her security, and, not inconceivably, to replace it with one of their own. As British and indeed German diplomats repeatedly explained to the German government, it was not the German naval program in itself that gave rise to so much alarm in Britain. It was the intention that lay behind it. If the status quo was to be maintained, the German challenge had to be met.

■

The naval race could quite easily have been ended on one of two conditions. Either the Germans could have abandoned their challenge, as had the French in the previous century, and acquiesced in British naval supremacy; or the British could have yielded as gracefully as they did, a decade or so later, to the United States and abandoned a status they no longer had the capacity, or the will, to maintain. As it was, they saw the German challenge as one to which they could and should respond, and their power position as one which they were prepared, if necessary, to use force to preserve. The British naval program was thus, like that of the Germans, a signal of political intent; and that intent, that refusal to acquiesce in a fundamental transformation of the power balance, was indeed a major element among the causes of the war. The naval competition provided a vary accurate indication and measurement of political rivalries and tensions, but it did not cause them; nor could it have been abated unless the rivalries themselves had been abandoned.

It was the general perception of the growth of German power that was awakened by the naval challenge, and the fear that a German hegemony on the Continent would be the first step to a challenge to her own hegemony on the oceans, that led Britain to involve herself in the continental conflict in 1914 on the side of France and Russia. "What made war inevitable was the growth of *Spartan* power," to reword Thucydides, "and the fear which this caused in *Athens.*" In the Great War that followed, Germany was defeated, but survived with none of her latent power destroyed. A "false hegemony" of Britain and France was established in Europe that could last only so long as Germany did not again mobilize her resources to challenge it. German rearmament in the 1930s did not of itself mean that Hitler wanted war (though one has to ignore his entire philosophy if one is to believe that he did not); but it did mean that he was determined, with a great deal of popular support, to obtain a free hand on the international scene.

With that free hand, he intended to establish German power on an irreversible basis; this was the message conveyed by his armament program. The armament program that the British reluctantly adopted in reply was intended to show that, rather than submit to the hegemonic aspirations they feared from such a revival of German power, they would fight to preserve their own freedom of action. Once again to recast Thucydides:

> Finally the point was reached when German strength attained a peak plain for all to see, and the Germans began to encroach upon Britain's allies. It was at this point that Britain felt the position to be no longer tolerable and decided by starting this present war to employ all her energies in attacking and if possible destroying the power of Germany.

What the Second World War established was not a new British hegemony, but a Soviet hegemony over the Euro-Asian land mass from the Elbe to Vladivostok; and that was seen, at least from Moscow, as an American hegemony over the rest of the world; one freely accepted in Western Europe as a preferable alternative to being absorbed by the rival hegemony. Rival armaments were developed to define and preserve the new territorial boundaries, and the present arms competition began. But in considering the present situation, historical experience suggests that we must ask the fundamental question: *What kind of competition is it?* Is it one between powers that accept the status quo, are satisfied with the existing power relationship, and are concerned simply to modernize their armaments in order to preserve it? Or does it reflect an underlying instability in the system?

My own perception, I am afraid, is that it is the latter. There was a period for a decade after the war when the Soviet Union was probably a status quo power but the

23. The Causes of Wars

Society may have accepted killing as a legitimate instrument of state policy. This sanctioned violence (war) can be justified by the need to keep one's country intact; however, using a weapon that can cause the destruction of the human race (suicide) can not be even a remotely logical choice.

4. WAR AND DEPRESSION

West was not; that is, the Russians were not seriously concerned to challenge the American global hegemony, but the West did not accept that of the Russians in Eastern Europe. Then there was a decade of relative mutual acceptance between 1955 and 1965; and it was no accident that this was the heyday of disarmament/arms-control negotiations. But thereafter, the Soviet Union has shown itself increasingly unwilling to accept the Western global hegemony, if only because many other people in the world have been unwilling to do so either. Reaction against Western dominance brought the Soviet Union some allies and many opportunities in the Third World, and she has developed naval power to be able to assist the former and exploit the latter. She has aspired in fact to global power status, as did Germany before 1914; and if the West complains, as did Britain about Germany, that the Russians do not *need* a navy for defense purposes, the Soviet Union can retort, as did Germany, that she needs it to make clear to the world the status to which she aspires; that is, so that she can operate on the world scene by virtue of her own power and not by permission of anyone else. Like Germany, she is determined to be treated as an equal, and armed strength has appeared the only way to achieve that status.

■

The trouble is that what is seen by one party as the breaking of an alien hegemony and the establishment of equal status will be seen by the incumbent powers as a striving for the establishment of an alternate hegemony, and they are not necessarily wrong. In international politics, the appetite often comes with eating; and there really may be no way to check an aspiring rival except by the mobilization of stronger military power. An arms race then becomes almost a necessary surrogate for war, a test of national will and strength; and arms control becomes possible only when the underlying power balance has been mutually agreed.

We would be blind, therefore, if we did not recognize that the causes which have produced war in the past are operating in our own day as powerfully as at any time in history. It is by no means impossible that a thousand years hence a historian will write—if any historians survive, and there are any records for them to write history from—"What made war inevitable was the growth of Soviet power and the fear which this caused in the United States."

But times *have* changed since Thucydides. They have changed even since 1914. These were, as we have seen, bellicist societies in which war was a normal, acceptable, even a desirable way of settling differences. The question that arises today is, how widely and evenly spread is that intense revulsion against war that at present characterizes our own society? For if war is indeed now *universally* seen as being unacceptable as an instrument of policy, then all analogies drawn from the past are misleading, and although power struggles may continue, they will be diverted into other channels. But if that revulsion is not evenly spread, societies which continue to see armed force as an acceptable means for attaining their political ends are likely to establish a dominance over those which do not. Indeed, they will not necessarily have to fight for it.

My second and concluding point is this: Whatever may be the underlying causes of international conflict, even if we accept the role of atavistic militarism or of military-industrial complexes or of sociobiological drives or of domestic tensions in fueling it, wars begin with conscious and reasoned decisions based on the calculation, made by *both* parties, that they can achieve more by going to war than by remaining at peace.

Even in the most bellicist of societies this kind of calculation has to be made and it has never even for them been an easy one. When the decision to go to war involves the likelihood, if not the certainty, that the conflict will take the form of an exchange of nuclear weapons from which one's own territory cannot be immune, then even for the most bellicist of leaders, even for those most insulated from the pressures of public opinion, the calculation that they have more to gain from going to war than by remaining at peace and pursuing their policies by other means will, to put it mildly, not be self-evident. The odds against such a course benefiting their state or themselves or their cause will be greater, and more *evidently* greater, than in any situation that history has *ever* had to record. Society may have accepted killing as a legitimate instrument of state policy, but not, as yet, suicide. For that reason I find it hard to believe that the abolition of nuclear weapons, even if it were possible, would be an unmixed blessing. Nothing that makes it easier for statesmen to regard war as a feasible instrument of state policy, one from which they stand to gain rather than lose, is likely to contribute to a lasting peace.

SARAJEVO

The End of Innocence

After fifty years of explanations, it is still difficult to see why a political murder in a remote corner of the Balkans should have set off a war that changed the world forever

Edmund Stillman

A few minutes before eleven o'clock in the morning, Sunday, June 28, 1914, on the river embankment in Sarajevo, Gavrilo Princip shot the archduke Franz Ferdinand and brought a world crashing down.

After fifty years and so much pain, Sarajevo is worth a pilgrimage, but to go there is a disappointing and somehow unsettling experience: this dusty Balkan city, in its bowl of dark and barren hills, is an unlikely setting for grand tragedy. Blood and suffering are endemic to the Balkans, but Sarajevo is so mean and poor. Why should an age have died *here*? Why did the double murder of an undistinguished archduke and his morganatic wife touch off a world war, when so many graver pretexts had somehow been accommodated—or ignored—in the preceding quarter-century? It was an act that no one clearly remembers today; indeed, its details were forgotten by the time the war it engendered was six months old. Nowadays, even in Sarajevo, few pilgrims search out the place where Princip stood that morning. Nearby, on the river embankment, only a dingy little museum commemorates the lives and passions of the seven tubercular boys (of whom Princip was only one) who plotted one small blow for freedom, but who brought on a universal catastrophe. Within the museum are faded photographs, a few pitiable relics of the conspirators, a fly-specked visitors' book. A single shabby attendant guards the memorials to a political passion that seems, well, naïve to our more cynical age. "Here, in this historic place," the modest inscription runs, "Gavrilo Princip was the initiator of liberty, on the day of Saint Vitus, the 28th of June, 1914." That is all, and few visitors to present-day Yugoslavia stop to read it.

There is so much that goes unanswered, even though the facts of the case are so well known: how the failing Hapsburgs, impelled by an unlucky taste for adventure, had seized Bosnia and Herzegovina from the Turks and aggravated the racial imbalance of the Austro-Hungarian Empire; how the southern Slavs within the Empire felt themselves oppressed and increasingly demanded freedom; how the ambitious little hill kingdom of Serbia saw a chance to establish a South-Slavic hegemony over the Balkans; and how Czarist Russia, itself near ruin, plotted with its client Serbia to turn the Austro-Hungarian southern flank. But there is so much more that needs to be taken into account: how Franz Ferdinand, the aged emperor Franz Josef's nephew, became his heir by default (Crown Prince Rudolf had committed suicide at Mayerling; Uncle Maximilian, Napoleon III's pawn, had been executed in Mexico; Franz Ferdinand's father, a pilgrim to the Holy Land, had died—most improbably—from drinking the waters of the Jordan); how the new heir—stiff, autocratic, and unapproachable, but implausibly wed in irenic middle-class marriage to the not-quite-acceptable Sophie Chotek—sensed the danger to the Empire and proposed a policy that would have given his future Slav subjects most of what they demanded; how the Serbian nationalists were driven to panic, and how the secret society of jingoes known as "The Black Hand" plotted Franz Ferdinand's death; how seven boys were recruited to do the deed, and how one of them, Gavrilo Princip, on the morning of June 28, 1914, shot Franz Ferdinand and his Sophie dead.

But why the mindlessness of the war that followed, the blundering diplomacies and reckless plans that made disaster inevitable once hostilities broke out? It is all so grotesque: great and shattering consequences without proportionate causes. When the inferno of 1914–18 ended at last, the

From Horizon, *Summer 1964. Reprinted by permission of Harold Ober Associates, Inc. Copyright ©1964 by Edmund Stillman.*

4. WAR AND DEPRESSION

broken survivors asked themselves the same question, seeking to comprehend the terrible thing that had happened. To have endured the inferno without a justifying reason—to be forced to admit that a war of such terror and scope had been only a blind, insouciant madness—was intolerable; it was easier to think of it as an unworthy or a wrongful cause than as a ghastly, titanic joke on history. After the event Winston Churchill wrote: "But there was a strange temper in the air. Unsatisfied by material prosperity the nations turned restlessly towards strife internal or external. . . . Almost one might think the world wished to suffer." Yet if this opinion had been widely accepted, it would have been a judgment on human nature too terrible to endure. And so a new mythology of the war grew up—a postwar mythology of materialist cynicism almost as contrived as the wartime propaganda fictions of the "Beast of Berlin" or the wholesale slaughter of Belgian nuns. It embraced the myths of the munitions manufacturers who had plotted a war they were, in fact, helpless to control; of Machiavellian, imperialist diplomacies; of an ever-spiraling arms race, when in fact the naval race between England and Germany had, if anything, somewhat abated by 1914. But no single cause, or combination of such causes, will explain the First World War. Neither the Germans, the Austrians, the Russians, the French, the Italians, nor the British went to war to fulfill a grand ambition—to conquer Europe, or the world, or to promote an ideology. They did not even seek economic dominion through war. The somber truth is that Western civilization, for a hundred years without a major war and absorbed in a social and technological revolution—progress, in short—turned on itself in a paroxysm of slaughter.

On both sides the actual war aims, so far as they were articulated at all, were distressingly small. Merely to humiliate Serbia and to "avenge" a man whose death few particularly regretted, the Austro-Hungarian Empire began a war which cost it seven million casualties and destroyed its fabric; to prevent a senile Austria-Hungary from gaining a precarious (and inevitably short-lived) advantage in the poverty-stricken western Balkans, imperial Russia lost more than nine million men—killed, wounded, or taken prisoner. To support an ally, and to avoid the public humiliation and anxiety of canceling a mobilization order once issued, Germany lost almost two million dead, Alsace-Lorraine, a third of Poland, and its growing sphere of influence in Central Europe and the Middle East. England, to keep its word to Belgium, committed eight million men to the struggle, and lost nearly one million dead. France, to counter its German enemy and to avenge the peace treaty it had accepted in 1870, endured losses of 15 per cent of its population and initiated a process of political decline from which it may not yet have emerged.

This was the price of World War I. Two shots were fired in Sarajevo, and for more than four years thereafter half the world bled. At least ten million soldiers were killed, and twenty million were wounded or made prisoners. But the real legacy of the war was something less tangible—a quality of despair, a chaos, and a drift toward political barbarism that is with us to this day. We have not recovered yet.

In the summer of 1914 the armies marched out to Armageddon in their frogged tunics, red Zouave trousers, and gilded helmets. Five months later they were crouching in the mud, louse-ridden, half-starved, frozen, and bewildered by the enormity of it all. "Lost in the midst of two million madmen," the Frenchman Céline was to write of the war, "all of them heroes, at large and armed to the teeth! . . . sniping, plotting, flying, kneeling, digging, taking cover, wheeling, detonating, shut in on earth as in an asylum cell; intending to wreck everything in it, Germany, France, the whole world, every breathing thing; destroying, more ferocious than a pack of mad dogs and adoring their own madness (which no dog does), a hundred, a thousand times fiercer than a thousand dogs and so infinitely more vicious! . . . Clearly it seemed to me that I had embarked on a crusade that was nothing short of an apocalypse."

The savagery of the war and the incompetence of the military commanders quickly became a commonplace. The generals proved wholly unprepared for quick-firing artillery, machine guns, field entrenchments, railroad and motor transport, and the existence of a continuous front in place of the isolated battlefield of earlier centuries. They were helpless in the face of a combat too vast, too impersonal, too technical, and too deadly to comprehend. Quite aside from their intellectual shortcomings, one is struck by the poverty of their emotional response. Kill and kill was their motto. No one in command was daunted by the bloodletting, it seems. No more imaginative battle tactic could be devised than to push strength against strength—attacking at the enemy's strongest point on the theory that one side's superior *élan* would ultimately yield up victory. Verdun in 1916 cost the French some 350,000 men and the Germans nearly as many; the German penetration was five miles, gained in a little more than three months. The Somme cost the Allies more than 600,000 casualties, the Germans almost half a million; the offensive gained a sector thirty miles wide and a maximum of seven deep in four and a half months.

That it was an insane waste of lives the combatants realized early, but no one knew what to do. The waste of honor, love, courage, and selfless devotion was the cruelest of all: at the first Battle of Ypres, in the opening days of the war, the young German schoolboy volunteers "came on like men possessed," a British historian records. They were sent in against picked battalions of British regulars who shot them

24. Sarajevo

to pieces on the slopes of Ypres with the trained rifle fire for which they were famous. The incident has gone down in German history as the *Kindermord von Ypern*—"the Slaughter of the Innocents at Ypres." No other phrase will do.

It was a strange world that died that summer of 1914. For ninety-nine years there had been peace in Europe: apart from the Crimean War, only eighteen months of all that time—according to Karl Polanyi—had been spent in desultory and petty European wars. Men apparently believed that peace was man's normal condition—and on those occasions when peace was momentarily broken, war was expected to be comprehensible and salutary, an ultimately useful Darwinian selection of the fittest to lead. To us, after the profuse horrors of mustard gas, trench warfare, Buchenwald, the Blitz, Coventry, and Hiroshima, to name only a few, this is incomprehensible naïveté. But that we have been disillusioned and have awaked to our condition is due to the events of 1914–18.

In the nineteenth century the belief in progress—automatic progress—went deep. The American anthropologist Lewis Morgan had sounded a note of self-confident hope for the entire age when he said, in 1877, "Democracy in government, brotherhood in society, equality in rights and privileges, and universal education, foreshadow the next higher plane of society to which experience, intelligence and knowledge are steadily tending." The emphasis here was on *steadily*: nothing could stop the onward march of mankind.

And the progress was very real. The age that died in 1914 was a brilliant one—so extravagant in its intellectual and aesthetic endowments that we who have come after can hardly believe in its reality. It was a comfortable age—for a considerable minority, at least—but it was more than a matter of Sunday walks in the Wienerwald, or country-house living, or a good five-cent cigar. It was an imposing age in the sciences, in the arts, even in forms of government. Men had done much and had risen high in the hundred years that came to an end that summer. From Napoleon's downfall in 1815 to the outbreak of war in 1914, the trend had been up.

"As happy as God in France," even the Germans used to say. For France these were the years of the *belle époque,* when all the world's artists came there to learn: Picasso and Juan Gris from Spain, Chagall and Archipenko from Russia, Piet Mondrian from the Netherlands, Brancusi from Romania, Man Ray and Max Weber from America, Modigliani from Italy. All made up the "School of Paris," a name which meant nothing but that in this Paris of the *avant-guerre* the world of the arts was at home.

"Paris drank the talents of the world," wrote the poet-impresario of those years, Guillaume Apollinaire. Debussy, Ravel, and Stravinsky composed music there. Nijinsky and Diaghilev were raising the modern ballet to new heights of brilliance and creativity. The year 1913 was, as Roger Shattuck puts it in *The Banquet Years,* the *annus mirabilis* of French literature: Proust's *Du Côté de chez Swann,* Alain-Fournier's *Le Grand Meaulnes,* Apollinaire's *Alcools,* Roger Martin du Gard's *Jean Barois,* Valéry Larbaud's *A. O. Barnabooth,* Péguy's *L'Argent,* Barrès's *La Colline inspirée,* and Colette's *L'Entrave* and *L'Envers du music-hall* appeared that year. "It is almost as if the war *had* to come in order to put an end to an extravaganza that could not have been sustained at this level." That was Paris.

Vienna was another great mongrel city that, like Paris, drank up talent—in this case the talents of a congeries of Austrians, Magyars, Czechs, Slovaks, Poles, Slovenes, Croats, Serbs, Jews, Turks, Transylvanians, and Gypsies. On Sunday mornings gentlemen strolled in the Prater ogling the cocottes; they rode the giant red Ferris wheel and looked out over the palaces and parks of the city; or they spent the morning at the coffeehouse, arguing pointlessly and interminably. It was a pleasure-loving city, but an intellectual one, too. The names of the men who walked Vienna's streets up to the eve of the war are stunning in their brilliance: Gustav Mahler, Sigmund Freud, Sandor Ferenczi, Ernst Mach, Béla Bartók, Rainer Maria Rilke, Franz Kafka, Robert Musil, Arthur Schnitzler, Hugo von Hofmannsthal, Richard Strauss, Stefan Zweig—these hardly begin to exhaust the list. (There were more sinister names, too. Adolf Hitler lived in Vienna between 1909 and 1913, an out-of-work, shabby *Bettgeher*—a daytime renter of other people's beds—absorbing the virulent anti-Semitism that charged the Viennese social atmosphere; so did Leon Trotsky, who spent his evenings listening contemptuously to the wranglings of the Social Democratic politicians at the Café Central.)

England was still gilded by the afterglow of the Edwardian Age: the British Empire straddled the earth, controlling more than a quarter of the surface of the globe. If the realities of trade had begun to shift, and if British industry and British naval supremacy were faced with a growing challenge from the United States and Hohenzollern Germany, the vast British overseas investments tended to hide the fact. England had its intellectual brilliance, too: these were the years of Hardy, Kipling, Shaw, Wells, the young D. H. Lawrence and the young Wyndham Lewis, Arnold Bennett, Gilbert Murray, A. E. Housman, H. H. Munro (Saki)—who would die in the war—and many others, like Rupert Brooke, Robert Graves, Siegfried Sassoon, and Wilfred Owen, who were as yet hardly known.

As for the Kaiser's Germany, it is melancholy to reflect that if Wilhelm II himself, that summer in 1914, had only waited —five years, ten years, or twenty—Germany might have had it all. But Wilhelm was shrewd, treacherous, and hysterical, a chronic bully whose mother had never loved him. His

4. WAR AND DEPRESSION

habitual style of discourse was the neurotic bluster of a small man who has had the bad luck to be called upon to stomp about in a giant's boots. Wilhelm II lived all his life in the shadow of "the Great Emperor," his grandfather Wilhelm I, who had created a united Greater Germany with the help of his brilliant chancellor, Prince Otto von Bismarck; he wanted to make the world stand in awe of him, but he did not know, precisely, how to go about it.

If only he could have been patient: Austria-Hungary was really a German satellite; the Balkans and the Middle East looked to Berlin; Germany's industrial hegemony on the continent was secure, and might soon have knocked Britain from her commanding place in the world's trade. By 1914, fourteen Germans had won Nobel Prizes in the sciences (by contrast, their nearest competitors, the French, had won only nine).

But the lesson is something more than a chapbook homily on patience. Wilhelm's personal anxiety merely expressed in microcosm the larger German anxiety about the nation's place in the world. Something strange lay beneath the stolid prosperity of the Hohenzollern Age—a surfeit with peace, a lust for violence, a belief in death, an ominous mystique of war. "Without war the world would quickly sink into materialism," the elder Von Moltke, chief of the German General Staff, had proclaimed in 1880; and he, his nephew the younger Von Moltke, and the caste of Prussian militarists they represented could presumably save the world from that tawdry fate. But this belief in war was not a monopoly of the Right: even Thomas Mann, spokesman of German humanism, could ask, in 1914, "Is not war a purification, a liberation, an enormous hope?" adding complacently, "Is not peace an element in civil corruption?"

There had been peace in the world for too long. From Berlin, in the spring of 1914, Colonel House wrote to Woodrow Wilson: "The whole of Germany is charged with electricity. Everybody's nerves are tense. It only requires a spark to set the whole thing off." People were saying: "Better a horrible ending than a horror without end." In expressing this spirit of violence and disorientation, Germany was merely precocious. It expressed a universal European malaise.

The malaise was evident everywhere—in the new cults of political violence; in the new philosophies of men like Freud, Nietzsche, and Pareto, who stressed the unconscious and the irrational, and who exposed the lying pretensions of middle-class values and conventions; and in the sense of doom that permeated the avant-garde arts of the prewar years. Typical of this spirit of rebellion was the manifesto set forth in 1910 by the Italian Futurist painters: it declared that "all forms of imitation should be held in contempt and that all forms of originality glorified; that we should rebel against the tyranny of the words 'harmony' and 'good taste' . . . ; that a clean sweep be made of all stale and threadbare subject matter in order to express the vortex of modern life—a life of steel, pride, fever, and speed . . ."

In England and France, as in Germany and Italy, the darker strain was there. When the war came, a glad Rupert Brooke intoned:

Now God be thanked Who has matched us with His hour.

A fever was over Paris as the spring of 1914 slipped into summer. Charles Péguy—Dreyfusard, Socialist, man of good will and reason, to his intellectual generation "the pure man"—had caught this other darker spirit as well. That spring he had written:

Heureux ceux qui sont morts dans les grandes batailles . . .
Happy are those who have died in great battles,
Lying on the ground before the face of God . . .

By September of that year he himself was dead.

No doubt we shall never understand it completely. What is absolutely clear about the outbreak of the First World War is that it was catastrophic: the hecatombs of dead, the appalling material waste, the destruction, and the pain of those four years tell us that. In our hearts we know that since that bootless, reckless, bloody adventure nothing has really come right again in the world. Democracy in government, brotherhood in society, equality in rights and privileges, universal education—all those evidences of "the next higher plane of society" to which experience, intelligence, and knowledge seemed to be steadily tending—gave way to mass conscription and the central direction of war, the anonymity of the trenches, the calculated propaganda lie: in short, between 1914 and 1918 Europe evolved many of the brutal features of the modern totalitarian state. And twenty-one years after the last shot was fired in the First World War, a second war came: a war of even greater brutality, moral degradation, and purposeful evil, but one where the issues at last matched the scale on which men had, a quarter-century earlier, blindly chosen to fight. Here was a deadly justice. That such a war should be fought at all was the direct outcome of the spiritual wasteland that the first war engendered.

Woodrow Wilson, greeting the Armistice, was able to proclaim to his fellow Americans that "everything" for which his countrymen had fought had been accomplished. He could assert that it was America's "fortunate duty to assist by example, by sober, friendly counsel, and by material aid in the establishment of a just democracy throughout the world."

But today we know that the poet Robert Graves more truly expressed the spirit of the nightmare from which the world awakened in 1918 when he wrote, "The news [of the Armistice] sent me out walking alone along the dyke above the marshes of Rhuddlan . . . cursing and sobbing and thinking of the dead."

Article 25

The DANGEROUS SUMMER of 1940

For a few weeks Hitler came close to winning World War II. Then came a train of events that doomed him. An eloquent historian reminds us that however unsatisfactory our world may be today, it almost was unimaginably worse.

John Lukacs

John Lukacs is Professor of History at Chestnut Hill College, Philadelphia, and the author of many books, including the recent *Outgrowing Democracy: A History of the United States in the 20th Century*

In the summer of 1940 Adolf Hitler could have won the Second World War. He came close to that. Had he won, we would be living in a world so different as to be hardly imaginable. So let us contemplate that dangerous summer. It was then that the shape of the world in which we now live began to take form.

There was a curious, abstract quality to the Second World War when it started. On the first day of September in 1939, Hitler's armies invaded Poland. In 1914 the Germans had gone to war not knowing what the British would do. In 1939 the British had given Poland a guarantee to deter Hitler, to make it clear that a German attack on Poland would mean a British (and a French) declaration of war against Germany. Until the last minute Hitler hoped that the British did not mean what they said. In a way he was right. The British and the French governments kept their word and declared war nearly three days after the German armies had driven into Poland. Yet the British and French armies did virtually nothing.

Before long the phrase "Phony War," invented by American journalists, came into the language. Poland was overrun: but in this war, it really was All Quiet on the Western Front. The French and the British troops spent the freezing winter that followed standing still, the French occasionally peering across the wooded German frontier from the concrete casemates of the Maginot Line. If not a phony war, it was a reluctant one.

There was a curious, abstract quality in the mood of the American people too. When the First World War broke out in Europe, not one in ten thousand Americans thought that their country would ever become involved in it. In 1914 the American people and their President, Woodrow Wilson, took a naive kind of pride in their neutrality. When, on September 3, 1939, Franklin Roosevelt addressed the American people, he said the United States would stay neutral: but Roosevelt then added that he could not "ask that every American remain neu-

141

4. WAR AND DEPRESSION

tral in thought as well." Most Americans were not. They abhorred Hitler, yet they had no desire to commit themselves on the side of Britain or France or Poland. They followed the conflict on their radios: it was exciting to hear the voices of famous correspondents crackling through the transatlantic ether from the blacked-out capitals of a Europe at war. Many Americans uneasily felt—felt, rather than said—that sooner or later their country would become involved in the war. They did not look forward to it.

Besides, the Phony War got curiouser and curiouser. It had started between Germany and Poland and Britain and France; but three months later the only fighting that was going on occurred in the snowy forests of Finland, a winter war between Finland and Russia. American sympathies for Finland arose. The British government noticed this. It was toying with the idea of coming to the aid of Finland, for many reasons, including the purpose of impressing American opinion. But the winter war came to an end. Churchill now wished to open a far-flung front against Germany, in Norway. Hitler forestalled him. On a freezing, raw morning in early April, his troops invaded Denmark and Norway. They conquered Denmark in a few hours and Norway in a few weeks.

Hitler's triumph in Norway—which he conquered nearly undisturbed by the British navy and largely unvexed by the hapless Allied troops put ashore and then withdrawn again—had an unexpected effect. The great portly figure of his nemesis had arisen—an old-fashioned figure of a man, whose very appearance rose like a spectral monument out of the historical mist. As a member of the Chamberlain government, Winston Churchill had been responsible for much of the Norwegian fiasco. Yet the representatives of the British people had had enough of Chamberlain's reluctant warfare. They helped Winston Churchill into the saddle of the prime ministership—by coincidence, on the very day when the German onslaught in Western Europe had begun.

It was the first of several great coincidences that summer: the kind of coincidences that people weaned on scientific logic dislike and others, with a touch of poetry in their souls, love. Or as the great Portuguese proverb says: God writes straight with crooked lines. But, as often happens in this world, we see the meaning only in retrospect. At the time, there was no guarantee that Churchill would last. He could have disappeared after a few weeks: a brave, old-fashioned orator, overtaken by the surging tide of the twentieth century, swept under by the wave of the future. When his horse is shot out under him, the best rider must fall.

On the tenth of May, at dawn—it was a radiant, beautiful morning, cloudless across Europe from the Irish Sea to the Baltic—Hitler flung his armies forward. They were the winged carriers of an astonishing drama. Holland fell in five days; Belgium in eighteen. Two days after the German drive had begun, the French front was broken. Another eight days, and the Germans reached the Channel. Calais and Boulogne fell. Dunkirk held for just ten days. Most of the British Expeditionary Force barely escaped; all their equipment was lost. Five weeks from the day they had started westward, German regiments were marching down the Champs Elysées. Three more days, and a new French government asked for surrender.

Here was a drama of forty days unequaled in the history of war for centuries, even by the brilliant victories of Napoleon. Hitler himself had a hand in designing that most astonishing of successful campaigns. He also had a hand in designing an armistice that the French would be inclined to accept.

He hoped that the United States would stay out of the war. His propaganda minister Joseph Goebbels ordered the toning down of anti-American items in the German press and radio. When the German army marched into an empty Paris, its commanders made a courtesy call on the American ambassador, who, alone among the envoys of the Great Powers, chose to stay in the capital instead of following the torn French government during its sorry flight to the south. The Hotel Crillon, headquarters of the German military command, was across the street from the American Embassy. The German general in charge received the American military and naval attachés at ten in the morning. He offered them glasses of what he described as "the very best brandy in the Crillon." His staff approached the American ambassador with calculated and self-conscious courtesies, to which William C. Bullitt responded with all the tact and reserve of a great envoy of classical stamp. Two months later Bullitt was back from France in his native city of Philadelphia, where, in front of Independence Hall, he made a stirring speech, calling the American people to rally to the British side against Hitler. His speech did not have much of a popular echo.

Hitler hoped that the British would think twice before going on with the war. Their chances, he said, were hopeless; and he repeated that he had no quarrel with the existence of the British Empire. He hoped that the British would make some kind of peace with him.

They didn't. Their savior Churchill had arisen; and behind Churchill—slowly, cautiously, but deliberately—rose the massive shadow of Franklin Roosevelt. In the summer of 1940—still a year and a half before Pearl Harbor and his declaration of war against the United States—Hitler already knew that his principal enemy was Roosevelt, whom he came to hate with a fury even greater than his hatred for Churchill (and, of course, for Stalin, whom he admired in many ways till the end).

Roosevelt and Churchill knew each other. More than that, they had, for some time, put their hopes in each other. For some time Franklin Roosevelt—secretly, privately, through some of his envoys, personal friends whom he trusted—had encouraged those men in London and Paris who were convinced that Hitler had to be fought. Foremost among these was Winston Churchill. In turn, Churchill knew what Roosevelt thought of Hitler; and he knew that what Britain needed was the support of the giant United States. The two men had begun to correspond, in secret. On the day German armor appeared on the cliffs across from Dover, an American citizen, an employee of the American Embassy in London, was arrested by detectives of Scotland Yard. This young man, Tyler Kent, was a convinced and committed isolationist. He knew of that secret correspondence and

25. The Dangerous Summer of 1940

had tried to inform pro-Germany sympathizers in London.

At that time—and for some dangerous weeks thereafter—Winston Churchill's position was not yet fixed in strength. He had, after all, a mixed reputation: yes, a great patriot, but an enthusiast for losing causes. He had been flung out of power during the First World War because of his advocacy of the failed Dardanelles campaign. There were many people within his own Conservative party who distrusted him. When, during the first eight weeks of his prime ministership, he entered the House of Commons, they sat on their hands. King George VI himself had not been quite happy to hand over the reins to him on that tenth of May. John Colville, Churchill's later faithful and admiring private secretary, reported in his diary that day that "this sudden coup of Winston and his rabble was a serious disaster and an unnecessary one.... They had weakly surrendered to a half-breed American whose main support was that of inefficient but talkative people of a similar type...."

On the dark first day of the Dunkirk evacuation, there was a near break between Churchill and the Foreign Secretary, Lord Halifax. Halifax wanted to consider at least the possibility of some kind of a negotiation with Hitler and Mussolini. Churchill said no. "At the moment our prestige in Europe was very low. The only way we could get it back was by showing the world that Germany had not beaten us. If, after two or three months, we could show that we were still unbeaten, our prestige would return. Even if we were beaten, we should be no worse off than we should be if we were now to abandon the struggle. Let us therefore avoid being dragged down the slippery slope...." But he himself was not so far from the edge of a slippery slope. All this looks strange and unreal now. But it is the task of the historian to see not only what happened but also what could have happened. At the end of May and throughout June 1940, the continuation of Churchill's brave position and leadership were still problematic. His great phrases in his great public speeches had not fallen into the void: but their meaning had yet to mature.

During that beautiful and deadly early summer of 1940, Franklin Roosevelt, too, had to contend with a difficult problem. This was the divided mind of the American people. We have heard much lately—because of nostalgic inclinations due to the trauma of a divided nation during the Vietnam War—about the Second World War having been a Good War, when this giant nation was united in purpose and in concept. Even after Pearl Harbor this was not exactly true. During the summer of 1940 it was not true at all. There was a small minority of Americans that was convinced the United States should abet and aid the nations warring against Hitler at almost any price. There was another, larger, minority of isolationists that wanted the United States to keep out of this war, at all costs. And there was a large and inchoate majority that did not like Hitler, and that was contemptuous of the Japanese, but their minds were divided: yes, the United States should oppose the enemies of democracy; no, the democracy of the United States should not engage in a foreign war. There were people who understood that these sentiments were contradictory. Others did not. Yet other Americans began to change their minds—slowly, gradually, at times imperceptibly. But not until after the dangerous summer of 1940.

There was a strange unreality in the American scene during the early summer. The few people from Europe and Britain who landed in New York during those dazzling May and June days found themselves in quite another world—in the gleaming lobbies of the great New York hotels, among the glistening stream of automobiles and taxis, before the glowing glass windows of the incredibly rich department stores, around which flowed the masses of a confident, prosperous, largely undisturbed American people. It was as if the astonishing speed of the devolving events in Western Europe was too fast to grasp. It was not until the fall of France that the startling new specter of a German Europe cohered. The press, for example, including the internationalist newspapers of the East Coast, had not really prepared people for that. Until the fall of Paris its reporters gave undue credit to the resistance of the French and British armies: for the wish is the father of the thought, in newspaperdom as well as elsewhere.

There was another problem. A difficulty between Churchill and Roosevelt had arisen. In their confidential correspondence Churchill was wont to sign himself "Former Naval Person." Yet, oddly, of the two, Roosevelt was more of a naval person. Even after the fall of France, he believed, and said, that "naval power was the key to history," that Hitler, because of his naval inferiority, was bound to lose this war. For the European theater, this was wrong in the long run. The internal-combustion engine had changed the nature of warfare; for the first time in five hundred years, armies could move faster on land than on the seas. Eventually Hitler's armies had to be destroyed on land, and mostly by the Russians. Had the German armies not been chewed up by the Russians, the Western allies, with all of their sea and air superiority, could not have invaded France in 1944.

What is more important, Roosevelt was wrong in the short run too. If worst came to worst, he thought, and told Churchill, the British navy could come across the Atlantic to fight on. But Churchill could not guarantee that. As early as May 15 he wrote Roosevelt that if American help came too late, "the weight may be more than we can bear." Five days later, when the Germans had reached the Channel, he repeated this: "If members of this administration were finished and others came in to parley amid the ruins, you must not be blind to the fact that the sole remaining bargaining counter with Germany would be the fleet, and if this country was left by the United States to its fate no one would have the right to blame those then responsible if they made the best terms they could for the surviving inhabitants." The day after Paris fell, Churchill let Roosevelt know that "a point may be reached in the struggle where the present ministers no longer have control of affairs and when very easy terms could be obtained for the British Islands by their becoming a vassal state of the Hitler empire." This was exactly what Hitler had in mind. As in the case of France, his plan called for a partial occupation of the British

143

4. WAR AND DEPRESSION

island, with the fleet in British ports but demobilized, and with a Germanophile British government somewhere within the reach of the German occupation forces.

Nevertheless, Roosevelt's inclinations were strong and clear. He tried to cajole and to warn Mussolini against entering the war on Hitler's side. Roosevelt knew that this kind of diplomacy represented another move away from neutrality and that Mussolini was still popular among the large Italian-American populations in the important cities of the East: but Roosevelt discounted that. When, on June 10, Mussolini chose to declare war on France and Britain, Roosevelt changed the draft of a speech he was to give at the University of Virginia in Charlottesville. He added a sentence: "The hand that held the dagger," he intoned, "has struck it into the back of its neighbor." Few phrases could be more unneutral than that. When he heard this, Churchill growled with satisfaction. But Roosevelt's hands were, as yet, not free.

He had to prepare himself for an unprecedented nomination for an unprecedented third-term election as President. And against him a new American coalition had begun to gather: it came to be called America First, composed by all kinds of men and women who thought, and said, that American support to Britain was illegal, futile, and wrong. A leader of this movement was Charles A. Lindbergh, a great American hero. Its actual members were recognizable, while its potential popularity was not measurable. It is wrong to consider America First as if it had been a fluke, a conventicle of reactionaries and extremists. There were all kinds of respectable Americans who opposed Roosevelt and who were loath to engage themselves on the British side. They included not only Herbert Hoover but John Foster Dulles, with whom the Lindberghs were dining on the evening the French asked for an armistice—in other words, surrender. Anne Morrow Lindbergh was about to publish her book about the spirit of the times, entitled *The Wave of the Future*, arguing, by no means crudely or unintelligently, that the old world of liberal individualism, of parliamentary democracy, was being replaced by something new, before our very eyes. Another book, from the hands of a young Kennedy, a Harvard undergraduate, was also in the making. Its conclusions were more cautious than Anne Lindbergh's, but some of its underlying suggestions were not entirely different. His father was Roosevelt's ambassador to Britain. Joseph P. Kennedy, Sr., was no admirer of Hitler, but he was a convinced isolationist who loathed Churchill and believed the British resistance to Hitler was futile. His son, John F. Kennedy, was a secret contributor to America First.

Then came the second great coincidence. On the twenty-second of June the French delegates signed their capitulation to Hitler. It was his greatest triumph —and the lowest point in Britain's fortunes in a thousand years. Yet, that very week, the British cause was lifted by an unexpected stroke of fortune, in Philadelphia of all places. There the Republican party had met in convention and nominated Wendell Willkie for their presidential candidate: and Willkie was not an isolationist. There had been many reasons to believe that the Republicans would nominate an isolationist: perhaps Robert A. Taft from Ohio or Arthur H. Vandenberg from Michigan. The Midwest, with its large German-American and Scandinavian-American populations, mostly Republicans, was strongly isolationist. Willkie came from Indiana; and after Hitler's invasion of Scandinavia, some of that Scandinavian-American Anglophobe isolationism began to melt away. Yet the isolationist conviction was still a strong, unchanneled current among the milling Republican delegates on the floor, in that boiling arena of Philadelphia's Convention Hall. But a carefully orchestrated and arranged effort, with the galleries chanting, "We want Willkie," carried the day.

None of this would be possible in our day of the mechanized primary system. It was still possible forty-six years ago. It was the achievement of the internationally minded, anti-populist, financial and social leadership of East Coast Republicans, of readers of the New York *Herald Tribune* over those of the Chicago *Tribune*, of Anglophiles over Anglophobes. The difference between the world view of Willkie and Roosevelt was one of degree, not of kind. Had the Republicans nominated an isolationist, Roosevelt would probably still have won, but the nation would have been sorely and dangerously divided; and Roosevelt would have been constrained to go slow, very slow; constrained to deny his very convictions and inclinations, to the mortal peril of the British, the sole remaining champions of freedom during that dangerous summer of 1940.

This Willkie business was a great help to Britain. Churchill knew that, and he had been smart enough to do nothing about it. He remembered the aggressive British propaganda in the United States during the First World War. "We shall not dance attendance at American party conventions." He let Hitler do the job of turning the sentiments of Americans around, so that their captain could begin to change the course of the mighty American ship of state from armed neutrality to defiance and war.

Hitler now dawdled—for one of the very few times during the war. Europe lay at his feet. He went off on a vacation, touring places in northern France where he had soldiered during the First World War. He made a short, furtive visit to an empty Paris at dawn. He suggested a European version of the Monroe Doctrine: Europe for the "Europeans," America for the Americans. He did not draft the directive for the invasion of Britain until the middle of July—and even then with some reluctance. On July 19 he made a long and crude speech, offering a last chance of peace to Britain. In London the German "peace offer" was let drop with an icy silence, somewhat like a blackmailing note left at the door of a proud old mansion.

A proud old mansion: but would it stand? Could it stand? Above the gray seas patrolled the pilots, across the soughing waves drove the British flotillas, watching. Were the Germans about to come? And the Americans? There was a trickle of war goods moving eastward across the Atlantic, propelled by a current of American sympathy: but sympathy was not yet resolution, and that current not yet a flood. The bombing of England that turned the hearts and minds of many Americans around had not yet begun. For six weeks after the fall of France, the Americans, as Churchill said later

25. The Dangerous Summer of 1940

to a confidant, "treated us in that rather distant and sympathetic manner one adopts toward a friend we know is suffering from cancer." There were many people in America—not only isolationists but men high in the Army general staff—who doubted whether Britain would or could hold out against Hitler. In some of the country clubs around Boston and Philadelphia and New York, the members went around to collect secondhand shotguns for the British, whose Home Guard was still bereft of weapons. Some of the Home Guard were given old golf clubs and sticks, presumably to hit prowling Germans on the head. If and when the invasion came, "you can always take one with you," Churchill had planned to say.

Then came the third coincidence, so enormous and shattering in its consequences that, even now, many people, including a number of historians, are unaware of its ultimate portent.

Six weeks had now passed since France had fallen; and Britain still stood, inviolate, increasingly aglow with the spirit breathed by Churchill's words. Franklin Roosevelt made up his mind. He took an important step. He brought in a few confidants who assured him that he, in his constitutional capacity as Commander-in-Chief, could go ahead. This was at the very end of July. Two days later Roosevelt announced to his cabinet that the United States would "sell directly or indirectly fifty or sixty old World War destroyers to Great Britain." Churchill had asked for such a deal in May. The destroyers were not, in themselves, as important as the gesture, the meaning of the act itself for the world. It meant *the* decisive departure from American neutrality. What Roosevelt did not know, and what Churchill did not know, was that, at the same moment, Hitler had taken his first decisive move in ordering the German army staff to plan for an invasion of Russia.

There was method in Hitler's madness. What did he say to the close circle of his commanders on that day? "England's hope is Russia and America." Against America he could do nothing. But "if hope in Russia is eliminated, America is also eliminated," he said. He was not altogether wrong. Eliminating Russia would destroy British hopes for an eventual conquest of Germany in Europe, and it would strengthen Japan's position in the Far East. In the United States it would also strengthen popular opposition to Roosevelt. There were many Americans who hated and feared communism: the elimination of communist Russia would make Roosevelt's continued intervention on the side of Britain increasingly futile and unpopular. Russia, Hitler said on July 31, 1940, was not yet "a threat." But he was not sure about his prospects of conquering England. Air warfare against England was about to begin; but "if results of the air war are not satisfactory, [invasion] preparations will be halted." So at the end of July 1940, Hitler, after some hesitation, began to consider invading Russia at the very moment when Roosevelt, after some hesitation, made his decision to commit the United States on the British side.

This last day of July in 1940 was not merely an important milestone. It was the turning point of the Second World War. There followed the climax of the Battle of Britain in the air, which, for Hitler, was indecisive. So far as the American people went, the bombing of Britain solidified their gradually crystallizing inclination to stand by the British. Britain held out; and in November 1940 Roosevelt easily won the majority of his people for a third term. That was the first American presidential election watched by the entire world. When Mussolini attacked Greece at the end of October, Hitler berated him: he ought to have waited until after the American election. When Hitler agreed to invite Stalin's minion Molotov, the Soviet commissar for foreign affairs, to Berlin, Stalin set the date of the visit after the American election.

What followed—Lend-Lease, the Selective Service Bill, the Marines sent to Greenland and Iceland, Roosevelt's order to the Navy to shoot at any appearance of Axis naval craft—was a foregone conclusion. Hitler was shrewd enough to order German commanders to avoid incidents with the United States at all costs. He did not want to furnish Roosevelt with the pretext of a serious naval incident. Eventually his Japanese allies were to accomplish what he was reluctant to do. Five hundred days after that thirty-first of July came another great coincidence. In the snow-covered wasteland before Moscow, the Russians halted the German army just when, in the sunny wastes of the Pacific, the Japanese attack on Pearl Harbor propelled the United States into the war. The Germans and the Japanese would achieve astounding victories even after that: but the war they could not win.

One year before Pearl Harbor, Roosevelt had announced that the United States would be the "arsenal of democracy." Churchill had told the American people: "Give us the tools, and we will finish the job." Did he mean this? We cannot tell. It was far from certain that Hitler could be defeated by the supply of American armaments alone. What was needed was the employment of immense American armies and navies in the field. And even that would not be enough. Hitler's defeat could not be accomplished without the armed might of Russia, whereby victory in Europe had to be shared with Russia.

Forty-six years later we have a government that neither remembers nor understands this. Churchill understood the alternative: either all of Europe ruled by Germany, or the eastern portion of it controlled by Russia. It was not a pleasant alternative. In world politics few alternatives are altogether pleasant. Yet half of Europe was better than none. Had it not been for Franklin Roosevelt during that dangerous summer of 1940, even this alternative would have been moot. Had the United States been led by an isolationist president in 1940, Hitler would have won the war.

SOCIAL OUTCASTS IN NAZI GERMANY

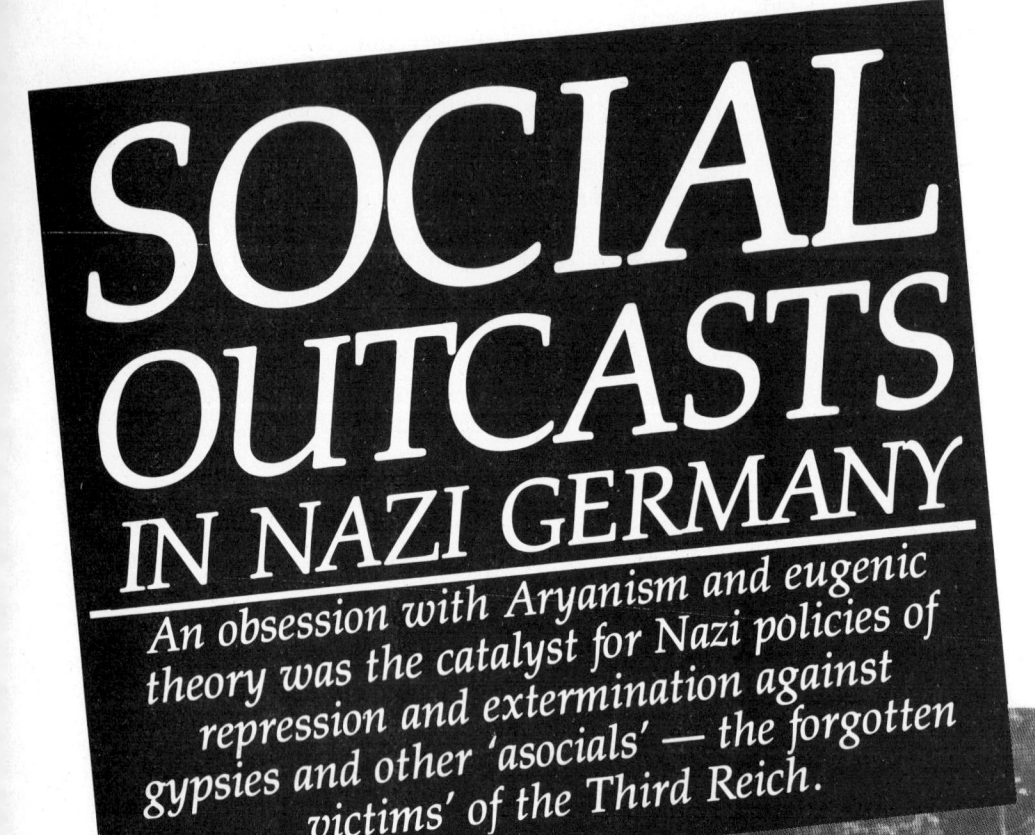

An obsession with Aryanism and eugenic theory was the catalyst for Nazi policies of repression and extermination against gypsies and other 'asocials' — the forgotten victims' of the Third Reich.

Jeremy Noakes

OF ALL NAZI ATROCITIES, THE extermination of the Jews has, rightly, commanded the most attention from historians and the general public. But this understandable preoccupation with the horrors of Nazi anti-Semitism has led people to overlook the fact that the Jews formed only one, albeit the major, target in a broad campaign directed against a variety of groups who were considered to be 'alien to the community' (*Gemeinschaftsfremd*), and who often were defined in biological terms. Only recently have historians begun to focus their attention on this hitherto neglected sphere of Nazi policy and action.

Nazism arose in the aftermath of defeat and revolution. In the view of its leaders, and notably of Hitler, the main cause of Germany's collapse had not been military defeat but the disintegration of the home front weakened by years of incompetent leadership, corroded by pernicious ideas of liberal democracy, Marxism and sentimental humanitarianism, and sapped by biological decline which was the result of ignoring the principles of race and eugenics. Their main domestic goal was to create out of the German people, riven by divisions of class, religion and ideology, a new and unified 'national community' (*Volksgemeinschaft*) based on ties of blood and race and infused with a common 'world view'. They believed this united national community would then possess the requisite morale to enable Germany to make a

A German gypsy family on the road in the 1920s.

bid for the position as a world power to which she had long aspired. The members of this national community, the 'national comrades' (*Volksgenossen*), were expected to conform to a norm based on certain criteria. A national comrade was expected to be of Aryan race, genetically healthy (*erbgesund*), socially efficient (*leistungsfähig*), and politically and ideologically reliable, which involved not simply passive obedience but active participation in the various organisations of the regime and repeated ges-

26. Social Outcasts in Nazi Germany

tures of loyalty (the Hitler salute, etc.).

On coming to power the Nazis were determined to discriminate against, or persecute, all those who failed to fulfill these criteria and were therefore regarded as being outside the national community. There were three main types of these outsiders which, although they overlap, can be conveniently considered as separate categories. Firstly, ideological enemies – those who propagated or even simply held beliefs and values regarded as a threat to national morale. Secondly so-called 'asocials' – the socially inefficient and those whose behaviour offended against the social norms of the 'national community'. And thirdly, the biological outsiders – those who were regarded as a threat because of their race or because they were suffering from a hereditary defect. It is with the last two of these categories that this article is concerned.

The third category, that of biological outsiders, consisted of two main groups: those considered undesirable because of their race (the non-Aryans), and those who were unacceptable on eugenic grounds because of hereditary defects which posed a threat to the future of the German race and/or rendered them socially ineffective. Although the racial and eugenic theories which defined these groups were in some respects distinct – not all eugenists were anti-Semitic for example – they shared common origins in biological theories of the late nineteenth century and a common perspective in viewing mankind primarily in biological terms. Individuals were not seen as possessing validity in themselves as human beings and were not judged in terms of their human qualities, but their significance was assessed first and foremost in terms of their physical and mental efficiency as members of a 'race' and they were seen primarily as collections of good or bad genes.

The theory of eugenics – the idea of improving the 'race' through the encouragement of selective breeding – had become increasingly influential in many countries during the 1920s and 1930s and Germany was no exception. It flourished against a background of concern about declining birthrates and particularly about the destruction of a generation of the healthiest members of the nation in the First World War. There was also growing concern about the impact of modern improvements in welfare, hygiene, and medical care in ensuring the survival of increasing numbers of those with hereditary defects who were thereby allegedly producing a deterioration of the race. Moreover, during this period it was fashionable to attribute many social ills to heredity – habitual criminality, alcoholism, prostitution, and pauperism. Even some on the Left were attracted by eugenics. They tended to make a sharp distinction between the 'genuine' working class and the *Lumpenproletariat*, the 'dregs' of society. Eugenics appeared to offer the prospect of eliminating the *Lumpenproletariat*, traditionally seen since Marx as the tool of reaction.

During the 1920s a number of doctors and psychiatrists in Germany began to propose a policy of sterilisation to prevent those with hereditary defects from procreating. Such a policy of 'negative selection' had already been carried out on a limited scale in the United States where the technique of vasectomy had been developed and was first applied by a prison doctor in 1899. With the economic crisis which began in 1929 such proposals gained increasing support among those involved in the welfare services, since they appeared to offer the prospect not only of substantial savings in the future but also of facilitating the release of some of those in institutional care without fear of their producing defective offspring. Towards the end of 1932 the Prussian authorities prepared a draft law permitting the voluntary sterilisation of those with hereditary defects. Those who drafted the law had felt obliged to make sterilisation voluntary since they believed that public opinion was not yet ready for compulsion. The logic of the eugenist case, however, required compulsion and, significantly, the Nazi medical experts who took part in the preceding discussions had demanded compulsion. The sterilisation issue was given priority by Hitler himself who overruled objections from his Catholic Vice-Chancellor, von Papen. On July 14th, 1933, within six months of its coming to power, the new regime had issued a Sterilisation Law ordering the sterilisation – by compulsion if necessary – of all those suffering from a number of specified illnesses which were alleged to be hereditary.

Apart from the moral issues raised by the question of compulsory sterilisation as such, the criteria used to define hereditary illness were in many respects exceedingly dubious. Thus, while there could be no doubt about the hereditary nature of some of the diseases specified, such as Huntingdon's Chorea, others such as 'hereditary simple-mindedness', schizophrenia, manic depressive illness, and 'chronic alcoholism' were not only more difficult to diagnose but their hereditary basis was much more questionable. Moreover, even if it were granted, the elimination of these diseases through the sterilisation of those affected was an impossible task in view of the role played by recessive genes in their transmission. Finally, although an impressive apparatus of hereditary courts was established to pass judgment on the individual cases, the evidence used to justify proposals for sterilisation sometimes reflected more the social and political prejudices of the medical and welfare authorities involved than objective scientific criteria. Thus a reputation for being 'work-shy' or even former membership of the Communist Party could be used as crucial supporting evidence in favour of sterilisation. From 1934 to 1945 between 320,000 and 350,000 men and women were sterilised under this law and almost one hundred people died following the operation. After the war few of those sterilised received any compensation for what they had suffered since they could not claim to have been persecuted on political or racial grounds. The new measure appears to have had at least tacit support from public opinion. It was only when people found members of their own families, friends and colleagues affected by it that they became concerned.

The Nazis claimed that sterilistion was an unfortunate necessity for those with hereditary defects and that once it was carried out the sterilised were thereby in effect restored to full status as 'national comrades'. In practice, however, in a society in which health, and in particular fertility, were key virtues the sterilised were bound

4. WAR AND DEPRESSION

to feel discriminated against, and the fact that they were forbidden to marry fertile partners underlined this point. However, for those who were not merely suffering from hereditary defects but were socially ineffective as well the future was far bleaker. Already in 1920 a distinguished jurist, Karl Binding, and a psychiatrist, Alfred Hoche, had together published a book with the title: *The Granting of Permission for the Destruction of Worthless Life. Its Extent and Form*. In this book, written under the impression of the casualties of the First World War, the two authors proposed that in certain cases it should be legally possible to kill those suffering from incurable and severely crippling handicaps and injuries – so-called 'burdens on the community' (*Ballastexistenzen*). This proposal assumed, first, that it was acceptable for an outside agency to define what individual life was 'worthless' and, secondly, that in effect an individual had to justify his existence according to criteria imposed from outside (i.e. he had to prove that his life was worthwhile). These assumptions were indeed implicit in the biological and collectivist approach to human life which had become increasingly influential after 1900.

With the take-over of power by the Nazis it was not long before this biological and collectivist approach began to be transferred from theory into reality. In addition to the sterilisation programme, this took the form, firstly, of a propaganda campaign designed to devalue the handicapped as burdens on the community in the eyes of the population and, secondly, of a programme of systematic extermination of the mentally sick and handicapped – the so-called Euthanasia Programme, a misleading title since the term 'euthanasia' was in fact a Nazi euphemism for mass murder.

The euthanasia programme began in the spring or early summer of 1939 when the parents of a severely handicapped baby petitioned Hitler for the baby to be killed. He agreed to the request and ordered the head of his personal Chancellery, Phillip Bouhler, to proceed likewise in all similar cases. Bouhler set up a secret organisation to carry out the programme which initially covered children up to three years old, later extended to twelve-sixteen years. By the end of the war approximately 5,000 children had been murdered either by injection or through deliberate malnutrition. In August 1939 Hitler ordered that the extermination programme be extended to adults, for which the *Führer*'s Chancellery set up another secret organisation. So large were the numbers involved – there were approximately 200,000 mentally sick and handicapped in 1939 – that a new method of killing had to be devised. Experts in the Criminal Police Department came up with the idea of using carbon monoxide gas. After a successful trial on a few patients, gas chambers were constructed in six mental hospitals in various parts of Germany to which patients were transferred from mental institutions all over the *Reich*. By the time the programme was officially stopped by Hitler in August 1941 under pressure from public protests some 72,000 people had been murdered.

During the next two years under a separate programme also run by the *Führer*'s Chancellery under the code number 14F13, the reference number of the Inspector of Concentration Camps, another 30-50,000 people were selected from concentration camps and gassed on the grounds of mental illness, physical incapacity, or simply racial origin, in which case the 'diagnosis' on the official form read 'Jew' or 'gypsy'. In the meantime, however, the majority of the personnel who had developed expertise in operating the gas chambers had been transferred to Poland and placed at the disposal of the SS for the death camps which opened in the winter of 1941-42. These notorious death camps – Belsen, Treblinka, Sobihor, Majdanek, and Auschwitz-Birkenau – were intended to destroy the other biological outcasts of Nazi Germany, the non-Aryans, of whom the Jews formed by far the largest group. However, the understandable preoccupation with the Holocaust has tended to divert attention from another group which came into this category – the gypsies. For they also suffered genocide at the hands of the Nazis.

Long before the Nazis came to power the gypsies had been treated as social outcasts. Their foreign appearance, their strange customs and language, their nomadic way of life and lack of regular employment had increasingly come to be regarded as an affront to the norms of a modern state and society. They were seen as asocial, a source of crime, culturally inferior, a foreign body within the nation. During the 1920s, the police, first in Bavaria and then in Prussia established special offices to keep the gypsies under constant surveillance. They were photographed and fingerprinted as if they were criminals. With the Nazi take-over, however, a new motive was added to the grounds for persecution – their distinct and allegedly inferior racial character.

Nazi policy towards the gypsies, like the policy towards the Jews, was uncertain and confused. Initially they were not a major target. With their small numbers – 30,000 – and generally low social status they were not seen as such a serious racial threat as the Jews. They were, however, included in the regulations implementing the Nuremberg Law for the Protection of German Blood and Honour of September 15th, 1935, which banned marriage and sexual relations between Aryans and non-Aryans. From then onwards they were the subject of intensive research by racial 'experts' of the 'Research Centre for Racial Hygiene and Biological Population Studies'. The aim was to identify and distinguish between pure gypsies and the part-gypsies (*Mischlinge*) who had been lumped together in the records of the Weimar police. Whereas in the case of the Jews the *Mischlinge* were treated as less of a threat than the 'full' Jews, among the gypsies the *Mischlinge*, some of whom had integrated themselves into German society, were treated as the greater threat. The leading expert on the gypsies, Dr Robert Ritter, insisted that:

> The gypsy question can only be regarded as solved when the majority of a-social and useless gypsy *Mischlinge* have been brought together in large camps and made to work and when the continual procreation of this half-breed population has been finally prevented. Only then will future generations be freed from this burden.

In December 1938 Himmler issued a 'Decree for the Struggle against the Gypsy Plague', which introduced a more systematic registration of gypsies based on the research of the racial experts. Pure gypsies received

26. Social Outcasts in Nazi Germany

brown papers, gypsy *Mischlinge* light blue ones and nomadic non-gypsies grey ones. The aim was 'once and for all to ensure the racial separation of gypsies from our own people to prevent the mixing of the two races, and finally to regulate the living conditions of the gypsies and gypsy *Mischlinge*'. After the victory over Poland the deportation of gypsies from Germany to Poland was ordered and in the meantime they were forbidden to leave the camps to which they were assigned and which were now in effect turned into labour camps. In May 1940 2,800 gypsies joined the Jewish transports to Poland. However, this deportation programme was then stopped because of logistical problems in the reception areas.

During 1941-42 gypsies and gypsy-*Mischlinge* were included in the discriminatory measures introduced against Jews within the Reich and they were also removed from the Armed Forces. However, while there was unanimous contempt for the gypsy *Mischlinge*, Nazi racial experts had a certain admiration for the way in which the pure gypsies had sustained their separate identity and way of life over the centuries, an achievement attributed to their strong sense of race. Dr Robert Ritter suggested that the 'pure bred' gypsies in Germany (*Sinti*) and in the German-speaking areas of Bohemia and Moravia (*Lalleri*) should be assigned to an area where they would be permitted to live according to their traditional ways more or less as museum specimens, while the remainder should be sterilised, interned, and subjected to forced labour. Himmler sympathised with this view and in October 1942 issued orders for appropriate arrangements to be made. However, he ran into opposition from Bormann and probably Hitler and so, on December 16th, 1942, he issued an order for the German gypsies to be transferred to Auschwitz. Between February 26th and March 25th, 1943, 11,400 gypsies from Germany and elsewhere were transported to a special gypsy camp within Auschwitz. Here, unlike other prisoners, they were able to live together with their families, probably to facilitate the medical experiments which were carried out in a medical centre established in their camp by the notorious Dr Mengele. Of the 20,000 gypsies in all transported to Auschwitz, 11,000 were murdered there, while the others were transferred elsewhere. At the same time, thousands of gypsies were being murdered throughout occupied Europe, notably by the *Einsatzgruppen* in Russia. It has been estimated that half a million European gypsies died at the hands of the Nazis. Of the 30,000 gypsies living in Germany in 1939 only 5,000 survived the war.

The gypsies offended against the norms of the 'national community' not only on the grounds of their non-Aryan character (although ironically since they had originated in India they could legitimately claim to be more 'Aryan' than the Germans!), but also on the grounds of their 'a-social' behaviour. The 'a-socials' formed another major category of social outcasts. The term 'a-social' was a very flexible one which could be used to include all those who failed to abide by the social norms of the national community: habitual criminals, the so-called 'work-shy', tramps and beggars, alcoholics, prostitutes, homosexuals, and juvenile delinquents. The Nazis introduced much tougher policies towards such groups, in some cases – as with the Sterilisation Law – implementing measures which had been demanded or planned before their take-over of power. Above all, there was a growing tendency for the police to acquire more and more control over these groups at the expense of the welfare agencies and the courts. It was the ultimate ambition of the police to take over responsibility for all those whom it defined as 'community aliens' (*Gemeinschaftsfremde*). To achieve this goal, in 1940 it introduced a draft 'Community Alien Law' which, after being held up by opposition from other government departments, was finally intended to go into effect in 1945. According to Paragraph 1.i of the final draft:

> A person is alien to the community if he/she proves to be incapable of satisfying the minimum requirements of the national community through his/her own efforts, in particular through an unusual degree of deficiency of mind or character.

The official explanation of the law maintained that:

> The National Socialist view of welfare is that it can only be granted to national comrades who both need it and are worthy of it. In the case of community aliens who are only a burden on the national community welfare is not necessary, rather police compulsion with the aim of either making them once more useful members of the national community through appropriate measures or of preventing them from being a further burden. In all these matters protection of the community is the primary object.

In September 1933, the Reich Ministries of the Interior and Propaganda initiated a major roundup of 'tramps and beggars' of whom there were between 300,000 and 500,000, many of them homeless young unemployed. Such a large number of people without fixed abode was regarded as a threat to public order. However, the regime lacked the means to provide shelter and work for such vast numbers. Moreover, there were advantages in having a mobile labour force which could if necessary be directed to particular projects. The Nazis, therefore, initially made a distinction between 'orderly' and 'disorderly' people of no fixed abode. Those who were healthy, willing to work, and with no previous convictions were given a permit (*Wanderkarte*) and were obliged to follow particular routes and perform compulsory work in return for their board and lodging. 'Disorderly' persons of no fixed abode on the other hand could be dealt with under the Law against Dangerous Habitual Criminals and concerning Measures for Security and Correction of November 24th, 1933, and the Preventive Detention Decree of the Ministry of the Interior of December 14th, 1937, which introduced the practice of preventive detention. Many tramps were also sterilised.

After 1936, as a result of the economic recovery, Germany faced a growing labour shortage and the regime was no longer willing to tolerate either numbers of people of no fixed abode or the 'work-shy'. Apart from their significance for the labour force, such people contradicted basic principles of the national community – the principle of performance and the principle of being 'integrated' (*erfasst-eingeordnet*). As one Nazi expert put it:

> In the case of a long period without work on the open road where he is

4. WAR AND DEPRESSION

entirely free to follow his own desires and instincts, he (the tramp) is in danger of becoming a freedom fanatic who rejects all integration as hated compulsion.

As a result, persons of no fixed abode increasingly came to be regarded as a police rather than a welfare matter. Even before 1936 some people designated as 'work-shy' had been sent to concentration camps forming the category of 'a-socials' who wore a black triangle. A big round-up had taken place before the Olympic games and in 1936 two of the ten companies in Dachau were composed of this category. In the summer of 1938 an even bigger round-up took place under the code word 'Work-shy Reich' in the course of which approximately 11,000 'beggars, tramps, pimps and gypsies' were arrested and transferred largely to Buchenwald where they formed the largest category of prisoner until the influx of Jews following the 'Night of Broken Glass' on November 8th. It has been estimated that some 10,000 tramps were incarcerated in concentration camps during the Third Reich of whom few survived the ordeal. This harsh policy towards the 'a-socials' appears to have been popular with many Germans and was welcomed by local authorities who were thereby able to get rid of their 'awkward customers'.

Having set up a utopian model of an ideologically and racially homogeneous 'national community', the Nazis increasingly sought an explanation for deviance from its norms not in terms of flaws within the system itself and its incompatibility with human variety but rather in terms of flaws which were innate within the individual. As an anti-type to the racially pure, genetically healthy, loyal and efficient 'national comrade', they evolved the concept of the 'degenerate a-social' whose deviance was *biologically* determined. As the Reich Law Leader, Hans Frank, put it in a speech in October 1938:

National Socialism regards degeneracy as an immensely important source of criminal activity. It is our belief that every superior nation is furnished with such an abundance of endowments for its journey through life that the word 'degeneracy' most clearly defines the state of affairs that concerns us here. In a decent nation the 'genus' must be regarded as valuable *per se*: consequently, in an individual degeneracy signifies exclusion from the normal *genus* of the decent nation. This state of being degenerate, this different or alien quality tends to be rooted in miscegnation between a decent representative of his race and an individual of inferior stock. To us National Socialists criminal biology, or the theory of congenital criminality, connotes a link between racial decadence and criminal manifestations. The complete degenerate lacks all racial sensitivity and sees it as his positive duty to harm the community or member thereof. He is the absolute opposite of the man who recognises that the fulfillment of his duty as a national comrade is his mission in life.

These ideas represent a variation on concepts which had emerged from research into so-called 'criminal biology' which had been going on in the Weimar Republic. Nor was this simply a matter of theory. For the Nazis had actually begun to apply the principles of criminal biology in the sphere of juvenile delinquency. This was another area in which the police usurped the responsibility of the welfare agencies and the courts. In 1939 they exploited the Preventive Detention Decree of 1937 to set up their own Reich Central Agency for the Struggle against Juvenile Delinquency and the following year established a Youth Concentration Camp in Moringen near Hanover. Perhaps the most significant feature of the camp was the fact that the youths were subjected to 'biological and racial examination' under the supervision of Dr Ritter, now the Director of the Criminal-Biological Institute of the Reich Security Main Office. Then, on the basis of highly dubious pseudo-scientific criteria, they were divided into groups according to their alleged socio-biological character and reformability. This process of socio-biological selection pioneered in Moringen was an integral part of the concept of the Community Aliens Law. Thus, according to the official justification of the Law:

The governments of the period of the System (Weimar) failed in their measures to deal with community aliens. They did not utilise the findings of genetics and criminal biology as a basis for a sound welfare and penal policy. As a result of their liberal attitude they constantly perceived only the "rights of the individual" and were more concerned with his protection from state intervention than with the general good. In National Socialism the individual counts for nothing when the community is at stake.

Defeat preserved Germans from being subjected to the Community Aliens Law and a future in which any deviation from the norms of the 'national community' would be not merely criminalised but also liable to be defined as evidence of 'degeneracy', i.e. biological inadequacy, for which the penalties were sterilisation and probably eventual 'eradication' (*Ausmerzen*) through hard labour in concentration camp conditions. The Third Reich's policy towards social outcasts stands as a frightful warning both against the application of pseudo-science to social problems and against the rationalisation of social prejudices in terms of pseudescience.

FOR FURTHER READING:
Gitta Sereny, *Into that Darkness* (Picador Books, 1977); D. Kenrick and G. Puxon, *The Destiny of Europe's Gypsies* (Chatto, 1972); J. Noakes, 'Nazism and Eugenics: The Background to the Nazi Sterilization Law of 14 July 1933' in R.J. Bullen et. al., eds., *Ideas into Politics. Aspects of European History 1880-1950* (Croom Helm, 1984); E. Klee, *'Euthanasie' im NS-Staat. Die 'Vernichtung lebensunwerten Lebens'* (Frankfurt, 1983); D. Peukert, 'Arbeitslager und Jugend-KZ: die Behandlung Gemeinschaftsfremder im Dritten Reich', in D. Peukert & J. Reulecke, *Die Reihen fast geschlossen. Beiträge zur Geschichte des Alltags unterm national sozialismus* (Wuppertal, 1981).

REBORN FROM HOLOCAUST

Michael Dillon

Michael Dillon teaches Chinese and Japanese in Tameside, Greater Manchester

ON the morning of August 6, 1945, *Enola Gay,* a Boeing B-29 Superfortress of the US Air Force, flew over the centre of Hiroshima and released the first atomic bomb ever to be used in action. It exploded in mid-air, 580 metres above the Industrial Promotion Hall. A clock, now in the city's museum, shows its hands fused to its face at 8.15, the precise time of the blast.

Up to a radius of 2500 metres almost everything was reduced to ashes; buildings 1000 metres further out were destroyed completely and there was substantial destruction much further away. People within 3.5 kilometres of the hypocentre suffered burns even if they survived the blast. Strangely, the Industrial Promotion Hall, though damaged, was left erect. It remains to this day, renamed the Atom Bomb Dome. It is still impossible to be certain about the total number of casualties but, according to the plaque at the foot of the Dome, more than 200,000 deaths can be attributed to the bomb.

Hiroshima's response to such catastrophic devastation was robust. In January 1946, just five months after Japan's surrender, a Reconstruction Committee was formed under a town planner, Toshio Nakashima, with the aim of rebuilding Hiroshima so that it should become the most modern city in Japan with 'wide streets, skyscrapers and open parks'. During that grim early period of reconstruction, a symbol gave the people cause for hope: two cherry trees that stood a little to the south of the Town Hall had been blackened by the explosion. One morning in April 1946, white blossoms suddenly appeared on the charred branches and thousands flocked to see them.

A brief walk around the city confirms the success of the 1946 plan. Like all Japanese cities razed during the war, Hiroshima today is a prosperous town built of steel, glass and concrete, and ablaze with neon signs at night. Anyone who did not know its history would not be able to guess what happened there.

Unlike most of Japan's largest cities, however, which seem to have developed without any overall sense of planning since the war, the central part of Hiroshima at least still retains much of the character of the pre-war city. The area that is now called Peace Park and encompasses that part of the city most completely devastated by the bomb, looks very similar to photographs taken of the same scene during the 1930s. Although the buildings and bridges have been rebuilt with modern materials, the essential shape of the old city has been preserved, as has the uninterrupted view of the mountains to the north.

The dominant feature of the Peace Park is the Atom Bomb Dome, a powerful reminder of that day 40 years ago. The Park also houses the Peace Memorial Museum and the A-Bomb Cenotaph, a marble tomb with the list of names of all known victims. Despite these reminders, the Park is a place of enjoyment and leisure: families and couples walk by the river and sit in the sun, while groups of school children queue up to be photographed in front of the Cenotaph. Beneath the central pillars of the museum, a group of *takenokozoku,* or 'bamboo-shoot kids', dressed as early 1960s rockers, jive around a cassette recorder.

Inside the museum, the atmosphere changes. Exhibits show in detail, through relics, diagrams, photographs and a scale model of the ruined city, the effect of heat, blast and radiation on people, buildings and everyday objects. Tape-recordings of survivors' voices and paintings of their impressions of the explosion personalize the tragedy, and exhibits from Nagasaki are a reminder that Hiroshima was not alone. However many photographs the visitors may have already seen, to stand in Hiroshima and see the remains of twisted metal, fused brick and stone and the imprint of a human shadow on a stone step produces an indescribable emotion. Commentary and captions in the museum are presented with commendable understatement, yet visitors walk around in stunned silence.

There are several ironies associated with the bombing. Although Hiroshima had been a military base

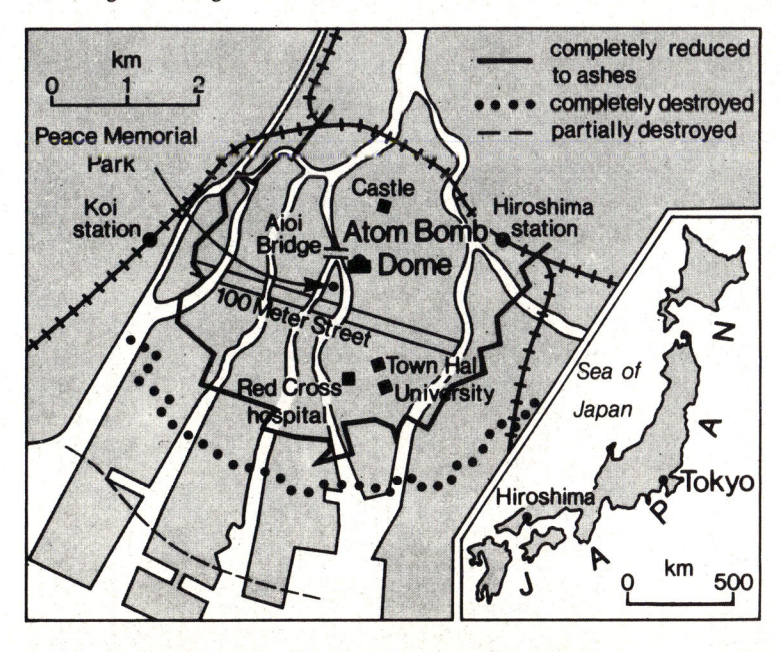

4. WAR AND DEPRESSION

since the war with China in 1894–5, it also had one of the highest concentration of devout Buddhists. They would have nothing to do with ritually impure aspects of daily life such as butchery, the leather trade, and the disposal of refuse or bodies. The small army of *eta* (outcasts) who performed these services was considered as unclean as the tasks themselves and were forced into ghetto areas, or *buraku*, outside the city centre. Thus they suffered less than the rest of the population.

The atom bomb itself produced a new class of outcasts, the *hibakusha*, 'the bombed', who have since undergone serious social and economic deprivation along with the physical or mental suffering. Thousands of horror stories could be told about the effect of the blast, fire and radiation on the victims, but a simple tale illustrates the depth of the psychological damage. Mrs Onoyo Yamamoto lost four of her children in the bombing, but her one-year-old son survived. Interviewed 26 years later, she said that her son had suffered no apparent physical ill effects from the explosion and had grown up and become engaged to be married. But his future parents-in-law, finding that his mother was a hibakusha, forced their daughter to break off the engagement.

Although the scars and the sadness remain, Hiroshima thrives economically. The population today is 900,000, many of them employed in Hiroshima's main industries: shipbuilding, machinery and automobile manufacture. One of Hiroshima's main contributions to the post-war economic miracle of Japan is the Mazda car plant, the single largest employer in Hiroshima. Occupying two million square metres, it claims to be the largest automotive plant in the world.

Mazda accounts for perhaps 25 per cent of the total industrial production of the city, employs 27,700 people directly, and a further 18,000 who work for the company via subcontractors. Four assembly lines run under centralized computer control which allows different models to be produced on each line. Almost 1.5 million vehicles are produced each year at a rate of one every 15 seconds. Seventy per cent of Mazda's production is exported.

HIROSHIMA has made an outstanding success of modernizing its city and its industries. It has the soaring buildings, wide avenues and open spaces planned in 1946. But the city authorities and the people are acutely conscious of their responsibility to warn others of the horrors that must not be repeated. Before I left Hiroshima, Mr Sakata Hiroo, of the International Relations Department of the Mayor's Office, told me that his department wanted every foreign visitior to take home something of the spirit of Hiroshima so that the world would never forget.

In October 1976, the commander of the original mission to bomb Hiroshima flew a restored B-29 bomber at an air display in Texas. The culmination of the entertainment was a mock atom-bomb drop from the aircraft, complete with a simulated mushroom cloud. Clearly, reminders are still necessary.

Lessons from a Lost War

What has Viet Nam taught about when to use power—and when not to?

> *The customary reward of defeat, if one can survive it, is in the lessons thereby learned, which may yield victory in the next war. But the circumstances of our defeat in Vietnam were sufficiently ambiguous to deny the nation [that] benefit.*
> —Edward N. Luttwak
> *The Pentagon and the Art of War*

Ten years after the fall of Saigon, the debacle in Southeast Asia remains a subject many Americans would rather not discuss. So the nation has been spared a searing, divisive inquest—"Who lost Viet Nam?"—but at a heavy price. The old divisions have been buried rather than resolved. They seem ready to break open again whenever anyone asks what lessons the U.S. should draw from its longest war, and the only one to end in an undisguisable defeat.

Was that loss inevitable, or could the war have been won with different strategy and tactics? Was the war fought for the right reasons? Did its aftermath prove or explode the domino theory? The questions are not in the least academic. They bear on the all-important problem of whether, when and how the U.S. should again send its troops to fight abroad.

Pondering these questions, Secretary of Defense Caspar Weinberger argues, citing Viet Nam, that "before the U.S. commits combat forces abroad, there must be some reasonable assurance that we will have the support of the American people and . . . Congress." Secretary of State George Shultz replies that "there is no such thing as guaranteed public support in advance." The lesson Shultz draws from Viet Nam is that "public support can be frittered away if we do not act wisely and effectively." And this open dispute between two senior members of the Reagan Cabinet is mild compared with the arguments among policy analysts, Viet Nam veterans and the public about what kinds of wars can be won or even deserve public support in the first place.

A number of experts doubt that the U.S. can evolve any common view of Viet Nam and its lessons for many years to come. Says Graham Martin, the last U.S. Ambassador to South Viet Nam: "I estimated at the end of the war that it probably would be at least two decades before any rational, objective discussion of the war and its causes and effects could be undertaken by scholars who were not so deeply, emotionally engaged at the time that their later perceptions were colored by biases and prejudices." William Hyland, editor of *Foreign Affairs* magazine, thinks an even longer perspective may be required: "We always want to make historical judgments two days after the fact. Historians need 100 years."

But the U.S. is unlikely to have anywhere near that much time to decide what lessons to draw from Viet Nam and how to apply them. The initial impulse after the American withdrawal was to avoid any foreign involvement that might conceivably lead to a commitment of U.S. troops. Scholars differ on how seriously this so-called Viet Nam syndrome inhibited an activist U.S. foreign policy, but in any case it is fading—witness the enthusiastic approval of the Grenada invasion in late 1983 (to be sure, that was a rare case in which the U.S. was able to apply such overwhelming force that it could not have failed to win quickly). Says Maine's Republican Senator William Cohen: "The legacy of Viet Nam does not mean that we will not send our sons anywhere. It does mean that we will not send them everywhere." Even some fervent doves agree that memories of Viet Nam should not keep the U.S. from ever fighting anywhere. Sam Brown, onetime antiwar leader who now develops low cost housing in Colorado, remains convinced that if it were not for the protests against U.S. involvement in Viet Nam that he helped organize, "we would have three or four other wars now." Even so, concedes Brown, some "wrong lessons" might be drawn, among them "the risk that we won't be prepared if our national interest is genuinely threatened."

But if the specter of Viet Nam no longer inhibits all thought of projecting U.S. military power overseas, it still haunts every specific decision. In the Middle East, Weinberger's fears of entrapment in a drawn-out conflict fought without public support caused him at first to oppose sending Marines to Lebanon and then to insist on their withdrawal after terrorist attacks left 266 U.S. servicemen dead. Shultz objected that the pullout would undercut U.S. diplomacy in the area, and still regards it as

---

> "I want to rail against wind and tide, kill the whales in the ocean, sweep the whole country to save people from slavery."
> —TRIEU AU,
> VIET NAM'S
> "JOAN OF ARC"
> A.D. 248

> "France has had the country for nearly 100 years, and the people are worse off than at the beginning."
> —FRANKLIN D.
> ROOSEVELT
> 1944

> "Kill ten of our men and we will kill one of yours. In the end, it is you who will tire."
> —HO CHI MINH
> 1946

4. WAR AND DEPRESSION

POWER
B-52 dropping bombs on guerrillas, 1966: Was it a matter of too much force, or not enough?

a mistake. But Ronald Reagan ordered the withdrawal anyway and won the approval of voters, even though critics portrayed the pullout as a national humiliation. The reason, suggests Democratic Political Analyst William Schneider, is that the President sensed the persistence of a popular attitude toward foreign military commitments that is summarized by the Viet Nam-era slogan "Win or Get Out." Says Schneider: "In Grenada we won. In Lebanon we got out. So much for the Viet Nam syndrome."

The Viet Nam experience colors almost every discussion of Central American policy. Nebraska Governor Bob Kerrey, who won a Congressional Medal of Honor and lost part of a leg fighting with the Navy SEAL commandos in Viet Nam, maintains that if memories of the ordeal in Southeast Asia were not still so strong, "we'd be in Nicaragua now." In Congress, Kerrey's fellow Democrats fret that the Administration's commitment to resist the spread of Marxist revolution throughout the isthmus could eventually bog down American troops in another endless jungle guerrilla war.

Reaganites retort, correctly, that while Viet Nam is halfway around the world and of debatable strategic importance to Washington, Central America is virtually next door, an area where U.S. interests are obvious. Moreover, the amounts Washington is spending to help the government of El Salvador defeat leftist guerrillas and to assist the *contra* rebels fighting the Marxist Sandinista government of Nicaragua are pittances compared with the sums lavished on South Viet Nam even before the direct U.S. military intervention there. Still, the Administration every now and then feels obliged to deny that it has any plan or desire to send U.S. troops to fight in Central America. Weinberger last November coupled his remarks about the necessity of popular support for any foreign military commitment with a pledge that "the President will not allow our military forces to creep—or be drawn gradually—into a combat role in Central America."

> "Master fear and pain, overcome obstacles, unite your efforts, fight to the very end, annihilate the enemy."
> —GENERAL GIAP
> 1954

> "I could conceive of no greater tragedy than for the U.S. to [fight] an all-out war in Indochina."
> —DWIGHT D. EISENHOWER
> 1954

> "You have a row of dominoes set up, you knock over the first one and [the last one] will go over very quickly."
> —EISENHOWER
> 1954

> "We do commit the U.S. to preventing the fall of South Viet Nam to Communism."
> —ROBERT MCNAMARA
> 1961

One of the few propositions about Viet Nam that commands near unanimous assent from Americans is the obvious one that the U.S. lost— and a growing number would qualify even that. Richard Nixon, in his new book, *No More Vietnams*, argues that "we won the war" but then abandoned South Viet Nam after the Communist North began violating the 1973 Paris accords that supposedly ended the fighting. Though the former President's self-interest is obvious, parts of his analysis are supported even by the enemy. U.S. Army Colonel Harry Summers Jr., who considers Viet Nam "a tactical success and a strategic failure," was in Hanoi on a negotiating mission a few days before Saigon fell. Summers recalls telling a North Vietnamese colonel, "You know, you never defeated us on the battlefield." The foe's reply: "That may be so, but it is also irrelevant." In essence, the U.S. was outlasted by an enemy that proved able and willing to fight longer than America and its South Vietnamese allies.

Given the weakness of South Viet Nam, the determination of the North and the extent of the aid it could count on from the Soviet Union and neighboring China, even some hawks concede that Hanoi's victory might have been inevitable. Says Military Analyst Luttwak: "Some wars simply cannot be won, and Viet Nam may have been one of them." Nonetheless, the main lesson they would draw from the war is that the U.S. threw away whatever chance for victory it may have had through blunders that must not be repeated.

The most detailed exposition of this view comes from Colonel Summers, whose book, *On Strategy: A Critical Analysis of the Vietnam War*, has become must reading for young officers. Summers argues that the U.S. should have sealed off South Viet Nam with a barrier of American troops to prevent North Viet Nam from sending troops and matériel through Laos and Cambodia to wage war in the South. Instead, he says, the U.S. "wasted its strength" fighting the guerrillas in the South, a hopeless task so long as they were continually reinforced from the North and one that American troops had no business trying to carry out in the first place. The U.S., he contends, should have confined itself to protecting South Viet Nam against "external aggression" from the North and left "pacification," the job of rooting out the guerrillas, to the South Vietnamese. By in effect taking over the war, the U.S. sapped the initiative and ultimately the will of its Southern allies to carry out a job only they could do in the end.

Luttwak carries this analysis a step further by pouring scorn on the tactics used in the South: "The jet fighter bombing raids against flimsy huts that might contain a handful of guerrillas or perhaps none; the fair-sized artillery barrages that silenced lone snipers; the ceaseless firing of helicopter door gunners whereby a million dollars' worth of ammunition might be expended to sweep a patch of high grass." This "grossly disproportionate use of firepower," says Luttwak, was not just ineffective; it alienated South Vietnamese villagers whose cooperation against the guerrillas was vital. At least equally important, "Its imagery on television was by far the most powerful stimulus of antiwar sentiment" back in the U.S. Former CIA Director William Colby agrees that the U.S. got nowhere as long as it tried to defeat guerrillas with massed firepower and only began to make progress when it shifted to a "people's war" in which the

28. Lessons from a Lost War

South Vietnamese carried the main burden of the fighting. By then it was too late; American public sentiment had turned irreversibly in favor of a fast pullout.

According to Hyland, "The biggest lesson of Viet Nam is that we need to have a much better notion of what is at stake, what our interests are, before we go into a major military undertaking." Weinberger voiced essentially the same thought last fall in laying down several conditions, beyond a reasonable assurance of public support, that must be met if U.S. troops are again to be sent into battle overseas: "We should have clearly defined political and military objectives, and we should know precisely how our forces can accomplish those." Other criteria: "The commitment of U.S. forces to combat should be a last resort," undertaken only if it "is deemed vital to our national interest or that of our allies," and then "with the clear intention of winning" by using as much force as necessary.

Weinberger's speech, delivered after he had talked it over with President Reagan, is the closest thing to an official Administration reading of the lessons of Viet Nam. But some rude jeers greeted the Weinberger doctrine. Luttwak, for example, called Weinberger's views "the equivalent of a doctor saying he will treat patients only if he is assured they will recover." Columnist William Safire headlined a scathing critique ONLY THE 'FUN' WARS, and New York Democrat Stephen Solarz, who heads the House Subcommittee on Asian and Pacific Affairs, pointed out, "It is a formula for national paralysis if, before we ever use force, we need a Gallup poll showing that two-thirds of the American people are in favor of it."

More important, what is a "vital interest"? To some Americans, the only one that would justify another war is the defense of the U.S. against a threat of direct attack. Decrying "this whole practice of contracting our military out just for the survival of some other government and country," Georgia Secretary of State Max Cleland, who lost an arm and both legs in Viet Nam, insists, "There is only one thing worth dying for, and that is this country, not somebody else's."

Diplomats argue persuasively that a policy based on this view would leave the U.S. to confront Soviet expansionism all alone. No country would enter or maintain an alliance with a U.S. that specifically refused to fight in its defense. But in the real world, an outright Soviet attack against a country that the U.S. is committed by treaty to defend is quite unlikely. The decision whether or not to fight most probably would be posed by a Communist threat to a friendly nation that is not formally an ally. And then the threat might well be raised not by open aggression but by a combination of military, political and economic tactics that Moscow is often adept at orchestrating and Washington usually inept at countering: the front groups, the street demonstrations, the infiltrated unions, the guerrilla units. One reason the U.S. sent troops to Viet Nam is that it lacked other alternatives to help its allies prevail against this sort of subversion. In fact, developing a capacity to engage in such political action and shadowy paramilitary activities might help the U.S. to avert future Viet Nams.

Merely defining U.S. interests, in any event, can prove endlessly complicated. Geography alone is no guide in an age of ocean-spanning missiles. Economics may be vital in some areas like the Persian Gulf, where the flow of oil must be maintained,

POLITICS

Defense Secretary McNamara brooding after troop call-up, 1965: Would Americans have backed a bigger war?

> "But it will be just like Berlin. The troops will march in; the bands will play; the crowds will cheer; and in four days everyone will have forgotten. Then we will be told we have to send in more troops."
> —JOHN F. KENNEDY 1961

> "There just isn't any simple answer. We're fighting a kind of war here that I never read about at Command and Staff College. Conventional weapons just don't work here. Neither do conventional tactics."
> —FROM GRAHAM GREENE'S *THE UGLY AMERICAN*

> "You let a bully come into your front yard, the next day he'll be on your porch."
> —LYNDON B. JOHNSON ON SEVERAL OCCASIONS

unimportant in others like Israel, where political and moral considerations are paramount. There may be times too when U.S. intervention, even if it seems justified, would be ineffective. Not much is heard these days of the once fashionable argument that in Viet Nam the U.S. was on the wrong side of history because it was fighting a nationalistic social revolution being waged by a regime that was, deep down, benign; Hanoi's brutality within Viet Nam and its swift move to establish hegemony over all of Indochina removed all doubt that the foe was and is not only totalitarian but imperialistic besides. Today, with the focus on Central America, the argument is often heard that economic and social misery have made leftist revolution inevitable. To those who maintain that revolution is the only way to progress, the counterargument is that whatever social and economic gains may be achieved by Communist takeovers usually carry an extremely high price tag: the establishment of tyranny.

About the only general rule that foreign-policy experts can suggest is not to have any general rule, at least in the sense of drawing up an advance list of where the U.S. might or might not fight. They still shudder at the memory of a 1950 definition of the U.S. "defense perimeter" in Asia that omitted South Korea—which promptly suffered an outright Communist invasion that took three years and 54,000 American lives to repel. Walt Rostow, who was Lyndon Johnson's National Security Adviser, recalls how the late Soviet Foreign Minister Andrei Vishinsky "told a group of Americans that we deceived them on Korea." Says Rostow: "I believe that's correct."

The decision on where American military intervention might be both necessary and effective can only be made case by case, based on a variety of factors that may be no easier to judge in the future than they were in Viet Nam: the nature and circumstances of war, the will and ability of the nation under attack to defend itself, the consequences of its loss. Any such debate is sure to revive another long buried but still unresolved con-

4. WAR AND DEPRESSION

troversy of the Viet Nam era: whether a Communist takeover of one country would cause others to topple like a row of dominoes. Hawks insist that this theory was vindicated by Communist triumphs in Laos and Cambodia after the fall of Saigon. Opponents point out that the Asian "dominoes" that most concerned the U.S.—Thailand, Burma, Malaysia, Singapore, Indonesia, the Philippines—have all survived as non-Communist (in several cases, strongly anti-Communist) societies. Rostow, now a professor of political economy at the University of Texas, offers a counterrebuttal. Those countries might have gone under if Saigon had fallen in 1965, he contends. The U.S. intervention in Viet Nam bought them ten years to strengthen their economies and governments and, says Rostow, "bought time that was used extremely well by Asians, especially Southeast Asians."

Be that as it may, the evidence would seem to argue against any mechanical application of the domino theory. It originated in the 1950s, when world Communism was seen as a monolithic force headquartered in Moscow, with Peking a kind of branch office. Today China, never really comfortable with its Hanoi "allies," has resumed its ancient enmity toward Viet Nam; both Washington and Peking are aiding guerrillas battling against the Soviet-backed Vietnamese in Kampuchea. That does not mean that the domino theory has lost all validity everywhere, but its applicability is also subject to case-by-case application.

The most bedeviling of all the dilemmas raised by Viet Nam concerns the issue of public support. On the surface it might seem to be no issue at all: just about everybody agrees that Viet Nam proved the futility of trying to fight a war without a strong base of popular support. But just how strong exactly? Rostow argues that the only U.S. war fought with tremendous public backing was World War II. He points out that World War I "brought riots and splits," the War of 1812 was "vastly divisive" and even during the War of Independence one-third of the population was pro-revolution, one-third pro-British and one-third "out to lunch." Rostow proposes a 60-25-15 split as about the best that can be expected now in support of a controversial policy: a bipartisan 60% in favor, 25% against and 15% out to lunch.

A strong current of opinion holds that Lyndon Johnson guaranteed a disastrously low level of support by getting into a long, bloody war without ever admitting (perhaps even to himself) the extent of the commitment he was making. Colonel Summers, who considers Viet Nam a just war that the U.S. could and should have won, insists that any similar conflict in the future ought to be "legitimized" by a formal, congressional declaration of war. Says Summers: "All of America's previous wars were fought in the heat of passion. Viet Nam was fought in cold blood, and that was intolerable to the American people. In an immediate crisis the tendency of the American people is to rally around the flag. But God help you if it goes beyond that and you haven't built a base of support."

At the other extreme, former Secretary of State Dean Rusk defends to this day the Johnson Administration's effort "to do in cold blood at home what we were asking men to do in hot blood out in the field." Rusk points out that the war began with impressive public and congressional support. It was only in early 1968, says Rusk, that "many at the grass-roots level came to the opinion that if we didn't give them some idea when this war would come to an end, we might as well chuck it." The decisive factor probably was the defection of middle-class youths and their parents, a highly articulate segment that saw an endless war as a personal threat—though in fact the burden of the draft fell most heavily on low-income youths.

Paradoxically, though, Johnson might well have been able to win public support for a bigger war than he was willing to fight. As late as February 1968, at the height of the Tet offensive, one poll found 53% favoring stronger U.S. military action, even at the risk of a clash with the Soviet Union or China, vs. only 24% opting to wind down the war. Rusk insists that the Administration was right not to capitalize on this sentiment. Says he: "We made a deliberate decision not to whip up war fever in this country. We did not have parades and movie stars selling war bonds, as we did in World War II. We thought that in a nuclear world it is dangerous for a country to become too angry too quickly. That is something people will have to think about in the future."

It certainly is. Viet Nam veterans argue passionately that Americans must never again be sent out to die in a war that "the politicians will not let them win." And by win they clearly mean something like a World War II–style triumph ending with unconditional surrender. One lesson of Viet Nam, observes George Christian, who was L.B.J.'s press secretary, is that "it is very tough for Americans to stick in long situations. We are always looking for a quick fix." But nuclear missiles make the unconditional-surrender kind of war an anachronism. Viet Nam raised, and left unsolved for the next conflict, the question posed by Lincoln Bloomfield, an M.I.T. professor of political science who once served on Jimmy Carter's National Security Council: "How is it that you can 'win' so that when you leave two years later you do not lose the country to those forces who have committed themselves to victory at any cost?"

It is a question that cannot be suppressed much longer. Americans have a deep ambiguity toward military power: they like to feel strong, but often shy away from actually using that strength. There is a growing recognition, however, that shunning all battles less easily winnable than Grenada would mean abandoning America's role as a world power, and that, in turn, is no way to assure the nation's survival as a free society. Americans, observes Secretary of State Shultz, "will always be reluctant to use force. It is the mark of our decency." But, he adds, "a great power cannot free itself so easily from the burden of choice. It must bear responsibility for the consequences of its inaction as well as for the consequences of its action."

—By George J. Church.
Reported by David S. Jackson/Austin and Ross H. Munro/Washington, with other bureaus.

"In the final analysis it is their war . . . We can help them . . . but they have to win it, the people of Viet Nam."
—KENNEDY
1963

"We are not about to send American boys 10,000 miles away to do what Asian boys ought to be doing for themselves."
—JOHNSON
1964

"Hell no, we won't go!"
—ANTIWAR CHANT
1965

"I'm not going to be the first President who loses a war."
—RICHARD NIXON
1969

"Peace is at hand."
—HENRY KISSINGER
1972

THE TWO THOUSAND YEARS' WAR

Walter Karp

AROUND THE TIME Republicans were vowing to "roll back Communism," a wise old college professor of mine suggested that his Humanities 1 class might get more out of Thucydides if it compared the Peloponnesian War to the ongoing struggle between America and Russia, then only recently named the Cold War. This, he assured us (quite needlessly), would not do violence to the great Athenian historian, since Thucydides himself believed that "human nature being what it is, events now past will recur in similar or analogous forms." Of the profundity of that remark Humanities 1 had not the slightest inkling. Nonetheless, analogies fell at our feet like ripe apples.

The combatants we identified readily. Authoritarian Sparta, ruling over a mass of terrified helots, was plainly the Soviet Union. Democratic Athens was America, of course. There were even neat correspondences between the two sets of foes. Sparta, as Thucydides tells us, was an insulated, agricultural, and sluggish state, rather like Russia. Athens, like America, was commercial, fast-moving, and far-ranging. "They are never at home," complained a Corinthian envoy to the Spartans, "and you are never away from it." In Athens and America, commerce and democracy seemed, 2,300 years apart, to have nurtured the very same kind of citizen. "I doubt if the world can produce a man," said great Pericles, "who, where he has only himself to depend upon, is equal to so many emergencies and graced by so happy a versatility as the Athenian." What the Athenians possessed, concluded Humanities 1, was Yankee ingenuity.

More striking than the analogies between past and present combatants were the resemblances between the two conflicts. In neither struggle do the enemies fight alone. Like America and the Soviet Union, Athens and Sparta are leaders of great confederations of inferior and subordinate allies. Similarly, they represent hostile political principles, Athens championing democracy, Sparta a traditional oligarchy. In the Peloponnesian War, as in the Cold War, the enemies are "ideological" foes. And neither is physically capable of winning. Sparta, with its invincible infantry, is so superior by land that Athens avoids pitched battles at all costs. Athens is so superior by sea that Spartan ships flee her peerless navy on sight. As a result, the Peloponnesian War, like the Cold War, is fought indirectly, peripherally, and spasmodically.

That was about as far as Humanities 1 got in its hunt for analogies between the ancient struggle for supremacy in Hellas and the ongoing struggle for supremacy in the modern world. Youth and ignorance doubtless limited our inquiry, but a greater handicap was the fact that the Peloponnesian War lasted twenty-seven years while the Cold War had not yet survived six.

THAT WAS NEARLY three decades ago, decades in which the struggle for supremacy between America and Russia did not cease for a single day. When I decided to reread Thucydides, the struggle was about to enter a new and more vigorous phase, under a newly elected president and a political faction that Thucydides would have unhesitatingly described as the war party. Two things struck me as I read: that the Cold War, now so long protracted, had come to resemble the Peloponnesian War more than ever and that in this resemblance lay a wholly unexpected vindication of political history, created by Thucydides, despised by the modern *eruditi*, and barely kept alive today by Grub Street hacks and doting amateurs.

The grounds for vindication are clear enough. Ancient Hellas and the modern world have nothing in common technologically, economically, or socially, none of those "factors" so dear to the hearts of the modern historian. If the ancient war and the modern war bear strong and essential resemblances, only political causes could have produced them; precisely those political causes that Thucydides' titanic genius found operating in the Peloponnesian War.

"Of the gods we believe, and of men we know," an Athenian envoy tells an ally of Sparta's, "that by a necessary law of their nature they rule wherever they can." Our nature as *political* beings is what Thucydides describes. Nothing compels men to enter the bright, dangerous arena of political action, but what lures them there—love of fame, power, glory, fortune, distinction—makes it fairly certain, a "law," that they will strive to rule over others. According to Pericles, Athenians, out of a love of splendid deeds and for the glory of their city, "forced every sea and land to be the highway of [their] daring." In doing so they also forged

4. WAR AND DEPRESSION

a far-flung empire, which they had to struggle continuously to maintain; for if men strive for dominion, others strive to resist it. "You risk so much to retain your empire," the Athenian envoy is told, "and your subjects so much to get rid of it."

In the striving to gain dominion and in the inevitable struggle to maintain it, men produce one thing with certainty—they "make" history. Such was Thucydides' great discovery. History is the story woven by men's deeds, and the political nature of man provides a completely intelligible account of the story. That is why the great Athenian dared to predict that the tragic events of the Peloponnesian War would one day recur in similar forms.

CONSIDER THE ORIGINS of the Peloponnesian War. Thucydides describes the petty squabbles that poison relations between certain allies of mighty Sparta and those of upstart Athens. The squabbles set in motion the great train of events, but, like Soviet–American squabbles over the Yalta accords, they are not, says Thucydides, the "real cause" of the war. "The growth of the power of Athens and the alarm which this inspired in Lacedaemon [Sparta] made war inevitable."

In 432 B.C. the Hellenic world reached a political condition that the modern world was to duplicate in 1945 A.D.—and with much the same result. Two superpowers, Athens and Sparta, have so completely absorbed all the available power in Hellas that any further gain by one appears a menacing loss to the other. Under such conditions no real peace is possible. Of course if men and states accepted the diminution of their power there would have been no Peloponnesian War (and precious little human history), but that is just what men and states do not accept.

War with Sparta is unavoidable, Pericles tells the Athenian assembly (it is pondering whether to accede to a Spartan fiat), because "we must attempt to hand down our power to our posterity unimpaired." Moral scruple has nothing to do with it. The Athenian empire "is, to speak somewhat plainly, a tyranny," says Pericles, referring to Athens' crushing subjugation of her nominal allies. "To take it [the empire] perhaps was wrong, but to let it go is unsafe." With respect to its unwilling allies, Athens resembles the Soviet Union and, like it, must expend a great deal of her strength keeping her "allies" down.

Because such tyranny is inherently unstable, Pericles urges his countrymen to fight a strategically defensive war and seek no "fresh conquests" in the course of it. The result of the Periclean policy reveals the extraordinary, history-making dynamism released by merely trying to hang on to one's own. Framed by a statesman of the highest genius, the policy scores a brilliant success and then leads Athens to its ultimate ruin.

To the astonishment of the Hellenic world, the newfangled Athenian navy, as Pericles foresaw, proves tactically superior to Sparta's great infantry, which the Athenians, safely walled up in their city, can avoid with impunity. Facing a foe so swift, so daring, so immune to injury, Sparta, after seven years of war, becomes deeply unnerved. "Being new to the experience of adversity," observes Thucydides, "they had lost all confidence in themselves."

Buoyed up by their unexpected triumphs over the traditional leader of Hellas, however, the Athenians fall prey to the fateful temptation inherent in all political action—rashness. Success "made them confuse their strength with their hopes," says Thucydides, providing, at least, a definition of political rashness that cannot be improved upon. After a Spartan garrison surrenders without a fight, something unprecedented in Spartan history, the Athenians are ripe for any daring folly; just as President Truman, blinded by General MacArthur's sweeping victory at Inchon, rashly attempted to conquer North Korea; and just as President Kennedy, puffed up by his Cuban missile triumph, was ripe for the Vietnam war—a confusion of strength and hope that drained the country of both.

The Peloponnesian War, like the Cold War, brings civil war and revolution in its wake. The political causes are the same in both cases. When states are at peace, hostile factions and classes within countries are willing to rub along together. But when the great powers are desperately competing for allies, domestic rivals are no longer willing to preserve internal peace. Popular leaders can call on the opposing power to put their domestic enemies to the sword; oligarchic factions, to set their own cities aflame.

Love of dominion, the desire for "the first place in the city" (never far from the surface in peacetime), convulses all Hellas in wartime. Men betray their own cities without scruple and cheer foreigners for killing their own countrymen. Political exiles, aided by foreign powers, wage ceaseless war against their own cities. The Peloponnesian War, which spawns a half dozen analogues of the Bay of Pigs and of Moscow-trained revolutionary brigades, blights the integrity of the city-state, just as the Cold War now erodes the integrity of the nation-state.

ATHENS IS by no means immune to the war's corrupting effects on domestic politics. At one point Athenians undergo a spasm of political paranoia that duplicates with remarkable fidelity the American McCarthy era. The causes here, too, are the same, as the sequence of events clearly shows. Shortly after the Spartan garrison's stunning surrender, Sparta humbly sues for peace, and the Athenians, a little out of breath themselves, reluctantly and ruefully accept. Thucydides regards the peace, which lasts six years, as a mere incident in a continuous war. It was, says Thucydides, "an unstable armistice [that] did not prevent either party doing the other the most effectual injury."

The chief reason for the instability is the emergence in Athens of a self-serving war party. Ten years have passed since the outbreak of war. Great Pericles is dead; new men have arisen with ambitions of their own, Pericles' own ward Alcibiades among them. The Periclean policy of deadlock, based on the determination to preserve past glories, does not content them. They want to win fresh glory for themselves, and with it, says Thucydides, "the undisturbed direction of the people." Their real complaint about the peace with Sparta is that it is an unambitious use of Athenian power (which is exactly what the American foes of détente believe).

Confusing strength with hope, the leaders of the war party think Athens can do far more than merely hold Sparta at bay; it can destroy Spartan

29. The Two Thousand Years' War

pretensions forever. Like the Republicans of 1951–52, the war party will accept, in effect, "no substitute for victory." Like millions of Americans in 1951–52, the Athenian people, "persuaded that nothing could withstand them," find deadlock exasperating. Why must irresistible Athens suffer the endless tensions of the unstable armistice? Is it possible that there are oligarchy-loving pro-Spartans in their midst?

A shocking act of impiety, analogous to the Alger Hiss trial, turns baseless suspicion into angry conviction: "oligarchical and monarchical" Athenians are conspiring to subvert the democratic constitution. The enraged citizenry demands arrests; blatant perjurers supply the evidence; nonconformists, including Alcibiades, fall prey to the mania. At the war's outset Pericles had proudly noted the extraordinary personal freedom enjoyed by Athenians, who "do not feel called upon to be angry with our neighbor for doing what he likes." Now those who live differently from their neighbors fall under suspicion of treason. A war begun to safeguard the power of a democracy profoundly corrupts democracy.

Firmly in control of a rapidly degenerating polity, the war party launches its grandiose plan to tilt the balance of power once and for all against the Spartans. Beyond the little world of Hellas, across the Ionian Sea, lie the broad island of Sicily and a dozen Greek colonial city-states. The Athenians, as Thucydides icily remarks, do not even know Sicily's size; they are ignorantly contemptuous of the island's colonial "rabble." Nonetheless, the self-vaunting, overconfident Athenians intend to conquer it and use that huge accession of imperial power to throw down Sparta itself. When an opponent of the enterprise warns Athenians of the enormous costs and hazards of a war so far from home, enthusiasm for the expedition grows even warmer.

In the seventeenth year of the Peloponnesian War, "by far the most costly and splendid Hellenic force that had ever been sent out by a single city" sets sail for faraway Sicily. Vietnam is but a pale analogy to what fortune inflicts on the great armada. Thucydides' account of its hideous, heartbreaking fate—how its leaders blundered, how its strength drained away, how its dauntless Athenian oarsmen, the backbone of the democracy, lost their nerve and their courage—is one of the great feats of historical writing. On the hostile shores of a distant island, before the walls of an underestimated enemy, the power of Athens crumbles away forever.

Since the Cold War continues with no end in sight, its story remains incomplete. Still, it seems fairly certain even now that the same principle that makes the Peloponnesian War intelligible, 2,300 years after its end, will make the Cold War intelligible to posterity: "Of the gods we believe, and of men we know, that by a necessary law of their nature they rule wherever they can."

The Retreat of the West

Following World War II the colonial empires ended and new nations fired with nationalism (also perhaps a Western legacy), liberalism, socialism, and sometimes capitalism came on the world stage. Between 1944 and 1980 ninety countries became independent. The United Nations started with fifty-one members and in 1980 it listed 152. When looking at what happened in Africa where the new nations often lacked economic balance, Westerners generally thought that nationalism had failed. In June, 1987, for example, the Central African Republic sentenced its former dictator, Jean-Bedel Bokassa, to be shot to death. He was responsible for over twenty murders and for spending $100 million for his coronation as emperor in 1977. The poor, landlocked republic had a population of only three million people. Michael Crowder points out that the condemnation by the West is made in the framework of eurocentric hopes. He says there have been accomplishments worth noting.

The legacy in South Africa, of course, was apartheid. There, the white minority, left from the earlier days of imperialism, controlled the country with laws and weaponry. Bhupinder Singh Liddar, a journalist from Canada, traveled through South Africa to witness the segregation first-hand. Liddar was dark skinned and sympathetic to the black South Africans. It seems that the liberalism of the West has been deeply planted in the black Africans, and Liddar feels that the nation is nearing the brink of a bloody revolt.

The most remarkable revolt against Western control came in India under the leadership of Mohandas Gandhi. He wanted independence for India, but chose nonviolent demonstrations to achieve his goal. He won, and India was split into two nations—one for Hindus and one for Moslems (Pakistan). In part, this triumph over British imperialism was due to the exhaustion of the British from World War II, and the fact that they were willing to close down their empire. In addition, Gandhi worked within a British frame of ethics; they too abhorred the bloodshed of the contest.

After the war, the British moved to get out of the Middle East and worked to set up the independent state of Israel. There was world sympathy for the Jews who had suffered during the holocaust, and the United Nations agreed to the establishment of a Jewish homeland. Unfortunately, there were Arabs already there who felt they had an equal claim to the land. In addition, Christians also had an interest in the area because of their heritage. There developed a three-way religious controversy. At the time of the creation of Israel, the Vatican wanted Jerusalem to remain under United Nations jurisdiction. Silvio Ferrari writes about this development in *The Middle East Journal*.

As it has turned out, the Middle East has suffered a series of wars between the Jews and Arabs, between Iran and Iraq, and between Afghanistan and the Soviet Union. Part of the reason for this is because of Islamic religious fervor which rejected both the capitalism of the West and the communism of the Soviet Union. Tom Hundley points out that outsiders often misread the motives of Islamic politicians. The inspiration of religion can still be powerful.

The Economist classified the Soviet Union at the time of the Iceland Summit as a third-class power in all but military proficiency. Historically the Soviets have the same sort of analysis problem the United States has with the Vietnam War. The Soviet problem, however, has to do with Joseph Stalin. He ruled the country from 1929 to 1953. His accomplishments include success in World War II and a degree of economic stability, but he was also involved in political annihilations and suppression. According to Stephen F. Cohen, the Soviets have yet to come to terms with the character of Stalin.

In their titanic struggle, both the US and the USSR can count victories and defeats. As "The New English Empire" brings out, though, one subtle triumph for the West is that English has become a world language. During its time of imperialism, the West exported its technology and ideas. Among the remnants of imperialism is the language. English has become the international language of science, technology, and diplomacy.

Looking Ahead: Challenge Questions
Why did the colonial empires come to an end?
What are the results of colonialism on both sides—colony and mother country?
Why was Gandhi successful? Is he an anomaly?
Why is the Middle East in turmoil?
Why is the memory of Stalin a problem for the Soviets?
What is the significance of English as a world language?

Unit 5

Article 30

Whose Dream Was It Anyway? Twenty-Five Years of African Independence

Michael Crowder

Michael Crowder is visiting Professor at the Institute of Commonwealth Studies, University of London.

When the Union Jack was lowered at midnight and the green white and green flag of Nigeria raised in its place on October 1st 1960, there was considerable optimism in the British press about the future of that erstwhile British colony. The leaders of its three political parties were all by their own declarations committed to the practice of liberal democracy Westminsterstyle. The constitution that enshrined the ideals of Westminster had been patiently negotiated over a decade between the British and the leaders of the three main political parties. The former colonial masters left with the warm words of the new Prime Minister ringing in their ears: 'We are grateful to the British officers whom we have known, first as masters, and then as leaders, and finally as partners and always as friends'.[1] Many stayed on under the new Nigerian leadership, particularly those in commerce and industry, especially as Nigerians had only taken over the political infrastructure of the state from the British. The economic infrastructure remained largely intact in the hands of big British firms like UAC. The prospects for the country seemed rosy with its apparently sound agricultural base and the promise of additional foreign earnings from its proved oil reserves. An optimism about Nigeria pervaded most of the British press for the next five years. The riots that were taking place in Tivland at the very time the new flag of Nigeria was being raised were conveniently ignored by many pressmen intent on conveying an appropriate euphoria to their British readers. Indeed, the Prime Minister of the Federation, Sir Abubakar Tafawa Balewa, remarked wryly on the adulation of the world's press that 'even some of the big nations of the world are expecting us to perform miracles and solve their problems for them'.[2] That adulation had indeed been fairly universal but *West Africa* did note that one foreign visitor to the Independence Celebrations did not share the 'general satisfaction and optimism' and that was Mr. Sisnev, the correspondent of *Trud*, but it concluded 'even if Nigeria sounds too good to be true, the Nigerian story is one of the most remarkable and creditable in the modern world'.[3] *Time* talked of Nigeria's 'impressive demonstration of democracy's workability in Africa'.[4]

Despite the many internal strains which the country experienced in its first few years of independence, including the suspension of the constitution of one of its three constituent regions and the jailing of the leader of the opposition for treason, the British press appeared to share the belief that as one Nigerian newspaper put it: 'Nigerians seem to have perfected the art of walking to the brink of disaster without falling in.'[5] Indeed the British Prime Minister and his officials were apparently so ignorant of the real breakdown of law and order in the country that in January 1966 they flew to Lagos to attend the Commonwealth Prime Ministers Conference on the Rhodesian question.[6] A day after they flew back to London, the Prime Minister of Nigeria was assassinated and the first military regime was installed. In the twenty years that followed, Nigeria has suffered four more military coups, at least one failed coup, a three year long civil war, a brief return to an elective form of government that made a mockery of liberal democracy, and an oil boom that permitted lavish spending and corruption on a massive scale, followed by the near bankruptcy of the country, which today is economically on its knees. As a result, Nigerians of all classes have developed a deep cynicism about their leaders, both civilian and military, and certainly have little faith in the liberal democracy and mixed economy that were the legacy of their colonial rulers.

I have chosen Nigeria as an example of the disillusion that has attended the first twenty-five years of independence not only among the former colonial rulers who transferred pow-

I am grateful to Lalage Bown and Roland and Irene Brown for helpful comments on a first draft of this paper which was originally presented in the series of lectures on Africa since Independence sponsored by the Yale University African Studies Program in Spring of 1986 under the title 'Things Fall Apart?'.

er but also among those who inherited that power, because it contains a quarter of the population of the African continent. Its experience has unhappily not been atypical but rather the norm for the majority of African countries.

The same optimism that attended Nigeria's independence attended that of the Francophone countries, and the British territories in East, Central and Southern Africa. In each case, what was transferred was a constitution inspired by the metropolitan model. All these states committed themselves in their national anthems and the mottoes on their coats of arms to variations of freedom, justice and equality.

Of all these states only one has realised the pious hopes of those who transferred power: Botswana, which alone has suffered no *coup* or *coup manqué* and has maintained intact its liberal democratic constitution in both spirit and practice.[7] The story everywhere else has been the same. Majority parties voted to establish one party states which western apologists were quick to justify as reflecting true African democracy encouraging the politics of consensus where two or multi-party democracy was divisive.[8] In reality, such moves usually proved but a cloak for the establishment of personal rule, as Jackson and Rosberg have put it.[9] Even military regimes that intervened were seen by optimists as mere correctives for temporary aberrance in the practice of democracy by young nations. Military coups were invariably staged in the name of cleansing the state, after which the soldiers would return to the barracks. And this they did in Sudan, Ghana, the former Upper Volta and Nigeria, only to fling wide the barrack gates again as it became clear that the politicians had learnt nothing except how to abuse power more successfully. The excesses of the second Obote regime in Uganda were reputedly greater than those of Amin himself.[10]

Coupled with the abuse of the inherited constitutions and the acquisition of personal power through manipulation of the ballot box or the barrel of the gun has been the expropriation of the resources of the state by the few and the apparent progressive immiseration of the masses as a result. The famines that have caught the world's attention in the past few years have increasingly been laid at the doors of the politicians and military leaders rather than nature. And yet, grasping at straws, westerners refuse to see their dreams shattered. Nigeria's return to democracy in 1979 was seen as a vindication by those who believed that Africans could and would adhere to the ideals of Western liberal democracy. Similar optimism attended the return to civilian rule under Obote, with the British government even helping to train the army he used to establish a worse record with Amnesty International than Amin.[11]

But by 1985, a quarter of a century after the *annus mirabilis* of African independence, the dream had been shattered and replaced by a profound disillusion whereby Africa had become the world's basket case, a permanent *mezzogiorno* for which there was little if any hope. Ghana and Uganda, the jewels in Britain's African colonial crown had, despite their extensive educated elites, sunk in the former case into an economic slough of despond and in the latter into anarchy. In the chanceries of the West, officials wished Africa would just go away and this has been reflected most dramatically in Britain, still the country with the largest investments in sub-Saharan Africa, which has reduced its support for the study of Africa to a level lower than it has been for the past twenty years.[12]

The universal wisdom has become that African independence has been an abysmal failure. Thus the conservative London *Daily Telegraph* in a recent editorial wrote that Uganda 'the one-time pearl of Africa can fairly be described as having become a symbol of everything that has gone wrong in that continent over the past 20 years or so. Since independence it has experienced violence (with hundreds of thousands killed), poverty, misgovernment on an enormous scale, and terrible suffering. Steadily the pillars of government, of law and even economic life have been destroyed. . . '.[13]

But is this not to judge the past twenty five years in terms of a dream manufactured in Europe not Africa, and a dream that took no cognisance either of contemporary African realities, nor, more important and less forgivable, of the legacy of colonial rule?

Was not this dream of a model Africa in which Africans would faithfully adhere to the liberal democratic institutions transferred at independence and uphold a mixed economy in which the interests of the ordinary people would be served in reality a pipe dream in the context of a plethora of states that had for the most part only been cobbled together fifty odd years before? Will not historians be kinder in their judgement of these sometimes unlikely states created by the colonial rulers when they come to assess the post independence period than the journalists and political scientists who wring their hands in despair today? Will they not judge the experience of independence in terms of the African experience of colonial rule, which has been undergoing serious revision by historians as the true secrets of the colonial rulers emerge from the archives? Will they not compare favourably the impressive economic transformations that even the most impoverished of African states in question have undergone since independence with the little that was done for them under colonial rule? Given the little attention that any of the European colonial powers gave to building national political and economic structures during the period of their rule will not historians of the future see the very survival of these states as something of an economic and political miracle?

In this essay, therefore, I want to try and project myself forward and see what sort of perspective historians may have on what so many see today as 'the African disaster'.

I suggest they will look at the developments of the past twenty five years as part of a continuum in which independence will not be seen as a historical dividing line. All that has happened in the past quarter of a century will be set much more firmly in the context of the colonial experience than is the custom for present-day political scientists and journalists to do. So I first want to examine how the colonial experience has affected the way Africa has developed over the past twenty-five years and I shall suggest that there are many more parallels to be found between the colonial state and the independent state than are usually conceded.

I believe that historians will consider that contemporary judgements about the so called failure of Africa are really judgements made in terms of a Eurocentric dream for an independent Africa in which liberal democracy would be the norm, a dream that was shared only by a few elitist politicians like the Danquahs,[14] who were pushed aside in the struggle for independence by politicians with mass following like Nkrumah. I shall suggest that most African politicians did not share this dream and at best thought as Nyerere did that liberal democracy would only be a slowly acquired habit,[15]

5. THE RETREAT OF THE WEST

and at worst like Nkrumah only paid lip service to it.[16]

Finally I believe that future historians will set against the obvious failures of independent African states the very real achievements they have made in comparison with the record of their colonial masters.

THE COLONIAL LEGACY

In considering continuities between the colonial period and independence, let us look at the sort of model the colonial state provided in terms of the *Daily Telegraph* editorial. The violence which the editorialist posited as characteristic of contemporary African states was no stranger to the colonial state. The many studies of resistance to colonial occupation have shown that for the most part the colonial state was conceived in violence rather than by negotiation. This violence was often quite out of proportion too the task in hand, with burnings of villages, destruction of crops, killing of women and children, and the execution of leaders.[17] Some military expeditions were so barbaric that they caused outrage in the metropolitan press, as did the Voulet and Chanoine expedition in Niger.[18] The colonial state was not only conceived in violence, but it was maintained by the free use of it. Any form of resistance was visited by punitive expeditions that were often quite unrestrained by any of the norms of warfare in Europe. The bloody suppression of the Maji Maji and Herero uprisings in German East and South West Africa are well enough known. The less known atrocities committed in the suppression of the Satiru revolt in Northern Nigeria by the Sultan of Sokoto's forces acting on commission for the British in 1906 were such that the missionary Walter Miller wrote that 'it would be worth Leopold of Belgium's while to pay ten thousand pounds to get hold of what we know of this'.[19] As Edward Lugard, brother of the British High Commissioner in Northern Nigeria, wrote: 'they killed every living thing before them', Women's breasts had been cut off and the leader spitted on a stake.[20]

Lest these be thought too distant events in the colonial record to have much bearing on the present, one must recall that a man aged eighteen at the time of Satiru, would only have been 72 at the time of Nigeria's independence. Furthermore, the use of violence to suppress protest continued throughout the colonial period and into the period of decolonisation. The bloody massacre of Tirailleurs Sénégalais protesting against delays in paying their benefits and effecting their demobilisation at Thiaroye in Dakar in 1944 sent shock waves throughout the French African empire,[21] as did the revelations about the brutal treatment of Mau Mau prisoners by the British at the Hola Camp in Kenya through the British African colonies.[22] The colonial state, it must be remembered, maintained troops for internal security, not for defence against external aggression. These armies were of course used for this latter purpose when the occasion arose, most notably in the two world wars where African soldiers experienced violence on an unprecedented scale.[23] So too did civilians when their territory became part of the theatre of war. As Terence Ranger wrote of the impact of the First World War on East Africa 'it was the most awe-inspiring, destructive and capricious demonstration of European 'absolute power' that Eastern Africa ever experienced'.[24] It must be remembered too that the colonial rulers set the example of dealing with its opponents by jailing or exciling them, as not a few of those who eventually inherited power knew from personal experience.[25] Indeed if the colonial state provided a model for its inheritors it was that government rested not on consent but force. Indeed when Nyerere was once pressed on the subject of preventive detention in his country he was quick to point out that Tanzania had inherited the practice from British colonial times.[26]

If we take up the second theme of the *Telegraph* leader, that of poverty, this was certainly no stranger during the colonial period. The colonial state was certainly not run for the benefit of its inhabitants. The roots of rural poverty, as Palmer and Parsons' volume of essays of that name on Southern Africa demonstrate, lie deep in the policies of the colonial powers.[27] In the white settler colonies the best land was appropriated from the African farmer who was crowded into less fertile reserves often with disastrous ecological results.[28] Where the main agent of exploitation was the African farmer, he was forced to produce the crops that the colonial rulers required rather than those he needed. Through taxation, compulsory crop cultivation, forced labour and requisition, and in the case of the Portuguese territories physical coercion, the farmer produced the cash crops that the big companies overseas required even at the risk of impoverishment of the land and famine. For many Africans taxation of any kind was a complete innovation. Many others had only paid indirect taxes. And where direct taxation was imposed, it was rarely, if ever, as high as that of colonial state, which at its most oppressive extracted taxes directly in the form of cash, labour and compulsory crop cultivation, and indirectly through duties on imported goods.[29] Robert Shenton in his recent book on *The Development of Capitalism in Northern Nigeria* has shown how British taxation policies designed to increase cultivation of cotton and groundnuts in some cases took up to 50% of a farmer's income from him and led to shortages of subsistence crops which in turn led to famines. As he shows, the colonial rulers themselves were fully aware of the consequences of their policies.[30] Similarly later colonial government marketing boards were used as a means of taxing further the potential earnings of the farmer. Yet critics of the independent African regimes seem to suggest that this neglect and exploitation of the farmer was new rather than a major legacy of colonial rule.[31]

Urban poverty and the slums associated with it were not a function of independent Africa but were established features of colonial rule. I recall arriving in Nigeria for the first time in 1953 and nearly retching as I crossed from the Mainland to Lagos Island by Carter Bridge, so rank was the stink from the slums beneath its piers. The bidonvilles of Dakar were a colonial creation of which Senghor was so ashamed that after independence he built a high wall around them so that visitors to his country should not see them as they entered Dakar from the airport.

The third theme in the *Telegraph* editorial is the misgovernment that has characterised independent African governments. Here again we must remind ourselves how little opportunity Africans had of participating in the machinery of government of the colonial state until a few years before its demise. In British Africa only a few chiefs under British indirect rule were allowed any initiative in the administration before 1945. Otherwise all Africans in the administration, whatever the colonial regime, fulfilled a purely subaltern role without executive initiative. As to legislative functions, again these were limited to local government under the system of indirect rule, and to a handful of elected Africans in Nigeria, Senegal and the Gold Coast. Generally in British and French Africa preparation for taking over the legislative, executive and administrative organs of the colonial state by Africans began only after the Second World War. Even where some effort was made to prepare African administrative cadres, they were often treated as second class members of the administration. In the 1950s, newly appointed African administrative officers in Uganda were specifically barred from access to the confidential files, a point that led to much bitterness on their part.[32] In many African countries not a few inhabitants exercised the right to vote for the first time at the elections that brought their independent governments to power.

The Congo perhaps provides the most notorious example of the lack of preparation for the transfer of the institutions of state, while Guinea provides a different kind of example, where the French actually tried to destroy the very fabric of that state before they departed. They even removed the books from the law library of the Ministry of Justice.[33] Yet the scuttling Belgians received surprisingly little blame in the press for the disasters of the Congo compared with the Congolese themselves. Surely historians of the future will be less preoccupied by the anarchy and savagery that flowed from independence than by the marvel of the survival of the Congo intact as the huge state of Zaire, however far the former corporal who is its current head of state may deviate from the standards of good government as conceived in Brussels, Paris or London.

If the Belgians only prescribed the medicine of democracy for their Congolese subjects on the eve of the transfer of power, we must recall that neither the Spaniards nor the Portuguese rulers of the day had any faith in this type of medication for their own peoples, let alone their African subjects. They had no qualms about their conviction that their states were based on force not consent.

No aspects of post-independence Africa has drawn more criticism by scholars and journalists of the West than the personal power exercised by its leaders. Again it is instructive to look at the colonial model. Colonial governors enjoyed very wide powers without brakes from below. Even in British Africa where some territories had legislative councils these were dominated by an official majority which could be relied on to vote as solidly for any new policy or programme introduced by the Governor as the legislators in today's one party states. In many territories the Colonial Governor ruled by decree or proclamation and even where he had an executive council his decision on policy was over riding since that council's members were all his officials. The Governor also enjoyed to the full the outward trappings of power, living in an imposing palace, driven in large limousines flying the flag, deferred to by all, and on ceremonial occasions dressed in cocked hat and plumes and a quasimilitary uniform. In the British territories, he alone was allowed to use red ink to minute or sign official documents.

This again was a model not lost on the inheritors of the colonial state. The model for the successors was invariably derived from that of the colonial masters. Thus ex-Sargeant Jean Bedel Bokassa modelled his coronation as Emperor of Central Africa on that of a former French corporal. Americans will recall Washington Irving's allegorical version of the European folk-tale about Rip Van Winkle. In Irving's version he becomes a Catskill villager who slumbers through the American Revolution to awake to the many changes that have taken place in his village. Among these is the new sign on the Inn. Before he slept it was a crude picture of George III. The uniform has now been changed and the name transmogrified from King George to George Washington.[34] For a more sinister comparison we might remember that the OGPU of the Russian revolutionary state had its direct antecedents in the Tsar's okhrana.

Another theme in the *Telegraph* leader is the destruction of the pillars of law in African societies. Again we must look back at the colonial model. In French Africa until 1946, all Africans but a few citizens were under a regime of administrative law whereby they were subject to summary justice with no right of appeal. In 1914 Lugard specifically outlawed the representation of defendants by lawyers in the magistrate's courts of the South where a British model judiciary had been installed, albeit with massive problems and defects. In The Congo and Portuguese territories, too, the Africans had no access to metropolitan style legal institutions. These existed only for the European inhabitants or in the case of the Portuguese territories the handful of *assimilados*. They were made available to Africans only on the eve of independence or immediately afterwards.

Again, what is remarkable is that so much of the trappings of spirit of these hastily implanted systems have survived rather than broken down. I am sure all were moved that out of the misery and anarchy that has bedevilled Uganda for the past decade and a half the apparent end should be marked by a bewigged and scarlet robed Chief Justice swearing in the new Conqueror-President Museveni—and what is more that it should have been a white Ugandan in a post that in Uganda has held few promises of retirement benefits.

The final point made by the *Telegraph* leader was that economic life had been destroyed. Of course in terms of exports and imports this has often been the case as countries like Nigeria have built up massive overseas debts, cannot afford imports and have neglected agricultural exports. But as Pius Okigbo, former economic adviser to the Nigerian Government, so forcefully pointed out in a recent lecture, the real problem is that the health of African economies is judged by the outside world in terms of the size of their imports and exports.[35] This too of course is a legacy of the colonial period when the colonial rulers were little concerned with measuring the African domestic economy but were principally interested in the size of its import-export economy. Thus during the Depression of the 1930s there was crisis for the colonial rulers whose income was reduced, for the import-export firms whose crops fetched abysmal prices on the world market, and for those African farmers who were involved in the sector of the agricultural economy. But for the subsistence crop producer and the craftsmen there was something of a boom.[36] Similarly in many countries that are apparently suffering in terms of their import-export economy, there is today something of an internal boom. If African leaders have tended to judge the health of their economies in terms of imports and exports, they are only following a colonial precedent.[37]

The colonial rulers, furthermore, hardly set a good example of operating the economy in the best interests of their subjects: profits were expatriated not invested in local industries, providing a parallel with, though here not a model for, the present salting of ill-gotten gains by African leaders in the banks of Switzerland and other safe havens of the Western

5. THE RETREAT OF THE WEST

world. We must recall too the price rings, the lack of local industrial development and the lodging of the assets of marketing boards in metropolitan banks before we talk too much about mismanagement of the economy by African successor states. As Ralph Austen has recently emphasised, Patrick Manning has demonstrated that considerable economic damage was done to Dahomey by the French 'who used it to subsidise less profitable French possessions, to fulfil their own ambitions, or to respond to the pressures of local European economic interests'.[38] As Austen further emphasises: 'The economic and political malaise afflicting the African continent today with such breadth and severity . . . must have deep roots in a past about which so little is generally known'.[39]

A final point concerning the colonial legacy to Independent Africa concerns the state structures that were handed over at independence. The borders of these states, it may be tedious to remind ourselves, were erected without reference to African realities in the chanceries of Europe. But having created them, colonial powers did little to foster a sense of national unity within them. The French territory of Upper Volta for instance was not created until 1920, was dismembered in 1932 and divided up among its neighbours, only to be re-established in 1947, thirteen years before it became independent, German Kamerun and Togo were divided between the French and British after the First World War, while, although the separate Protectorates of Northern and Southern Nigeria were amalgamated by Lugard in 1914, it was a token amalgamation which did not truly bring them into a meaningful relationship with each other.[40] The two French federations of Equatorial and West Africa were broken up by the French against the wishes of the majority of the constituent colonies on the eve of independence. Furthermore it has been argued, convincingly, that the system of indirect rule, employed by the British, was a divisive one in that it emphasised the integrity of the pre-colonial political unit as against the new colonial state. And up until the mid-forties there were still powerful advocates in the Colonial Office who saw the native authorities as the building blocks of independence.[41]

This has been a deliberately selective view of the colonial past but, I hope, a corrective one that the Cassandras of contemporary Africa would be advised to take into account.

WHOSE DREAM WAS IT ANYWAY?

We come now to my second theme: how far did Africans share the dream of the colonial rulers for Africa? In the first place, it has to be remembered that the liberal democratic ideal was espoused only by the British and French for their African colonies. Though at home the Belgians shared these ideals, they only very belatedly suggested that they might be appropriately transferred to their colonial subjects.[42] In both Spain and Portugal liberal democracy had succumbed many years since to Fascist regimes, so for their overseas subjects there was not even a metropolitan model of democracy to aspire to. In the case of the Portuguese their African colonies were considered integral parts of the metropolis and, far from instruments of power being transferred to African subjects, control of the state was seized by them by force of arms. There was thus no obligation placed on the victors to maintain any particular form of government.[43]

In all the French Black African states, with the exception of Guinea, and in all the British African states, including Zimbabwe, the transfer of power was negotiated and made conditional on the acceptance of a liberal democratic constitution inspired by the metropolitan model. What we have to ask ourselves is how far the African parties to these negotiations were ideologically committed to these constitutions? In Francophone and Anglophone Africa educated Africans soon learnt that the pen was mightier than the sword in dealing with their particular colonial masters and turned the democratic ideals and institutions of their masters against them and asked why they espoused democracy at home and denied it abroad. The Senegalese politician Lamine Gueye in his autobiography recalls the irony of the 'Liberté, Egalité et Fraternité' emblazoned on the offices of a colonial administration which practised none of these three virtues as far as their African subjects were concerned.[44] An educated chief like Tshekedi Khama in the then Bechuanaland Protectorate skilfully manipulated British press, parliament and public opinion to block measures of the local administration to which he was opposed. But if we examine his own life closely we find that while he was keen on his own rights, and went to great lengths to defend them, he was none too careful with respect to those of his own subjects.[45] David Williams has hypothesised that the emirs in Northern Nigeria finally agreed to back self-government and independence under the Sardauna of Sokoto because they believed he would be less insistent on the implementation of democracy than the British showed clear signs of being if they continued administering their country any longer.[46]

African leaders may have skilfully pressured the British and French to transfer their models and when finally they agreed to do so accepted them as a condition of gaining independence, just as Nkrumah had to accept a final election as a precondition of independence for Ghana.[47] But did this mean that they implicitly believed in them as anything other than as a means to an end? The answer is surely 'No'. Only thus can we explain the rapid dismantling of these constitutions in form or spirit by nearly all who were party to the independence agreements. A few days after Ghana's independence, Nkrumah gave a press conference in which he assured the world's press that 'We shall help [other African states] by our example of successfully working a parliamentary democracy'.[48] But within a few days more he had moved into Christiansborg Castle, the seat of the colonial governors, arranged for his own portrait to appear on currency and postage stamps, and started on the road to the acquisition of unchecked personal power. The commitment to liberal democracy thereafter tended to be the exclusive concern of the opposition, but how shallow this was may be illustrated by the example of Siaka Stevens of Sierra Leone. His All People's Congress (APC) had campaigned against the ruling Sierra Leone People's Party (SLPP) in part on the basis that it was abusing democracy. Having won the election despite heavy rigging by the Government, and finally acceding to power several coups later, Stevens set about creating the one party state that the SLPP had not quite dared to. It is clear that for all but a few leaders—Seretse Khama of Botswana and Dauda Jawara of The Gambia being the notable exceptions—the commitment to liberal democracy was a transitory one. Nor of course were the military who succeeded them so committed, coming from a very different tradition of dealing with people.

Was it not a staggering piece of arrogant paternalism that the European powers should prescribe for their African dependencies a model that had had such a chequered career on their own continent and criticise them for failing to work it? African leaders were for the most part aware of the many attacks on democracy experienced by Europe during the years that they had been under its tutelage. They had seen how weak democracies could be in the face of a determined fascist leader like Mussolini. Not all were convinced by their masters' condemnations of Hitler. It is not for nothing that a fair number of African boys were named Adolf in the early forties.[49] But democracy remained, in the eyes of the Western press, the panacea for Africa. Thus there was general rejoicing at Nigeria's return to civilian rule in 1979 and general hostility to the military coup that brought it to an end in December 1983, even though there was rejoicing by the general population at the demise of a corrupt and increasingly oppressive regime. A former Labour Minister in the British Foreign Office concerned with Africa, Ted Rowlands, was reported by *West Africa* as appearing to be calling for economic sanctions against Nigeria for 'abandoning democracy'.[50] While the *Daily Express* referring to the new military ruler, General Buhari, wondered whether the Queen 'will take this despot's hand'.[51]

What African leaders surely appreciated more perceptively than those who wished liberal democratic constitutions on them was that liberal democracy had only worked in those countries of Europe where there was relative lack of inequality, a deep-rooted sense of national identity, and a consensus as to the ideal model for the government of the state. Where, as in Zimbabwe, such conditions did not obtain, and where there were two major ethnic groups vying for power, the operation of the liberal democratic constitution became very close in character to the operation of democracy in Northern Ireland. There was certainly genuine belief on the part of those African leaders who advocated the one-party state, however much later they were to pervert it to their own ends, that it would be less divisive than the two-party model of the British or the multi-party model of the French.[52] Nor were African leaders particularly committed to the equitable distribution of resources that their election manifestos promised and their talk of African socialism may have suggested. Since the means to independence was to be through the ballot box, they had necessarily to persuade the electorate by offering to implement programmes that would benefit them. With independence won, the behaviour of African politicians has differed little from that of the majority of office-seekers in promoting personal advancement and profit, with some pork barrelling for their homeboys. Africans were much more hard-nosed, realistic and even cynical about what independence portended. Rosy dreams were left to the departing colonial masters and the metropolitan press. Indeed as *West Africa* remarked almost petulantly at Ghana's independence celebrations 'the Accra crowds were much less demonstrative than expected'.[53] Its then editor, David Williams, tells the story of Sir Milton Margai who was overseeing the arrangements for the independence service in the Freetown Cathedral. When the Bishop suggested he might like to give a second thought to the choice of one hymn which contained what he felt was the inappropriate second verse: 'Though the darkness deepens, Lord with me abide'. 'Exactly' replied Sir Milton.[54] David Williams also tells of how journalists at Nigeria's independence had to file their stories three hours before the ceremonial lowering of the Union Jack in order to have their stories on the British breakfast table. All wrote of the dancing in the streets that followed the raising of the Nigerian flag. In fact when David Williams and a fellow-journalist toured the streets after the midnight ceremonial they met only desultory groups wending their way home. His colleague shouted out of the car: 'Dance, Dammit, you're meant to be dancing'.[55] To be fair, however, to the British, it must be remembered that the democratic dream was more enthusiastically supported in the corridors of Whitehall than in the offices of the District Officers who, as Sylvia Leith-Ross has shown in her memoirs of Nigeria, were much more apprehensive of its application to the societies among which they worked.[56]

I would like to conclude with the more positive assessment of the last quarter century of African history that I believe will be accorded by historians of the future. I need not record the failures of Africa—these can be read about daily in the papers.

AFRICAN ACHIEVEMENT

I am convinced that historians of the future will find much more to the credit of Africa than current press punditry and academic despondency at present will admit. And I think that their judgement will be made in the context of the colonial record.

Here it is instructive to listen to Julius Nyerere's recent justification *pro vita sua* made just after he relinquished the Presidency of Tanzania.[57] It is instructive not least because Tanzania is usually cited as one of Africa's worst basket-cases in economic terms. In 1961, he recalled, on the eve of independence and after nearly seventy years of colonial rule only 486,000 children were in primary school. Today there are over three and a half million, in his own words 'a tremendous achievement unmatched anywhere else in Africa'. In 1961 80% of the adult population was illiterate. Today, according to the Tanzanian Government, 85% can read and write. In 1961 only 11% of the population had access to clean water— today, Nyerere claims, nearly 50% have access to clean water within 450 yards of their homes. The availability of health services, particularly in the rural areas has improved out of all recognition. The ratio of doctors to population has been reduced from 1:830,000 to 1:26,000. The mortality rate of infants has nearly halved while life expectancy for adults has risen from 35 to 51.

Of course all this was achieved at a tremendous cost to the economy with the accumulation of massive international debts. We know that in many African countries these debts have been amassed not through genuine attempts at betterment of the lives of the people but by large scale squandering of resources and corruption. Two points have to be made about the debts of African countries. In many cases they were built up in a genuine attempt to make up for the sad development record of the colonial governments. We should also remind ourselves that some of the spectacular failures in African development were part of development plans concocted largely in the metropole to buttress the colonial state, for instance the notorious Tanganyika groundnut scheme and the Gambia poultry project. Moreover, in the post-colonial era, many African development plans and projects were the outcome of advice by foreign experts.[58]

The financial strains experienced by the post-independence governments have also been due to a sometimes over-zealous concern to improve the inadequate communications systems left by the colonial powers and to build the foundations of

5. THE RETREAT OF THE WEST

an industrial infrastructure that would make them less dependent on supplies from the First World. Much more directly responsible for these economic problems are facts such as these: in 1979, as Nyerere put it, Tanzania was paying nine times as much for its oil though using less than before the oil crisis began. To buy a seven ton truck in 1981 his country had to produce four times as much cotton, three times as many cashew nuts, ten times as much tobacco, and three times as much coffee as five years earlier.[59]

As Nyerere complained at the Cancun North-South summit in 1981:

> Our balance of payment difficulties are enormous and getting greater. This is not because we are trying to live as though we were rich. It is because our already low income is constantly being reduced because of our participation in international trade. . . . We find ourselves always selling cheap and buying dear . . . we are asking for a chance to earn our living in the international system.[60]

I believe that historians will also see these problems in this perspective, and I believe that, in the context of the colonial legacy and the economic vicissitudes of independence (whether self-inflicted or brought about by the caprices of the world market), they will marvel that by and large the post-colonial state in Africa has remained intact, often despite the machinations of erstwhile colonial powers or the conflicting interests of East and West as in the cases of Biafra, Chad and Angola. They will marvel that the map of Africa has remained largely the same as it was at independence and that there have been so few wars between the post-colonial states though they were left with so many of the problems that in Europe have been the cause of war: ill-defined frontiers, split ethnic groups and so forth. In the thirty years period 1914-1944, as we know, Europe was ravaged by two major wars, as a result of which the boundaries of Europe were twice redrawn. In the thirty year period following the independence of Sudan in 1956, there has been marginal readjustment of the African map, and surprisingly little interstate hostility and when it has broken out it has usually been quickly resolved. Many potentially explosive situations have been defused by the little-known but often highly effective Conciliation Committee of the Organisation of African Unity.

Against the internal violence of Chad and Uganda we must set the large number of African countries where such violence has been minimal, and remember that even the three year lonng Biafran civil war in Nigeria came to an end without recrimination and in a spirit of reconciliation on the part of the victors that was without precedent in Europe or the Americas. We must also recall that when for instance South Africans use the examples of Uganda or Chad to argue against the transfer of power to their own African majority, the surprising thing is that the most secure group in Africa since independence has in fact been the whites themselves. We must further remind ourselves that some of the most extreme forms of violence perpetrated in post-colonial Africa have been by the whites of Rhodesia and South Africa.

If it seems that I have presented this case as though it were that of a defence lawyer, this has been deliberate. Africa has in a very real sense been on trial for the desperate situation in which she has found herself twenty-odd years after independence. The blame for this situation has almost universally been placed upon African leaders. I have tried to show that blame properly should be divided between these leaders and their colonial predecessors. I have also tried to show that the criteria by which Africa is being judged are Eurocentric ones. Finally I have suggested that historians of the future will set against the many failures of African leaders since independence their very real achievements which the Western press so often ignores. I rest my case.

FOOTNOTES

1. Sir Abubakar Tafawa Balewa, Speech made on Independence Day, 1 October 1960 in *"But always as Friends": Northern Nigeria and the Cameroons, 1921-1957*, (London, George Allen and Unwin, 1969), Frontispiece.
2. *West Africa* 19 November 1960.
3. *ibid.*
4. *ibid.*
5. See Michael Crowder *The Story of Nigeria* (London, Faber, 1978), p. 259.
6. To be fair the usually well informed magazine *West Africa* raised no alarm in its columns either on the eve of the Conference nor during it, even though its own representative 'Griot' was touring the country at the time.
7. See Michael Crowder 'Botswana and the Survival of Liberal Democracy in Africa' in Prosser Gifford and Wm. Roger Louis eds. *African Independence: the Origins and Consequences of the Transfer of Power in Africa* (Newhaven: Yale University Press) (forthcoming).
8. See for example James S. Coleman and Carl G. Rosberg Jr. eds. *Political Parties and National Integration in Tropical Africa* (Berkeley and Los Angeles, University of California Press, 1964), especially their 'Introduction'.
9. Robert H. Jackson and Carl G. Rosberg *Personal Rule in Africa. Prince, Autocrat, Prophet, Tyrant.* (Berkeley, Los Angeles and London, University of California Press, 1982.
10. The first indications that this might be the case came to public attention as a result of the Namugongo massacre of May 1984, when both Baganda Muslims and Christians were murdered, thus giving it a genocidal character. I am grateful to Michael Twaddle for this reference.
11. See comments on the Amnesty International Report in *The Times* 28 June 1985.
12. See Michael Twaddle 'The State of African Studies' *African Affairs* 85, 340, July 1986 especially p. 444 and Richard Hodder-Williams, 'African studies: back to the future', *African Affairs* 85, 341. October 1986, pp. 593-604, with their gloomy prognoses for the future.
13. 'Agony in East Africa'. Editorial in *Daily Telegraph* 28 January 1986.
14. See L.H. Ofosu-Appiah *The Life and Times of Dr. J.B. Danquah*, (Accra, Waterville Publishing House, 1974), in particular Danquah's letter of protest against the Removal Order served on him, 12 March 1948, p. 61, in which he wrote that 'the people directly charged with the administration of Government should be directly responsible to the people, with power in the people to change the personnel of Government when they feel that the Government or Cabinet of the day had failed them, or served its time. This constitutional goal I am pledged to pursue without flinching. . .'
15. Julius K. Nyerere interviewed by William E. Smith in 'A Reporter at Large: Transition'. *New Yorker*, 3 March 1986.
16. On the very day of Independence Nkrumah was presenting himself as a committed democrat.
17. See H.L. Wesseling 'Colonial Wars and Armed Peace, 1870-1914' *Itinerario V*, 1981, 2, pp. 53-69.
18. See Finn Fugelstad *A History of Niger 1850-1960* (Cambridge, Cambridge University Press, 1983), p. 61.
19. Walter Miller to Sir Frederick Lugard, 24 September 1907 in Rhodes House Library, Oxford, Mss. Brit. Emp. s. 62. 'Lugard Papers'. Cited in Robert Shenton *The Development of Capitalism in Northern Nigeria* (London, James Currey, 1986), p. 27.
20. *ibid.* Edward Lugard to Sir Frederick Lugard. 21 May 1908.
21. Myron Echenberg ' "Morts pour la France": the African Soldier in France during the Second World War' *Journal of African History*, 26, 4, 1958, p. 376.
22. It also convinced Britain's new Colonial Secretary, Iain Macleod, that 'swift change was needed in Kenya'. Quoted in Jeremy Murray-Brown *Kenyatta* (London, George Allen and Unwin, 1972), p. 299. See also A. Marshall Macphee *Kenya* (London, Ernest Benn, 1968), pp. 151-3.
23. See for example the special issues of the *Journal of African History* on the two world wars: 'World War I and Africa', 19, 1978, No 1; and 'World War II and Africa', 26, 1985, No 4. David Killingray and Richard Rathbone

eds. *Africa and the Second World War* (London, Macmillan, 1986).

24. T.O. Ranger *Dance and Society in Eastern Africa 1890-1970: the Beni Ngoma* (London, Heinemann, 1975), p. 45.

25. For instance Jomo Kenyatta of Kenya, Hastings Banda of Malawi, Kwame Knrumah of Ghana, Sultan Mohammed V of Morocco, Seretse Khama of Bostwana.

26. William P. Smith 'A Reporter at Large'.

27. Robin Palmer and Neil Parsons eds. *The Roots of Rural Poverty in Central and Southern Africa* (London, Heinemann, 1977).

28. For instance Robin Palmer *Land and Racial Domination in Rhodesia*, (London, Heinemann, 1977) but see also Paul Mosley *The Settler Economies: Studies in the Economic History of Kenya and Southern Rhodesia 1900-1963* Cambridge, (Cambridge University Press, 1983) where he expresses reservations about the conventional view of settler economies in Africa.

29. While it is difficult to calculate the relative burden of taxation imposed on their subjects by those pre-colonial policies which raised revenue through direct taxes and that exacted by the colonial state, it is significant that many inhabitants of pre-colonial polities that did impose direct taxation in cash or kind, for example in Niger, French Soudan and Chad, were forced to migrate in order to earn enough to pay their taxes. See Elliott P. Skinner *The Mossi of the Upper Volta* (Stanford, Stanford University Press, 1964), pp. 156-8 for the early impact of taxation by the French on the Mossi, who were later to be one of the chief suppliers of migrant labour in West Africa.

30. See in particular Chapter 6 of Shenton *The Development of capitalism in Northern Nigeria*.

31. See Robert H. Bates, Essays on the Political Economy of Rural Africa (Cambridge, Cambridge University Press, 1983), especially Part III, though he has trenchant criticisms of the effect of the colonial agricultural regime on the peasant.

32. Personal Communication from Professor Lalage Bown based on direct observation in the Eastern Province of Uganda 1955-60.

33. Personal communication from Irene Brown. Most of the examples of what the French did on leaving Guinea are not published but fall into the category of 'on dit que'. See, however, Claude Rivière *Guinea: the Mobilisation of a People* (Ithaca, Cornell University Press, 1977), p. 83, where he says of the departing French that some destroyed equipment before they left, others carried away files, while one group of soldiers set fire to their barracks.

34. Marcus Cunliffe 'The Cultural Patrimony of the United States' in Prosser Gifford ed. *The Treaty of Paris (1793) in a Changing States System* (Lanham, Maryland, University Press of America and Washington D.C., Wilson Center, 1985), p. 177.

35. Pius Okigbo 'The Nigerian Economy in the next decade: possibilities of self-reliance'. St. Antony's College Oxford, African Affairs Seminar, 13 March 1986. Discussion.

36. See S.M. Jacobs 'Report on Taxation and Economics of Nigeria', 1934 in Rhodes House Library Mss. Afr. t. 16 where he writes '. . . Nigeria in *all internal respects* has not suffered from an economic depression. Her production of yams, cassava, fish, corn, and her exchange of all her produce goes on as before'. Quoted in Shenton *The Development of Capitalism in Northern Nigeria* p. 101.

37. The health or otherwise of a colonial economy was measured almost exclusively in terms of imports and of agricultural and mineral exports since there was little attempt by the colonial authorities to assess the volume of production of food crops for local consumption or of locally manufactured goods, for example cloth, pots and iron work.

38. This point from Patrick Manning's *Slavery, Colonialism and economic Growth in Dahomey, 1640-1960* (Cambridge, Cambridge University Press, 1982), (see especially Chapter 10) is made by Ralph Austen in 'African Economies in Historical Perspective', *Business History Review,* Spring 1985, p. 103.

39. Austen in *ibid* p. 101.

40. See Michael Crowder 'Lugard and Colonial Nigeria: Towards an Identity' *History Today* 36, February 1986, pp. 23-29.

41. R.D. Pearce *The Turning Point in Africa: British Colonial Policy 1938-1948* (London, Frank Cass), 1982, especially Chapter 3.

42. Crawford Young *Politics in the Congo: Decolonisation and Independence* (Princeton, New Jersey, Princeton University Press, 1965), Chapters 3 and 4.

43. In Guinea-Bissau, for instance, the PAIGC carried out a General Election in the liberated zones in 1972 two years before the Portuguese recognised the independence of its former colony, an independence which the Guinea-Bissau leaders had anyway effectively proclaimed in September 1973. See Basil Davidson 'Portuguese-speaking Africa' in *Cambridge History of Africa* 8 (Cambridge, Cambridge University Press, 1984), p. 788-9. Another example would be the Algerian Revolution though here there was a deliberate move to revalidate many of the institutions and much of the legislation of the erstwhile colonial regime because the FLN had failed to build political institutions of its own during the long and bitter struggle with the French. See Clement Henry Moore 'The Maghrib' in *ibid.* pp. 580-82.

44. Lamine Gueye *Itinéraire africaine* (Paris, 1966), p. 79.

45. See Michael Crowder 'Tshekedi Khama: Statesman' in R.F. Morton and Jeff Ramsay eds. *Botswana: Making of a Nation* (Gaborone, Longman) (forthcoming).

46. David Williams: Personal Communication.

47. Ofosu-Appiah *Danquah* pp. 130-1.

48. *West Africa* 16 March 1957.

49. I have come across one Nigerian named Hitler, a Motswana named Mussolini, and been told of two sons of a Togolese called respectively Bismarck and Goebbels.

50. *West Africa* 16 January 1984.

51. Cited in *ibid*.

52. Julius Nyerere immediately comes to mind. Another example is Mamadou Dia, the former Prime Minister of Senegal.

53. *West Africa* 16 March 1957. 'Ghana takes it calmly'. Two and half years later *West Africa* used a similar headline 'Lagos takes it calmly' for its report on the independence celebrations of Nigeria.

54. David Williams: Personal Communication.

55. *ibid.*

56. Sylvia Leith-Ross *Stepping Stones: Memoirs of Colonial Nigeria, 1907-1960* (London, Peter Owen), 1983, in particular Section V covering the years 1951-55.

57. Interview with William E. Smith 'A Reporter at Large'.

58. See the admirable critique of the role of foreign experts in African development in Paul Richards *Indigenous Agricultural Revolution* (London, Hutchinson University Library for Africa), 1985.

59. Julius Nyerere in interview with William E. Smith 'A Reporter at Large'.

60. *ibid.*

VISIT TO SOUTH AFRICA

Bhupinder Singh Liddar

Bhupinder Singh Liddar is an Ottawa writer associated with Parliamentary Liaison.

In a world where freedom is becoming increasingly rare, our country today is a symbol of the expansion of freedom, of the upholding of freedom of religion and free enterprise, sustained by equal rights before an independent judiciary.

This statement by the State President of South Africa, P.W. Botha, at the opening session of the "Parliament" boggles the mind, filled as it is with the television images of violence, riot and general unrest that has gripped that unhappy country. The President was not speaking to the foreign news media but to the elected white parliamentarians of the Republic of South Africa.

Referring to the victims of violence and unrest, the State President further stated in that same speech, "Allow me once again to express my sympathy with the suffering of all those affected"—knowing full well that more than half of those were Blacks killed by police.

These are some examples of what has come to be termed double-speak or "Bothaspeak!"

An opportunity presented itself to me recently to travel to this land where Botha-as-freedom contrasts sharply with Black unrest. Where does the reality lie? Having been born in Kenya and having spent many years there, as well as in independent Zimbabwe, I felt a compelling desire to seek an answer to this question. I knew I did not have to go to South Africa to know what "apartheid" was all about. We experienced shades of it in Kenya and up until recently Rhodesia operated the same regime under Ian Smith. Separateness along racial lines—separate schools, separate residential areas, separate cemeteries, separate hospitals, and disparities such as higher wages for the Whites than non-Whites for the same job—and certain jobs (including that of writing parking tickets) reserved for Whites!

The most deceptive argument presented by the pro-status quo South Africa observers is that the situation is "complicated," and that one really has to go to South Africa to fully understand it. This line of appeal was used to invite Canadian parliamentarians and business leaders to show them the "good" life of the African. Many were convinced of the "civilizing" efforts of the South African regime and of its righteousness.

TOURIST IN SOUTH AFRICA

It was from Harare that I flew to Johannesburg by Air Zimbabwe. There are frequent daily flights by Air Zimbabwe and South African Airways between the major cities of these neighboring states. An active South African commercial office exists in Harare in a building decked with a South African flag. There is also considerable cooperation between the railways of the two countries, because of geohistorical factors.

The man who sat next to me was a young white student of pharmacy in South Africa who had been visiting friends and relatives in Zimbabwe. He and his family belong to those who, upon Zimbabwe attaining independence, decided to pack up and head south. He seemed concerned that about 3,550 Whites were leaving South Africa every month as a result of recent unrest. What were his impressions of Zimbabwe? He was impressed with the progress Zimbabwe had been able to make and the cordial race relations that existed. A number of South African Whites were concerned about being conscripted into the army to fight yet another liberation army and were contemplating returning to Zimbabwe. A familiar experience of talking with white South Africans outside their country is the degree of misinformation they can accumulate and disseminate.

This young white pharmacy student told me confidently that all universities were open to all races. Technically he was right, except that a non-White who wishes to attend a predominantly white university has to obtain a ministerial permit. A couple of days later I read in the papers that the Minister of Education had declared four universities now open to all races, thereby dropping the permit requirement to gain entry. There remain other universities, however, to which non-Whites still cannot gain admission. Discrimination permeates education at the primary and secondary school levels too. For instance in the 1983-84 fiscal year, per capita spending was approximately $992 for Whites, $653 for Indians, $341 for Coloreds and $141 for Blacks. This disparity in spending on education leads to obvious results released recently on illiteracy rates for South Africans over the age of fifteen: 33 percent for Blacks, 15.5 percent for Coloreds, 7.6 percent for Indians and 0.72 percent for Whites. While this progressive announcement was being

31. Visit to South Africa

made, another report appeared alongside, stating that "the quota system which pegs the number or percentage of other race's students which may be admitted to white universities will still remain in force."

The South African government has strategically designated residential areas along racial lines, so that it makes it easy for the government to argue against mixed schools. The government, of course, has no intention of integrating schools, but can use the pretext of geographical proximity of schools to residential areas to pursue the policy of separateness.

In Kenya, prior to independence, and in Zimbabwe under the Smith regime, a similar policy of separation of schools on racial lines was pursued. Upon attaining independence or majority rule schools in both countries were made multiracial. This greatly contributed to racial harmony. Policies of racial segregation were practised by the English in Kenya and Rhodesia. In Rhodesia's case one could not find a more English-sounding name to lead the country than "Smith." It is, therefore, ironic when one hears English-speaking apologists in South Africa blaming the Dutch settlers or Afrikaners exclusively for the ills of apartheid. After all, the English-speakers make up 40 percent of the white population.

APARTHEID EVERYWHERE

Now back to arrival at Johannesburg airport. A British Airways jumbo was landing, and departures to Mauritius, Malawi, Botswana, Luxembourg and France were listed for the day. From the plane one gets into the bus driven by a white woman in her forties. The Immigration Officer points out that since I have a visa stamped to visit Kenya during the onward journey he would not stamp it, but affix one of the stick-on visas. This is to avoid any complication in being allowed into Kenya.

The Immigration and Customs Officers are Whites, while the bag-handlers and porters are Blacks. The bank where I cash traveller's cheques is staffed by Whites only. I board the airport bus to Johannesburg driven by a Black with all shades of people on board.

Into Johannesburg—a bustling metropolis. We go past the exhausted gold mines, now packed away into neat rectangular piles. These piles of dust that were once gold seemed to symbolize the exhaustion of the ruling regime.

Once in downtown Johannesburg one begins to notice the double-decker buses (not painted red!) with white passengers and single blue-grey colored buses carrying black passengers and driven by Blacks. The sidewalks are shared by all races—on equal footing for once!

Whites and Blacks mingle freely in downtown stores. Only Whites are allowed to own businesses in the downtown area known as the CBDA, Central Business District Area. This is the case with all major centers. These were the areas effectively boycotted during last Christmas season. White shopkeepers became aware of their reliance on the spending-power of the Blacks as a result of this exercise. You hardly met any storeowner who did not feel the pinch. An extended and a more effective boycott at Christmas this year is being feared by businessmen. One does, however, run across a shop or two being operated by an Asian. How did he manage to secure the store in this restricted area? Well, he bought it in the name of a White and paid him a nominal fee for the use of his name! There is no manifestation of hatred or violence in the streets but there is certainly a sense of nervousness and bitterness. There is tension.

SEPARATE BUSES, BUT SHARED TRAINS

One day I decide to visit an acquaintance in Pretoria, who once was stationed in Ottawa. There are regular bus and train connections between Johannesburg and Pretoria, the seat of the executive branch of the government. (The legislative capital is Cape Town.)

I go down to the Johannesburg train station to inquire about train departures and to obtain a ticket to Pretoria. I buy a newspaper from the vendor and engage in a conversation about changes that are being brought about. The charming newspaper vendor points to the pedestrian mall adjoining the railway station. It was once forbidden territory to non-Whites but they can now walk there. In our brief encounter he nervously tells me that the townships (areas where Blacks live) are very politicized and there is a lot of political activity there. He points to a restaurant across the street where he was not allowed to enter because of the color of his skin. He hopes that will change—though he does not sound as though it will happen soon. I go past a coffee shop in the railway station complex which has a prominently displayed sign "Whites only." As I enter the train station, I realize that the place is divided on racial lines. There are separate entrances to the station for Whites and non-Whites. Inside the railway station is another coffee shop with a sign hanging in the window (like the closed and open sign) which states "Whites only." Someone, probably a black man, washes that window every day with that hideous sign hanging as an ugly reminder of the rules of the game. As I proceed towards the information desk I encounter another sign over a door "General Waiting Room—Whites Only!"

On to the information counter staffed by Whites. Asked to proceed to the ticket counter. Staffed by Whites. I buy my ticket to Pretoria and proceed to the turnstiles manned by tough-looking white women. I run down the stairs to the platform. As usual, I think I shall miss the train. It is departure time. As soon as I get to the platform I am confronted by a string of coaches each clearly marked "Whites only." What do I do? I say to myself, "I am not White." I have made it so far because the authorities must have bestowed upon me the dubious honor of being a Mediterranean!

There are only Whites in the coach I am in. Even the ticket examiner is White. Nothing seems to have changed since the days of Gandhi! We are on our way to Pretoria. At every station I notice toilet facilities marked "Men—White only." Later on after one of our stops at a suburban station I see a few Blacks on the platform. I stick my head out of the window and notice that the front section of the train is for Blacks—and they even have a black ticket examiner! The Whites and Blacks enter and leave the train through separate entrances and exits. At one station a black woman runs to board the train. She misses the train not because she is too far from it, but because she is too far from the coaches for the Blacks up front. She dared not have jumped into the coaches for the Whites. Here she is in a country where her people

5. THE RETREAT OF THE WEST

Apartheid is still very pronounced in South Africa. The only people this couple will encounter when they travel will be white.

make up 71 percent of the population of 32.5 million, but a mere 17 percent (the Whites) are dictating the lives of the rest of the population and making laws affecting every little detail of their lives. Colored (mixed race) make up 9 percent of the population, while Asians account for 3 percent.

GETTING AN EARLY START

At one train station we pick up a large number of school children—boys and girls in their late teens. I wondered about these white children and their world-view. They live in white suburbs, socialize with white families only, board a train with "Whites only" coaches to school, attend exclusively white schools, play with white friends, attend church with white congregations and their only contact with a black African is with their gardener or cook at home or the nanny who brought them up! The Whites do not only want to maintain their exclusivity but also their social superiority. Yet they want to be known as Africans. They have, however, never lived as though they belong to Africa. The school children could have been coming out of any British public school. They are Africans of convenience. The color of their skin assures them a secure job after graduation.

The same pattern of separate waiting room for "Whites" is repeated at Pretoria railway station. I walk down to see the acquaintance at the Government's Bureau of Information. It is a 7-storey building in downtown Pretoria. From the time I enter and the time I leave I do not see a single non-White in the building. My acquaintance talks about the universities being open to all races.

31. Visit to South Africa

He mentions universal citizenship being extended to all South Africans. It is merely an attempt to cover up the failure of the policy of establishing "independent" homelands with respective citizenships. The Blacks are now being restored their right to citizenship of South Africa. The homelands of Transkei, Bophutatawans, Venda and Ciskei were merely labor pools for South Africa and not economically viable entities.

The Immorality Act forbidding interracial marriages has been scrapped. The question arises: if an interracial couple were to get married and want to settle down, where would they live? In a black area? A white area? While my acquaintance rattles off the government record, I casually mention my dilemma earlier in the afternoon when I stood facing a coach marked "Whites only" and having the option of either hopping the train or missing it altogether—in which case I would not have seen him at the appointed time. He shyly informs me that the railway system is still segregated along racial lines.

On my way back to the bus station I walked into a government building to inquire for directions to the bus terminal. I see one black man among hordes of Whites leaving the building. I encounter a young soldier at the front desk who, having also finished the day, volunteers to walk with me for a few blocks towards the bus terminal. He is young looking. He tells me he had been in the army for six years. He is concerned about the "terrorist" activity of the ANC (African National Congress) reaching the urban centres. Only last year the ANC had stuck a sub-power station in Pretoria.

Urban political violence has many Whites worried. Once the downtown business areas become vulnerable to bomb attacks the white community will no longer feel that it is invincible.

While Pretoria is a clean and organized city, there is an air of distance from reality. As in Ottawa, civil servants pour out in droves, from lines at the bus stops and within a short period the city core begins to look deserted. At the bus stops there are benches marked "WHITE BUS PASSENGERS ONLY." The buses are exclusively for Whites and driven by white bus drivers!

AN ASIAN VIEW

One evening we drive south from Johannesburg to Lenasia—Land of Asia! This place is home to about 200,000 Asians. Asians working in downtown Johannesburg have to make about a 30-kilometre trip each way by car or take the train. As one drives along the highway to Lenasia one sees the signs for Soweto. Immediately one is filled with images of funerals, rock-throwing and clenched fists. One becomes a little nervous. We approach closer. One sees rows of neatly arranged houses. Smiling children. No funeral or a demonstration today. One crosses the highway to Lenasia and one sees opulence. This is no Soweto. One sees street lights, while back across the highway there are those overhead lights that light up whole areas. The meaning is clear: the Asians are the buffer zone between the Blacks and the Whites. The display of material well-being is a daily reminder to residents of Soweto across the highway, while the luxury of the Whites is hidden away in the northern parts of Johannesburg.

I spend the evening with an Asian family. The sons tell me that a growing number of Asians, especially the young ones, are identifying with the political goals of the ANC and the black majority. I am told once again that the House of Delegates for Asians does not have the confidence of the Asian community. Only 4 percent of the eligible voters cast their votes.

A tricameral Parliament was created under a new Constitution which came into force in late 1984. Under the new arrangement Whites are represented by a House of Assembly, Coloreds by a House of Representatives and Asians by a House of Delegates. The majority of the population—the Blacks—have no elective chamber.

The Lenasia family informs me that no substantial reforms have taken place. There is a lot of talk to appease the international community, but no action is being taken on the domestic front. One of the sons went to watch a rugby match with some of his white coworkers earlier this year. He, not being White, was turned away from sitting with his white coworkers.

There is almost universal feeling that the situation in South Africa is going to get much worse before it improves. There is no immediate danger of civil war but it is approaching. The feeling is that unless the international community—especially the West—undertakes to bring about a negotiated settlement through the aegis of an international constitutional conference, South Africa is poised on the brink of a bloodbath unlike any yet seen on the continent.

GANDHI
A Twentieth-Century Anomaly?

John Broomfield
John Broomfield is professor of history.

Early one misty morning in January, 1941, a bearded figure, dressed as a Muslim, slipped away from a house on a Calcutta back street to begin what has become an epic journey in modern Indian history. Eluding the police and ultimately the British military on the frontier, he made his way across North India into Afghanistan, where he arranged with difficulty to be taken to Moscow and on to Berlin. There he persuaded the Nazis to provide him with the resources to raise an Indian regiment, which he hoped would spearhead the armed liberation of his homeland. When it appeared that the Japanese were likely to reach India before the Germans, he made another journey, by submarine, to Southeast Asia, there to raise an Indian National Army. His troops saw action against the British in Burma before their leader died in an air crash in 1945.

This heroic figure was Subhas Chandra Bose, and his life story is in many ways typical of the twentieth-century revolutionary nationalist. Western-educated, with a university degree, he went in his late teens to the imperial metropolis, London, to compete successfully for a place in the ruling Indian Civil Service. At the moment of triumph, however, he renounced the opportunity and returned to India to join the new mass movement of resistance to British rule. In his twenties he organized militant youth brigades, reaching the height of his popularity during the civil disobedience campaigns from 1930 to 1932. He advocated the violent overthrow of the British and led paramilitary formations in displays of opposition to their imperialism. He was arrested, imprisoned, and externed for long periods, but from his jail cell in exile he continued to exhort his countrymen to rise in revolt against their oppressors.

In Bose we can see the likeness of many other twentieth-century revolutionaries: Mao, Ho, and Sukarno in Asia; Kenyatta in Africa; Madero and Castro in Latin America; Venizelos, Husseini, and Grivas in the Eastern Mediterranean; Trotsky, De Valera, Tito, and Hitler in Europe. All were practitioners of the politics of militant confrontation, and all earned their periods of imprisonment or exile. All shared an ambition to mobilize sectors of their societies to effect the overthrow of perceived imperialisms, internal or external. All were attracted by military styles of organization and discipline, and all had faith in the efficacy of violence.

How striking the contrast if we consider Mohandas Karamchand Gandhi. During that same civil disobedience campaign of 1930 in which Subhas Bose led his young stormtroopers against the police, we find Gandhi on his Dandi salt march: a walk of 200 miles through village India to the seacoast to make salt, as a symbolic gesture of resistance to British rule. What a quaint figure we see in the photographs: a skinny, knobbly-kneed little man, dressed in a loin cloth, granny glasses perched on his nose, barefoot, setting forth with only a walking stick to assist him on a trek that would daunt most men of sixty. Here was a man leading a great political movement with watch cries of truth, love, self-suffering, abstinence, and nonviolence. Surely anomalous watch cries for the twentieth century, with its dynamic emphasis upon revolutionary uprising and violence. Perhaps Gandhi is an anomalous figure in this century? "In an era that takes matters of religious faith lightly," Susanne Rudolph has written, "it is difficult to consider a man who is suspected of saintliness." Yet it is Gandhi, not Subhas Chandra Bose or the many other Indian proponents of violence, who is best known outside, as well as inside, India.

Let us recap the main features of Gandhi's life to draw out the characteristics of his ideals and achievement. He was born in Kathiawar, an isolated northwestern peninsula, where his father was a princely state official. The

32. Gandhi

> "My experience," Gandhi wrote, "has shown me that we win justice quickest by rendering justice to the other party."

environment in which he was raised was one of orthodox Hinduism, and he was strongly influenced by the quietous principles of Vaisnavism and Jainism. His was an educated but not, we may fairly say, an intellectual family. He was put into that most favored of professions for the nineteenth-century Indian elites, the law, and, as few Indians in that century could hope to do, he was enabled to go to Britain in 1887 for extended legal education.

Gandhi's first months in London were cold, lonely, and uncomfortable (as his photographs of the period suggest: flannel suit, starched shirt, Victorian high collar, and all). It was not until he abandoned his legal studies and began to associate with a vegetarian, pacifist group that he discovered some warmth and friendship in that alien city. It was in this company that he rubbed shoulders with such European minds as Tolstoy, and with the American Thoreau. The mixed metaphor of shoulders and minds is appropriate, for Gandhi does not appear to have gained any deep understanding of these thinkers. They influenced him, but mainly by reinforcing established beliefs. The basis of his philosophy is to be sought within his own Indian traditions.

In 1891, having belatedly resumed his legal studies and passed the bar examinations, Gandhi returned to Bombay, where he was an instant and spectacular failure as a barrister. Rising in court to plead his first case, he found himself at a loss for words, and he was quickly demoted to office paper work. In 1893 his firm received a lucrative but routine request for legal counsel from a member of the Indian community in the Transvaal. The partners looked around for their most dispensable clerk — and dispatched Mr. Gandhi.

The experience in South Africa, though in origin so humdrum, was to work a transformation in Gandhi's life — a transformation so spectacular that it may be compared with that of Saul on the road to Damascus. Gandhi arrived in South Africa to be met with racial discrimination of a kind he had never experienced in India and Britain. It shook his faith in the fundamental justice and goodwill of the British imperial system. For a time he was at a loss for a course of action, but finally in May, 1894, goaded by the imminent disenfranchisement of his compatriots in Natal, he formed the Natal Indian Congress. The inarticulate young lawyer was gone; in his place stood an outspoken and courageous crusader against racial injustice.

For the next twenty years, up to the outbreak of the First World War, Gandhi worked in South Africa. In this land far from India, step by step, he fashioned his new revolutionary technique, to which he gave the name *satyagraha:* "soul force," which he contrasted with "brute force." His basic principle was *ahimsa:* non-violence. Non-violence in thought as well as deed, for Gandhi drew on a philosophical tradition that does not recognize that hard distinction between thought and action with which we are familiar in the West. Angry thoughts injure the thinker as well as those against whom they are directed. So Gandhi insisted that love, not hatred, must be the guiding principle of political, as well as personal, action. One must empathize with one's adversary, seeking the good in him and his cause, and trying to eradicate whatever is evil — in self or opponent. The aim in politics, Gandhi emphasized, is to help one's opponent escape his error, as much as to advance one's own cause. The objective must be to heal social wounds, to establish a new basis for reconciliation and positive political action in the future, not to antagonize and polarize. "My experience," he wrote, "has shown me that we win justice quickest by rendering justice to the other party."

This did not mean that injustice from others should go unresisted. Indeed, Gandhi emphasized that non-violent resistance to oppression was a duty. Urging his fellow Indians in South Africa to united action in defense of their communal rights, his call was: "Not to submit; to suffer." Again he drew upon the traditions of his native Gujarat in applying to politics a technique of moral suasion used there in familial and mercantile disputes. The method was for the aggrieved party to shame his adversary and win sympathetic support for his cause by display of self-abnegation, most commonly fasting. With this model in mind, Gandhi devised a succession of non-violent confrontations with the South African authorities. The issues were diverse, and time and place varied greatly, but there was a common aim: to provide those in power with opportunities to demonstrate the injustice of their regime by forcing them to retaliate against limited, non-violent and symbolic acts of protest.

Gandhi achieved a surprising number of victories, but the long-term gains for the South African Indian community were negligible. For this reason the real significance of this period of Gandhi's work must be sought in the experience it gave him: as an organizer, tactician, and publicist. His trips to India and Britain in search of finance and support provided enduring contacts for his later work with the Indian National Congress, and the attention his movement attracted in the press assured him of fame among politically-aware Indians. He left South Africa in 1914 after a striking success against the Union Government. His opponent of many years, the Minister of the Interior, Jan Smuts, breathed a sigh of relief. "The saint has left our shores," he wrote. "I sincerely hope forever." It proved to be so.

Gandhi in India had bigger fish to fry — if one may use so inappropriate a metaphor for a vegetarian! The Indian nationalist movement to which he returned, and in which he was clearly determined to play a role, had developed rapidly in the preceding decade. If, for comparison's sake, we use the familiar categories of American Black nationalism, the Indian movement had developed from its late nineteenth-century NAACP stage, of a liberal

> For Gandhi it was a dictum of politics that an unjust regime is bound to enlarge the area of conflict by its over-reactions to protest.

5. THE RETREAT OF THE WEST

union of right-thinking people, through a period of marches and sit-ins, to economic campaigns to "Buy Black," accompanied by cultural revivalism ("Black is Beautiful"), and finally to the revolutionary call to arms: "Burn, Baby, Burn." As one might expect, such radical developments had split the Indian National Congress. Growing disunity and the failure of the Congress leaders to win mass support had convinced many nationalists of the need for a structural reorganization of their movement.

Into this situation Gandhi came with striking advantages. He had an established public reputation, but, unlike other prominent figures, he was free of factional identification. Moreover, he was an experienced organizer, with his own patented technique of agitational politics. Circumspect as ever, he bided his time. He spent the war years extending his network of political contacts, but steadfastly resisted the temptation to be drawn into their factional squabbles. He chose his own distinctive point of entry into the Indian political arena, initiating a peasant *satyagraha* against the British indigo planters of northern Bihar in 1918. The indigo industry he attacked was uneconomic and had been maintained only by blatant exploitation of the peasant cultivators. His *satyagraha* was a rapid and complete success, and its publicity precipitated him into the front rank of nationalist leaders.

For Gandhi it was a dictum of politics that an unjust regime is bound to enlarge the area of conflict by its over-reactions to protest. The months following his Bihar movement seemed to prove him right. Disturbed by industrial and peasant unrest, and with a weather-eye on Bolshevik successes in Russia, the government of India insisted upon arming itself with legislation to extend its war-time powers of summary action against suspected conspirators. Gandhi responded with a call to the Congress to organize nation-wide *hartals* (general strikes). April, 1919, brought mass protests in many cities of northern and western India, and, when violence erupted in the Panjab, a jittery British administration retaliated brutally. In the bitter aftermath, Gandhi was able to persuade the Congress to accept his blueprint for reorganization and his leadership of a mass campaign of non-cooperation.

It is instructive to observe the elements Gandhi emphasized in the program he advanced, for it will give some measure of the principles that were to guide his three decades of political work in India. In the first place he proposed that all participation in the activities and institutions of British Indian government should cease, and that Congressmen should devote themselves to the construction of national institutions: "a government of one's own within the dead shell of the foreign government." Resistance, non-violent and symbolic, might be offered to particular acts of British oppression, but the really important work was in national reconstruction. For the nation as for the individual, Gandhi taught, salvation could be gained only by internal reformation. Society had to be rid of its evils, especially those of dissension and human exploitation. As a first step he called for reconciliation between religious communities, and he took up the Khilafat issue as a means of cementing Hindu-Muslim unity. He also demanded that caste barriers be broken down and that the untouchables be accepted into the body of Hinduism. Congressmen of all castes should work with the Harijans (the "Children of God," as Gandhi called them) to help them rise from their degradation.

Similarly, there had to be an end to economic oppression. Gandhi was adamant that self-government for India would be a travesty if the mass of people were not freed from the exploitation of capitalists, landholders, and money-lenders. The nationalist movement had to be the people's movement, to benefit the mass of the people. He insisted that Congress demonstrate its concern for the welfare of the Indian poor by adopting a program of economic rehabilitation. Congressmen should leave their urban professions and go into the villages to start cottage industry. The local manufacture of cotton cloth should be revived. The spinning wheel should become the symbol of India's new life, and the wearing of *khadi* (homespun) a gesture of the nation's rejection of imperialism.

In its initial states in the early months of 1921, the first non-cooperation movement was a remarkable success. The unprecedented numbers participating in the agitation — Muslims as well as Hindus — raised serious alarm among British officials. To the perplexity of many of his colleagues in the Congress hierarchy, however, Gandhi seemed to value opportunities for confrontation with the government less than those for popular or political education and social reform. His insistence on continually shifting the focus of the movement, and his prohibition of what to others seemed logical areas of agitation, e.g., industrial disturbances, frustrated even some of his closest followers. In part these shifts reflected his mature judgment of the need to keep the British off-balance; in part they were the product of a determination to maintain his personal domination of the movement; but, most of all, they reflected his deep concern to preserve non-violence. It was the conviction that he had failed to do this that led to his sudden call in February, 1922, for an end to the agitation.

Gandhi initiated two other great campaigns and a host of minor actions in the years before independence. Always he put major emphasis on ethical considerations, insisting doggedly that he alone must be their arbiter. Always he was unpredictable in his tactical decisions and in his timing of the final withdrawal. As a consequence, there were some who became totally exasperated with his leadership — Subhas Chandra Bose being amongst the most outspoken. We need not follow Gandhi step by step through these years, but we must surely ask: how could he retain his following despite such apparently eccentric political behavior? The question is the more intriguing when we realize that on a number of occasions he withdrew from active politics for five or more years at a time and yet was still able to emerge at his chosen moment to resume the leadership of the national movement.

One answer is that Gandhi was a phenomenal scribbler, a fact readily verified by a count of the number of volumes of his *khadi*-bound collected works, now threatening to engulf all but the largest libraries. His polemical writings filled his own newspaper and the columns of many others, year in and year out. He produced books on politics, religion, social organization, and his own life. During his great campaigns, his scribbled battle orders poured from every halting place; and from his *ashram* during his years of retreat the flow of advice, praise, cajolery, and (forgive the heresy) moralizing never ebbed. Gandhi knew the value of a good communication system, and he spared neither himself nor his assistants in his efforts to keep in touch.

He also knew the value of good lieutenants. It is paradoxical that while Gandhi was not particularly responsive to criticism (being too assured of the quality of his own judgment), he was willing to tolerate strong differences of opinion amongst his associates. Indeed it should be put more positively: he worked hard (often through painfully devised compromises) to prevent disagreements over ideology or strategy from driving able men and women out of the Congress.

As these two points suggest, Gandhi was an organizer *par excellence*. We should not be misled by the sainthood conferred upon him by popular mythology into thinking of him as some impractical, dreamy visionary. This was the man who took the ramshackle Indian National Congress of the second decade of the century, and rebuilt it as an effective nationwide organization, extending from a full-time working central executive, link-by-link, to representative committees in virtually every district of British India. At the high points of participation during the civil disobedience campaigns, the formal organization reached even to the villages. Though periodically weakened by the removal to prison of its office-bearers, it survived to provide independent India with a nationwide institution parallel to, and reinforcing, the governmental structure.

Another of Gandhi's personal attributes — one which he undoubtedly shared with other great politicians — was extraordinary physical and mental stamina. The seemingly frail old man could outwalk, outsit, and outtalk others half his age. We have amusing accounts from the second Round Table Conference in London of British Cabinet Ministers wilting perceptibly as Mr. Gandhi, calmly and quietly, talked on into the small hours of the morning. His slow, tireless methods drove foes, and sometimes friends as well, to distraction.

Lastly, Gandhi had what we can only describe as an amazing mass appeal. He was known to, and revered by, millions in urban and rural India, like no other figure in historic times. Wherever he went, the news of his coming spread far beyond the reach of the mass media. How could this be? The easy thing to say is: because of his charisma. But that is no answer, merely a rephrasing of the statement about his mass appeal. Gandhi was a master of symbolism, and here we may have a key. To say he was "a master of symbolism" is to make him sound more manipulative than I would intend. Rather, he had a keen sense of the political, social, and ethical fitness of a variety of symbols and symbolic acts.

Let us take some examples: The Dandi salt march of 1930, already mentioned, was one of his most brilliant, yet simple, symbolic successes. All humans need salt, and in many places in India salt can be produced with the simplest equipment, or even scraped up from dried pools or marshes. The British Indian government, however, levied a tax on salt and prohibited its unlicensed production. Obviously an attack on this restriction would be universally popular and would serve as an indictment of a regime that taxed the basic needs of its pitifully poor colonial population. Brilliant in conception; equally brilliant in execution: a long march through village India, gathering thousands of supporters, drawing the attention of the world press to the moment by the sea when the imperial policemen would be forced to arrest India's most revered leader, and unmanageable numbers of his adherents, simply for lighting a fire and heating a pan of salt water.

Gandhi's choice of the spinning wheel and *khadi* to represent the revitalized Congress was a similar attempt to find symbols that would have emotive appeal across the many levels of Indian society. To the urban professional classes it was a call for a return to a more pure and traditional way of life. Discarding imported cloth offered them a way to make a visible sacrifice for the cause, while striking a blow at British economic domination. It also offered them an opportunity (not welcomed by all) for a symbolic union with the masses by donning common garb. For the peasantry, the spinning wheel was among the most sophisticated of their familiar instruments of production, and one which had frequently provided a marketable product to supply an income above their minimum needs. For generations past the sale of homespun had brought them a few good times and good things, but all too often of late their spinning wheels had lain unused, unable to compete with factory-made goods. In Gandhi's symbols they saw the promise of a restoration of a more just order.

Gandhi himself was a living symbol. His lifestyle expressed a traditional philosophy. To many he appeared as a humble ascetic, the pure man of the soil, fearless of his environment, because his own physical survival meant little to him. Confident and courageous, yet devoid of all defensiveness, even the defensiveness of blustering arrogance. This idealized stereotype owed much to the Indian tradition of the ascetic leader, a tradition in which Gandhi himself believed implicitly. He was at pains to project the image of the *brahmachari* (celibate). Although his rejection of worldly comforts was sometimes ostentatious (a puckish disciple is credited with the comment: "You have no idea how much it costs to keep Mahatmaji in the style of poverty to which he has become accustomed"), there can be no question that he was thoroughly sincere in his conviction that strength came through a renunciation of sensual indulgence. He accepted traditional Indian theories of physiology and psychology, which hold that the bodily essences giving physical, mental, and moral strength are dissipated through such outpourings as sex and anger, but increased by pure foods, particularly vegetables and milk products, and through disciplined meditation. Gandhi shared this belief with the vast majority of his fellow Hindus. They saw that he was a disciplined *brahmachari*, and they had no difficulty in understanding the source of his superior stamina and moral virtue.

He earned for himself the title *Mahatma*: a great soul. It is a title he disclaimed, but significant nonetheless, for it suggests a link with an Indian tradition of religious leadership that has been disregarded in measuring Gandhi's impact on twentieth-century India. This is the tradition of the religious ascetic combining spiritual instruction for a

5. THE RETREAT OF THE WEST

peasant community with the leadership of that community in rebellion against its oppressors: against (in Eric Hobsbawm's words) the "special form of brigand," the government, and against the lesser, but regrettably more familiar brigands: tax collectors, policemen, landlords, and moneylenders. Many Hindu folk tales and many of the most popular epics concern such rebel *gurus*, leading the fight against injustice. In more recent times, under Muslim rule and in the nineteenth century, there are many recorded cases of religious teachers, *sufis* and *bhaktas* particularly, providing leadership for local revolt. Gandhi could easily be understood by the peasant community as a great leader, a *mahatma*, in this tradition of protest.

As Eric Wolf has observed in *Peasants:* "Simplified movements of protest among a peasantry frequently center upon the myth of a social order more just and egalitarian than the hierarchical present." By attacking the hierarchical present, by symbolizing a resistance to the economic oppressions worked by intrusive modern technology and its accompanying innovations in the organization of labor, by using the language and symbolism of the popular Hindu tradition, Gandhi mobilized rural mass India in a way that would never have been possible had independence from Britain been the sum total of the Indian nationalist movement. It was his genius to have seen the need, and to have provided the means, to link together the urges of India's peasant masses with the struggle to expel the foreigner.

Here we touch the tragic core of Gandhi's life. He used symbolism brilliantly. He was a master of emotive religious imagery and the historical myths associated with his religion. But in a multi-religious and multi-cultural society, such an emphasis on one tradition, even if it is an unconscious emphasis expressed through a lifestyle, must inevitably give offense to some groups. We cannot be surprised, given the structure of Indian thought in the twentieth century, that attempts at mass mobilization would involve the use of Hindu symbols, but equally we must expect the alienation of non-Hindu communities, most notably the Muslims, a quarter of all Indians before 1947. The Muslims felt increasingly threatened by Indian nationalism, and the Mahatma — for all his non-violence — was not a reassuring figure. Gandhi devoted his last ten years to a struggle to heal the wounds opened between Islam and Hinduism in the mass political movements of the century. It was tragic irony that he should be assassinated in 1948 by a Hindu nationalist who blamed him for the concessions to the Muslims that made possible Pakistan.

Let us return to the original question: was Gandhi a twentieth-century anomaly? Certainly he was out of step with much else in the twentieth century, but he was intentionally so. It was not that he was unaware of what was occurring around him. He emphasized "soul force" as a counter to what he saw as the omnipresent, twentieth-century brute force. He emphasized non-violence for a society he believed to be far too violent. He was not saying, as many have mistakenly suggested, that non-violence was *the* Indian tradition. Rather, he lamented that India had many violent traditions, and he warned his contemporaries not to let those traditions dominate. He charged them to take the most noble of their traditions — non-violence — and to work to ensure its dominance of their national life.

This invites the retort that he had little success: India, after Gandhi, remains a violent place. Similarly, many will question the general effectiveness of non-violence as an agitational strategy, and they can cite numerous instances of its failure. It would be foolish to suggest that non-violent movements are always victorious, but that claim could scarcely be made for violent struggles either. Perhaps, if we could draw up a score sheet, we would find that failure was no more frequent in non-violent agitations, and I suspect we would discover that in the former, means less often distorted ends.

What Gandhi contributed with *satyagraha* was an alternative model of revolutionary action. He extended the range of political options available to the twentieth-century activist. This was no mean achievement.

Perhaps Gandhi was an anomaly in another way: as a traditionalist leader in a modern world. Not so, I would argue. If we properly understand our twentieth-century world, we shall expect to find traditionalist leaders all about us. Such understanding, however, has been made difficult by the false dichotomy many social scientists (and journalists in their wake) have drawn between tradition and modernity. Modernization, we have been told, implies moving away from the traditional. On the contrary, I would argue that tradition is not something dispensed with as one becomes modern. Tradition is the cement that binds society together. If it is hard and inflexible, it may prevent change, or change may crack the cement and shatter the society. This has happened, but rarely. Usually the cement is flexible, for tradition is a malleable commodity. In the hands of traditionalist leaders it can be bent and reshaped in adapting the society to modern demands. Insight comes from understanding and interpreting the continuity of tradition: the strengths or weaknesses of diverse traditions for various social and political purposes. Because of our acceptance of the false dichotomy between tradition and modernity, we have equated modernization with change and neglected the equally valid equation between tradition and change. We have been taught to regard traditionalist leaders as reactionaries, when in fact many, like Gandhi, have been vigorous proponents of change. Frequently they have been most effective "modernizers," for they have understood the importance of presenting change in comprehensible, i.e., traditional, forms.

There is a final point to be made about Gandhi's relevance to the twentieth century. He recognized the critical need to deal with the problems of the peasantry — still a majority of the world's population, though so often treated as an anachronistic survival. I have already pointed to his attempts to evolve an economic program for the Indian nationalist movement that would relieve the economic hardships and social dislocations inflicted on peasant communities by industrialization. Through his criticism of urban elitism in the Congress, and, more im-

> Far from being an anomaly in his twentieth-century world, Gandhi was wrestling (however unsuccessfully) with a crucial problem of that world: the construction of an economic and political order in which the peasantry could have a full role.

portantly, through his own labors in rural reconstruction, he attacked the dysfunctional and debilitating status inferiority imposed upon the cultivator by the cult of urban civilization. In his reverence for the tradition of the village *panchayet* (council of elders), and in his utopian hopes for the ultimate withering away of the central state structure, he faithfully reflected the peasantry's hostility to that "cold monster," the state, whose baffling complexity grew with every advance in communications technology. In his insistence that the Congress not become the inheritor of the institutions of British administration, he was trying to prevent in India what has happened almost everywhere else in the ex-colonial world: the transfer of the power to exploit the peasantry from an urban-centered imperialist regime to an urban-centered nationalist regime. Far from being an anomaly in his twentieth-century world, Gandhi was wrestling (however unsuccessfully) with a crucial problem of that world: the construction of an economic and political order in which the peasantry could have a full role.

ates
The Vatican, Israel and the Jerusalem Question (1943-1984)

Silvio Ferrari
Silvio Ferrari is a Professor at the Faculty of Jurisprudence of the University of Parma.

On October 19, 1984, when the new Egyptian Ambassador to the Vatican presented his credentials, Pope John Paul II restated his conviction that "the religious identity of Jerusalem, and in particular the common monotheistic tradition, can provide a way to promoting a coming together among all those who feel the Holy City to be their own. This is fundamental for a just peace in the region of the Middle East. . . ."[1]

The Pope's words reflect a conviction which, with different emphases and in different forms, has characterized the teaching and statements of all Popes from the end of the Second World War onwards.

The Vatican and the Palestine Question (1943-1948)

The Vatican's firm opposition to a National Home for the Jews being created in the Holy Land, expressed several times in the 1920s during the polemic surrounding the decision to give Great Britain the Palestine mandate, was reiterated in the clearest and most unmistakable terms between the summer of 1943 and the summer of 1944, when the Second World War was clearly going the Allies' way. On June 22, 1943, the Apostolic Delegate in Washington received instructions from the Vatican Secretary of State to inform the US government that Catholics throughout the world "could not but be wounded in their religious pride should Palestine be handed over to the Jews or placed virtually under their control."[2] Similar but less hawkish opinions expressed by Mgr. Angelo Roncalli, later Pope John XXIII,[3] show that the Vatican Secretary of State's line met with approval of the Vatican diplomats most actively involved in helping the Jews, and lead us to the conclusion (backed up by other documents)[4] that the Vatican's opposition to the creation of a Jewish State in the Holy Land was not caused by anti-semitic feeling but rather by the Vatican's determination to protect Catholic interests in Palestine.

The Vatican's aversion to a "Jewish Home" did not mean it favored Arab domination in the Holy Land. In a meeting with Myron C. Taylor, President Roosevelt's personal representative to the Pope in April 1944, the Vatican Secretary of State expressed the Vatican's concern over the plan to create a Pan-Arab Confederation (the Arab League) in the Middle East, which put the Christian community's future in an uncertain and precarious position.

The Vatican held that the Great Powers' intervention to ensure that "the basic legislation of the planned Confederation would clearly give non-Muslims freedom of opinion, freedom of worship and parity with Muslims as regards civil rights and duties"[5] was a *sine qua non* for making this plan "at least partly acceptable."

Clearly, a fear that either Arab or Jewish domination would prejudice Catholic interests in Palestine lay behind the Vatican's concern over the Holy Land's future. These interests, the Vatican believed, would be better protected by a solution where "neither Jews nor Arabs, but a Third Power, should have control in the Holy Land."[6] Either a continuation of the British Mandate (or a mandate given to another Christian power) or the internationalization of all Palestine under UN supervision were consequently favored by the Vatican. Either solution meant that control of the Holy Land would be safely in Christian hands and that the danger of the Arab-Jewish conflict degenerating into open war and the concomitant threat of irreparable destruction to the Holy Places would be averted.

Between 1945 and 1947 this proposed solution to the Palestine question, clearly the most acceptable for the majority of Catholics, was warmly supported by Archbishop Spellman of New York and his closest collaborator for Palestine affairs, Mgr. Thomas J. McMahon.[7] Although undoubtedly sharing their opinion, the Vatican decided to make no public statement about a plan which was firmly opposed by both the Arab countries and the Jewish Agency. The Vatican decided it was more advisable to follow an extremely reserved line and avoid any official statement of its position on the Palestine conflict.

The Vatican was forced to review this policy in April 1947, when Great Britain decided to submit the Palestine issue to the UN. As there was now no chance of Britain's mandate in the Holy Land being extended and because doubts were growing regarding the wisdom of entrusting

---

This paper uses the following abbreviations: ASMAE = Ministere degli Affari Esteri, Roma, Archivio Storico Diplomatico; CZA = Central Zionist Archives, Jerusalem; FO = Public Record Office, London, Foreign Office Papers; ISA = Israel State Archives, Jerusalem; NA = National Archives, Washington, D.C., Record Group 59, Central Files of the Department of State.

Palestine to UN administration for fear of easing Soviet penetration in the Middle East, the Vatican was faced with an alternative: a divided Holy Land as the result of the creation of a Jewish State and an Arab State or the creation of a single state in Palestine representing both sides but with an Arab majority, considered to be the lesser evil as compared with the creation of a Jewish State.

The first solution was decidedly unappealing to Catholics and was openly criticized by Spellman ("The Catholic Church strongly opposes any form of partition, primarily on the ground that the whole of the land is sacred to Christ").[8] Leading officials in the Vatican Secretary of State's Office agreed in principle with these opinions but failed to make them official only because of the Vatican's policy of reserve, which counselled against any over-precise public statements that might well have conflicted with Jewish aspirations for national independence.

The creation of a single Arab-controlled state in Palestine was openly supported by the Middle Eastern Catholic community and, more discreetly, by missionary organizations working in the Holy Land. In Rome these positions were greeted favorably in some ecclesiastical circles close to the Sacred Oriental Congregation, highly aware of the implications of the Palestine question for the future of Catholic activities throughout the Middle East:[9] but, despite the pressure placed on the Pope by these groups and despite the existence of objectively significant factors favoring the Arabs, the Vatican State Secretary's Office did not pronounce itself in favor of an Arab State in Palestine although it knew perfectly well that, generally, Catholic communities and most ecclesiastical authorities preferred this solution to the division of the Holy Land. This reticence is explained (a) by the belief that the Arab proposals, opposed by both the US and the USSR, would not have been approved by the UN General Assembly and, (b) in particular, by the Vatican's hopes for the internationalization of Jerusalem, which was an important feature of the plan to divide Palestine approved in the summer of 1947 by the majority of the United Nations Special Committee on Palestine (UNSCOP).

Originally, it would seem, the Vatican appeared to be seeking safeguards that did not necessarily mean making Jerusalem a "corpus separatum."[10] But it is equally obvious that the Vatican was extremely pleased when this solution received the support of the majority of UNSCOP. The Vatican felt it gave the best protection possible to the Holy Places and the Catholic community in Palestine and, in addition, satisfied a number of spiritual ideals (a legal and institutional framework embodying the universal meaning of the Holy Places) and political ideals (preventing Jerusalem from becoming part of a Jewish or Arab State) that were deeply rooted in the Catholic world.

It was thus the possibility of obtaining an international *status* for Jerusalem that led the Vatican Secretary of State's Office not to oppose the plan to divide the Holy Land in 1947, although the Vatican avoided openly opposing the idea of creating a single Arab-controlled State in Palestine for fear of compromising the good relationships with Arab countries or exposing the Catholic Church to dangerous consequences should the UN have favored the latter solution. It is, therefore, correct to say that, in this decisive year in the Middle East question, the Vatican "was not opposed to the creation of a Jewish State, if the division of Palestine ensured Jerusalem's internationalization."[11] Apart from the observations of the Jewish Agency,[12] this is confirmed by the Latin American vote (highly influenced by the Vatican's position) at the UN General Assembly on November 29, 1947. The Latin American countries, together with other Catholic countries like Belgium, France, Luxembourg, and the Philippines, were hardly likely to vote so overwhelmingly for the division of the Holy Land unless they knew that the Vatican did not oppose this solution.[13] Despite some hesitancy and uncertainty, caused in the winter of 1947-48 by the Vatican's interest in the US proposal to drop the plan to divide the Holy Land and to place the whole of Palestine under UN "temporary trusteeship,"[14] this position was never subsequently abandoned.

The Vatican, Israel and the Internationalization of Jerusalem (1947-1953)

On December 29, 1947, the UN General Assembly accepted the proposal by the majority of UNSCOP and approved the division of Palestine into an Arab State and a Jewish State. At the same time it established that Jerusalem and its environs were to constitute a "corpus separatum" directly under UN control. But the war that broke out in the Holy Land in the months immediately after this decision prevented its implementation and once again dramatically brought to light the problems facing the Holy Places and Jerusalem, occupied in the course of hostilities by Jordanian and Israeli troops, who respectively took up positions in the "old city," where the majority of the Holy Places were to be found, and the "new city," where much of the city's administration was concentrated.

Faced with protracted Israeli and Jordanian occupation, which threatened to undermine the plans for Jerusalem's internationalization contained in the November 29, 1947, Resolution, and with a debate imminent in the UN on the Palestine question, the Vatican decided to state its position in the clearest of terms. On October 24, 1948, Pius XII published the encyclical *In multiplicibus curis*, in which he argued for the expediency of giving "an international character to Jerusalem and its vicinity [. . .] as a better guarantee for the safety of the sanctuaries under the present circumstances."[15]

Various considerations lay behind the decision to publish the encyclical which ended the strategy of silence followed until then by the Vatican. Most notable among these was acute concern over the damage suffered by the Catholic sanctuaries and institutions in the Holy City and the hope that, once internationalized, Jerusalem might become the place where thousands of Palestinian refugees (including a sizeable contingent of Christian Palestinians) would wish to settle.[16]

Special mention must also be made of the pressures exerted by France on the Vatican, since France hoped that by exploiting the opportunities opened up by the international administration of Jerusalem it would regain some of the influence it previously had in the Middle East as watchdog of Catholic interests. To this end, Robert Schuman, the French Foreign Minister, gave the French Ambassador to the Vatican instructions to "demander au Souverain Pontife de prendre officiellement position en faveur de l'internationalisation de Jérusalem et des Lieux Saints."[17]

5. THE RETREAT OF THE WEST

The failure in fall 1948 of a mission to Rome undertaken by two Israeli emissaries[18] and the failure of Mgr. McMahon's visit to Palestine a few months later,[19] led the Vatican to renew its demands for an international regime for Jerusalem. These failures also induced the Pope to publish a second encyclical (*Redemptoris Nostri*) inviting the Catholic world to rush to the defense of the Holy Places and the internationalization of Jerusalem.[20]

The Pope's appeal was immediately taken up by the Catholics in many parts of the world, particularly in France and the United States. In the United States, Cardinal Spellman approached President Truman directly and from May to August 1949 there was a protracted exchange of letters between the two, by means of which Spellman hoped to convince Truman of the "necessity of placing Jerusalem and its environs beyond the control of any local group."[21]

Despite a second mission by McMahon to Palestine in the summer of 1949 and a final attempt in Rome in November 1949 undertaken by Jacob Herzog,[22] the Vatican and Israel failed to reach agreement and they began the 4th session of the UN General Assembly in open disagreement on the Jerusalem question.

The debate on this occasion centered on three different proposals. The first was the Palestine Conciliation Commission's proposal suggesting Israel and Jordan should each govern the two zones into which Jerusalem was divided as a result of the fighting in 1948 and that a UN Commissioner should be appointed with the task, among other things, of protecting the Holy Places.[23] The second was put forward by Sweden and Holland and proposed to limit UN activity to the protection of the Holy Places, not far removed from the "functional" internationalization of Jerusalem that the Israel government had stated it was willing to implement on several occasions (the most recent being a memorandum to the UN on November 15, 1949).[24] The third proposal was supported by Australia, which proposed a return to the principle of Jerusalem's territorial internationalization favored in Resolution 181 (II) of November 29, 1947.

The Australian draft resolution, fiercely contested by Israel and opposed among the Great Powers by the US and the UK, was supported by the Arab bloc (save Jordan), the Communist bloc (which saw the internationalization of Jerusalem as a chance to enter Middle East politics) and the majority of Catholic countries, no doubt heavily influenced by the Vatican. At the end of a heated debate[25] this heterogeneous coalition managed to obtain sufficient votes for the Australian resolution to be approved, and with it the reaffirmation of the principle of territorial internationalization for Jerusalem.

This outcome has been attributed in various quarters to a "terrific last minute exercise of Catholic pressure." The *Palestine Post* reported that "papal nuncios in almost every UN state visited heads of government with result that almost identical cables received by Latin American and other delegations ordering them to support Australian resolution."[26] The documents that it has been possible to consult do not contain any decisive confirmation of this thesis.[27] There can be no doubt, however, that the Vatican did everything in its power to support Jerusalem's territorial internationalization. Had the Australian resolution been rejected, the General Assembly would probably have approved the project for the "functional" internationalization proposed by Sweden and Holland. It would have been a very serious blow to the Vatican, which would have been forced, by the will of the UN, to accept a solution that it had refused on every occasion it was proposed by the Israelis in the course of direct negotiations.

The vote taken on December 9, 1949, reaffirming the General Assembly's will to internationalize Jerusalem territorially, further stiffened Israel's and Jordan's positions. They intensified their negotiations to find an agreement based on Jerusalem's division and accelerated the process of integrating the sections of Jerusalem they controlled into their respective States. The Israeli Parliament proclaimed Jerusalem its capital and transferred its headquarters and main government offices there. The King of Jordan, worried by the rise of dangerous rivalry with Amman, merely appointed a Supreme Custodian of the Holy Places in Jerusalem.[28]

In 1950 new discussions and negotiations took place, at first centering on the Garreau plan which proposed the internationalization of a limited area of Jerusalem (but including all the Christian Holy Places),[29] and, subsequently, on a draft statute drawn up by the Trusteeship Council following guidelines contained in the resolution of December 9, 1949, which had reaffirmed the internationalization of all Jerusalem. The Vatican monitored the debate on Jerusalem very carefully, letting its own observations be known on various occasions, but did not significantly shift its position from the one it had taken the previous year.[30]

Neither of the proposals mentioned above (nor the proposal subsequently put forward by Sweden and Belgium) managed to gather sufficient consensus to obtain the approval of the UN General Assembly, which completed its work in December 1950 without adopting any resolution regarding Jerusalem.

An attempt to reopen the UN debate, undertaken by the Philippine delegate in 1952, and the polemic sparked off the following year by the transfer of the Israeli Ministry of Foreign Affairs to Jerusalem did not modify a situation, which, despite the hopes cherished in various Israeli and Christian quarters[31] was not unblocked even by Paul VI's journey to the Holy Land in 1964.

A Statute for Jerusalem: The Position of the Vatican After 1967

Jerusalem's unification under Israeli control in 1967 sparked a resumption of the debate which had produced no significant result since the beginning of the 1950s. At first, the Vatican forcefully and clearly re-affirmed its traditional position based on the territorial internationalization of the entire city. On June 9 the Vatican official spokesman, Mgr. Vallainc, stated that "the UN resolutions of November 1947 were and are in accord with the wishes of the Holy See"[32] and a few days later the Vatican observer at the UN circulated a document declaring that the Vatican was "convinced that the only solution which offers a sufficient guarantee for the protection of Jerusalem and of its Holy Places is to place that city and its vicinity under an international regime," further stating that "the term 'internationalization' in its proper sense means a separate

33. The Vatican, Israel and the Jerusalem Question

territory, a 'corpus separatum' subject to an international regime."[33] Inspired by the Vatican, a group of Latin American countries presented a draft resolution on June 30 designed to support the internationalization of Jerusalem, but this did not obtain a sufficient majority to be accepted by the General Assembly[34] (which indicated that the majority of the nations represented at the UN no longer considered this solution viable).

In the same month, while the Israeli government was appeasing fears expressed in many quarters regarding the fate of the Holy Places,[35] a number of meetings were held in Rome between Ehud Avriel, the Israeli Ambassador to Italy, and Vatican officials (including the Pope) which led to the decision to receive an Israeli emissary in the Vatican bearing a message from Eshkol for Paul VI[36] and to send a Vatican representative immediately afterwards to Israel "to get first hand knowledge of the situation and the attitude of the local authorities."[37] At the end of this mission a joint communiqué, signed by Mgr. Angelo Felici and Jacob Herzog on July 11, recorded that discussion had taken place regarding "a number of possible formulae [...] that might be taken into consideration for the purposes of an acceptable solution of the important issue connected with the Holy Places," and added that "the conversations will continue."[38] Shortly after a statement circulated by the Israeli Foreign Ministry further stated that the parties had discussed the possibility of drawing up a statute for the Holy Places, "without prejudice to the acquired rights of the various communities" based "on a satisfactory legal formula designed to give the Holy Places a statute comparable, in rights and immunity, to that of diplomatic missions."[39]

The difficulty associated with the attempt to continue to seek successfully the territorial internationalization of Jerusalem after the failure of the Latin American resolution at the UN, and the Israeli government's willingness to open negotiations regarding the status of the Holy Places led the Vatican to reconsider its position.

From August 1967 the demand for a special internationally guaranteed statute for Jerusalem and the Holy Places was no longer accompanied by the customary references to the territorial internationalization of the city, making it much more elastic and indefinite. This was to a certain extent made explicit by Paul VI in an important allocution on December 22, 1967, which indicated the two features that the Vatican considered "essential and impossible to evade" in any solution to the problem of Jerusalem and the Holy Places: "The first concerns the Holy Places properly so called and considered as such by the three great monotheistic religions, Judaism, Christianity and Islam. It is a matter of guaranteeing freedom of worship, respect for, preservation of and access to the Holy Places, protected by special immunities thanks to a special statute, whose observation would be guaranteed by an institution international in character, taking particular account of the historic and religious personality of Jerusalem. The second aspect of the question refers to the free enjoyment of the legitimate civil and religious rights of persons, residences and activities of all communities present on the territory of Palestine."[40]

With this speech, the Pope indicated what features needed to be incorporated in any formula replacing that of Jerusalem's territorial internationalization, on which the Vatican no longer insisted. There were three such features:

(a) the protection of the Holy Places and the historical and religious character of the city;

(b) the international nature of the statute which would have to be applicable to both the Holy Places and Jerusalem;

(c) guarantees regarding the civil and religious rights of the communities in Palestine.

Great care needs to be exerted for a proper interpretation of the Vatican's reference to the need to protect the "historical and religious personality" of Jerusalem (as well as the Holy Places) included in Paul VI's speech, a criterion repeatedly upheld since then.[41] This criterion implicitly contained a refusal to accept a solution based merely on the extraterritorial nature of the Holy Places, which, although adequately protecting the Holy Places themselves could not provide any guarantee against changes (as a result of town-planning and architectural innovations for example) which might irredeemably impair the sacred character of the entire city. These concerns regarding the Old City of Jerusalem were echoed in UNESCO Resolution 3.343 (October 1968) which referred to the "patrimoine culturel" comprising not only the Holy Places but the entire Old City as well and which stressed its value "pour l'humanité tout entière."

It is not hard to guess the reasons which led the Pope to clarify the Vatican's position in these terms. As already mentioned, the demand for Jerusalem's internationalization had been put forward by the Vatican as a result of a number of political contingencies (which by 1967 had been superseded) and two fundamental requirements, namely the need to ensure the presence of a significant Christian community in Palestine and the need to protect the Holy Places. Both needs could be satisfied, in the Vatican's opinion, only by a legal committment involving the international community. With his December 22 speech Paul VI wished to clarify beyond a shadow of a doubt that while the Vatican was prepared to abandon Jerusalem's territorial internationalization and consider alternative solutions (which, moreover, were not specified), it was not prepared to compromise on the basic requirements that had led it in 1948-50 to request a "corpus separatum." These requirements would have to be satisfied in any new formula put forward.

It is sufficient to compare Paul VI's words with the statements which were being made at the same time by Israeli government officials to see the clear-cut divergence between the two positions. According to Israeli Foreign Minister Abba Eban "the international interest in Jerusalem has always been understood to derive from the presence of the Holy Places": the problem was therefore "to assure the universal character of the Holy Places"[42] by means of mechanisms guaranteeing control by the various religious communities. But this approach, which underlay the Israeli government's proposal for extraterritoriality for the Holy Places in the 1967 negotiations, was in no way considered satisfactory by the Vatican because it gave no guarantee as regards the two issues about which it felt most keenly, namely the survival of the Catholic community in Palestine and the protection of the sacred character of Jerusalem from which, in the Vatican's opinion, the problem of the Holy Places could not be extrapolated and isolated. Hence the difficulty which quickly led to the breakdown of the talks between Israel and the Vatican (which

183

5. THE RETREAT OF THE WEST

a meeting between Eban and Paul VI in October 1969 could not overcome). This breakdown became definitive at the beginning of 1971, when the Pope sent a letter to the Israeli President. In this letter he stated that he could not subscribe to any agreement with a country that the Vatican did not recognize (and could not recognize while a state of war existed in the Middle East) and rejected the Israeli offer to recognize "the Pope as the representative of all the Christian groups."[43]

Shortly afterwards the differences between the Vatican and Israel, no longer hidden by the existence of negotiations, were brought into the open in a polemic over changes in Jerusalem's town plan. On the grounds that Jerusalem was firstly the capital of Israel and that the interests of the international community were restricted to the Holy Places, the Israeli authorities drew up a city development plan which envisaged, through expropriating land belonging for the most part to the Arab population, construction around the city of a ring of new quarters designed to house Jewish immigrants.[44] On March 22, 1971, the *Osservatore Romano* (which was echoed in the following months by other leading Catholic newspapers) severely criticized the plan, taking it as an example of a policy designed to cause the "slow suffocation" of the "minority communities" and to imprint "Jerusalem with a particular character prejudicial to non-Jewish members of the population, both Christian and Moslem. These are being forced in the name of city planning to retreat into increasingly smaller confines, and ultimately to seek elsewhere a future which the climate of their homeland no longer makes available to them." These projects, the Vatican newspaper concluded, confirmed "the need for an international juridical instance which would truly guarantee the unique character of Jerusalem and the rights of the minority communities in the City."[45]

It is probable that this sharply defined Vatican position was influenced by appeals and pressures coming from the Middle East Christian community which from 1970 onwards had dramatically underlined the danger of the "Judaization" of Jerusalem.[46] In any case the *Osservatore Romano's* intervention was in keeping with the line that the Vatican followed after 1967, designed to uphold the universal significance of Jerusalem (as well as the Holy Places) and to protect the future of the local Christian community, whose dangerous decline in numbers had been commented upon by Paul VI.[47]

The conflict that grew up around the Jerusalem development plan, which involved other Christian confessions as well[48] and which went on throughout 1971[49] did not alter the Vatican's official stand. The Pope once again clarified this in December 1971, "confirming the need for a special internationally guaranteed statute fully providing for the pluralistic and very special nature of the Holy City, and for the rights of the various communities based there and who look upon it, and come together there, as their spiritual center."[50]

In later years, Paul VI's statements on Jerusalem stressed the growing concern for the fate of the Christian communities in Palestine, threatened by an exodus repeatedly criticized by Catholic Church leaders (but contested by the Israeli government).[51] His statements—linked to progress in ecumenism that had occurred in the 1960s and 1970s—also developed more fully the theme of religious pluralism in Jerusalem, the Holy City for the three great monotheistic religions.[52] Both of these considerations led to the continuance, indeed the strengthening, of the Vatican's basic demand: a special internationally guaranteed statute which would ensure the sacred and universal character of Jerusalem.

The 1970s passed, therefore, with no particularly significant change in the Vatican's position on Jerusalem while relations between the Vatican and Israel, although undergoing periods of tension,[53] slowly but steadily improved and were strengthened by the happy outcome of the delicate Notre Dame de France question,[54] by the visit of Mgr. Giovanni Benelli (a leading figure in the Vatican Secretary of State's Office) to Israel in 1972, and by Moshe Dayan's visit to the Vatican a few years later.[55]

President Sadat's historic journey to Jerusalem in November 1977, followed the year after by the Camp David agreements, at least partially unblocked the impasse in which all the previous initiatives designed to resolve the Middle East conflict peacefully had foundered. Although the differences separating Egypt and Israel over Jerusalem remained unresolved, the Vatican could not overlook the possibility that during the course of the diplomatic negotiations between these two countries the question of Jerusalem might find a stable outcome. This explains the care attributed to the reiteration of the Vatican's position, firstly in a confidential message sent to both sides in 1977,[56] secondly in John Paul II's speech to the UN General Assembly in 1979, where he reaffirmed, in keeping with Paul VI's previous statements, the "hope for a special statute that, under international guarantees [. . .] would respect the particular nature of Jerusalem"[57] and finally in a very detailed note drawn up by the Vatican's Permanent Observer at the UN.

This document reaffirmed the customary demand for "a special statute, internationally guaranteed for Jerusalem" but this demand was placed in the context of a more specifically religious speech in which priority was given to "the intention [. . .] to preserve and guarantee to the Holy City its identity as a religious center, unique and outstanding in the history of the world, in such a way that it may become a stable place of encounter and concord for the three great monotheistic religions." In the Vatican's opinion this implied "above all, the recognition of an historical and religious pluralism, to be put into practice by according all of the three religions, in their particular expression as communities, full enjoyment of their respective rights, excluding positions of predominance and, indeed, favoring the prospect of a useful human and religious dialogue." The theme of equal rights, both religious and civil, for all three communities present in Jerusalem was further considered in the final part of the document, which mentioned the need "to define the territory and list the Holy Places, as well as provide for the guarantees and for the supervision which the international community will have to give to the 'statute' and for the juridical form of this committment and of the accord of the interested parties."[58]

The interest and novelty of this document does not lie in the solution it proposes, which was in keeping with the solutions put forward after 1967. Rather, the novelty lies in the importance attributed to the need to guarantee equal rights for the Christian, Hebrew and Muslim communities so that religious pluralism (the fundamental characteristic of Jerusalem making it so special) could blossom and initiate dialogue and collaboration among the confessions. In this respect (perhaps as a result of the careful protection that had been afforded to them by the Israeli government, as the Vatican had recognized on a number of occasions) the question of the Holy Places lost the paramount significance that it had previously had and became a detail in a design which aimed at making Jerusalem the place where the three major monotheistic religions could work together in the future precisely because of the historical memories of its past.

The elasticity shown when indicating the legal framework of the special statute for Jerusalem and the hint at the need "to define the territory" to which it would apply (which could be interpreted in the sense that the Vatican did not require its extension to the entire city) prompted prominent Catholics and Catholic groups to forward proposals and suggestions designed to give more precise content to the guidelines coming from the Vatican. In February 1980, in particular, a document was circulated (which was "Vatican inspired" according to the Times of London). This document proposed that the special statute for Jerusalem was to be guaranteed by "a conjunction [...] of several Western States with a traditional interest in (Christianity in) the Holy Land such as Greece (for Greek Orthodox), Italy, France, Britain and the United States as overall guarantor of agreements in the area."[59] The purpose of this proposal was to prevent any traditionally atheistic countries from participating in the protection of the Holy Places, and also to prevent the Soviet Union and the Eastern Bloc States from profiting from UN involvement in the system of international guarantees for Jerusalem and gaining influence in the Middle East, but it is likely that the document the Times published put forward opinions coming from the Catholic community in Palestine rather than the Vatican Secretary of State's Office.

A few months later, in an article published shortly before the Israeli Parliament declared Jerusalem to be the "whole and united" capital of the Jewish State,[60] the Osservatore Romano avoided encouraging such solutions and merely stressed both the inadequacy of guarantees based on unilateral initiatives by one State and the inadequacy of "bilateral agreements between one or more States." (Perhaps this was an indirect reference to the risk of a solution negotiated between Israel and a number of Arab countries, excluding "Christian" countries.) The Osservatore Romano once again stressed the need for an "appropriate legal system, guaranteed by some higher international authority" which the Osservatore Romano apparently associated with the UN.

Certainly the Vatican's position—once again reaffirmed in the apostolic letter recently published by John Paul II[61]—seems to be marked by great flexibility regarding the legal framework of the special statute for Jerusalem and perhaps even regarding the geographical area in which it would be implemented, whereas a much firmer position was maintained regarding the demand that it should be international in nature and be designed to have three functions. These three functions are (a) protection with complete equality of the religious and civil rights of the communities in Palestine, (b) the safeguarding of the sacred character of Jerusalem and protection of the Holy Places, (c) the encouragement of dialogue and collaboration between the believers in the three monotheistic religions.

The divergence from the Israeli proposals, which can be summed up as the offer of extra-territoriality for the Holy Places,[62] is still great. But within the context of an overall settlement for the Middle East conflict, which will undoubtedly require a great effort at mutual understanding by all the parties involved, it is legitimate to hope that a meeting-point may be found.

Footnotes

1. See Osservatore Romano, October 20, 1984.
2. Luigi Maglione, Vatican Secretary of State, in a letter to Amleto Cicognani, Apostolic Delegate in Washington, May 18, 1943, in Actes et Documents du Saint-Siège relatifs à la seconde guerre mondiale, v. IX, (Città del Vaticano: Libreria Editrice Vaticana, 1975), p. 302. This line was reaffirmed when Churchill visited the Vatican. See Actes, v. XI, (Città del Vaticano, 1981), pp. 509-10.
3. See Angelo Roncalli (then Apostolic Delegate in Istanbul) in a letter to Maglione, Sept. 4, 1943, in Actes, v. IX, p. 469.
4. See Actes, v. XI, p. 510.
5. Maglione in a letter to Cicognani, Jan. 18, 1944, in Actes v. XI, p. 101; Cicognani in a letter to Myron C. Taylor, April 11, 1944, in E. Di Nolfo, Vaticano e Stati Uniti 1939-1952 (Milan: Angeli, 1978), pp. 299-300.
6. John V. Perowne in a letter to B.A.B. Burrows, Jan. 19, 1948, FO 371/1175; ; Perowne, British Plenipotentiary Minister to the Vatican, was passing on thoughts of Mgr. Giovanni Montini, then Acting Secretary of State and later Pope Paul VI.
7. See for example Thomas J. McMahon, "Threat to the Holy Places," in Sign, June 1945.
8. George Wadsworth, US Ambassador to Iraq, memorandum for Loy W. Henderson, Jan. 13, 1947, NA 867N.01/1-3047.
9. See Giuseppe Soragna (Italian Ambassador to the Holy See) to Ministry of Foreign Affairs, May 8, 1948, ASMAE, Palestine, b. 10, f. 2; see also G. De Vries, Cattolicismo e problemi religiosi nel prossimo Oriente (Roma: La Civiltà Cattolica, 1944), p. 48.
10. See the official statements made by UNSCOP by the Custodia di Terra Santa, by far the most important Catholic organization working in Palestine, and by the Catholic Near East Welfare Association, whose president was Spellman and whose national secretary was McMahon (UN Document A/364/Add.3, oral evidence given by the Custodia di Terra Santa representative, July 5, 1947 and UN Document A/364/Add.1, CNEWA memorandum, June 5, 1947). The Vatican was certainly aware of these initiatives.
11. D. Lazar, "French Catholics and the Struggle for Israel 1945-1950," in Christian Attitudes on Jews and Judaism, October 1971, p. 12.
12. See D. Horowitz, State in the Making (New York: Knopf, 1953), pp. 296-97.
13. On the Latin American countries' attitudes see Edward B. Glick, Latin America and the Palestine Problem (New York: Herzl Foundation, 1958), pp. 78-122; E. Kaufman, Y. Shapira, J. Barromi, Israel-Latin American Relations (New Brunswick: Transaction Books, 1979), p. 151 ss.
14. See M. Kaufman, "A Trust Betrayed: The American Trusteeship Proposal for Palestine in 1948," in The Jewish Journal of Sociology, June 1983, pp. 5-32. On the reverberations the U.S. initiative had in the Vatican see S. Ferrari, "The Holy See and the postwar Palestine issue: the internationalization of Jerusalem and the protection of the Holy Places," in International Affairs, 1984, pp. 265-67.
15. L'Osservatore Romano, Oct. 24, 1948.
16. For a detailed analysis of the reasoning behind the encyclical see S. Ferrari, "The Holy See," pp. 267-70.
17. W. d'Ormesson, "Pie XII tel que je l'ai connu," in Revue d'histoire diplomatique, 1968, pp. 15-16; see also William C. Burdett, US Consul in Jerusalem, in a telegram to the Secretary of State, Nov. 5, 1948, NA 867N.404/11-548; Perowne in a letter to Ernest Bevin, Oct. 25, 1948, FO 371E/13963. On the Palestine policy of France see D. Amson, "La diplomatie française et le problème de Jérusalem. Un chemin tortueux," in Nouveaus Cahiers, 28, Spring 1972, pp. 35-44; Burdett in a telegram to the Secretary of State, Nov. 9, 1948, NA 867N.01/11-948.
18. For this mission see Walter Eytan (Director-General of the Israeli Ministry for Foreign Affairs) in a telegram to Uriel Heyd, Sept. 15, 1948, ISA 130.09/2308/1; Jacob Herzog (Director of the Department for Christian Communities, Israeli Ministry of Religious Affairs) in a letter to Moshe

5. THE RETREAT OF THE WEST

Shertok, Sept. 29, 1948, in Y. Freundlich (ed.), *Documents on the Foreign Policy of Israel*, v. I, Jerusalem 1981, p. 654; Franklin C. Gowen (Special Assistant to Myron Taylor) in a letter to the Secretary of State, Nov. 2, 1948, NA 766A.67N/11-248; Giuseppe Soragna in two letters to the Ministry of Foreign Affairs, Oct. 16, 1948 and Jan. 8, 1949, ASMAE, Holy See, b. 13, f. 5. The two Israeli delegates were Jacob Herzog and Chaim Wardi.

19. On McMahon discussions see Burdett's telegram to the Secretary of State, Jan. 4, 1949, NA 867N.01/1-449; James G. McDonald (US Special Representative in Israel) in a letter to the Secretary of State, Jan. 11, 1949, NA 867N.01/1-1149.

20. See *Osservatore Romano*, April 17, 1949.

21. Francis J. Spellman in a letter to Harry S. Truman, June 10, 1949, NA 867N.404/6-1449; the entire correspondence was published by S. Ferrari, *Il Vaticano e la questione di Gerusalemme nel carteggio Spellman-Truman*, in *Storia contemporanea*, April 1982, pp. 285-320.

22. See S. Ferrari, "The Holy See," pp. 277-81.

23. See UN Document A/973 and A/973/Add.1. The Palestine Conciliation Commission (with representatives from France, the US and Turkey) had been set up under Resolution 194 (III) of the UN General Assembly. Among its tasks was drawing up "detailed proposals for a permanent international regime for the Jerusalem area."

24. See UN Document A/AC/31/L.34. Regarding the policy of the Israeli government—which would have been willing also to accept a solution based on the internationalization of the old city of Jerusalem (then in Jordanian hands)—see *Israel and the United Nations* (New York: Manhattan Publ. Co.: 1956), p. 128 ss.

25. Regarding the UN debate and the proposals put forward in 1949 and 1950 see H.E. Bovis, *The Jerusalem Question 1917-1968* (Stanford: Hoover Institution Press, 1917), p. 70 *et seq* and J. Le Morzellec, *La question de Jérusalem devant l'Organisation des Nations Unies* (Bruxelles: Bruylant, 1979), p. 212 *et seq*.

26. The *Palestine Post* article is summarized in a telegram of Burdett to the Secretary of State, Dec. 9, 1949, NA 867N.00/12-949.

27. For indirect confirmation see Thomas F. Power (member of the US mission to the United Nations) in a letter to Dean Rusk, Dec. 12, 1949, NA 501BB.Palestine/12-1249 and in particular Abba Eban in a telegram to Walter Eytan, Dec. 14, 1949, ISA 130.09/2329/17.

28. For a more detailed exposition of these events and, in general, the action taken by the Vatican to internationalize Jerusalem between 1947 and 1949 see S. Ferrari, "The Holy See."

29. Garreau was the President of the UN Trusteeship Council.

30. See William Godfrey (Apostolic Delegate in the UK) in a letter to William Strang, Jan. 25, 1950, FO EE1018/23; Perowne in a letter to G.W. Furlonge, Feb. 20, 1950, FO EE1018/32, Sept. 21, 1950, FO EE/1018/135, and Oct. 13, 1950, FO EE1018/158.

31. See Marcel J. Dubois, "The Catholic Church and the State of Israel after 25 Years," in *Christian News from Israel*, Spring 1973, p. 218.

32. *Osservatore Romano*, June 10, 1967; for other statements to the same effect see W. Zander, *Israel and the Holy Places of Christendom* (London: Weidenfeld & Nicolson, 1971), p. 111.

33. *New York Times*, June 24, 1967; see also articles published by the *Osservatore Romano* on June 11 and, in particular, July 6, 1967.

34. See *Yearbook of the United Nations*, 1967, pp. 208-11; p. Pastorelli, "La S.Sede e il problema di Gerusalemme," in *Storia e Politica*, March 1982, p. 86; *Jerusalem Post*, June 26, 1967.

35. See the statements made by Eshkol and Wahrhaftig to the leaders of the religious communites present in Israel and the rapid approval of the *Law for the Protection of the Holy Places*. W. Zander, *Israel*, pp. 101-05; J. Le Morzellec, *La question*, pp. 417-24.

36. The emissary was Jacob Herzog, who reached the Vatican on June 30, 1967 (*Jerusalem Post*, July 2 and Nov. 24, 1967); regarding Herzog's subsequent visits to the Vatican see P.E. Lapide, *Brennpunkt Jerusalem. Eine israelische Dokumentation* (Trier: Spee, 1972), pp. 342-43.

37. *Promemoria on Jerusalem and the Holy Places*, released by the Vatican Secretary of State's Office in August 1967. [B. Collin, *Pour une solution au problème des Lieux Saints* (Paris: Maisonneuve et Larose, 1974), p. 147]; the Vatican's representative was Mgr. Angelo Felici (see *Jerusalem Post*, July 7 and 12, 1967 for this mission).

38. *Christian News from Israel*, July 1967, p. 22; see, however, the rather more cautious *Promemoria* mentioned in note 37.

39. Undated typewritten manuscript kept in the Israeli Foreign Affairs Ministry's Library; see also on the same matter *Jerusalem Post*, Nov. 24, 1967; M. Benvenisti, *Jerusalem. The Torn City* (Jerusalem: Isratypeset, 1976), p. 267.

40. *Acta Apostolicae Sedis*, 1968, pp. 25-26.

41. See for example the allocutions of June 24, December 23, 1971 and Dec. 22, 1973 (*Osservatore Romano*, June 25, December 24, 1971 and Dec. 22, 1973).

42. UN Document A/6753, July 10, 1967; see the letter addressed by Eban to the UN Secretary General on April 30, 1968 (UN Document 5/8565 and A/7089), the speech given to the UN General Assembly on Sept. 19, 1969 and the statements made to the *Jerusalem Post* on June 25, 1967.

43. M. Benvenisti, *Jerusalem*, p. 268. Only a few aspects of the negotiations which took place between Israel and the Vatican are known: in particular, it is not clear whether, in the course of these negotiations, the Vatican represented other Christian denominations as well (see *Jerusalem Post*, July 12, 1967; *Ma'ariv*, July 12, 1967) or whether a modification of the *status quo* as regards the Holy Places to the benefit of the Catholic Church was contemplated (as claimed by Benvenisti, *Jerusalem*, pp. 266-68). On the attitude of other Christian communities, who were afraid that an agreement between the Vatican and Israel might pass over their heads, see W. Zander, *Israel*, p. 111 *et seq*.

44. See T. Prittie, *Whose Jerusalem?* (London: Muller, 1981), p. 119 *et seq*; A.M. Goichon, *Jérusalem. Fin de la ville universelle?* (Paris: Maisonneuve et Larose, 1976), p. 85 *et seq*.

45. *Osservatore Romano*, March 22, 1971. See also on the same matter *La Civiltà Cattolica*, 1971, II, pp. 429 *et seq* and 538 *et seq*; III, p. 111 *et seq*; *Tablet*, March 27, April 13, and 10, 1971; *La Croix*, April 2, 1971 and the evidence of the two Catholic representatives to the *Near East Subcommittee of the US House of Representatives* (*The Christian Century*, October 6, 1971, pp. 1205-10).

46. See for example the acts of the First World Conference of Christians for the Support of Palestine, which took place in May 1970 (*Pour la Palestine*, Paris 1972), the letter from the Jordanian bishops sent to Paul VI, Atenagora and Ramsey (*IDOC Internazionale*, Feb. 1972, pp. 4-5) and King Hussein's letter to Paul VI in April 1971 (*Le Monde*, April 7, 1971).

47. *Osservatore Romano*, Dec 15/16, 1969.

48. See the Anglican Primate's statements (*Times*, Dec. 20, 1971; T. Prittie, *Whose Jerusalem?* p. 106).

49. For the developments of this polemic see J.L. Ryan, "The Catholic Fund and the Problem of Israel and Jerusalem," in *Jerusalem. The Key to World Peace* (London: Islamic Council of Europe, 1980), pp. 64-66.

50. *Acta Apostolicae Sedis*, 1972, p. 38; see also the assurances Herzog was given by the Apostolic Delegate to Jerusalem (*Jerusalem Post*, March 28, 1971) and the comments made by the Vatican delegate to UNESCO (*New Outlook*, Dec. 14, 1971, p. 35 *et seq*.).

51. See in particular the apostolic exhortotion dated March 25, 1974 (*Acta Apostolicae Sedis*, 1974, p. 117 *et seq*.), the document of the Eastern Congregation dated Jan. 9, 1975 and more recently, the intervention by the Vatican observer at the International Conference on the Palestine Question (*France—Pays Arabes*, October 1983, p. 26); for the opposite point of view see Eban's speech to the Knesset dated June 30, 1971 and O. Stendal, "Christians in Jerusalem (1948-1971)," in *Christian News from Israel*, 1971, p. 52 *et seq*. The growing importance of this theme in determining Israeli policy on Jerusalem is stressed by W. Zander, "Holy Places and Christian Presence in Jerusalem," in *New Middle East*, July 1971, pp. 18-20 and Y. Moubarac, "La question de Jérusalem," in *Revue d' études palestiniennes*, 1983, p. 66 *et seq*. See also the article by Daphne Tsimhoni "Demographic Trends of the Christian Population in Jerusalem and the West Bank 1948-1978" in the Winter 1983 issue of the *Middle East Journal*, vol. 37, pp. 65-88.

52. See for example the speech by Paul VI on December 22, 1973 (*Osservatore Romano*, December 22, 1973).

53. Thus, in 1974, the arrest and conviction of Mgr. Capucci, followed by the award of John XXIII's prize to UNESCO which shortly before had approved a document which deemed Zionism and racism to be the same thing. Two years later the final declaration of the Christian-Islamic Conference in Tripoli, subsequently partially retraced by the Vatican, and the Vatican's vote in favor of the Declaration of Principles adopted by the UN Habitat (Human Settlements) Conference in Vancouver, which referred to a previous UN General Assembly Resolution defining Zionism as a form of racism. In 1977 finally, a statute was passed in the Knesset limiting missionary organizations' activity in Israel.

54. In 1970, the French Congregation of the Assumptionist Fathers sold the Notre Dame de France Convent to the Hebrew University. This was a huge complex overlooking the walls of the old city. The Vatican contested the sale in the Israeli Courts, arguing that the sale had not received the necessary prior authorization provided for under Canon Law. But before proceedings were completed, an out-of-court settlement was

33. The Vatican, Israel and the Jerusalem Question

reached whereby the Hebrew University (after discreet encouragement by the Israeli government) resold Notre Dame to the Vatican.

55. Some disagreement did occur during Golda Meir's meeting with Paul VI in January 1973. On these episodes and those indicated in the previous note see the two articles by M.J. Dubois in *Christian News from Israel*, 1973, pp. 261-25 and 1979, pp. 12-14 and 63-65. Improvement in Vatican-Israeli relations is mentioned, in addition to Dubois, by J. Herzog, *A People that Dwells Alone* (London: Weidenfeld and Nicolson, 1975), p. 110.

56. See *Le Monde*, Dec. 14, 1977. The message was transmitted by Mgr. Monterisi to the heads of the Israeli and Egyptian delegations meeting in Cairo.

57. *Osservatore Romano*, October 4, 1979.

58. UN Document S/13679, Dec. 4, 1979. In the last part of the document "suitable guarantees" were called for as regards the Holy Places in Palestine which were not in Jerusalem.

59. *The Times*, Feb. 6, 1980. The need for an international agreement stipulating guarantees and rights for the three major religious communities in Palestine had already been pointed out by the *Tablet* on July 28, 1979, by the *Associated Christian Press Bulletin* in Feb. 1980 and once more by the *Tablet* on March 8, 1980.

60. See *Osservatore Romano* for July 1, 1980, where the seriousness of "any unilateral act tending to modify the Holy City's *status*" is stated.

61. See *Osservatore Romano*, April 20, 1984.

62. See finally S. Berkowitz, Proposals for the "Political Status of the Holy Places Within the Context of a Peace Treaty," in *Jerusalem. Aspects of Law* (Jerusalem: The Institute for Jerusalem Studies, 1980), p. 10 *et seq.*

Islam Religion Has Potential to Reshape World

Tom Hundley
Knight-Ridder Newspapers

Wearing blue tennis shoes, fatigues and a red headband that proclaims "Nobody is greater than God," Mustafa Haidari, a 22-year-old Iranian foot soldier in the legions of Ayatollah Khomeini, explained that he is "fighting to uphold the dignity of Islam."

In the last five weeks alone, tens of thousands of Iranian soldiers have been slaughtered on the marshy flatlands along the Shatt al Arab waterway in a holy war between Iraq and Iran that has dragged on for 6½ years. But for Haidari, who is serving his second tour on this battlefield, death is an invitation.

"The people of Iran," he explained, "respect the blood of martyrs."

Martyrs, holy wars, suicide bombings and hijackings—ever since a mob of students seized the U.S. Embassy in Tehran seven years ago, Americans have been buffeted by a bewildering succession of headlines linked to the "Islamic fundamentalism" of Mustafa Haidari and the Iran of Ayatollah Khomeini.

Even today, the headlines are often dominated by the latest kidnappings in Beirut, and yet another American presidency is paying a heavy price for getting too close to Iran, the eye of this whirlwind.

But what is happening in the Moslem world is something far more profound than religious fury or the revival of a 1,400-year-old faith. That is the message that emerges from interviews with specialists as well as with ordinary people across the Islamic heartland.

From Morocco to the Philippines, from the Sudan to Yugoslavia, there is a growing sense among the world's 850 million Moslems that their traditional Islamic values are under attack from alien ideologies—specifically, from the competing secular ideologies of the United States and the Soviet Union.

The response has been a powerful resurgence of religious sentiment fueled by a belief that Islam offers an alternative to the "materialistic capitalism" of the West and to the "godless communism" of the Soviet Union.

Because Islam's appeal transcends ethnic and national boundaries, and because its basic ideological foundations are already deeply imbedded in one-fifth of the world's population, the Islamic movement's potential for reshaping global politics is enormous.

Often characterized in the West as Islamic fundamentalism, it is actually a broad-based but highly fragmented social movement aimed at bringing the political systems of Moslem countries in line with deeply held personal beliefs.

On another battlefield in another holy war a thousand miles from the Persian Gulf war, Malik Mujahid Nazir expresses the depth of his beliefs with certainty: "If we die fighting the Russians, we will be awarded paradise."

But Nazir, a barrel-chested man with a ferocious black beard, is confident that his Khugani tribesmen will defeat the Soviet troops that have been occupying their lands in Afghanistan since 1979.

Fourteen hundred years of history and divine will are on the side of the Afghan rebels known as the mujahideen, he tells a visitor to the dusty refugee camp at the foot of the Hindu Kush mountains on the Pakistan border.

"At the time of our Holy Prophet, the Moslem armies were able to overcome enemies who greatly outnumbered them. It is our faith that those who stand in the way of Allah will be defeated."

Sipping from a bottle of Coca-Cola, ignoring the swarming flies that have invaded the camp's mud- and dung-walled guest house, Nazir explains why he and the Afghan rebels are so driven by their faith.

"We call our resistance jihad (holy war) because the Russians have attacked our beliefs. They are taking away our Islamic traditions and trying to convert Afghanistan to communism," Nazir says through an interpreter.

"The Russians also want to destroy the purdah system and permit the free mixing of males and females. We believe such things generate many vices. They want to make it possible for a father to sleep with his daughter."

These sentiments might sound simplistic or naive to a Western audience, but among the world's Moslems they would strike a responsive cord.

Viewed against this background, it is easy to understand why Marvin Zonis of the University of Chicago's Middle East Institute has called the Islamic movement "the single most impressive polit-

34. Islam

ical ideology which has been proposed in the 20th century since the Bolshevik Revolution."

Palpable signs of the Islamic movement's strength can be seen throughout the Moslem world.

In Iran, the Islamic revolution has been relentless. Each week thousands of young men heed the call for volunteers to fight Iraq in a war that has been portrayed as a struggle against the enemies of Islam.

Portraits of the Supreme Guide, Ayatollah Khomeini, hang in every public place. Revolutionary Guards, identifiable by their drab olive parkas, seem to be in charge of running everything from the Tehran airport to the ever-expanding cemetery reserved for the war's martyrs on the southern outskirts of the city.

Iran has been totally transformed by the reign of the ayatollahs, while elsewhere in the Islamic world, newspapers seem to be devoting much more space to Islamic affairs. Television is crowded with religious programming. And ever greater numbers of pilgrims are inspired to visit the holy shrines in Mecca and Medina.

In smart sections of Cairo, boutiques featuring "Islamic fashions" are doing a brisk business as more women return to the hijab, the modest head-covering. Beards, a Moslem sign of piety, are undergoing a revival among young men.

Alcohol, once freely available in Pakistan, may now be consumed only by foreigners—after they fill out two forms in triplicate swearing that they are not Moslems. Under Islamic law, violators face public flogging. Kuwait, which once turned a blind eye to the private use of alcohol by foreigners, has recently cracked down.

Mosque construction is booming. Turkey had 20,000 mosques at the end of World War II; today it has 72,000, outpacing population growth by 40 percent despite the government's official policy of secularization. Bahrain, a compact nation with only 250,000 citizens, has more than a thousand mosques. Saudi Arabia, a nation of 9 million, which already has 20,000 mosques, recently announced plans to add 2,000 more. Even the Soviet Union, whose southern region is populated by 44 million Moslems, has tolerated a mild surge in new mosques.

Perhaps the most telling sign of the Islamic movement's strength is its popularity among the educated. At universities, administrators say students are flocking to Islamic studies programs. They are pressuring the universities to "Islamicize" the curricula of traditional fields such as economics and law—that is, to teach them in accordance with Moslem religious traditions. And at many campuses, male and female students have demanded to be segregated by sex.

"I don't like it, but we are surrounded," said Ahmed el-Shafti, an economics professor at Cairo University. "This religious sentiment is widespread among the young. It's serious and you cannot ignore it or repress it. We have to come to terms with it."

Iran remains the symbolic heart of the Islamic movement. Although the perceived extremism of Ayatollah Khomeini and the excesses of his theocratic regime have tarnished Iran's reputation in the eyes of much of the Moslem world, the 1978-79 Iranian revolution remains the one shining triumph of Islam over the West in the modern era.

The Iranian experience, though closely identified with the Moslem minority Shiite sect, was a jolt of adrenaline shot through the entire body of Islam. Moslems everywhere began to assert themselves with militant determination against regimes that they view as repressive, corrupt and anti-Islamic. The result has been a continuing string of violent confrontations:

• Before 1978, Lebanon's Shiites were politically irrelevant even though they were the largest of that country's many religious cantons. Today, Shiite militias control west Beirut and most of southern Lebanon. One Shiite faction, the Hizballah, Party of God, has orchestrated a string of deadly attacks against U.S. targets and continues to hold a number of kidnapped Westerners.

• In Egypt, Islamic extremists in the army gunned down President Anwar Sadat; five years later, the government of Hosni Mubarak is still rooting out extremist elements within the military.

• In Saudi Arabia, the monarchy was stunned in 1979 when Mecca's Grand Mosque, Islam's holiest shrine, was seized by extremists whose proclaimed mission was to cleanse Islam of the corruption of the royal family.

• In Syria, President Hafez Assad laid siege to one of his own cities in an effort to crush an Islamic fundamentalist movement. Thousands were killed, but the fundamentalists remain the single biggest threat to the regime's stability.

• In Pakistan, seven years after a mob burned the U.S. Embassy, opposition politicians continue to press the Islamic government of Mohammad Zia ul Haq to distance itself from the United States.

The Islamic world, the locus of so much unrest, is of vital strategic interest to the United States: Egypt is the linchpin of U.S. efforts to resolve the Arab-Israeli conflict, the Persian Gulf states contain 60 percent of the world's proven oil reserves, and Pakistan is considered a "front-line state" in the struggle to contain Soviet expansion.

But successive U.S. administrations have attempted to deal with the Islamic movement as an element of superpower rivalry, rather than come to grips with it as an independent force. U.S. embassies in Moslem countries have become isolated fortresses bristling with anti-terrorism devices—a stark symbol of the failure to heed the depth and intensity of the Islamic movement.

This failure has been costly: 52 Americans held hostage in Iran for more than a year, 68 killed in embassy bombings in Beirut and Kuwait, 241 Marines killed in Beirut by a suicide bomber, and more than a dozen Americans kidnapped in Lebanon over the last three years, eight of whom are still being held.

The continued misreading by U.S. policymakers of the politics of the Islamic movement, its key players and what motivates them is one of the more obvious factors in the controversy over the Reagan administration's secret arms sales to Iran.k

Because only the excesses of the Islamic movement tend to make news in the United States, many Americans equate it with violence and fanaticism. But fanatics and extremists represent only the fringe.

Islam, in fact, emphasizes economic and social justice. From the beginning, the faith of Muhammad strove to improve the lot of society's have-nots: women, slaves, orphans and the poor.

For strict Moslem fundamentalists, distinctions between U.S. capitalism and Soviet communism are irrelevant. As American scholar Daniel Pipes, director of Foreign Policy Research Institute in Philadelphia, has observed, "The two Western cultures are alike—and different from Islam—in many ways. Men wear pants, women wear skirts and everyone sits on chairs. The intelligentsia in both countries listen to the same classical music, attend the same plays, and admire the same oil paintings."

"Mr. Reagan and Mr. Gorbachev are the same face," says Maulana Noorani, a Pakistani cleric. "America and Russia both want to destroy Islam. We must resist. We must make Islam the third superpower."

Stalin's Afterlife

Stephen F. Cohen

Stephen F. Cohen is director of Russian Studies at Princeton and author of Bukharin and the Bolshevik Revolution, *now in paperback (Oxford University Press). He is the editor of* Political Diary, *a collection of* samizdal *writings, published by Norton.*

It has been called the "accursed question," like serfdom in prerevolutionary Russia. Stalin ruled the Soviet Union for a quarter of a century, from 1929 to his death at the age of 73 in 1953. For most of these years, he ruled as an unconstrained autocrat, making the era his own—*Stalinshchina*, the time of Stalin. The nature of his rule and the enduring legacy of Stalinism have been debated in the Soviet Union for more than another quarter of a century, first in the official press and since the mid-1960s in *samizdat*. And yet it remains the most tenacious and divisive issue in Soviet political life.

Stalinism was, to use a Soviet metaphor, two towering and inseparable mountains: a mountain of national accomplishments alongside a mountain of crimes. The accomplishments cannot be dismissed. During the first decade of Stalin's leadership, memorialized officially as the period of the first and second five-year plans for collectivization and industrialization, a mostly backward, agrarian, illiterate society was transformed into a predominantly industrial, urban, and literate one with many of the benefits of a modern welfare state. For millions of people the 1930s were a time of willingly heroic sacrifice, educational opportunity, and upward mobility. In the second decade of Stalin's rule, the Soviet Union destroyed the mighty German invader, contributing more than any other nation to the defeat of fascism; it also acquired an empire in Eastern Europe, and became a superpower in world affairs.

But the crimes were no less mountainous. Stalin's system of mass terror—arrests, torture, deportations, and executions by the NKVD or MGB (as the political police was variously known), and the murderous forced labor camps of the Gulag archipelago—victimized tens of millions of innocent men, women, and children for more than 20 years. Judged only by the number of victims, and leaving aside the important differences between the two regimes, Stalin's policies created a holocaust greater than Hitler's. Twenty million deaths resulted from his forcible collectivization of the peasantry in 1929-33 and the terror that continued almost unabated against officialdom and society alike until 1953. This figure does not include millions of unnecessary casualties that can be blamed on Stalin's negligent leadership at the beginning of World War II, or the eight million souls (a conservative estimate) who languished in Soviet concentration camps every year between 1939 and 1953.

Yet today most Soviet officials and ordinary citizens, probably the great majority, still speak mostly, or even only, good of Stalin. It is true, of course, that official censorship has deprived many citizens of a full, systematic account of what happened. But much of the story did appear, however elliptically, in Soviet publications by the mid-1960s. Moreover, most adult survivors must have known or sensed the magnitude of the holocaust, since virtually every family lost a relative, friend, or acquaintance. Why then don't most people share the unequivocal judgment once pronounced, even in censored Soviet publications, that "there is no longer any place in our soul for a justification of his evil deeds"?

Two categories of Soviet citizens had an intensely personal interest in the Stalin question after 1953: victims of the terror and those who had victimized them. Most of the victims were dead, but many remained to exert pressure on high politics. Millions of people had survived—some for 20 years or more—in the camps and in remote exile. Most of these, perhaps seven or eight million, were freed after Stalin's death. They began to return to society, first in a trickle in 1953 and then in a mass exodus in 1956. To salvage what remained of their shattered lives, the returnees required, and demanded, many forms of rehabilitation—legal exoneration, family reunification, housing, jobs, medical care, pensions. Their demands were shared by millions of relatives of those who had perished in the terror. The community of victims had direct and indirect access to the high leadership. Returnees from the camps became members, and even heads, of various party commissions set up after 1953 to investigate the Gulag system, the question of rehabilitations, and specific crimes of the Stalin years. Quite a few returnees resumed high positions in military, economic, scientific, and cultural life. Some returnees had personal access to repentant Stalinists in the leadership (such as Khrushchev), whom they lobbied and influenced. And other returnees, such as Aleksandr Solzhenitsyn, made their impact in different ways.

Their adversaries were no less self-interested, and far more powerful. The systematic victimization of so many people had implicated millions of other people, party and state officials who had participated in the repressions, hundreds of thousands of NKVD personnel who arrested, tortured, executed, and guarded prisoners, and the plethora of petty informers and slanderers who fed on the crimson madness. Millions of other people were implicated by having profited (often inadvertently) from the misfortune of victims. They inherited the positions, apartments, possessions, and sometimes even the wives of the vanished. Generations built lives upon a holocaust. The remote specter of retribution was enough to unite millions who had committed crimes, and also those who only felt some unease about their lives, against any revelations about the past.

Unavoidably, Stalin became a symbol for both the friends and foes of change, reformers and conservatives inside the Soviet bureaucracy. Khrushchev set the pattern in the 1950s. His official de-Stalinization efforts after 1956 were stymied by deeply ingrained popular attitudes. The expression "cult of Stalin's personality" became, after 1953, an official euphemism for Stalinism, but it had a powerful resonance. For more than 20 years, Stalin had been glorified publicly in grotesquely extreme ways. His name, words, and alleged deeds were trumpeted at every level and in every corner of the country. His photographed, painted, bronzed, and sculpted likeness were everywhere. The cult became a religious phenomenon. When the government assaulted the Stalin cult, first obliquely and then with revelations that portrayed "the father of the peoples" as a genocidal murderer, it caused a crisis of faith. For every person who repudiated Stalin and what he represented, there were others who could not make the psychological adjustment.

By removing the autocrat who had dominated the system, Stalin's death was the first act of de-Stalinization. It also dealt an irreparable blow to the divinity of the cult: gods do not suffer brain hemorrhages, enlargement of the heart, and high blood pressure. The second important act of de-Stalinization came from the people who had been most constantly vulnerable to the terror, those who had risen highest under it. Khrushchev spoke for the whole ruling elite when he said "All of us around Stalin were temporary people." Even Politburo membership had provided no protection. Several had been shot, one as recently as 1950; the wife of another (Molotov) was in prison camp; and the whole Politburo had come under Stalin's morbid suspicion toward the end. The experience of living so long under a terroristic and capricious ruler united his successors (except one), probably for the last time, on a major reform: the partial dismantling of the powerful terror machine and the restoration of the Communist party to primacy in the political system. By April 1953, Stalin's last terror scenario, the "Doctors' Plot," had been disavowed. By June the political police

35. Stalin's Afterlife

had been brought under party control; the chief, Lavrenti Beria, had been arrested along with a few henchmen; and a few hundred prominent camp inmates had been released.

None of these partial repudiations of the past extended publicly to Stalin himself, except by inference. The revised version of his official reputation that emerged in 1953-54, and prevailed until 1956, was still highly laudatory. Though no longer the "driver of the locomotive of history," Stalin was still the "great continuer of V. I. Lenin's immortal cause" who had led the party and the country in all victories since the 1930s, including the destruction of "enemies of the Party and of the people." But this reformulation of Stalin's greatness was unstable. Stalin's reduced status ironically posed a grave danger for his successors by elevating Marxism-Leninism and the party system to joint responsibility with him for all of the deeds of the past, including the bad ones.

The era of official anti-Stalinism began the night of February 24-25, 1956, with Khrushchev's dramatic "secret" speech to a closed session of the 20th Party Congress. Speaking for four hours before about 1500 hastily reassembled delegates, in effect the country's ruling elite, Khrushchev delivered a stunning blow to the official myth of Stalin as a great and benevolent leader. He assailed Stalin's autocratic rule with vividly detailed accounts of the dictator's personal responsibility for "mass repressions," torture, "monstrous falsifications," and his own glorification. And he flatly blamed Stalin for a succession of Soviet disasters in World War II. Khrushchev's words, spiked with long quotations from pleading, agonized letters written by tortured victims in their jail cells, were plain and rarely euphemistic. Nor was the speech really secret. Although never published in the Soviet Union, it was read to thousands of official meetings across the country over the next few weeks. Its general contents became widely known.

But Khrushchev's indictment of the dead tyrant was sharply limited in three ways. Its gravamen was Stalin's dictatorial regime over the party and his "mass terror against party cadres" and other political elites; it maintained silence about the millions of ordinary people who had perished. Second, Khrushchev dated Stalin's criminal misdeeds from 1934. This left out Stalin's forcible collectivization of 1929-33. Finally, Khrushchev avoided the question of widespread criminal responsibility and punishment by defining the abuses narrowly in terms of Stalin and a small "gang" of accomplices, who already were exposed and punished.

Nevertheless, reports of Khrushchev's denunciation of "mass repressions" were enough to trigger shock waves across the Soviet empire in Eastern Europe and tumultuous dissension elsewhere in the international communist movement. These events brought a strong reaction in high Soviet circles against Khrushchev's

5. THE RETREAT OF THE WEST

radical revelations and led to a still more "balanced" evaluation when the first public resolution on the Stalin question, adopted by the Central Committee on June 30, finally appeared on July 2, 1956. Though eclipsed in the early 1960s, this document was resuscitated by Khrushchev's successors more than 10 years later. The long resolution condemned the "harmful consequences of the cult of personality," but in terms so euphemistic and self-defensive that Stalin's "many lawless deeds" seemed to add up to little more than "certain serious mistakes," which, the resolution implied, were "less important against the background of such enormous successes. . . ." Further shock waves of anti-Stalinism, especially the uprisings in Poland and Hungary in October and November 1956, reinforced this considerable rehabilitation of Stalin's reputation. Within a year, Khrushchev himself was promoting the "two sides" of Stalin, of which the "positive" now seemed ascendant.

Meanwhile, the past continued to generate anti-Stalinist heat outside the apparatuses of power. Millions of camp inmates freed since 1956 were now visible, and sometimes clamorous, reminders of the holocaust. Khrushchev's 1956 speech had roused a segment of the intelligentsia. A more dramatic cultural "thaw" in 1956-57 allowed guarded public discussion of past Stalinist abuses and existing ones. The "camp theme," as it later became known, forced its way tentatively but persistently into Soviet fiction and poetry in the character of the vanished and the returnee. Names unmentioned for decades crept slowly back into textbooks, monographs, encyclopedias, journals, and newspapers, though the fate of their possessors was mentioned only elliptically. All of these ghosts were loose in the country by 1960-61.

A repentant Stalinist himself, Khrushchev seemed always divided on the Stalin question, even in the memoirs he dictated privately after his fall, hating and admiring Stalin almost in the same breath, rounding on radical anti-Stalinists whom he had previously encouraged. But ultimately Khrushchev's resolve "to root out this evil" grew and gained the upper hand. "Some people are waiting for me to croak in order to resuscitate Stalin and his methods," he said in 1962. "This is why, before I die, I want to destroy Stalin and destroy those people, so as to make it impossible to put the clock back."

Khrushchev and his supporters unveiled a second, and more radical, version of official anti-Stalinism at the 22nd Party Congress in October 1961. The assault on the Stalin cult at the 22nd Congress differed from Khrushchev's speech at the 20th Congress in important ways. Above all, it was public. For almost two weeks during the anniversary month of the October revolution, daily newspapers and broadcasts riveted public attention on "monstrous crimes" and demands for "historical justice," as speaker after speaker related lurid details of mass arrests, torture, and murder that had been carried out in every region of the country. Impassioned Party Congress resolutions ordered Stalin's body removed from the Lenin Mausoleum on Red Square and stripped his name from thousands of towns, buildings, and monuments across the country. The criminal indictment of Stalin's rule was so harsh and sweeping that it obscured his "positive side" altogether.

Most dramatically, Khrushchev and his allies at the Congress made criminal accusations against living political figures, implying the possibility of trials for crimes of the past. The specter of such trials, inflated by references to "numerous documents in our possession" and Khrushchev's call for "a thorough and comprehensive study of all such cases rising out of the abuse of power," sent tremors of fear through the thousands, or millions, who bore "direct personal responsibility." Anti-Stalinists took full advantage of the new dispensation. Virtually every criticism of Stalinism that appeared later in *samizdat* was anticipated in official publications of the early 1960s. The result was an impressive body of revelations about the three main episodes of Stalin's rule: collectivization, the great terror, and World War II.

Stalin's reputation as the great generalissimo of 1941-45, as he titled himself and which became the linchpin of his cult, was the most thoroughly assaulted. Successors to the military corps he had slaughtered took belated revenge. Official histories, monographs, memoirs, and novels portrayed Stalin as a leader who had decapitated the armed forces on the eve of war, who had ignored repeated warnings of the German invasion and thus left the country undefended in June 1941, who had deserted his post in panic during the first days of combat, and whose capricious strategy later caused major military disasters. The vaunted generalissimo became a criminally incompetent tyrant who bore personal responsibility for millions of casualties. For millions of veterans who had fought with Stalin's name on their lips, this part of the anti-Stalin campaign was probably the most resented. It was the first to be undone after Khrushchev's fall.

The Stalinist terror and concentration camp system inspired an even more dramatic body of historical exposé. The most famous example is Solzhenitsyn's *One Day in the Life of Ivan Denisovich*, published in 1962. But there were many novels, short stories, biographies, memoirs, films, and plays about the terror, which produced a fairly unvarnished picture of the 20-year holocaust.

The magnitude of the unfolding picture shattered the legend that only Stalin and a few accomplices had been guilty. Publicizing the camps meant publicizing the conduct of millions. Face-to-face confrontations between victims and their former tormentors were portrayed in literature and on the stage, suggesting the menace of people who, as Yevtushenko put it, "hate this era of emptied prison camps."

35. Stalin's Afterlife

If the camp theme was traumatic, the subject of the forcible collectivization of 125 million peasants in 1929-33 was potentially even more dangerous. Every thoughtful citizen knew that collectivization had been a special national tragedy; it had destroyed not only Soviet agriculture but the traditional life and culture of peasant Russia. But the legitimacy of the existing collective farm system, a still unworkable and largely unreformed foundation of the whole economic system, rested wholly on the Stalinist legend of collectivization as a spontaneous, voluntary, and benevolent process of the peasant masses themselves.

By the mid-1960s, Soviet scholars (as well as novelists of village life) had chipped away at this legend by itemizing Stalin's peremptory, coercive measures in the winter of 1929-30, which had unleashed the assault on the countryside, and by revealing suggestions of the mass violence, deportations, and famine that followed.

A sweeping reaction soon surged up against this kind of de-Stalinization. From higher reaches of power, anti-Stalinism seemed to be out of control. It was challenging the official axiom that Stalinism had been only "an alien growth" and not indigenous to the system for 20 years. By arguing that the "essence of the cult of personality is blind admiration for authority," anti-Stalinists were threatening the existing system of authoritarian control. Alarmed professional managers of the political system launched a counter-campaign, based on a "heroic-patriotic theme," for deference to authority. They denounced "dismal compilers of memoirs, who...unearth long-decayed literary corpses."

There was also a broad reaction against de-Stalinization from below, from decent people who were not evil neo-Stalinists but who naturally composed the Soviet conservative majority. For them, ending the terror and making limited restitutions was one thing; desecration of the past and radical reforms in the Soviet order, for which they had sacrificed so much, was quite another.

It is impossible to document the part played by the Stalin question at the Central Committee meeting that overthrew Khrushchev in October 1964. Official explanations made public at the time of his ouster did not hold de-Stalinization against him. The main charges that Khrushchev himself had grown increasingly autocratic and capricious, and that his bolder reforms were hastily conceived, were substantially true. Nevertheless, Khrushchev was brought down by a conservative swing in official and popular attitudes against his 10-year reformation, of which de-Stalinization had been a substantial part.

The powerful resurgence of pro-Stalinist sentiment since 1964 is reflected in the career of Aleksandr Solzhenitsyn. In 1964, he was nominated for a Lenin Prize, the Soviet Union's highest literary honor, for his prison camp story *Ivan Denisovich*; 10 years later, he was arrested and deported from the country.

At first Khrushchev's downfall encouraged both anti-Stalinists and neo-Stalinists in official circles. New anti-Stalinist publications appeared, rehabilitations of Stalin's victims continued, and in October 1965 the leadership legislated a major (and ill-fated) program of economic reform. At the same time, however, influential figures, including Brezhnev himself, began to issue authoritative statements refurbishing Stalin's reputation as a wartime leader, eulogizing the 1930s while obscuring the terror, and suggesting that Khrushchev's revelations had "calumniated" the Soviet Union. Behind the scenes, an assertive pro-Stalin lobby, proud to call itself "Stalinist," took the offensive in 1965 for the first time in several years, apparently with Brezhnev's support. Anti-Stalinists were demoted, censorship was tightened, new ideological strictures were drafted, already processed rehabilitations were challenged, and subscriptions to anti-Stalinist journals were prohibited in the armed forces.

The decisive battle in officialdom was over by early 1966. Within 18 months of Khrushchev's overthrow, official de-Stalinization was at an end. In February 1966, two prominent writers, Andrei Sinyavsky and Yuli Daniel, were tried and sentenced to labor camps for publishing their "slanderous" (anti-Stalinist) writings abroad. The public trial, with its self-conscious evocation of the purge trials of the 1930s, was a neo-Stalinist blast against critical-minded members of the literary intelligentsia. Meanwhile a campaign began against anti-Stalinist historians.

These events gave birth to the present-day dissident movement and *samizdat* literature. The growing conservatism and neo-Stalinist overtones of the Brezhnev regime drove anti-Stalinists from official to dissident ranks and gave the movement many of its most prominent spokesmen, such as Andrei Sakharov, Roy and Zhores Medvedev, and Solzhenitsyn.

Some dissidents believed that their protests prevented a full rehabilitation of Stalin at the 23rd Party Congress in March 1966, where his name was hardly mentioned. If so, it was a small victory amidst a rout. The policies of the Brezhnev government grew into a wide-ranging conservative reaction to Khrushchev's reforms. The defense of the status quo required a usable Stalinist past. Increasingly, only the mountain of accomplishments was remembered in rewritten history books and the press.

By 1969 Stalin had been restored as an admirable wartime leader; serious criticism of collectivization was banned; rehabilitations were ended and some even undone; and intimations that there had been a great terror grew scant. Indeed, people who criticized the Stalinist past could now be prosecuted for having "slandered the Soviet social and state system."

Fresh from this triumph, neo-Stalinist officials began a campaign for the full rehabilitation of Stalin's reputation in connection with the 90th anniversary of

5. THE RETREAT OF THE WEST

his birth in December 1969. Pro-Stalin articles and novels appeared regularly throughout the year. Plans for a grand rehabilitation were aborted at the last moment. The memorial article that finally appeared in *Pravda* on December 21 was carefully balanced. It credited Stalin's "great contribution"; but it also condemned his "mistakes," which had led to "instances" of "baseless repressions." But this still marked the first official commemoration of Stalin's birthdate in 10 years. Shortly thereafter a flattering marble bust was placed on his gravesite just behind the Lenin Mausoleum.

Anti-Stalinist voices in the official press became fewer and fainter after 1969. In official mass circulation publications, Stalin's reputation soared in the 1970s. Though no longer the subject of religious worship, he became, once again, a wise statesman and benefactor of the people. Historians were told by a high official, "*all*—and I repeat, *all*—stages in the development of our Soviet society must be regarded as 'positive.'" Nor was neo-Stalinist sentiment merely an artifice manufactured above. Ordinary people began to restore privately manufactured replicas of his likeness to their homes, kiosks, and dashboards.

A coarser, more ominous form of pro-Stalinism also emerged. Some official publications—including a spate of historical novels that seem to appeal to a popular craving for real history—began to justify Stalin's terror of the 1930s as a "struggle against destructive and nihilistic elements." Epithets and ideological justifications of the terror years—"enemies of the Party and of the people," "alien elements," "fifth column," and "rootless cosmopolitans"—crept back into various kinds of literature. As the centenary of Stalin's birth approached in 1979, neo-Stalinist officials campaigned again for a full-scale official glorification unblemished by carping references to Stalin's "mistakes."

Stalinist opinion today among high officials is easy to understand. For them, the generalissimo on his pedestal continues to symbolize and protect their power. But as a broad popular phenomenon, today's pro-Stalin sentiment is something different, even an expression of discontent. It is part of the widespread resurgence of Russian nationalism, to which Stalin linked the fortunes of the Soviet state in the 1930s and 1940s, and which has reemerged today as the most potent ideological factor in Soviet political life. In this haze of nationalist sentiment, Stalin joins a long line of great Russian rulers stretching back to the early czars.

Pro-Stalin sentiment also is a reflection of contemporary problems. Liberalizing trends and other changes in the 1950s and 1960s unsettled many lives and minds; the open discussion of long-standing social problems made them seem new. By the mid-1960s, many officials and citizens saw a reformed, partially de-Stalinized Soviet Union as a country in crisis. Economic shortages, inflation, public drunkenness, escalating divorce rates, unruly children, cultural diversity, complicated international negotiations—all seemed to be evidence of a state that could no longer manage, much less control, its own society. And all cast a rosy glow on the Stalinist past as an age of efficiency, low prices, law and order, discipline, unity, stability, obedient children, and international respect.

By now there is little to counteract this revised folk version of the past. As anti-Stalinists were silenced by censorship, another generation, raised by parental followers of the cult, grew up thinking that Stalin had arrested "20 or 30 people" or "maybe 2000."

Official censorship can mute the controversy, postpone the historical reckoning, and allow another generation to come of age only dimly aware (though not fully ignorant) of what happened during the Stalin years. But events after Stalin's death demonstrate that making the past forbidden serves only to make it more alluring, and that imposing a ban on historical controversy causes that controversy to fester, intensify, and grow politically explosive.

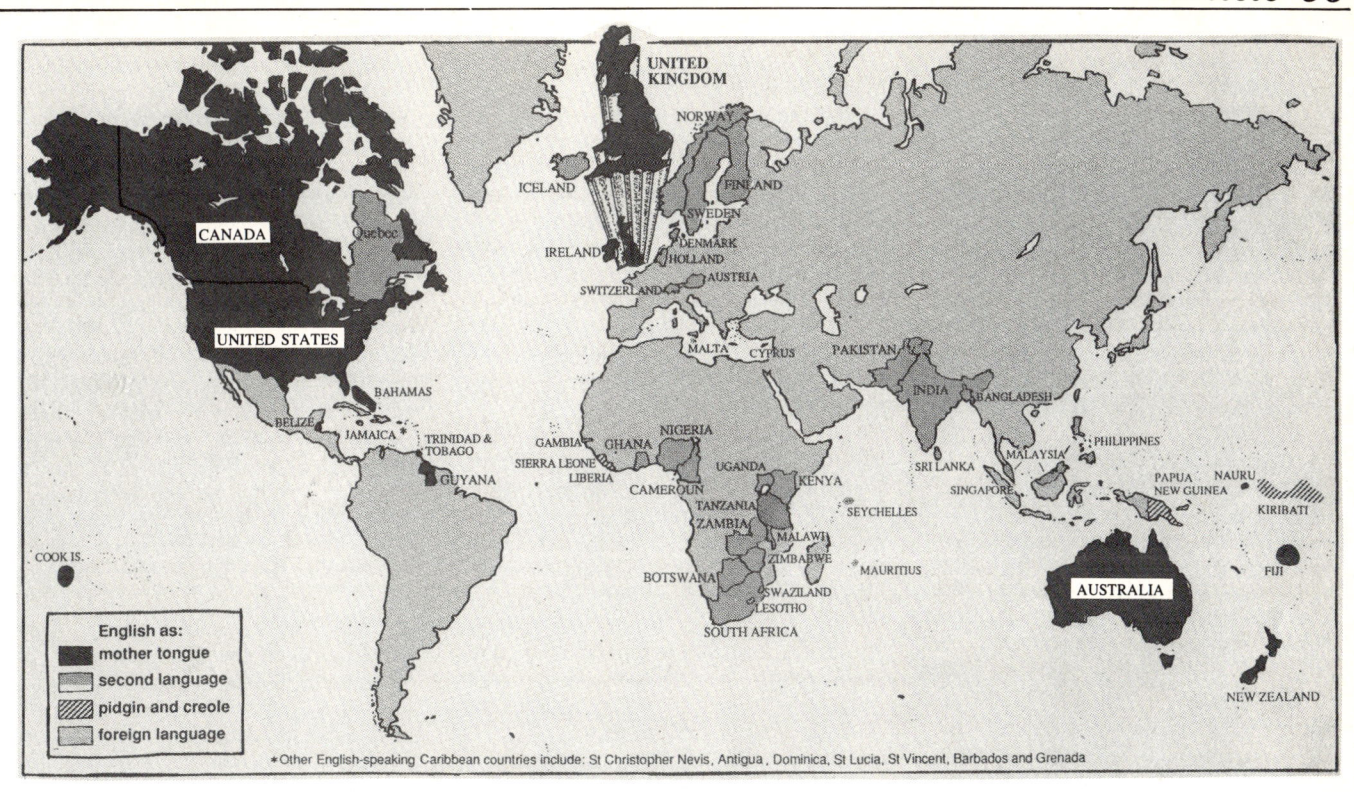

The new English empire

English is the first truly universal language wider in its scope than Latin was or Arabic and Spanish are. These five pages examine why

The worldwide spread of English is remarkable. There has been nothing like it in history. Spanish and French, Arabic and Turkish, Latin and Greek have served their turn as international languages, in the wake of the mission station, the trading post or the garrison. But none has come near to rivalling English.

Four hundred years ago, English was the mother tongue of 7m speakers tucked away on a foggy island in Western Europe. Today, about 330m people throughout the world speak it as a mother tongue. That leaves it a distant second to Guoyo (Mandarin Chinese), which is estimated to have 750m speakers. But in international diffusion and acceptance, English is in a class of its own. Add to its 330m mother-tongue speakers the same number using English as a second language (ESL) and the same number again with reasonable competence in English as a foreign language (EFL), and you approach 1 billion English speakers.

As an official language, English serves more than 40 countries; French serves 27, Arabic 21 and Spanish 20. English is the language of international shipping and air travel. It is one of the two working languages of the United Nations (French is the other). And it has become the language of both international youth culture and science (two-thirds of all scientific papers are published in English).

Its appeal is irresistible: advancement in the civil or diplomatic service almost anywhere will be aided by a good grasp of English; preliminary trade negotiations between a Hungarian and a Kuwaiti will probably be conducted in English; half of all foreign-language courses in the Soviet Union are English courses; and a quarter of China's 1 billion people is engaged in studying English, in one way or other.

English, then, is a world language. What befits it for that role? It is chiefly, of course, thanks to the power of Britain in the nineteenth century and America in the twentieth. But English has spread far beyond its spheres of political influence in a way that French and Spanish have not. Luckily, English fits its role well, thanks to the structure of the language.

English is relatively easy to pronounce: it has few of the tongue-knotting consonant-clusters of Russian or the subtle tone-shiftings of Chinese. The basic syntax is fairly straightforward, too. Words can be readily isolated (Turkish words cannot), and they are relatively "stable" (having few of the inflections of Russian). English dispensed long ago with informal vocatives (*du, tu*) and with the gender-system (*der, die, das*; *le, la*) that most other European languages rejoice in and most students of them despair at.

The Roman alphabet is supple and economical (more efficient than the Arabic alphabet; easier to learn than the ideography of Chinese). The problem is spelling, which, for historical reasons, is out of kilter with pronunciation. *Ough* can be pronounced in at least seven different ways (*though, rough, thought, cough, hiccough, plough, through*).

The huge vocabulary, on the other hand, is no drawback to its use as a world language, though many people have sought to disqualify it on that ground. No one needs Shakespeare's command of the language for everyday communication. The more adept speaker can always adjust his register to suit the less adept.

English, in short, is easy to speak badly—and that is all that is required of a world language, if what you mean by a world language is an attenuated code, a means of transmitting and receiving simple information. English is the official language of the European Free Trade

5. THE RETREAT OF THE WEST

Association, composed of six countries none of which has English as a mother tongue. Its secretary-general says: "using English means we don't talk too much, since none of us knows the nuances."

As a means of more complex social exchange, however, English is, on the face of it, less well suited to being a true world language. Here, its vast vocabulary does begin to prove a formidable obstacle. Idioms—as in all languages—confront the learner with their opacity. English is particularly well endowed with idioms: *a dark horse*, *a horse of a different colour*, *hold your horses* and *from the horse's mouth*. And English has the added irritation of a plethora of phrasal and prepositional verbs. *Put someone down*, *put someone up*, *put up with someone*, *put someone up to something*: such "simple" phrases are much harder for students to grasp than the corresponding "advanced" vocabulary (*humiliate someone*, *accommodate someone*, *tolerate someone* and *incite someone to something*).

More recondite still is idiom itself—the deep, sometimes unanalysable determinants of natural construction and usage. Why is it acceptable to say "You'll succeed provided that you prepare sufficiently" but not "You'll fail provided that you prepare insufficiently"? Why do people say "a *very* affected lady"; "*much* affected by your kindness", and "*greatly* affected by a change in pressure"? Why should "I haven't got a clue" mean "I don't know" but "You haven't got a clue" mean "You're a fool"?

Whose English?
Even in England, "standard English" has always been a will-o'-the-wisp. True, the language of south-eastern England began to acquire its prestige in Chaucer's time and, by the early days of the BBC, was so well established that the job of a radio announcer was closed to anyone whose accent was regional or not upper-middle class. But many linguists now reject the notion of a blanket uncountable noun "English", with its suggestion of a relatively homogeneous language. They use instead the unlovely term "Englishes" which, in effect, challenges the very notion of an ideal English *tout court*.

Englishes are:
- **Pidgins and creoles.** Pidgins are makeshift. They started as elementary systems of communication between traders, explorers or soldiers and suppliers, guides or slaves. The outsider's language—the "base" language—usually contributes 80% or more of the vocabulary, often in distorted form. *Pidgin* itself probably began life as a pidgin English word for *business*, hence the expression "That's not my pigeon". Syntax and pronunciation are often simplified by the constraints of the local vernacular.

A creole is a pidgin that has become a mother-tongue and developed into a sophisticated and well equipped language. The main fully-fledged English creoles are broad Creole in Jamaica, Krio in Sierra Leone and Tok Pisin in Papua New Guinea. English pidgins and creoles fall into two families: the Atlantic (in West Africa, the Caribbean, and parts of Nicaragua, Florida and Georgia); and the Pacific (spoken by Australian Aborigines, in Papua New Guinea and other Pacific islands, and formerly along the coast of China).

Educated creole speakers can shift back and forth along a kind of linguistic spectrum that stretches to standard English; their shift is mimicked by the communities as a whole. If the experience of black American English during the nineteenth century is anything to go by, all creole speakers may be drifting towards standard English (though, as if in rearguard action, a distinctive and energetic creole literature is emerging in both the Atlantic and Pacific families).

- **English as a foreign language.** EFL is big business. American universities offer PhDs in the teaching of it. In Britain, it earns dollops of foreign currency and goodwill. There is a quiet war going on between Britain and America over the international EFL market, with Australia increasing its share of EFL-teaching.

The plum, China, has fallen to Britain: the BBC's "Follow Me" is probably the most widely followed teaching course in history. But the most lucrative market, Western Europe, seems to be changing from British English to American. The countries of Latin America keep faith with the American variety; even the partial-exception is swinging away from its traditional preference for British English; that odd-man-out is, or was, Argentina.

It is impossible to be sure how many foreigners "know" English; 330m is a convenient speculation (though whatever number you choose, it is certainly rising rapidly every year). The reason is that the "linguistic spectrum" is wider in EFL than in any other kind of English. At one end lie the excited unintelligibiiities of a souvenir-seller in Siena or Sao Paulo: at the other, the accented, but serene, fluency of a teacher from Tel Aviv or Tübingen.

- **English as a second language.** This is the English of the Commonwealth, the Philippines, Pakistan, and of American Hispanics, Québecois, black South Africans, Afrikaners and so on. ESL is usually modelled on British English rather than American. The Philippines is the main exception; Liberia and Sierra Leone are partial exceptions.

English acts as an instrument of national unity, a relatively neutral *lingua franca*. Tribal rivalries can be allayed more easily when neighbouring peoples—Hausas, Yorubas and Ibos, for instance—can speak the same language. Understanding

---

Pay attention on your language

ESL is the most diverse form of English. "Mother-tongue interference" changes standard English—and ESL-speakers have an enormous number of mother tongues. Even within a single community, not all local ESL peculiarities will hold good for all speakers; or, even, for any one speaker. An Indian professor is unlikely to omit the word *is* when lecturing to a university class; but might well do so when rebuking the *dhobi wallah* for inattention to the laundry.

With those qualifications, some common features of ESL are:

- **Pronunciation.** Many consonants are hard for ESL speakers to distinguish or reproduce. Speakers from south Asia, for instance, tend to use the *v* and *w* sounds interchangeably. *It vas a wery vet veekend in Nowember* is how a dull British or American ear might register a statement made by an Indian. An Indian might also confuse the sounds of *k* and *g*, or *p* and *b*—*gruel and baneful* for *cruel and painful*—and so would an African, though often in the opposite direction: *picketed and crumpling* for *bigoted and grumbling*. Consonant clusters are often broken up by an "epenthetic" vowel—*spot* comes out as *si-pot* in Kashmir—or reduced: *bend* and *bent* and *burnt* are often sounded as *ben* in African English. Vowels are no easier. *Cutting* and *curtain* both sound like *cotton* in West Africa (and the Caribbean) and like *kettin* in East and southern Africa. The slurred or neutral vowels of standard English are seldom heard in ESL. In West Africa, *gorilla* sound something like *go'-rill-o'*. Jamaica, to a Jamaican, is *juh-mée-kuh*. And the stress-system of ESL often goes against that of mother-tongue English. ESL imitating indigenous African and Asian languages tends to have a smoother "syllable-timed" rhythm, closer to that of French than to the "stress-timed" undulations of standard English. When ESL speakers do add stress, accordingly, it is often in an unconventional position; *imitáting*, *pósition*, *capítalist*.
- **Vocabulary.** Standard English words may be extended in meaning; in parts of Africa, *carpet* might also be used to refer to a linoleum floor-covering, and *bluffing* can be used to mean "showing off". Standard English forms might be distorted; Indian English has *dissentment* for *dissent*. African and Indian English are much given to pluralising uncountable English nouns: *funs*, *slangs* and so on. In India, you might buy *two breads* or put *two woods* on the fire.

36. The New English Empire

(comprehension) breeds understanding (tolerance).

As the sun set on the British Empire, each newly independent country had to commit itself to an official language. English was usually entrenched as the language of education, the law and the civil service. Sometimes, it could be edged out—as in Tanzania by Swahili (a *lingua franca* anyway) and in Pakistan by Urdu (another *lingua franca*, though one spoken as a mother tongue by only 5m of the country's 90m inhabitants compared with 60m who use Punjabi as theirs). But such edging-out has not proved easy. Malaysia imposed Bahasa Malaysia (a standardised form of Malay) as a national language in the 1960s. Not only was this of doubtful fairness to the Chinese and Tamil minorities, it has also meant that young Malays, educated in Bahasa Malaysia to secondary school and beyond, are finding it hard to get places at English-speaking universities abroad.

India, with a dozen or more main indigenous languages, and more than 150 languages in all, resolved at independence to establish Hindi as its sole official national language by 1965. Hindi is the mother tongue of about a third of the population. But in 1965, the government conceded that English should, for the time being, remain an "associate official language". Professional advancement and social prestige among middle-class urban Indians still depend upon skill in English. In the southern states, where the indigenous languages are unrelated to Hindi, many people are reluctant to learn the northerners' tongue when it is more useful (and no harder) to learn English.

Indian English shows how one variety of the language can take on a life of its own while still remaining comprehensible to speakers of standard English (indeed, British English continues to coexist with the new indigenous form). Just as Australia, with its robust cultural self-confidence, has ceased looking over its linguistic shoulder at London, so India can now fairly lay claim to possessing a separate English (in a way that Nigeria, say, cannot yet do). Indian English occurs in writing, not just in speech, and might be adopted even by an author accustomed to writing standard British English.

The influence of Indian English is felt far beyond the Indian subcontinent. Foreign students studying at Indian colleges take it home with them. Thousands of Indian teachers elsewhere in Asia and in Africa spread it abroad. School and college textbooks are written in Indian English—they are even sometimes "translated" into Indian English from British and American English. This pleads eloquently on behalf of English's claim to be a true international language, not just a national language used internationally.

● **English as a mother tongue.** A Scot might say "Will I write a letter of complaint?" where an Englishman or North American would say "Should I write a letter of complaint?" Scots also, like South Africans, may say "Where do you stay?" when asking where you live. A Miami Beach realtor (estate agent), if she ever had occasion to refer to a hot-water bottle, might call it a *haat wáa-derr báa-dill*. A Cockney shop assistant (salesclerk) calls hers a '*o*' *wáw-uh bó-oo*. Cornishmen and Newfoundlanders speak of farmers as *varmers*.

The broadest divide in mother-tongue English lies between British English and American English. There are systematic differences of spelling (*colour/color, manoeuvre/maneuver*) and of pronunciation (*hostile* [Britons and Canadians distinguish it from *hostel*] and *ballet*). There are "morphological" differences: *aluminium/aluminum, zip/zipper, at a loose end/at loose ends*. Above all, there are lexical and idiomatic differences—*drawing pin/thumbtack, unit trust/mutual fund*.

These are straightforward enough. But the same word may have different meanings on different sides of the Atlantic (see table). Or a word or phrase may have a common transAtlantic meaning, but have an additional sense in one variety that it lacks in the other. In British English, *majority* does service for a "relative majority" as well as for an "absolute majority". In American English, it means only an "absolute majority"; a "relative majority" is a *plurality*.

This asymmetry is best demonstrated by words or phrases that have suffered "semantic taint" on one side of the Atlantic but not on the other. A *rubber* refers to an eraser in British English; in American English, to a condom. An American sociological study called "Women on the Job" had to be retitled when published in Britain.

Such differences take only a little application to identify and remember. But other subtleties are harder to master—even to define. Wilde's dictum about "two great countries divided by a common language" applies mostly to this twilight zone. Two examples must suffice, both tentative. First, the "register" of the word *toilet*: it seems to have a coarser ring to it in American English. Second, the size of a *pond*: in British English, any pool of water wider than about 40 yards would probably be called a *lake*; American English, on the other hand, provides for much larger ponds.

Noah Webster and H. L. Mencken both thought that British and American English were diverging. That may have been true once, but is no longer. The changes can be traced by comparing the various vocabularies to do with communication. Before 1776, sailing terms were almost identical in both American and British English. In the nineteenth and early twentieth centuries, in a proud

---

New words might be created from English elements. In West Africa, a *been-to* is a person who has been overseas. In India, to *airdash* is to fly from place to place. And so-called "calquing" (an element-by-element translation of an indigenous idiom or compound word) flourishes: *plenti han* (plenty hands) for *centipede*; *grass-bilong paul* (grass belong fowl) for feathers.

Words that are archaic or regional in British English may be part of the mainstream vocabulary of both ESL and West Indian creole (where *buss* is used to refer to a kiss, and *bubby* to a breast). In India, the police might *nab a miscreant*, or you might greet a friend with the question "How is your good self?", and show him your new *timepiece*.

Most conspicuous of all, to the outsider, are those words taken unselfconsciously into ESL from the speaker's mother tongue, whether to designate western things or purely local ones. In India, the *mali* (gardener) might sleep on a *charpoy* (string bed).

● **Syntax.** The word *him* or *im* might be used (as in Jamaican creole) to cover the forms *he, him, his* and even *she* and *her*. Among proficient speakers, articles and basic verbs may be left out (especially if the mother tongue lacks or habitually omits them). *We are going to see new hotel this morning*, a Nigerian architect might tell his draughtsmen.

Word-order is often unconventional. It may remain uninverted in a direct question—"What you will do if I go away?"—or be irregularly inverted in an indirect question: "He asked why are you are wanting to go away?" A frequent ESL feature, in both Asia and Africa, is the use of unvarying tags at the end of a sentence: "He is a very clever boy, isn't it?"

The subtleties of the English tense system seldom correspond to those of an ESL- or EFL-speaker's mother tongue. Hence such common constructions in south Asia, as: "When you will come and help me here, I can get finished." "I am telling you—I am not knowing how to help you." And the randomness of English pronouns gives rise to many defiant local preferences. Standard adverbs may be omitted; in West Africa, you might hear "The taxi will pick me at 10 o'clock". Or one may be inserted where standard English has none, or be substituted for the standard one. In India, a politician might *voice out a protest*, and the press might urge people to *pay attention on this protest of his*.

197

5. THE RETREAT OF THE WEST

assertion of linguistic independence, American English chose to go its own way: hence the differences in *railway/railroad* vocabulary (*goods train/freight train, sleepers/cross-ties*) and in *motor car/automobile* terms (*boot/trunk, wing/fender*). But technical vocabularies are coming together again. Aerospace terminology has fewer transAtlantic variations than that of motor cars; computer terminology shows hardly any differences at all. America's *program* and *disk* have ousted Britain's traditional *programme* and *disc*.

The current "convergence" of British and American Englishes is mainly the result of British adoption of American usages. The American pronunciation of *suit*, *lute* and *absolute* has almost ousted the traditional standard British pronunciation with its *y*-sound after the *s* or *l*. (Curiously, *pursuit* remains resolutely *pur-syóot* in British English and *nuclear* showed no signs of going *nóo-clear*).

In vocabulary and meaning, too, American English calls the shots. The American sense of *billion* has been widely adopted in Britain. Many American imports to Britain have been quietly absorbed: *teenager, babysitter, commuter; striptease, brainwash, streamline; lean over backwards, fly off the handle, call the shots*. Even *stiff upper lip* seems to be American in origin.

Estas neniu alternativo

As a world language, English has two half-serious rivals and one serious alternative. The two half-serious rivals are Esperanto and Basic English.

Esperanto, 100 years old in 1987, has around 100,000 fluent speakers in some 85 countries; as many as 8m people have a smattering. It is one of the oldest of such "constructed languages" and is certainly the best survivor. Four or five others have got beyond the linguistic drawing-board and between five and 35 more have been devised. Esperanto's syntax and sound system are both regular and simple; its vocabulary is largely European. More than 10,000 publications have been produced in Esperanto; these include not just technical studies and works of non-fiction but some creative writing, too, especially poetry.

Most experts agree that Esperanto has nowhere to go. Why should a non-Anglophone student devote language-learning time and resources to Esperanto rather than to English? Esperanto is so Eurocentric in its vocabulary and structure that it cannot claim to be much freer of cultural bias than English is. In any case, the culture inherent in English is part of its appeal: at least a few novice students of EFL look forward to the treasures of Shakespeare, Mark Twain and Yeats. And those language students who have less exalted ambitions—refining their appreciation of Bob Dylan's lyrics, following "Dynasty" without the subtitles, securing the local McDonald's franchise, emigrating to America—have even less reason to be diverted from their English studies.

Basic English, devised in the 1930s, enjoyed only a brief vogue. It is a slimmed-down English, with 850 core words and a moderately simplified syntax. It could, perhaps, rival Esperanto in ease of acquisition. But radical changes to English grammar would be needed, and so would a drastic reform of spelling. But the less like English Basic English becomes, the less likely it is to gain acceptance.

The real alternative to English as a world language is the interpreting machine. One day, perhaps, there will be a portable black box—the size of a largish pocket calculator?—with flawless powers of voice recognition and simultaneous translation. Put it on the desk between you and your Japanese counterpart, and let talks proceed.

A new kind of colonisation

English has a happily eclectic vocabulary. Its foundations are Anglo-Saxon (*was, that, eat, cow*) reinforced by Norse (*sky, get, bath, husband, skill*); its superstructure is Norman-French (*soldier, Parliament, prayer, beef*). The Norman aristocracy used their words for the food, but the Saxon serfs kept theirs for the animals. Its decor comes from Renaissance and Enlightenment Europe: sixteenth-century France yielded up *etiquette, naive, reprimand* and *police*; Italy provided *umbrella, duet, bandit* and *dilettante*; Holland gave *cruise, yacht, trigger, landscape* and *decoy*. Its elaborations come from Latin and Greek: *misanthrope, meditate* and *parenthesis* are all first attested during the 1560s; in this century, English adopted *penicillin* from Latin, *polystyrene* from Greek, and *sociology* and *television* from both. And English's ornaments come from all round the world: *slogan* and *spree* from Gaelic, *hammock* and *hurricane* from Caribbean languages, *caviar* and *kiosk* from Turkish, *dinghy* and *dungarees* from Hindi, *caravan* and *candy* from Persian, *mattress* and *masquerade* from Arabic.

Redressing the balance of trade, English is sharply stepping up its linguistic exports. Not just the necessary *imotokali* (motor car) and *izingilazi* (glasses) to Zulu; or *motokaa* and *shillingi* (shilling) to Swahili; but also *der Bestseller, der Kommunikations Manager, das Teeshirt* and *der Babysitter* to German; and, to Italian, *la pop art, il popcorn* and *la spray*. In some Spanish-speaking countries you might wear *un sueter* to *el beisbol*, or witness *un nocaut* at *el boxeo*.

Indeed, a sort of global English wordlist can be drawn up: *airport, passport, hotel, telephone; bar, soda, cigarette; sport, golf, tennis; stop, OK*, and increasingly, *weekend, jeans, know-how, sex-appeal* and *no problem*. The presence of so many words to do with travel, consumables and sport attests to the real source of these exports—America.

Foreign governments rarely welcome this lexical dumping. Is there a secret clause in the constitution of the Fifth Republic which requires a French president to protest at the defilement of his noble language by *les anglicismes*? According to one calculation, *Le Monde* perpetrates an anglicism once every 166 words—not just the established *le dancing, le parking* and *le camping*, but now *le fast food, le hot money* and *le jumbo jet*. The recommended alternatives for these phrases—*prêt-à-manger, capitaux fébriles* and *le gros-porteur*—seem to lack a certain *je ne sais quoi*. More important, they miss the point: that things and ideas American should be American in name, too, if you want to preserve the nation's "linguistic integrity". French cultural traditions are under threat more from fast food the thing than from *fast food* the phrase.

While French presidents protest, there is no record of an American president or a British prime minister complaining at the defilement of English by the infiltration of gallicisms. (Indeed, the word *gallicism* is much rarer in English than *anglicisme* is in French; there is no term at all for the obverse of *franglais*).

Note, however, two caveats in dealing with *anglicismes*. First, they are not always recent: *le biftek* goes back to at least 1807, *le snob* to 1857 and even *le self-made man* to 1878. (English, note, has two useful near-synonyms for that last phrase—namely, *parvenu* and *nouveau riche*.) Second, *anglicismes* do not always mean what they appear to mean. *Un smoking* is not a smoking jacket but a dinner jacket; *un egghead* means an idiot and *un jerk*, a good dancer.

36. The New English Empire

Although most transAtlantic lexical traffic runs eastwards, *central heating* and *weekend* crossed the Atlantic from east to west before 1900. They have been followed by *miniskirt, opposite number, hovercraft, the Establishment, smog, brain drain* (appropriately) and, probably, *gay,* in the sense of homosexual.

The future of English

Mr Robert Burchfield, who recently retired as chief editor of the "Oxford English Dictionary", once suggested that the varieties of English (ESL as well as mother-tongue English) might one day become separate languages, just as Latin, after the fall of the Roman Empire, broke up into French, Italian, Spanish, and so on. Almost 100 years before Mr Burchfield, another language scholar, Henry Sweet, wrote:

> In another century . . . England, America and Australia will be speaking mutually unintelligible languages.

Such a divergence did not occur then because, though communications were slow in those days, language changed slowly, too. Such a divergence is not likely to take place in the next 100 years

The exchange rate

British	American
camp bed	cot
cot	crib
fruit machine	slot machine
slot machine	vending machine
waistcoat	vest
vest	undershirt

because, though language is changing faster today, so, are communications, and hence mutual linguistic influences.

True, a few new dialects might develop, joining the ranks of English creoles that are unintelligible to most mainstream English speakers. British and American English are never likely to become indistinguishable but they are never likely to become mutually unintelligible either. Indian English will remain widely comprehensible elsewhere. It is precisely because of its international intelligibility that English is so earnestly courted by governments and citizens alike.

This does not mean English is in the process of unbuilding the Tower of Babel, as the extreme proponents of a universal language want. Equivocation, lies and babble flourish as much in communities united by one language as they do in those divided by two. Nor is English replacing other languages, as opponents of its spread fear. For the most part, it is supplementing them, allowing strangers to talk to each other. A more temperate and useful role this—and one that English fulfils creditably and deservedly, in all its variety of varieties.

World Problems and Interdependence

Unit 6

One of the unpredicted benefits of space exploration has been the view of our own planet from outside our atmosphere. It has given us the concept of "spaceship earth" and impressed us with the thought that all humanity has a responsibility for the well-being of the planet. Many of our problems are now global ones, and what we do may have worldwide consequences.

One issue of concern is population growth. We have now reached five billion people and are on our way to six billion at the turn of the century. Unchecked growth may eventually lead to a scarcity of resources for feeding all of the people. On the other hand, there may be an element of panic in respect to the so-called "population explosion." Nick Eberstadt reviews the current situation and concludes that the reaction of leaders is more important than the size of the population and its growth rate.

The Chinese who have over a billion people in their country embarked on an ambitious one child per family program which has been remarkably successful in slowing their growth. Greater longevity because of better care of the elderly, however, has prevented them from stopping the growth entirely. Within China, and elsewhere in the world, the urbanization process has continued. At the turn of the century one-half the world's people will live in cities and eighty percent of the growth will be in the Third World. Mexico City and Sao Paulo will be megacities with populations of twenty-five million or more. There will be massive problems of food supply, water, sanitation, and air pollution. China, as Richard Kirkby notes, has avoided urban slums by a state commitment to welfare and an effort to control the move of population from the country to the city.

In Brazil thirty years ago, the government built a "new town," a completely planned city for their capital. The futuristic planning of Brasilia failed to meet the much heralded expectations, but it was not a total failure either. Paul Forster offers a reappraisal of the city. Part of the difficulty with Brasilia was that the planners did not consider carefully the characteristics of the society. There were exquisitely crafted roads for automobiles, for example, in a society which had few cars. Planning for future urban growth is an easily predicted need for the world.

As the world population increases, the need for conservation of all kinds will increase. On a world scale a small fearless organization called Greenpeace currently has brought the world's attention to saving whales and seals. It also has struck at polluters and countries involved in nuclear testing to bring attention to the ecological damage.

Human rights are also attracting more attention in this modern world of interdependence. Some ninety countries have endorsed the United Nations pledge to end discrimination against women, yet, the patriarchy still stands. Nobuko Hashimoto reports that women in Japan, for example, receive but half the pay men earn. In China the government wants marriage based upon love, free choice, and equality. This is contrary to societal traditions and, consequently, the divorce courts, reported by Tamara K. Hareven, reflect the stress between the old and the new attitudes.

To note another aspect of global concern, there is the problem of AIDS. It is a frightening disease of extraordinary mortality. Although epidemiologists know a great deal about the virus—a tribute to recent medical technology—there is no cure for this new plague. Matthew Allen Gonda explores the history of the disease.

The naturalist John Muir once said that when you tug at a single thing in nature, you will find it attached to the rest of the world. So it is also with the human species. Lewis Hanke comments about the need to learn about the rest of the world. The earth is filled with wonders and perils and we should know its history for our own salvation and inspiration.

Looking Ahead: Challenge Questions

What are the major problems in the world today?

What are the complications in population control?

Why is there a move to the cities? What will this mean for the future?

Both terrorists and Greenpeace interfere with the rights of others. What is the difference between them?

Why is it so difficult for women to gain equal rights in Japan? In China?

Why is AIDS a global problem? Why was it not contained in Africa?

Of what use is world history?

Population and Economic Growth

The world's population, increasing by more than one million human beings a week, reached a total of five billion in 1986. Since the time of Thomas Malthus (1766–1834), scholars and philosophers have worried that population growth, if unchecked, would doom mankind to famine, disease, and dire poverty. Today, that threat seems acute among some of the rapidly growing peoples of the Third World. Here, Harvard's Nick Eberstadt examines the diverse economic effects of the much-publicized "population explosion." His surprising conclusion: The size and growth rate of a poor country's population are seldom crucial to its material prospects. What matters most, he contends, is how well a society and its leaders cope with change.

THE THIRD WORLD

Nick Eberstadt

Nick Eberstadt, is a Visiting Fellow at the Harvard University Center for Population Studies and a Visiting Scholar at the American Enterprise Institute for Public Policy Research. Born in New York City, he received a B.A. from Harvard (1976), an M.Sc. from the London School of Economics (1978), and is a doctoral candidate at Harvard's John F. Kennedy School of Government. His most recent book is Poverty & Policy in Marxist-Leninist Countries *(forthcoming).*

The world's poorer nations are in the midst of an unprecedented "population revolution." The revolution is occurring not in the delivery room, but in the minds of men who run governments. In Africa, Asia, and Latin America, political leaders of the Left and Right have variously agreed that one thing is crucial: shaping the size and growth rate of their populations.

These officials, along with many Westerners, have come to embrace the idea that slowing the birthrate in the Third World is essential to economic progress, and, indeed, will foster rapid modernization. As early as 1967, President Lyndon B. Johnson endorsed this view. "Five dollars in family planning aid," he said, "would do more for many less-developed countries than $100 of development aid."

Family planning programs, directed by governments and implemented on a massive scale, seemed feasible only after the 1957 invention of the birth control pill by Gregory Pincus, an American scientist at the Worcester Foundation for Experimental Biology. Third World governments, however, were long reluctant to make population control a top priority: They rebuffed U.S. efforts to win backing for the idea at the 1974 United Nations (UN) World Population Conference in Bucharest. A delegate from Communist China, the planet's most populous nation, declared that "the large population of the Third World is an important condition for the fight against imperialism." Many Third World delegates argued that Washington and its well-to-do Western allies were simply trying to divert attention from their obligations to the poor nations. To Washington's chagrin, the conference voted, as an Algerian delegate put it, "to restore the paramountcy of development over the matter of negatively influencing fertility rates."

A Plea for Modesty

"After the brouhaha of Bucharest, however," recalls Charles B. Keely, of the Population Council in New York, "the population establishment, led by the United Nations Fund for Population Activities, set about its business; and soon family planning programs and a government role in them became the accepted wisdom in most developing nations."

Today, with UN encouragement, more than 40 Third World regimes, including the governments of six of the world's 10 largest nations, are developing or implementing "population plans." Overall,

37. Population and Economic Growth

some 2.7 billion people live under regimes committed to carrying out such policies. They comprise about three-quarters of the population of the less-developed regions of the earth, and nearly three-fifths of the entire world population.

In the past, national governments often performed tasks with demographic consequences—the regulation of immigration, for example, or the eradication of communicable diseases. But the demographic impact of such efforts was always secondary to their intended purpose (e.g., the preservation of national sovereignty, the promotion of public health). The policy of harnessing state power to the goal of altering the demographic rhythms of society per se suggests a new relationship between state and citizen.

In South Asia, for example, General Hossain Mohammad Ershad's regime in Bangladesh is committed to reducing the fertility rate of the nation's 95 million people to 2.5 births per family by the year 2000. In West Africa, the government of Ghana (pop. 13 million) is aiming for 3.3 births per family. Parents in Bangladesh, however, seem to be having an average of six children and Ghana's parents an average of perhaps seven children. Statistics on Third World nations are unreliable, but the families of Bangladesh today appear to be as large as ever, and Ghanaians seem to be having *bigger* families than in the recent past. If Bangladesh and Ghana are to attain their targets, both governments must oversee a 50 percent reduction in their people's fertility during the next 15 years.

How such a radical alteration of personal behavior in so intimate a sphere—the bedroom—is to be achieved is not clear. But if these governments are serious about meeting their goals, they will need to resort to direct, far-reaching, and possibly even forceful intervention into the daily lives of their citizens. Among the nations that already have turned to coercion is India, where hundreds of thousands of men and women were sterilized against their will during the mid-1970s.

Unfortunately for the ordinary people in all of the 40 countries devoted to activist population plans, their governments have acted on the basis of a serious misconception.

The fact is that there is much less to the "science" of population studies than most politicians realize or proponents concede.

Do slower population gains *cause* economic development, or vice versa?

What other factors are involved?

None of the studies done by population specialists answer these questions. In the same year that Lyndon Johnson voiced his faith in family planning, Simon Kuznets, Harvard's late Nobel laureate in economics, called for "intellectual caution and modesty" on population issues. Scholarship, he declared, "is inadequate in dealing with such a fundamental aspect of economic growth as its relation to population increase." Kuznets's plea was, as we know, largely ignored.

I
THE PERILS OF DEMOGRAPHY

Writers and thinkers have debated the "population question" for centuries. Plato argued that the ideal community would limit itself to exactly 5,040 citizens; Aristotle warned that overpopulation would "bring certain poverty on the citizens, and poverty is the cause of sedition and evil." John Locke, on the other hand, suggested in 1699 that large numbers were a source of wealth. In 1798, Thomas Malthus, the spiritual father of today's pessimists, published *An Essay on the Principle of Population*, the famous treatise in which he argued that population would inevitably outstrip "subsistence." During the 1930s, John Maynard Keynes and other economists warned that *falling* birthrates would exacerbate unemployment, erode living standards, and spark a food crisis—precisely the threats that pundits see in today's high birthrates in the Third World.*

Few of the basic issues in this centuries-old debate have been resolved. One lesson that can be drawn from the recurring arguments, however, is that the population question has usually engaged man's fervor more than his intellect.

That is not surprising. After all, the debate involves many matters of deep personal conviction. To talk about population issues is to touch upon the nature of free will; the rights of the living and the unborn; the roles of the sexes; the obligation of the individual to his society or to his God; the sanctity of the family; society's duties to the poor; the destiny of one's nation or one's race; and the general prospects of mankind.

These are fundamentally questions of conscience or creed, not of science. Avowed political ideology is not always a reliable indicator of a country's stance on "population policy." Communist China's "one-child" policy, with its harsh penalties for large families, represents the contemporary world's most drastic current effort to curb population growth [see box, p. 211]. But Prime Minister Lee Kuan Yew of Singapore, who governs a nominally open society with a nominally democratic government, has embraced policies with many of the same precepts.

Around the world, today's campaign against "overpopulation" resembles nothing so much as a religious crusade. Faith, far more than facts, inspires the politicians and intellectuals, North or South, who fervently believe that they have found a "magic bullet" solution to the problems of economic development.

This zeal emerges in the messianic pronouncements of some of today's most influential thinkers on population control. They often evoke the specter of a population apocalypse—and justify the enormous sacrifices they favor by holding out the prospect of demographic salvation. Thus, Stanford biologist Paul Ehrlich began his 1968 best seller *The Population Bomb* with the prophetic words: "The battle to feed all of humanity is over. In the 1970s the world will undergo famines—hundreds of millions of people will starve to death in spite of any crash programs embarked upon now."

Changing the Date

That dire prediction was echoed in 1972 by an international group of researchers gathered under the aegis of the Club of Rome. Their much-publicized report, *The Limits to Growth*, predicted a population "collapse" more devastating than that caused by the Black Death in medieval Europe unless global ecological and population trends were reversed. A feat of that magnitude presumably could only be accomplished with far-reaching and praetorian social controls. And in 1973, Robert McNamara, then president of the World Bank, warned that "the threat of unmanageable population pressures is very much like the threat of nuclear war.... Both threats can and will have catastrophic consequences unless they are dealt with rapidly and rationally."

Few of these true believers are nonplused when events prove them wrong. Like disappointed prophets of the millennium, they simply move the day of reckoning forward or refashion their dire predictions in terms too vague to be disproved.

In recent years, faith in such prophets has waned somewhat in Western official and academic circles. In 1986, for example, the U.S. National Research Council, which had published an alarmist assessment of global population trends in 1971, issued a much more sober-minded study, *Population Growth and Economic Development: Policy Questions*. Family planning programs, it concluded, "cannot make a poor country rich or even move it many notches higher on the scale of development."

But Third World governments are still attracted by the prospect of "scientifically" advancing their national welfare through population control. And Charles Keely's "population establishment"—at the UN, in academe, and in numerous private think tanks in America and Western Europe—is still sounding the alarm. Almost always, popular journalism reflects their convictions. "The consequences of a failure to bring the world's population growth under control are frightening," *Time* declared in 1984. "They could include widespread hunger and joblessness.... heightened global instability, violence, and authoritarianism."

Population studies cannot be expected to provide solutions to such problems. Just as no one would demand that historians create a unified "theory of history," it is asking too much of demographers to expect them to provide overarching "laws of population." For all the

---
*Among the less-heralded intellectual forebears of today's "science" of population studies are the 19th-century social Darwinists, who warned that "inferior" nations, ethnic groups, or social classes might outprocreate their betters. Toward the turn of the century, an English anthropologist named Francis Galton founded the pseudoscience of eugenics, claiming that he could identify individuals and entire "races" endowed by heredity with superior qualities. One eugenicist, Madison Grant, president of the New York Zoological Society, urged America to "take all means to encourage the multiplication of desirable types and abate drastically the increase of the unfit and miscegenation by widely diverse races."

6. WORLD PROBLEMS AND INTERDEPENDENCE

mathematical rigor of some of its investigations, population studies is a field of social inquiry, not a natural science. Researchers may uncover relationships between population change and prosperity, poverty, or war in particular places at particular times, but none of these findings can be generalized to cover the world at large.

Indeed, it is difficult even to forecast the long-term growth rates of human populations with any accuracy. During the 1920s, Raymond Pearl, one of America's leading population biologists, predicted that U.S. census-takers would not count 200 million Americans until the start of the 22nd century. In fact, the United States passed that mark during the 1960s. During the 1930s, France's foremost demographers agreed that the French population was certain to fall between five and 30 percent by 1980. However, despite the losses it sustained during World War II, France's population *rose* by about 30 percent.

An Embarrassment of Theories

Some long-range estimates of population trends have been quite accurate. But long-term forecasts for particular regions or countries are still frequently wrong. In 1959, for example, the UN's "midrange" prediction envisioned India's 1981 population at 603 million, too low by nearly 20 percent.

Despite improvements in the software and computers that demographers use, it is actually getting harder to foresee the demographic future. One reason is that new medicines and public health programs have enabled even the poorer nations to make deep cuts in their death rates quickly and inexpensively—if their governments choose to spend the money.

The unpredictable "human factor" also affects fertility. In England and Wales, it took almost 80 years during the 19th and early 20th centuries for the birthrate to fall by 15 points, from about 35 to 20 births per 1,000 people. Following World War II, Japan experienced a 15-point drop between 1948 and 1958 without any aggressive government intervention, and birthrates may have dropped by 20 points in China during the 1970s.

So every nation follows its own path: Personal choice and national culture seem stronger influences than any pat structural parameters of social science.

Low fertility, for example, is often said to go hand in hand with high levels of health. Yet life expectancy in contemporary Kenya, where women now seem to bear more than eight children on average, is almost exactly equal to that of Germany during the mid-1920s, when that country's total fertility rate was only 2.3 children per woman. Nineteenth-century France experienced a drop in fertility even though the nation's death rates were considerably higher than those in Bangladesh today.

Another demographic truism is that people in poor nations have more children than those in wealthier lands. The limits of that generalization are suggested by the World Bank's *World Development Report 1985*. According to those statistics, Zimbabwe's level of output per capita and its birthrate are *both* about twice as high as the corresponding measures in Sri Lanka.

Demographers have, in a sense, an embarrassment of theories. As historian Charles Tilly puts it, they offer "too many explanations in general terms which contradict each other to some degree, and which fail to fit some significant part of the facts."

There is also a "fact" problem, evident, for example, in the treatment of Somalia in the *World Development Report 1985*. The report presents an estimate of 5.1 million for Somalia's 1983 population—implying a margin of error of 100,000, or about two percent. It also puts Somalia's birthrate at 50 per 1,000 for both 1965 and 1983—again implying a two percent margin of error. The unhappy surprise is that Somalia has no registration system for births whatsoever, and has never conducted a census. The World Bank's numbers were essentially invented: guesses dignified with decimal points.*

Somalia, of course, is an extreme example. Almost every modern nation has by now conducted at least one census of its people. Even so, it would be a mistake to take for granted the precision of estimates by the World Bank or by the many other international organizations that publish them. Only about 10 percent of the Third World's population lives in nations with near-complete systems for registering births and deaths. And the published economic data on most poor nations are even less reliable.

What Is Overpopulation?

Nevertheless, the general outlines of the population trends that some scholars and political leaders call a "crisis" are not hard to sketch. Until the 20th century, births and deaths were roughly balanced in most of the Third World, with both at relatively high levels. During this century, improved sanitation and health care have cut death rates dramatically, especially among children, while birthrates have stayed relatively high. As a result of these changes, the Third World did indeed experience a "population explosion," growing from two billion souls in 1960 to 3.6 billion in 1985, according to the UN's best estimates.

Based on the West's experience, some specialists assume that Third World birthrates will now begin to fall until a new equilibrium between births and deaths, and more stable population growth, is achieved. That interpretation seems consistent with current trends, for example, in many of the nations of Latin America. But it is far from clear that such a "demographic transition" will occur quickly or even of its own accord. That uncertainty has spurred political leaders from Karachi to Mexico City to try to curb "overpopulation" by government action.

But what is overpopulation? There are no workable demographic definitions. Consider these possible indicators:

• *A high birthrate.* The U.S. birthrate during the 1790s was about 55 per 1,000 people, more than 20 points higher than the latest World Bank estimates of the birthrates for India, Vietnam, Indonesia, or the Philippines.

• *A steep rate of natural increase (births minus deaths).* By this measure, the United States was almost certainly overpopulated between 1790 and 1800. Its annual rate of natural increase then was

---

MEXICO

"Poor Mexico, so far from God, so close to the United States," mourned President Porfirio Diaz a century ago. Yet the proximity that he lamented has, in one way, proved a godsend to his successors and to millions of Mexicans.

Every year, an estimated one to six million *mojados* (wets) illegally cross the Rio Grande in search of work on farms or in factories. After saving the lion's share of their earnings for a few months, most return to their villages; later, they head north again. The unemployment rate in Mexico officially averages 8.5 percent, but "underemployment" is said to reach 40 percent. In a land of some 79 million people, the working-age population grows by 3.2 percent annually.

Those statistics, argue many U.S. scholars and politicians, are all one needs to know about the causes of illegal immigration. "With unemployment increasing and hundreds of thousands of field hands moving illegally into the United States, the crisis nature of Mexico's annual population increase became evident" in 1972, writes Marvin Alisky, an Arizona State University political scientist. The "crisis" prompted Mexico's government to mount an expensive family planning campaign, publicized in a TV soap opera, "Maria la Olvidada" (Maria the Forgotten One), a victim of her husband's machismo. Officials were helped by the Mexican Catholic Church, which broke with Rome to implicitly endorse the program. With their priests' consent, millions of Mexicans felt free to begin using modern contraceptives. Within 10 years, overall annual population growth slid from an estimated 3.6 percent—very high for such a relatively prosperous nation—to 2.3 percent, or about the same rate as in Egypt.

•

The fact is that many Mexicans would trek north even if there were no "population pressure." One big reason: Wages in the United States are three times as high as those in Mexico.

Even so, the illegal influx probably would be smaller were it not for Mexico's long series of wrong turns in economic policy. In some ways, Mexico is one of Latin America's success stories, with a record of rapid economic growth since World War II surpassed only by Brazil's. But growth has not created a corresponding number of jobs. During the 1960s, the Mexican economy expanded by more than six percent annually; yet, according to one study, its demand for labor rose by only 2.3 percent per year.

Under President Miguel Alemán Valdes (1946–52), Mexico, like many other Third World nations, adopted a policy of "import substitution," seeking

---

*Over the years, the World Bank also issued seemingly precise data on Ethiopia. In 1985, after Ethiopia conducted its first census, the Bank was obliged to drop its estimate of the nation's birthrate by 15 percent and to boost its figure for Ethiopia's population by more than 20 percent.

37. Population and Economic Growth

three percent—almost exactly the rate that the World Bank ascribes to Bangladesh today, and considerably higher than the rates prevailing in Haiti and India. Today, population is growing faster in the United States than it is in Cuba, Eastern Europe, or the Soviet Union, all of them in economic torpor.

- *Population density*. By this measure, in 1980 France was more overpopulated than Indonesia, and the United Kingdom was in worse shape than India. The world's most densely populated nation in 1980: Prince Rainier's Monaco.
- *The "dependency ratio" (the proportion of children and the elderly to the "working-age" population)*. According to 1980 World Bank data, the world's *least* overpopulated lands were crowded Singapore and the United Arab Emirates, where immigration was helping to achieve an ultrarapid population growth rate of 11 percent a year.
- *Poverty*. Inadequate incomes, poor health, malnutrition, overcrowded housing, and unemployment are the unambiguous images of poverty. But it is a profound error to equate these social and economic ills with problems of population. Upon closer examination, it becomes clear that many of these Third World woes are closely related to ill-advised government policies, such as those that discriminate against farmers in favor of city dwellers or stifle private initiative. More generally, what are often mistaken for "population problems" are usually manifestations of state-imposed restrictions that prevent ordinary individuals from pursuing what they see as their own welfare and the welfare of their families.

II

THE POOREST OF THE POOR

The catchall term "Third World" conceals at least as much as it reveals about the 133 nations it encompasses. Any classification that lumps together Hong Kong and Chad, or Iran and Jamaica, or Cuba and South Africa, loses much of its meaning. Even within a single country, social, cultural, and economic differences can be profound. India, for example, has a single central government, but at least six major religions, six alphabets, and a dozen major languages. Life expectancy is thought to be 20 years greater in Kerala, India's healthiest state, than in impoverished Uttar Pradesh. The fertility rates in these two states of India differ by almost three children per woman.

Such variations, to say nothing of the dubious social and economic statistics available for many less-developed countries, suggest that the best way of gaining some insight into the population question may be to examine a few specific cases.

Let us begin by looking at the most troubled populations of the modern world: the nations at the low end of the national income spectrum. By the reckoning of the World Bank's *World Development Report 1984*, eight of the 34 nations that the Bank classifies as "low-income economies" were poorer in terms of gross national product (GNP) per capita during the early 1980s than they were in 1960. The unhappy eight were: Chad, Nepal, Zaire, Uganda, Somalia, Niger, Madagascar, and Ghana.

By the World Bank's estimate, these nations had a total of over 90 million inhabitants in 1982. Between 1960 and 1982, their economies grew, albeit slowly. Population, however, increased faster—indeed, the rate of population increase is said to have *accelerated* in five of the nations. The Bank's estimates of population growth range from just under two percent annually in Chad to more than three percent a year in Niger.

War, Politics, Chaos

Do these numbers mean that rapid population growth dragged these nations deeper into poverty?

Not necessarily. For one thing, many of the statistics that point to a drop in GNP per capita are suspect or contradictory. Take the numbers for Niger: According to the *World Development Report 1984*, the former French West African colony's GNP per capita fell by about 29 percent between 1960 and 1982. According to other tables in the same report, however, private consumption per capita in Niger *increased* by about three percent during the same years, investment per capita jumped by over 35 percent, and government spending maintained a steady share of GNP. The only logical conclusion: GNP per capita must, in fact, have gone up.

Another set of figures from the same report supports that conclusion. Based on what the report's authors say about the growth of Niger's exports (which include uranium, peanuts, and cotton) and the share of its GNP derived from them, one comes to the conclusion that Niger's GNP per capita *grew* by almost six percent annually between 1960 and 1982. That would add up to a cumulative jump of 240 percent during those years.

What, in truth, are the correct numbers for Niger? It is impossible to tell from the World Bank's figures.

Let us ignore such inexactitudes for the moment, however, and accept the World Bank estimates of growing poverty in these eight nations as accurate. Would they allow us to conclude that population growth was to blame? No. The figures show only that their economies grew more slowly than population, not *why* they did.

Although the World Bank estimates that the rate of natural increase in these eight nations quickened between 1960 and 1982, the speedup, according to Bank numbers, was chiefly the result of a drop in death rates. In other words, their people suffered less sickness and disease. How could that have reduced their productivity?

The cause of the economic woes of these countries must lie elsewhere. In three of the eight nations—Chad, Somalia, and Uganda—the explanation seems clear enough. Chad has been convulsed by unending civil war since the late 1960s, with Libya joining in; Uganda remains in chaos even though Idi Amin's barbarous eight-year rule ended in 1979; Somalia has been fully mobilized for war against Ethiopia for nearly a decade. (The Somali government claims that it spends "only" 14 percent of GNP on defense; U.S. defense outlays are 6.5 percent of GNP.) Politics can fully account for the misfortunes of these three African nations. There seems to be no need in these cases to resort to demographic explanations.

---

to nurture steel, chemicals, and other industries to reduce the need to buy manufactured goods from abroad.

Alemán and subsequent presidents imposed stiff tariffs on foreign goods, exempting only the foreign-made tools and machinery that Mexico's infant industries needed to get started. They offered cheap loans to Mexican entrepreneurs. Bowing to labor union pressure, the government also required industrial employers to contribute heavily to new pensions, schooling, and profit-sharing programs for their workers.

All of these measures artificially boosted the cost of labor relative to capital, encouraging Mexico's industrialists to replace workers with machinery.

At the same time, protectionism eased competitive pressures on Mexican factory managers, especially those in state-run enterprises, to control costs and improve quality. Mexico's exports suffered; more jobs were lost. To make matters worse, the government neglected Mexican agriculture, which employed the bulk of the nation's workers. As the wage gap between farmers and factory workers widened, many Mexicans deserted the countryside, subsisting in the city slums without work or in marginal occupations—shining shoes, peddling fruit or flowers—in the hope of landing the elusive "high-paying job." The population of greater Mexico City soared to 17 million.

Paradoxically, the discovery of vast new oil reserves in Mexico in 1976 hurt its basic economic health. As in Nigeria and Venezuela, swelling oil revenues made it easy to import foreign products without relying on exports of domestic goods to pay the bills. Succumbing to the "oil syndrome," President José Lopez Portillo (1976–82) went on a spending spree, borrowing heavily, expanding the government payroll, and boosting industrial subsidies.

Today, five years after world oil prices began to fall, Mexico is $98 billion in debt. Despite its continuing promises of reform to the World Bank and other lenders, the government of President Miguel de la Madrid Hurtado appears to have done little to relieve the productivity-constricting restraints it has imposed upon the national economy.

Encouraging citizens to seek jobs in the United States may simply be seen, in Mexico City, as a substitute for taking painful economic measures at home.

—*N. E.*

6. WORLD PROBLEMS AND INTERDEPENDENCE

What about the difficulties of Ghana, Madagascar, Nepal, Niger, and Zaire (formerly the Belgian Congo)?

Many development economists argue that rapid population growth retards economic progress by slowing the accumulation of capital needed to build factories, harbors, and roads. However, if the World Bank's figures are accurate, low investment was not a major problem in four out of these five stricken nations.

In Nepal, Zaire, and Niger, the investment ratios for 1983 were all reckoned at 20 percent or more—higher than those in many advanced industrial nations, including the United States (17 percent). Indeed, a number of Third World nations with higher rates of population growth and lower investment ratios outperformed this trio.

Ghana is the only one of the five suffering from capital scarcity today. But that was not always so. By the World Bank's reckoning, Ghana's gross domestic investment ratio in 1960 was 24 percent—more than twice as high as the 1960 estimates for Singapore or South Korea.

If the World Bank's numbers are correct, the economies of these five countries have been afflicted by an extremely low ratio of growth to investment. In other words, heavy capital outlays yielded very meager dividends. (Madagascar's ratio of economic growth to investment appears to be only half the U.S. rate; Zaire's seems to be less than a third as high as Spain's; Ghana's during the 1960s and '70s was about one-tenth that of South Korea.) To find out what has been going wrong in these countries, one must inquire into the economic policies of their political leaders.

A Reign of Error

Take Ghana. During the late 1950s and early '60s, it was one of a select group of nations (including Burma, Chile, and Egypt) that economists were touting as bright prospects in the Third World.

After the West African nation gained its independence from Britain in 1957, Kwame Nkrumah, the charismatic new prime minister, quickly embarked on an ambitious "reform" program. Casting aside such economic considerations as competitiveness and productivity, he decided to seek prosperity by political means. "The social and economic development of Africa," he declared, "will come only within the political kingdom, not the other way round."

Nkrumah aimed to transform Ghana into a prestigious industrial power at all costs. The nation's long-successful small farmers were to foot the bill.

Nkrumah forced the farmers to sell their cocoa, the nation's chief export, at a fixed price to the government, which then sold it abroad at a profit. The proceeds were poured into Nkrumah's industrial development schemes.* By the late 1970s, long after Nkrumah, the self-styled "Redeemer," had been deposed, Ghana's small cocoa farmers were getting less than 40 percent of the world price for their crop—an effective tax of over 60 percent. Not surprisingly, Ghana's cocoa output and cocoa exports plummeted.

As these new policies made their mark on agriculture, Nkrumah took aim at industry. Shortly after independence, he nationalized the nation's foreign-owned gold and diamond mines, cocoa-processing plants, and other enterprises. Ghana's new infant industries were also state-owned. The result was inefficiency on a monumental scale. According to one study, between 65 percent and 71 percent of Ghana's publicly owned factory capacity lay idle 10 years after independence.

To cut the price of imported goods, Nkrumah allowed the Ghanaian cedi to rise in the world currency markets. Unfortunately, that also drove up the price of the products Ghana was trying to sell overseas. The nation's trade balance tilted deeply into the red.

Under these diverse pressures, the nation's visible tax base began to shrink, even as the government budget swelled. Foreign aid did not solve the problem. Deficit spending increased: By 1978, tax revenues paid less than 40 percent of the government's budget. Inflation spiraled, climbing by over 30 percent a year during the 1970s, according to the World Bank. With annual interest rates fixed by law at levels as low as six percent (to reduce the cost of capital), it made no sense for Ghanaians to put their money in the bank.

By 1982, only one percent of Ghana's GNP was devoted to investment. Black Africa's most promising former colony had become an economic disaster.

So Ghana's current economic travails can be explained without recourse to demographic theory. The nation's parlous economic straits are the result of Accra's 29-year reign of error. Rapid population growth may have compounded the woes caused by mismanagement, or it may have eased these pressures somewhat by creating a better-educated, healthier, and potentially more productive work force. It may have done both. But its overall impact on the course of events does not seem to have been great.

Food for the Hungry

The most haunting evidence of a Malthusian crisis in Africa—a growing number of hungry mouths to feed and ever-diminishing resources—is the images of hunger and starvation that regularly appear on TV news broadcasts. The U.S. Department of Agriculture estimates that farm output per capita in Black Africa dropped by nine percent between 1969–71 and 1979–81. In one African country after another, write Lester R. Brown and Edward C. Wolf of the Worldwatch Institute, "demands of escalating human numbers are exceeding the sustainable yield of local life-support systems—croplands, grasslands, and forests. Each year, Africa's farmers attempt to feed 16 million additional people."

In this bleak view, population pressures are pushing people into marginal lands, which are eventually reduced to desert by overgrazing and deforestation. Indeed, the evidence of food shortages and famine in the nations of the Sahel—from Senegal in the west to the Sudan in the east—is undeniable.

But does all of this mean that population growth per se is causing food shortages in sub-Saharan Africa?

In fact, none of the nations with the poorest records of farm output—Ghana, Mozambique, Uganda (where output per capita dropped by more than 30 percent between 1969–71 and 1979–81), and Angola (where it fell by more than 50 percent)—is in the drought-stricken Sahel. Several African nations have creditable records of improving farm productivity, and they are right next door to the nations with the most severe problems: Prosperous Kenya is contiguous to Uganda, Mozambique adjoins Zimbabwe (formerly Rhodesia), and a common border unites Ghana and the flourishing Ivory Coast. Since the climates and population growth rates of these nations were broadly similar, something else must have been at work.

In the overwhelming majority of cases, the food crisis in Black Africa has obvious political and economic causes. In Uganda, Mozambique, and Angola, coups or revolutions were followed by continuing domestic violence, persecution of minority groups, and, as in Ghana, destructive economic policies. In Ethiopia, where mass starvation has reached its most tragic proportions, the fault lies largely with the

POPULATION GROWTH AND POVERTY

POPULATION GROWTH RATE, 1973–1983 (per year)

- ☐ One percent to less than two percent
- ▨ Two percent to less than three percent
- ■ Three percent or more
- ▦ No data

THE WORLD'S TEN POOREST COUNTRIES
Based on 1983 GNP per capita

1. Ethiopia
2. Bangladesh
3. Mali
4. Nepal
5. Zaire
6. Burkina Faso (formerly Upper Volta)
7. Burma
8. Malawi
9. Uganda
10. Burundi

---
*Nkrumah also received generous aid from abroad during his 10-year rule, including $145.6 million in economic assistance from the United States.

forced collectivization of farming and other cruel and disastrous accomplishments of a 12-year-old Marxist regime, now headed by Mengistu Haile Mariam, turning an ordinary drought into a deadly famine. But Ethiopia is only one of the most extreme cases. During the decades since independence, more and more regimes in Black Africa have adopted misguided policies that have variously restricted trade, discouraged farm production, and depressed local industry.

III
THE 'LITTLE DRAGONS'

On the basis of demographic criteria alone, four of the most likely candidates for severe "population problems" after World War II were Singapore, Hong Kong, Taiwan, and South Korea. As they entered the 1950s, they were among the most densely peopled lands in the world. There were almost four times as many people per square mile in Taiwan as in mainland China; South Korea's population density was nearly twice as high as India's.

These crowded lands were blessed with comparatively little in the way of oil, coal, iron, or other natural resources. Hong Kong and Singapore imported even their drinking water. All four had high fertility levels during the early 1950s: six births per woman was the lowest level. During the period from 1950 to 1980, population grew faster in Taiwan (2.7 percent per year), Hong Kong (2.7 percent), and Singapore (2.9 percent) than in the world's less-developed countries as a whole (an estimated 2.3 percent). South Korea, despite suffering perhaps one million deaths during the Korean War, still grew by an average rate of about two percent annually.

Dependency ratios were high, with the young and the elderly vastly outnumbering workers. Twenty-five years ago, unemployment and underemployment were still pervasive. The signs of poverty and even destitution—sprawling city slums, malnutrition, unemployment—were everywhere.

Many observers expected nothing but grim futures for these impoverished lands. In 1947, General Albert Wedemeyer, dispatched from Washington to assess South Korea's prospects, reported: "Basically an agricultural area, [it] does not have the overall economic resources to sustain its economy without external assistance.... It is not considered feasible to make South Korea self-sustaining."

Such judgments proved almost ludicrously wrong. Today, Singapore, Hong Kong, Taiwan, and South Korea are known as Asia's "little dragons." In all four lands, GNP per capita quadrupled between 1960 and 1980, despite rapid population growth. Unemployment (and, with the exception of South Korea, underemployment) have virtually disappeared. Despite an "adverse" balance of "dependent" age groups to working-age population, each society sharply increased domestic investment per capita. Despite high ratios of population to arable land, measured malnutrition was virtually eliminated. Even without a wealth of natural resources, all four have emerged as major export centers and commercial entrepôts.

What explains these success stories? Edward K. Y. Chen, an economist at the University of Hong Kong, has attempted a breakdown of the "sources of growth" for the four from the late 1950s through 1970. By his accounting, increased "inputs" of capital and labor alone explain less than half the growth of Taiwan, Singapore, and South Korea and barely more than half of Hong Kong's. Improvements in "total factor productivity" (net output per unit of net expenditure) account for the remainder. In short, the economies of the little dragons were simply more efficient than were those of other less-developed nations.

Not that they all found a *single* success formula. Hong Kong's economy is freewheeling and lightly regulated, while Taiwan's Nationalist government owns a number of inefficient large enterprises. South Korea blocks most foreign investment and runs constant balance of payments deficits, while Singapore holds more foreign currency reserves than does oil-rich Kuwait. Hong Kong is a British colony, Singapore a nominal parliamentary democracy, and South Korea a virtual dictatorship. But there are common elements in their success: "outward-looking" export-promotion policies, including reduction of barriers against imports, minimal restraints on interest rates, subsidies to encourage production for foreign markets, and an openness to the adoption of technology from abroad.

The relationship between population change and economic development in the little dragons is more ambiguous. During their decades of astonishing economic growth, all four enjoyed rapid fertility declines. (Rates now range from two children per woman in Hong Kong and Singapore to just under three in South Korea.) Many development specialists credit state-sponsored family planning programs with bringing birthrates down in these countries. But, as we have seen, that explanation may not suffice.

A Nobel Prize winner, Paul Samuelson of the Massachusetts Institute of Technology, once observed that there are always two plausible, and opposite, answers to any "common sense" question in economics. So it is with the effects of population growth.

Such growth may impose costly new burdens on a government, or it may expand the tax revenue base. It may cause food shortages, or it may speed the division of labor by which farm productivity is increased. If it tends to increase unemployment by adding new workers to the labor pool, it also tends to reduce the danger of insufficient consumer demand that so troubled Keynes and many other Western economists during the Great Depression of the 1930s.

The overall impact of population change on a society seems to depend on how the society deals with change *of all kinds*. Indeed, coping with fluctuations in population is in many ways less demanding than dealing with the almost daily uncertainties of the harvest, or the ups and downs of the business cycle, or the vagaries of political life. Societies and governments that meet such challenges successfully, as the little dragons did, are also likely to adapt well to population change. Those that do not are likely to find that a growing population "naturally" causes severe, costly, and prolonged dislocations.

AROUND THE WORLD, 1973–1983

The world's poorest countries do not have its fastest-growing populations. Most destitute is Ethiopia, with a GNP per capita of $120, and a population growth rate equal to Hong Kong's.

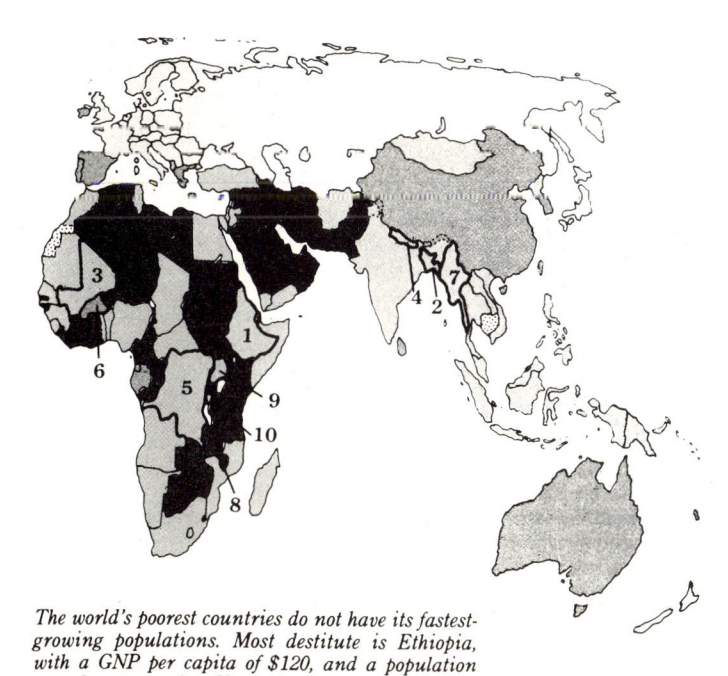

IV
HUMAN CAPITAL

Spinning the globe offers a broad perspective on the impact, or lack of impact, of population change. One can also "come down to earth" to examine the behavior of individuals and their families.

Much of today's alarm over population growth springs from simple arithmetic. Every newborn child shrinks the wealth per person of his family and his nation. In a sense, he begins life as a debit in the national ledger.

During his lifetime, the child will require food, clothing, school-

6. WORLD PROBLEMS AND INTERDEPENDENCE

ing, and medical attention. But there is no guarantee that he will be able to "repay" his debt during his working life. And if his homeland is developing rapidly, his debt actually grows larger, because the cost of raising children soars and the length of their dependency increases as the economy demands more skilled and educated workers.

During the late 1950s and early 1960s, development scholars, notably Ansley J. Coale and Edgar M. Hoover of Princeton, crafted influential economic models that demonstrated that, beyond some ideal point, additional births would indeed impose an intolerable economic burden on society. These "excess" children, they warned, would, in effect, be "living off capital," draining their societies of savings and investment desperately needed to fuel economic growth.

Getting Rich

Economists have since recognized the limitations of these models. Coale, Hoover, and their colleagues made a number of questionable assumptions. Among them: that economic growth results solely from the accumulation of capital; that the rate of return on capital is fixed; and that education, health care, and all other forms of human consumption bear no productive returns.

Today, the old argument has reappeared in a new, albeit more cautious, form. Some development scholars now contend that Third World governments are in effect subsidizing the births of too many children. How? By providing free services, such as public education, that make it cheaper for families to raise children but increase society's costs.

The Soviet Union offers a fascinating example of how such "externalities" work. To prevent any upsurge of unrest in its Muslim republics, Moscow is spending millions of rubles to provide schools, jobs, and health care for its Muslim citizens. Children are indeed a "bargain" for Muslim parents. Not surprisingly, total fertility in Soviet Central Asia remains in the vicinity of six births per woman—higher than the World Bank's current estimates for neighboring Iran, or nearby Pakistan and India. In this case, the development scholars appear to be right about externalities.

Yet such dramatic gaps between public and private costs rarely occur. Only serious failures of the market mechanism, or, as in the Soviet Union, political decisions, make them possible. In either case, such policies are costly. Except under extraordinary circumstances, they cannot be sustained for long—certainly not long enough to have pronounced effects on childbearing patterns.

Another cause of worry among population specialists is the tendency of poor people to have more children than rich people. If the poor and the well-to-do also have nearly the same death rates, as is now the case in most countries, it makes sense to expect that poverty will spread and the gaps between rich and poor widen.

As it happens, however, the record of modern history does not bear out these fears. In Western nations where the poor have borne more children than the well-to-do for a century or more, long-term economic growth has not slowed. And economists' measures of income distribution, though imperfect, give no indication that the gaps in the West between rich and poor have widened over the long term. In fact, most studies suggest that they are narrower today than they were a century ago.

The data on wealth and poverty in the Third World are even less reliable than comparable statistics on the West, but careful long-term studies have been made of two countries, India and Taiwan. The results show no clear evidence of increased inequality in either nation since World War II, despite population growth, and there is a hint of reduced inequality in Taiwan.

The modern world has witnessed two general, though not universal, trends. First, the productivity of individuals has climbed steadily, enough not only to cover rising standards of living, but also to add to national wealth. That is what has happened in North America and Western Europe over the past four or five generations, despite wars and recessions. And these improvements were not financed by "dipping into capital": Assets per capita in these societies are vastly greater today than they were a century ago.

Thus, over the generations, the people in these societies produced more than they consumed. The pattern was repeated during the rapid climb of Japan and Israel into the ranks of economically advanced nations. Following close on the heels of these industrial

A Taiwanese farmer plants his field using a rice transplanter. By allowing crop prices to rise and dispersing industry throughout the countryside, Taiwan has avoided many of the pitfalls of economic development.

powers are Asia's little dragons and an encouraging number of other Third World countries.

Their success highlights the second general trend of the post–World War II era. Despite the rhetoric of Third World partisans in the "North-South" debate, the history of the past 25 years shows that it is possible for the poor, as well as the rich, to become richer. In fact, the productivity of the poor can rise more rapidly than that of the rich. But certain things have to happen.

Adding Value to Time

In his now-classic studies of economic growth, Simon Kuznets discerned two distinctive features of the economic development of the West between the beginning of the 19th century and the middle of the 20th. The first was that increases in GNP could not be explained simply by the growth of population and the accumulation of physical capital. Secondly, he found that while dividends from capital and other property (e.g., farmland) grew as economies developed, the share of GNP from wages, salaries, and earnings grew even more rapidly. Long-term economic development, Kuznets concluded, depended much less on building factories, power plants, and other capital stock than on the improvement of "human capital"—the ability of human beings to put to work a growing body of knowledge, research, and technology.

Theodore W. Schultz, Nobel laureate in economics at the University of Chicago, refined this notion of human capital. In a series of studies beginning during the 1950s, he showed that government outlays on education, health, and nutrition were not unproductive "consumption," as some economists had defined them to be. Usually, these investments in human beings bore productive returns—often very high ones.

Originally trained as an agricultural economist, Schultz had observed that even in impoverished, "backward" societies, poor people tended to make the most of whatever resources were available to them. He argued that even penniless men and women with nothing to invest but their time would often behave like entrepreneurs. The process of economic development, he argued, is in large part the extension of human choice made possible by the rising value of human time. Time, after all, is the single resource that is absolutely fixed in quantity, nonrenewable, and impossible to trade or save.

By helping their people to improve their health and gain better schooling, for example, governments increased the value of human time, and thus of human capital.

Poor people and poor nations can actually enjoy a paradoxical edge in building up human capital. Because of what the late Alexander Gerschenkron of Harvard called the "advantages of backwardness," they can climb the "learning curve" of economic development much more quickly than the pioneers in other societies who preceded them. Whether by importing penicillin invented and manufactured in the West, or by borrowing the technology for manufacturing com-

37. Population and Economic Growth

A CONTRARY VIEW

The nations of the West achieved prosperity despite rapid population growth. Can the Third World follow the same path, without imposing government-sponsored family planning programs? Sharon L. Camp, vice president of the Population Crisis Committee, writing in Population *(Feb. 1985), argued that the West's experience does not apply to the Third World:*

During Europe's [18th–19th century] population explosion, annual rates of population growth rose from about 0.5 percent to about 1.5 percent. In contrast, Third World countries now have higher birthrates and lower death rates than did Europe, and their annual rate of population increase is about 2.4 percent (excluding China). Some African countries are growing by three to four percent a year—a population doubling time of just over 20 years. The analogy with historical Europe is thus suspect....

The post–World War II population explosion in less-developed countries is largely the result of a precipitous drop in death rates spurred primarily by a revolution in public health and improved response to food crises. The speed and magnitude of these changes are unprecedented. In 18th- and 19th-century Europe, by contrast, death rates declined slowly in response to rising standards of living and remained relatively high compared to current rates in many developing countries....

•

The reverse is true of birthrates. During Europe's Industrial Revolution, cultural and other factors kept birthrates well below the biological maximum. Marriage was delayed to the mid-twenties and not uncommonly to the late twenties. Significant numbers of adults did not marry at all or did not survive their reproductive years. In most Third World countries today, marriage is nearly universal and the majority of women are married by their late teens. Although maternal and infant deaths take a large toll, it is not unusual to find women in developing countries who have been pregnant a dozen times and have eight to 10 living children....

Not only are Third World countries growing two to three times faster, many are starting from a much larger population base than did European countries at a comparable stage of economic development. In most developing countries, population density on arable land is at least three times higher than in 19th-century Europe and rural population growth is twice as rapid despite massive urbanization. The combination of a larger population base and a more rapid rate of growth means that the total number of people added to the Third World's population in the last decade alone exceeds the total increase in Europe's population over the whole of the 19th century.

---

puter chips, they can reap at relatively low cost the advantages that others paid dearly for. This is precisely what Japan and the little dragons did during their post–World War II economic "catch-up."

Demographic events can profoundly influence when and where this catch-up occurs. Migration is an obvious example. When they move from countryside to city, or from one nation to another, most families pursue economic advantages. The Nigerian who leaves his farm for the city of Lagos makes a personal economic calculation. But by putting himself where his time can be used more productively (e.g., in a factory), he enhances national wealth. In the same way, America's immigrants have added vastly to the nation's affluence (and their own) by fleeing lands where, among other things, their labor was less productively employed.

Small-Family Formula

Another important economic event is the recent fall in mortality rates in many less-developed nations. Coming largely as a result of improvements in nutrition, hygiene, and health care, the drop can be seen as an enormous deposit in the human capital "bank." Not only will the productive working lives of many people be lengthened, but the returns from further "social investments" can be higher. Healthy children, after all, can profit more from extra schooling than can malnourished children.

The economic implications of changes in fertility are more ambiguous. Few parents decide whether or not to have children solely on considerations of profitability. If Western parents did so, they would be childless.

On the other hand, personal choices are always constrained by what is economically feasible. And the economics of the family vary enormously from place to place. In the West, where the economic value of human time is high, preparing a child for adult life is a lengthy and expensive proposition. It consumes a great deal of time that many parents could otherwise devote to work, and few will call upon their young for financial help in their old age. It is not surprising, then, that Western parents tend to have small families.

In a farming society such as Kenya, on the other hand, children may start working in the fields at an early age and help support their parents long after they reach adulthood. In such societies, where the costs of raising a child are low and the benefits high, it may not be financially punitive to have large families. In India, there is a saying: "One son is no sons." In short, parents may have different views of the family than do their political leaders or their governments' technocrats, a fact worth remembering.

V
FAMILY PLANNING

The Third World's population is considered to be "exploding," despite the fact that governments in all but 27 of these 133 nations promote the use of modern contraceptives among their people, and often distribute them at little or no charge.

The political energy and financial resources expended on these family planning programs are considerable. By the World Bank's estimate, Third World governments spend more than $2 billion annually on such efforts. (The actual purchasing power is probably much greater than dollar figures indicate.) International organizations, Western governments, and charitable institutions also make substantial contributions. Between 1969 and 1984, they added another $7 billion (in 1982 dollars). In some less-developed countries, e.g., Bangladesh, governments spend more on family planning programs than on all other health-related services combined.

What do such programs, and national population policies, actually accomplish? How do they affect current living standards and the prospects for economic development?

Today's national family planning bureaucracies are in the business of subsidizing and promoting the use of birth control pills, intrauterine devices (IUDs), condoms, diaphragms, and other modern contraceptives. These methods are not necessarily more effective than some old approaches to family planning: On grounds of effectiveness alone, nothing can improve upon total abstinence or infanticide. Of course, modern contraception is much more acceptable than these extreme alternatives, and it is also more reliable than some widely used traditional techniques of birth control (such as coitus interruptus, the rhythm method, or drinking native contraceptive potions). Moreover, by making it easier to exercise choice, modern contraception reduces unwanted pregnancies that can cause sickness and death among mothers and infants—notably by preventing closely spaced births. So a voluntary family planning effort can be a useful public health service, one of many government activities that can increase choice, reduce mortality, augment human capital, and improve the well-being of individuals and families.

It is not so clear, however, that voluntary family planning always delivers the big reductions in "unwanted" births that Third World governments seek.

Family planning workers from Nepal to Kenya have discovered that making modern contraceptives available to all does not by itself stimulate a revolution in attitudes toward family size. In Kenya, for example, total fertility appears to have *increased* from under six children per couple to more than eight despite nearly 20 years of officially sponsored family planning efforts.

As Lord Peter Bauer of the London School of Economics has observed, people of all nations are quick to buy Western-style cosmetics, soft drinks, and transistor radios. In most Third World countries, birth control pills, IUDs, and diaphragms are just as available, but are in much less demand.

In the Third World, Bauer writes, "the children who are born are generally desired. They are certainly avoidable. To deny this amounts to saying that Third World parents procreate heedless of consequences. This view treats people with... contempt."

Indeed, in many parts of the globe, truly effective family planning might actually *increase* the birthrate. In Zaire, Gabon, and other nations of sub-Saharan Africa, for example, families have demonstrated little interest in modern contraception, but considerable concern about *infertility*. In these societies, a wife who cannot bear

6. WORLD PROBLEMS AND INTERDEPENDENCE

children faces an unenviable fate. Increasing parents' "freedom to choose" will always serve the purposes of parents, whatever the preference of the government and its advisors.

Of course, the thrust of most family planning efforts in less-developed countries over the past generation has been antinatalist. And the principal international institutions supporting these programs, including the World Bank and the U.S. Agency for International Development, remain firmly in favor of reducing birthrates.

Unquestioning faith in this goal has led some of the world's poorest governments to pour extraordinary amounts of money into family planning. In 1980, for example, the World Bank estimates that Ghana's family planning program spent $68 per contraceptive user, Nepal's $69. The Bank's data also suggest that government outlays for *all other* health programs totaled only $20 per family in Ghana and $8 in Nepal. In these and other poor nations, government officials seem to believe that birth control yields tremendous benefits.

The Bottom Line

That faith extends even into the academic world. Only a handful of researchers have attempted to *measure* the impact of family planning against a "control group" (i.e., a similar population which lacks the service)—standard practice in the health sciences. The few properly conducted studies do not reveal many differences in fertility decline between "control" and "experimental" groups.

In a little-noticed 1984 study, Donald J. Hernandez, a demographer at Georgetown University, attempted to disentangle the effects of family planning efforts from "natural" declines in fertility. Among the nations he examined were four that have been widely hailed as exemplars of successful family planning programs: Two little dragons, Taiwan and South Korea, as well as Costa Rica and Mauritius.

In Mauritius, he found, family planning might have pushed birthrates down by as much as three to six points over 10 years. However, because of shortcomings in his own methodology, Hernandez cautioned against ascribing too much meaning to this calculation.

In Taiwan, South Korea, and Costa Rica—where Hernandez felt that his methodology would produce more reliable results—he estimated that family planning efforts brought birthrates down only by between 0.1 and 1.6 points over periods ranging from four to 11 years. Hernandez rightly concluded that family planning programs may be able to speed the fall of birthrates somewhat where this decline has begun on its own. But such programs experience "little success and considerable failure in initiating fertility reductions independently of socioeconomic and other indigenous factors."*

One sure way to bring birth trends down is to resort to Draconian measures, as several governments have done. But insofar as they have coerced involuntary behavior out of parents, these governments generally have reduced—not raised—standards of living.

A case in point is Romania's radical effort to *increase* fertility during the 1960s. The nation's Communist leaders had long been concerned that declining birthrates (by that time below the net replacement level) would exacerbate the nation's troublesome labor shortages. In 1966, one year after taking the helm of the Romanian Communist Party, Nicolae Ceauşescu announced a series of measures designed to raise the national birthrate. The most important of these was a sudden restriction of access to abortion, at that time Romanians' principal means of birth control.

Taken unawares by the change in rules, Romanian parents had many more children that year than they had been planning. Romania's crude birthrate in 1967 jumped to 27 per 1,000—almost double the 1966 rate of 14 per 1,000. But as parents reverted to traditional methods of contraception (e.g., rhythm, withdrawal, abstinence), fertility dropped back toward the pre-1966 level. Between 1967 and 1972, the crude birthrate fell from 27 to 18.

But Romania is still paying for its artificial birthrate "blip." Infant mortality jumped and maternal death rates more than doubled between 1966 and 1967. Ceauşescu's edict also created a peculiar bulge in the Romanian age structure. To accommodate the needs of this "cohort" as it passed through the different stages of childhood and youth, Bucharest has been forced to create and then close down kindergartens, elementary schools, and health clinics—a costly proposition. Entirely apart from the damage done to Romanians' physical health, Bucharest's demographic shock may well have done more to retard the pace of economic progress than to hasten it.

Singapore has taken a more constant approach to population policy, and with the opposite end in view. Lee Kuan Yew, Singapore's prime minister since 1959 and the chief architect of its economic success, seems to be deeply impressed by some of the arguments of the prewar eugenicists. "We are getting a gradual lowering of the general quality of the total [world] population," Lee fretted in 1973. "Over the long run this could have very serious consequences for the human race."

For the island republic of Singapore, he sought "zero, possibly even negative [population] growth. Then we can make up for it with selective immigration of the kind of people we require to run a modern higher technology society."

Penalizing Big Families

Lee's vision of the solution was specific. "We must," he said, "encourage those who earn less than $200 a month [then about half of Singapore's households] never to have more than two [children]" so that Singapore might as its economy progressed be spared a "trend which can leave our society with a large number of the physically, intellectually, and culturally anemic."

In August 1972, Lee's government announced a new policy of "social disincentives against higher order births," to take effect the following year. Among the many disincentives were restrictions on maternity leaves for mothers bearing a third or higher-order child and the elimination of family tax deductions for children born fourth or later, as well as official discrimination against these children in public school placement.

The demographic impact of these strictures is unclear. It is true that since 1975—the third year of the "social disincentives" policy—Singapore's fertility rate has fallen. But the rate was already dropping before 1973, and Lee's new edicts do not appear to have hastened the speed of its fall.*

While the demographic consequences of Singapore's population sanctions are murky, some of the social and economic effects are unmistakable. Lee's program has reduced the living standards of Singaporeans who choose to have large families, widening income gaps in the nation. It has also created a new disadvantaged minority: the youngest children born to large families since August 1973.

Under Lee's law, these youngsters stand last in line for spots in the nation's desirable schools and universities, an important consideration in a society that places a premium on schooling. How the new "undesirables" will finally fare, and how their fate will affect Singapore, remains to be seen. The eldest are only 13 years old today.

VI

THE VALUE OF A LIFE

What, finally, can be said with confidence about the impact of population change on social and economic development in the Third World? As we have seen, much less than partisans in the population debate currently claim. So it may be appropriate to conclude with a few observations distinguished more by their tentativeness than by their insight.

First, population growth (or decline) is a relatively slow form of social change. A rate of population increase of four percent a year is extremely high; four percent price inflation a year is, today, generally

---

*Some family planning advocates claim that there is an enormous unmet need for birth control in the Third World, which only a 50 percent boost in outlays can satisfy. That claim is based on the results of surveys showing that many women say they want no more children or wish to delay the birth of their next child, and also say they are not using modern contraceptives. The researchers ignore the fact that many of these women may be using traditional birth control methods. In any case, Western survey methods are rarely reliable—especially among poor, uneducated people in less-developed nations. Moreover, the interrogators never put their questions to men, who, in many societies, have the final say in such matters.

*During the decade before the disincentives were announced, Singapore's birthrate dropped from 22 per 1,000 people to 17 per 1,000. Since 1973, Singaporeans *have* had smaller families. In 1980, fourth and higher-order births accounted for about seven percent of all live births—as against more than 28 percent in 1970. But this pattern was not distinctly different from those in comparable countries. In Hong Kong, which imposes no penalties for having large families, only nine percent of all births in 1980 were children born fourth or later.

37. Population and Economic Growth

CHINA

"Every stomach comes with hands attached," Chairman Mao once said in explaining his laissez-faire attitude toward population growth. In 1982, Beijing's census-takers counted one billion stomachs, nearly double the number in 1949, when Mao took power.

Mao's successors, led by Deng Xiaoping, had already rejected Mao's benign view. In 1979, they launched an ambitious population control program, calling on every couple to have a single child. "Husband and wife," declared the new constitution of 1982, "have a duty to practice family planning."

The intensity of China's "one-child" campaign has varied over time and from locale to locale. Billboards, newspapers, and radio broadcasts trumpet the message. Beijing offers economic rewards (e.g., cash awards and free medical care) to parents who agree to stop having children after their first child, and penalties (e.g., fines equalling 15 percent of family income for seven years) for those having a second child. At the height of the campaign in 1983, Beijing ordered the sterilization of one spouse in every couple with more than one child. Reports of forced abortions in China began reaching the West [see "The Mosher Affair," *WQ*, New Year's '84].

Deng has put population control near the top of the Chinese political agenda because he and his colleagues blame the nation's economic woes—occasional food shortages, unemployment, lackluster economic growth—on its vast human numbers. But studies by Western economists point directly at China's official policies—such as Mao's 1958 Great Leap Forward and the Cultural Revolution of the 1960s. According to K.C. Yeh of the Rand Corporation, for example, the overall efficiency of Chinese industry and agriculture fell by more than 25 percent between 1957 and 1978. If China had merely matched *India's* improvements in productivity during those years, its output per capita in 1978 would have been two-thirds greater than it was.

In the short term, Deng's "one-child" policy will surely work. Fertility, which had already dropped sharply during the 1970s, has continued to decline. By 1984, the Chinese population was growing by only 1.1 percent annually.

What price China will pay for this success is not yet entirely clear. Smaller families by themselves mean a lower quality of life for couples who desire more children. And, in the nation's fields and rice paddies, one-child families find themselves short-handed—especially if the child is a girl. Female infanticide seems to be on the upswing among China's peasants.

Moreover, limiting couples to one child may not be in the best interests of the country's future elderly population. China's parents must be asking themselves today: Will Beijing keep its promise to provide for them in their old age, when *their* child (and spouse) may be supporting four grandparents?

—*N. E.*

For nations that cope poorly in general, any quickening of the pace of change—including the rate of demographic change—is likely to cause difficulties. Yet adapting to novel conditions is in itself an integral part of modern economic development for any society. Development is in a sense a learning process. To the extent that population growth stimulates this learning process, it can accelerate a society's material progress.

Second, demographic change since World War II has typically been both benign and relatively favorable to economic growth. It has come about chiefly because of dramatic improvements in human health, lengthening the life expectancy of people all over the globe. Better health, moreover, can help augment human capital, which is the ultimate basis of economic productivity. Increasing human capital alone does not assure material progress; such progress depends on many other things, including the priorities governments place on developing and utilizing human talents. But it does make it *possible* to quicken the pace of economic advance.

Third, to assume, as many academics and public officials do, that preventing the birth of poor people will help eliminate poverty appears to be a fundamental error. Mass affluence is the result of human productivity and human organization, and it is not at all clear that these factors would be enhanced by falling birthrates, or, for that matter, by rising birthrates.

To make the economic case for aggressive population control, demographers and economists would have to show, in effect, that the cost of raising a child born in a particular society would be greater than his lifetime economic "value." That would be an extraordinarily difficult task. Economists and corporate executives constantly go astray in estimating the economic value of such relatively simple things as machinery, factories, and dams. Imagine how much more difficult it would be to determine the value of an unpredictable, living human being, or to have decided, in 1955, whether a baby born in Ghana was "worth" more than one born in South Korea.

Such population controls, in any realistic sense, would be fruitful *only* if no new technologies were ever created, societies did not change, and individuals were given few options in shaping their futures. That kind of world would be incompatible with the very essence of economic development, which is the successful management of change, and, ultimately, the extension of human choice.

There is little chance that enforced family planning in the Third World or elsewhere will yield benefits without great social costs and a sacrifice of human freedom. This approach reflects, as Peter Bauer notes, a contempt for ordinary people. In most of the countries where they have been tried, population policies, "soft" or "hard," have amounted to little more than attempts to solve through demographic tinkering economic problems that can, in fact, be traced to misguided governmental policies. To make a reduction of the birthrate the focus of so many high hopes is to divert attention and political energy from the real sources of poverty and lagging economic growth in many countries of the Third World.

considered to be blessedly low. And, for all the uncertainties of long-term population forecasting, *annual* shifts in the size and composition of a national population can be predicted with far greater accuracy than can changes in inflation, unemployment, the gross national product, or crop harvests.

BACKGROUND BOOKS

POPULATION AND ECONOMIC GROWTH

"The scourges of pestilence, famine, wars, and earthquakes have come to be regarded as a blessing to overcrowded nations, since they serve to prune away the luxuriant growth of the human race." So wrote the Christian theologian Tertullian during the second century A.D., when the earth's population was only about 300 million—or six percent of what it is today (five billion).

Tertullian's observation, and the book in which it appears—Garrett Hardin's **Population, Evolution and Birth Control** (W. H. Freeman, 1964, cloth; 1969, paper)—remind the reader that the Reverend Thomas R. Malthus (1766–1834) was not the first writer to reflect on the hazards of under- or overpopulation. Hardin pulled together a rich menu on the subject—everything from Han Fei-Tzu's fifth-century B.C. observations on fecundity and prosperity to the government of India's 1962 birth control campaign slogan: "Don't postpone the first, don't hurry up the second, and don't go in for the third."

Malthus's **Essay on the Principle of Population** (1798; Penguin, 1970, paper only) still stands as the single most influential work on population. The English economist's argument is well known: "It may be safely asserted," Malthus wrote, "that population, when unchecked, increases in a geometrical progression [whereas] the means of subsistence, under circumstances most favorable to human industry, could not possibly be made to increase faster than in an arithmetical ratio."

Thus Malthus, as Swedish sociologist Gunnar Myrdal observed 142 years later, "shifted the blame for misery from Society to Nature, from environment to heredity." Myrdal believed that a prudent society could control its own destiny. But in **Population: A Problem for Democracy** (Harvard, 1940), Myrdal foresaw a conflict in democratic countries between private wants (whether to have children) and public needs (to boost or limit population). "The population question," he predicted,

211

6. WORLD PROBLEMS AND INTERDEPENDENCE

"will dominate our whole economic and social policy for the entire future."

Myrdal's prognosis was at least partly correct. The immediate post–World War II years saw the appearance of several population "scare books." William Vogt's **Road to Survival** (William Sloane, 1948), for example, stressed what would become an oft-repeated theme: the interdependence between human beings and their planet. "An eroding hillside in Mexico or Yugoslavia," Vogt said, "affects the living standard and probability of survival of the American people." Vogt also alerted Americans to the increasing multitudes of "Moslems, Sikhs, Hindus (and their sacred cows)," whose populations ballooned due to "untrammeled copulation."

Paul R. Ehrlich's **Population Bomb** (River City, rev. ed., 1975, cloth; Ballantine, rev. ed., 1976, paper) dramatized the threat of overpopulation for the next generation of Americans. Only some five million people, Ehrlich estimated, had inhabited the planet in 6000 B.C. Doubling every 1,000 years, the world's population reached 500 million by A.D. 1650, and then began to accelerate rapidly. It doubled again in just 200 years, hitting one billion by 1850, and reached two billion by 1930. Should the world's population continue to grow by two percent annually (doubling every 35 years), Ehrlich warned, 60 million billion people (or 100 for every *square yard* of the globe's surface) would be swarming the earth by the year 2900.

Ehrlich also publicized many of the environmental hazards commonly associated with overpopulation and industrialization—such as the "greenhouse effect"—all well known today. A slight warming of the globe, resulting from an overabundance of carbon dioxide in the atmosphere, generated by the burning of fossil fuels, could melt the polar ice caps, raising ocean levels by some 250 feet. Asked Ehrlich: "Gondola to the Empire State Building, anyone?"

More recent works on the "population problem" are less apocalyptic, for several reasons. As Rafael M. Salas, executive director of the United Nations Fund for Population Activities, points out in **Reflections on Population** (Pergamon, 2nd ed., 1986), the *rate* of population growth worldwide has dropped dramatically, from 2.03 percent in 1970–75 to 1.67 percent in 1980–85. Demographers now expect the globe's population to hit 6.1 billion by A.D. 2000, and level off at 10.2 billion by the end of the next century. And, "despite rapid population growth," as the National Research Council's scholarly **Population Growth and Economic Development** (National Academy, 1986, paper only) observes, "developing countries have achieved unprecedented levels of income per capita, literacy, and life expectancy over the last 25 years."

Much current research focuses on the environmental (rather than the economic) effects of population growth. The best, most comprehensive surveys include **State of the World 1986** by Lester Brown et al. (Norton, 1986, cloth & paper); the World Resources Institute's **World Resources 1986** (Basic, 1986, cloth & paper); and economist Robert Repetto's **Global Possible** (Yale, 1985, cloth & paper). All of these works emphasize that the "state of the world" varies from country to country. Two of the 23 scientists and environmentalists who contributed to Repetto's book, for example, found that the rate of annual deforestation ranges from a safe 0.6 percent of all woodlands in the Congo and Zaire to a dangerous four to six percent in the Ivory Coast and Nigeria. Limiting population, Repetto says, is just one way to help preserve world resources. Governments, he stresses, must also provide better management of land, forests, and waterways. Underdeveloped countries, meanwhile, need easier access to credit, new technologies, and small-scale investment.

Indeed, these three books suggest that the "spaceship earth" approach to population and development problems may be misguided. As former *New York Times*man Pranay Gupte writes in his highly readable **Crowded Earth** (Norton, 1984), "people do not live on the 'globe' but in villages and towns, within the walls of their houses or shacks or tenements."

Gupte spent 14 months traveling through 38 impoverished countries around the world to discover how ordinary people cope in overpopulated and underdeveloped communities.

He spoke, for example, with Ibrahim Mesahi, a grocery store owner in bustling downtown Lagos. The population of Nigeria's capital shot up, largely through in-migration, from 1.4 million in 1970 to 3.6 million in 1985. But Gupte found that Mesahi had no interest in birth control, at least not for himself. "I need all the help I can get," explained Mesahi. "I have 10 boys and one girl... with my children, at least I can watch them. They are honest."

The author, however, still favors population education programs. "When it is demonstrated to people that 'small is beautiful,'" he says, "their choice will be for small families, not large ones."

CHINA GOES TO TOWN

Richard Kirkby describes the changing pattern of urban growth in China since 1949

Dr Richard Kirkby is an urban planner and an independent consultant on China

CHINA is often cited as one of the world's great agrarian nations. Yet in its long history of civilization, China has also been a nation of great and sophisticated cities. Witness, for example, the economic, social and cultural complexities of Hangzhou which dazzled Marco Polo 700 years ago. When, in the 1840s, unwelcome visitors from the West began to come to China in large numbers, they found what was probably a more highly urbanized society than existed at the time in Europe. But unlike Europe, the Chinese city had never developed an independent purpose founded on commercialism which could lead to a process of industrialization and challenge the fabric of rurally-based feudal rule.

The modern history of China's urbanization begins with the growth of those cities which expanded in the late 19th century as industrial and port centres serving the needs of foreigners. Prominent among them were Shanghai and Tianjin. These developments remained peripheral and by the declaration of the People's Republic in 1949, only one-tenth of China's half billion population were considered urban. The Chinese Communist Party (CPC) has presided over an industrial revolution comparable in scale and pace only to that of the Soviet Union in the early 1930s.

From the late 1950s to the late 1970s, reliable population figures for China were entirely lacking. The image which China sought to project during this period was one of vigorous industrial growth without the urbanization associated with capitalist, or indeed, Soviet industrial revolutions. The attempt to eradicate the distinction between town and country, as called for by Marx and Engels, was sometimes claimed as an achievement in Mao's China.

Yet the information now available shows that the development process since 1949 has echoed the experience of other industrially-developing countries, industrialization being accompanied by dramatic growth in its urban population. What is peculiar to the Chinese experience is the erratic course of that growth. And China has not industrialized without a price being paid by the rural population. From the mid-1950s until the late 1970s the relation between levels of agricultural and industrial prices did not alter much in the peasants' favour. Neither was there much overall improvement in rural per capita consumption. The notion that the Maoist development model was intrinsically anti-urban and pro-rural is no longer acceptable.

With the exception of the Great Leap Forward period of the late 1950s the Chinese government has shown extreme caution regarding the pace of growth of the non-agricultural population. The CPC was conscious that its hegemony might well be threatened if it were unable to adequately house, employ, defend, control and above all, feed its urban citizens. Thus an essential feature of China's planned economy has been the array of administrative controls over personal mobility.

During the early 1950s, pressure on the cities led to the introduction of a residence monitoring system overseen by local police stations. Without urban household registration, it was not easy to survive in the cities, for access to housing, employment and most vitally, food rations would be denied.

SPORADICALLY from the early 1950s on, these controls were complemented by the 'sending down' campaigns which thrust huge numbers of unwanted peasant migrants, urban officials, and particularly school leavers from the urban system.

The most drastic period of expulsion occurred during the 1960s, when up to 20 million people who had left agriculture during the Great Leap Forward (1958-9) were returned to their villages. And in the years of the Cultural Revolution (1966-76), perhaps 16 million urban youths were sent down to the people's communes and to the state farms of the peripheral provinces. Measures to control migration, and, periodically, to decant huge numbers of urban dwellers down the hierarchy of settlements, were always intended to serve, rather than confound, the essentially urban-based industrialization process by keeping the cities both politically and economically manageable.

To make sense of the eccentric urbanization process in the People's Republic of China it is first necessary to understand the basis of Chinese urban statistics of the 1980s. These give rise to two main measures of urban-ness, both of which enumerate population in those settlements administratively designated as towns (*zhen*) and municipalities (*shi*). The distinction between the two series of data is that the larger, more broadly-defined one (which has enjoyed official status since the 1982 census), includes all the population resident in the urban districts of the shi whether they be agricultural or non-agricultural in terms of household registration. The more restricted series used before 1982 excluded the registered agricultural population within shi districts.

A further complicating factor in analyzing China's overall urban population is that since 1958, municipalities of a certain rank have been able to annex surrounding rural counties.

6. WORLD PROBLEMS AND INTERDEPENDENCE

Neither data series includes the population of the countries annexed by municipalities. This process has been accelerated in recent years so that today in many provinces all the counties fall under municipal jurisdiction. Definite administrative control by a city over its hinterland is necessary in order to ensure the supply of grain, vegetables and industrial inputs (including labour).

Study of both series of data showing urban growth since 1949 reveals the same main features. Rapid growth in the 1950s accompanied the first stage in the nation's industrialization. By the end of the 1950s, the Great Leap Forward propelled millions out of agriculture and by 1960 China's urban population had more than doubled on its 1950 figure (61.9 million to 130 million using the more restricted data series). There was an equally dramatic decline in the urban population between 1965 and 1975 leading to a very slow rate of growth of urban population. However the last decade has witnessed rapid urbanization.

This latest sudden surge in the process of urbanization is a consequence of several related factors. Many of those expelled, including the majority of the young people sent down during the Cultural Revolution, managed to return to the urban areas. Second, delayed marriages by many of these returnees have exaggerated the fact that they themselves are a disproportionate section of the urban population, being the result of a bulge in the birth rate in the mid 1950s. The result has been a rise in the natural rate of population increase since the early 1980s despite the well-known 'one child' policy of the present period. The last factor has been the relaxation of the state controls on population mobility. Vast numbers of rural dwellers have entered the urban areas, though in the larger centres they might not directly achieve any permanent status and be incorporated in official statistics.

There is also a strong element of statistical exaggeration behind the surge in urbanization in the 1980s as the larger data series, first used as the official measure in the 1982 census, has been greatly affected by the recent enthusiasm of the Chinese authorities for chartering new urban places. In 1976 there were just 189 shi, while today there are over 300.

DESIGNATIONS of towns has been even more dramatic, particularly since 1984 when criteria were changed nearly doubling the number of zhen to more than 6000. As a consequence, the official figure for China's aggregate urban population was swollen from 241.28 to 330.06 million in a single year (1983-84). With registered agricultural persons making up almost half of the new total, the current official measure of urban-ness looks decidedly arbitrary.

The pressure on the cities of recent years has highlighted the need for an effective national urbanization strategy going far beyond the sloganizing of the Cultural Revolution. By the early 1980s, Chinese urbanists were expressing great concern about the slow pace of growth of the small centres, and the increasing share of the nation's urban population and economic activities accounted for by the very large cities. Numerous studies pointed out that in 1953, China only had nine cities of more than one million inhabitants and 16 cities of from 0.5 to one million inhabitants. By 1982 these had increased to 20 and 28 respectively. If the larger measure of urban-ness is used (including the agricultural households in the immediate urban peripheries) then we could speak of 38 'million cities' and a further 47 of from 0.5 to one million inhabitants, between them accounting for 75 per cent of the national urban total.

The Chinese experience has been that the larger the urban centre, the worse the condition of housing, infrastructure, and the prospects for future expansion. Yet state economic policies since 1978 have threatened to swamp the existing cities with farmers

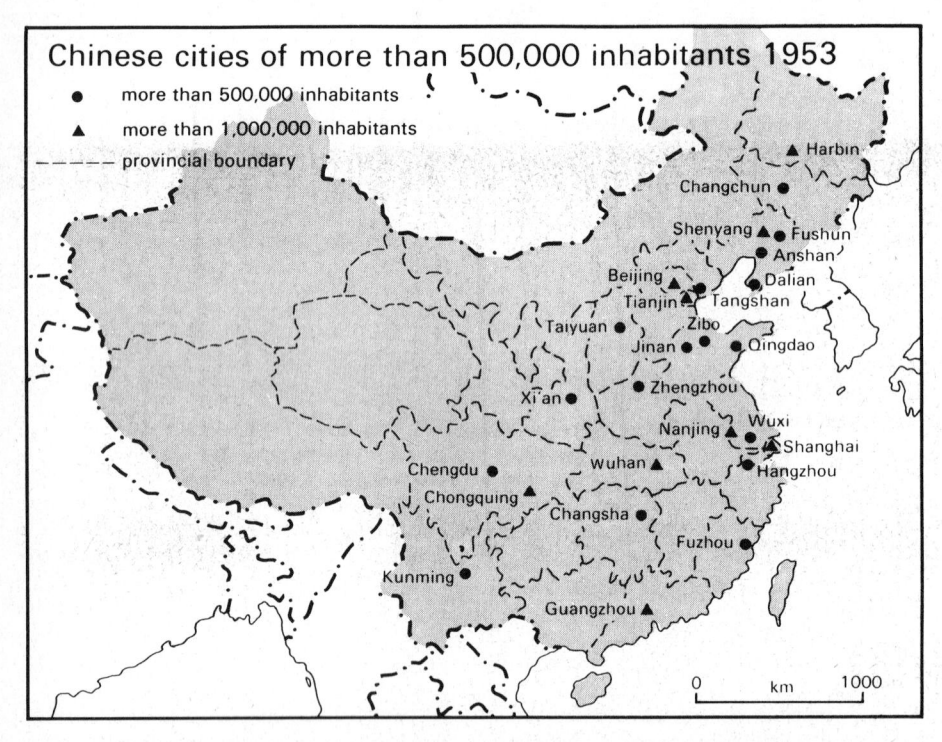

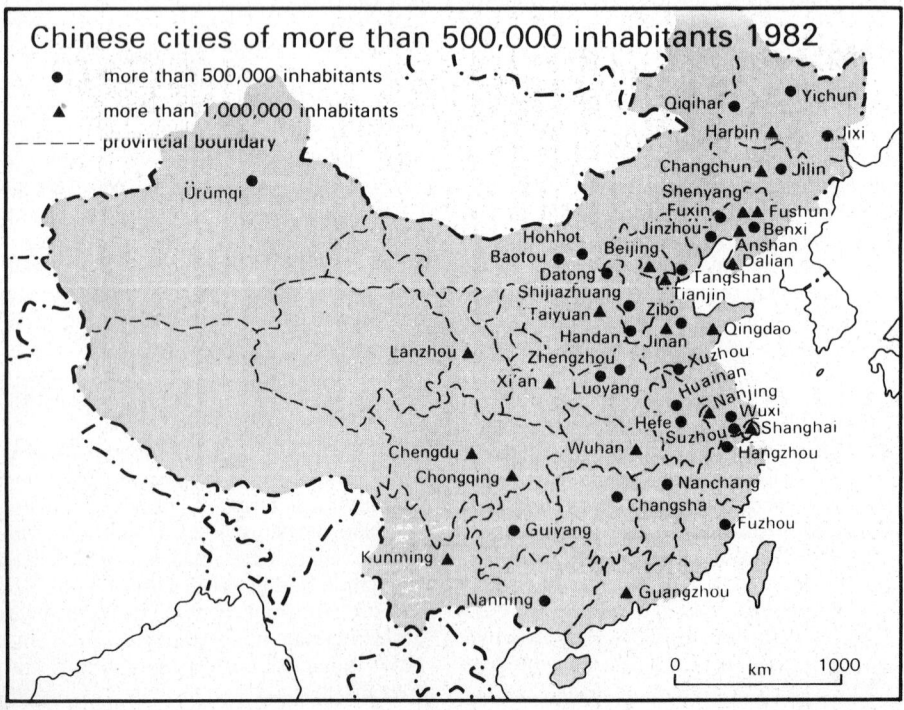

38. China Goes to Town

The urbanization process in China has been remarkable mainly in one respect; their commitment to welfare has meant that the mass urban squalor of capitalist industrial revolutions has been absent in China.

leaving the land. The swift demise of the familiar system of collective agriculture (the people's communes) revealed a situation of substantial rural overemployment. Suddenly, one third of the rural workforce (more than 100 million agricultural workers) were said to be surplus to the requirements of crop production.

OVERALL, in the three decades from 1949 onward, a virtual doubling of population combined with a steady net loss of land to construction projects had reduced the per capita cultivable area by almost half.

The potential pressures on the cities which these facts suggest led in 1980 to the formulation of a strategic policy for ubanization to: 'Strictly control the development of the large cities (above 0.5 million), rationally develop medium-sized cities (from 0.2 - 0.5 million) and vigorously promote the development of the small cities and towns'. This seemed to express no more than a pious hope in a period of slackening controls over migration, and of greater emphasis on the benefits to productivity of urban-industrial concentration.

In an effort, however, to prove that a small towns policy was viable, it became *de rigeur* for every writer on the subject to speculate on the capacity of China's tens of thousand of small rural townships (including the now more than 6000 zhen, and the 54,000 former seats of the people's communes) to absorb the hundreds of millions unwanted in crop production. A copious literature has proclaimed the virtues of a 'Chinese road to urbanization' founded on the development of small towns.

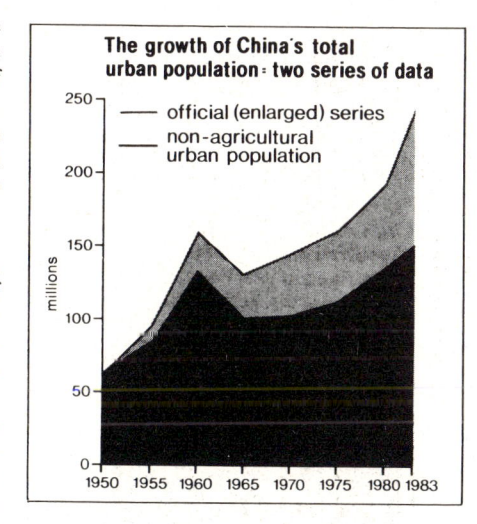

In the event, the experience of the past six years has indeed shown the enormous potential for expansion of China's small rural settlements. For instance, in 1982 rural enterprises employed around 31 million, two-thirds of them in manufacturing and processing. Just three years later, the village and township enterprise workforce had doubled to 60 million. In those eastern areas of the country, particularly the provinces of Jiangsu, Zhejiang and Shandong where pressure on the land is greatest, the new industries have managed to absorb the rural workforce displaced from crop growing. The extraordinarily rapid growth of China's industrial output since 1979 is due in large measure to the expansion of the rural industry sector.

The remarkable development of rural industry has not been without problems, for most of the small enterprises lack management expertise, technology and workforce skills (a recent survey showed that they averaged only nine skilled workers per thousand). Frequently they are forced out of business by state decree or simply by competition from large-scale and efficient big city plants. A major problem lies in their emission of pollutants and few rural centres are developing according to any unified spatial or economic plan.

Over the past five years official policy towards rural industries can be described as one of benign neglect. Today, however, it is recognized that if the small settlements which play host to rural enterprises are to provide a viable location for the hundreds of millions who are expected to leave agriculture in the

6. WORLD PROBLEMS AND INTERDEPENDENCE

years ahead, positive intervention from state agencies will be necessary. Measures currently under proposal are a limitation of small-scale manufacturing to certain activities, the systematic training of rural school leavers in science and technology, and above all the further development of the economic web which links smaller industrial producers to larger ones. Industrial plants in large centres will be encouraged to provide capital, cast-off equipment and expertise to subsidiary rural-based units. In the rural areas surrounding the larger cities, this is already widespread.

China is currently facing a revolution in employment and population distribution of historic proportions. Transition from an agricultural to an industrial society without wholesale uprooting of vast numbers of peasants from their native places will require strong national policies in support of small town development.

To date, the urbanization process in China has been remarkable mainly in one respect; a strong state commitment to welfare has meant that the mass urban squalor of capitalist industrial revolutions has here been absent. Yet the scale, pace and distributional features of urban growth have not been so different from elsewhere. If the small town/small industries strategy can be successfully sustained, however, we can anticipate a truly novel pattern of urbanization; the hundreds of millions displaced from the soil will not be forced to the fringes of the large cities, but will settle to a new life in the myriad townships of the Chinese countryside.

CAPITAL OF DREAMS

Paul Forster looks at the past, and the prospects, of Brasilia

Paul Forster
Paul Forster is a freelance photo-journalist

At the beginning of March this year, scaffolding once again decorated the facade of the Ministry of Justice in Brasilia, Brazil's futuristic capital. Surprisingly, workmen were not repairing the notorious marble tiles, added to the 'egalitarian' concrete during the recent 21 years of military dictatorship, but removing them. The architect, Oscar Neimeyer, was pleased and the popular press proclaimed another democratic triumph, albeit minor, for the year-old-civilian government.

Only a month before, a combined ministry building and cultural centre was commissioned despite a self-imposed one year moratorium on federal construction projects and the estimated US$15-20 million cost. The architect, again, is to be Niemeyer who was given seven months to complete the plans.

No stranger to haste or public discussion, Neimeyer, now 79, first arrived on the rolling upland plains of Brazil's *planalto* in November 1956. No plans had been finalized for the new capital; the site was 125 kilometres from the nearest railway, 640 km from the nearest paved road and 190 km from the nearest airport. Gravel and sand were available not too far away, but timber was 1200 km distant and steel, 1600 km. In the face of all this, Brasilia had to be inaugurated on April 21, 1960, because President Juscelino Kubitschek was obliged by law to step down in October of that year and he was determined to leave a new capital as his personal memorial.

The plan was audacious but not new. The first recorded demand for an inland Brazilian capital was in 1789. In 1821 Jose Bonifacio de Andrade e Silva, the patriarch of Brazilian independence announced that a central city would encourage 'the prompt circulation of government communications and the commercial development of the Empire of Brazil'. The name Brasilia first appeared in 1822 and in 1833 an Italian priest, Dom Bosco, had his famous dream: 'Between the 15th and 20th parallels, where a lake had formed, a great civilisation will be born'.

In 1889 Brazil became a republic and in the first constitution of 1891, Article Three read: 'From now on, an area of 14,400 square kilometres will belong to the government for the creation of a new capital'. Possible sites were surveyed in 1892 and Theodore

Brasilia, although built more than 20 years ago, still retains the futuristic look that made it so startling in 1960. The roof of the National Congress building attracts the public to the 'dome' of the Federal Senate and the 'cup' of the Deputies Chamber.

6. WORLD PROBLEMS AND INTERDEPENDENCE

Roosevelt, visiting the western edge of the planalto in 1913 wrote: 'Any sound northern race could live here; and in such a land, with such a climate, there would be much joy of living'. A symbolic cornerstone was placed in 1922 and in 1934 President Getulio Vargas included "The capital of the republic will be transferred to a centrally-located point in Brazil' in his new constitution. Still, very little actually happened until January 1953 when Vargas, again President, announced the final demarcation for the new city: 15°30' to 17° South and 46°30' to 49°30' West. In 1954, Donald J. Belcher and Associates of Ithaca, New York won the contract for the aerial survey of the site, but later that year Vargas committed suicide.

Juscelino Kubitschek won the ensuing contest for the presidency narrowly, and made plans for a massive expansion of the economy. When asked about Brasilia he replied: 'I will implement the constitution'. Brasilia wouuld symbolise his efforts 'to provide the nation with a foundation for economic development and a stable and democratic political order', but it would have to be finished before his term of office expired, as the next incumbent would have little enthusiasm for finishing a project so strongly associated with the previous regime. In 1956 Kubitschek formed NOVACAP (Companhia Urbanizadora da Nova Capital) headed by Dr Israel Pinheiro da Silva. Rio's *Correio da Manha* commented: 'The limit of insanity! A dictatorship in the desert! and *O Globo* succinctly: 'Madness!'; but Kubitschek sensed that the time was right: 'The capital is moving, and anyone who tries to stop it will be lynched by the people'.

Rio de Janeiro, the old capital city, certainly had its problems: population growth had stretched the housing and transport facilities beyond the possibilities of its physical geography. Even J.O. de Meria Perna, in an essay published by the Brazilian Institute of Geography and Statistics in 1958, pointed out that: 'A centrally located capital . . . might make Brazil more conscious of her role in the Americas . . . and turn the elites from their nearly exclusive interest in Europe' and that 'as Rio is so untypical of most of Brazil, a move to Brasilia might put the politicians more in touch with the real problems of the country'. What actually prompted the move though, apart from Kubitschek's megalomania, was the fact that for the first time Brazil's construction and communications industries were equal to the task.

So was Kubitschek's old friend Oscar Niemeyer. He had worked with Le Corbusier from 1937 to 1943 on the Ministry of Education and Health building in Rio. When Kubitschek called on Niemeyer in September 1956, his office was dealing with more than sixty commissions from all over the world. In the same month NOVACAP held a competition judged by an international panel which included Niemeyer, to determine the plan for the new city. The sketchy but inspired plan of Lucio Costa was selected out of 26 entries.

Costa was a modernist, the movement so effectively promoted by Le Corbusier, who opened his seminal book *The City of Tomorrow* (1924) with the sentence 'A town is a tool'. Costa's plan laid out the city co-axially in the shape of an aeroplane. The body, or Monumental Axis, would house the government buildings, the cathedral and the banking, cultural and entertainment areas, while the residential zones, the embassies, hotels and churches would be in the 'wings' — the Residential Axis. Road junctions were to be eliminated, pedestrians separated from traffic, and heavy goods vehicles separated from cars. The 'superblock' accommodation units were to be surrounded by greenery and would be 'no higher than a mother could call to a playing child'. Furthermore there was to be 'no undue and undesirable stratification of society': senators and their chauffeurs were to live in the same buildings. Never before had the principles of the Modern Movement been applied so completely and on so great a scale.

Forty thousand men were drafted to the area, mainly from the poor and drought-stricken northeast, and immediately began working around the clock in a spirit of wild pioneering. Kubitschek orated and raised money. He had planned that the city would pay for itself through the sale of rapidly

Brasilia was originally planned to contain a centre on an intimate scale, giving life and human quality to the core of the city. However, the main roads now effectively divide up the centre.

39. Capital of Dreams

The W3 road runs up to the area called the 'Monumental Axis', containing government buildings, cultural centres and banks.

$600 million before the inauguration.

Six months later Kubitschek stood down and Janio Quadros was returned with the biggest majority ever accorded a Brazilian President. He broadcast to the nation: 'We must pay back nearly two billion dollars in foreign loans during my five year term alone. All this money, spent with so much publicity, we must now raise — bitterly, patiently, dollar by dollar, cruzeiro by cruzeiro . . .' Niemyer recorded at the time: 'We felt, deeply, that our work in Brasilia was paralysed' and moved to Israel. From 1961 to 1974 he returned to Brazil only occasionally.

INITIALLY Brasilia failed: there was no immediate transfer of government activity and the haste with which the project had been completed became evident. The air-conditioning in the legislative halls refused to work, only four of the 11 ministry buildings were usable and one half of all federal employees were officially 'without residence'. Quadros accomplished little before his chaotic resignation in May 1962. He was succeeded by his Vice-President, Joao Goulart, who regarded Brasilia as an extravagant, anti-social waste of resources and the prime initiator of Brazil's inflationary spiral. The city and the dream were ready to flounder.

In April 1964 a military coup brought General Castelo Branco to the helm. He was torn between 'the folly of finishing Brasilia and the crime of abandoning her', but decided to persevere; the monumental emphasis suited the military mentality and the new programmes of discipline and reform. The administration of the city was reformed and a new municipal prefecture, Co-ordination and Development of Brasilia, took over all the main planning responsibilities. Niemeyer and Costa remained as token members on an advisory council, but their left-wing views ensured that their opinions were received with little sympathy. After Niemeyer recieved the Lenin Peace Prize, one official announced that 'The place for a Marxist architect is in Moscow' and his distinctive plan for Brasilia's airport was replaced by one produced by the Ministry of Aeronautics.

Brasilia has had no shortage of critics. When Simone de Beauvoir visited Brasilia in 1963 with Jean-Paul Sartre, she wrote: 'What possible interest could there be in wandering around the six or eight storey quadra and superquadra . . . exuding the same air of elegant monotony'; and the Journal of the Royal Institute of British Architects published an ironic quiz of photographs taken in Brasilia's 'satellite' towns under the title of 'The Moon's backside'. There has however, been little analysis of why the new capital was less than perfect.

Lewis Mumford, in a 1962 article entitled 'Yesterday's City of Tommorrow', suggested that the principles proposed by Le Corbusier in the 1920s and 1930s were simplistic and already out of date by the time they were

appreciating plots of land, but this failed and he was forced to inject funds (raised abroad and from the emission of paper *cruzeiros*) through various government agencies. As Niemeyer himself put it: '. . . there prevailed an enthusiasm we had never before encountered, a determination and sporting spirit that got round every difficulty'.

As April 21, 1960, approached the pace became more and more frenetic: 2000 steel lamp posts were installed in one day, overnight 722 houses were painted and as *The Times* of April 21 reported: 'As midnight approached (on the 20th) . . . workers were still busy preparing buildings for occupants, planting grass and trees and laying pavings'. Exactly three years, one month and five days after the selection of the masterplan, a reported 150,000 people turned up for the inauguration ceremonies; 5000 dignitaries scrambled for the 150 first-class rooms available; 5000 troops and 10,000 workers paraded and 38 tons of fireworks were ignited.

When the smoke cleared, the critics were for a moment silenced: an infrastructure of roads was complete, as were the Presidential Palace, the Brasilia Palace hotel, the Supreme Court, the Palace of the Planalto, the National Congress, 11 government ministries, 94 apartment blocks, 500 one-storey houses, 222 two-storey houses and their local schools and shops. Most importantly, but almost overshadowed by the construction of the city, the first Latin American highway between the Atlantic and the Pacific had been pushed 3200 km through the Matto Grosso and 2200 km of road linked Brasilia to Belem on the mouth of the Amazon.

Kubitschek had lived up to his campaign promise of 'fifty years progress in five' as far as Brasilia was concerned, but at what cost? Niemeyer's now famous reply to Max Lock's question about the cost of the Presidential Palace: 'I do not know. How should I know?' sums up the attitude of the planners. Lincoln Gordon, the American Under-Secretary of State and ex-ambasador to Brazil made the most informed assessment when reporting to the House of Representatives in 1966: US

219

6. WORLD PROBLEMS AND INTERDEPENDENCE

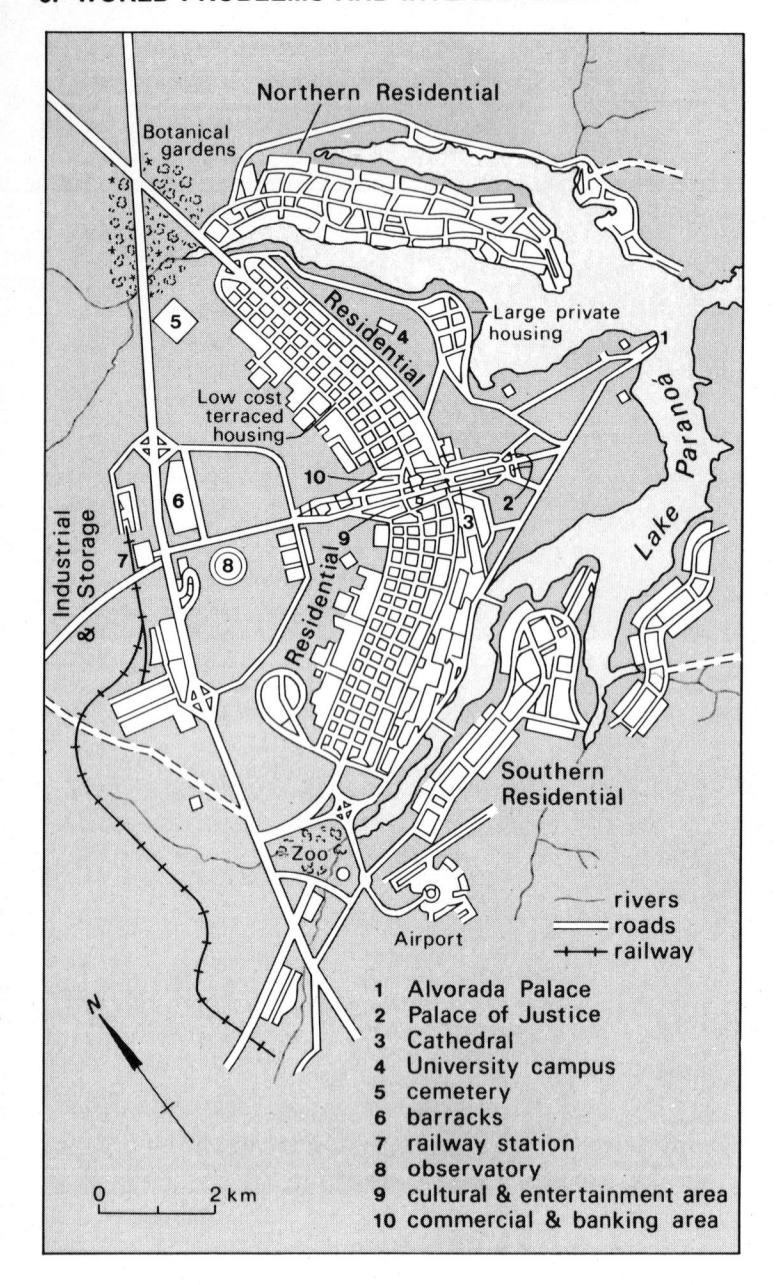

[Map of Brasília with legend:
- Northern Residential
- Botanical gardens
- Residential
- Large private housing
- Low cost terraced housing
- Industrial & Storage
- Southern Residential
- Zoo
- Airport
- Lake Paranoá
- rivers, roads, railway

1 Alvorada Palace
2 Palace of Justice
3 Cathedral
4 University campus
5 cemetery
6 barracks
7 railway station
8 observatory
9 cultural & entertainment area
10 commercial & banking area]

realized in Costa's plan: 'Le Corbusier overemphasized the new mechanical facilities and equated urban progress with geometrical order, rectilinear planning and mechanized bureaucratic organization'. Costa also patently failed to make any long-range provisions for the future growth of the Federal District, but since the inception of the *Plano piloto* the problem has been compounded by total absence of any large-scale conception of urban design. This may well have resulted from the edging out of Niemeyer and Costa by a military regime unsympathetic to their ideals, and has certainly resulted in all Brasilia's major problems.

In 1976, 400,000 middle and upper income people lived within Costa's original plan, while an estimated 600,000 lower income people inhabited the so called 'satellite' towns, which did not appear on the prize-winning design and consisted of ramshackle shanties and gridiron 'aid' projects. At the very centre of the city, Costa had envisaged an area 'resembling the streets and squares of Venice', which was 'to be small in scale with a visual complexity giving colour and life to the centre and offsetting the vast Monumental Axis'. Kubitschek, however, had dealt with the large and costly elements of the plan first and ignored the small-scale; and by the time development of the city centre did take place, the area had been zoned and divided by large roads in direct contradiction of the pilot plan.

Similarly, the area planned for exclusive residential houses on the south side of the lake has been developed in a haphazard fashion and the north side of the lake, planned as a series of parks and public places, has been occupied by private clubs, effectively cutting the city off from the lake. George Balcome, who visited Brasilia in 1960 on a Leverhulme travel grant, suggested that Costa's social ideas were too far ahead of the existing patterns of Brazilian society.

On a smaller, more practical level, the shops in the residential areas open onto the service roads and not onto the apartment blocks as was intended, and there is a distinct shortage of the street-corner bars and markets that are such an important feature of Brazilian life elswhere. The trees designed to screen the apartments from the road are generally missing and many of the open-plan ministries have been partitioned with plywood.

The local residents, one feels, have come to terms with the place. Ministerial assistants complain of still having to live in hotels though, and shop assistants face a long uncomfortable bus journey to and from their 'satellite' homes. Well-to-do professionals appreciate the smooth mechanics of life in Brasilia and realize the advantages for their children.

BRASILIA is not the egalitarian paradise its planners had dreamt of, nor is it a particulariy pleasant town; it will take more than a new cultural centre to make up for the vacuum that is the city centre. Perhaps if they had taken note of Frank Lloyd Wright, who wrote in 1932 that 'Architectural values are human values or they are not valuable', the city would be more suitable for pleasant living rather than efficient working.

It must not be forgotten though that Brasilia is still not finished. Niemeyer has plans to design a public library and a museum of Indian life, but it is the wastelands between the buildings, the pedestrian tracks around the traffic interchanges and the general lack of municipal care and detail that really let the place down. Still, children do play in the open spaces around their apartment blocks, as they were intended to do, and due to the sheer speed with which the city was conceived and built, it represents a particular moment in the history of architecture on a scale which is undeniably stunning.

Brasilia's greatest triumph though, is not to be seen in Brasilia at all but in the states of Goias and Minas Gerais and in the towns of Belo Horizonte, Manaus and Belem where the new capital has increased prosperity and provided new opportunities for study and jobs — the objectives of the very oldest of the proposals to provide Brazil with a new inland capital.

THE ZEAL OF DISAPPROVAL

Michael Brown

Michael Brown is the author of The Toxic Cloud, *a book to be published by Harper & Row.*

It began on the high, hostile seas in French Polynesia, in an official "forbidden zone." A tiny band of Canadian ecologists, calling themselves Greenpeace, had been demonstrating against atmospheric atomic bomb testing. But none had made it to an actual test site. None had even caught a glimpse of a mushroom cloud.

Now, David McTaggart was practically in the target zone.

The year was 1972. The sea roiled with warships. Any moment, McTaggart says, he expected "scorching walls of heat, blinding unearthly light, shock waves coming across the water like freight trains."

McTaggart and a two-man crew had made the 3,000-mile voyage from New Zealand to the atoll of Mururoa on McTaggart's 38-foot ketch, *Vega*. Now officers from France's Centre d'Experimentations Nucleaires du Pacifique were urgently trying to shoo them away so the test weapon could be detonated.

A disenchanted Canadian construction magnate who dropped out to become a South Pacific vagabond, McTaggart had read a small item in a New Zealand newspaper about a group calling itself "Greenpeace" and decided to lead the protest. He did it almost as a dare, as a sailing adventure. Suddenly, though, the adventure turned dangerous. McTaggart was approaching 40 and his birthday candle could be ten megatons.

Spotting the dirigible carrying the bomb, McTaggart and his crew managed to delay the test by maneuvering into the fallout zone. But they were soon rammed from behind by a minesweeper and forced to leave the area. A year later, when McTaggart tried again to disrupt a nuclear test at Mururoa, French commandos boarded his ketch and clubbed him so severely that they left him partially blind.

Thus was born Greenpeace International, arguably the world's most effective ecological organization. McTaggart has been its guiding spirit since 1973 and became its first elected chairman in 1979. With his leadership, the group has grown into a network of chapters in 17 countries, with 250 paid staffers and 1.5 million contributing members. Its boats range from England's North Sea to Antarctica. It practices a brand of environmentalism unique in an otherwise staid field—what McTaggart calls "non-violent direct action."

Their method works, but clearly carries some risks. Publicity over McTaggart's 1973 beating forced France to halt atmospheric testing. Last year, French secret service agents created an international scandal when, bent on preventing a protest against underground nuclear tests at Mururoa, they blew a hole in the Greenpeace ship *Rainbow Warrior,* sinking the vessel and killing a photographer who was on board. The embarrassment reached the highest levels of the French government, forcing François Mitterand's defense minister to resign. France has since paid New Zealand $7 million in compensation and apologized for the sabotage—and is being sued by Greenpeace.

Since McTaggart assumed leadership, Greenpeace members have landed in Siberia and challenged a Russian whaling ship in dinghies. They have parachuted from an Ohio smokestack to protest acid rain, plugged a chemical-effluent pipe in New Jersey, and attempted to plug radioactive-waste pipes in England. The group was a major force in halting the dumping of radioactive materials in the ocean. It was also instrumental in reducing the annual slaughter of Canadian harp seal pups by 90 percent and in pressuring the International Whaling Commission to vote a moratorium on commercial whaling.

McTaggart and his group are determined to protect the earth, the oceans, and all living beings—including humans—from man's depredations. Their name defines their ultimate goal: a restored and healthy world, peaceful and green. In its pursuit, they will tackle any promising target, from a national government to a single fishing boat. Their methods are eclectic and frequently improvisational: At one point, they spray-painted harp seal pups green to make the pelts unsalable. "The only rule we have is nonviolence," says McTaggart. "And boy, you can go a long way with that."

6. WORLD PROBLEMS AND INTERDEPENDENCE

Greenpeace's international headquarters are on the top two floors of a post-World War II building in the ancient town of Lewes, set in the sedate, hilly countryside of Sussex, south of London, England. It is a peaceful place with winding, cobbled streets, and sheep grazing along the nearby rail line.

Inside, 20 or so young workers (the average Greenpeacer is about 30) monitor projects around the globe. In the large room outside the modest executive offices, under a row of clocks showing the time around the world, Roger Wilson, project coordinator, and a couple of assistants map strategy for a permanent Antarctic base. Starting a few months ago, some Greenpeacers began living there year round. Greenpeace has declared Antarctica a "world park" in an effort to block exploitation of this last unsettled continent and, typically, it plans to take whatever action seems appropriate. According to the executive director, John Frizell, this is the first time they have attempted to head off significant damage before it's done. "If we see something we should take direct action on, we will," says Wilson.

The four (Wilson will remain at headquarters) will observe Russian fishing in coastal waters, particularly of Antarctic cod, which, says Greenpeace, has been decimated. They will also keep an eye on the American base at McMurdo Sound, where, they say, radiation may have remained when a nuclear power station was dismantled, and leaking oil drums have in the past been allowed to pollute the environment. "Our goal is to make our voice there very hard to ignore," says Frizell. "We don't want Antarctica torn to pieces."

> *Greenpeace dates to 1970, when a handful of Canadians met to protest American hydrogen bomb tests in the Aleutian Islands.*

Greenpeace staff members are as free-spirited as McTaggart. Like him, he says, they are "a little frustrated with the political and legal system." Frustrated enough to work for half the pay they could get elsewhere. Frustrated enough to row in dinghies out to a ship about to dump nuclear wastes and hold steady directly under the waste-laden derricks. Or to board another nuclear-waste ship. Or to lash themselves to whaling harpoons. And that boldness is matched by a certain cleverness: One Greenpeacer became a client of Lloyd's of London to gain access to a maritime computer that tracked Japanese whaling ships.

Dressed in plaid and denim, with shaggy hair or beards, these young ecologists exude the old idealistic zeal last seen among anti-Vietnam protesters. Many of them are scientists: Alan Pickaver, coordinator of the ocean ecology program, has a doctorate in microbiology and lectured at Trinity College. Frizell did his graduate work in biochemistry.

In the communications room, secretaries tap into computer terminals or review telex sheets. On the wall behind them is an oil painting of a lonely ship on a hazy night. The calm ends with the appearance of David McTaggart from behind an inner door. He swirls with energy, his eyes busy and piercing blue. "There's a mayor in Italy who's trying to keep nuclear reactors out of his village," he says excitedly. "Let's send him a telex. He's just a little guy and he could use our support. He's ready to go to bloody jail."

McTaggart did not invent Greenpeace; it dates to 1970, when a handful of Canadians (only a few of whom are with the organization today) met to protest American hydrogen bomb tests in the Aleutian Islands. But McTaggart is its real founder and, to a large extent, he personifies the organization. His early adventures with French authorities put Greenpeace on the map, attracting much attention, and much of its early funding. At 55, McTaggart is balding, with gray hair tufting out over his ears. And though he runs a multimillion dollar operation that routinely tangles with corporate giants and heads of state, there is little pretension about him. He doesn't mention that his supporters include celebrities ranging from George Harrison to Carl Sagan. He wears a turtleneck under an open-necked shirt and, like the rest of the Greenpeacers, a pair of jeans.

The organization he has put together is a bit old-fashioned for the 1980s. It resembles the peace groups that formed and re-formed during the '60s and early '70s. In part, its growth has been haphazard and serendipitous. "New staff members are just pulled in," says the serious, lanky Frizell. "At first, they volunteer. When their savings run out, Greenpeace gives them a salary." A Canadian himself, Frizell grew up in a small town that was heavily polluted by a wood-pulp mill. In 1976, impressed by Greenpeace's antiwhaling campaign, he walked into the Vancouver office and volunteered. He opened mail and responded to phone calls, and eventually he, too, was put on salary.

Offices get started, says Frizell, "when the energy is there." In Midland, Michigan, Diane Hebert is a one-woman office, with a copy machine in her basement. Last year, upset over pollution in her neighborhood, she volunteered to investigate allegations that the nearby Dow Chemical Company plant was emitting dioxin into a nearby river. The resulting action by Greenpeacers, who plugged 15 pipes, became a public-relations triumph. When a Dow official spread a false rumor that a woman protester had venereal disease, his tactic backfired: The story was reported across the country, and the company apologized.

Collecting information is among Greenpeace's strong suits. In the U.S., they make regular use of the Freedom of Information Act. With continually updated intelligence, they can exploit opportunities for action whenever the timing and location seem right—and staff members or competent volunteers are on hand.

Swift action demands some form of organization, though, as does rapid growth, and seven years ago McTaggart formed the Greenpeace Council and Board to oversee the far-flung offices and activities. Of the 17 member countries, ten have voting rights on the council, which meets yearly to discuss budgets and campaigns. The Greenpeace board has five members: two from Europe; two from Canada, the United States, Australia, New Zealand; and McTaggart—a continent unto himself. Communicating by telex and telephone, and frequently dropping by Lewes, members of the board make day-to-day decisions.

The money for all this comes mainly from membership contributions: "We don't report to anybody, only to all those people who give us ten dollars," says McTaggart. Celebrities lend their names and their moral support, but, McTaggart emphasizes, virtually all donations are under $1,000. The Lewes base and the international campaigns, such as those against whaling and ocean dumping, are financed by overseas branches,

40. The Zeal of Disapproval

Collecting information is among Greenpeace's strong suits . . . they make regular use of the Freedom of Information Act.

which donate 20 percent of their gross income. To raise money, the branches mainly rely on membership, contributions, supplemented by concerts, and T-shirt sales.

It's 6:30, about quitting time, and along with Frizell and Pickaver, McTaggart repairs to the nearby White Hart Inn for a few pints of bitter—the dark British ale. The small pub is a favorite of McTaggart's, perhaps because the inn once was a watering place for another freethinker, Thomas Paine.

"Get a load of this," McTaggart says with amusement. "Ten million readers in the Soviet Union!" He passes around an article, translated from Russia's *Literaturnaya Gazeta*, which details the French crisis over the *Rainbow Warrior* months after it has vanished from American and English front pages.

Greenpeace's suit over the incident is being arbitrated in Geneva. Greenpeace is represented by a team of *pro bono* lawyers led by Lloyd Cutler, former special counsel to President Jimmy Carter. It's hard to put a price on *Warrior* (named for an Indian legend), a 417-ton trawler that McTaggart and his crew had spent months renovating by hand. "It was our first major boat," McTaggart says solemnly. "To replace it will be very hard."

Soon after he heard about the loss of *Warrior*, McTaggart slipped into France to try to learn just who had sunk it. He used an assumed name and switched hotels every night. "I found out that it was indeed a military operation," he says. "At one point things got very heavy and I had to disappear for a few days." His caution was hardly paranoiac: Greenpeace's office in New Zealand had been infiltrated by a French spy and the organization's phones have regularly been tapped. The administrators often speak obliquely on secure lines.

At first McTaggart didn't believe the French had done it. "I thought, 'they couldn't be that stupid!' I mean, after beating me up in 1973, that was the final blow." He's still infuriated that Jeane Kirkpatrick, former United States ambassador to the United Nations, said France had a right to do it. "Never in history has an ally sent spies into another ally's port and sunk an ally's boat!" he says.

It's not unusual for McTaggart to visit five or more countries in a month. He doesn't live in Lewes. Instead, he commutes from home a safe distance away, in Stockholm, Sweden. Why Stockholm? McTaggart moved there last year; he hints that he is afraid English authorities might put a lien against any property he held in the United Kingdom, as he has battled the British government too: In 1983 the U.K. fined Greenpeace £50,000 for trying to stop radioactive effluents coming from a pipeline into the Irish Sea.

Those wastes came from the world's first commercial nuclear reprocessing plant, the government-owned Sellafield installation near Seascale. In the wake of Greenpeace's protest, authorities discovered that radiation had contaminated nearby beaches and admitted that among children in a nearby town leukemia occurred at ten times the national average. Plutonium was even found in local vacuum cleaners.

The Sellafield plant was fined for its environmental transgressions, but only a fraction of that paid by Greenpeace, McTaggart notes bitterly. To add injury to insult, several of his men were irradiated when a sudden plume of scum poured from the pipe.

Warrior may be gone, but Greenpeace has no shortage of boats. One is currently taking chemical samples with a gas chromatograph up and down the Rhine River. An oceangoing tug has taken the Greenpeace group to Antarctica, and McTaggart's old ketch, *Vega*, is still in service. And there is a scheme afoot to send a surveillance boat equipped with sonar gear to the Mediterranean to keep track of Soviet and American submarines operating there. Greenpeace aims to discourage both by broadcasting news of their comings and goings. The goal is "a nuclear-free Mediterranean," McTaggart says in his rat-a-tat-tat cadence, his eyes fully ablaze. "Why not?"

Boats are only one part of the Greenpeace fleet. A hot-air balloon used in antinuclear protesting was held for two years by East Germany; recently, it crossed the border into the Nevada nuclear test site. "In England," says McTaggart, "we used a double-decker bus to climb Big Ben."

They drove it right up to the building, then extended a ladder through the rooftop hatch, climbed up, and unfurled a banner protesting nuclear arms.

Protests against nuclear wastes and weapons have obviously remained a Greenpeace priority, and sometimes the group goes beyond protest. One of *Rainbow Warrior's* last voyages, directed by Steve Sawyer, now executive director of Greenpeace U.S.A., was a mercy mission to the Marshall Islands and the atoll of Rongelap. Residents there were said to have suffered thyroid nodules, leukemia, miscarriages, and stillbirths because of American bomb tests at nearby Bikini in the 1950s. The children had played in the radioactive fallout, and reports say that visiting American scientists stay away from the coconuts, giant clams, and choice lobsters, apparently wary of contamination by strontium 90 and cesium 137. Greenpeace moved all 304 residents to Mejato, a safer island.

McTaggart developed his deep feelings for the environment as a boy in Vancouver, British Columbia. His family summered on a beautiful bay, where McTaggart often watched whales. At 17, he began working in construction; at 21, he founded his own firm. "I designed villages that protected the trees, and I built a ski area where as few trees as possible were cut down and the roads weren't cleared of snow," he recalls.

Thanks to his construction business, McTaggart soon rose to vice president of a development corporation, in charge of a 400-acre ski resort in the Sierra east of San Francisco. But his career was shattered when, in 1968, a gas leak blew up the ski lodge. McTaggart helped rescue two workers. "My stride had been broken," he says. "I decided the hell with it. In the end, I got tired of the cold-bloodedness of the business."

He had the urge to go to sea. With what little he had in cash after the resort accident, he bought *Vega* and roamed from port to port—until he saw that fateful news story on the Canadian protesters, and set out for the French nuclear test at Mururoa.

What offended him as much as anything about the French was that, contrary to international law, they had declared thou-

Whaling is the issue that most infuriates McTaggart. "Man doesn't need to kill whales, period," he says.

6. WORLD PROBLEMS AND INTERDEPENDENCE

"Anybody who is really trying to do anything gets a lot of heat, a lot of criticism."

sands of square miles of international waters off-limits during the nuclear tests. When *Vega* was rammed, says McTaggart, "I went back to my brother's house in Vancouver and I sat down and started my own little war with France," a stubborn legal and public-relations battle to recover his losses.

When publicity over the Mururoa protests began to bring in donations, he set up a bank account in West Vancouver. "There was still no real organization," he says. "When I went to Paris for the court case [he had accused the French government of piracy] I started a chain-letter-type thing for more support. I built up a mailing list of two or three thousand people." And with that letter network came the real formation of what is now known as Greenpeace.

By 1975, Greenpeace had started protesting against whaling. The numbers were compelling. At the turn of the century the oceans contained about 200,000 blue whales, some as long as 90 feet and weighing over 100 tons—the largest mammals on the planet. Eight decades later, the survivors may number as few as 1,000, although estimates vary widely.

Whaling is the issue that most infuriates McTaggart. "Man doesn't need to kill whales, period," he says. "I don't think we have a right to go around wiping out animals. It's been proven that a blue whale can hear 3,000 miles. Fifty million years it took for evolution to get that organized! Sperm whales dive down to depths that submarines can't. They have conversations, they joke, laugh, and have a good time. They're not in competition with us. What right do we have to wipe them out?"

In one Greenpeace tactic to obstruct whalers, members would position a fast, highly maneuverable dinghy between a factory ship and its quarry—despite the whalers' firing 250-pound explosive harpoons over the heads of the Greenpeace crew. But it was probably by organizing boycotts against whaling countries and lobbying long and hard at the International Whaling Commission (IWC) that Greenpeace pressured the IWC to vote for an indefinite moratorium on commercial whaling. The ban was supposed to go into effect this year, but several countries, including Japan and Norway, are ignoring the deadline. "There are very few victories," sighs McTaggart. "You never win outright."

Greenpeace's tactics may regularly alienate large segments of any given public. "But the group fills a need," says John Adams, executive director of the comparatively conservative Natural Resources Defense Council. "It provides an outlet for frustrations that develop because the system doesn't take care of problems. Anybody who is really trying to do anything gets a lot of heat, a lot of criticism."

Out in the Lewes High Street, a fog blows in from the English Channel, and the flint walls of the nearby old castle are drenched in cold rain. In the office, McTaggart drowsily rubs his eyes. His right one is still blurry from the French attack 13 years ago. "I have a 50 percent chance of getting acute glaucoma," McTaggart says.

He is currently remarried and the father of a three-year-old girl. That's made him think of spending more time in Stockholm, but as yet he shows no signs of relaxing his pace. Greenpeace is still trying to stop the killing of dolphins in tuna fishermen's nets and the decimation of pilot whales in the Faeroe Islands. The group has launched a campaign against Star Wars, the Strategic Defense Initiative, that will rely on the mailing of articles and satirical cartoons reproduced from the world press. McTaggart recently helped establish a new chapter in Italy, and there is a drive to open offices in Third World countries. The American chapter has discussed a trip down the Mississippi River to block chemical effluent pipes, and recently visited Louisiana to protest incineration of hazardous wastes near the Mississippi River. There are also plans to protest drift-net fishing in the Pacific Ocean. And seal killings off Canada are once more on the rise. And after that?

"We will keep close to the edge," McTaggart says. "I don't predict too far into the future—I'll be surprised if we don't get it in two or three years."

" 'Get it?' "

He nods. He believes that, somehow, Greenpeace may itself be driven to extinction by the governments it so ably offends. He is vague about how this might happen: "We're just a little group of people," he says, "and governments have a strange way of operating."

McTaggart won reelection recently as chairman by the Greenpeace board and the odds are that he will be at the helm. "He is controversial in certain circles of the organization, but he has been the driving force behind it, and he is much more important than any other single individual," says Steve Sawyer.

Rainbow Warrior lies in an Auckland berth, awaiting burial at sea. Although she was refloated after the bombing, *Warrior* will never be seaworthy again. The plan is to clean her of pollutants and sink her in 100 feet of water off the New Zealand coast to take up new duty as an artificial reef—a haven for the marine life she campaigned to save.

JAPANESE WOMEN IN A MALE SOCIETY

Bound by tradition,
women struggle to take on responsibility at work
while society still expects them to leave
their jobs for family life

Nobuko Hashimoto
Special to The Christian Science Monitor

Tokyo

YUKO Murakami is a top postgraduate art student at Tokyo University, one of Japan's most prestigious universities.

Last year she applied for one of 16 positions available at a private television network. There were 15 openings for men, but only one for women. Out of 2,500 female applicants, Ms. Yuko was among the top three women candidates for the one job. She was finally turned down, she believes, because another woman with an influential relative got the position.

"It made me mad to think that if I were a man, I would have gotten in with 15 possibilities. But perhaps it's just as well. Had I gotten in, I'd probably be serving tea now," observes Yuko, who has opted to continue her career in art.

In 1980 Japan signed a United Nations pledge to eliminate discrimination against women during the "UN Decade for Women: Equality, Development, and Peace," which started in 1976. This year Japan is rushing to make some of the promised changes. Despite the various noises being made and the Equal Opportunity Bill being discussed in the Diet (parliament), many Japanese — especially women — say the social attitudes are slow in changing.

In a country where industry is dominant, the female work force has long been considered secondary and only complementary to that of men. In actual numbers, working women are on the increase, however, accounting for 38 percent of the work force today, and 60 percent of working women are married, according to a

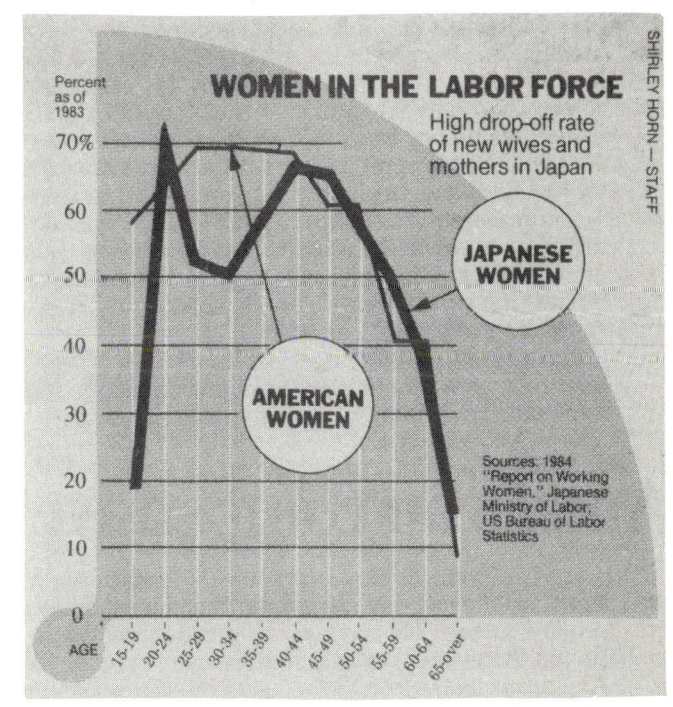

6. WORLD PROBLEMS AND INTERDEPENDENCE

recent study on women by the Hakuhodo Institute of Life and Living (HILL), a private research institute.

However, the actual quality and condition of women's jobs remain poor, making women a "useful and inexpensive source of labor for most companies," according to a report in the Nihon Keizai Shimbun, a financial daily.

Studies show that starting salaries for Japanese women are close to that of men. According to the Ministry of Labor, the starting salaries for women with four-year college degrees is 93.9 percent that of men.

But the gap widens with the years. In Japan, as many other Western countries, women's salaries are about half those of men. According to a June 1983 study by the Labor Ministry, by the time women reach their peak salaries (between ages 54 and 59), they are earning 51.6 percent of what men make during their peak salary years (45 to 49).

In 1983, for the first time in 20 years, working wives outnumbered housewives, the HILL study notes. "A typical working woman is no longer a young single woman working several years until she gets married. She is, instead, a middle-aged woman who reenters the work force now that her children are in school."

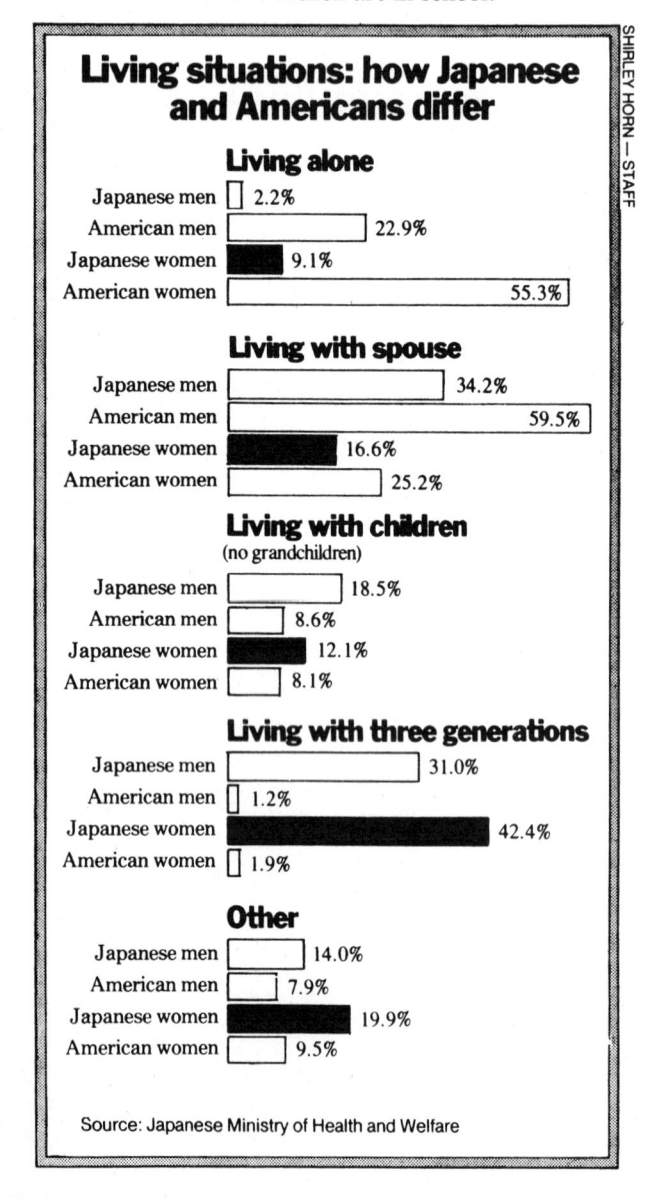

Living situations: how Japanese and Americans differ

Living alone
- Japanese men: 2.2%
- American men: 22.9%
- Japanese women: 9.1%
- American women: 55.3%

Living with spouse
- Japanese men: 34.2%
- American men: 59.5%
- Japanese women: 16.6%
- American women: 25.2%

Living with children (no grandchildren)
- Japanese men: 18.5%
- American men: 8.6%
- Japanese women: 12.1%
- American women: 8.1%

Living with three generations
- Japanese men: 31.0%
- American men: 1.2%
- Japanese women: 42.4%
- American women: 1.9%

Other
- Japanese men: 14.0%
- American men: 7.9%
- Japanese women: 19.9%
- American women: 9.5%

Source: Japanese Ministry of Health and Welfare

SHIRLEY HORN — STAFF

The number of working women over age 35 has increased mainly because these women are willing to work part time. More and more Japanese corporations are hiring female part-timers because they are more experienced and less expensive than full-time, younger high-school graduates.

According to Sohyo, Japan's major labor organization, 20 percent of female workers are part-timers working under poorer conditions than full-time women workers. Most are between the ages of 35 and 49, and they usually work six-hour days, five days a week, earning an average hourly pay of 561 yen (about $2.35). This is approximately 76 percent of the average pay of full-time working women.

Not only is the pay low, but companies rarely give protection or compensation. These women can be fired on short notice, and they usually don't get employment insurance, bonuses, or holiday pay. Even under these conditions, most work part time for about 3½ years.

Even with more women getting higher education, and more seeking jobs, many Japanese still harbor the image of women as homemakers. "To be intelligent, educated, and to have a responsible job creates problems for women, especially when looking for a husband," says Yuko, who is still single at 25. (The average Japanese woman gets married at age 25.)

Most companies still have policies that reflect prewar attitudes that women mainly want to get married and will quit when they reach marriageable age three or four years after they leave school, the HILL study says.

In fact, many companies expect women to leave once they are married. As a chief representative of the Federation of Employers' Associations, or Nikkeiren, said in a recent article, "I didn't oppose when my wife first started working, but I said very clearly that she must first take care of the house." Three months later his wife left her job.

If some women persist in their jobs even after they marry, they are encouraged to quit after they have their first child. "As mothers, they are expected to take on full responsibility of raising their children," says the HILL survey.

Once in their jobs, women face other obstacles. Even if they are university graduates, they are expected to make tea for their male colleagues. Many firms still put women in uniforms, and women complain that they're not taken seriously enough to get responsible jobs.

One young woman, Yoshiko, says in the HILL report: "There is a woman in our section. She's been there for years and she tells me I should not mind doing the menial tasks around the office. If I stick to it, she tells me, eventually I'll be able to do more responsible work. But I feel I can't wait around. I want to do something more challenging."

But employers say they can't take women seriously if they don't have staying power. What's more, they complain that the women often abuse their rights. One bank executive notes, "Every woman has the right to take menstrual leave, but most of the time we discover that the women took off the extra days to go skiing."

Why then are working women on the increase? What most of these women seem to be seeking, the HILL report suggests, is not so much extra income as a sense of fulfillment by doing something useful beyond their housework. For similar reasons volunteer jobs are becoming popular, as are cultural centers.

How the proposed Equal Opportunity Bill will change the present situation remains to be seen. The bill states that employers should strive for equal opportunity in recruiting workers. It also says that employers should not subject women to any "discriminatory treatment in regard to retirement or dismissal" and that marriage and pregnancy should not be considered grounds for dismissal or early retirement.

Many feminists are opposed to the draft of the bill becuse it is too "watered down," as former Labor Minister Misoji Sakamoto himself admits.

There is no mention of penalty to help enforce these guidelines. Feminists are against losing their guarantees of menstrual leave and protection from working overtime and on night shifts. Vice-Foreign Minister Mayumi Moriyama, recently appointed as the second woman to take up the post in 36 years, said recently: "We can't change everything overnight, but the working environment will eventually change to make it easier for women to have jobs and to keep them."

The employers' federation Nikkeiren is expected to oppose the bill, saying it would escalate costs, which would then burden the Japanese economy and industry.

Even the labor unions aren't expressing strong support for the proposed equality bill. One writer, Taro Yayama, expressed this general sentiment in a recent article: "The law may very well destroy the lifetime employment system and the seniority wage system — the very basis of the stability of Japanese society and the source of power of Japanese corporations."

Article 42

DIVORCE, CHINESE STYLE

TAMARA K. HAREVEN

Tamara K. Hareven, a professor of history at Clark University, is a Fulbright Scholar and a visiting research professor at Doshisha University, Kyoto, and at Keio University, Tokyo. Hareven is also a research associate at the Center for Population Studies at Harvard University and the founding editor of The Journal of Family History. *She received a B.A. in history from Hebrew University in Jerusalem in 1961, an M.A. from the University of Cincinnati the following year, and a Ph.D. from Ohio State University in 1965. Hareven is the author of* Family Time and Industrial Time *(1982), and she is working on a social history of the American family. Hareven carried out the research for this article while she was a distinguished visiting scholar of the National Academy of Science's Committee on Scholarly Communication with the People's Republic of China.*

ZHENHUA AND SHUQIN WERE SITTING ON OPPOSITE sides of the aisle, their backs to the audience, facing a long empty table. Shuqin was fiddling with a piece of paper—her marriage certificate. She was suing Zhenhua for divorce. One September day Shuqin had taken her clothes and her quilt, and with her sister's help had moved out of her husband's family home. Now, two years later, her case was about to be heard in the Hongkou People's District Court in Shanghai, one of thousands of local courts of this type. A slight twenty-eight-year-old woman with short black hair, Shuqin worked as a statistician in a government office. She came to court wearing beige slacks and a patterned blouse. Zhenhua, Shuqin's slim, tall, thirty-one-year-old husband, worked as a laborer on Shanghai's waterfront. Wearing khaki pants and a blue cotton Mao jacket, he sat slouching forward, as if folded into himself. On the floor next to him rested a thick black plastic bag with two handles, of the type that men all over China carry with them.

Noise generally fills public places in China, but the austere courtroom of the Hongkou ("Mouth of the Rainbow") district was silent. The leaders of the couple's neighborhood committee sat along the wall to the right of the official table. Representatives of their work units sat along the opposite wall. Three judges entered. The scales of justice were embroidered in gold on their military hats and the epaulets of their dark-gray cotton uniforms.

The judges positioned themselves behind the table, facing the couple. Almost in unison they took off their hats and placed them on the table in a neat row, each hat in front of its owner, with the visor and the emblem facing the public. First the chief judge, a woman in her fifties, sat down. A somewhat younger male judge took his place on her right, and a female judge in her late twenties sat on the chief judge's left. The trial was ready to begin.

The judges' theatrical entrance underscored the solemnity of the divorce proceedings and the importance attached to them in the People's Republic of China. Divorce was effectively made legal in China by the Marriage Law of 1950, which was designed to liberate men and women from forced marriages and to provide relief for women being abused by their husbands and in-laws. (About 70 percent of the divorce petitions filed since the law was passed, a year after the Communists came to power, have been filed by women.) In 1953 the number of divorces granted reached a record 1.17 million. The number fell dramatically during the Cultural Revolution, but following the introduction in 1981 of a new marriage law, it has been rising again. The new law for the first time in Chinese history recognizes alienation of affection as grounds for divorce (providing that mediation has failed). About half a million divorces have been granted each year since the new law went into effect—still a relatively small number when considered in proportion to the population, of a billion. (In the United States, which has a population of 240 million, there are around 1.2 million divorces each year.) Despite the unprecedented liberality of the new law, divorce proceedings remain arduous. The drawn-out mediation process and the constant pressures to which a couple is subjected by local leaders and the courts are in themselves sufficient to discourage many couples from considering divorce.

The integrity of the family is a cornerstone of Chinese social policy. "Society and family in China depend on each other like a larger river on a little one," a leading authority on Chinese family law told me recently. "When the little rivers are full of water, the large river is also full. When the little rivers are polluted, they also pollute the larger one." In the case of Zhenhua and Shuqin, and in another recent case that I was given the rare privilege of observing, the court hearings illuminated Chinese family and community life, caught as it is between the forces of individualism and those of community, during a period of rapid social change.

THE CHIEF JUDGE OPENED THE PROCEEDINGS WITH an announcement that the judges, along with the neighborhood-committee leaders and the work-unit representatives, had done all they could to mediate and bring about a reconciliation. But they had failed. The judges had worked closely with the local leaders, and the chief judge certified that she and her colleagues were familiar with all the details of the case.

The chief judge asked Shuqin why she wanted a divorce. Shuqin told her story: When she and Zhenhua met, they were both very poor. Zhenhua had just returned from forced labor in the countryside. They were introduced by

42. Divorce, Chinese Style

a go-between and fell in love. After a year-long courtship, Zhenhua and Shuqin were married, in April of 1981, and Shuqin moved into Zhenhua's crowded household, which included his parents and four sisters. Since their marriage, Shuqin said, she had tried and tried to get along with her husband, but they had experienced numerous "contradictions." She said that she had repeatedly asked the leaders of her work unit and the neighborhood committee for help, but that she had been unsuccessful in resolving the contradictions between herself and Zhenhua.

The judges explored the nature of these contradictions by questioning both Shuqin and Zhenhua. The first conflicts had occurred over the wedding itself. Zhenhua wanted a simple wedding, but Shuqin wanted to invite many friends to a large dinner, according to the current fashion. Shuqin had her way, but as a result they had to borrow 1,000 yuan (ten times the average laborer's monthly wage) from one of Zhenhua's sisters to pay for the dinner. After their marriage Zhenhua used his wages to repay the debt, but Shuqin kept her own pay. The fact that Shuqin did not contribute her wages to the common kitty became a sore point with the family, especially since she gave ten yuan a month to her mother, despite Zhenhua's insistence that she give only five yuan.

Next the judge brought up the matter of an abortion that Shuqin had had, and asked Shuqin to tell the court about it. Her voice trembling with embarrassment, Shuqin said that she had gotten pregnant by Zhenhua before their marriage. In China premarital sex is still considered a serious transgression, and until several years ago it was severely punished. After her marriage Shuqin wanted to get an abortion. Although his mother approved of it, Zhenhua objected. Shuqin went ahead anyway. Zhenhua never forgave her. But the abortion was not the cause of their estrangement, Shuqin insisted.

The fight that precipitated the breakup of the marriage resulted from Shuqin's struggle to maintain some privacy in her husband's home. Privacy is rare in China, not only because of overcrowding but also because of the traditional Chinese view that individual lives do not exist separately from the life of the community. Shuqin and Zhenhua, like the majority of other Shanghai residents, lived in cramped quarters. Many couples actually postpone marriage because they cannot find a room of their own. The Hongkou district, once the "concession" area controlled by the Japanese, is one of the most densely populated in Shanghai. In its narrow alleys old Japanese wooden houses and dilapidated European stucco mansions, now subdivided into multiple dwellings, stand side by side with mammoth tenements and small shacks. Several unrelated families often share the same kitchen, which may consist of little more than a stove and a wok. They may also share a toilet, and a water faucet in the common entry hall. Bathing is often done at public baths, or at the place of work. In warm weather family life spills out onto the sidewalks and into the alleys. People bring out small stoves, tables, chairs, and cots. They cook and eat outside, play with their children, sew and do repair work, all in close proximity. Under these conditions family fights can hardly remain private.

Zhenhua and Shuqin began by quarreling over the television, several months after their wedding. One evening, much to Zhenhua's chagrin, Shuqin locked the door to their room in order to keep his oldest sister out. The sister, who had been accustomed to sewing and watching television in that room, continued to do so after their marriage. Shuqin requested that she stop using the room because she habitually "left it in a mess." The sister threatened to take "her" TV away. Shuqin insisted that the TV stay, believing that Zhenhua owned it. The sister claimed that the TV was her own. Shuqin kept asking her husband who really owned the TV, but he never responded. As long as it was not clear who owned it, Shuqin said, she would not part with it.

Watching TV is almost the only form of entertainment available to a typical family in China. Until recently the TV was the star of the "three technologies," its supporting cast being the electric fan and the radio–tape deck. (The brightest stars now are the washing machine and the refrigerator.) A TV is still considered so precious that in most households it is clad in an embroidered velvet or silk cover when not in use.

The argument escalated. One evening Zhenhua's sister came home, pounded on the table, and shouted at Shuqin, "If you don't like to stay here, you can go back to your parents!" Neighbors rushed in "to help." Shuqin's mother and sister, who lived down the block, also came to her rescue. Several days later Shuqin hid the TV. After Zhenhua found it, Shuqin hid its plug. When Zhenhua found the plug, Shuqin hid the activating button. Zhenhua asked for the button four times, and Shuqin refused to give it to him. Zhenhua openly sided with his family.

The next day Shuqin's mother-in-law gave her two months' worth of food coupons: she was being expelled. Food coupons are given to each registered family, or *hukou*, for the purchase of subsidized rice and grain. After Shuqin joined her husband's family, her registration was changed to his *hukou*. Giving the coupons to Shuqin meant, Go away and do your own cooking. Shuqin sought the help of the neighborhood leaders. On their advice she returned to her mother-in-law and said, "If you want me to do the cooking by myself, give me the coupons for two persons, and I'll cook for my husband." Her mother-in-law said nothing. When Zhenhua returned from work, Shuqin gave him her coupons and said, "You should take a stand." But Zhenhua kept silent.

Next Zhenhua's mother and sister came into Shuqin's room and scolded her for not contributing her wages and for wanting to borrow money in order to buy a wedding present for her sister. They used "dirty words" and ordered her to leave. Shuqin rushed to Zhenhua's workplace and told him that his mother and sister had ordered her out of the house. Zhenhua said nothing. That evening Shuqin's father came to see Zhenhua. He asked Zhenhua why he and his daughter were quarreling. Again Zhenhua was silent. Shuqin's father reaffirmed that he was not responsible for his daughter anymore. He told Zhenhua that when

6. WORLD PROBLEMS AND INTERDEPENDENCE

he had permitted Shuqin to eat at his home occasionally, he had been unaware of the couple's conflicts. "Now that I know you have a quarrel, I will not allow my daughter to eat in my house anymore." But despite her father's seeming resolve, the following day Shuqin moved back to her parents' home.

"Your conflict was with your husband's family, not with your husband," the chief judge said to Shuqin. "Why did you leave him?"

"Because my husband did not make an effort to solve the contradictions," Shuqin said.

The male judge, reminding Shuqin that her family consisted of *two* persons, asked, "Why did you leave if your husband did not want you to?"

Shuqin said that she knew Zhenhua did not want her to leave but that she had no choice. "Because my husband's family ordered me to," she said.

There were discrepancies between Zhenhua's and Shuqin's testimony, which made it impossible to determine how persistent Zhenhua really was in trying to get Shuqin back.

"Your husband wanted you back, so he came to your workplace and to your home at night," the male judge said. "Your husband did not completely sit with folded arms. Why did you not return after he asked you to?"

Shuqin replied that in fact Zhenhua *was* sitting with folded arms. During the quarrels she had told Zhenhua in tears, "Your family has a quarrel with me. You should not sit with folded arms. If I was mistaken, you should criticize me, or if they are wrong, you should tell them."

Zhenhua told the court that on the advice of the neighborhood leaders he took a gift to Shuqin's family during the mid-autumn festival. He and the leaders arrived at her home around 8:00 P.M. Shuqin's father was not there, and Shuqin was asleep. Zhenhua said, "I want to take my wife home. I have nothing to do with her parents." But the leaders advised him that, given the late hour, he should try another time. After that Zhenhua and Shuqin met for two hours at the Huangpu River Park. On Sundays and summer evenings the park teems with young couples. Several couples share each bench and seek to maintain a discreet distance from one another. According to Zhenhua, Shuqin asked him whether she could return to his home, and he said yes. But Zhenhua recounted that she never came. Zhenhua and Shuqin did not meet again for two years.

Finally the judges tried to pin Zhenhua down as to who actually owned the TV. After many evasive replies Zhenhua admitted that his sister had bought the TV with her own money. The chief judge now held Zhenhua responsible for the escalation of the fighting, because he had kept the truth from his wife.

THE JUDGES INDICATED THAT THE TIME FOR THEIR decision had arrived. The chief judge asked Shuqin whether she wanted a divorce.

"Yes," Shuqin said.

"You have lived apart for two years," the chief judge said. "Can you still be reconciled?"

"No," Shuqin said. She said she had attempted a reconciliation for a long time. The work unit and the neighborhood leaders had also tried their best. But Zhenhua was "cold-blooded." While insisting that she admit her mistakes, he refused to take a stand on his family's conduct. Bursting into tears, Shuqin told the court that when her father-in-law died—this had happened about a year earlier—she asked Zhenhua's permission to return, but Zhenhua's family refused. She had even asked the leaders of Zhenhua's work unit to intercede on her behalf. But his relatives stood firm. They blamed Zhenhua's father's death on Shuqin and said that his last words were not to let her come back.

Did Shuqin still wish to be reconciled? the judge asked again. "No," she replied in a tearful voice. The judge then addressed the same question to Zhenhua. In his evasive style Zhenhua said that they had lived apart for two years and some months. "Do you still have feelings?" asked the judge. There was no basis left for the marriage, Zhenhua replied; the feelings were lost.

In their testimony the leaders of the neighborhood committee and the work units confirmed that all hope was gone. They had done everything they could but all mediation routes were exhausted. The role that the neighborhood committees and the work units play in the court is an extension of their function as moral guardians and mediators in the community. They implement government policy in the workplace, neighborhood, and family. The work-unit committee registers marriages, provides some housing, and distributes food coupons and contraceptives. The neighborhood committee, consisting primarily of retired workers, mostly women, serves without pay. It enforces birth-control policy and investigates disputes among neighbors and within families. Both committees mediate cases and bring them to court as a last resort.

This type of mediation, which has its origins in ancient Chinese practice, is frequently used in China to settle disputes. In 1983, seven million domestic disputes of various kinds were settled through mediation by local committees. The committees wield considerable power over people's lives in cases of internal family quarrels, adultery, and pregnancy. Since people cannot change jobs and housing on their own initiative, falling out of grace with committee leaders is tantamount to being ostracized. The committees can intervene, unsolicited. They "persuade" people through persistent moral pressure and public shaming. During a visit to a neighborhood in Beijing, I asked a committee member in charge of family planning how it was possible to force a woman to get an abortion. "We don't force her," the leader said. "We talk to her again and again until she agrees."

Following the testimony from the committee leaders the chief judge announced that the court would be prepared to grant a divorce once the matter of property was settled. In the division of property the judges followed the principle that each person should keep those objects that he or she had brought into the marriage or paid for during the marriage. The judge established that Shuqin had brought to Zhenhua's house her own clothes, eight quilts, four pillows, two blankets, and a lamp. Zhenhua said that at the time of the marriage he had owned a bed, two bed boxes, a writing table, a sofa, two small tables, two chairs, and a glass box. Zhenhua, who had been passive and evasive in discussions of personal relations, became suddenly aggressive regarding property issues.

In a dispute over who had paid for quilt covers, Shuqin finally admitted that Zhenhua had. The judge ordered her to return the covers. Zhenhua also insisted that Shuqin return three wooden buckets that he had bought in the countryside. "Do not raise such a small thing," Shuqin responded with embarrassment. But the judge intervened: "Don't say this is a small thing." In response to Zhenhua's demand that Shuqin return the wedding photos, Shuqin proposed to cut each photo in half. "Don't do that," the chief judge said. "You have to continue to live as good neighbors." She also advised Zhenhua to instruct his mother and sister to stop quarreling with Shuqin. Zhenhua insisted that Shuqin pay the three-yuan court fee, because she had initiated the suit. It was irrelevant who sued, the judge said, but Shuqin had already offered to pay.

The chief judge announced the verdict. According to the marriage law of 1981, the couple would be divorced by mutual consent. Neither party could be married again until after receiving the certificate of divorce. The judge commended the neighborhood and work-unit leaders for their efforts, and again asked for their opinions. The leaders concurred with the verdict. They also advised Shuqin not to rush back into marriage. As silence descended again over the courtroom, the judges picked up their hats in unison and walked out, followed by the local leaders. The audience, consisting of relatives and neighbors, erupted into loud conversation.

Shuqin and Zhenhua walked out separately. As Zhenhua passed the front row, he cast a curious glance at me, the foreign observer, who had, he knew, been sitting behind his back but whose face he had not seen. He smiled in embarrassment, revealing his buck teeth. He then moved on, carrying his black bag. Shuqin was free now from oppression by her husband's family and from a marriage that had lost its meaning. In reality she had gained very little freedom. She would continue to live in poverty in her parents' home. Given the stigma attached to divorce in China, and the competition from younger women, she would find it almost impossible to remarry. As a single person, she had no place in the community's social life. She was now part of the large pool of women whose inability to find a husband has recently become a source of anxiety to the Chinese leadership.

T**HE SOCIAL AND ECONOMIC CIRCUMSTANCES OVER** which Zhenhua and Shuqin had little control, and which eventually figured in the destruction of their marriage, were not unique to their lives. Their poverty and dependence on Zhenhua's family locked them into conflict. From the beginning they were deprived of the opportunity to nurture their separate existence as a couple. By joining her husband in his family home Shuqin continued a time-honored Chinese tradition. While the socialist regime has attempted to replace the patriarchal family with one based on equality and mutual respect, regardless of sex or age, the ghost of "feudal" family relationships has lingered.

A considerable number of sons in China still bring their brides into their parents' households. This practice is especially common in the countryside, where arranged marriages and other traditional family customs have persisted despite the communal organization of production. Recently the introduction of the new "individual responsibility" system—a limited free-market system for small farmers and craftsmen—has encouraged the return of married sons and their families to the parental home, because their labor can be essential to maximizing family profit.

In urban areas residential patterns are more diverse: some couples live with the wife's parents instead of the husband's, depending on housing space, proximity to a workplace, and compatibility. In the large cities young couples tend increasingly to reside near their parents rather than with them. A recent survey of households in Beijing, Tienzin, and Shanghai found that about half the couples in each of these cities live in "nuclear" families. In such cases, however, nuclear families do not reside in separate, private housing. Because of housing shortages, the young couples typically share a flat with several other families, who are not relatives.

Most of the older couples I interviewed in Beijing and Shanghai said that nowadays married children who stay with parents do so mainly as a convenience rather than out of filial piety. Several public officials with whom I spoke predicted that once housing and child-care needs are met, most young people will prefer to live separately, in the hope of avoiding the predicament that drove Shuqin and Zhenhua apart.

After the courtroom emptied, I met with the judges and the president of the district court to discuss the case. As what were evidently customary bottles of orangeade were served, the judges relaxed and unbuttoned their uniform jackets, the women revealing colorful blouses underneath.

First the judges wanted to assure me that they and the local leaders had worked very hard to save Zhenhua and Shuqin's marriage. Judges in China interpret divorce law conservatively. They distinguish carefully between the use of divorce to liberate people from bondage and its "abuse" in the service of individual whim or a new romance. Accordingly, one judge explained, the courts are guided by four major criteria for divorce: whether the conflict followed a "rash" marriage; the quality of the relationship; the causes and depth of the conflict; and the prospects for reconciliation. The courts are particularly conservative when children are involved.

Zhenhua's and Shuqin's case, the male judge said, was clear-cut before it even came to court. It could have been

6. WORLD PROBLEMS AND INTERDEPENDENCE

settled in the work-unit committee's meeting room and then registered with the Marriage Division of the Bureau of Civil Affairs, as is customary for uncontested divorces. Why, then, the lengthy testimony about painful personal matters? The chief judge replied that since Shuqin had seen fit to bring suit, the court had wanted to affirm in public that all reconciliation efforts had failed. Thus the court served as a theater for public education—as it had also done in traditional China. In a society where public shaming continues to be a method of social control, the story of Zhenhua and Shuqin would be a lesson to others.

Because the judges had determined early on that the quarrel was primarily between Zhenhua's family and Shuqin rather than between the husband and wife, I asked, had the local leaders, during their efforts to save the marriage, considered finding separate housing for the couple? "No, this is not done here," one of the judges said. "We could not separate the son from his family." The new ideology and traditional customs can make strange, uncomfortable bedfellows.

Couples in China are caught between the authorities' traditional commitment to the integrity of the family, on the one hand, and the rather more recent and limited emphasis on individualism and affection, on the other. Personal feelings are respected only as long as they serve the higher goals of family and community. Happiness is not a goal in itself.

In this respect, the case of Fuchang and Liyin, in the Changning district of Shanghai, provides a counterpoint to that of Zhenhua and Shuqin. Fuchang, twenty-nine years old, was suing his wife, Liyin, two years his junior, for divorce. Both were laborers, and they had met by chance at a movie. They were married in April of 1981, after a six-month courtship. They had a twenty-two-month-old son. Fuchang had just been discharged from the military when he met Liyin. She was "plain-looking" and did not wear fine clothes. But he decided to marry her, over his parents' objections, because he was "too poor to choose." Liyin said that she had seen marriage as an opportunity to have her own family after a hard life in her parents' home. She had lost her mother when she was six and had had to raise her younger brother, who ended up a delinquent.

Fuchang accused Liyin of deceit: at the time of their marriage she had promised him a certain sum of money and a good apartment from her work unit. Neither had materialized, and they lived in a run-down apartment in an industrialized, working-class area. He said also that Liyin was a poor housekeeper and that she had gone to the movies with a male co-worker. Liyin denied these accusations. The major problem, she said, was Fuchang's unwillingness to treat her as an equal. When she obeyed him, all was fine, but when she expressed a contrary opinion, all hell broke loose. Fuchang had been sympathetic to her family problems during their courtship, but after their marriage he did not allow her to invite her father to dinner. He also prevented her from giving some money to her brother, who had just returned from a reform camp.

In February of 1982, following a violent quarrel, Fuchang took the television set and moved to his parents' house, while Liyin and her infant remained in the apartment. The quarrel had broken out when Liyin returned from work one evening and found a "girlfriend" of Fuchang's visiting their home. Fuchang had brought this woman along to visit Liyin in the hospital after their child was born. At that time the woman in the neighboring bed told Liyin that she had seen Fuchang's companion place her hand on his thigh. When Liyin saw the guest, she concealed her jealousy and chastised Fuchang ostensibly for not serving "proper dishes" to company. Fuchang told her to mind her own business; he was master of this house and it was his responsibility to look after his guests. Liyin then asked the woman to leave. In response Fuchang threw a bowl at Liyin, and blood started gushing from her forehead. Fuchang moved out that evening. The couple had been living apart ever since.

According to Fuchang, Liyin visited him several times after this. Each visit ended in a quarrel. On one occasion Liyin stormed into Fuchang's workplace and broke a window. Another time, when their baby was sick, she left him at Fuchang's parents' house and poured the baby's medicine out on the floor. On a third occasion she showed up clutching a bottle of DDT and threatening to commit suicide. At this Fuchang called the neighborhood committee. Mediation commenced.

Liyin told the court that she would not consent to a divorce. She still had feelings, she said. She was sure that if she and Fuchang could develop mutual trust and respect, the marriage could be saved. If they were reconciled, she would do her best to keep house. Nor could Liyin believe that Fuchang's feelings were all gone. Once after their separation, when Fuchang had fallen and hurt his arm, he had allowed Liyin to hold his hand and to comfort him. But when she asked him to move back home, he refused. Overcome by the memory, Liyin broke down crying in the courtroom. The child could not live without his father, she said between sobs. In his sleep he often cried out, "Papa! Papa!"

Fuchang's lawyer (lawyers were provided because the divorce was contested), a balding, middle-aged man, used the only point of law he could latch onto: the couple should be granted a divorce on the grounds of a rash marriage. Liyin's lawyer, a wiry woman in her fifties, delivered an animated speech in reply. "In our country women have equal rights in political and cultural life," she said. But Fuchang had not treated Liyin as an equal. Liyin's lawyer recommended that both partners undergo self-criticism and try to revive the good feelings that they had once had.

Fuchang insisted again that his feelings were dead. But Liyin said she was convinced that he still had some tenderness left. Fuchang turned to Liyin directly and shouted, "I have no more feelings for you!" Facing the judges, he said, "You cannot force me to feel a certain way." Even if they denied him a divorce, he said, he still would not have any feelings for Liyin. "Why should he say such insulting things to me?" Liyin asked, and she broke down crying.

42. Divorce, Chinese Style

The chief judge declared a recess in order to offer the couple one more opportunity for a reconciliation. During the recess, with the crowd milling around them, Liyin and Fuchang exchanged only a few words before Liyin started screaming and rushed out of the courtroom. Some relatives and work-unit leaders followed Liyin and ushered her into the far corner of the courtyard, where they spoke intensely with her, in the presence of one judge.

Meanwhile, inside the courtroom, Liyin's lawyer verbally assaulted Fuchang. "You must embark on self-criticism! You must admit your own shortcomings!" she shouted repeatedly. Fuchang kept saying that he had no shortcomings, that it was all his wife's fault. Two older women from the neighborhood committee kept trying to protect Fuchang: "Leave him alone. He is a good boy. He is a good boy."

The court reconvened after forty-five minutes. The judge accused the husband of violating the principles of equality, warned him against wife-beating, and ordered him to continue to support his child. The court denied Fuchang a divorce, because in its view there were no grounds. Fuchang was charged the three-yuan court fee. Both parties had the right to appeal the case to a higher court. Fuchang's lawyer said later that he intended to do that.

Did the judges feel that they had accomplished anything by denying a divorce when one party so emphatically wanted one? They explained that they were unable to grant a divorce because Liyin still claimed to have feelings. Even though the judges had some doubts as to her sincerity, the law was on Liyin's side, especially because of the child.

Could they really get this couple to live together again? I asked. "Yes!" the judges said; so long as the couple were not divorced, they would have further opportunity for mediation. Even if there is a mere one-percent chance, the judges said, the court will make a hundred-percent effort to reconcile the couple.

Like Zhenhua and Shuqin, Fuchang and Liyin had not had the opportunity to establish an independent marriage. Familial obligations and economic constraints kept them from developing an egalitarian love relationship. They were barely able to spend time alone.

Young people in China are now facing a paradox. The socialist regime wants to foster marriages based on free choice, love, and equality. But the young men and women have neither the experience nor the role models to develop such relationships. The custom of dating is not yet widespread in China. Most couples still meet through parentally arranged introductions. Their relations are formal, even when they are alone. The many young couples hugging in public are already engaged. Otherwise they would not be embracing in broad daylight. The Communist Party has launched an appeal to various local organizations to introduce matchmaking facilities. Meanwhile, the Young Socialist League and the All China Women's Federation have established "marriage introduction centers," which are supported by the municipalities as well. But these "marriage factories" in Beijing and Shanghai have not been notably successful, in part because potential candidates are often too shy to register.

ACCORDING TO LI CHENG, THE PRESIDING JUDGE OF the civil division of the Beijing Supreme People's Court, a recent poll indicates that 60 percent of China's young married people lack "real and spontaneous" love for their spouses. Among their reasons for marriage, the respondents said, were that they had "reached the age" and that "one had to be married sooner or later." These are, perhaps, traditional reasons. But there are also signs of change. The All China Women's Federation has embarked on a nationwide campaign to teach young people the meaning of love and equality in marriage, through film and study sessions. The honeymoon, meanwhile, is becoming popular for the first time, and honeymooners can be spotted at many of the major tourist sites, especially in favorite resorts like Suchou and Hangchow. Wearing a colorful suit with a corsage, and a lacy hat, the new wife poses for her husband's black-and-white snapshots in front of famous fountains and pavilions. Even the materialistic rewards of marriage have changed. The dowry chest is back in fashion (along with the wedding veil), but the dowry now comes from both sets of parents, and marriage partners typically have definite expectations as to what each side should contribute—expectations that at times may undermine "feelings."

Contemporary attitudes toward the family in China—among ordinary people and those who rule them—remind one somewhat of the Puritans' attitudes in seventeenth-century New England. The Puritan family was viewed as a "little commonwealth"—a miniature version of an ideal society. Like the Puritan elders, the rulers of the People's Republic consciously use the family as an agent of reform and of morality. They endorse public intervention in family affairs and they subordinate, to the extent that they can, the individual to the larger community. At the same time, the government has come to recognize the importance of "feelings" in maintaining social cohesion and strong family ties.

No one can predict precisely how the constellation of forces in China—of long-standing tradition and conformity on the one hand, and of emergent individualism, consumerism, and romance on the other—will change the dynamics of the Chinese family. It remains to be seen whether China can succeed in having it both ways.

The Natural History of AIDS

The disease may have existed in isolated humans for thousands of years

Matthew Allen Gonda

Matthew Allen Gonda, Ph.D., is head of the Laboratory of Cell and Molecular Structure, Program Resources, Inc., at the National Cancer Institute–Frederick Cancer Research Facility. He has authored numerous scholarly papers on retroviruses, most recently on the AIDS virus.

In 1984, a previously unknown virus was isolated from human blood. Named HTLV-III (human T-cell lymphotropic virus type III), the virus selectively attacked a specific group of white blood cells crucial to the body's immune response. Soon generally recognized as the causative agent of acquired immunodeficiency syndrome, or AIDS, the virus was later discovered to have an affinity for infecting cells of the brain as well.

Although the AIDS disease process has proved to be enormously complex and often baffling—there is no complete parallel for it among the other viral diseases of humans—we have learned a great deal about the virus's molecular biology and structure in a very short time. Structurally and biochemically, HTLV-III belongs to the retrovirus family, a unique subgroup of viruses found not only in humans but also in many animals, from reptiles to primates. Like other viruses, retroviruses don't always cause disease in their hosts.

Also like other viruses, retroviruses are not really living organisms. Lacking the machinery and the energy-generating capabilities to manufacture progeny, they are perhaps best described as infectious chemicals made up of a sticky protein coat encapsulating a genome (the DNA or RNA blueprint for constructing more viruses). Incapable of growth and division on their own, viruses exploit the cells of living organisms to perform these functions for them. Infection occurs when, via highly specific receptors on its protein coat, a virus attaches itself to and penetrates a susceptible cell. Once inside, it is read and reproduced by the host's manufacturing machinery. Sometimes the cell is killed during virus replication; but before its demise, it has released a new generation of viruses into the host's system.

Retroviruses have evolved a particularly effective variation on this parasitic theme. Unusual because their genomes are composed of RNA (in most living things, including most viruses, genomes are composed of DNA), retroviruses also possess a gene for a unique enzyme, reverse transcriptase. When the retrovirus attaches itself to and penetrates a cell, reverse transcriptase transcribes the retrovirus's genetic information from RNA into DNA. The host, often perceiving this new DNA to be its own genetic material, integrates it into its own chromosomes. Once in this new habitat, the retrovirus may be reproduced or it may remain dormant for weeks, months, or even years. The virus stays in the chromosomes for the life of the cell, that is, until the cell has been killed by the infection, eliminated by the immune system, or removed after senescence. The association is permanent; every time host cells reproduce, they also reproduce retrovirus DNA, even in the absence of new virus.

Some mouse and chicken retroviruses have assured themselves of even longer relationships with their hosts. Because in a past event they infected and were integrated into the host's germ cells (that is, sperm and egg or their precursor cells), they are now automatically transmitted to the next generation of host animals without an infectious cycle. There are no known methods of eliminating these so-called endogenous viruses.

Other retroviruses are exogenous—that is, acquired from the outside. The AIDS virus, passed from person to person (or from pregnant woman to fetus) via infected blood or body fluids, is of this type. Exogenous or endogenous, however, retrovirus infections have one feature in common; infected individuals remain infected (though not necessarily ill) for life.

Before the discovery of the AIDS virus,

43. The Natural History of AIDS

only two other retroviruses had ever been isolated in human beings. These—the human T-cell leukemia viruses, HTLV-I and II—belong to the oncovirus subfamily of retroviruses, so called because they are oncogenic (tumor producing in their host). Like the AIDS virus, they attack T-4 lymphocytes, the white blood cells that begin the immune reaction. The question therefore arose early as to whether the AIDS virus was also an oncovirus. At first, the idea seemed plausible, because of the properties shared with the the leukemia viruses, the most prominent of which was their affinity for T-cells. In addition, the AIDS virus was suspected of causing Kaposi's sarcoma, a rare cancer of the skin's blood vessels, from which many AIDS victims suffer. Further investigation, however, made it clear that HTLV-III did not directly cause Kaposi's sarcoma. Rather, the tumors were arising opportunistically because of the underlying immune deficiency, just as they do in organ-transplant patients who are given immunosuppressive drugs.

If the AIDS virus was not an oncovirus, what was it? Investigators began to look for similarities in the two other known retrovirus subfamilies—the lentiviruses and the spumiviruses. (There was also the possibility that it belonged to a new group of retroviruses not previously identified.) The spumiviruses, or foamy viruses, although they had not been thoroughly studied, were ruled out quickly; they were not known to cause disease, and structurally, they differed sharply from both the leukemia viruses and from the AIDS virus.

Important clues to the identity of the virus were already apparent, however. Most important was that the AIDS virus did not cause cancerous proliferations but instead brought about cell-killing (cytolytic) events. This cytolytic propensity is one of several distinguishing properties of the lentiviruses. Called "slow" viruses for their slow but persistent rate of replication, the lentiviruses eventually induce debilitating diseases, although years may pass between the initial infection and the onset of symptoms. Since the AIDS virus also is associated with the slow evolution of a lethal debilitating disease, this was a second family resemblance. Firmer evidence came from electron microscope pictures; HTLV-III strikingly resembled the visna virus, a lentivirus that infects sheep.

Lentiviruses had been isolated from a variety of ungulates—sheep, goats, horses, cows—that have been closely associated with humans for thousands of years. Visna virus—grouped with maedi and progressive pneumonia viruses, two related retroviruses of sheep—was the first lentivirus to be isolated and the first to be intensively studied. *Visna*, the Icelandic word for "wasting," was the name given to the sheep disease when it suddenly appeared in Iceland in the 1930s. Like the AIDS virus, visna virus induces a complicated disease syndrome. The signs in sheep included lymphadenopathy (infected lymph nodes), encephalitis (brain inflammation), wasting, and susceptibility to infections, the most common of which was an acute pneumonia caused by a bacterium that probably resided in Icelandic sheep populations before visna virus came along.

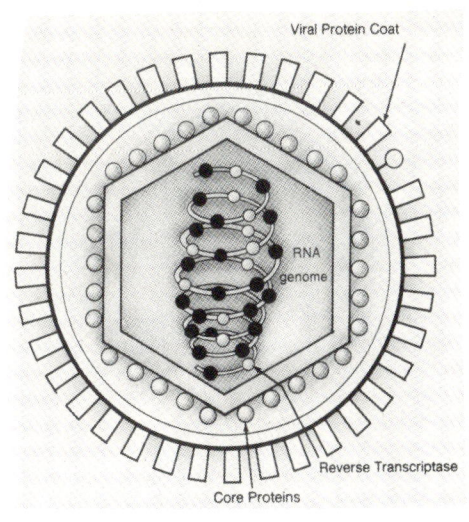

Lentiviruses that have since been identified in other animals induce a variety of disease syndromes. Caprine (goat) arthritis encephalitis virus, which is genetically very closely related to visna, causes crippling arthritis, paralysis, and encephalitis in goats. Horses are vulnerable to a lentiviral agent called equine infectious anemia virus, which causes intermittent anemia, bouts of fever, and immune-complex glomerulonephritis, an inflammatory disease of the kidneys occurring secondary to the infection. The lentivirus of cows, bovine visnalike virus, also affects the lymph system and causes persistent lymphocytosis, an excessive production of white blood cells.

When observed under an electron microscope, all of the lentiviruses, including the AIDS virus, share a common physical structure. Each infects cells of the immune system, although the specific target cell and the level of interference with the host's immune response differ from species to species. Visna and caprine arthritis encephalitis viruses seem to attack the large white blood cells, the monocytes and macrophages. These cells normally de-

General retrovirus structure
Joe LeMonnier

vour foreign bacteria and cellular debris and are a first line of defense against infection. Besides attacking the T-cells, HTLV-III also infects monocytes and macrophages, as well as antibody-producing lymphocytes. Whether other cells of goats and sheep are affected by lentiviruses is not known, since their immune systems have not been as intensively studied as that of humans.

Further analysis of the relationship between the AIDS virus and visna virus awaited direct comparison of their genetic sequences. For if it could be proved that the AIDS virus is genetically related to the lentiviruses, some of the disease's mysterious processes would begin to make sense. DNA hybridization using cloned DNAs of the viruses, an effective way of grossly estimating genetic relatedness, revealed that the AIDS virus and the lentivirus resemble one another even on the very basic level of their DNA sequences. Of the several genetic likenesses investigators saw, the most dramatic was the similarity in the gene for coding reverse transcriptase. This gene, in fact, has changed the least in the evolution of retroviruses, and virologists now depend upon it to determine phylogenetic information for the group. Overall, the AIDS virus and visna virus had significantly more DNA sequences in common than either did with any oncovirus tested, including HTLV-I and HTLV-II.

By this time it was evident that HTLV-III and visna virus were close cousins. But the question of whether HTLV-III was also related to other lentiviruses awaited testing of other representative species. Equine infectious anemia and caprine arthritis encephalitis virus were subsequently cloned and showed an equal amount of likeness with HTLV-III. Clearly, the AIDS virus was a lentivirus.

Final confirmation came from DNA sequencing, which allows nucleotide-by-nucleotide comparisons of the reverse transcriptase gene and the rest of the virus genome. (Each nucleotide represents a single letter of the genetic code.) It demonstrated that the genomes for HTLV-III and lentiviruses were similar in organization and coded for similar sets of genes in the same order and location. This information was important, because sequencing determines how the virus is assembled, how it works, and what it looks like.

In 1985, not long after the structural and genetic studies were reported, another

6. WORLD PROBLEMS AND INTERDEPENDENCE

important clinical manifestation of AIDS was recognized. Physicians began to realize that neurological signs and symptoms that they had been seeing in AIDS patients—chronic meningitis, dementia, encephalopathy, loss of motor coordination, and paralysis—were caused directly by the AIDS-virus infection. The findings suggested that HTLV-III was attracted to brain cells as well as to white blood cells. In retrospect, in view of the virus's demonstrated close association with the visna and caprine retroviruses—both of which cause neurological disease—the findings should not have been that surprising.

A great deal was being discovered about HTLV-III, but much of it boded ill for the development of a vaccine. On the one hand, since the virus was exogenous (transmitted from outside), there was an inherent "weakness" in its replicative cycle that could be exploited. Uninfected persons could theoretically be protected via vaccination, as has been done with other horizontally transmitted viral diseases, such as measles, mumps, and smallpox. But the AIDS virus is a retrovirus, and to date an effective vaccine has been made for only one retrovirus, feline leukemia virus, a cancer-causing retrovirus of cats. Although this vaccine has not totally contained the disease—probably because some apparently healthy cats had already been infected—its existence at least raises the possibility that a successful human retrovirus vaccine can also be developed.

Normally, the host immune system counters infection by making protective antibodies that are specially adapted to adhere to and destroy a specific attacking virus. Lentiviruses, however, have developed novel strategies to avoid elimination by the host. Visna virus and equine infectious anemia virus, for example, undergo rapid changes in the gene responsible for their characteristic protein coat. This capacity for rapid change, called antigenic drift, produces variants of the virus that are not recognized by the host's protective antibodies, which were effective in neutralizing the original strain. The variant viruses thus escape destruction and can continue to infect and, sooner or later, to induce a new cycle of disease. (An analogous process takes place in the envelope of the influenza virus and has created a major stumbling block in obtaining a single effective flu vaccine.)

Caprine arthritis encephalitis virus has another means of evading destruction. It evokes a very weak immune response; the antibodies that do respond seem to do so only halfheartedly and do not kill the virus. The AIDS virus seems to act similarly in this respect, and even though antibodies are present, they do not appear to prevent severe disease or predict survival for the patient. Additionally, the envelope gene of HTLV-III is quite variable, indicating that both of the mechanisms described may be at work.

Effective vaccines have not been made for any lentiviruses, so that producing an AIDS vaccine is no trivial task. Any knowledge gained about lentivirus disease in animals will contribute to the effective control of AIDS.

HTLV-III was presumably introduced into the United States in the 1970s, and AIDS was first recognized clinically in 1981. Although no one knows whether the HTLV-III-induced syndrome is a new disease or where it came from, serologic data are now accumulating to suggest that the virus was in Africa at least a decade before it came to the United States, probably via Haiti. What we don't know is whether the virus was present in humans before the first documented evidence or whether it came from an animal reservoir.

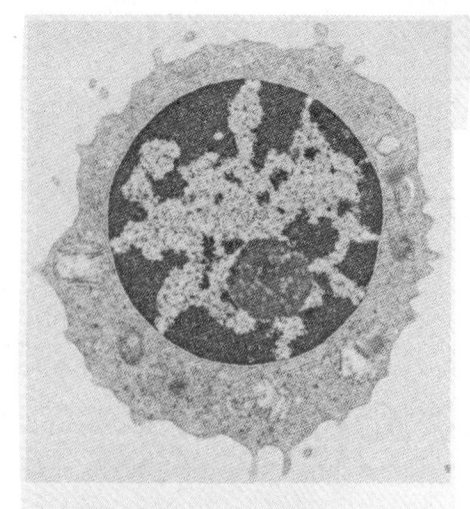

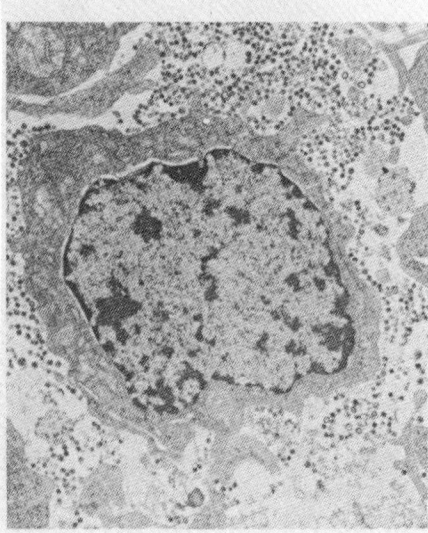

Top: A normal T-4 lymphocyte. Bottom: A T-4 lymphocyte that has been attacked by the AIDS virus.
Kunio Nagashima and Matthew Gonda

We can only speculate on these possibilities. If the virus was widely present in humans before that time, it must have gone through a genetic change that made it more pathogenic. But there are no data at present to substantiate the coexistence of pathogenic and nonpathogenic forms of the virus. It is hard to believe that the nonpathogenic version could have died out in the few years since giving rise to a pathogenic form.

Another possibility is that there exists a lentivirus family group in animals that resembles the AIDS virus even more closely than already identified lentiviruses and that a virus in this group gave rise to a human variant. A newly isolated virus, called STLV-III (simian T-lymphotropic virus type III), causes an AIDS-like syndrome in the macaque monkey. The simian virus resembles the AIDS virus in growth characteristics and structure, and it is attracted to similar cells. These data suggest that STLV-III may also be a lentivirus. Moreover, the presence of strongly cross-reactive antibodies to STLV-III in the blood of apparently healthy wild African green monkeys suggests that the virus is not disease producing in one species and quite pathogenic when it is transmitted to another—in this case, the macaque.

How close is the relationship between the simian virus and the AIDS virus? There is at least the possibility of a monkey retrovirus giving rise to a human variant. Human leukemia virus type I, for instance, has a correlate in a simian virus (simian leukemia virus type I), to which it is remarkably similar in terms of DNA. There have been no direct comparisons of the AIDS-virus DNA and its simian counterpart, but serological analyses have provided some evidence that the AIDS virus may be closer to STLV-III than it is to other lentiviruses. However, the two are not nearly so closely related as the human leukemia virus type I and the simian leukemia virus type I. Even if STLV-III crossed from monkeys to humans, it is unlikely to have diverged so much in such a short time, to become HTLV-III.

A better analogy may be found in the sudden appearance of visna virus in sheep, first described by Bjorn Sigurdsson, a physician. Before 1933, visna was unknown in Iceland. That year, the government purchased twenty karakul sheep from a farm near Halle, Germany, where a visnalike virus was endemic. (The disease in Germany was less severe than what was later seen in Iceland.) When the sheep arrived in Iceland, they were put into quarantine for several weeks and then distributed to farms scattered all over the country. At least two of the introduced breed apparently carried the infection at the time of quarantine because by 1935, there were outbreaks in two widely separated districts. Until 1939, however, no one realized that the disease was an entirely new entity. The losses were enormous. Between 1939 and 1952 at least 150,000 animals died of the infection.

Between 1949 and 1951 all the sheep in the southern part of the island were destroyed in an attempt to control the virus, and ultimately the disease was brought under control. It is now known that visna can be easily transmitted from ewe to kid during feeding, especially through the virus-laden immune cells found in the colostrum, the fluid secreted by the mammary glands before milk appears. Chance abrasions of the skin or mucous membranes are other possible modes of entry, as are the bites of blood-sucking insects, which are implicated in the spread of equine infectious anemia. It could also be that centuries of isolation made Icelandic sheep particularly susceptible to visna.

If HTLV-III is not a new virus, has not recently jumped into the human species from an animal reservoir, and is not a mutation of a known nonpathogenic virus, what plausible explanation can account for its sudden appearance in humans? Drawing on the parallels with visna, we can make some educated guesses. It is possible that the virus has existed in humans in central Africa for hundreds of thousands of years, but that it resided in an isolated population. Such isolated groups may have coadapted with the virus, lessening the severity of the infection and allowing for mutual coexistence. The persistence of HTLV-III in this scenario may lie in old customs such as scarification and the sharing of needles used for body marking. Parallels exist in the spread of kuru, a slow-acting and fatal viral disease of the nervous system. Kuru is found only in a specific tribe in New Guinea and is spread exclusively by rites associated with cannibalism.

Demographic factors, too, may have a bearing on the spread of AIDS. In the past thirty years, Africa's tribal and geographical boundaries have broken down as individuals moved toward cities for a variety of reasons. Such changes could have brought an infectious agent into contact with previously unexposed populations, both international and local, and the devastating effects of the virus would have been felt more readily, as when visna virus was introduced to Iceland.

Such a pattern of sudden virulence has often been seen when other pathogens have reached unexposed peoples. Examples include the fatal measles epidemic in the Faroe Islands (1781) and the Fiji Islands (1875), and the devastating effects of smallpox on American Indian populations after contact with Europeans in the sixteenth century. Anthropological studies in central Africa may provide further insights into such a scenario.

Fortunately, the AIDS virus, unlike smallpox or measles, is not easily transmitted, and unlike some other retroviruses, it cannot be transmitted from generation to generation. Therefore, even in the absence of a vaccine, we can expect that preventive measures already in place can effectively prevent the spread of the disease.

The Importance of Learning About the Rest of the World: What Would Emerson Say Today?

Lewis Hanke

Lewis Hanke, Professor of Latin American History, Emeritus, University of Massachusetts, Amherst, is the general editor of the 5-volume Guide to the Study of United States History Outside the U.S., 1945-1980. *His many other publications include the* Handbook of Latin American Studies *(coeditor),* Aristotle and the American Indians: A Study of Race Prejudice in the Modern World, Modern Latin America: Continent in Ferment, *and* Do the Americans Have a Common History? *He is currently at work on an edition of the writings of Waldo Gifford Leland (1879-1966).*

Ralph Waldo Emerson delivered a oration before the Phi Beta Kappa Society at Cambridge, Massachusetts, on August 31, 1837, on the role of "The American Scholar" in the life of a nation then only half a century old. It was a fighting speech, a call to action for American scholars, which has become one of the most famous of all exhortations to university students on those solemn occasions such as tonight when we are saluting and honoring that small band of graduates who have distinguished themselves during their years at the University of Massachusetts in Amherst.*

Emerson was then a relatively young man in his early thirties, and only at the beginning of his many publications which would make him, at his death in Concord in 1882, the foremost writer and thinker in the United States who exerted more intellectual influence at home and in the Old World than any other American. In his Phi Beta Kappa oration, Emerson in effect called for a Declaration of Intellectual Independence. The time had come, he declared, for the new nation to make its own contribution to the world. He looked forward to the time "when the sluggard intellect of this continent will look from under its iron lids and fill the postponed expectation of the world with something better than the exertions of mechanical skills. Our day of dependence, our long apprenticeship to the learning of other lands, draws to a close."

*These remarks were delivered in 1982 on the occasion of receiving new members of the Phi Beta Kappa chapter at the University of Massachusetts, Amherst.

If Emerson were with us today, he might well feel that the challenge he made then has been met to some extent at least—whether measured in the large number of different kinds of colleges and universities, in the size and quality of our libraries, in the effort to develop art and music, or in the number of Nobel Prize winners who are American citizens.

But he would probably not be content with the world today, any more than we are. Which one of the current pressing problems would he focus on? There are so many to choose from—the tragedy now unfolding in the South Atlantic, the fundamental question of what to do with the nuclear giant that man has created but has not yet learned how to control, the impasse in the Middle East between the Arabs and the Israelis which may lead to a bloody confrontation at any time, the silent but terrible struggle that is going on all over the world today, and in all countries, to provide adequate food and decent living conditions for all people. In attempting to select which crisis to present tonight, I have decided to follow the advice Emerson gave in "Self-Reliance": "Trust thyself: every heart vibrates to that iron string." This powerful essay urging us to use our own experience is full of those lapidary phrases which characterize the style of his writings: "Believe your own thought, believe that what is true for you in your private heart is true for all men."

Therefore my remarks are directed tonight to "The Importance of Learning About the Rest of the World." Let me begin with my senior year at Northwestern University in Illinois, which began in the fall of 1923, not

44. Learning About the Rest of the World

quite 60 years ago. The history department announced at that time a new program of "Honors in History." Being an eager youth from a small town in Ohio, I yearned for recognition and determined to compete. The history department had not established any regulations for the new program, but my professor had a casual approach. Select a good book, and we will examine you on it, he said. In looking over the new acquisitions in the university library, I came upon *The Life of Caleb Cushing* by Claude M. Fuess, published in 1923. It was a two-volume opus, which I hoped would impress the examining committee with my willingness to scale heights. Besides, the author was the headmaster of Andover Academy, then as now a prestigious institution in the East—and in those days the academic world in the Middle West still looked upon institutions on the Eastern seaboard as *the* centers of education.

One chapter in the life of this Massachusetts statesman was his negotiation of the first U.S. treaty with China in 1844. He served in many positions, including responsible public service posts, during his long career—a tutor in Harvard College, member of the House of Representatives from Massachusetts, Justice of the Supreme Court of Massachusetts. But his experience with the wily Chinese seemed to me an excellent illustration of how a shrewd Yankee lawyer met and conquered the Oriental diplomats. To prepare for this task Cushing seriously researched the history and culture of China, and even studied the Manchu language so that when his imposing fleet reached the Portuguese island of Macao near Hong Kong, he was well prepared. He dispatched a formal note to Governor General Ching of the Kwang Tung and Kwang Se provinces stating his authority and the purpose of his mission and announcing that he was on his way to Peking, as he had been appointed by President John Tyler as Envoy Extraordinary and Minister Plenipotentiary to the court of the Emperor of China.

Cushing was all prepared to proceed to Peking to deliver a letter from President Tyler to the Emperor, and in order to meet what was believed to be the rigors of ceremonial at the court, he had on the ready a blue coat with gilt buttons, richly embroidered, a white vest, white pantaloons with a gold stripe down the seam, and a large hat with a white plume. Governor Ching in Whampoa seemed in no hurry to meet Cushing, or to forward his plans to go to Peking. In the first of many leisurely communications he assured the New Englander that the Emperor was "in the enjoyment of happy old age and quiet health," and there was no mention at all of a possible visit to see the Emperor. These were the days when the Chinese Mandarins considered all non-Chinese as inferior beings and termed them "barbarians." Chinese scholars did not bother to learn foreign languages, though a few were deputed to study English and French as an unpleasant but necessary public duty for practical purposes, in the same way that certain persons had to serve as sewer cleaners.

The correspondence dragged on for months. Finally, Cushing announced that he was going to Peking to treat directly with the Emperor. This bold action brought favorable results. Though the Chinese Commissioner Kiyeng, who arrived from Peking to negotiate a treaty, sent Cushing a letter with the title of the United States on a lower line than that of the Chinese Empire, the alert Cushing detected this deceitful cunning, indignantly protested, and the Oriental envoy apologized. Finally, on July 3, 1844, there was formally signed in Macao the Treaty of Wang Hisa which opened five Chinese ports to American merchants, settled many disputed points on tariffs and trade regulations, and established the important principle of "extraterritoriality." The usual exchange of gifts was omitted because Cushing had been forbidden to offer or to accept gifts. Commissioner Kiyeng, however, insisted on organizing a "repast" in his honor, which turned out to be an elaborate banquet. As a preliminary each guest was given a kind of teapot filled with a hot and potent drink called *samchou*. The guests were expected to pour out a cup of this potent beverage, raise it in both hands, rise, nod to the friend whom he wished to compliment, and then empty the cup, taking care to expose the inside so that everyone might observe that its contents had all been consumed.

Cushing proved to be rather successful in this exercise, as he had had plenty of practice in this sort of activity in Massachusetts drinking bouts. Afterwards there was a four-hour dinner beginning with fruit and ending with soup. In between, guests were served such native delicacies as birds' nests, sea-snails, roof of hog's mouths, and sea-weed, as well as turkeys, hams, and roasted pigs. At frequent intervals the pledging of eternal friendship in long draughts of *samcho* was continued, and the Americans had no means of escaping these responsibilities. Cushing survived even this, but he did confess to a "slight langour" the following morning. Finally, Cushing sent to Kiyeng a copy of President Tyler's letter to the Emperor, and received in return some Tartar cheese cakes. Commissioner Cushing returned to the United States conscious of a mission well done, to the praise of his countrymen. He had upheld the honor of the United States, had protected its national interests—all this despite the dilatory and unhelpful tactic of the Chinese officials who clearly were opposed to any treaty with Americans. (For more information on this episode, see the 448-page dissertation by Jeffrey Robert Biggs, "The Origins of American Diplomacy with China: The Cushing Mission of 1844 and the Treaty of Wang-Hsia" (The George Washington University, 1975).)

A few years after my graduation from Northwestern University in 1924, I chanced to read a monograph produced by a Chinese historian based on Chinese manuscript records concerning the negotiations conducted by Cushing's manuscripts which Claude M. Fuess did not have access to, as his biography rests upon forty large boxes of letters and newspaper clippings which Cushing's family had made available for his research. The Chinese records told an entirely different story from the account derived from the boxes of Cushing material. When the Emperor learned that the Yankee "barbarian" actually proposed to visit him in Peking, the Emperor decided that under no circumstances could the American envoy be permitted to pollute the Imperial Court. The Governor was informed that his own head would be cut off if he allowed such a visit, and Commissioner Kiyeng was despatched from Peking to Macao with instructions to sign a treaty with Cushing!

You will not be surprised to learn that these dramati-

6. WORLD PROBLEMS AND INTERDEPENDENCE

cally different explanations for the Treaty of Wang Hisa made a deep impression on me in the early years of my study of history. Indeed, after concentrating on the history of Latin America for over fifty years after graduation from Northwestern, I happened to visit in 1977 that Portuguese island of Macao where in 1844 Commissioners Cushing and Kiyeng had signed the treaty. The Temple of Wang Hisa still stood there, and the table on which the treaty was signed is preserved as a tourist attraction. I discovered that the details of that curious episode of Chinese-American history were fresh in my mind, and I wondered how many other events in the history of the United States were also misinterpreted in our textbooks and monographs because the historians depended upon incomplete evidence.

From this point it was an easy transition to speculating what kind of history foreign authors wrote about the United States. To my surprise, I could not find any volume analyzing what had been produced on the United States outside the United States since World War II. Although in the nineteenth century Alexis de Tocqueville had written his classic study *Democracy in America* and Lord Bryce had published his *American Commonwealth*, there was little serious interest abroad in United States history until after World War II had demonstrated the power and influence of the United States. Then a considerable development took place with the assistance of the Fulbright Program and support from our foundations and our universities.

After leaving Macao in 1977, I returned to Amherst to study this subject. By now I was a retired professor, and after half a century on Latin America history felt there was a need for a change. With the help of the National Endowment for the Humanities and various other foundations, and with the strong logistical support of the University of Massachusetts I am now in the fifth year of my present project on United States history abroad. It should be completed next year, and in 1984 the American Historical Association will publish a three-volume *Guide to the Study of United States History outside the U.S., 1945-1980* as a part of the centenial commemoration of the establishment of the AHA.*

Some 300 foreign historians in 55 countries are now preparing material for the *Guide*, which aims to make United States historians aware of how our history is taught abroad and to provide information on scholarly books, articles, and dissertations on United States history produced abroad. There will be a report on archival materials and manuscripts on United States history in the many repositories in foreign nations. There is already a significant and growing number of scholars scattered around the world who are professionally concerned with and academically competent in teaching and research on American history. It is likely that *all* historians concerned with the American experience will have their perspective broadened when they become more aware of the contributions in other parts of the world, and there certainly will be somewhat different interpretations in the same way that the Chinese documents provided new information on the true reasons for the signing of the Treaty of Wang Hisa in 1844.

I expect that most of the selected annotated bibliography will consist of items on the economic, intellectual, political, and social aspects of our past. But other subjects will be included too—such as art, biography, business, cinema, education, medicine, music, sport, and war—so long as they are primarily historical in scope and treated in chronological fashion.

American literature has aroused much interest in many countries—in some countries more attention is paid to it than to history—and literary studies with a historical content will therefore merit special attention. Many articles, books, and dissertations have been prepared outside the United States on the history of American literature, distinct in purpose and approach from works on purely literary topics and aspects such as aesthetics and criticism. To be included in the *Guide*, items should have a definite connection with the cultural, political, or social aspects of literature in a chronological setting.

The editorial, human, and political problems involved in dealing with so many different kinds of editors in so many countries are too numerous to be mentioned here. The socialistic countries alone present a particular kind of relationship; suffice it to say that we have editors in Bulgaria, Czechoslovakia, East Germany, Hungary, Poland, Romania, and the Soviet Union. And everywhere the editors exhibit that distinctive characteristic of scholars—they are individuals, often with strongly developed personalities. I will not dwell on my experiences with my overseas colleagues, except to remark that in my office in 716 Herter Hall I already have a rich archive of correspondence and memoranda which I hope to use as the basis for my eventual memoirs, possibly posthumous. So far as I know, this is the first international project of its kind, and it is based upon the professional, and may I add unpaid, labors of the editor and of those 300 foreign editors.

To return to my subject—"The Importance of Learning about the Rest of the World." We who study and teach at the University of Massachusetts have every right to be proud of the international spirit and dimensions of this institution. It was the first President, William Clark, who in 1876 established the University of Sopporo on the island of Hokkaido in northern Japan. Through the years the University has been the home of many foreign students, and still is. Most languages are taught here from Armenian and Arabic to Chinese, Polish, Portuguese, Russian, and many others. The director of our international program, Dr. Barbara Burn, is playing an important role on the national scene in the President's Commission on Foreign Languages and International Studies, and has been instrumental in developing opportunities for many of our students and professors to go abroad, and for many foreign scholars to come here. Let us remember also that our university—like other American institutions—has welcomed many foreign scholars to our faculty, and our students have benefited from their presence. This situation may be contrasted with the laws of other countries which restrict such appointments. For example, in France only French citizens can teach history regularly in its universities.

---

*Those who have prepared reference works will not be surprised to learn that the *Guide* did not actually appear until 1985 when it was issued by Kraus International Publications, and then in an edition of five volumes.

44. Learning About the Rest of the World

There is no place for complacency, however. We may recognize that universities have a unique influence in helping our people to learn more about the world. We may rejoice that thus far our individual scholars have been relatively free to learn and to teach foreign languages and about foreign cultures. But we cannot and must not forget that it is always difficult to find the funds to keep these programs going. This year the attack upon funds for international programs was particularly aggressive, and only through the combined force of educators, foreign-affairs specialists, former exchange scholars, and members of Congress of both parties was it possible to beat back the budget-cutters in Washington.

One of those who has fought strongly through the years, first as a member of the House of Representatives from Indiana and now as President of New York University, is John Brademas. If Ralph Waldo Emerson were alive today, would he not fully agree with Brademas that "there is a special responsibility on the part of the colleges and universities of the United States to help educate the American people about the other peoples of the world—who after all, populate most of it"?

We cannot presume to say how Emerson would view the chaotic and dangerous world in which we live today, so different from the studious life he pursued in the quiet village of Concord in the nineteenth century. Nevertheless, I venture to suggest that he would be pleased to know that the United States is learning more about how other countries interpret its history, but that he would also argue that we should know more about their history and their values. Americans can remain ignorant of the world only at their peril.

Certainly Emerson, and everyone who has enjoyed the experience of studying at a university, would agree with John Brademas as he quoted the terse but eloquent words of Senator William Fulbright, who helped to establish in 1946 a government program that has enabled 45,000 Americans to study and teach abroad, and 80,000 scholars from over 100 countries to do the same in the United States.

Senator Fulbright declared: "Education is a slow-moving but powerful force. It may not be fast enough or strong enough to save us from catastrophe, but it is the strongest force available."

Index

Acquired Immune Deficiency Syndrome (AIDS), 234-237
Africa: effect of independence on countries of, 162-169; *see also,* South Africa; West Africa
agriculture: use of genetic engineering in, 40-46; Soviet, 193
AI, *see* artificial intelligence
AIDS, 234-237
amendments, to US Constitution, 87, 88
analytic rationality, as cause of wars, 130, 132
Anglo-Zulu War, causes and consequences of, 99-101
anti-Stalinism, and Nikita Khrushchev, 191-194
apartheid, 170, 171, 172
Arabs, and Vatican's position on Palestine question, 180, 181
Armistice, and World War I, 140
arms race, 133, 134
art, in nineteenth century France, 119-127
artificial intelligence, 47-49
Artificial Intelligence: The Search for the Perfect Machine (Stevens), 48
asocials, treatment of, by Nazis, 146-150
astronomy: and Tycho Brahe, 13-14; and Copernicus, 13; and kinds of electromagnetic waves, 16; and Galileo, 14, 15, 18-23; and Herschel, 16; and Kepler, 14; and Isaac Newton, 15, 17, 25-26; during post-Restoration period, 24-30
astrophysics, 17
atomic bomb, and rebuilding Hiroshima, 151-152
Aurangzeb, Emperor of Moghul Empire, 110, 112, 114, 115
Austro-Hungarian Empire, and World War I, 137, 138

Bach, Johann Sebastian, 69-73
Bangladesh, impact of agricultural innovations in, 42
Basic English, as world language, 198
Beagle, voyage of, and Darwin's work as geologist, 31-36
Bernhardt, Sarah, 119-127
Bethe, Hans, 17
Bible, Luther's translation of, 56
Bill of Rights, 87, 88
biotechnology, and deciphering the code in DNA, 37-39
Boers, and Anglo-Zulu War, 99-101
Brahe, Tycho, 13-14
Brasilia, 217, 220
Brazil, history and future of Brasilia, 217-220
Britain: and colonial rule in Africa, 162-169; factory vs. domestic system of production in, 6-12; and South African apartheid, 170-172; women's rights in eighteenth century, 81-85; and World War I, 131, 133, 139, 140; and World War II, 134, 141-145
British Raj, in India, 109

Camp David agreements, 184
camp theme, and anti-Stalinism, 192, 193
cancer, molecular biology's contribution to understanding of, 38
Catholic Church: condemnation of Galileo by, 18-23; Luther's challenge of, 54-58
Central America, influence of Vietnam experience on US policy in, 154, 155

Cetshwayo, and Anglo-Zulu War, 100-101
Child, Josiah, 110, 111, 112
China: divorce in, 228-233; population control in, 211, 214; urban growth in, 213-216
Churchill, Winston, and World War II, 142-145
civil rights, and Supreme Court, 89
Cold War, resemblance of, to Peloponnesian War, 157-159
collectivization, and Stalinism, 192, 193
colonial rule, British, in Africa, 162-169
comets, and Edmund Halley, 17, 29
Community Alien Law, and Nazi treatment of asocials, 149, 150
computer-aided instruction, 49
computers, and artificial intelligence technology, 47-49
concentration camps, Soviet, 190
Constitution, of United States, 86-88
Copernicanism, Galileo's support of, 18-23
Copernicus, Nicolaus, 13, 18
coral reefs, Darwin's geological research on origin of, 31-36
corporation, Adam Smith's views on, 63
cottage industry, vs. factory system, 6-12
Clive, Robert, 109, 110, 113
Crick, Francis, 37
Cultural Revolution, 213, 214

Darwin, Charles, as a geologist, 31-36
demography, problems of, in predicting population trends, 203, 204, 205
Denmark, and World War II, 142
deoxyribonucleic acid, *see* DNA
dependency ratio, 205, 207
de-Stalinization, 193, 194
Dialogue on the Two Chief Systems of the World (Galileo), 20-21, 22
diplomacy, in seventeenth and eighteenth centuries, 95-97
discrimination: of Nazis against gypsies and asocials, 146-150; and South Africa, 170-173; Supreme Court decisions regarding, 89
diving bell/helmet, Halley's contributions to design of, 28
divorce, in China, 228-233
DNA, deciphering the code in, 37-39
domino theory, and Vietnam War, 156

East India Company, empire of, in India, 109-115
economic growth, and population, 202-212
economics, contribution of Adam Smith to, 59-64
Egyptian astronomers, 14
Ehrlich, Paul, 202, 212
electromagnetic radiation, new efforts to analyze, 16
Emerson, Ralph Waldo, 238
emotions, computers with, 48
Engels, 67, 68
English: as a foreign language (EFL), 196; as a second language (ESL), 195; as a universal language, 195-199
environmentalism, and Greenpeace, 221-224
Equal Opportunity Bill, in Japan, 225, 227
equal protection clause, of Fourteenth Amendment, 89
Esperanto, as world language, 198
Essay on the Principle of Population (Malthus), 211

eugenic theory, Nazi, and treatment of gypsies and other asocials, 146-150
Europe: and World War I, 131, 133, 137-140; and World War II, 141-145; *see also,* European state system
European state system, 92-98
Euthanasia Programme, and Nazi Germany, 148
evolution of species (Darwin), 33, 36
expert systems, 48
ex suppositione, Galileo's reasoning, 21, 22

factory: impact of artificial intelligence technology in, 47-49; vs. domestic system of production, 6-12
family planning: and population control in China, 211, 214; and Third World, 209, 210; and world population, 202
Federalists, and ratification of US Constitution, 86
feminism, Mary Wollstonecraft as first spokesperson for, 81-85
Ferdinand, Franz, assassination of, 137
fertility, and economic growth, 208, 209
food production, use of genetic engineering in, 40-46
food shortages, and population growth, 206, 207
Fourteenth Amendment, Supreme Court decisions regarding, 89
France: and colonial rule in Africa, 166; and internationalization of Jerusalem, 181-182; nineteenth-century Paris, 119-127; in seventeenth century, 93, 94; and World War I, 138-140; and World War II, 141-145
Frederick the Great, 132
Frere, Bartle, 99-101
Freud, Sigmund, myths and realities of life of, 74-80

Galileo: 14, 15; trial of, and Catholic church's condemnation of, 18-23
Gandhi, Mahatma, ideals and achievements of, 174-179
genes: and achievements in molecular biology, 37-39; *see also,* genetic engineering; genome
genetic engineering: 39; and the Green Revolution, 40-46
genome, 234
geocentric theory, of Ptolemy, 18
geology, Darwin's contribution to, 31-36
Germany: impact of Martin Luther on, 55-56; and Nazi atrocities against gypsies and asocials, 146-150; and World War I, 131, 133, 138-140; and World War II, 134, 141-145
Ghana: 166; explanation of poverty in, 206
Godwin, William, 85
Graves, Robert, 140
Great Leap Forward, 213, 214
great powers, emergence of, 92-98
Great War, *see* World War I
Greek astronomers, 14
Greenpeace International, goals and achievements of, 221-224
Green Revolution, 40-46
gypsies, treatment of, by Nazis, 146-150
gypsy *Mischlinge,* 149

Hale Observatory, telescope at, on Mount Palomar, 15-16

Halley, Edmund: 17; contribution of, to mathematics and science, 24-30
handicapped people, killing of, by Nazis, 148
hegemony, 134, 135
heliocentric theory, of Copernicus, 13, 18
helium, discovery of, 17
Herschel, William, 16
Hiroshima, rebuilding of, after atomic bomb, 151-152
Hitler, Adolph: 190; treatment of gypsies and asocials under, 146-150; and World War I, 139; and World War II, 141-145
Hohenzollern Age, and Germany, 140
Holy Land, 180, 181
Holy Places, and internationalization of Jerusalem, 183
Hong Kong, and relationship of poverty to population, 207
HTLV-II, and AIDS, 234, 235
HTLV-III, 236
hut tax controversy, 106-107

India, power of East India company in, 109-115
Inkatha, 101
internationalization of Jerusalem, Vatican position on, 181, 182
Iran, and Islamic fundamentalism, 189
Islamic fundamentalism, 188-189
Italy: as origin of diplomacy, 95, 96; and World War I, 140

Japan: feudal, 116-118; and rebuilding of Hiroshima after atomic bomb, 151, 152; working women in, 225-227
Jerusalem, Vatican position on internationalization of, 181, 182
Jews: Luther's views on, 57; and Nazi atrocities, 146; and Vatican's position on Palestine question, 180, 181
judicial review, origin of power of, 88
"Just in Time Manufacturing," 47

Kepler, Johannes, 14, 18
Khomeini, Ayatollah, 188, 189
Khrushchev, Nikita, 190, 191, 192
Kingsley, Mary, empathy of, with African cause, 102-108
knowledge of world, importance of, 238-241

labor: impact of artificial intelligence technology on, 47-49; female and child, 8, 11; female, in Japan vs. US, 225-227
labor camps, and Stalinism, 190
learning, importance of, about the rest of the world, 238-241
lentiviruses, AIDS as, 235
Limits of Growth, The (Club of Rome), 203
literature, on women's rights, 81-85
Louis XIV, 93, 94
Luther, Martin, 54-58
Lyell, Charles, influence of, on Charles Darwin, 32-35

Madison, James, 86, 87
Maginot Line, 141
Malthus, Thomas, 202, 203, 211
maps, Halley's contribution to navigation, 27
Marbury v. Madison, 88
Marx, Karl, critique of Payne's biography on, 65-68

Marx (Payne), 65-68
mass production, domestic vs. factory, 6-12
Mayan astronomers, 14
McTaggart, David, and Greenpeace, 221-224
medicine: and scorn of Freud by medical profession, 76-77; molecular biology's contribution to, 37-39
Mendel, Gregor, 37
Mexico, and population growth, 204
Middle East: 132, 138, 184; and Islamic fundamentalism, 188, 189; and Vatican's opinion on Palestine question, 180, 181
military coups: in African countries, 163; and Nigeria, 162
military intervention, American, and Vietnam, 153-156
Mischlinge, gypsy, 149
Moghul Empire, vs. East India Company, 109-115
molecular biology, contributions of, to science and medicine, 37-39
money, role of, in Freud's Vienna, 78
Moslem fundamentalists, 188, 189
mother tongue, English as, around world, 195, 196, 197, 198
Mount Palomar, telescope at Hale Observatory on, 15-16
mujahideen, 188
music, impact of Bach on, 69-73

national comrades: and Nazism, 146, 147; and sterilization, 147, 148
nationalism, Russian, 194
natural-language systems, of computers, 49
navigation, Halley and methods of, 27
Nazism, development of, 146, 147
"necessary and proper" clause, of the US Constitution, 88
negative selection, and sterilization of people with hereditary defects, 147
Nepal, 205, 206
Neptune, discovery of, 16-17
neutrality, US, in World War II, 141, 142
Newton, Isaac: 15, 17; association of, with Edmond Halley, 25-26
Nicaragua, 154
Niger, explanation for poverty in, 205, 206
Nigeria, effect of independence on, 162, 163, 164, 166
North American Indians, practice of astronomy by, 14
North vs. South, in number of publishing scientists, 50-51
Norway, and World War II, 142
nuclear waste, and Greenpeace, 223
nuclear weapons, and Greenpeace, 223, 224
Nuremburg Law, 148
Nyerere, Julius, 163, 167, 168

one-child campaign, and China, 211, 214
On the Origin of Species (Darwin), 35, 36
On the Revolutions of the Celestial Spheres (Copernicus), 13, 18
overpopulation, 204, 205

Paris, nineteenth-century, 119-127
Payne, Robert, 65-68
Peace Park, in Hiroshima, 151, 152
Pearl Harbor, 142, 143, 145

Peloponnesian War, resemblance of, to Cold War between US and Russia, 157-159
"Phony War," 141, 142
pidgins, and English language, 196
Pluto, discovery of, 17
Poland, and World War II, 141
"poorhouse neurosis," 78-79
Pope Leo X, and Martin Luther, 54-56
population: in China, 211; and economic growth, 202-212; and poverty, 205-207; and urban growth in China, 213-216
Population: A Problem for Democracy (Myrdal), 211
Population Bomb (Erlich), 212
Population, Evolution and Birth Control (Hardin), 211
poverty: and fertility, 208; and population growth, 205-207
"power packs," 49
pre-World War I, arts and sciences in, 139, 140
Principia (Newton), 25, 26
Principles of Geology (Lyell), 32, 33, 34, 35
problem-solving, use of artificial intelligence technology for, 47-49
Protestant-Catholic split, and Martin Luther, 54-58
Prussia, seventeenth-century, 94, 95
psychoanalysis, 76-78
purdah system, 188

Rainbow Warrior, 221, 223, 224
raison d'état, 93
Reconstruction Amendments, 88
religion, and Islamic fundamentalism, 188-189
retrovirus, AIDS as, 234, 235
ribosome, 37
rice, genetic breeding of, 41-42
"right to privacy," Supreme Court on constitutional, 89
RNA, 37
Roe v. Wade, 89
Roosevelt, Franklin: 180; and World War II, 141-145
Russia, seventeenth-century, 94, 95

scientists, number of publishing, in North vs. South, 50-51
seal pups, harp, and Greenpeace, 221
sexual behavior, in Freud's Vienna, 78
Shelley, Percy Bysshe, 85
Shiites, 189
Shultz, George, 153, 156
Singapore, 207, 210
Smith, Adam, 59-64
Solzhenitsyn, Aleksandr, 192, 193
South Africa: 170-173; Zulu of, 99-101
Soviet Union: and Afghanistan, 188; and the Cold War, 157-159; and Third World, 208; and Vietnam War, 155; and World War II, 134, 136, 145
spectroscopy, 17
Stalin, Josef, 190-194
sterilization, and Nazi Germany, 147, 148, 149
Sterilization Law, 147, 149
Stevens, Lawrence, 48
Stonehenge, as astronomical observatory, 14
Study of War, A (Wright), 131
Summers, Harry, 154, 156

superstition, during post-restoration period, 29
Supreme Court: landmark decisions of, 88-89; origin of power of judicial review of, 88

Tanzania, 167
taxation, Adam Smith's views on, 62
telescope: and Galileo's astronomical observations, 15, 18-19; at Mount Palomar, 15-16
Third World: 136; and family planning, 209-210; population and economic growth in, 202-212
Thirty Years' War, 92-93
Thucydides, 130, 131, 133, 157
transmutation, *see* evolution of species
Trotsky, Leon, 139
Truman, Harry, 182

underdeveloped countries, promise of Green Revolution for, 40-46
United Nations: and internationalization of Jerusalem, 181, 182; and world population, 202
United States: and the Cold War, 157-159; and sterilization, 147; and Vietnam syndrome, 153; and World War II, 141-145
universal gravitation law (Newton), 15, 25, 28

universal language, English as, 195-199
Uranus, discovery of, 16
urban growth, and China, 213-216
urban poverty, and colonial rule in Africa, 164

Vatican: and internationalization of Jerusalem, 181-183; and Palestine Question, 180, 181
Vienna: of Freud's time, 78-80; and World War I, 139
Vietnam War, lessons to be learned from, 153-156
Vindication of the Rights of Woman (Wollstonecraft), 83, 85
violence, and colonial rule in Africa, 164
Visna virus, 235
vocabulary, of English language and role as world language, 195, 196, 197, 198

war: and analytic rationality, 130, 132; causes of, 130-136; Peloponnesian and Cold, 157-159; Vietnam, 153-156
Watson, James, 37
Wealth of Nations, The (Smith), 59-64
Weinberger, Caspar, 153, 154
West Africa, nineteenth-century image of Mary Kingsley's, 102-108
West African Studies (Kingsley), 107
Western Europe: and World War I, 132; and World War II, 134

whaling, and Greenpeace International, 222, 223, 224
wheat, genetic breeding of, 41-42
Wilson, Woodrow, 140, 141
Wollstonecraft, Mary, 81-85
women: Mary Wollstonecraft on rights of, 81-85; in workforce, 8; in workforce in Japan vs. United States, 225-227; *see also,* women's rights
women's rights: and Mary Kingsley's empathy with African cause, 102-108; and Supreme Court, 89; Mary Wollstonecraft as first spokesperson for, 81-85
working women, in Japan, 225-227
world, importance of learning about other countries of the, 238-241
world language, English as, 195-199
world population, effect of, on economic growth, 202-212
World War I, 130, 131, 133, 137-140, 141, 166
World War II, 133, 134, 140, 190, 192
Wright, Quincy, 131, 132

Youth Concentration Camp, 150

Zulu, and Anglo-Zulu War, 99-101

Credits/Acknowledgments

Cover design by Charles Vitelli

1. The Industrial and Scientific Revolution
Facing overview—Dover *Pictorial Archives* Series. 6—from *The Textile Manufactures of Great Britain*, by George Dodd, London, 1844. 8—(top) from *Book of English Trades*, London, 1804; (bottom) from *Cotton Manufacture in Great Britain*, by Edward Baines, London, 1835. 9—(left top and bottom) from *The Book of English Trades*; (right top) from *Days at the Factories*, by G. Dobb, London, 1843; (right bottom) from *Penny Magazine*, November 1944. 10-12—Mansell Collection. 14—Peabody Museum, Harvard University. 15—The Bettmann Archive. 16—National Aeronautics & Space Administration. 19—Smithsonian Institution Libraries. 20—Pitti Collection, Italy. 22—(top) Ann Ronan Picture Library; (bottom) Rare Book Collection, Perkins Library. 25—by courtesy of the Master & Fellows of Magdalene College, Cambridge. 26—Ann Ronan Picture Library. 27—Mansell Collection. 29—Ann Ronan Picture Library. 36—Andrew Tomko.

2. The Cultural Ferment of the West
Facing overview—The National Gallery of Art. 86—in the collection of the Corcoran Gallery of Art, Museum purchase, Gallery Fund. 88—The New York Public Library.

3. The Extension and Domination of the West
Facing overview—The National Gallery of Art. 102, 104—by courtesy of the Royal Commonwealth Society. 106—by courtesy of P.H. Rivers Museum, University of Oxford. 109—by courtesy of the India Office Library & Records. 111—HT map by Ken Wass. 112—by courtesy of the India Office Library & Records. 113—Mansell Collection.

4. War and Depression
Facing overview—The American Red Cross. 135—United Nations/photo by Sygma. 146—from *Die Zigeuner*, by Hermann Arnold, Freiburg, 1965.

5. The Retreat of the West
Facing overview—United Nations/photo by J. Isaac. 172—UN photo.

6. World Problems and Interdependence
Facing overview—United Nations. 208—Government Information Office. 215—UN photo/T. Chen.

ANNUAL EDITIONS: WORLD HISTORY, VOL. II
1500 to 20th Century
Article Rating Form

Here is an opportunity for you to have direct input into the next revision of this volume. We would like you to rate each of the 44 articles listed below, using the following scale:

1. **Excellent: should definitely be retained**
2. **Above average: should probably be retained**
3. **Below average: should probably be deleted**
4. **Poor: should definitely be deleted**

Your ratings will play a vital part in the next revision. So please mail this prepaid form to us just as soon as you complete it.
Thanks for your help!

We Want Your Advice

Annual Editions revisions depend on two major opinion sources: one is our Advisory Board, listed in the front of this volume, which works with us in scanning the thousands of articles published in the public press each year; the other is you—the person actually using the book. Please help us and the users of the next edition by completing the prepaid article rating form on this page and returning it to us. Thank you.

Rating	Article	Rating	Article
	1. Cottage Industry and the Factory System		25. The Dangerous Summer of 1940
	2. From Astronomy to Astrophysics		26. Social Outcasts in Nazi Germany
	3. Galileo's Science and the Trial of 1633		27. Reborn from Holocaust
	4. Halley and Post-Restoration Science		28. Lessons from a Lost War
	5. Darwin as a Geologist		29. The Two Thousand Years' War
	6. Life's Recipe		30. Whose Dream Was It Anyway? Twenty-Five Years of African Independence
	7. The Green Revolution		
	8. Artificial Intelligence: A New Reality		31. Visit to South Africa
	9. Scientists Go North		32. Gandhi: A Twentieth-Century Anomaly?
	10. Luther: Giant of His Time and Ours		33. The Vatican, Israel and the Jerusalem Question (1943-1984)
	11. Scotland's Greatest Son		
	12. Marx: His Death and Resurrection		34. Islam: Religion Has Potential to Reshape World
	13. The Body of Bach		
	14. Freudian Myths and Freudian Realities		35. Stalin's Afterlife
	15. The First Feminist		36. The New English Empire
	16. Making It Work		37. Population and Economic Growth: The Third World
	17. The Emergence of the Great Powers		
	18. The Struggle for Land		38. China Goes to Town
	19. West Africa's Mary Kingsley		39. Capital of Dreams
	20. The East India Company and the Emperor Aurangzeb		40. The Zeal of Disapproval
			41. Japanese Women in a Male Society
	21. Southern Barbarians and Red Hairs in Feudal Japan		42. Divorce, Chinese Style
			43. The Natural History of AIDS
	22. Sarah Bernhardt's Paris		44. The Importance of Learning About the Rest of the World: What Would Emerson Say Today?
	23. The Causes of Wars		
	24. Sarajevo: The End of Innocence		

(cont. on next page)

ABOUT YOU

Name_____ Date_____
Are you a teacher? ☐ Or student? ☐
Your School Name _____
Department _____
Address _____
City _____ State _____ Zip _____
School Telephone # _____

YOUR COMMENTS ARE IMPORTANT TO US!

Please fill in the following information:

For which course did you use this book? _____
Did you use a text with this Annual Edition? ☐ yes ☐ no
The title of the text? _____
What are your general reactions to the Annual Editions concept?

Have you read any particular articles recently that you think should be included in the next edition?

Are there any articles you feel should be replaced in the next edition? Why?

Are there other areas that you feel would utilize an Annual Edition?

May we contact you for editorial input?

May we quote you from above?

WORLD HISTORY, VOL. II

BUSINESS REPLY MAIL
First Class   Permit No. 84   Guilford, CT

Postage will be paid by addressee

The Dushkin Publishing Group, Inc.
Sluice Dock
Guilford, Connecticut 06437

No Postage
Necessary
if Mailed
in the
United States